ISSUES FOR DEBATE
IN SOCIAL POLICY

SELECTIONS FROM CQ RESEARCHER

SAGE

Los Angeles | London | New Delhi
Singapore | Washington DC

For information:

SAGE Publications, Inc.
2455 Teller Road
Thousand Oaks, California 91320
E-mail: order@sagepub.com

SAGE Publications Ltd.
1 Oliver's Yard
55 City Road
London EC1Y 1SP
United Kingdom

SAGE Publications India Pvt. Ltd.
B 1/I 1 Mohan Cooperative Industrial Area
Mathura Road, New Delhi 110 044
India

SAGE Publications Asia-Pacific Pte. Ltd.
33 Pekin Street #02-01
Far East Square
Singapore 048763

Printed in the United States of America

Library of Congress Cataloging-in-Publication Data

Issues for debate in social policy: selections from CQ researcher.
 p. cm.
Includes bibliographical references and index.
ISBN 978-1-4129-7941-2 (pbk.)
 1. United States—Social policy—1993- I. CQ researcher.
HN59.2.I798 2010
320.60973—dc22   2009023868

This book is printed on acid-free paper.

09 10 11 12 13 10 9 8 7 6 5 4 3 2 1

Acquisitions Editor:	Kassie Graves
Editorial Assistant:	Veronica Novak
Production Editor:	Laureen Gleason
Typesetter:	C&M Digitals (P) Ltd.
Cover Designer:	Candice Harman
Marketing Manager:	Stephanie Adams

Contents

Annotated Contents

Middle-Class Squeeze: Is More Government Aid Needed?

Millions of families who once enjoyed the American dream of home ownership and upward financial mobility are sliding down the economic ladder — some into poverty. Many have been forced to seek government help for the first time. The plunging fortunes of working families are pushing the U.S. economy deeper into recession as plummeting demand for goods and services creates a downward economic spiral. A consumption binge and growing consumer debt beginning in the 1990s contributed to the middle-class squeeze, but the bigger culprits were exploding prices for necessities such as housing, medical care and college tuition, cuts in employer-funded benefits and, some say, government policies that favored the wealthy. President Barack Obama has promised major aid for the middle class, and some economists are calling for new programs — most notably national health coverage — to assist working Americans.

Vanishing Jobs: Will the President's Plan Reduce Unemployment?

The news is grim and getting grimmer. The jobless rate recently hit 8.1 percent — the highest level in a quarter-century. American workers lost 651,000 jobs in February alone. All told, more than 12.5 million Americans are jobless — including 2.9 million who have been unemployed for at least 27 weeks. The nation is banking on the Obama administration's newly enacted, $787 billion "economic stimulus" bill to spark job growth through government spending on infrastructure projects and other programs. Conservatives argue that the spending won't help, and some liberals say the magnitude of the crisis calls for still more stimulus money. The huge spending measure also includes funds to encourage states to expand eligibility for unemployment insurance, though some governors are resisting on the grounds that their states will wind up footing future bills. With no quick turnaround predicted, creating or saving jobs will remain the top priority for President Barack Obama and the millions of citizens counting on his administration's rescue plan.

Mortgage Crisis: Should the Government Bail Out Borrowers in Trouble?

More than 2 million borrowers will lose their homes to foreclosure because of subprime mortgage lending in recent years. With the housing market booming, lenders enticed many lower-income people into buying homes they couldn't afford by offering adjustable-rate mortgages (ARMs) with temptingly low initial teaser interest rates. Many loans didn't require down payments or documented proof of income. Moreover, with real-estate prices rising many homeowners used the higher value of their homes to get second mortgages to pay for extras like remodeled kitchens. But this year the housing market crashed and the party ended: The low teaser loans reset at higher interest rates, and many borrowers defaulted on their new, higher mortgage payments. When the dust settles, investors who bought mortgage-based securities stand to lose $160 billion or more. Congress and the Bush administration are debating how to help borrowers keep their homes and whether tough, new lending standards are warranted.

Gender Pay Gap: Are Women Paid Fairly in the Workplace?

More than four decades after Congress passed landmark anti-discrimination legislation — including the Equal Pay Act of 1963 — a debate continues to rage over whether women are paid fairly in the workplace. Contending that gender bias contributes to a significant "pay gap," reformists support proposed federal legislation aimed at bringing women's wages more closely in line with those of men. Others say new laws are not needed because the wage gap largely can be explained by such factors as women's choices of occupation and the amount of time they spend in the labor force. Meanwhile, a class-action suit charging Wal-Mart Stores with gender bias in

pay and promotions — the biggest sex-discrimination lawsuit in U.S. history — may be heading for the Supreme Court. Some women's advocates argue that a controversial high-court ruling last year makes it more difficult to sue over wage discrimination.

Women's Rights: Are Violence and Discrimination Against Women Declining?

Women around the world have made significant gains in the past decade, but tens of millions still face significant and often appalling hardship. Most governments now have gender-equality commissions, electoral gender quotas and laws to protect women against violence. But progress has been mixed. A record number of women now serve in parliaments, but only 14 of the world's 193 countries currently have elected female leaders. Globalization has produced more jobs for women, but they still constitute 70 percent of the world's poorest inhabitants and 64 percent of the illiterate. Spousal abuse, female infanticide, genital mutilation, forced abortions, bride-burnings, acid attacks and sexual slavery remain pervasive in some countries, and rape and sexual mutilation have reached epic proportions in the war-torn Democratic Republic of the Congo. Experts say without greater economic, political and educational equality, the plight of women will not improve, and society will continue suffering the consequences.

Reproductive Ethics: Should Fertility Medicine Be Regulated More Tightly?

Nadya Suleman, an unemployed, 33-year-old, single mother from Southern California, felt her six children weren't enough. Last January, after a fertility doctor implanted six embryos she had frozen earlier, Suleman gave birth to octuplets — and was quickly dubbed "Octomom." Many fertility experts were shocked that a doctor would depart so far from medical guidelines — which recommend implantation of only one, or at most two, embryos for a woman of Suleman's relatively young age. Although multiple births often do result from in vitro fertilization (IVF) and other assisted-reproduction technologies, the number of multiples has dropped over the past few years, they point out. Other analysts note, however, that government statistics show a large percentage of clinics frequently ignore the guidelines on embryo implantation. In response, lawmakers in several states have introduced proposals to increase regulation of fertility clinics.

Domestic Poverty: Is a New Approach Needed to Help the Poorest Americans?

Despite sweeping welfare reforms in the 1990s and generally healthy economic growth in recent years, domestic poverty remains intractable. Moreover, signs are emerging that so-called deep poverty is growing sharply — most significantly among children. U.S. poverty is fueled by a long list of problems, including Katrina's devastation, immigration, the growing income gap between rich and poor, the subprime mortgage fallout and education disparities. Conservatives say solutions must emphasize personal responsibility, higher marriage rates and fewer out-of-wedlock births. Liberals focus on the negative effects of government budget cuts for antipoverty programs, tax cuts benefiting the wealthy and the need for more early-childhood-development programs. The Democratic Congress is making poverty a priority issue, as are some of the presidential candidates. President Bush himself acknowledged the gap between rich and poor, raising hopes that a bipartisan effort would be found to reduce poverty.

Hunger in America: How Bad Is the Problem?

New government statistics show that amid the nation's prosperity 31 million Americans — including 12 million children — suffer from hunger or face the risk of hunger. Most are minorities and single moms with children. Food-bank operators say that as housing costs continue to rise and wages stagnate, many working families with children are forced to line up at food banks to feed their families. Meanwhile, participation in the federal food stamp program has declined by more than 7 million persons over the past three years. Skeptics say the decline proves that the hunger problem is exaggerated, but advocates for the hungry blame the lower participation on tightened eligibility criteria and red tape. Indeed, they say overcoming skepticism about hunger is one of the biggest problems they face.

Welfare Reform: Are Former Welfare Recipients Better Off Today?

The destitution among children and single mothers that liberals predicted when welfare was overhauled in 1996 has not come to pass. Conservatives credit the sweeping welfare reforms with a historic rise in employment among former welfare mothers. But many remain in poverty. When welfare reform comes up for reauthorization in Congress next year, Republicans will argue for trimming funding, since half as many people are on welfare. But Democrats will argue for generous funding to help those still unable to work and to assist new workers with child care and other work expenses. More aid may be forthcoming, now that welfare mothers have become the "working poor" — a group the American public is far more willing to help.

Social Security Reform: How Should America's Retirement System Be Saved?

Social Security has provided a guaranteed income for retirees, widows and disabled individuals for almost 70 years. But unless changes are made to the taxpayer-funded system, Social Security will begin paying more in benefits than it collects in payroll taxes in about 15 years. That's when the retirement of millions of baby-boom workers will overwhelm the system's pay-as-you-go funding mechanism. Moreover, by 2052, the program's trillion-dollar trust fund is expected to run dry. Experts continue to debate the seriousness of the program's problems and the best way to strengthen it. Three years ago, President Bush called for bolstering Social Security funding by allowing workers to invest part of their payroll contributions in personal investment accounts. Democratic presidential candidate Sen. John Kerry opposes privatization. Regardless of who wins this fall's presidential election, Social Security reform is likely to figure high on the legislative agenda next year.

Child Welfare Reform: Will Recent Changes Make At-Risk Children Safer?

The U.S. child welfare system is designed to protect the nation's children, but in recent years it has been rocked by horror stories of children who were physically and sexually abused and even murdered. More than 900,000 children were maltreated in 2003 — and some 1,300 died. But a nationwide reform movement offers hope for the future. Welfare agencies across the country are focusing more on keeping families together and quickly moving the nation's 500,000 foster children into permanent homes. Although the foster care rolls are dropping, unadopted foster teens still must struggle with a lonely transition to adulthood after leaving the system. No state program has passed a federal review, but states are hitting improvement targets in follow-up checks. Meanwhile, social workers continue to complain that they are underpaid and overworked. And Congress is divided over a Bush administration plan that would give states more flexibility in using federal funds but end the guarantee of federal support for every foster child.

Universal Coverage: Will All Americans Finally Get Health Insurance?

Some 45 million Americans lacked health insurance in 2005—a number that has been climbing for two decades. Every month, about 2 million Americans become uninsured, at least temporarily, as lower-paying service jobs with minimal benefits replace union-dominated manufacturing jobs with health benefits — undercutting the nation's employer-based coverage system. Health costs — rising faster than wages or inflation — also push employers to drop coverage. Past legislative proposals for universal coverage relied heavily on government management, drawing fatal opposition from physicians and insurance companies. But now consensus may be forming around proposals requiring most Americans to buy private insurance with public assistance. Republican governors in California and Massachusetts back such plans, as does former Sen. John Edwards, the first presidential hopeful to announce what's expected to be a slew of universal-coverage proposals in the coming 2008 election.

Wounded Veterans: Is America Shortchanging Vets on Health Care?

Early this year, *The Washington Post* exposed shockingly substandard treatment for wounded veterans at Walter Reed Army Medical Center's outpatient facilities. Follow-up investigations soon turned up evidence that problems extended beyond shabby conditions at the military's top-drawer hospital. On the battlefield, military surgeons are saving many more lives than ever before. But once they return home, men and women recovering from sometimes devastating war injuries confront a red-tape jungle of laws and regulations. Moreover, many wait months for treatment or benefits, and some even have had reenlistment bonuses withheld after wounds forced them out of active service. A history of disgraceful treatment of veterans of past wars, including the Vietnam conflict, looms over the issue. Amid the present uproar, a presidential panel on military and veterans' health care has called for far-reaching changes, but some critics say changes need to go deeper if the country is to live up to its promises to its troops.

Ending Homelessness: Is the Problem Solvable?

More than 2 million Americans are homeless during the course of a year, and the number is rising. About 40 percent are families with children, 30 percent are substance abusers, 23 percent are severely mentally ill and 10 percent are veterans. Advocates blame the growing problem on the sluggish economy, Congress' refusal to raise the minimum wage, rising unemployment and stricter welfare-eligibility requirements. The Bush administration declared a commitment to ending chronic homelessness in 10 years and is pressing Congress to pass the Samaritan Initiative, which would provide $70 million for housing and attendant care specifically for the chronically homeless. Critics say the proposal does not go far enough because the chronically homeless represent only 10–20 percent of the problem. Meanwhile, although new research clearly shows that homelessness can indeed be solved, no consensus yet exists on a comprehensive approach to rooting out the causes of the problem.

Caring for the Elderly: Who Will Pay for Care of Aging Baby Boomers?

Nearly 70 percent of those turning 65 this year will need long-term care (LTC) in their lifetimes; 20 percent will need it for five years or longer. But — unlike most other industrialized nations — the United States has no public or private insurance infrastructure to pay for LTC. Those needing years of care will have to impoverish themselves before Medicaid will pay for it. But state officials say Medicaid — intended as a health-care safety net for poor children — could be bankrupted by rising LTC costs as the baby boom generation ages, and the number of people over age 85 soars from around 5 million to 21 million by 2050. Meanwhile, understaffing, low pay and poor working conditions at nursing homes put residents at risk of life-threatening malnutrition and bed sores. As an alternative, states and nonprofits are offering more home- and community-delivered care, but LTC experts say the alternatives may not be any safer.

Aging Baby Boomers: Will the 'Youth Generation' Redefine Old Age?

In January, the oldest baby boomers will turn 62 — and become eligible to collect Social Security benefits. For the next 18 years, a member of the baby boom generation — the 78 million Americans born between 1946 and 1964—will reach that age every eight seconds. Boomers have long been famous for their desire to stay or at least act young. What will they be like as seniors? Many predict they will reshape the nation's view of old age, as healthier boomers continue to work and stay active longer than their parents. Others worry that the vast expansion of the nation's senior population will put unaffordable strains on government entitlement programs like Social Security and Medicare. Still others worry boomers could upset the economy as they begin spending down their assets all at once. Boomers have left their imprint on every stage of American life they've passed through, and there's no reason to think that the senior years will be any exception.

Race and Politics: Will Skin Color Influence the Presidential Election?

The once unthinkable could happen this November: A black man may win the presidency. When freshman Illinois Sen. Barack Obama was born in 1961, African-Americans couldn't vote in parts of the United States. Now, as Obama prepares to accept the Democratic nomination in August, he is running slightly ahead of his presumptive Republican opponent, Arizona Sen. John McCain, a 71-year-old Vietnam War hero. First dogged by questions of whether he was "black enough," Obama now faces doubts about whether racial prejudice will prove a major obstacle to his historic campaign, especially among white working-class voters. Nonetheless, Obama is likely to benefit from changes in the country's demographic makeup, which is growing less white as immigration diversifies. At the same time, younger voters are showing notably less racial prejudice than older generations. Meanwhile, some top Republicans acknowledge the GOP needs to appeal to a broader range of voters if McCain is to win.

The Obama Presidency: Can Barack Obama Deliver the Change He Promises?

As the 44th president of the United States, Barack Hussein Obama confronts a set of challenges more daunting perhaps than any chief executive has faced since the Great Depression and World War II. At home, the nation is in the second year of a recession that Obama warns may get worse before the economy starts to improve. Abroad, he faces the task of withdrawing U.S. forces from Iraq, reversing the deteriorating conditions in Afghanistan and trying to ease the Israeli-Palestinian conflict. Still, Obama begins his four years in office with the biggest winning percentage of any president in 20 years and a strong Democratic majority in both houses of Congress. In addition, as the first African-American president, Obama starts with a reservoir of goodwill from Americans and people and governments around the world. But he began encountering criticism and opposition from Republicans in his first days in office as he filled in the details of his campaign theme: "Change We Can Believe In."

Preface

Keeping students up to date on timely policy issues can be challenging given the range of issues, changing administrations and the volatile political economy. Furthermore, finding readings that are student friendly, accessible and current can be an even greater challenge. Now *CQ Researcher,* CQ Press and SAGE have teamed up to provide a unique selection of articles focused on social policy, specifically for courses in Social Welfare Policy and Social Policy. This collection aims to promote in-depth discussion, facilitate further research and help students formulate their own positions on crucial issues.

This first edition includes seventeen up-to-date reports by *CQ Researcher,* an award-winning weekly policy brief that brings complicated issues down to earth. Each report chronicles and analyzes executive, legislative and judicial activities at all levels of government. This collection was carefully crafted to cover a range of issues from the mortgage crisis, to women's rights, child welfare reform, aging baby boomers, the Obama Presidency and much more. All in all, this reader will help your students become better versed on current policy issues and gain a deeper, more critical perspective of timely and important issues.

CQ RESEARCHER

CQ Researcher was founded in 1923 as *Editorial Research Reports* and was sold primarily to newspapers as a research tool. The magazine was renamed and redesigned in 1991 as *CQ Researcher.* Today, students are its primary audience. While still used by hundreds of journalists and newspapers, many of which reprint portions of the reports, the *Researcher's* main subscribers are now high school, college and public libraries. In 2002, *Researcher* won the American Bar Association's coveted Silver Gavel award for magazine excellence for a series of nine reports on civil liberties and other legal issues.

Researcher staff writers—all highly experienced journalists—sometimes compare the experience of writing a *Researcher* report to drafting a college term paper. Indeed, there are many similarities. Each report is as long as many term papers—about 11,000 words—and is written by one person without any significant outside help. One of the key differences is that writers interview leading experts, scholars and government officials for each issue.

Like students, staff writers begin the creative process by choosing a topic. Working with the *Researcher's* editors, the writer identifies a controversial subject that has important public policy implications. After a topic is selected, the writer embarks on one to two weeks of intense research. Newspaper and magazine articles are clipped or downloaded, books are ordered and information is gathered from a wide variety of sources, including interest groups, universities and the government. Once the writers are well informed, they develop a detailed outline, and begin the interview process. Each report requires a minimum of ten to fifteen interviews with academics, officials, lobbyists and people working in the field. Only after all interviews are completed does the writing begin.

CHAPTER FORMAT

Each issue of *CQ Researcher,* and therefore each selection in this book, is structured in the same way. Each begins with an overview, which briefly summarizes the areas that will be explored in greater detail in the rest of the chapter. The next section chronicles important and current debates on the topic under discussion and is structured around a number of key questions, such as "Does corporate social responsibility really improve society?" or "Does corporate social responsibility restrain U.S. productivity?" These questions are usually the subject of much debate among practitioners and scholars in the field. Hence, the answers presented are never conclusive but detail the range of opinion on the topic.

Next, the "Background" section provides a history of the issue being examined. This retrospective covers

important legislative measures, executive actions and court decisions that illustrate how current policy has evolved. Then the "Current Situation" section examines contemporary policy issues, legislation under consideration and legal action being taken. Each selection concludes with an "Outlook" section, which addresses possible regulation, court rulings and initiatives from Capitol Hill and the White House over the next five to ten years.

Each report contains features that augment the main text: two to three sidebars that examine issues related to the topic at hand, a pro versus con debate between two experts, a chronology of key dates and events and an annotated bibliography detailing major sources used by the writer.

ACKNOWLEDGMENTS

We wish to thank many people for helping to make this collection a reality. Tom Colin, managing editor of *CQ Researcher,* gave us his enthusiastic support and cooperation as we developed this edition. He and his talented staff of editors and writers have amassed a first-class library of *Researcher* reports, and we are fortunate to have access to that rich cache. We also wish to thank our colleagues at CQ Press, a division of SAGE and a leading publisher of books, directories, research publications and Web products on U.S. government, world affairs and communications. They have forged the way in making these readers a useful resource for instruction across a range of undergraduate and graduate courses.

Some readers may be learning about *CQ Researcher* for the first time. We expect that many readers will want regular access to this excellent weekly research tool. For subscription information or a no-obligation free trial of *CQ Researcher,* please contact CQ Press at www.cqpress .com or toll-free at 1-866-4CQ-PRESS (1-866-427-7737).

We hope that you will be pleased by this edition of *Issues for Debate in Social Policy.* We welcome your feedback and suggestions for future editions. Please direct comments to Kassie Graves, Acquisitions Editor, SAGE Publications, 2455 Teller Road, Thousand Oaks, CA 91320, or kassie.graves@sagepub.com.

—The Editors of SAGE

Contributors

Thomas J. Billitteri is a *CQ Researcher* staff writer based in Fairfield, Pa., who has more than 30 years' experience covering business, nonprofit institutions and public policy for newspapers and other publications. His recent *CQ Researcher* reports include "Campaign Finance," "Human Rights in China" and "Financial Bailout." He holds a BA in English and an MA in journalism from Indiana University.

Marcia Clemmitt is a veteran social-policy reporter who previously served as editor in chief of *Medicine & Health* and staff writer for *The Scientist.* She has also been a high-school math and physics teacher. She holds a liberal arts and sciences degree from St. John's College, Annapolis, and a master's degree in English from Georgetown University. Her recent reports include "Climate Change," "Health Care Costs," "Cyber Socializing" and "Prison Health Care."

Mary H. Cooper specializes in defense, energy and environmental issues. Before joining the *CQ Researcher* as a staff writer in 1983, she was Washington correspondent for the Rome daily newspaper *l'Unità.* She is the author of *The Business of Drugs* (CQ Press, 1990) and holds a B.A. in English from Hollins College in Virginia. Her recent reports include "Smart Growth," "Exporting Jobs," "Weapons of Mass Destruction" and "Bush and the Environment."

Karen Foerstel is a freelance writer who has worked for the *Congressional Quarterly Weekly Report* and *Daily Monitor, The New York Post* and *Roll Call,* a Capitol Hill newspaper. She has published two books on women in Congress, *Climbing the Hill: Gender*

Conflict in Congress and *The Biographical Dictionary of Women in Congress.* Her most recent *CQ Global Researcher* report was "China in Africa." She has worked in Africa with ChildsLife International, a nonprofit that helps needy children around the world, and with Blue Ventures, a marine conservation organization that protects coral reefs in Madagascar.

Sarah Glazer is a New York freelancer who specializes in health, education and social-policy issues. Her articles have appeared in *The Washington Post, Glamour, The Public Interest* and *Gender and Work,* a book of essays. Glazer covered energy legislation for the Environmental and Energy Study Conference and reported for United Press International. Her recent reports include "Cell Phone Safety" and "Faith-Based Initiatives." She graduated from the University of Chicago with a BA in American history.

Alan Greenblatt is a staff writer at *Governing* magazine. He previously covered elections, agriculture and military spending for *CQ Weekly,* where he won the National Press Club's Sandy Hume Award for political journalism. He graduated from San Francisco State University in 1986 and received a master's degree in English literature from the University of Virginia in 1988. His recent *CQ Researcher* reports include "Sex Offenders" and "Pension Crisis."

Kenneth Jost is a graduate of Harvard College and Georgetown University Law Center. He is the author of the *Supreme Court Yearbook* and editor of *The Supreme Court from A to Z* (both CQ Press). His previous reports include "Electing the President," "Presidential Power" and "The Bush Presidency."

Peter Katel is a *CQ Researcher* staff writer who previously reported on Haiti and Latin America for *Time* and

Newsweek and covered the Southwest for newspapers in New Mexico. He has received several journalism awards, including the Bartolomé Mitre Award for coverage of drug trafficking, from the Inter-American Press Association. He holds an AB in university studies from the University of New Mexico. His recent reports include "Mexico's Drug War" and "Future of the Military."

Kathy Koch—assistant managing editor of the *CQ Researcher* and managing editor of the *CQ Global Researcher*—previously covered environmental legislation for *CQ Weekly* and has reported for newspapers in South Florida. She also has freelanced extensively in Asia and Africa for various U.S. newspapers, including *The Christian Science Monitor* and *USA Today.* She graduated in journalism from the University of North Carolina at Chapel Hill.

Tom Price is a Washington-based freelance journalist who writes regularly for the *CQ Researcher.* Previously he was a correspondent in the Cox Newspapers Washington Bureau and chief politics writer for the *Dayton Daily News* and *The Journal Herald.* He is the author of two Washington guidebooks, *Washington, D.C., for Dummies,* and the *Irreverent Guide to Washington, D.C.* His work has appeared in *The New York Times, Time, Rolling Stone* and other periodicals. He earned a BS in journalism at Ohio University.

William Triplett recently joined the *CQ Researcher* as a staff writer after covering science and the arts for such publications as *Smithsonian, Air & Space, Nature, Washingtonian* and *The Washington Post.* He also served as associate editor of *Capitol Style* magazine. He holds a BA in journalism from Ohio University and an MA in English literature from Georgetown University.

Middle-Class Squeeze

Is More Government Aid Needed?

Thomas J. Billitteri

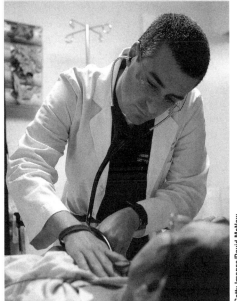

Affordable health care for all Americans is a key element of the budget recently announced by President Barack Obama, along with other policies aimed squarely at helping the middle class. Nearly half of home foreclosures in 2006 were caused, at least partly, by financial issues stemming from a medical problem, according to the advocacy group Families USA. Above, emergency room physician Jason Greenspan cares for a patient in Panorama City, Calif.

From *CQ Researcher*,
March 6, 2009.

Cindy Dreeszen, 41, and her husband may have seemed like unlikely visitors to the Interfaith food pantry last month in affluent Morris County, N.J., 25 miles from New York City. Both have steady jobs and a combined income of about $55,000 a year. But with "the cost of everything going up and up" and a second baby due, the couple was looking for free groceries.

"I didn't think we'd even be allowed to come here," Ms. Dreeszen told *The New York Times*. "This is totally something that I never expected to happen, to have to resort to this."[1]

Countless middle-class Americans are thinking similar thoughts these days as they ponder their suddenly fragile futures.

Millions of families who once enjoyed the American dream of upward mobility and financial security are sliding rapidly down the economic ladder — some into poverty. Many are losing their homes along with their jobs, and telling their children to rethink college.[2] And while today's economic crisis has made life for middle-class households worse, the problems aren't new. Pressure on the middle-class has been building for years and is likely to persist long after the current recession — now 14 months old — is over.

The middle class "is in crisis and decline," says sociologist Kevin Leicht, director of the Institute for Inequality Studies at the University of Iowa.

"Between wages that have been stagnant [in inflation-adjusted terms] since the middle of the 1970s and government policies that are weighted exclusively in the direction of the wealthy, the only thing that has been holding up most of the American middle class is access to cheap and easy credit."

No official definition of the "middle class" exists. (*See sidebar, p. 12.*) But most Americans — except perhaps the very richest and poorest — consider themselves in that broad category, a fact not lost on Washington policy makers.

Indeed, President Barack Obama announced a 10-year budget on Feb. 28 that takes direct aim at the challenges facing America's middle class and the growing concentration of wealth at the top of the income scale.[3] Key elements of the plan include shifting more costs to the wealthiest Americans and overhauling health care to make it more affordable.[4]

In further recognition of the importance of the middle-class, Obama has named Vice President Joseph R. Biden to chair a new White House Task Force on Middle Class Working Families. It will examine everything from access to college and child- and elder-care issues to business development and the role of labor unions in the economy.[5]

Vice President Joseph Biden, chair of the new White House Task Force on Middle Class Working Families, listens to a presentation on creating "green" jobs at the University of Pennsylvania on Feb. 27, 2009. President Obama directed the panel to examine issues such as access to college, business development and the role of labor unions in the economy.

"Talking about the middle class is the closest that American politicians and maybe Americans are willing to go to emphasize the fact that we have growing inequality in this country," says Jacob Hacker, a political scientist at the University of California, Berkeley, and a leading social-policy expert. "A very small proportion of the population is getting fabulously rich, and the rest of Americans are getting modestly richer or not much richer at all."

What's at stake goes far beyond economics and family finances, though, experts say. "A large middle class, especially one that is politically active, tends to be a kind of anchor that keeps your country from swinging back and forth," says sociologist Teresa Sullivan, provost and executive vice president for academic affairs at the University of Michigan and co-author of *The Fragile Middle Class: Americans in Debt.* What's more, she says, "there are typical values that middle-class families acquire and pass on to their children," and those values "tend to be very good for democracy."

Right now, though, the middle class is under threat.

In a study of middle-class households, Demos, a liberal think tank in New York, estimated that 4 million families lost their financial security between 2000 and 2006, raising the total to 23 million. Driving the increase, Demos said, were declines in financial assets, then-rising housing costs and a growing lack of health insurance.[6]

"In America the middle class has been a lifestyle, a certain way of life," says Jennifer Wheary, a co-author of the study. "It's been about being able to have a very moderate existence where you could do things like save for your retirement, put your kids through school, get sick and not worry about getting basic care. And those kinds of things are really imperiled right now."

In another study, the Pew Research Center found this year that "fewer Americans now than at any time in the past half-century believe they're moving forward in life."[7]

Among the findings:

• Nearly two-thirds of Americans said their standard of living was higher than that of their parents at the same age, but more than half said they'd either made no progress in life over the past five years or had fallen backward.

• Median household income rose 41 percent since 1970, but upper-income households outperformed those in the middle tier in both income gains and wealth accumulation. The median net worth of upper-income families rose 123 percent from 1983 to 2004, compared with 29 percent for middle-income families.

• Almost eight in 10 respondents said it was more difficult now for those in the middle class to maintain their standard of living compared with five years ago. In 1986, 65 percent felt that way.

Lane Kenworthy, a sociology and political science professor at the University of Arizona who studies income inequality and poverty, says "the key thing that's happened" to the middle class over the past three decades "is slow income growth compared to general economic growth." Moreover, Kenworthy says a bigger and bigger portion of economic growth has accrued to the wealthiest 1 percent, whether the measure is basic wages or total compensation, which includes the value of employee-sponsored and government benefits.

Even the economic boom leading up to today's recession has proved illusory, new Federal Reserve data show. While median household net worth — assets minus debt — rose nearly 18 percent in the three years ending in late 2007, the increase vanished amid last year's drastic declines in home and stock prices, according to the Fed's triennial "Survey of Consumer Finances." "Adjusting for those declines, Fed officials estimated that the median family was 3.2 percent poorer as of October 2008 than it was at the end of 2004," *The New York Times* noted.[8]

A hallmark of middle-class insecurity reflects what Hacker calls "the great risk shift" — the notion that government and business have transferred the burden of providing affordable health care, income security and retirement saving onto the shoulders of working Americans, leaving them financially stretched and vulnerable to economic catastrophe.

"Over the last generation, we have witnessed a massive transfer of economic risk from broad structures of

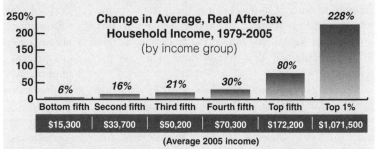

Income Gap Getting Wider

The gap between the wealthiest Americans and everybody else grew to its widest point since at least 1979.* The top 1 percent of households received 70 times as much in average after-tax income as the bottom one-fifth and 21 times as much as the middle one-fifth — in both cases the widest gaps on record. From 1979-2005, the top 1 percent saw its income rise 228 percent compared to a rise of only 21 percent for the middle one-fifth of Americans.

Change in Average, Real After-tax Household Income, 1979-2005
(by income group)

	Bottom fifth	Second fifth	Third fifth	Fourth fifth	Top fifth	Top 1%
Change	6%	16%	21%	30%	80%	228%
Average 2005 income	$15,300	$33,700	$50,200	$70,300	$172,200	$1,071,500

* Data go back only to 1979.

Source: Arloc Sherman, "Income Inequality Hits Record Levels, New CBO Data Show," Center on Budget and Policy Priorities, December 2007

insurance, including those sponsored by the corporate sector as well as by government, onto the fragile balance sheets of American families," Hacker wrote. "This transformation . . . is the defining feature of the contemporary American economy — as important as the shift from agriculture to industry a century ago."[9]

The challenge of solving the problems facing the American middle class will confront policy makers for years to come. Some experts say the key is growth in good jobs — those with good pay, good benefits and good, secure futures. Others argue that solving the nation's health-care crisis is the paramount issue.

One thing is certain, experts say: Leaving the fate of the American middle class to chance is not an option.

"We're believers in hard work, and we're increasingly in a situation where the difference between whether or not a middle-class family prospers comes down to luck, says Amelia Warren Tyagi, co-author of *The Two-Income Trap: Why Middle-Class Mothers and Fathers Are Going Broke.* "And that's an idea that makes us really uncomfortable."

Here are some of the questions that policy makers and average Americans are asking about the middle class:

Is a stable middle class a thing of the past?

First lady Michelle Obama remembers what some call the good old days of middle-class security.

"I am always amazed," she told a gathering, "at how different things are now for working women and families than when I was growing up. . . . When I was growing up, my father — as you know, a blue-collar worker — was able to go to work and earn enough money to support a family of four, while my mom stayed home with me and my brother. But today, living with one income, like we did, just doesn't cut it. People can't do it — particularly if it's a shift-worker's salary like my father's."[10]

Brookings Institution researchers noted in 2007 that two-thirds of American adults had higher family incomes than their parents did in the late 1960s and early '70s, but a third were worse off. Moreover, they pointed out, the intergenerational gains largely stemmed from dual paychecks in families.[11]

"Men's earnings have grown little, if at all," while those of women "have risen along with their greater involvement in the work world," they said. "So, yes, today's families are better off than their own parents were. . . . But they are also working more and struggling with the greater time pressures of juggling work and family responsibilities."[12]

At the same time, many economists say the earnings of middle-class working families have not kept pace with gains by the wealthy. They point to Congressional Budget Office data showing that from 1979 through 2005, the average after-tax income of the top 1 percent rose 228 percent, compared with 21 percent for the middle fifth of the population. For the poorest fifth, the increase during the 25-year period was just 6 percent.[13]

Emmanuel Saez, an economist at the University of California, Berkeley, concluded last year that those in the top 1 percent of income distribution captured roughly half of the overall economic growth from 1993 to 2006, and almost three-fourths of income growth in the 2002-2006 period.[14]

"It's the very top of the economic ladder that's pulled away from the rest," Berkeley political scientist Hacker says. "Depending on which source you look at, it's the top 1 percent, or the top one-half of 1 percent, or the top one-tenth of 1 percent that's really received the lion's share of the gain in our economy overall. . . . It would be one thing if we saw middle-class Americans hold onto or even expand their wealth and economic security. But they're more in debt and less secure than they were 20 years ago."

The reasons the middle class is running in place or falling behind can be elusive, though. Kenworthy of the University of Arizona cites a litany of factors — technological changes in the workplace, globalization of trade and the outsourcing of jobs overseas, declining influence of labor unions, slow growth in the proportion of workers with at least a high-school diploma and a stagnant minimum wage — that have helped dampen the economic progress of the middle class. But, he says, social scientists and economists don't have a "good handle on which matter most."[15]

John Schmitt, senior economist at the Center for Economic and Policy Research, a liberal think tank, disputes the notion that technology and globalization are immutable forces

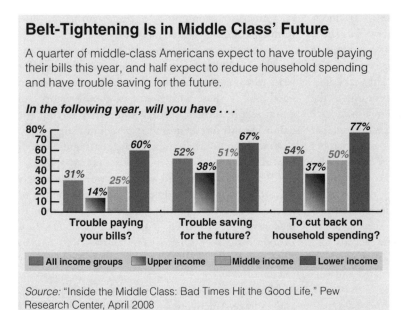

Belt-Tightening Is in Middle Class' Future

A quarter of middle-class Americans expect to have trouble paying their bills this year, and half expect to reduce household spending and have trouble saving for the future.

In the following year, will you have . . .

Trouble paying your bills? — All income groups 31%, Upper income 14%, Middle income 25%, Lower income 60%

Trouble saving for the future? — All income groups 52%, Upper income 38%, Middle income 51%, Lower income 67%

To cut back on household spending? — All income groups 54%, Upper income 37%, Middle income 50%, Lower income 77%

■ All income groups ■ Upper income ■ Middle income ■ Lower income

Source: "Inside the Middle Class: Bad Times Hit the Good Life," Pew Research Center, April 2008

that have, in themselves, hurt the middle class. "We've had technological growth at a rapid pace in the United States from the early 1800s," he says, and after World War II the country saw "massive technological innovation," including the introduction of computers.

Those "were huge, potentially disruptive innovations, but we had a social structure that had a lot of protections and guarantees for workers," including "a decent minimum wage, significant union representation" and a strong regulatory framework.

"The real story is that we've made a lot of decisions about economic policy that have had the effect of shifting the playing field toward employers and away from workers at a whole lot of levels," Schmitt says.

As that shift occurred, job security has suffered, many economists say.

In a recent study, Schmitt found that the share of "good jobs" — those paying at least $17 per hour and offering health insurance and a pension — declined 2.3 percentage points in the 2000-2006 business cycle, far more than in comparable periods in the 1980s and '90s. A "sharp deterioration" in employer-provided health plans was a "driving force" in the decline of good jobs, which was most pronounced among male workers, he found.[16]

Meanwhile, career employment — employment with a single employer from middle age to retirement — is no longer the norm, according to researchers at Boston College. Only half of full-time workers ages 58 to 62 are still with the same employer for whom they worked at age 50, they found.[17]

And manufacturing — long a bedrock of middle-class lifestyles — has shrunk from about a third of non-farm employment to only 10 percent since 1950.[18]

Still, interpretations of income and other economic data can vary widely among economists, depending on their political viewpoint. While not diminishing the severe pressures many in the middle class are feeling right now, some conservative economists have a more optimistic view of the jobs issue and long-term middle-class gains in general.

In a study last year, James Sherk, Bradley Fellow in Labor Policy at the Heritage Foundation, challenged the notions "that the era of good jobs is slipping away" and that workers' benefits are disappearing.[19]

"Throughout the economy, jobs paying high wages in fields requiring more education are more available today than they were a generation ago, while low-wage, low-skill jobs are decreasing," he wrote. And, he added, "employer-provided health insurance and pensions are as available now as they were in the mid-1990s. Worker pension plans have improved significantly, with most employers shifting to defined-contribution pensions that provide workers with more money for retirement and do not penalize them for switching jobs."

In an interview, Sherk said that while many middle-class families are struggling today, over the long term they have not, on average, fallen behind overall growth in the economy. Average earnings have risen in step with productivity, he said.

But others are not sanguine about the status of the middle class, long-term or otherwise.

"For quite some time, we've had a sizable minority of the middle class under enormous strain and on the verge of crisis, and since the recent meltdown the proportion of middle-class families in crisis increased exponentially," says Tyagi, who co-authored *The Two-Income Trap* with her mother, Harvard law Professor Elizabeth Warren, chair of a congressional panel overseeing last fall's $700 billion financial bailout. "Many families teetering on the uncomfortable edge have been pushed over."

Is overconsumption at the root of the middle class' problems?

In a recent article about the collapse of the Florida real estate market, *New Yorker* writer George Packer quotes a woman in Cape Coral who, with her husband, had built a home on modest incomes, borrowed against its value, spent some of the money on vacations and cruises, and then faced foreclosure after her husband was laid off.

"I'm not saying what we did was perfect," the woman said. "We spent our money and didn't save it. But we had it, and we didn't see that this was going to happen."[20]

Such vignettes are commonplace these days as the economy plummets and home foreclosures soar. So, too, is the view that many middle-class consumers brought trouble to their own doorsteps by overconsuming and failing to save.

Thomas H. Naylor, a professor emeritus of economics at Duke University and co-author of *Affluenza: The All-Consuming Epidemic*, says the vulnerability of the

Being Middle Class Takes More Income

The minimum income needed for a three-person household to be considered in the middle class was about 40 percent higher in 2006 than in 1969.

Economic Definition of Middle-class Household of Three
(in constant January 2008 dollars)

Year	Income
1969	$31,755 to $63,509
1979	$37,356 to $74,712
1989	$41,386 to $82,771
1999	$45,920 to $91,841
2006	$44,620 to $89,241

Source: "Inside the Middle Class: Bad Times Hit the Good Life," Pew Research Center, April 2008

middle class has been "enhanced by [its] behavior." He blames both consumer excess and the influence of advertising and media.

"On the one hand, consumers have done it to themselves. They've made choices to spend the money," Naylor says. "On the other hand, they've had lots of encouragement and stimulation from corporate America. The big guns are aimed at them, and it's very difficult to resist the temptation."

Pointing to the Federal Reserve's recent "Survey of Consumer Finances," Nobel laureate and *New York Times* economic columnist Paul Krugman wrote that the fact that "the net worth of the average American household, adjusted for inflation, is lower now than it was in 2001" should, at one level, "come as no surprise.

"For most of the last decade America was a nation of borrowers and spenders, not savers. The personal savings rate dropped from 9 percent in the 1980s to 5 percent in the 1990s, to just 0.6 percent from 2005 to 2007, and

household debt grew much faster than personal income. Why should we have expected net worth to go up?"

But, Krugman went on to say, until recently Americans thought they were getting wealthier, basing their belief on statements saying their homes and stock portfolios were appreciating faster than the growth of their debts.[21]

In fact, many economists say the picture of consumer behavior and household savings is far more complex than simple theories of overconsumption suggest.

President Obama weighed in at a press conference in early February, saying, "I don't think it's accurate to say that consumer spending got us into this mess." But he added that "our savings rate has declined, and this economy has been driven by consumer spending for a very long time. And that's not going to be sustainable."

Schmitt, of the Center for Economic and Policy Research, contends that what has hurt the middle class the most are steep cost increases of necessities, not spending on luxuries. "There's a lot of argument about overconsumption, but my argument is that consumption of basic necessities is not subject to big price savings," he says. "Housing, education, health care — those are much more expensive than they used to be. That's where people are feeling the pinch."

Housing prices doubled between the mid-1990s and 2007.[22] Average tuition, fees and room-and-board charges at private four-year institutions have more than doubled since 1978-79, to $34,132.[23] And growth in national health expenditures has outpaced gross national product (GNP) growth every year at least since the late 1990s.[24]

One study found that among adults earning $40,000 to $60,000, the proportion of adults spending 10 percent or more of their income on health care doubled between 2001 and 2007, from 18 percent to 36 percent.[25]

"Health care is the epicenter of economic security in the United States today," says Hacker, the University of California political scientist. "It's not the only thing impinging on families finances, but it's one of the areas where the need is greatest."

Economist Robert H. Frank, author of *Falling Behind: How Rising Inequality Harms the Middle Class*, argues that as the wealthiest Americans have acquired bigger and more expensive houses and luxury possessions, their behavior has raised the bar for middle-class consumers, leading them to spend more and more of their incomes on bigger houses and upscale goods.

While some of the spending may be frivolous, he says, many consumers have felt compelled to keep up with rising economic and cultural standards — and often for practical reasons: Bigger, more expensive homes typically are in neighborhoods with the best schools, and upscale clothing has become the norm for those who want to dress for success.

"There are people you could say have brought this on themselves," Frank says of the troubles middle-class families are now facing. "If you've charged a bunch of credit cards to the max [for things] that aren't really essential, is that your fault? You bet. But most of it I don't think is. You need a decent suit to go for a job interview. You can buy the cheap suit, but you won't get the call-back. You can break the rules at any turn, but there's a price for that."

In their book on two-income middle-class families, Tyagi and Warren attacked the "rock-solid" myth that "middle-class families are rushing headlong into financial ruin because they are squandering too much money on Red Lobster, Gucci and trips to the Bahamas."[26]

In fact, they wrote, after studying consumer bankruptcy data and other sources, "Today, after an average two-income family makes its house payments, car payments, insurance payments and child-care payments, they have less money left over, even though they have a second, full-time earner in the workplace," than an average single-earner family did in the early 1970s.[27]

One-paycheck households headed by women are among the most vulnerable. In an analysis of 2004 Federal Reserve Board data, the Consumer Federation of America found that the 31 million women who head households had median household income of $22,592, compared with $43,130 for all households. And women on their own had a median net worth of less than $33,000 compared with about $93,000 for all households.[28]

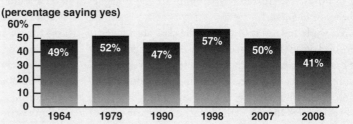

Fewer Americans Say They Are Better Off

The percentage of Americans who said they were better off in 2008 than they were five years earlier dropped to 41 percent in 2008, the lowest confidence level since 1964.

Are you better off now than you were five years ago?

(percentage saying yes)

Year	1964	1979	1990	1998	2007	2008
%	49%	52%	47%	57%	50%	41%

Source: "Inside the Middle Class: Bad Times Hit the Good Life," Pew Research Center, April 2008

Are aggressive new government programs needed to bolster the middle class?

Last year, former Republican Rep. Ernest Istook of Oklahoma criticized then-presidential candidates Hillary Clinton and Obama for arguing that "America is a place where the middle class is repressed" by rising income inequality, stagnating wages, soaring medical and college costs and other woes.

"For both candidates," wrote Istook, a Heritage Foundation fellow, "the answer to all these problems is a rush of new government programs." He pointed to Heritage Foundation studies arguing that wage-growth data have been understated and that the poor are doing better than they were 14 years earlier.

"Convincing Americans that they need government to do all these things," he wrote, "hinges on convincing them that they are victims in need of rescue. . . . It's not enough for America's left to show sympathy for victims of real tragedies like 9/11 or Katrina. Now they must elevate every challenge into a crisis, provoking a sense of desperation that more and bigger government is the answer."[29]

Yet that is not how many policy advocates view the question of government help for the middle class. The pressures weighing on working families — heightened by the current economic crisis — are so great, they argue, that bold government action is needed to keep working Americans from further economic harm.

"We talk about the big financial institutions as too big to fail," says University of California political scientist Hacker. "But most Americans have until recently been apparently viewed as too small to save."

Without policy changes, including ones that make education and health care more affordable and help people build assets, "instability is going to stay," argues Wheary of Demos.

Yet, while the needs of the middle class are a favorite rhetorical device for politicians, they often disagree about the best way to advance those interests. This year's $787 billion stimulus package, which emerged from a cauldron of partisan bickering, is a case in point.

President Obama, speaking to employees of Caterpillar Inc. in February, said the stimulus plan is "about giving people a way to make a living, support their families and live out their dreams. Americans aren't looking for a handout. They just want to work."[30] But Rep. John A. Boehner of Ohio, a key Republican opponent of the president's recovery plan, said it "will do little to create jobs, and will do more harm than good to middle-class families and our economy."[31]

An overhaul of health-care policy is a key priority for many policy experts. Families USA, an advocacy group supporting affordable health care, pointed to research showing that nearly half of home foreclosures in 2006 were caused, at least partly, by financial issues growing out of a medical problem.[32]

Also key, many liberal policy analysts say, is solving what they see as a growing pension crisis, made more perilous for middle-class workers by the Wall Street crash. (*See sidebar, p. 14.*) Rep. George Miller, D-Calif., chairman of the House Education and Labor Committee, says private retirement-savings vehicles like 401(k) plans "have become little more than a high-stakes crap shoot. If you didn't take your retirement savings out of the market before the crash, you are likely to take years to recoup your losses, if at all."[33]

And crucial to the future of the middle class, many experts say, are sound policies for job creation and retention.

"The major policy change we need is to decide that good steady jobs with good wages are a family value," says Leicht of the University of Iowa. "It's good jobs at good wages that last — that's the Rosetta Stone."

Leicht says "our entire system of consumption is built around the idea that you accumulate a lot of debts when you're young, then you get a steady job and your income steadily rises and you gradually pay off your debt as you age." But nowadays, he says, the average job lasts only four to five years. "If you're constantly starting over, you never get out of the hole."

Leicht wants to see a 25 percent break on corporate taxes for businesses that create "high-quality jobs" — ones lasting at least five years and paying at least 30 percent above the median income of a family of four, which in 2007 was $75,675, according to the U.S. Census Bureau.

Kenworthy, the University of Arizona sociologist, advocates temporary "wage insurance" that would "prop up your earnings for a little while if you lost your job and took a new one that paid considerably less."

Not counting the current economic crisis, Kenworthy says, "there really isn't a problem in the United States with long-term unemployment. Most people are able to get a job within six months." Even so, he adds, such jobs often come "at a lower salary."

BACKGROUND

Evolving Concept

During the 2008 presidential campaign, the Rev. Rick Warren, pastor of giant Saddleback Church in Lake Forest, Calif., asked Democrat Obama and Republican John McCain to define "rich."

Obama said that "if you are making $150,000 a year or less as a family, then you're middle class, or you may be poor. But $150 [thousand] down you're basically middle class." He added, though, that "obviously, it depends on [the] region and where you're living." McCain answered the question another way, saying — perhaps with tongue in cheek — that as a definition of rich, "if you're just talking about income, how about $5 million?"[34]

Besides helping to open a window on the candidates' views and personalities, the exchange underscored how highly subjective social and economic class can be.

That's nothing new. For centuries, the concept of a "middle class" has been evolving.

"The middle class first came into existence in early modern Europe as a new social class for which the economic basis was financial rather than feudal — the system in which the nobility owned land and others (serfs, peons) worked it," according to Andrew Hoberek, an associate professor of English at the University of Missouri, Columbia, and author of *The Twilight of the Middle Class: Post World War II American Fiction and White-Collar Work.*[35]

In the United States, the term "middle class" didn't start showing up until the 1830s or 1840s, says Jennifer L. Goloboy, an independent scholar.[36] But years earlier, she says, a segment of the population began to embrace values that would come to define the American middle class, including diligence, frugality, self-restraint and optimism.

"The early republic was such an aspirational time, and it was disproportionately young," Goloboy says. "These young people came to the cities hoping for the best, and they clung to ideas of how they would make it. That's sort of the root of middle-class values. They believed that if they held to these values they were middle class, even if they were not necessarily successful yet."

As the American economy matured in the 20th century, industrialization both nurtured and threatened the nation's budding middle class. Pioneering automaker Henry Ford helped nurture it by paying high wages and encouraging mass consumption of his cars. But the gap between rich and poor remained wide, and industrialization made life precarious for the working class when jobs disappeared.

"The paramount evil in the workingman's life is irregularity of employment," Supreme Court Justice Louis D. Brandeis wrote in 1911.[37] Historian David Kennedy noted that Brandeis' view "was echoed in Robert and Helen Merrell Lynd's classic study *Middletown* a decade later, when they cited 'irregularity of employment' as the major factor that defined the difference between the life trajectories of the working class and the middle class."[38]

During the Great Depression of the 1930s, unemployment soared to 25 percent, and many Americans fell from middle-class stability into destitution. But from the ashes of the Depression came President Franklin D. Roosevelt's New Deal program, which *New York Times* columnist Krugman says created the modern middle class.[39]

"Income inequality declined drastically from the late 1930s to the mid-1940s, with the rich losing ground while working Americans saw unprecedented gains," he wrote.[40]

Consumerism at Its Finest

Some economists say the higher cost of necessities like health care, rather than spending on luxury items like big-screen TVs or new cars, has hit consumers hardest. Moreover, Americans' personal savings rate from 2005 to 2007 was just 0.6 percent — down from 9 percent in the 1980s — with household debt growing faster than personal income.

The New Deal "made America a middle-class society," Krugman wrote this year in *Rolling Stone* magazine. "Under FDR, America went through what labor historians call the Great Compression, a dramatic rise in wages for ordinary workers that greatly reduced income inequality. Before the Great Compression, America was a society of rich and poor; afterward it was a society in which most people, rightly, considered themselves middle class."[41]

After World War II, the U.S. economy blossomed, aided by the GI Bill, which helped millions of former service members buy homes and get college educations. In 1946, construction began on Levittown, one of a series of massive housing developments that became national models of middle-class suburbia.

The postwar boom helped spawn the contemporary notion of the American Dream — a home, a car or two (or three), a good job, paid vacation and a comfortable suburban lifestyle. By 1960, median family income was 30 percent higher in purchasing power than a decade earlier, and more than 60 percent of homes were owner-occupied, compared with 44 percent just before World War II.[42]

Downward Slide

But many economists say the good times began to wane in the 1970s, and for a variety of reasons that can be difficult to untangle. The shift away from manufacturing toward a service economy helped erode middle-class security, as did the increasingly competitive nature of globalization, many economists say. Some also cite the declining power of unions. In 1979, 27 percent of employed wage-and-salary workers in the United States were covered by a collective bargaining agreement, but that figure has steadily declined over the years. It stood at less than 14 percent in 2008.[43]

In remarks tied to formation of his middle-class task force, Obama said, "I do not view the labor movement as part of the problem; to me it's part of the solution. We need to level the playing field for workers and the unions that represent their interest, because we know that you cannot have a strong middle class without a strong labor movement."[44]

Hacker, the University of California political scientist, says that "employers at one time were encouraged by unions, the federal tax code and their own competitive instincts to provide very strong guaranteed benefits to many of their workers in the form of defined-benefit pension plans [and] good health insurance coverage."

But, he says, "over the last generation the work force has changed, and the competitive environment in which employers have operated changed in ways that have made it much less attractive for many employers to provide such

benefits. There used to be a kind of implicit long-term contract in many workplaces, enforced in part by unions, that is no longer there. So it's much more of a free-agent economic culture, which means that it's good for some workers but imposes a lot more risk on all of them."

Many conservatives disagree, though, on the role of unions in helping the middle class. "Numerous studies have shown that unions are not the answer to increasing prosperity for American workers or the economy," the U.S. Chamber of Commerce stated in a paper on the issue. It added: "Organized labor's claims that unionization is a ticket to the middle class cannot be squared with data showing that increased unionization decreases competitiveness and leads to slower job growth."[45]

Besides the issue of union influence, critics often cite Reagan-era economic policies, which included cuts in tax rates for those in upper-income brackets, as contributing to inequality and hurting the middle class.

The criticism is not universal. George Viksnins, a professor emeritus of economics at Georgetown University, argues that so-called Reaganomics was a plus for the middle class. "Perhaps the most significant positive aspect of the Reaganomics program of lower taxes and regulatory reforms is the tremendous increase in employment," he wrote.[46] In an interview, he said that "lowering marginal tax rates held out a lot of hope for young members of the middle class that they might get to keep some of the income" they earned "and didn't need to work quite as hard in sheltering it."

But others see the Reagan years differently. "Yes, there was a boom in the mid-1980s, as the economy recovered from a severe recession," Krugman, the Nobel economist and *Times* columnist, wrote. "But while the rich got much richer, there was little sustained economic improvement for most Americans. By the late 1980s, middle-class incomes were barely higher than they had been a decade before — and the poverty rate had actually risen."[47]

The University of Iowa's Leicht is highly critical of another legacy of the 1980s: deregulation of the banking industry, which he says set the stage for a massive increase in easy credit. The explosion in consumer lending that began in the 1980s helped millions of working Americans buy homes and cars, Leicht acknowledges, but he says the credit binge has come back to haunt the middle class now as home-foreclosure rates and personal bankruptcies soar.

CHRONOLOGY

1800-1929 *Industrial age shifts employment from farm to factory, setting stage for rise of middle class.*

October 1929 Stock market crash marks end of a speculative bubble on Wall Street.

1930-1970 *Great Depression sends unemployment soaring, President Roosevelt crafts New Deal social and economic legislation and postwar boom spurs growth of middle class.*

1933 Unemployment rate reaches 25 percent; Congress passes flood of New Deal legislation.

1935 President Franklin D. Roosevelt signs Social Security Act into law.

1939 Food Stamp program starts.

1944 Roosevelt signs Servicemen's Readjustment Act, or GI Bill, into law; by 1952, the law backed nearly 2.4 million home loans for World War II veterans, and by 1956 nearly 8 million vets had participated in education or training programs.

1946 Construction starts on New York's Levittown, one of three low-cost post-World War II residential communities that would come to define middle-class suburbia.

1960 Median family income is 30 percent higher in purchasing power than a decade earlier, and more than 60 percent of homes are owner-occupied, compared with 44 percent just before World War II.

1970-1995 *Oil shocks, inflation, foreign competition, and other changes mark tougher era for middle-class Americans.*

1979 U.S. manufacturing employment peaks at 21.4 million workers.

1981 President Ronald Reagan fires 11,000 striking members of the Professional Air Traffic Controllers Organization, helping to weaken the power of organized labor; Reagan persuades Congress to pass largest tax cuts in U.S. history.

1981-82 Severe recession rocks U.S. economy, sending the unemployment rate to 10.8 percent, the highest since the Great Depression.

Oct. 19, 1987 Dow Jones Industrial Average loses 23 percent of its value.

1996-Present *Home ownership peaks, and consumer spending soars, but good times end as home values plummet, financial institutions collapse and nation sinks into recession.*

1996 Congress ends 60-year welfare entitlement program, imposing work requirements and putting time limits on cash benefits.

1997 Federal minimum wage raised to $5.15 an hour.

2000 Federal poverty rate falls to 11.3 percent, lowest since 1974.

2001-2006 Housing prices in many cities double, and home-equity loans help lead to soaring consumer spending.

2004 Home-ownership rate peaks at 69 percent.

2008 Federal minimum wage rises to $6.55 an hour; it is set to increase to $7.25 effective July 24, 2009. . . . U.S. seizes Fannie Mae and Freddie Mac, Lehman Brothers files for bankruptcy and Washington Mutual collapses in biggest bank failure in history. . . . President George W. Bush signs $700 billion financial rescue bill but recession deepens.

2009 President Barack Obama announces budget seeking to aid middle class and forms Middle Class Task Force headed by Vice President Joseph Biden; first meeting focuses on "green jobs." . . . Federal unemployment rate rises to 7.6 percent in January (12.6 percent for African-Americans and 9.7 for Hispanics). . . . Labor Department says employers took 2,227 "mass layoff actions" in January, resulting in nearly 238,000 job cuts; from December 2007 through January 2009, mass layoff events totaled more than 25,700. . . . Claims for unemployment benefits exceed 5 million for first time in history. . . . Home foreclosures are reported on 274,399 U.S. properties in January, up 18 percent from January 2008.

What Does 'Middle Class' Really Mean?

Does the definition include income? Number of cars in the garage?

At his first White House press conference, President Barack Obama promised tax relief for "working and middle-class families." But what, exactly, does it mean to be in the "middle class"?

No official definition exists. Politicians, journalists and pundits freely use the term, often without attaching a precise meaning to it. And in opinion polls, most Americans — uncomfortable defining themselves as "rich" or "poor" — place themselves in the category of the middle class, even if their incomes reflect the outer limits of wealth or poverty.

In a report last year, the Pew Research Center noted that the term "middle class" is both "universally familiar" and "devilishly difficult to pin down."

"It is both a social and economic construct, and because these domains don't always align, its borders are fuzzy," Pew said. "Is a $30,000-a-year resident in brain surgery lower class? Is a $100,000-a-year plumber upper middle class?"

In a national survey of more than 2,400 American adults, Pew asked people to define themselves. It found that 53 percent said they were middle class. But, Pew said, "behind the reassuring simplicity of this number lies a nest of anomalies."

For example, it said, 41 percent of adults with annual household incomes of $100,000 or more said they were middle class, as did 46 percent of those with household incomes below $40,000. And of those in between, roughly a third said they were not middle class.

"If being middle income isn't the sole determinant of being middle class, what else is?" Pew added. "Wealth? Debt? Homeownership? Consumption? Marital status? Age? Race and ethnicity? Education? Occupation? Values?"[1]

Christian Weller, an associate professor of public policy at the University of Massachusetts, Boston, and a fellow at the liberal Center for American Progress, says that often, people count the number of cars in a garage or the square footage of a house to judge another person's economic standing. But, he says, "that's not really how people perceive and define middle class. . . . One part of middle class is an aspirational definition: 'I'll be able to send my kids to college, I'll be able to create a better future for my children, and do I have a secure lifestyle right now?'

"That goes beyond just simply having a good job," he says. "That means, do you have health insurance coverage, do you have enough savings, do you own your own home, do you

have retirement savings?" And, Weller adds, "By all those measures middle-class security has been eroding substantially."

Many economists look at the concept of a middle class through the lens of household-income data gathered by the federal government. Median household income was $50,233 in 2007, the latest year for which data are available.[2] That was the midpoint in the distribution, with half of households having more income and half less.[3]

The government also separates household income into five "quintiles," from lowest to highest. Some might consider "middle class" to mean only the third quintile — the one in the very middle — with incomes between $39,101 and $62,000. But many economists consider that view to be too cramped. Some count the third and fourth quintiles, with an upper limit of $100,000 in household income in 2007. Among the broadest definitions of middle class is one encompassing the three income quintiles in the middle, from $20,292 to $100,000.

Of course, using household income to measure the middle class has its own problems. For example, a family might seem solidly middle class based on its income, but parents may be toiling at two jobs each to raise their income level into the middle tier of the distribution tables. They might make good incomes but lack health insurance, putting them and their children at risk of a catastrophic financial collapse. Or they may live in a high-cost region of the country, where a supposed middle-class income of around $50,000 or $60,000 a year simply can't cover the bills.

One thing is certain, say those who have studied the American middle class: Its survival is crucial to the nation's future.

"It is the heart of the country, it's the heart of our democracy, it's the heart of our economy, it's the heart of our population," says Amelia Warren Tyagi, co-author of *The Two-Income Trap: Why Middle-Class Mothers and Fathers Are Going Broke.* "So while it may not be easy to define with precision, it's extremely important."

---

[1] Paul Taylor, et al., "Inside the Middle Class: Bad Times Hit the Good Life," Pew Research Center, April 9, 2008, p. 3, http://pewsocialtrends.org/assets/pdf/MC-Middle-class-report.pdf.

[2] U.S. Department of Commerce, Bureau of the Census, "Historical Income Tables — Households," www.census.gov/hhes/www/income/histinc/h05.html.

[3] In 2007, the United States had about 116,783,000 households.

"Starting in about the mid-1980s, we decided as a nation, through a number of mechanisms, that being loaned money was a perfect substitute for being paid it as long as you could buy things that represented middle-class status like houses and cars," Leicht says.

Impact of Globalization

Like the impact of so-called supply-side Reaganomics, the effects of globalization and trade policy are often hotly debated. While some argue they have, on balance, helped the U.S. economy, others say they have undermined middle-class security. (*See "At Issue," p. 17.*)

In his 2006 book *War on the Middle Class*, CNN anchor Lou Dobbs wrote "[i]n their free-trade fervor, Republicans and Democrats alike, most economists, certainly corporate leaders, and business columnists assure us that the loss of millions of jobs to other countries is the inevitable result of a modern global economy. The result, they promise us, will be a higher standard of living for everyone in America — and especially for the rest of the planet."

But Dobbs went on to say that millions of U.S. manufacturing jobs already had vanished and that many more jobs — including millions of white-collar service positions — were expected to do so in coming years, with the information-technology industry leading the way. "The free-trade-at-any-price enthusiasts once promised us that all those millions of people who lost their positions in manufacturing would find even better ones in the tech industry. But today no one is saying which industry will be the source of replacement for those jobs lost to outsourcing."[48]

C. Fred Bergsten, director of the Peterson Institute for International Economics, appearing on the PBS show "The NewsHour with Jim Lehrer," said studies by his organization have shown that the U.S. economy is $1 trillion a year richer as a result of globalization during the past 50 years.

Nonetheless, Bergsten said "there are losers . . . , costs . . . [and] downsides" to globalization and that the United States "has done a very poor job" in dealing with

Middle Class Enjoys Some of 'Life's Goodies'

More than two-thirds of middle-class Americans enjoy at least three of "life's goodies," such as high-speed Internet and more than one vehicle, according to the Pew Research Center. But half as many middle class as wealthy Americans have vacation homes, household help and children in private school.

Percentage of Americans who have. . .

Item	All incomes	Upper income	Middle income	Lower income
Cable or satellite service	70%	80%	71%	62%
Two or more cars	70	83	72	57
High-speed Internet	66	80	67	50
High-definition or flat screen TV	42	59	42	28
Young child in private school	15	31	14	6
Paid household help	16	36	13	7
A vacation home	10	19	9	4

Source: "Inside the Middle Class: Bad Times Hit the Good Life," Pew Research Center, April 2008

those problems. "You lose your health care when you lose your job. Unemployment insurance is miserably inadequate. Trade-adjustment assistance works, but it doesn't even cover [service] workers who get outsourced, and it's inadequate."

But Thea Lee, policy director and chief international economist at the AFL-CIO, who also appeared on the PBS program, was more critical of globalization than Bergsten. "We've had the wrong kind of globalization," she said. "It's been a corporate-dominated globalization, which has not really served working people here or our trading partners very well. . . . We've seen this long-term, decades-long stagnation of wages and growth of wage inequality in the United States even as we've been in a period of tremendous economic growth, productivity growth, technological improvements and increase in globalization."[49]

However one may interpret the economic history of recent decades, few observers would disagree that the middle class is now caught in the greatest economic downdraft in generations.

"We've really had an erosion of economic security and economic opportunity," and it occurred "very rapidly" after 2001, says Christian Weller, an associate professor of public policy at the University of Massachusetts,

Economic Meltdown Batters Retirement Plans

Reform proposals call for limiting risk to workers.

The economy may look bleak for millions of middle-class Americans, but for those in or near retirement, it's downright scary.

Experts say the steep downturns in stock and real estate values, along with soaring layoffs among older workers, have left millions worrying that they won't have enough income to see them through their golden years. And the crash has underscored what critics see as the weaknesses of 401(k) accounts — tax-advantaged plans that require employees to assume the primary responsibility for building and managing their retirement nest eggs.

"The collapse of the housing bubble, coupled with the plunge in the stock market, has exposed the gross inadequacy of our system of retirement income," Dean Baker, co-director of the Center for Economic and Policy Research, a liberal think tank in Washington, told a House committee in February.[1]

At the same hearing, Alicia H. Munnell, director of the Center for Retirement Research at Boston College, said the center's National Retirement Risk Index, which projects the share of households that will not be able to maintain their living standard in retirement, jumped from 31 percent in 1983 to 44 percent in 2006 and rises to 61 percent when health-care expenses are factored in.

Munnell said that in the two years following the stock market's peak on Oct. 9, 2007, the market value of assets in 401(k) retirement plans and Individual Retirement Accounts fell roughly 30 percent. For people ages 55 to 64, she said, median holdings in 401(k) plans went from a modest $60,000 or so in 2007 to $42,000 at the end of 2008.[2]

Critics have long warned of serious faults in the nation's private system of retirement savings. The number of so-called defined-benefit plans, which provide for guaranteed pensions, has been shrinking, while defined-contribution plans like 401(k)s have risen from supplemental savings vehicles in the early 1980s to what they are now: the main or sole retirement plan for most American workers covered by an employer-sponsored retirement plan.[3]

Jacob S. Hacker, a political scientist at the University of California in Berkeley, said the historical "three-legged stool" of retirement security — Social Security, private pensions and personal savings — is now precarious.

"The central issue for retirement security is . . . the risk," he told a congressional hearing last fall. "Retirement wealth has not only failed to rise for millions of families; it has also grown more risky, as the nation has shifted more of the responsibility for retirement planning from employers and government onto workers and their families.[4]

Several proposals have surfaced for revamping the retirement system, some bolder than others.

Teresa Ghilarducci, a professor at the New School for Social Research in New York, wants Congress to establish "Guaranteed Retirement Accounts," in which all workers not enrolled in an equivalent or better defined-benefit pension plan would participate. A contribution equal to 5 percent of each worker's earnings would go into an account each year, with the cost shared equally between worker and employer. A $600 federal tax credit would offset employees' contributions.

Money in the accounts would be managed by the federal government and earn a guaranteed 3 percent rate of return, adjusted for inflation. When a worker retired, the account would convert to an annuity that provides income until death, though a small portion could be taken in a lump sum at retirement. Those who died before retirement could leave only half their accounts to heirs; those who died after retiring could leave half the final balance minus benefits received.[5]

Boston, and a fellow at the liberal Center for American Progress.

After a "five-year window" of employment and wage growth during the late 1990s, Weller says, pressure on the middle class began accelerating in 2001. "There are different explanations, but one is . . . that after the 2001 recession [corporate] profits recovered much faster than in previous recessions, to much higher levels, and corporations were unchecked. They could engage in outsourcing and all these other techniques to boost their short-term profits, but obviously to the detriment of employees. I think what we ended up with was very slow employment growth, flat or declining wages and declining benefit coverage."

The plan has drawn criticism. Paul Schott Stevens, president and CEO of the Investment Company Institute, which represents the mutual-fund industry, called it "a non-starter."[6] Jan Jacobson, senior counsel for retirement policy at the American Benefits Council, said, "We believe the current employer-sponsored system is a good one that should be built on."[7]

But Ghilarducci told the AARP Bulletin Today that "people just want a guaranteed return for their retirement. The essential feature of my proposal is that people and employers would be relieved of being tied to the financial market."[8]

Hacker advocates an approach called "universal 401(k)" plans. The plans would be available to all workers, regardless of whether their employer offered a traditional retirement plan. All benefits would remain in the same account throughout a worker's life, and money could be withdrawn before retirement only at a steep penalty, as is the case with today's 401(k) plans. The plans would be shielded against excessive investments in company stock, and the default investment option would be a low-cost index fund that has a mix of stocks and bonds. Over time, the mix would change automatically to limit risk as a worker aged.

At age 65, government would turn a worker's account into a lifetime annuity that guarantees a flow of retirement income, unless the worker explicitly requested otherwise and showed he or she had enough assets to withstand market turmoil.

Employers would be encouraged to match workers' contributions to the plans, and government could give special tax breaks to companies offering better matches for lower-paid workers.[9]

Teresa Ghilarducci, a professor at the New School for Social Research, says Congress should establish "Guaranteed Retirement Accounts" for workers not enrolled in similar pension plans.

teresaghilarducci.org

Says Hacker, "We have to move toward a system in which there is a second tier of pension plans that is private but which provides key protections that were once provided by defined-benefit pension plans."

[1] "Strengthening Worker Retirement Security," testimony before House Committee on Education and Labor, Feb. 24, 2009, http://edlabor.house.gov/documents/111/pdf/testimony/20090224DeanBakertestimony.pdf.

[2] "The Financial Crisis and Restoring Retirement Security," testimony before House Committee on Education and Labor, Feb. 24, 2009, http://edlabor.house.gov/documents/111/pdf/testimony/20090224AliciaMunnellTestimony.pdf.

[3] Ibid. For background, see Alan Greenblatt, "Pension Crisis," *CQ Researcher*, Feb. 17, 2006, pp. 145-168, and Alan Greenblatt, "Aging Baby Boomers," *CQ Researcher*, Oct. 19, 2007, pp. 865-888.

[4] "The Impact of the Financial Crisis on Workers' Retirement Security," testimony before House Committee on Education and Labor field hearing, San Francisco, Oct. 22, 2008.

[5] For a detailed explanation, see, Teresa Ghilarducci, "Guaranteed Retirement Accounts: Toward retirement income security," Economic Policy Institute, Briefing Paper No. 204, Nov. 20, 2007, www.sharedprosperity.org/bp204/bp204.pdf.

[6] Stevens and Jacobson are quoted in Doug Halonen, "401(k) plans could be facing total revamp," Financial Week, Oct. 29, 2008.

[7] Ibid.

[8] Quoted in Carole Fleck, "401(k) Plans: Too Risky for Retirement Security?" AARP Bulletin Today, Dec. 17, 2008, http://bulletin.aarp.org/yourmoney/retirement/articles/401_k_plans_too_risky_for_retirement_security_.html.

[9] See Jacob S. Hacker, The Great Risk Shift (2006), pp. 185-187. See also Testimony before House Committee on Education and Labor, Oct. 22, 2008, op. cit.

And overlaid on all of that, Weller says, was the unprecedented boom in housing.

Even before the housing bubble burst, though, the middle class was on shaky ground, as Weller noted in an article early last year. In 2004, fewer than a third of families had accumulated enough wealth to equal three months of income, he found. And that was counting all financial assets, including retirement savings, minus debt.[50]

"For quite some time," says *Two-Income Trap* co-author Tyagi, "we've had a sizable minority of the middle class under enormous strain and on the verge of crisis, and since the recent meltdown the proportion of middle-class families in crisis increased exponentially.

"Many families teetering on the uncomfortable edge have been pushed over. I really see the [home] foreclosure crisis as front and center in this. We can't overestimate how important home ownership is to the middle class is, and what a crisis losing a home is."

CURRENT SITUATION

Narrowing the Gap

Joel Kotkin, a presidential fellow at Chapman University in Orange, Calif., and author of *The City: A Global History,* wrote recently that "over the coming decades, class will likely constitute the major dividing line in our society — and the greatest threat to America's historic aspirations."[51]

With the gap between rich and poor growing and even a college degree no assurance of upward mobility, Kotkin wrote, President Obama's "greatest challenge . . . will be to change this trajectory for Americans under 30, who supported him by two to one. The promise that 'anyone' can reach the highest levels of society is the basis of both our historic optimism and the stability of our political system. Yet even before the recession, growing income inequality was undermining Americans' optimism about the future."

Obama's legislative agenda, along with his middle-class task force, aims to narrow the class gap. But the deep recession, along with a partisan divide on Capitol Hill, could make some of his key goals difficult and costly to reach.

In announcing his budget, Obama did not hesitate to draw class distinctions between "the wealthiest few" and the "middle class" made up of "responsible men and women who are working harder than ever, worrying about their jobs and struggling to raise their families." He acknowledged that his political opponents are "gearing up for a fight" against his budget plan, which includes tax cuts for all but the richest Americans, universally available health-care coverage and other policies aimed squarely at the middle class. Yet, he said, "The system we have now might work for the powerful and well-connected interests that have run Washington for far too long, but I don't. I work for the American people."[52]

Republicans also are invoking middle-class concerns in expressing their opposition to Obama's budget. Delivering the GOP response to Obama's weekly address, Sen. Richard Burr, R-N.C., said the budget would require

the typical American family to pay $52,000 in interest alone over the next decade.[53]

"Like a family that finds itself choking under the weight of credit-card balances and finance charges," said Burr, "the federal government is quickly obligating the American people to a similar fate.

The stimulus package signed by the president in February includes payroll-tax breaks for low- and moderate-income households and an expanded tax credit for higher-education expenses. But costly overhauls of health and retirement policies remain on the table.

Douglas W. Elmendorf, director of the Congressional Budget Office, told a Senate budget panel in February that without changes in health-insurance policy, an estimated 54 million people under age 65 will lack medical insurance by 2019, compared with 45 million this year. The projection "largely reflects the expectation that health-care costs and health-insurance premiums will continue to rise faster than people's income."[54]

Meanwhile, the abrupt collapse of the global financial markets has decimated middle-class retirement accounts. Between June 30 and September 30 of 2008, retirement assets fell 5.9 percent, from $16.9 trillion to $15.9 trillion, according to the latest tally by the Investment Company Institute, which represents the mutual-fund industry.[55]

In announcing his middle-class task force, Obama said his administration would be "absolutely committed to the future of America's middle class and working families. They will be front and center every day in our work in the White House."[56]

The group includes the secretaries of Labor, Health and Human Services, Education and Commerce, plus the heads of the National Economic Council, Office of Management and Budget, Domestic Policy Council and Council of Economic Advisors.[57]

According to the White House, the task force will aim to:

- Expand opportunities for education and lifelong training;
- Improve work and family balance;
- Restore labor standards, including workplace safety;
- Help to protect middle-class and working-family incomes; and
- Protect retirement security.

Has U.S. trade and globalization policy hurt the middle class?

YES
Thea Lee
Policy Director, AFL-CIO

Written for *CQ Researcher*, March 2, 2009

The middle class is not a single entity — nor is trade and globalization policy. The clothes we wear, the food we eat, the air we breathe, the jobs we have, the places we choose to live — all are affected by trade and globalization policy, but in many different ways.

I would argue, nonetheless, that U.S. trade and globalization policy has failed the middle class in numerous ways. It has eroded living standards for a large majority of American workers, undermined our social, environmental, consumer safety and public health protections, exacerbated our unsustainable international indebtedness, weakened our national security and compromised our ability to innovate and prosper in the future.

Most significant, especially during this global downturn, the negative impact of globalization on American wages should be a top concern — both for policy makers and for business. Economists may disagree about the magnitude of the effect, but few would dispute that globalization has contributed to the decades-long stagnation of real wages for American workers.

The Economic Policy Institute's L. Josh Bivens finds that the costs of globalization to a full-time median-wage earner in 2006 totaled approximately $1,400, and about $2,500 for a two-earner household. It only makes intuitive sense that if the point of globalization is to increase U.S. access to vast pools of less-skilled, less-protected labor, wages at home will be reduced — particularly for those workers without a college degree. And this impact will only grow in future years, as trade in services expands. We won't be able to rebuild our real economy and the middle class if we can't figure out how to use trade, tax, currency and national investment policies to reward efficient production at home — not send it offshore.

That is not to say, however, that trade and globalization in themselves are inherently pernicious. U.S. globalization policies in recent decades prioritized the interests of mobile, multinational corporations over domestic manufacturers, workers, farmers and communities. At the same time, they undermined prospects for equitable, sustainable and democratic development in our trading partners.

If we are going to move forward together in the future, we need to acknowledge that our current policies have not always delivered on their potential or their promise — particularly for middle-class workers. If new trade and globalization initiatives are to gain any political momentum, we will need deep reform in current policies.

NO
C. Fred Bergsten
Director, Peterson Institute for International Economics

Written for *CQ Researcher*, March 2, 2009

The backlash in the United States against globalization is understandable but misplaced. Despite widespread and legitimate concerns about worsening income distribution, wage stagnation and job insecurity, all serious economics studies show that globalization is only a modest cause of these problems. In the aggregate, globalization is a major plus for the U.S. economy and especially for the middle class.

An in-depth study by our nonpartisan institute demonstrates that the U.S. economy is $1 trillion per year richer as a result of global trade integration over the last half-century, or almost $10,000 per household. These gains accrue from cheaper imports, more high-paying export jobs and faster productivity growth. The American economy could gain another $500 billion annually if we could lift the remaining barriers to the international flow of goods and services.

Of course, any dynamic economic change, like technology advances and better corporate management, affects some people adversely. The negative impact of globalization totals about $50 billion a year due to job displacement and long-term income reductions. This is not an insignificant number, but the benefit-to-cost ratio from globalization is still a healthy 20-to-1.

The United States could not stop globalization even if it wanted to. But it must expand the social safety net for those displaced while making sure that our workers and firms can compete in a globalized world.

The Obama administration and the new Congress have already begun to shore up these safety nets through the fiscal stimulus package. Unemployment insurance has been substantially liberalized. Sweeping reform of the health care system has begun. Most important, Trade Adjustment Assistance has been dramatically expanded to cover all trade-impacted workers and communities.

We must also remember that globalization has lifted billions of the poorest citizens out of poverty. No country has ever achieved sustained modernization without integrating into the world economy, with China and India only the latest examples. The flip side is that products and services from these countries greatly improve the purchasing power and an array of consumer choices for the American middle class.

Fears of globalization have expanded during the current worldwide downturn. But strong export performance kept our economy growing through most of last year, and global cooperation is now necessary to ignite the needed recovery.

Soaring home foreclosures and job losses are battering middle class families. Home prices doubled between the mid-1990s and 2007, prompting many families to borrow against the higher values and take out cash for vacations and other expenditures. When values began plummeting, families with job losses and limited or no savings found themselves underwater.

The group's first meeting, on Feb. 27, focused on so-called green jobs.

Jared Bernstein, Vice President Biden's chief economist and a task force member, told *The Christian Science Monitor* that the group "has a different target" than the recently enacted $787 billion economic-stimulus plan, which includes huge government outlays with a goal of creating millions of jobs. "It's less about job quantity than job quality," Bernstein told the *Monitor* in an e-mail. "Its goal is to make sure that once the economy begins to expand again, middle-class families will reap their fair share of the growth, something that hasn't happened in recent years."[58]

Biden expressed a similar sentiment in an op-ed piece in *USA Today.* "Once this economy starts growing again, we need to make sure the benefits of that growth reach the people responsible for it. We can't stand by and watch as that narrow sliver of the top of the income scale wins a bigger piece of the pie — while everyone else gets a smaller and smaller slice," he wrote.[59]

In late January, as he pushed Congress to pass the stimulus plan, Obama said that not only would the task force focus on the middle class but that "we're not forgetting the poor. They are going to be front and center because they, too, share our American Dream."

Cash-Strapped States

Cash-strapped state governments are on the front lines of dealing with the swelling ranks of the nation's poor. States are struggling to handle a rising number of Americans in need of welfare assistance as the economy weakens — some of them middle-class households pushed over the financial edge by job losses and home foreclosures.

Despite the economic collapse, 18 states reduced their welfare rolls last year, and the number of people nationally receiving cash assistance was at or near the lowest point in more than four decades, a *New York Times* analysis of state data found.[60]

Michigan, with one of the nation's highest unemployment rates, reduced its welfare rolls 13 percent, and Rhode Island cut its by 17 percent, the *Times* said.

"Of the 12 states where joblessness grew most rapidly," the *Times* said, "eight reduced or kept constant the number of people receiving Temporary Assistance for Needy Families, the main cash welfare program for families with children. Nationally, for the 12 months ending October 2008, the rolls inched up a fraction of 1 percent."

While the recession has devastated households across the demographic spectrum, it has been especially hard on minorities. The overall unemployment rate in January stood at 7.6 percent, but it was 12.6 percent for African-Americans and 9.7 percent for Hispanics. The rate for whites was 6.9 percent. What's more, unemployment among minorities has been rising faster than for whites.[61]

The crash of the auto industry, among the most spectacular aspects of the past year's economic crisis, has devastated African-Americans.

About 118,000 African-Americans worked in the auto industry in November 2008, down from 137,000 in December 2007, the start of the recession, according to researchers at the Economic Policy Institute, a liberal think tank.[62]

"One of the engines of the black middle class has been the auto sector," Schmitt, told *USA Today* in January. In the late 1970s, "one of every 50 African-Americans in the U.S. was working in the auto sector. These jobs were the best jobs. Particularly for African-Americans who had migrated from the South, these were the culmination of a long, upward trajectory of economic mobility."[63]

For those living in high-cost urban areas — whether black, Hispanic or white — the strain of maintaining a middle-class standard of living is especially acute. According to 2008 survey data by the Pew research organization, more than a fourth of those who defined themselves as middle class who lived in high-cost areas said they had just enough money for basic expenses, or not even that much, compared with 16 percent living in low-cost metropolitan areas.[64]

In New York City, the nation's biggest urban area, people earning the median area income in the third quarter of 2008 could afford only about 11 percent of the homes in the metro area — the lowest proportion in the country — according to the Center for an Urban Future, a Manhattan think tank. To be in the middle class in Manhattan, according to the center's analysis, a person would need to make $123,322 a year, compared with $72,772 in Boston, $63,421 in Chicago and $50,000 in Houston.[65]

"New York has long been a city that has groomed a middle class, but that's a more arduous job today," said Jonathan Bowles, the center's director and a co-author of the report. "There's a tremendous amount of positives about the city, yet so many middle-class families seem to be stretched to their limits."[66]

OUTLOOK

Silver Lining?

No cloud is darker over the middle class than the deepening recession. "Everything points to this being at least three years of a weak economy," Nobel economist Krugman told a conference in February sponsored by several liberal groups.[67]

The economic crisis, he said, is "out of control," and "there's no reason to think there's any spontaneous mechanism for recovery. . . . My deep concern is not simply that it will be a very deep slide but that it will become entrenched."

Still, Krugman said, "If there's any silver lining to [the crisis], it's reopening the debate about the role of public policy in the economy."

Many liberals argue that policy changes in such areas as health-care coverage and higher-education benefits offer avenues for lifting middle-class families out of the economic mire and that getting medical costs under control is a key to the nation's long-term fiscal health. But many conservatives oppose more government spending. Advancing major reforms amid partisan bickering and a budget deficit inflated by bailouts, recession and war will be difficult.

University of Arizona political scientist Kenworthy says focusing policy changes on people living below the poverty level could be "easier to sell politically" and would still benefit those in higher income brackets.

"For example, think about the minimum wage," he says. Raising it "has an effect further up the wage distribution. The same with the earned-income tax credit," a refundable credit for low and moderate working people and families. "If it's made more generous, it has effects a bit further up. The same with health care."

As Washington grapples with potential policy changes, the plunging economy is forcing many middle-class consumers to live within their means. Many see that as a good thing.

"I certainly think some of the entitlements we have come to expect, like two homes, a brand-new car every couple of years, college education for all the kids, a yacht or two, expensive vacations — some of this will need to be reoriented," says Georgetown University's Viksnins. "Some reallocation of people's priorities is really necessary."

Yet, long-term optimism hasn't vanished amid the current economic gloom. "We will rebuild, we will recover and the United States of America will emerge stronger than before," Obama declared in an address on Feb. 24 to a joint session of Congress.

Viksnins says he is "utterly hopeful" about the future of the middle class.

And Sherk, the Heritage Foundation labor-policy fellow, says that "as long as your skills are valuable, you're going to find a job that pays you roughly at your productivity.

"For people in jobs disappearing from the economy, it's going to mean a substantial downward adjustment in standard of living," Sherk says. But "those in the middle class who have some college education, or have gone to a community college or have skills, broadly speaking, most will wind up on their feet again."

NOTES

1. Julie Bosman, "Newly Poor Swell Lines at Food Banks," *The New York Times*, Feb. 20, 2009, www.nytimes.com/2009/02/20/nyregion/20food.html?scp=1&sq=newly%20poor&st=cse.

2. For background, see the following *CQ Researcher* reports: Marcia Clemmitt, "Public Works Projects," Feb. 20, 2009, pp. 153-176; Kenneth Jost, "Financial Crisis," May 9, 2008, pp. 409-432; Thomas J. Billitteri, "Financial Bailout," Oct. 24, 2008, pp. 865-888; Marcia Clemmitt, "Mortgage Crisis," Nov. 2, 2007, pp. 913-936, and Barbara Mantel, "Consumer Debt," March 2, 2007, pp. 193-216.

3. For background see Kenneth Jost, "The Obama Presidency," *CQ Researcher*, Jan. 30, 2009, pp. 73-104.

4. Jackie Calmes, "Obama, Breaking 'From a Troubled Past,' Seeks a Budget to Reshape U.S. Priorities," *The New York Times*, Feb. 27, 2009, p. A1. For background, see the following *CQ Researcher* reports: Marcia Clemmitt, "Rising Health Costs," April 7, 2006, pp. 289-312, and Marcia Clemmitt, "Universal Coverage," March 30, 2007, pp. 265-288.

5. For background, see the following *CQ Researcher* reports: Thomas J. Billitteri, "Domestic Poverty," Sept. 7, 2007, pp. 721-744; Alan Greenblatt, "Upward Mobility," April 29, 2005, pp. 369-392; and Mary H. Cooper, "Income Equality," April 17, 1998, pp. 337-360.

6. Demos and Institute on Assets & Social Policy at Brandeis University, *From Middle to Shaky Ground: The Economic Decline of America's Middle Class, 2000-2006* (2008).

7. Paul Taylor, *et al.*, "Inside the Middle Class: Bad Times Hit the Good Life," Pew Research Center, April 9, 2008, http://pewsocialtrends.org/assets/pdf/MC-Middle-class-report. pdf, p. 5.

8. Edmund L. Andrews, "Fed Calls Gain in Family Wealth a Mirage," Feb. 13, 2009, www.nytimes.com/2009/02/13/business/economy/13fed.html?ref=business. The study is by Brian K. Bucks, *et al.*, "Changes in U.S. Family Finances from 2004 to 2007: Evidence from the Survey of Consumer Finances," *Federal Reserve Bulletin*, Vol. 95, February 2009, www.federalreserve.gov/pubs/bulletin/2009/pdf/scf09.pdf.

9. Jacob S. Hacker, *The Great Risk Shift* (2006), pp. 5-6.

10. Quoted in Ta-Nehisi Coates, "American Girl," *The Atlantic*, January/February 2009.

11. Julia B. Isaacs and Isabel V. Sawhill, "The Frayed American Dream," Brookings Institution, Nov. 28, 2007, www.brookings.edu/opinions/2007/1128_econgap_isaacs.aspx.

12. *Ibid.*

13. Arloc Sherman, "Income Inequality Hits Record Levels, New CBO Data Show," Center on Budget and Policy Priorities, Dec. 14, 2007, www.cbpp.org/12-14-07inc.htm. The CBO report is "Historical Effective Federal Tax Rates: 1979 to 2005," www.cbo.gov/doc.cfm?index= 8885. Figures are inflation adjusted and are in 2005 dollars.

14. Emmanuel Saez, "Striking it Richer: The Evolution of Top Incomes in the United States," University of California, Berkeley, March 15, 2008, http://elsa.berkeley.edu/~saez/saez-UStopincomes-2006prel.pdf.

15. For background, see the following *CQ Researcher* reports: Pamela M. Prah, "Labor Unions' Future," Sept. 2, 2005, pp. 709-732; Brian Hansen, "Global Backlash," Sept. 28, 2001, pp. 761-784; Mary H. Cooper, "World Trade," June 9, 2000, pp. 497-520; Mary H. Cooper, "Exporting Jobs," Feb. 20, 2004, pp. 149-172; and the following *CQ Global Researcher* reports: Samuel Loewenberg, "Anti-Americanism," March 2007, pp. 51-74, and Ken Moritsugu, "India Rising," May 2007, pp. 101-124.

16. John Schmitt, "The Good, the Bad, and the Ugly: Job Quality in the United States over the Three Most Recent Business Cycles," Center for Economic and Policy Research, November 2007, www.cepr.net/documents/publications/goodjobscycles.pdf.

17. Alicia H. Munnell and Steven A. Sass, "The Decline of Career Employment," Center for Retirement Research, Boston College, September 2008, http://crr.bc.edu/images/stories/ib_8-14.pdf.

18. Richard Florida, "How the Crash Will Reshape America," *The Atlantic*, March 2009, www.theatlantic.com/doc/200903/meltdown-geography.

19. James Sherk, "A Good Job Is Not So Hard to Find," Heritage Foundation, June 17, 2008 and revised and updated Sept. 2, 2008, www.heritage.org/research/labor/cda08-04.cfm.

20. George Packer, "The Ponzi State," *The New Yorker*, Feb. 9 and 16, 2009.

21. Paul Krugman, "Decade at Bernie's," *The New York Times*, Feb. 16, 2009, www.nytimes.com/2009/02/16/opinion/16krugman.html?scp=1&sq=decade%20at%20bernie's&st=cse.

22. Federal Housing Finance Agency, "U.S. Housing Price Index Estimates 1.8 Percent Price Decline From October to November," Jan. 22, 2009, www.ofheo.gov/media/hpi/MonthlyHPI12209F.pdf.

23. College Board, "Trends in College Pricing 2008," http://professionals.collegeboard.com/profdownload/trends-in-college-pricing-2008.pdf.

24. Department of Health and Human Services, Centers for Medicare and Medicaid Services, www.cms.hhs.gov/NationalHealthExpendData/downloads/tables.pdf.

25. Sara R. Collins, *et al.*, "Losing Ground: How the Loss of Adequate Health Insurance Is Burdening Working Families: Findings from the Commonwealth Fund Biennial Health Insurance Surveys, 2001-2007," Commonwealth Fund, Aug. 20, 2008, www.commonwealthfund.org/Content/Publications/Fund-Reports/2008/Aug/Losing-Ground-How-the-Loss-of-Adequate-Health-Insurance-Is-Burdening-Working-Families-8212-Finding.aspx.

26. Elizabeth Warren and Amelia Warren Tyagi, *The Two-Income Trap* (2003), p. 19.

27. *Ibid*, pp. 51-52.

28. Press release, "'Women on Their Own' in Much Worse Financial Condition Than Other Americans," Consumer Federation of America, Dec. 2, 2008, www.consumerfed.org/pdfs/Women_America_Saves_Tele_PR_12-2-08.pdf.

29. Ernest Istook, "Land of the free and home of the victims," Heritage Foundation, Feb. 29, 2008, www.heritage.org/Press/Commentary/ed022908b.cfm.

30. "Remarks by the President to Caterpillar Employees," Feb. 12, 2009, www.whitehouse.gov.

31. Foon Rhee, "Partisan spat continues on stimulus," Political Intelligence blog, *The Boston Globe*, Feb. 17, 2009, www.boston.com/news/politics/political intelligence/2009/02/partisan_spat_c.html.

32. Fact Sheet, "The Hidden Link: Health Costs and Family Economic Insecurity," Families USA, January 2009, www.familiesusa.org/assets/pdfs/the-hidden-link.pdf. The research cited by Families USA is by Christopher Tarver Robertson, *et al.*, "Get Sick Get Out: The Medical Causes of Home Mortgage Foreclosures," *Health Matrix Vol. 18*, 2008, pp. 65-105.

33. Reuters, "U.S. may need new retirement savings plans: lawmaker," Feb. 24, 2009, www.reuters.com/article/domesticNews/idUSTRE51N5UM20090224.

34. Lynn Sweeton, "Transcript of Obama, McCain at Saddleback Civil Forum with Pastor Rick Warren," *Chicago Sun Times*, Aug. 18, 2008, http://blogs.suntimes.com/sweet/2008/08/transcript_of_obama_mccain_at.html.

35. Quoted in Jeanna Bryner, "American Dream and Middle Class in Jeopardy," www.livescience.com, October 9, 2008, www.livescience.com/culture/081009-middle-class.html.

36. See Jennifer L. Goloboy, "The Early American Middle Class," *Journal of the Early Republic*, Vol. 25, No. 4, winter 2005.

37. Quoted in David Kennedy, *Freedom From Fear* (1999), p. 264.

38. *Ibid.*

39. For historical background, see *CQ Researcher Plus Archive* for a large body of contemporaneous coverage during the 1930s and 1940s in *Editorial Research Reports*, the precursor to the *CQ Researcher*.

40. Paul Krugman, "The Conscience of a Liberal: Introducing This Blog" *The New York Times*, Sept. 18, 2007, http://krugman.blogs.nytimes.com/2007/09/18/introducing-this-blog/.

41. Paul Krugman, "What Obama Must Do: A Letter to the New President," *Rolling Stone*, Jan. 14, 2009, www.rollingstone.com/politics/story/25456948/what_obama_must_do.

42. James T. Patterson, *Grand Expectations* (1996), p. 312.

43. Barry Hirsch, Georgia State University, and David Macpherson, Florida State University, "Union Membership, Coverage, Density, and Employment

Among All Wage and Salary Workers, 1973-2008," www.unionstats.com.

44. "Remarks by the President and the Vice President in Announcement of Labor Executive Orders and Middle-Class Working Families Task Force," Jan. 30, 2009, www.whitehouse.gov/blog_post/Todaysevent/.

45. U.S. Chamber of Commerce, "Is Unionization the Ticket to the Middle Class? The Real Economic Effects of Labor Unions," 2008, www.uschamber.com/assets/labor/unionrhetoric_econeffects.pdf.

46. George J. Viksnins, "Reaganomics after Twenty Years," www9.georgetown.edu/faculty/viksning/papers/Reaganomics.html.

47. Paul Krugman, "Debunking the Reagan Myth," *The New York Times*, Jan. 21, 2008, www.nytimes.com/2008/01/21/opinion/21krugman.html?scp=1&sq=%22Debunking%20the%20Reagan%20Myth%22&st=cse.

48. Lou Dobbs, *War on the Middle Class* (2006), p. 112.

49. Transcript, "In Bad Economy, Countries Contemplate Protectionist Measures," "The NewsHour with Jim Lehrer," Feb. 19, 2009, www.pbs.org/newshour/bb/business/jan-june 09/trade_02-19.html.

50. Christian Weller, "The Erosion of Middle-Class Economic Security After 2001," *Challenge*, Vol. 51, No. 1, January/February 2008, pp. 45-68.

51. Joel Kotkin, "The End of Upward Mobility?" *Newsweek*, Jan. 26, 2009, p. 64.

52. "Remarks of President Barack Obama, Weekly Address," Feb. 28, 2009, www.whitehouse.gov/blog/09/02/28/Keeping-Promises/.

53. "Burr delivers GOP challenge to Obama's budget," www.wral.com, Feb. 28, 2009, www.wral.com/news/local/story/4635676/.

54. Statement before the Committee on the Budget, U.S. Senate, "Expanding Health Insurance Coverage and Controlling Costs for Health Care," Feb. 10, 2009, www.cbo.gov/ftpdocs/99xx/doc9982/02-10-HealthVolumes_Testimony.pdf.

55. Investment Company Institute, "Retirement Assets Total $15.9 Trillion in Third Quarter," Feb. 19, 2009, www.ici.org/home/09_news_q3_retmrkt_update.html#TopOfPage.

56. Quoted in Jeff Zeleny, "Obama Announces Task Force to Assist Middle-Class Families," *The New York Times*, Dec. 22, 2008.

57. Cited at www.whitehouse.gov/blog_post/about_the_task_force_1/.

58. Mark Trumbull, "Will Obama's plans help the middle class?" *The Christian Science Monitor*, Dec. 24, 2008.

59. Joe Biden, "Time to put middle class front and center," *USA Today*, Jan. 30, 2009.

60. Jason DeParle, "Welfare Aid Isn't Growing as Economy Drops Off," *The New York Times*, Feb. 2, 2009.

61. See Bureau of Labor Statistics, "The Employment Situation: January 2009," www.bls.gov/news.release/empsit.nr0.htm.

62. Robert E. Scott and Christian Dorsey, "African Americans are especially at risk in the auto crisis," Economic Policy Institute, Snapshot, Dec. 5, 2008, www.epi.org/economic_snapshots/entry/webfeatures_snapshots_20081205/.

63. Quoted in Larry Copeland, "Auto industry's slide cuts a main route to the middle class," *USA Today*, Jan. 20, 2009, www.usatoday.com/money/autos/2009-01-20-blacks-auto-industry-dealers_N.htm.

64. D'Vera Cohn, "Pricey Neighbors, High Stress," Pew Social and Demographic Trends, May 29, 2008, www.pewsocialtrends.org/pubs/711/middle-class-blues.

65. Jonathan Bowles, *et al.*, "Reviving the City of Aspiration: A study of the challenges facing New York City's middle class," Center for an Urban Future, Feb. 2009, www.nycfuture.org/images_pdfs/pdfs/CityOfAspiration.pdf.

66. Quoted in Daniel Massey, "City faces middle-class exodus," *Crain's New York Business*, Feb. 5, 2009, www.crainsnewyork.com/article/20090205/FREE/902059930.

67. Krugman spoke at the "Thinking Big, Thinking Forward" conference in Washington on Feb. 11 sponsored by *The American Prospect*, the Institute for America's Future, Demos and the Economic Policy Institute.

BIBLIOGRAPHY

Books

Dobbs, Lou, *War on the Middle Class*, Viking, 2006.
The CNN broadcaster argues that the American government and economy are dominated by a wealthy and politically powerful elite who have exploited working Americans.

Frank, Robert H., *Falling Behind: How Rising Inequality Harms the Middle Class*, University of California Press, 2007.
The Cornell University economist argues that most income gains in recent decades have gone to people at the top, leading them to build bigger houses, which in turn has led middle-income families to spend a bigger share of their incomes on housing and curtail spending in other important areas.

Hacker, Jacob S., *The Great Risk Shift*, Oxford University Press, 2006.
A professor of political science argues that economic risk has shifted from "broad structures of insurance," including those sponsored by corporations and government, "onto the fragile balance sheets of American families."

Uchitelle, Louis, *The Disposable American*, Alfred A. Knopf, 2006.
A New York Times business journalist, writing before the current economic crises threw millions of workers out of their jobs, calls the layoff trend "a festering national crisis."

Articles

Copeland, Larry, "Auto industry's slide cuts a main route to the middle class," *USA Today*, Jan. 20, 2009, www.usatoday.com/money/autos/2009-01-20-blacks-auto-industry-dealers_N.htm?loc=interstitialskip.
The financial crisis in the auto industry "has been more devastating for African-Americans than any other community," Copeland writes.

Gallagher, John, "Slipping standard of living squeezes middle class," *Detroit Free Press*, Oct. 12, 2008, www.freep.com/article/20081012/BUSINESS07/810120483.
America's middle-class living standard "carried generations from dirt-floor cabins to manicured suburban subdivisions," Gallagher writes, but it "has sputtered and stalled."

Kotkin, Joel, "The End of Upward Mobility?" *Newsweek*, Jan. 26, 2009, www.newsweek.com/id/180041.
A presidential fellow at Chapman University writes that class, not race, "will likely constitute the major dividing line in our society."

Samuelson, Robert J., "A Darker Future For Us," *Newsweek*, Nov. 10, 2008, www.newsweek.com/id/166821/output/print.
An economic journalist argues that the central question confronting the new administration is whether the economy is at an historic inflection point, "when its past behavior is no longer a reliable guide to its future."

Weller, Christian, "The Erosion of Middle-Class Economic Security After 2001," *Challenge*, Vol. 51, No. 1, January/February 2008, pp. 45-68.
An associate professor of public policy at the University of Massachusetts, Boston, and senior fellow at the liberal Center for American Progress concludes that the gains in middle-class security of the late 1990s have been entirely eroded.

Reports and Studies

Bowles, Jonathan, Joel Kotkin and David Giles, "Reviving the City of Aspiration: A study of the challenges facing New York City's middle class," *Center for an Urban Future*, February 2009, www.nycfuture.org/images_pdfs/pdfs/CityOfAspiration.pdf.
Major changes to the nation's largest city have greatly diminished its ability to both create and retain a sizeable middle class, argues this report.

Schmitt, John, "The Good, the Bad, and the Ugly: Job Quality in the United States over the Three Most Recent Business Cycles," *Center for Economic and Policy Research*, November 2007, www.cepr.net/documents/publications/goodjobscycles.pdf.
The share of "good jobs," defined as ones paying at least $17 an hour and offering employer-provided medical insurance and a pension, deteriorated in the 2000-2006 business cycle.

Sherk, James, "A Good Job So Hard to Find," *Heritage Foundation*, June 17, 2008, www.heritage.org/research/labor/cda08-04.cfm.

Job opportunities have expanded the most in occupations with the highest wages, the conservative think tank states.

Taylor, Paul, et al., "Inside the Middle Class: Bad Times Hit the Good Life," *Pew Research Center*, April 2008, http://pewsocialtrends.org/assets/pdf/ MC-Middle-class-report.pdf.
The report aims to present a "comprehensive portrait of the middle class" based on a national opinion survey and demographic and economic data.

Wheary, Jennifer, Thomas M. Shapiro and Tamara Draut, "By A Thread: The New Experience of America's Middle Class," *Demos and the Institute on Assets and Social Policy at Brandeis University*, 2007, www.demos.org/pubs/ BaT112807 .pdf.
The report includes a "Middle Class Security Index" that portrays how well middle-class families are faring in the categories of financial assets, education, income and health care.

For More Information

Brookings Institution, 1775 Massachusetts Ave., N.W., Washington, DC 20036; (202) 797-6000; www.brookings .edu. Independent research and policy institute conducting research in economics, governance, foreign policy and development.

Center on Budget and Policy Priorities, 820 First St., N.E., Suite 510, Washington, DC 20002; (202) 408-1080; www .cbpp.org. Studies fiscal policies and public programs affecting low- and moderate-income families and individuals.

Center for Economic and Policy Research, 1611 Connecticut Ave., N.W., Suite 400, Washington, DC 20009; (202) 293-5380; www.cepr.net. Works to better inform citizens on the economic and social choices they make.

Center for Retirement Research, Boston College, 140 Commonwealth Ave., Chestnut Hill, MA 02467; (617) 552-1762; www.crr.bc.edu. Researches and provides the public and private sectors with information to better understand the issues facing an aging population.

Center for an Urban Future, 120 Wall St., 20th Floor, New York, NY, 10005; (212) 479-3341; www.nycfuture.org. Dedicated to improving New York City by targeting problems facing low-income and working-class neighborhoods.

Consumer Federation of America, 1620 I St., N.W., Suite 200, Washington, DC 20006; (202) 387-6121; www.consumerfed.org. Advocacy and research organization promoting pro-consumer policies before Congress and other levels of government.

Dēmos, 220 Fifth Ave., 5th Floor, New York, NY 10001; (212) 633-1405; www.demos.org. Liberal think tank pursuing an equitable economy with shared prosperity and opportunity.

Heritage Foundation, 214 Massachusetts Ave., N.E., Washington, DC 20002; (202) 546-4400; www.heritage .org. Formulates and promotes public policies based on a conservative agenda.

Middle Class Task Force, 1600 Pennsylvania Ave., N.W., Washington, DC 20500; (202) 456-1414; www.white-house.gov/strongmiddleclass. Presidential task force headed by Vice President Joseph R. Biden working to raise the living standards of middle-class families.

Pew Research Center, 1615 L St., N.W., Suite 700, Washington, DC 20036; (202) 419-4300; www.pew research.org. Provides nonpartisan research and information on issues, attitudes and trends shaping the United States.

U.S. Chamber of Commerce, 1615 H St., N.W., Washington, DC 20062; (202) 659-6000; www.uschamber .com. Business federation lobbying for free enterprise before all branches of government.

2

Vanishing Jobs

Will the President's Plan Reduce Unemployment?

Peter Katel

The line of job-seekers stretches around the block and back again at a Feb. 11 federal jobs fair in Atlanta. As the nation's financial/housing crisis has expanded into all economic sectors, employment has become the No. 1 issue for millions of Americans. President Barack Obama says the economic stimulus package Congress passed in February will "create or save" 3.6 million jobs, but skeptics doubt it will work.

From *CQ Researcher*,
March 13, 2009.

A layoff last year knocked Duane Simmons' life off its foundation. "I don't hold it against nobody," the 62-year-old machinist says, without apparent bitterness, "because the same thing is happening everywhere."

Indeed, in February alone, a record 651,000 Americans lost their jobs, pushing the unemployment rate to 8.1 percent — the highest in 25 years — and the number of unemployed workers to 12.5 million. A whopping 4.4 million jobs have been lost just since the December 2007 start of The Great Recession — as *The New York Times* calls the current economic crisis.[1]

Simmons' troubles began when Kennametal, a global metal-working, mining and tool company, bought Manchester Tool Co. of New Franklin, Ohio, where Simmons had labored for 33 years — virtually his entire working life. Kennametal quickly closed the plant where Simmons worked.

He moved his family to Newton, N.C., but his hopes for a new job have failed to materialize. Back home in Ohio, Simmons' $900-a-month home mortgage proved too heavy a burden, and soon the house was in foreclosure. The pressure of other debts forced Simmons and his wife into bankruptcy. And once his 26 weeks of unemployment insurance were exhausted, the couple began dipping into savings to pay rent and other expenses, with a little help from their son.

As the financial crisis last year expanded into all sectors of the economy, jobs and joblessness became the No. 1 issue for millions of Americans. A poll conducted for The Associated Press in mid-February showed that 47 percent of respondents were worried

AP Photo/Atlanta Journal-Constitution/Rich Addicks

about losing their jobs, and 65 percent knew someone who had been laid off.[2]

The pace and scale of layoffs accelerated in early 2009, with Jan. 27 an especially bleak day: Companies announcing big layoffs that day included Home Depot (7,000), Caterpillar (20,000), Texas Instruments (1,800) and Sprint Nextel (8,000). All in all, the first month of the year saw 598,000 jobs evaporate.[3] Then in February General Motors eliminated 10,000 more jobs, even though struggling carmakers had already cut their workforce in 2006-2008 by 80,000, using buyouts and early retirements.[4]

Each layoff announcement accelerates the economic decline that President Barack Obama and his team of economic advisers is struggling to reverse. "Without jobs, people can't earn," he said in mid-February at the signing ceremony in Denver for the $787 billion American Recovery and Reinvestment Act — the so-called economic stimulus bill — designed to "create or save" 3.6 million jobs. "And when people can't earn, they can't spend. And if they don't spend, it means more jobs get lost. It's a vicious cycle."[5]

Critics — even some liberals — say more needs to be done. "The Obama administration is . . . trying to mitigate the slump, not end it," wrote Princeton University economist Paul Krugman, winner of the 2008 Nobel Prize in economics and an influential *New York Times* columnist. "The stimulus bill, on the administration's own estimates, will limit the rise in unemployment but fall far short of restoring full employment."[6]

But White House Chief of Staff Rahm Emanuel dismissed the idea that a bill sized to Krugman's satisfaction could have gotten through Congress. "How many bills has he passed?" Emanuel carped in *The New Yorker.*[7]

In fact, despite Obama's call for bipartisanship, every single Republican in Congress — save for three senators — voted against the stimulus legislation, which includes billions of dollars to finance public-works spending. Many GOP leaders are denouncing the sweeping measure on the grounds that increased government spending alone won't end the job losses.

"It's filled with social policy and costs too much," said Mississippi Gov. Haley Barbour. "You could create just as many jobs for about half as much money."[8]

But other Republican governors, especially those in hard-hit states, backed the president. "I think he's on the right track," said Gov. Charlie Crist of Florida, which lost more than a quarter-million jobs last year.[9]

Nationally, layoffs are eliminating jobs far beyond blue-collar workers like Simmons in the ever-shrinking manufacturing sector. The financial-services industry is shedding so many workers that in New York City — the nation's financial capital — Mayor Michael Bloomberg has announced a $45 billion retraining program for pink-slipped investment bankers.[10]

"I have competitors closing up shop and going to live with their parents," says a financial software specialist in the New York area whose own contracts with banks and hedge funds have vaporized.

Newspapers and magazines, already reeling because millions of readers are going to the Web for free news, are laying off thousands of reporters and editors as advertising, the lifeblood of the news business, slows to a trickle. Newspapers have cut more than 3,000 jobs already this year, after slashing more than 15,000 in 2008, according to "Paper Cuts," a layoff monitor.[11]

"I'd like to stay in journalism," says journalist William Triplett, who recently lost his job as Washington correspondent

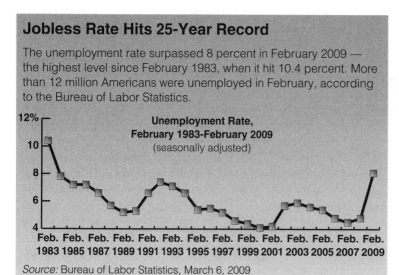

Jobless Rate Hits 25-Year Record

The unemployment rate surpassed 8 percent in February 2009 — the highest level since February 1983, when it hit 10.4 percent. More than 12 million Americans were unemployed in February, according to the Bureau of Labor Statistics.

Unemployment Rate, February 1983-February 2009
(seasonally adjusted)

Source: Bureau of Labor Statistics, March 6, 2009

for *Variety*, the entertainment-news daily. "But I don't know if I can make a sustainable living at it."

Major law firms have laid off 6,598 lawyers and staff members since Jan. 1, 2008 — more than half of them since the beginning of this year.[12]

Health care is one of the only sectors of the economy adding jobs, according to the U.S. Bureau of Labor Statistics: It showed a 30 percent increase in employment between February 2008 and February 2009.[13]

With few exceptions, the impact of the stimulus legislation has yet to be felt. In early March, state officials and politicians across the country were still drawing up lists of projects they planned to start with the new funds.

Meanwhile, Americans who have been laid off or who fear layoffs have cut back on shopping — forcing more layoffs in retail and manufacturing. Consumer spending fell 4 percent in the second half of 2008 after rising steadily for more than 20 years, the Commerce Department reported in March, and savings rose to 5 percent of disposable income in January — a 14-year high.[14]

"People who lose their jobs are going to be spending less," says Heidi Shierholz, a labor economist at the Economic Policy Institute, a liberal think tank. "For people hanging onto jobs in this climate, there is enormous economic insecurity. If you have the opportunity to build yourself a little cushion, putting off big-ticket purchases, now is the time you're going to do it — which further pushes out the recovery, until we get people feeling confident again."

But economists say the vicious cycle of layoffs, reduced spending and business retrenchment or outright failure won't wind down for some time. The Federal Reserve's influential Open Market Committee, which sets interest rates, concluded in late January that unemployment will "remain substantially above its longer-run sustainable rate at the end of 2011, even absent further economic shocks."[15]

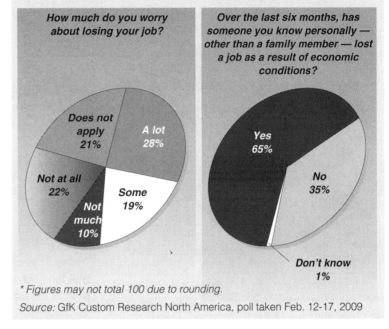

Almost Half of Americans Worry About Job Loss

Forty-seven percent of Americans currently have some concern over losing their job due to economic conditions. Nearly one-third say they worry a lot. Sixty-five percent say they know somebody — other than a family member — who has lost a job due to the recession.

How much do you worry about losing your job?

- Does not apply 21%
- A lot 28%
- Not at all 22%
- Some 19%
- Not much 10%

Over the last six months, has someone you know personally — other than a family member — lost a job as a result of economic conditions?

- Yes 65%
- No 35%
- Don't know 1%

* Figures may not total 100 due to rounding.

Source: GfK Custom Research North America, poll taken Feb. 12-17, 2009

As the economic meltdown continues — worldwide as well as within the United States — references to the Great Depression of the 1930s are increasing. In late February, Mark Zandi, chief economist of Moody's Economy.com, told *The New York Times* it was becoming more likely that the recession could turn into a "mild depression."[16]

His "mild" qualifier is rooted in historical reality. Americans haven't reached anywhere near an early-1930s level of misery. By 1932, the year Franklin D. Roosevelt was elected president, the unemployed "lived in the primitive conditions of a preindustrial society stricken by famine," a leading historian of the era wrote.[17]

In fact, conservatives cite statistics showing that today's 8.1 percent unemployment rate has not even reached the level of the 1981-1982 recession, when the jobless rate reached 10.1 percent.[18] "We've had worse recessions," says James Sherk, a labor policy fellow at the Heritage Foundation. "This is not the most painful, so far."

Michigan Had Highest Unemployment Rate

Michigan had the nation's highest unemployment rate — 11.6 percent — in January, largely due to the faltering auto industry. The South was among the hardest-hit regions, with many states at or above the nation's 7.6 percent jobless rate in January.

Unemployment Rate by State, January 2009
(not seasonally adjusted)

0.0-3.9%	
4.0-5.9%	
6.0-7.9%	
8.0-9.9%	
10.0% +	

Source: Bureau of Labor Statistics

unusually high unemployment.[21] But only 37 percent of laid-off workers receive benefits, in part because some states exclude part-time and temporary workers.[22] And some Republican Southern governors — including Bobby Jindal of Louisiana — say they'll refuse stimulus money tied to expanding UI eligibility, which they claim will unfairly burden states in later years. (*See "Current Situation," p. 39.*)

Even some former full-time workers are excluded from extra benefits. In his new home state of North Carolina, machinist Simmons says he couldn't get coverage past the standard 26 weeks because he had started withdrawing money from his 401(k) retirement fund. "I found afterward that I can't get unemployment and the 401(k) at once," he says. "It's my fault."

But Heather Boushey — a senior economist at the liberal Center for American Progress, which has close ties to the Obama administration — points out that there are 5 million more people unemployed compared to a year ago. "This is the largest annual jump in the number of unemployed since the U.S. Bureau of Labor Statistics began tabulating this data just after World War II," she writes.[19]

Roosevelt's New Deal — a set of programs designed to stimulate the economy, create publicly financed jobs and regulate business and financial practices — dented unemployment but hardly ended it. By 1940, the year before the United States entered World War II, 14.6 percent of workers were unemployed — well below 1933's catastrophic level of 25 percent but above the annual rates since then.[20]

Economists and historians are still arguing about the New Deal's effectiveness in countering the Depression. (*See "Background," p. 32.*) But not in dispute is the social safety net created by the Roosevelt administration, including unemployment insurance (UI).

In 2008, laid-off workers received more than $43 billion in UI payments, including $34 million in "extended benefits" designed to counteract the effects of

Will the economic stimulus bill create or save 3.6 million jobs, as promised?

Reversing the worsening unemployment trend is among the Obama administration's top goals — and biggest challenges — and the president's careful language shows his keen awareness of the strength of the current he's trying to reverse.

"We passed the most sweeping economic recovery package in history, to create or save 3.5 million new jobs," Obama told a "fiscal responsibility summit" at the White House on Feb. 23, apparently a slip of the tongue, since the earlier-stated goal has been 3.6 million jobs.[23]

The oft-used "create or save" phrase makes clear that the president is not promising to create 3.6 million new jobs. But if companies start hiring again in big enough numbers to move the jobless rate in a healthy direction, Obama will be able to take credit for saving jobs, even if the unemployment rate doesn't reach an ideal level. "We've already lost 3.6 million jobs," says economist Boushey at the Center for American Progress. "So saving or creating that many jobs would just get us back to where we were. It seems like a reasonable goal."

But Harvard University economist and blogger N. Gregory Mankiw, who served as chairman of the White House Council of Economic Advisers under President George W. Bush, ridiculed Obama's careful expression as "political genius." "You can measure how many jobs are created between two points in time. But there is no way to measure how many jobs are saved. Even if things get much, much worse, the president can say that there would have been 4 million fewer jobs without the stimulus."[24]

However adroitly Obama finesses his goal, the deeper question remains: Will his economic rescue package turn back the tide of job cuts? In the broadest terms, the "stimulus" is designed to revive the economy by pumping federal dollars into public-works projects, funding "green" energy projects such as manufacturing and installing solar panels, repairing the transportation infrastructure and extending broadband Internet access to rural areas.[25]

Also included are $400 tax credits for those earning less than $75,000 a year — calculated to put an extra $8 in the weekly paychecks of people still working. A household living on one minimum-wage salary would get additional tax credits amounting to $1,200 for a family of four. "Cutting taxes for working families helps to create jobs because these families are the most likely to spend the money," the White House said.[26]

Obama's approach reflects criticism of the effectiveness of a 2008 Bush administration $600 cash rebate to taxpayers earning less than $75,000. Recipients tended to save the money rather than spend it on goods and services.

The Economic Policy Institute's Shierholz, calls the Obama plan well-conceived. "There is no way you can spend $800 billion in a well-targeted way and not have it make a huge difference. This is a big help," she says. (The institute's former director, Jared Bernstein, is now economic policy adviser to Vice President Joseph R. Biden.)

Shierholz acknowledges the stimulus will take a long time to help most working families. In fact, like some other left-of-center policy experts, she suggests Obama is aiming too low. While the goal of creating or saving 3.6 million jobs may equal the number lost since the recession began, she says, it doesn't include jobs for the 127,000 people, on average, who enter the job market every month. "The working-age population is always growing," she points out.

But Lee E. Ohanian, an economics professor at the University of California, Los Angeles (UCLA), argues that the recovery package is unlikely to produce meaningful results because it isn't aimed at the banks' unwillingness to lend money. "The key impediments to recovery lie in the financial system," he says. Nothing in the recovery bill makes banks more likely to lend money, he argues.

Moreover, he says, the largely unspent Bush tax rebates bode ill for the Obama tax cuts. "It's not a bad idea to put money back into people's hands," he says, "but advertising it as a way of increasing consumer spending flies in the face of the evidence."

But some in grass-roots America say the Obama plan meets the common-sense test. In Atlanta, activist Cindia Cameron cited plans by her city's mayor to spend public-works money on projects at Atlanta's Hartsfield-Jackson International Airport and other infrastructure and to hire 200 police officers. "I am expecting that to happen," said Cameron. "People will be doing work that I'll be able to see."[27]

Cameron, national organizing director of 9to5, which campaigns for better conditions for low-wage female workers, said she's hearing some optimism — though tempered — from job-seekers. "People we know who are looking for jobs are looking for light on the horizon and are counting on the fact that this money will be coming through. There's now four applicants for every job, maybe soon there'll be only three."

Still, skeptical economists cite the magnitude of the crisis and the fact that hiring usually doesn't pick up until the end of a recovery. "All the evidence we have is that the economy is going down," says Rebecca M. Blank, a specialist in poverty and unemployment at the Brookings Institution. "The stimulus plan may pause things for a while. But the economy is rocky enough that I wouldn't want to say with any degree of certainty that we'll see job growth soon."

Is retraining for new skills the best option for laid-off workers?

The new recovery act includes nearly $4 billion for job training, including retraining "dislocated" workers who need new skills demanded in the modern workplace. In funding that program, Congress and the administration are relying on a strategy politicians often turn to in hard times.

In 1962, the John F. Kennedy administration had Congress enact a $435 million retraining program for workers whose jobs were endangered by a wave of imports flooding the country due to lower tariffs. But Arnold R. Weber, a University of Chicago economist who studied the programs, found that retraining was more complicated than politicians made it sound.

Writing in the wake of a recession that had cost 900,000 jobs, Weber warned: "Retraining programs are not likely to increase the total number of job opportunities in the economy. Large-scale, persistent unemployment ultimately can only be dissipated by maintaining the appropriate levels of aggregate demand and production." In fact, he concluded, "training activities are most effective in an economic climate of full employment."[28]

But Weber also acknowledged that on an individual level, retraining could indeed help workers upgrade their skills to become more employable. Over the decades that followed, the technological changes that rolled through the American workplace made the idea of retraining appealing to politicians and workers.

Industrial employees, especially, are keenly aware of the effects of technological modernization. "I didn't go on machines with computer-operated controls," says Mitchell Rice, 62, a former coworker of Duane Simmons at Manchester Tool Co. "I thought it was better for younger people to get on those machines; I didn't have much time left to work."

Essentially, Rice skipped his chance at retraining. He hadn't figured on being laid off at age 61, while still capable of working and still dependent on his pay and benefits.

Retraining advocates do not claim that new skills will benefit every laid-off worker or that employees nearing retirement age are all good retraining prospects. But retraining offers possibilities for those with the aptitude to re-learn jobs currently in high demand, or likely to be.

"The average age of apprentices in this country has risen to the late 20s," says Robert I. Lerman, an economics professor at American University in Washington who specializes in apprenticeship and other skill-building programs. "Even somebody in their 40s, if they want to get into 'green' jobs, can take a carpentry apprenticeship."

That approach can let apprentices learn a wide variety of skills, Lerman says. For example, someone who apprenticed on retrofitting homes with energy-saving insulation can also work on commercial buildings.

The realization that learning new skills isn't a panacea makes skeptics view retraining as merely an individual option. Some note that an unemployed person might as well learn new skills, because he or she has more to gain than to lose by doing so.

"Outside of the health sector, there isn't a sector that isn't shrinking right now," says Blank of Brookings. "The only reason to think about retraining . . . is to think in the long run. The opportunity cost to do some additional skills-building is very low."

But for many people, the practical obstacles may be too great, she adds. For example, "Very few people who are unemployed can afford to pay college tuition," she says.

Boushey of the Center for American Progress says the recovery act, with its green-jobs emphasis, will allow entire communities to push for retraining that would provide a big enough labor pool to attract new employers. In rust-belt areas where housing prices fell even before they did elsewhere, she says, "Many people can't afford to move, so they need jobs to come to them. This is one of the least-discussed, most challenging problems in the labor market right now."

In effect, retraining gives communities a chance to bet on what new industry will come into their region. The notion of retraining as a purely individual possibility "doesn't do a lot for a person living in a community where a GM plant just shut down and they can't sell their home," she says. "You need solutions that recognize this is a community problem."

But the University of California's Ohanian says trying to predict what industries will take off, and where, is a huge challenge. Instead, he advocates tax credits and other incentives for individuals wanting to retrain. "In the last 25 years we've seen a world of haves and have-nots develop," he says. "Receiving an education above and beyond high school is essential to succeeding in today's economy."

As to what skills laid-off workers should try to acquire or expand, Ohanian says he would leave it up to the individuals. "We know that people, for the most part, make pretty good decisions in terms of the educational opportunities they want to pursue."

Should unemployment insurance be extended beyond what the recovery act allows?

Unemployment insurance, which strings a safety net under some laid-off Americans, was created in 1935 as part of the Roosevelt administration's New Deal. The economic stimulus bill signed by Obama on Feb. 17 authorizes state governments to extend the time limits and eligibility standards for UI payments, which are limited in some states. UI standards are set by state governments, which pay the full cost of the basic program, financed primarily through taxes on employers.

The basic UI program provides 26 weeks of payments to those who lose their jobs through no fault of their own. Payments — calculated at 50 percent of an individual worker's past salary — average $293 a week, or about 35 percent of the average nationwide weekly wage.[29]

The federal government imposes its own employer UI tax, which funds some unemployment extensions enacted during recessions. For instance, in 1970, Congress authorized states to extend UI benefits an additional 13 weeks when unemployment is high — such as now. Last year, Congress added 20 more weeks, plus an extra 13 weeks for states with exceptionally high unemployment.[30]

The stimulus bill expands the program yet again, by shifting the entire cost of the 2009-2010 "extended benefits" program to the federal government and by covering more unemployed workers. It also adds $25 to each unemployment check in 2009-2010.[31]

Because states' eligibility standards and payments vary widely, the number of laid-off workers receiving the benefit — and how much they get — differs enormously from state to state. For example, 69 percent of jobless workers in Idaho in June, 2008, were receiving unemployment insurance but only 18 percent in South Dakota.[32]

Layoffs Accelerated in 2008

In the fourth quarter of 2008, more than half a million workers lost their jobs in "mass" layoffs — involving at least 50 people at one company — nearly 75 percent more than in the same period in 2007. In 2008 overall, nearly 1.4 million people lost their jobs in mass layoffs.

Jobs Lost in Mass Layoffs, 2007 and 2008

(No. of workers)

- Oct.-Dec. 2007: 301,592
- Oct.-Dec. 2008: 508,859
- **Fourth Quarter Layoffs***
- 2007: 965,935
- 2008: 1,383,553
- **Total Layoffs***

* Lasting at least 31 days

Source: "Extended Mass Layoffs in the Fourth Quarter of 2008 and Annual Totals for 2008," Bureau of Labor Statistics, February 2009

The Government Accountability Office (GAO) reported in 2007 that low-wage and part-time workers are more than twice as likely to lose their jobs, but only half as likely to receive unemployment benefits. In 1995-2003 (the most recent year for which full data are available), the GAO found that 55 percent of higher-wage workers who lost their jobs collected UI, compared to only 30 percent of low-wage workers employed the same length of time.[33]

The GAO hypothesized that the discrepancy in UI participation was due to declining union strength (because union members are well-informed about benefits) and the migration of manufacturing to states with stricter UI eligibility.

Given the current economic climate, demands for further UI extensions are certain to arise. "That's why it's called a safety net," says the Economic Policy Institute's Shierholz. "We have these programs to help maintain living standards, because for most people there is nothing to rely on but the labor market."

Moral or humanitarian reasons aside, Shierholz echoes a widely held belief that UI stimulates the economy in bad times because recipients immediately spend the money. "You get money into the hands of the long-term unemployed," she says. "Their savings have been depleted; they're most likely to spend UI on necessities in their local economies."

Conservative economists like the Heritage Foundation's Sherk argue that extending UI helps keep unemployment rates high by giving unemployed workers an incentive not to move to higher-employment states. "Workers spend less time looking for jobs and are less willing to make adjustments," Sherk says. "It's human nature, it's understandable. I'm not blaming them for it." (See "At Issue," p. 41.)

Sherk concedes that there are humanitarian reasons for extending UI, but he rejects the thesis that helping unemployed workers pay their bills benefits the economy as a whole. "You can't simply assume that every UI dollar goes into new spending," he says, citing a Heritage study he helped conduct. It concluded that any spending is offset by the effects of higher unemployment and by the taxes paid to support the UI payments.[34]

But University of California economist Ohanian — who questions both the likely impact of the Obama stimulus and the New Deal itself — argues that UI provides far more bang for the buck than other stimulus measures. "It's a more direct approach than expanding various federal expenditures in areas with high unemployment," he says.

Moreover, the classic economic argument that extending UI gives people an incentive not to look hard for work becomes less relevant in recessions as severe as the present one, Ohanian says. "It is really hard to find a job right now," he says.

Nevertheless, others warn, UI shouldn't be extended indefinitely. "You've got to mix the carrot and the stick," says Tim Duy, director of the Oregon Economic Forum at the University of Oregon and a former Treasury Department economist. "You don't want to starve people back into the labor force, but you want to give them some support."

Duy says 26 weeks of unemployment insurance isn't enough in the present circumstances. "Fifty-two weeks is certainly better, and should it be another 26 weeks on top of that, I probably wouldn't lose any sleep," he says. "But you can certainly slip from being too stingy to too generous."

BACKGROUND
Fighting the Depression

Massive unemployment was the hallmark of the world's most profound economic crisis. In the years after the U.S. stock market crashed in 1929, millions of jobs vanished as the entire global manufacturing and trading system nearly ground to a halt. Officially, the U.S. unemployment rate reached 25 percent by 1933, but estimates of the actual rate ranged as high as 50 percent.[35]

Even at the more conservative level, about 12 million working-age Americans lacked jobs (the country's population then was about 126 million). With federal unemployment insurance still two years away, hundreds of thousands of destitute jobless Americans relied on soup kitchens set up by charities.

Starving Chicago teachers who hadn't been paid for months were fainting in their classrooms; 5,000 banks had collapsed, wiping out 9 million savings accounts; crops rotted in fields as farmers lost their land or their customers. "Many believed that the long era of economic growth in the Western world had come to an end," wrote historian William E. Leuchtenburg in a classic study of the New Deal.[36]

President Herbert Hoover's response to the crisis was widely considered inadequate given the scale of the disaster. A federal construction program in 1931, for example, was designed to employ just 100,000 men. But Hoover rebuffed calls for more muscular measures, including a massive expansion in public-works projects.

"The problem of unemployment cannot be solved by any magic of appropriations from the public treasury," the President's Organization on Unemployment Relief declared on Dec. 22, 1931. The federal government's role was simple, the panel said: "Stop borrowing except to meet unavoidable deficits, balance our budgets and live within our income."[37]

Not surprisingly, the armies of homeless people living in makeshift settlements mockingly called them "Hoovervilles."[38]

Given Hoover's weak efforts, the tide of joblessness swamped local efforts. In 174 cities, donations to "community chest" federations — the precursors to the United Way — increased 15 percent from 1930 to 1931. In Philadelphia alone, charitable "relief" spending soared 404 percent between September 1930 and September

CHRONOLOGY

1929-1945 *Great Depression brings record unemployment; New Deal programs offer some relief.*

1931 As unemployment grows, President Herbert Hoover refuses to expand public-works programs.

1933 Unemployment hits 25 to 50 percent, and Franklin D. Roosevelt launches New Deal to restart economy and create jobs.

1935 Unemployment insurance is created to protect laid-off workers.

1937 Unemployment falls to 14.3 percent as New Deal programs kick in.

1938 Unemployment rebounds to 19 percent after Roosevelt retreats from some New Deal policies.

1941 Massive war buildup begins.

1942 Jobless rate falls to 4.7 percent.

1948-1962 *Postwar boom sees expanding economy and stable employment.*

1948 Congress supports Textile Workers Union effort to force a textile company to partly rescind a layoff.

1956 Federal government begins building Interstate Highway System.

1962 Congress passes $435 million worker-retraining program as foreign products appear in U.S. marketplace.

1970s-1990s *U.S. economy begins changing in response to massive foreign imports, outsourcing by U.S. firms, decline of unions and wave of mergers and acquisitions.*

1970 Congress extends unemployment insurance for high-unemployment periods.

1973 Oil producers' embargo ends era of cheap, plentiful petroleum — further weakening many U.S. employers.

1977 Youngstown Sheet & Tube shuts down a plant, laying off 5,000 steel workers — underscoring the weakening of U.S. manufacturing.

1981 Newly inaugurated President Ronald Reagan fires 11,500 air traffic controllers' union members — and dissolves the union — for violating federal anti-strike law.

1982 Worst post-war recession sends unemployment rate to 10.8 percent.

1984 Jack Welch becomes chairman of General Electric, lays off 25 percent of payroll over three years.

1988 New owner of RJR Nabisco lays off 50,000 employees — more than half the workforce.

1992 Unemployment reaches 7.4 percent during 1991-1992 recession.

1997 New technology spurs rapid growth, jobless rate falls to 4.6 percent.

2000s *Economy resumes growth after brief recession, but continuing employment lag prompts concern; "Great Recession" ends recovery.*

2002 Unemployment rate climbs back to 6 percent.

2003 Concern grows over "jobless" recoveries.

2005 Unemployment drops to 4.8 percent, but number of "discouraged" ex-workers remains high.

December 2007 Current recession begins.

2008 Plummeting real estate prices trigger economic meltdown, resulting in 3.6 million layoffs.

2009 President Barack Obama signs $787 billion "stimulus" bill, claiming it will "save or create" 3.6 million jobs. . . . States begin deciding which projects to fund with stimulus money, but some Southern GOP governors vow to forego money that would force them to pay higher long-term unemployment benefits. Jobless rate hits 8.1 percent at end of February; recession has cost 4.4 million jobs.

1931. In Chicago, the increase was 267 percent, and in New York, 125 percent.

Roosevelt took office on March 4, 1933, embarking immediately on an accelerated campaign to launch programs — known collectively as the New Deal — to put people back to work.[39]

Along the way, the New Deal reshaped the relationship between citizens and the government, and between the government and the economy. "Who can now imagine," wrote the late Arthur Schlesinger Jr., a leading historian of the New Deal, "a day when America offered no Social Security, no unemployment compensation, no food stamps, no Federal guarantee of bank deposits, no Federal supervision of the stock market, no Federal protection for collective bargaining, no Federal standards for wages and hours, no Federal support for farm prices or rural electrification, no Federal refinancing for farm and home mortgages, no Federal commitment to high employment or to equal opportunity — in short, no Federal responsibility for Americans who found themselves, through no fault of their own, in economic or social distress?"[40]

However, the New Deal was controversial at the time, and the economic debate surrounding its effectiveness has gotten a second wind in the present crisis. UCLA's Ohanian and Harold L. Cole of the University of Pennsylvania contend the New Deal prolonged the Great Depression. Writing in *The Wall Street Journal* recently, they blame the Roosevelt administration's promotion of "fair competition" codes in all industries — which encouraged trade associations to set industry-wide wages — with suppressing competition, forcing prices and wages up. "We have calculated that manufacturing wages were as much as 25 percent above the level that would have prevailed without the New Deal," they write, which "prevented the normal forces of supply and demand from restoring full employment."[41]

Advocates of massive government intervention say FDR's later retreat from aggressive spending prevented the New Deal from further improving the employment picture. "After winning a smashing election victory in 1936," writes Nobel Prize-winning economist Krugman, "the Roosevelt administration cut spending and raised taxes, precipitating an economic relapse that drove the unemployment rate back into double digits."[42]

The real engine of recovery, economists of all political stripes agree, was World War II, with its massive government-directed industrial production.

Boom and Gloom

The economic growth that started during the war continued for about three decades after combat ended in 1945. The prolonged expansion included rising education levels, as returning veterans used the new G.I. Bill to continue their educations; pent-up demand for consumer products, such as cars, kitchen appliances and clothing; and major public-works projects.

The signature public works undertaking was the massive Interstate Highway System, launched in 1956 and conceived by President Dwight D. Eisenhower. The system speeded up deliveries between manufacturers and markets while making it easier for ordinary Americans to strike out for new jobs in new territories.[43]

All the construction, production and consumption made jobs plentiful and easy to retain. In fact, writes Louis Uchitelle, an economic correspondent for *The New York Times*, there was a widespread belief that business had a duty to avoid layoffs. He points to what happened in 1948 in Nashua, N.H., when the community's biggest employer, a textile manufacturer, announced it would close two mills, laying off 3,500 workers.

The Textile Workers of America union fought back. A Senate subcommittee investigated the company, effectively forcing it to keep one mill open. City and state officials then attracted other employers to the city, and all the laid-off employees eventually found other work.[44]

Uchitelle cites a 1954 study that paints an employment picture nationwide that's scarcely recognizable today. Among employees changing jobs, he writes, "quitting was the norm; layoffs were an infrequent occurrence." And even laid-off employees found satisfactory new jobs.[45]

Nevertheless, even in relatively stable times, the fortunes of individual companies and industries rose and fell, sometimes affecting the economy as a whole. The country experienced six recessions from 1948-1975, lasting from eight to 16 months, according to the National Bureau of Economic Research.[46]

But even during these downturns, unemployment generally remained below worrisome levels. During the quarter-century from 1945 to 1970, unemployment climbed above 5 percent during only eight years.[47] However, the conditions that were conducive to decades of relatively high job security began changing in the early 1970s.

In 1971, the global system of currency exchange rates that initially promoted U.S. exports collapsed. Then the 1973 oil embargo against the United States by the Organization of Petroleum Exporting Countries marked the end of the era of cheap oil and relatively cheap foreign-made products — especially from Japan.

But Japanese exports began improving in quality, providing major competition to U.S. companies. In many cases, the U.S. companies surrendered. The steel industry led the way in 1977, when the big Youngstown Sheet & Tube steelmaker announced it would close a mill in Youngstown, Ohio, putting 5,000 workers on the street — considered a major layoff at the time. President Jimmy Carter arranged loan guarantees to workers who wanted to modernize the plant and run it themselves, but that plan failed. More steel plants closed in 1979, at a cost of 13,000 jobs.

Reagan and Reaganism

Characterized by his admirers as a visionary who guided the United States to new economic heights, and by his detractors as a promoter of winner-take-all capitalism that ultimately damaged the economy, President Ronald Reagan took office in 1981 vowing to create a new relationship between government and the economy.

Regulatory supervision of business declined (continuing a trend begun by Reagan's Democratic predecessor, Carter), unions lost clout, and "marginal" income tax rates — the rate imposed on a taxpayer's highest earnings — were cut from 70 percent to 28 percent.[48]

In one of his first moves, Reagan took on organized labor — a major player in national politics at the time. In 1981, when the nation's air traffic controllers went on strike for higher pay and shorter hours, Reagan fired all 11,500 members of the controllers union — who had defied a legal ban on work stoppages by federal employees — and hired permanent replacements.[49]

Steven Greenhouse, labor reporter for *The New York Times*, concludes in a recent book that Reagan's groundbreaking move was crucial to further weakening the already-challenged unions. "Companies now warned workers," Greenhouse writes, "that if they went on strike they might permanently lose their jobs." Unions now represent 12.4 percent of the U.S. workforce — and only 7.6 percent of the nongovernmental workforce — down from 20 percent in 1983.[50]

Reagan pushed his agenda at a time of rising fear and anxiety over foreign competition. Concern among businessmen and workers about cheap foreign imports forced Reagan — in actions rarely recalled today — to sign the Worker Adjustment and Retraining Notification Act. The 1988 law required companies with 100 or more workers to give 60 days' warning of any layoff of more than 500 employees. Today, Uchitelle reports, the law technically remains in force but has been so weakened with exemptions as to become irrelevant.[51]

Also often forgotten, Reagan's two terms were marked by import quotas on steel, textiles and other products, designed to buy time for U.S. manufacturers to build up their competitive edge. The outcome was greater efficiency with fewer workers in some companies and industries — and complete retreat in others.

For example, late-20th-century America's major contribution to the world economy, the personal computer, was in nearly all cases manufactured abroad. From 1973 to 2007, the nation's manufacturing workforce shrank from 24 percent to 10 percent of all non-agricultural employees.[52]

As the transformation of U.S. industry escalated, corporations began reaping profits less from manufacturing and more from buying or merging with other companies. In the process, they downsized or shuttered insufficiently profitable operations and reaped the benefits in the form of higher stock prices. The symbol of the new business model was General Electric Chairman Jack Welch. He took the top job in 1981 and within three years had laid off 118,000 employees — 25 percent of the workforce.[53]

Meanwhile, buyers of companies — known as "corporate raiders" — were financing acquisitions with "junk" bonds, so called because they were rated too risky for regular investors. They also carried high interest rates, which left the raiders so loaded with debt that their first moves invariably involved layoffs to cut expenses. RJR Nabisco, for example, was bought by Wall Street financier Henry R. Kravis in 1988. To pay down the borrowed portion of the $25 billion purchase price, he sold parts of the company and laid off some 50,000 employees — more than half the payroll.[54]

Critics decried the lavish rewards for speculators, contrasted with what they saw as shabby treatment of employees. The new business model, they said, was an

Behind the Grim Statistics, Grim Stories, Real People

"I can't imagine how I'd do it if I didn't live at home."

Behind the depressing unemployment statistics lie grim stories of people dealing — some better than others — with sudden, equally grim changes in their lives.

For Elaine Moore Kane, 47, losing her $15-an-hour data-entry job at the Fulton County Courthouse in Atlanta has left her getting by on what she can "rake, scrape and borrow — and God's grace." Her condo is in foreclosure, and she expects her car to be repossessed any day.

Kane readily acknowledges that, technically speaking, she quit her job to care for her 72-year-old mother, who has dementia, diabetes and asthma. Although the recently passed economic stimulus bill includes an unemployment insurance "modernization" program that would cover her situation, she's ineligible.

Kane has been in the workforce for a long time, having worked as a hotel clerk and a home health-care aide, among other jobs. But she's never faced such a drought of openings. "I frequent the Department of Labor for job searches. I try to create opportunities," she says, in a hopeful tone.

For now, Kane at least has a roof over her head. As a caregiver, she's authorized to live in her mother's government-subsidized apartment. But Kane's resources extend virtually no further.

Mitchell Rice — a 62-year-old machinist laid off last year after nearly a lifetime's work at Manchester Tool Co. of Akron, Ohio — would seem to have far more in the way of specialized experience. But, he says, "There doesn't seem to be anything out there."

Rice does receive unemployment insurance, but he and his wife are paying the full $630 monthly cost of health insurance under COBRA — the program that allows laid-off workers to keep their coverage if they pay for it. Under the stimulus bill, the federal government will pay 65 percent of COBRA participants' costs, but Rice says he was told he was ineligible. "I'm going to contact a congressman or someone," he says.

"You go through a period where you're real upset," Rice says of the layoff. "Then you realize you're not going to have a job anymore."

At age 36, Savoie Lockhart of Atlanta is not in a position to quit trying. But she's not having much luck. "I haven't been able to find anything," says Lockhart, who worked for more than eight years as a human resources officer for Wayne Farms, a poultry-processing company. The firm closed the plant where Lockhart had worked.

Now, the 401(k) account that represented Lockhart's savings is nearly tapped out. Getting by — barely — on $300 a week in unemployment insurance, Lockhart was planning to move out of her $855-a-month apartment into one renting for $500.

On the positive side, Lockhart has a son in college, on a full football scholarship at the University of Louisiana at Monroe. Another son, though, is still in high school. "I'm going to have to apply for financial aid and see how things go," she says.

---

ultimately self-defeating style of capitalism in which big profits created by paper transactions were favored over the production of goods and services and the reliable, good-paying — usually unionized — jobs it provided.

"While the rich got much richer, there was little sustained economic improvement for most Americans," Nobel Prize-winner Krugman wrote.[55]

From the other side of the political fence, the view couldn't differ more. "Reagan's record includes sweeping economic reforms and deep across-the-board tax cuts, market deregulation and sound monetary policies to contain inflation," Peter B. Sperry, then of the Heritage Foundation, wrote in 2001. "His policies resulted in the largest peacetime economic boom in American history and nearly 35 million more jobs."[56]

Jobless Recoveries

Months after taking office, Reagan was greeted by the start of one of the two longest recessions in the postwar

Lockhart had worked her way up into human resources even though she lacked professional certification in the field. Now her job search is hindered by both the dismal economy and the missing credential.

"The Internal Revenue Service was going to be doing some hiring," Lockhart says. "I had an interview, and went a second time and they took [identification] pictures and signed us up for a training class. A week before training was supposed to start, they sent me an e-mail that because of budget constraints, they weren't going to hire my group."

As for medical insurance, "Thank God, I haven't been sick," Lockhart says.

Many laid-off workers may be thinking about going back to school for more credentials, but that doesn't guarantee job stability either. In Bedminster, N.J., Patrick McCloskey, whose Ph.D in genetics and molecular biology enabled him to work for universities and biotech companies, has been jobless for a year. And he's learning that a lot of Ph.Ds, JDs and MBAs are unemployed as well.

"As I network I certainly run into more people than I expected who find themselves on the wrong end of a pink slip," he says, "more than I expected in the sense that my network tends to be fairly highly credentialed."

Still, McCloskey, 45, is upbeat. "I know it's going to be a hard search," he says. "But . . . at the end of the day, I'll find a job." For now, though, he lacks health insurance. "I considered getting catastrophic coverage. It's prudent for me to do so. But it's also prudent for me to pay my mortgage."

Despite a Ph.D in genetics and molecular biology, Patrick McCloskey, of Bedminster, N.J. — is still unemployed after losing his $125,000-a-year job in the pharmaceutical industry a year ago.

Another doctorate-holder in the same field, Roger Barthelson, 54, expects to lose his job in June as an assistant research scientist at the University of Arizona, Tucson, a state institution where he went to work after years in academia and the biotech industry. Both industry and academia, he says, hire Ph.Ds from abroad — who are generally lower-paid than Americans — which keeps salaries low. But he has nothing against foreign scientists, he adds.

If a funding shortfall eliminates his $42,000-a-year job, Barthelson says he and his wife could cope on her salary from a medical instruments firm. "We would have to cut back on expenditures," he says, "and we would not be putting away for retirement."

He shares the frustration of other scientists. "Why aren't we using our capabilities instead of having us sit around without resources to do what we're trained to do?" he asks.

Young people with fewer responsibilities are naturally better equipped to cope with the bleak job climate. In New York, Brian Pitre, 23, lost his first post-college job, at a two-person marketing agency. But as he looks for another position, his living circumstances are easing the hardship. "I can't imagine how I'd do it if I didn't live at home."

Thanks to his parents, Pitre can live comfortably on the UI checks he expects to receive soon. He certainly doesn't feel singled out by misfortune.

"I could count on more than two feet and hands the number of people I know who are laid off," he says. "Every day it seems like someone is getting the ax. We're all in the same boat."

U.S. economy, both lasting 16 months. The "Reagan recession" began in July 1981 and ran until November 1982.

Judged the most serious, until then, of all post-war recessions, the early-'80s recession pushed unemployment to a rate yet to be reached during the present crisis: 10.8 percent. Employment began picking up in 1984, but the unemployment rate didn't hit bottom until Reagan was almost out of office — in late 1988 — when it declined to 5.3 percent.[57]

Still, as Sperry notes, steady job growth marked Reagan's tenure, and the recovery stands as one of the pillars of the Reagan legend — evidence that his political-economic doctrine yielded positive results. But behind the falling unemployment rate, a trend emerged that later would prove problematic.

Two Bureau of Labor Statistics economists noted in analyzing employment trends in 1985 that the manufacturing sector continued shrinking, shedding about 200,000 jobs from 1984 to 1985. Meanwhile, the so-called service

What Will Happen to the American Workplace?

Three books offer early insights into the future of jobs.

Some of the leading indicators of hard times in the U.S. workforce came in the form of a trio of books by newspaper reporters — themselves members of a hard-hit sector of the economy.

In 2006, *The Disposable American: Layoffs and Their Consequences*, by Louis Uchitelle, an economics reporter for *The New York Times*, chronicled the decline of the dependable job and reliable employer. Two years later, labor reporter Steven Greenhouse, another Timesman, followed with *The Big Squeeze: Tough Times for the American Worker*, and Peter Gosselin, then the national economics correspondent of the *Los Angeles Times*, published *High Wire: The Precarious Financial Lives of American Families*.

The books focus on different dimensions of the labor market. But the writers — who all started out in a pre-Web world when newspapers and magazines thrived — draw parallel conclusions: American workers, whether blue- or white-collar, are getting less for the investment of their labor — including job security — than employees received during the flush quarter-century after World War II.

Disparities in income — documented by Greenhouse from government statistics — accompanied a growing disregard for employees, the books argue.[1] In the three accounts, workers are increasingly treated as interchangeable commodities to be overworked, outsourced or laid off virtually at will.

"No one is going to outlaw layoffs . . . from long-lived jobs by legislative fiat," Gosselin writes. Thus, "we need to decouple employment from many of the safety-net programs that employers have provided."[2]

Health-care coverage, for example, shouldn't end with a layoff, he argued. That position reflects, at least in principle, Obama's stance. Gosselin now has joined the administration as a speechwriter for Treasury Secretary Timothy F. Geithner.[3]

Uchitelle and Greenhouse remain at *The Times*. Their books compiled dozens of tales of life in workplaces where pressures on employees, by the authors' accounts, are rising at the same time that protection against job loss is disappearing.

Much like Gosselin, Uchitelle says workers need better cushioning against job loss than today's unemployment insurance offers. He also favors government discouragement of layoffs. "If we do manage to diminish layoffs, we will have taken a big step toward repairing a larger framework," he wrote. "Stable jobs and sufficient incomes in stable communities are powerful equalizers."[4]

---

sector was expanding, especially non-bank credit agencies. "This growth is tied to recent banking deregulation, which has lowered barriers to entry and encouraged growth and competition in the savings and lending industry," they concluded.[58]

Another trend emerged in the 1990s and continued into the 2000s. After eight-month recessions that opened each decade, recoveries were marked by a far slower return to low unemployment than had been the case in earlier business cycles. By 2003, the "jobless recovery" began to worry at least one top government economist: Federal Reserve Chairman Ben S. Bernanke, then a member of the Fed's Board of Governors. His conclusion: Businesses needed fewer workers.

At the time, the unemployment rate stood at 5.8 percent. But by rough calculation, he said, that left about 3.5 million fewer people working than was necessary for a healthy economy. He concluded that as companies learned to use new technology, they could do more with fewer workers. And American goods production continued to decline as imports accounted for more than one-quarter of manufactured products consumed by Americans — about double the foreign share in the 1980s, Bernanke said during a 2003 speech in Pittsburgh.[59]

"If (as some have argued) the jobless recovery is in part the result of an unusually high pace of structural change, then the degree of longer-term mismatch between workers' skills and the available jobs may have increased,"

The reporters' conclusions fall broadly within the Democratic policy universe. Conservatives, though, have largely refrained from confronting the authors directly. The two leading conservative magazines, *National Review* and the *Weekly Standard*, didn't review any of them.

In fact, the only mention came in a mocking squib in *National Review* in 2006, when unemployment was running at 4.6 percent. "He [Uchitelle] tries to debunk the idea that the economy has been creating about 200,000 new jobs each month," the unsigned entry said. "After his debunking, it turns out that the claim is, well, true. But the numbers allegedly conceal a problem. The pace of new hiring has not been very fast; the reason . . . is that fewer people are being fired or quitting their jobs. This might not look like bad news to most people."[5]

Since then, the news changed. In today's climate, conservatives are campaigning against broadening social protections and heavier regulation of business, both advocated by the three reporters. For conservatives, these measures amount to European-style socialism, hence contrary to American political tradition.

Writing in *The Wall Street Journal*, two leading conservative policy experts argued that Obama's push for universal health coverage bodes ill. "It will . . . put America on a glide path toward European-style socialism," wrote Peter Wehner, a former deputy assistant to President George W. Bush, and Rep. Paul Ryan, R-Wis. "We need only look to Great Britain and elsewhere to see the effects of socialized health care on the broader economy. Once a large number of citizens get their health care from the state, it dramatically alters their attachment to government. Every time a tax cut is proposed, the guardians of the new medical-welfare state will argue that tax cuts would come at the expense of health care — an argument that would resonate with middle-class families entirely dependent on the government for access to doctors and hospitals."[6]

Making a broader argument, Canadian conservative Mark Steyn wrote in *National Review* that the dangers of the European-style socialism — including "job-for-life security that he sees in Obama's policies — run even deeper. "When the state 'gives' you plenty," he warned, "when it takes care of your health, takes cares of your kids, takes care of your elderly parents, takes care of every primary responsibility of adulthood — it's not surprising that the citizenry cease to function as adults: Life becomes a kind of extended adolescence."[7]

Whether that vision or the three journalists' views predominate may determine what happens to the American workplace.

---

[1] Steven Greenhouse, *The Big Squeeze: Tough Times for the American Worker* (2009 edition), p. 40.

[2] Peter Gosselin, *High Wire: The Precarious Financial Lives of American Families* (2008), p. 318.

[3] Michael Calderone, "Dem exclusive? Reporters jump ship," *Politico*, Feb. 18, 2009, http://news.yahoo.com/s/politico/20090218/pl_politico/18971.

[4] Louis Uchitelle, *The Disposable American: Layoffs and Their Consequences* (2007 edition), p. 207.

[5] "The Week," *National Review*, April 10, 2006.

[6] Peter Wehner and Paul Ryan, "Beware of the Big-Government Tipping Point," *The Wall Street Journal*, Jan. 16, 2009, http://online.wsj.com/article/SB123207075026188601.html.

[7] Mark Steyn, "Prime Minister Obama: Will European statism supplant the American Way?" *National Review*, March 23, 2009.

Bernanke said. Ultimately, he drew a more optimistic conclusion, forecasting strong employment growth in 2004 and beyond.[60]

In fact, employment rose only slowly. It wasn't until January 2005 that the share of Americans with jobs reached its early-2001 level. But the number of discouraged job-seekers who had stopped looking for work — 416,000 — remained higher than before the 2001 recession, according to the Bureau of Labor Statistics.[61]

Meanwhile, some companies were prospering. And many cash-rich companies were using their money to buy other firms, often leading to layoffs. For example, Oracle Corp. bought PeopleSoft Inc. for $11 billion in late 2004, laying off 5,000 employees.[62]

Economists and businesspeople saw no mystery in the seeming paradox of booming business and slow employment. Drew Brousseau, managing director S. G. Cowen, an investment firm, told *The Los Angeles Times*: "A lot of the information industries that are drivers of growth these days are not as person-intensive as manufacturing."[63]

CURRENT SITUATION

Spending the Money

Lawmakers and bureaucrats throughout the country are meeting to decide where to spend the billions of dollars in stimulus funds heading to state capitols.

According to administration estimates, the American Recovery and Reinvestment Act of 2009 will "create or save" anywhere from 8,000 jobs in Wyoming to 396,000 in California.[64] In New York, officials representing nearly two-dozen agencies are hunkered down in Albany combing through hundreds of proposals from cities and counties vying for a chunk of the $24.6 billion the state will receive (estimated jobs impact: 215,000). By the first week in March, the proposals added up to $41.8 billion worth of projects — almost twice as much as the state will get.[65]

"Things have been so bleak for so long, where there was no money for any kind of project," said lobbyist Steven B. Weingarten, who represents several transportation agencies. "Once they saw there was money on the table, they said, 'We need to take a shot, any way we can.' "[66]

To abide by Obama's promise to keep the spending "transparent," a government Web site lists approved transportation-related projects certified by governors as meeting federal standards. By early March, 21 states and Puerto Rico had posted certifications for projects that would spend their portion of the $27 billion being made available for road and bridge work.[67]

A separate pot of $8.4 billion is destined for public transit projects, with New York taking the lion's share at $1.2 billion, and California $1 billion.[68]

Inevitably, the reality that many projects won't be funded is colliding with the ambitions of the politicians involved. Obama's hometown mayor, Richard Daley of Chicago, has been criticized because, by early March, he hadn't announced plans for spending his city's share of Illinois' $9 billion in stimulus funds (estimated jobs impact: 148,000).

"We did not put that out publicly," Daley said in early February, "because once you start putting it out publicly, you know, the newspapers, the media is going to be ripping it apart."[69]

Not surprisingly, Daley's critics had a field day contrasting that policy with the Obama promise of transparency. "In a normal city, such wish lists would be transparent, and the public would have a chance to comment, and if it chooses, to rip it apart," wrote Dennis Byrne, a Chicago commentator. He added that, apart from Obama himself, top aides including Chief of Staff Emanuel are Chicagoans.[70]

Of course, Chicago isn't the only place where public interest in job creation is intense. In Georgia (estimated jobs impact: 106,000), the director of Georgia State University's Economic Forecasting Center warned that tough times are likely to get tougher. The state would lose 143,000 jobs this year, said Rajeev Dhawan, who expects the stimulus bill to hasten recovery by only a few months. "After the last recession, we made up [jobs] we lost in about three years," he said. "This time, it is going to be a while."[71]

Governors' Resistance

After nearly unanimous Republican opposition to the stimulus legislation, GOP governors are split on whether to take all the money destined for their states.

One Southern faction doesn't object to building roads and infrastructure, but they do oppose taking funds contingent on expanding eligibility for unemployment insurance. Nationwide, states are being offered $7 billion for the first-year costs of expanding state unemployment insurance programs.

"You're talking about temporary federal spending triggering a permanent change in state law," Louisiana Gov. Jindal said in explaining why he wouldn't accept some $99 million in UI money.[72]

Barbour of Mississippi, Mark Sanford of South Carolina and Rick Perry of Texas agreed. "I remain opposed to...burdening the state with ongoing expenditures long after the funding has dried up," Perry told Obama in a letter.[73]

Their objections reflect longstanding conservative opinion that extending unemployment insurance discourages the jobless from seeking work. But another Southern Republican governor, Crist of Florida, favors taking the UI expansion funds along with the rest.[74] And Western and Midwestern GOP governors, including Arnold Schwarzenegger of California, also plan to take all the stimulus money.

At least one Southern GOP governor has changed his mind about accepting the UI money. "The changes we believe will be required in state law are feasible and relatively minimal," said Georgia Gov. Sonny Perdue.[75]

One of the changes Jindal and his colleagues don't like would make laid-off employees who've worked less than a year eligible for UI. Another would enlarge the pool of UI-eligible jobless workers by including unemployed part-time employees and those who quit work for major family reasons, including domestic violence; workers who qualify for benefits but need more money to cover dependent family members' needs; and laid-off workers who require extra benefits in order to get training in new skills.[76]

Does extending unemployment benefits boost joblessness?

YES James Sherk
Bradley Fellow in Labor Policy
Heritage Foundation

NO Heather Boushey
Senior Economist
Center for American Progress

Written for *CQ Researcher*, March 2009

Written for *CQ Researcher*, March 2009

Congress has increased the time laid-off workers can collect unemployment insurance (UI) payments to almost a year. Unfortunately these extended benefits have unintended consequences: They keep unemployed workers out of work longer and increase the unemployment rate.

Economic research conclusively demonstrates that extending the time unemployed workers can collect UI payments extends the time those workers stay unemployed. Dozens and dozens of studies reach the same conclusion.

It's not that unemployed workers enjoy being on the dole. Yes, some abuse the system, but most unemployed workers want to work. UI makes the need to find a new job less pressing. A recent study found that workers spend three times more time looking for work when their UI benefits expire than they do when they can rely on benefits. So while most UI recipients want a job, they do not look as intently as they would without government benefits.

This is a problem because workers are not replaceable cogs in the corporate machine. Employers need workers with unique skills: A laid-off Wall Street financier's talents do little for a software engineering firm. One worker or job is not just as good as another. It takes time and effort for employees to find jobs that put their unique skills to good use. Without that effort workers stay unemployed longer, regardless of economic circumstances.

Studies show that UI increases the time workers stay jobless by about the same amount in both recessions and booms. In both good times and bad, workers need to take the time to search for jobs that match their unique abilities. Twenty weeks of added payments — what Congress passed — causes the typical UI recipient to stay unemployed between three and four weeks longer.

This reduces the competition for jobs for everyone else, but not by much. The reduced competition for jobs from workers on UI will enable workers without benefits to find jobs five days faster than they otherwise would.

As a result, extended UI benefits increase the total unemployment rate. Heritage Foundation calculations show that the current extended benefits have increased the unemployment rate by more than 0.2 percentage points.

Good intentions aside, extended UI benefits do not help the economy.

Faltering job creation and lower consumption are keeping the unemployment rate high. Providing extended unemployment insurance (UI) benefits is boosting consumption — and thus helping to create jobs.

Employers have shed nearly 3.6 million jobs since December 2007, and about 11.1 million workers were unemployed by the end of 2008, yet there were only 2.7 million job openings — more than four unemployed workers for every available job.

The argument that unemployment insurance increases the unemployment rate hinges on two hypotheses: If the unemployed did not have benefits to rely on everyone would find a job, and unemployment benefits do not effectively stimulate the economy. On both counts, the evidence undermines these hypotheses.

Even if every worker with unemployment benefits took an extra week to job search, jobs will not go unfilled. Workers are lining up — even in 20-degree weather — to apply for jobs. In New York City, a job fair that had never attracted more than 2,000 people saw 5,103 show up last week. In Columbus, Ga., nearly 800 people lined up to fill about 150 positions for a new restaurant opening at the National Infantry Museum and Soldier Center at Patriot Park.

Around the nation, these stories are disturbingly common. Quite simply, there are not enough jobs to go around. Further, fewer than half of the unemployed workers nationwide receive UI benefits. For every worker receiving benefits, there's one without benefits who is ever more desperate to find a job. Consequently, no job goes unfilled for very long.

Unemployment benefits are a well-targeted economic stimulus. The 5.1 million workers who receive unemployment benefits can maintain their spending, which boosts their local economies. And, in general, research shows that without unemployment benefits recessions are longer and deeper.

Benefits flow to communities with the highest unemployment rates. To receive benefits, a worker must have been steadily employed during the previous year, been laid off through no fault of their own, be able and available for work and actively searching for work. In communities where many unemployed workers fit these criteria, the local economy is certainly in trouble.

Eliminating or reducing unemployment benefits will not create jobs and will reduce consumption. In these hard economic times, unemployment benefits are providing an important bulwark against poverty for millions of families while helping to keep local economies afloat.

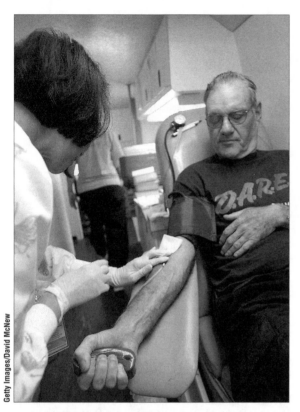

Getty Images/David McNew

The health-care industry is one of the only economic sectors adding jobs, according to the U.S. Bureau of Labor Statistics. Employment in health-care jobs jumped 30 percent within the last year, largely because of the growing number of aging Americans.

The recovery act adopted the new catagories wholesale from a separate bill, the Unemployment Insurance Modernization Act (UIMA), introduced in 2009 by Rep. James McDermott, D-Wash. Conservative lawmakers objected to expanding UI to cover all of the unemployed, not simply those who are laid off.

In early January, Senate Minority Leader Mitch McConnell, R-Ky., had said he "might" support expanding UI to part-time workers. But he went on to anticipate objections by Jindal and other GOP governors. "Do we, in the name of stimulus, want to make long-term, systemic changes?" McConnell asked.[77]

An advocate of UI expansion, Rick McHugh, Midwest coordinator of the New York-based National Employment Law Project, calls the objections groundless. States whose governors are resisting the changes and the money that

comes with them — Texas, Mississippi and Louisiana — "run stingy programs," he says, by paying minimum benefits and charging companies low unemployment insurance taxes. "They can keep taxes low because they're shifting the burden so that unemployed workers, their families, communities and charities bear the burden of unemployment instead of the taxpayers."

The average weekly unemployment benefit in Louisiana is $209.12, and it's $182.74 in Mississippi. In Texas, where the UI average is somewhat higher at $302.94, only 25 percent of the unemployed qualify for benefits.[78]

Layoff Alternatives

As the economy keeps shrinking — taking jobs with it — some employers are trying to stave off layoffs by cutting pay or cutting hours. Furloughs, or involuntary unpaid leaves — a traditional cost-cutting move in heavy industry, such as automobile manufacturing — have spread to universities, state governments and high-tech companies.

"Had we not done this, we would have had to lay off about 1,000 administrative personnel," Matt McElrath, human-resources chief for Arizona State University, told *The Wall Street Journal* after the college ordered staff to take furloughs of nine to 15 days by the end of June. The unpaid leaves responded to an $88 million budget cut by the Arizona legislature.[79]

California and Maryland state governments also ordered furloughs, as did Clemson University, Gulfstream Aerospace and the newspaper companies Media General and Gannett.

Some management experts say furloughs are better than layoffs in some ways. "Companies are . . . much more wary of the damage layoffs can cause, and the risks to their ability to rebound when the economy turns around if they cut too deeply," said John Challenger, chief executive of the outplacement consulting firm Challenger, Gray & Christmas.[80]

But when it comes to cutting pay instead of hours, other experts report mixed emotions in the executive suite. "Usually, companies say they prefer layoffs to pay cuts," Yale economics Professor Truman Bewley said. "It gets the misery out the door."[81]

Clearly, the United States isn't South Korea, where layoffs are nearly taboo. In late February, officials of Korean industry groups, unions, civic organizations and government ministries committed to a "grand bargain for social unity" — meaning that companies won't lay off workers, unions will accept lower or frozen wages and the government will grant tax breaks to companies that hold to the bargain. "We have to go through this together," Shim Hoyong, a factory worker for Shinchang Electrics Co., said. "If one disappears, it's awkward and uncomfortable."[82]

Furloughed Americans speak in much the same way, even in the absence of grand bargains. "I've gone through several rounds of layoffs, and those were much worse," a Gannett journalist told Reuters. "Once you've seen your friend laid off, you'd much rather do the furlough."[83]

OUTLOOK

The 'Great Recession'

The global sweep and intensity of the "Great Recession" is prompting economists and policy experts to ponder further structural changes to the economy and the workplace that until now have been considered unimaginable. In fact, conditions are deteriorating so quickly and with such force that old certainties are eroding.

For instance, there is renewed interest in "outsider" theorists such as Nikolai Kondratieff, a Russian economist of the early Soviet period who was executed in 1938, at the height of the Stalinist purges. Kondratieff held that capitalist economies run in 50-year cycles ending in depressions. The theory gets little notice in prosperous times. But an economic historian, David Colander of Middlebury College in Vermont, told *The New York Times*: "A good profession should take its outsiders more seriously. The worst thing for policy makers is to think they are right."[84]

For the moment, the economists that policy makers traditionally consult are scratching their heads. "If consumer demand is going to lag, what's that going to mean and how long will that go on?" asks Harry Holzer, an economist and professor of public policy at Georgetown University's Public Policy Institute. "And there are two other trends — baby boomers retiring, which in one sense is good, but if assets remain depressed they won't be able to retire; and the growing job outsourcing to India and China, which will tend to slacken the labor market."

'Slackening' is economist jargon for declining demand for workers — a development that bodes ill for job-seekers.

President Obama has said repeatedly that making the U.S. health-care industry more efficient could help American companies deal with international competitors in countries that provide subsidized universal health care and thus do not have the same high health insurance costs that saddle U.S. companies.

Boushey, the senior economist at the Obama-friendly Center for American Progress, says the health care industry — the only sector of the U.S. economy not shedding jobs — could remain strong even if its costs come down. "We spend almost twice as much of GDP on health care as other advanced economies," she says. "That extra money . . . could be spent on something else."

Echoing administration strategy, Boushey also suggests that development of environmentally friendly — "green" — energy industries could attract workers from the hard-hit manufacturing sector. But how soon wind, solar and other energy alternatives can compete with fossil fuel suppliers remains an open question.

Consequently, over the next several years, industrial workers are likely to continue to suffer the effects of global competition. "People may have to get used to job opportunities that, at least for awhile, aren't as lucrative as the ones we're losing," says Ohanian of UCLA. "Either they'll be unemployed, or they will make as much as 40 percent to 50 percent less than they've been making."

They may also find themselves settling for jobs they might never have considered before. In Perry Township, near Canton, Ohio, Edison Junior High School recently announced an opening for a janitor's job, paying $15 to $16 an hour, plus benefits. By the March 9 deadline, the school system had received 835 applications.[85]

Industries hit by forces other than global competition — such as the news media — are likely to feel the same effects, Ohanian says. "I feel for you guys," he adds.

If many elements of the future remain uncertain, opinion is unanimous that real estate-fueled credit binges are over. "We're not going to have people using their homes as ATMs because we thought the value of homes was going up," says economist Shierholz of the Economic Policy Institute. "We have this big gap in the economy that was being fueled by something that is not coming back."

The shrinking consumer credit sector won't affect all segments of society equally, says Duy of the Oregon Economic Forum. "The housing and credit boom were supportive of persons with lower educational levels and skill sets," he says. "We're not going to have an easy time transitioning those people into jobs."

Ripple effects will negatively affect small businesses, he predicts. At one time, Duy says, "Lots of people could start a small boutique and sell $600 pairs of shoes to people making $30,000 a year. Those days are in the past, most likely. What do those people do?"

The answer would interest millions of Americans. But, like much else about the future of jobs in the United States, it's not an answer that anyone has at the moment.

NOTES

1. "Employment Situation Summary," U.S. Bureau of Labor Statistics, March 6, 2009, www.bls.gov/news .release/empsit.nr0.htm. Also, Jack Healy, "651,000 Jobs Reported Lost in February," *The New York Times*, March 6, 2009, www.nytimes.com/2009/ 03/07/business/economy/07jobs.html?_r=1&hp.

2. "The AP-GfK Poll," GfK Roper Public Affairs and Media, Feb. 12-17, 2009 (interview dates), http:// surveys.ap.org/data%5CGfK%5CAP-GfK% 20Poll%20Topline%20021809.pdf.

3. Jack Healy, "62,000 Jobs Are Cut by U.S. and Foreign Companies," *The New York Times*, Jan. 27, 2009, www.nytimes.com/2009/01/27/business/ economy/27jobcuts.html?partner=rss. "Employment Situation Summary," *op. cit.*

4. Kendra Marr, "GM Slashing 10,000 jobs," *The Washington Post*, Feb. 11, 2009, p. D2; Bill Vlasic, "Ford is Pushing Buyout Offers to Its Workers," *The New York Times*, Feb. 26, 2008, p. A1.

5. "Remarks by the President and Vice President at Signing of the American Recovery and Reinvestment Act," White House, Feb. 17, 2009, www.whitehouse .gov/the_press_office/Remarks-by-the-President- and-Vice-President-at-Signing-of-the-American- Recovery-and-Reinvestment-Act/.

6. Paul Krugman, "Who'll Stop the Pain?" *The New York Times*, Feb. 19, 2009, www.nytimes .com/2009/02/20/opinion/20krugman.html.

7. Ryan Lizza, "The Gatekeeper," *The New Yorker*, March 2, 2009, www.newyorker.com/reporting/ 2009/03/02/090302fa_fact_lizza?currentPage=all.

8. Robert Pear and J. David Goodman, "Governors' Fight Over Stimulus May Define G.O.P.," *The New York Times*, Feb. 23, 2009, www.nytimes

.com/2009/02/23/us/politics/23governors.html? scp=1&sq=Governors'FightOverStimulus&st=cse.

9. "Regional State Employment and Unemployment Summary," Bureau of Labor Statistics, Jan. 27, 2009, www.bls.gov/news.release/laus.nr0.htm.

10. Patrick McGeehan, "City Plans to Retrain, and Retain, Laid-Off Wall Streeters," *The New York Times*, Feb. 18, 2009, www.nytimes.com/2009/02/19/ nyregion/19bankers.html.

11. See "paper cuts" (blog), updated frequently, http:// graphicdesignr.net/papercuts/? page_id=1088.

12. "Layoff Tracker," updated March 4, 2009, http:// lawshucks.com/layoff-tracker.

13. "Employees on nonfarm payrolls by industry sector and selected industry detail," U.S. Bureau of Labor Statistics, March 6, 2009, www.bls.gov/news.release/ empsit.t14.htm.

14. Kelly Evans, "Shoppers' New Frugality Hurts Business," *The Wall Street Journal*, March 3, 2009, http://online .wsj.com/article/SB123600014821809081.html.

15. "Minutes of the Federal Open Market Committee," Jan. 27-28, 2009, www.federalreserve.gov/mone- tarypolicy/files/fomcminutes20090128.pdf.

16. Peter S. Goodman, "Sharper Downturn Clouds Obama Spending Plans," *The New York Times*, Feb. 27, 2009, www.nytimes.com/2009/02/28/business/ economy/28recession.html?scp=3&sq=depression& st=cse.

17. William E. Leuchtenburg, *Franklin D. Roosevelt and the New Deal, 1932-1940* (1963), pp. 1-29.

18. "Labor Force Statistics from the Current Population Survey," U.S. Bureau of Labor Statistics (updated regularly), http://data.bls.gov/PDQ/servlet/ SurveyOutputServle.

19. Heather Boushey, "For Workers, The Grim News Just Keeps Coming," Center for American Progress, March 6, 2009, www.americanprogress.org/ issues/2009/03/grim_news.html/print.html.

20. "Employment status of the civilian noninstitutional population, 1940 to date," Bureau of Labor Statistics, updated annually, ftp://ftp.bls.gov/pub/special.requests/ lf/aat1.txt.

21. "UI Data Summary for United States," Department of Labor, updated quarterly, http://workforcesecurity

.doleta.gov/unemploy/content/data_stats/datasum 08/DataSum_2008_4.pdf.

22. Maurice Emsellem, *et al.*, "Helping the Jobless Helps Us All: The Central Role of Unemployment Insurance in America's Economic Recovery," Center for American Progress Action Fund, November 2008, www.americanprogressaction.org/issues/2008/ pdf/unemployment_insurance.pdf.

23. "Opening Remarks at Fiscal Responsibility Summit," transcript, *The New York Times*, Feb. 23, 2009, www .nytimes.com/2009/02/23/us/politics/23text-summit.html?scp=5&sq="createorsave" &st=cse.

24. Greg Mankiw, "Create or Save," Greg Mankiw's Blog, Feb. 19, 2009, http://gregmankiw.blogspot .com/2009/02/create-or-save.html.

25. For background, see Marcia Clemmitt, "Public-Works Projects," *CQ Researcher*, Feb. 20, 2009, pp. 153-176.

26. "American Recovery and Reinvestment Act: A Progressive Plan to Create Jobs and Help Families," The White House, Feb. 17, 2009, www.whitehouse .gov/assets/documents/Recovery_Act_Working_ Families_2-17.pdf. Also see, James Oliphant, "Stimulus package tax credit should mean $8 to $10 a week," *Los Angeles Times*, Feb. 18, 2009, p. A8.

27. For Atlanta Mayor Shirley Franklin's plans see Eric Stirgus, "Franklin wants Perdue to take stimulus money," *Atlanta Journal-Constitution*, Feb. 26, 2009, www.ajc.com/metro/content/metro/stories/2009/ 02/26/franlin_perdue_ stimulus.html.

28. Arnold R. Weber, "Retraining the Unemployed," University of Chicago, Graduate School of Business, undated (early 1960s), p. 16, www.chicagogsb.edu/ faculty/selectedpapers/sp4.pdf.

29. Emsellem, *et al.*, *op. cit.*

30. "Emergency Unemployment Compensation (EUC) Extended," Department of Labor, Feb. 17, 2009, http://workforcescecurity.doleta.gov/unemploy/ supp_ac.asp. Also, "Question & Answer: The Economic Recovery Bill's New "Extended Benefits: State Option," National Employment Law Project, Feb. 16, 2009, www.nelp.org/page/-/UI/eb.report .feb.09.pdf?nocdn=1.

31. *Ibid.*

32. Emsellem, *et al.*, *op. cit.*, p. 17.

33. "Unemployment Insurance: Low-Wage and Part-Time Workers Continue to Experience Low Rates of Receipt," Government Accountability Office, September 2007, www.gao.gov/new.items/d071147.pdf.

34. James Sherk and Karen A. Campbell, "Extended Unemployment Insurance — No Economic Stimulus," Heritage Foundation, Nov. 18, 2008, pp. 5-6, www .heritage.org/research/economy/cda08-13.cfm.

35. For background, see Jane Tanner, "Unemployment Benefits," *CQ Researcher*, April 25, 2003, pp. 369-392. Also, "Report on the American Workforce," Bureau of Labor Statistics, 2001, pp. 4-5, www.bls .gov/opub/rtaw/rtawhome.htm#introduction.

36. Leuchtenburg, *op. cit.*, pp. 1-29.

37. G. B. Galloway, "Relief of Unemployment," *Editorial Research Reports*, Dec. 28, 1931, available in *CQ Researcher Plus Archives*.

38. Photos of some Hoovervilles can be seen at Hoovervilles, Photograph Collage, The Library of Congress, Sept. 26, 2002, http://memory.loc.gov/ learn/features/timeline/depwwii/depress/hoovers .html.

39. Leuchtenberg, *op. cit.*

40. Arthur Schlesinger Jr., "The 'Hundred Days' of FDR," *The New York Times*, April 10, 1983, Sect. 3, p. 1.

41. Harold L. Cole and Lee E. Ohanian, "How Government Prolonged the Depression," *The Wall Street Journal*, Feb. 2, 2009, http://online.wsj.com/ article/SB123353276749137485.html.

42. Paul Krugman, "Franklin Delano Obama?" *The New York Times*, Nov. 10, 2008, p. A29.

43. "Welcome to the Eisenhower Interstate Highway Web Site," undated, www.fhwa.dot.gov/interstate/ homepage.cfm.

44. Louis Uchitelle, *The Disposable American: Layoffs and Their Consequences* (2007), pp. 43-45. Unless otherwise indicated, the remainder of this subsection is drawn from this book.

45. *Ibid.*

46. "U.S. Business Cycle Expansions and Contractions," National Bureau of Economic Research, updated Dec. 1, 2008, www.nber.org/cycles. The private, nonprofit, nonpartisan NBER is the national authority on when recessions begin and end.

47. Uchitelle, *op. cit.*; and "Employment status of the civilian noninstitutional population, 1940 to date," Bureau of Labor Statistics, undated, www.bls.gov/cps/cpsaat1.pdf.

48. "The Great Expansion — How It Was Achieved and How It Can Be Sustained," Joint Economic Committee, April, 2000, staff report, p.11, http://chuckskipton.com/uploads/growth_v4_-_no_cover.PDF.

49. Steven Greenhouse, *The Big Squeeze: Tough Times for the American Worker* (2009), pp. 81-82.

50. *Ibid.* Union membership numbers come from "Union Members Summary," U.S. Bureau of Labor Statistics, Jan. 28, 2009, www.bls.gov/news.release/union2.nr0.htm.

51. Uchitelle, *op. cit.*, p. 138.

52. Marlene A. Lee and Mark Mather, "U.S. Labor Force Trends," *Population Bulletin*, June 2008, Population Reference Bureau, pp. 7-8, www.prb.org/pdf08/63.2uslabor.pdf.

53. Uchitelle, *op. cit.*, pp. 132-134.

54. *Ibid.*, pp. 140-141.

55. Paul Krugman, "Debunking the Reagan Myth," *The New York Times*, Jan. 21, 2008, www.nytimes.com/2008/01/21/opinion/21krugman.html.

56. Peter B. Sperry, "The Real Reagan Economic Record: Responsible and Successful Fiscal Policy," Heritage Foundation, March 1, 2001, www.heritage.org/Research/taxes/bg1414.cfm.

57. "Labor Force Statistics from the Current Population Survey," Bureau of Labor Statistics, http://data.bls.gov/PDQ/servlet/SurveyOutputServlet?data_tool=latest_numbers&series_id=LNS14000000; also see Richard M. Devens Jr., "Employment and unemployment in the first half of 1988," Bureau of Labor Statistics, www.bls.gov/opub/mlr/1988/08/art 3full.pdf.

58. Susan E. Shank and Patricia M. Getz, "Employment and unemployment: developments in 1985," Bureau of Labor Statistics, February 1986, pp. 6-8, www.bls.gov/opub/mlr/1986/02/art1full.pdf.

59. "Remarks by Governor Ben S. Bernanke, Global Economic and Investment Outlook Conference," Nov. 6, 2003, www.federalreserve.gov/boarddocs/speeches/2003/200311062/default.htm.

60. *Ibid.*

61. Emy Sok, "Lower unemployment in 2005," Bureau of Labor Statistics, March 2006, p. 10, www.bls.gov/opub/mlr/2006/03/art1full.pdf.

62. *Ibid.*

63. Nicholas Riccardi, "Economy's Growing, but Where Are the New Jobs?" *Los Angeles Times*, Feb. 15, 2005, p. A1.

64. "American Recovery and Reinvestment Act: State-by-State Jobs Impact," The White House, Feb. 13, 2009, www.whitehouse.gov/assets/documents/Recovery_Act_state-by-state_jobs_2-131.pdf.

65. Nicholas Confessore, "Amid Albany's Budget Crisis, A Rush to Spend U.S. Billions," *The New York Times*, March 5, 2009, p. A1. Also, "New York's Guide to the American Recovery and Reinvestment Act," undated, www.economicrecovery.ny.gov/index.htm.

66. Confessore, *ibid.*

67. "Certifications Required by Sections 1201, 1511 and 1607 of the American Recovery and Reinvestment Act of 2009," http://testimony.ost.dot.gov/ARRAcerts.

68. "$8.4 billion for Public Transit," recovery.gov, March 5, 2009, www.recovery.gov/?q=node/202.

69. Dan Mihalopoulos, "Daley refuses to release stimulus project list," "Clout Street" (*Chicago Tribune* political blog), Feb. 4, 2009, http://newsblogs.chicagotribune.com/clout_st/2009/02/daley-refuses-to-release-stimulus-project-list.html.

70. Dennis Byrne, "Daley's great, big hush-hush," *Chicago Tribune*, March 3, 2009, p. A25.

71. Michael E. Kanell, "2011 turnaround seen for Georgia," *Atlanta Journal-Constitution*, Feb. 26, 2009, p. B1.

72. Jan Moller, "Jindal rejects federal aid for jobless," *Times-Picayune* (New Orleans), Feb. 21, 2009, p. A1.

73. Michael Luo, "Jobless Angry at Possibility of No Benefits," *The New York Times*, Feb. 26, 2009, www.nytimes.com/2009/02/27/us/27govs.html.

74. Robert Pear and J. David Goodman, "Governors' Fight Over Stimulus May Define G.O.P.," *The New York Times*, Feb. 22, 2009, www.nytimes.com/2009/02/23/us/politics/23governors. html?partner=rss&emc=rss.

75. James Salzer, "Perdue cuts deep, won't refuse funds," *Atlanta Journal-Constitution*, March 4, 2009, p. A1.

76. "The Unemployment Insurance Modernization Act: Filling the Gaps in the Unemployment Safety Net While Stimulating the Economy," National Employment Law Project, Jan. 30, 3009, http://nelp.3cdn.net/c763952a5b73e8852c_3iim6sj65.pdf.

77. "This Week," transcript, ABC News, Jan. 4, 2009, http://abcnews.go.com/ThisWeek/story? id=6573506&page=1.

78. "Unemployment Insurance Data Summary," Department of Labor, http://workforcesecurity. doleta .gov/unemploy/content/data_stats/datasum08/Data Sum_2008_4.pdf.

79. Dana Mattioli and Sara Murray, "Employers Hit Salaried Staff With Furloughs," *The Wall Street Journal*, Feb. 24, 2009, http://online.wsj.com/article/SB123542559566852689.html.

80. Andrea Hopkins, "Unpaid furloughs a trend for U.S. white-collar jobs," Reuters, Feb. 25, 2009, www .reuters.com/.

81. Mary Ann Podmolik, "More companies, such as Acco Brands, turning to pay cuts to avoid more layoffs," *Chicago Tribune*, Feb. 17, 2009, www.chicagotribune. com/business/chi-tues_ pay_cuts0217feb17,0,3374713 .story.

82. Evan Ramstad, "Koreans Take Pay Cuts to Stop Layoffs," *The Wall Street Journal*, March 3, 2009, p. A1.

83. Hopkins, *op. cit.*

84. Kyle Crichton, "Economic Lessons From Lenin's Seer," *The New York Times*, Feb. 14, 2009, www.nytimes .com/2009/02/15/weekinreview/15crichton.html.

85. Benjamin Duer, "More than 800 apply for school janitor's job," CantonRep.com, March 9, 2009, www.cantonrep.com/archive/x1593365705/More-than-800-apply-for-school-janitor-s-job.

BIBLIOGRAPHY

Books

Epstein, Lita, *Surviving a Layoff: A Week-to-Week Guide to Getting Your Life Back Together, Adams Media*, **2009**.
A professional retirement planner advises the newly laid-off on how to deal with their circumstances and bounce back.

Krugman, Paul, *The Return of Depression Economics and the Crisis of 2008, W. W. Norton*, **2008**.

One of the Bush administration's toughest critics — now chiding Obama from the left — the Nobel Prize-winning economist and *New York Times* columnist analyzes the financial meltdown, its causes and possible solutions.

Woods, Thomas E., *Meltdown: A Free-Market Look at Why the Stock Market Collapsed, the Economy Tanked, and Government Bailouts Will Make Things Worse, Regnery*, **2009**.
A conservative libertarian argues that government bailouts will delay economic recovery.

Articles

Aeppel, Timothy, and Justin Lahart, "Lean Factories Find It Hard to Cut Jobs Even in a Slump," *The Wall Street Journal*, **March 9, 2009, p. A1.**
U.S. manufacturing is so automated and efficient, laying off highly trained workers is difficult.

The Associated Press, "Buffett Says Nation Will Face Higher Unemployment," *The New York Times*, **March 9, 2009, www.nytimes.com/aponline/2009/03/09/business/AP-Buffett-Economy.html.**
Respected businessman Warren Buffett says the short-term future looks grim.

Baum, Geraldine, "It's Web 101 for this experienced intern," *Los Angeles Times*, **March 6, 2009, www .latimes.com/news/printedition/front/la-na-senior-intern6-2009mar06,0,3173555.story.**
As the media industry implodes, a former six-figure-salaried editor becomes an unpaid Web site intern to learn new skills.

Frayter, Karina, "IBM to laid-off: Want a job in India?" *CNN*, **Feb. 5, 2009, http://money.cnn.com/2009/02/05/news/companies/ibm_jobs/.**
In a reflection of how many operations IBM has moved abroad, the company is offering laid-off workers a chance to keep working — in another country.

Gerencher, Kristen, "Helping us through tough times," *MarketWatch*, **Oct. 23, 2008, www.marketwatch.com.**
A financial journalist discusses the growing psychological toll as the pace of layoffs continues unabated.

Leonhardt, David, "Job Losses Show Breadth of Recession," *The New York Times*, **March 4, 2009, www .nytimes.com/2009/03/04/business/04leonhardt.html.**

An economics correspondent reports that the pain of lay-offs has spread wide, both geographically and demographically, though non-college graduates are especially affected.

Luo, Michael, "Months After Plant Closed, Many Still Struggling," *The New York Times*, Feb. 9, 2009, www.nytimes.com/2009/02/10/us/10factory.html.
Laid-off workers attempt to rebuild their lives.

Neil, Martha, "February Free Fall: Major Law Firms Lay Off Another 2,000-Plus Attorneys and Staff," *ABA Journal*, Feb. 26, 2009, http://abajournal.com/news/february_ freefall_firms_ax_attorneys_freeze_pay.
The American Bar Association continues its coverage of major layoffs at big law firms, a new development in the upper reaches of the profession.

Reports and Studies

Dubay, Curtis, et al., "Economic Stimulus Pushed by Flawed Jobs Analysis," *Heritage Foundation*, Jan. 28, 2009, www.heritage.org/research/economy/wm2252.cfm.
Three conservative analysts say tax cuts will create more jobs than government spending.

Jacobson, Louis, et al., "Estimating the Returns to Community College for the Study of Labor (IZA)," February, 2004, *Federal Reserve Bank of Chicago*, December 2002, www.chicagofed.org/publications/workingpapers/papers/wp2002-31.pdf.
Three economists say taking math and science in community colleges improves potential earnings of laid-off workers.

Lerman, Robert I., "Are Skills the Problem? Reforming the Education and Training System in the United States," *Upjohn Institute for Employment Research*, 2008, www.american.edu/cas/econ/faculty/lerman/Ch2Lerman.pdf.
An advocate of expanding apprenticeship programs examines the consequences of education and job-training systems that don't reflect the varied ways in which people learn.

Vroman, Wayne, "Unemployment Insurance: Current Situation and Potential Reforms," Urban Institute, Feb. 3, 2009, www.urban.org/UploadedPDF/411835_unemployment_insurance.pdf.
An economist for a liberal think tank recommends steps to keep states' unemployment trust funds — the source of most benefits — healthy.

For More Information

Economic Policy Institute, 1333 H St., N.W., Suite 300, East Tower, Washington, DC 20005; (202) 775-8810; www.epi.org. Think tank with ties to organized labor and the Obama administration that places a heavy emphasis on job-related issues.

The Heritage Foundation, 214 Massachusetts Ave., N.E., Washington, DC 20002; (202) 546-4400; www.heritage.org. Conservative think tank issuing regular analyses and commentaries on the economy and unemployment.

National Employment Law Project, 75 Maiden Lane, Suite 601, New York, NY 10038; (212) 285-3025; www.nelp.org. Advocacy organization for workers and the unemployed providing information on unemployment insurance and other issues.

NewMajority.com; www.newmajority.com. Organization for dissident Republicans formed by former George W. Bush speechwriter David Frum that urges the party to rethink its positions on the economy.

U.S. Bureau of Labor Statistics, 2 Massachusetts Ave., N.E., Washington, DC 20212; (202) 691-5200; www.bls.gov. Statistical arm of the Department of Labor providing data about all aspects of employment and unemployment.

W. E. Upjohn Institute for Employment Research, 300 S. Westnedge Ave., Kalamazoo, MI 49007; (269) 343-5541; www.upjohninst.org. Nonpartisan think tank specializing in various aspects of employment and labor, including unemployment insurance.

This house in Pasadena, Calif., is among thousands around the country being sold after the owners defaulted on their mortgages. An estimated 2.2 million borrowers will lose their homes to foreclosure, largely because they had subprime mortgages. Congress and the Bush administration are debating how to help borrowers keep their homes and whether tough, new lending standards are warranted.

From *CQ Researcher*, November 2, 2007.

Mortgage Crisis

Should the Government Bail Out Borrowers in Trouble?

Marcia Clemmitt

When retired Chicago office administrator Delores King refinanced her house in 2004, she didn't expect to end up with "a mortgage that's thousands of dollars more than I started with" and payments that "have nearly doubled in two years."

"I have refinanced before, but I've never seen anything like this," King told a Senate Banking panel earlier this year.[1]

King's loan became unaffordable after its initial low interest rate reset to a higher rate and several unexpected, extra fees kicked in. King says her mortgage broker "rushed me through" the loan closing and never explained the mortgage's unusual features. King is one of millions of Americans in mortgage trouble in 2007, and her tale of an apparently "easy" loan that turns catastrophic is all too common, Eric Stein, senior vice president of the Center for Responsible Lending, in Durham, N.C., told a House subcommittee in September.

An estimated 2.2 million families will lose their homes to foreclosure because of a spate of "reckless" mortgage lending in recent years, Stein said. Today's foreclosure levels are the "worst they've been in at least 25 years," said Stein. Moreover, he said, "Millions of other families . . . will be hurt by declines in property values spurred by nearby foreclosures."[2]

The worst problems are concentrated in areas with slow economies, where cheap land encouraged a building frenzy, and in popular places like Phoenix and Florida, where floods of retirees and other new residents heated up the housing market.

Lower-income people are most at risk, but others will also feel pain. "Executives who built second homes out in the Carolinas" with 2- or 3-percent-interest loans that are about to reset to higher

Subprime Foreclosures Affect All Regions

In most of the states, 11-15 percent of the subprime mortgage loans made in 2006 will be foreclosed. In at least a half-dozen states, the failure rate is projected at up to 24 percent. The nation is experiencing the highest foreclosure rate since the Great Depression, according to the Center for Responsible Lending.

Source: www.responsiblelending.org

rates "will have trouble, too," says Robert Schultz, a home-building consultant in Boca Raton, Fla.

Still in question is whether the crunch will spread beyond housing and drag the nation into recession.

"I think the worst is over," wrote Jeremy Siegel, a professor of finance at the Wharton School, in early October. "Everyone is going to say, 'There is going to be a big bomb and . . . a hedge fund . . . is going to go under' " because it invested in mortgage-backed securities that are now defaulting. "Well, we haven't heard anything recently and . . . no news is good news. We are slowly returning to normal here."[3] Others see deeper housing troubles and recession ahead.

"A recession happens every decade, but this is going to be bigger" than usual "because the debt is so extreme," says Peter Cohan, president of a management-consulting and venture-capital firm in Marlborough, Mass. Builders will be hard hit as well as "insurance, furniture, paint and building-supply companies," he says.

Mortgage lenders and insurers are taking big losses, and some — including New Century Financial, the country's second-largest subprime lender — have gone bankrupt as recent loans began defaulting and the housing market slows.[4]

Several large investment funds and banks have already taken billion-dollar hits from losses on defaulting mortgages. Last summer big investment bank Bear Stearns put up over $3 billion to save one of its hedge funds that faced huge losses on mortgage investments.[5] Late last month financial giant Merrill Lynch announced an $8-billion loss on mortgage securities, over $3 billion more than the company had anticipated only weeks earlier.[6]

A combination of easy money, loose lending standards and real-estate bidding wars that sent home prices soaring contributed to today's problems.

The current crisis comes from a "confluence of factors, and if you looked at each individually, it wouldn't be a big problem," says Robert Rainish, a professor of finance at the University of New Haven.

The development in the 1990s of investment instruments known as mortgage-backed securities tempted even cautious investors to buy mortgages, Rainish says.

The so-called securitization of mortgages boosted homeownership by enabling banks and other lenders to sell mortgages, thus raising capital to make additional housing loans. With so much mortgage money available, however, "an incredible ramp-up" of riskier mortgages occurred "in a very short period," says Rainish.

The highest-risk mortgages — known as subprimes — were usually offered to people with poor credit histories at higher interest rates than ordinary mortgages. "Virtually nonexistent before the mid-1990s, subprimes accounted for a fifth of all new mortgages by 2005," said Robert J. Shiller, a Yale University professor of economics and finance.[7]

By 2006, another formerly limited mortgage class was being offered to people with poor credit scores — often without requiring documented proof of income — as lenders sought to write as many mortgages as possible to boost their own bottom lines. Virtually unheard of a decade earlier, subprime and so-called Alt-A loans accounted for $1 trillion of the nation's mortgage debt by 2006, says Rainish.

"People who didn't qualify for credit to rent could get credit to buy a house," says real-estate developer Robert Sheridan, of River Forest, Ill.

Many of the new loans had no or very low down payments and were adjustable-rate mortgages (ARMs) with low initial interest rates that would have to be refinanced later, when rates were much higher.

"You couple easy money with the fact that a lot of people were not astute enough to understand" the risks involved in their loans, and "it was a train wreck waiting to happen," says Schultz.

Compounding the problem, the high number of would-be new buyers drove house and condo prices far above what was traditionally thought to be affordable. And the easy mortgage money encouraged hopeful homeowners as well as speculators as they bid up prices to unprecedented levels.

Pre-boom, median home prices typically equaled about 2.5 times the buyer's median income. Today, they're about 4.5 times income, and much higher in some regions, says Rainish. "That's a housing bubble."

Trouble was inevitable when we simultaneously "made home ownership the American dream and then allowed prices to grow way beyond the rate of growth of the rest of the economy," says Corey Stone, CEO of Pay Rent, Build Credit, an Annapolis-Md.-based company that helps consumers repair bad credit histories.

"The average American today can't afford to buy a home at current prices," says Robert Hardaway, a professor of law at the University of Denver. "The average home in California costs $500,000. You can't afford that home." But easy initial mortgage terms made many buyers believe they could, which led to today's record defaults and foreclosures.

Now Congress is contemplating restrictions on risky mortgages.

For example, regulators should impose an " 'ability-to-repay' standard" for all loans made to people with poor

Mortgages Are Widely Purchased

Mortgages held by homeowners are sold to institutional investors in many sectors of the U.S. economy and abroad. The large number of investors, and the fact that many know little about the mortgage market, has led lenders to greatly increase the number and riskiness of mortgages they offer.

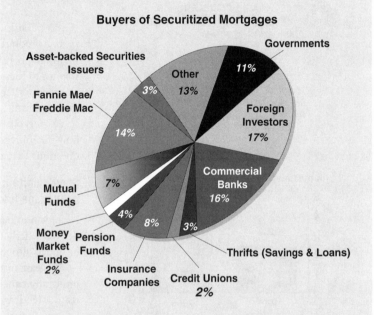

Buyers of Securitized Mortgages

Governments 11%
Asset-backed Securities Issuers 3%
Other 13%
Foreign Investors 17%
Fannie Mae/ Freddie Mac 14%
Commercial Banks 16%
Mutual Funds 7%
Money Market Funds 2%
Pension Funds 4%
Insurance Companies 8%
Credit Unions 2%
Thrifts (Savings & Loans) 3%

Source: "Mortgage Liquidity du Jour: Underestimated No More," Credit Suisse, March 12, 2007; Federal Reserve

credit histories, Martin Eakes, CEO of the Center for Responsible Lending, told the Senate Banking Committee in February. ARMs "now make up the vast majority of subprime loans, and they have predictable and devastating consequences for . . . homeowners," who may lose their houses when interest rates change, he said.[8]

The Federal Reserve Board (the Fed) — which governs the nation's banking system and money supply — has cut interest rates on bank-to-bank loans to encourage lenders and investors spooked by rising mortgage-default rates to get back in the financial game.

Lower Fed rates would not directly translate into lower mortgage interest. However, by making it easier for banks to get money, "the Fed is signaling, 'Let's restore confidence and get the economy started again,' " says Philip Ashton, an assistant professor of urban planning and policy at the University of Illinois, Chicago.

Housing Costs Swamp Millions of Families

The number of working families paying more than half their income for housing nearly doubled from 1997 to 2005. The increase reflects the rise in housing prices and the larger number of low-income people who obtained mortgages.

Families Paying More Than Half Their Income for Housing

(in millions)

Source: "The Housing Landscape for America's Working Families," Center for Housing Policy, August 2007

The rate cuts get mixed reviews as a strategy to ease the mortgage mess and credit freeze, since many experts partly blame low Fed interest rates in the early 2000s for helping fuel recent excesses.

Meanwhile, states, localities and the federal government — as well as private lenders and the giant Federal National Mortgage Corporation (Fannie Mae) — are making funds and loans available to help struggling homeowners stay put. For example, in hard-hit Cleveland, Cuyahoga County will fund loans to struggling homeowners using $3 million in penalties collected for late payment of property taxes.[9]

And under pressure to stop the bleeding, the nation's biggest mortgage lender, Countrywide Financial Corp.,

announced in October that it will restructure about 82,000 mortgages to make them more affordable.[10]

But some economists criticize such "bailouts" as unwise tinkering with economic markets.

"Individuals need to be responsible for their own borrowing," says Marvin Goodfriend, a professor of economics at Carnegie Mellon University's Tepper School of Business and a research economist with the Federal Reserve Bank of Richmond. That means much more financial education for everyone, he says. The government, the private sector, and nonprofit groups should step up to the task but haven't yet, he says. "People need to hear another voice besides the voice that's saying, 'No money down.'"

As nervous homeowners and investors wait to see how the mortgage crunch plays out, here are some of the questions that are being asked:

Should certain kinds of risky home loans be banned?

As large numbers of mortgages go into default, Congress debates whether some mortgage-lending practices should be ended altogether.

"At least in the vast majority of situations, and definitely any time federal money is involved," some of the riskiest lending practices should be banned, says Robert Losey, chairman of the Department of Finance at American University in Washington, D.C. For example, "there should be a requirement for significant down payments" for most loans, a tradition that's gotten lost, Losey says. "If someone makes no down payment, they have nothing to risk" and are more likely to walk away from the mortgage if the going gets tough, he says.

Some recent mortgages also have limited requirements for borrowers to document their income and assets — or don't require them at all.

"Oversight should limit or eliminate no-doc [no-documentation] loans," says Sandra Phillips, an assistant professor of finance at Syracuse University. "There should have been a crackdown on these lenders who were originating mortgages based on nonexistent and inflated equity," she says.

It's also become common practice for lenders to certify that borrowers are equipped to pay off adjustable-rate mortgages (ARMs) based on whether they have enough income to pay the loans' initial, low "teaser" rates. Critics call for ARMs to be sold only to borrowers who show they will be able to make payments when interest resets to a higher rate.

The Treasury Department and other federal agencies recommended in October 2006 eliminating ARMs that certify only that borrowers can pay the low, initial rates. According to the agencies, analysis "of borrowers' repayment capacity should include an evaluation of their ability to repay the debt by final maturity at the fully indexed rate."[11]

But many in the mortgage industry protest that strict rules will stifle innovation in lending and keep many people from getting mortgages.

"While it may sound reasonable to require that all borrowers contending for" ARMs "be qualified at the fully indexed rate . . . such an approach will lock some borrowers out of the home of their dreams and deprive them of lower payments," Douglas O. Duncan, senior vice president for research and business development at the Mortgage Bankers Association, told a Senate panel in February. "The magic of today's market is that the widest range of borrowers can get the widest spectrum of loans."[12]

"We cannot agree that underwriting to the fully indexed rate is the correct standard in all situations," said Sandor Samuels, an executive managing director of Countrywide Financial. Many "homeowners who will need to refinance will not be able to qualify under such a standard," and "many first-time homebuyers who can currently purchase a home will no longer . . . qualify . . . under the proposed guidelines," he said. "This will materially reduce housing demand . . . and delay the housing recovery."[13]

The National Association of Mortgage Brokers (NAMB) "believes the problem of rising foreclosures is complex and will not be corrected by simply removing products from the market," said NAMB President Harry Dinham.

Indeed, the availability of subprime mortgages helped push homeownership to an all-time high of about 69 percent of families in the last few years.[14]

Rules can be significantly tightened without banning some kinds of mortgages altogether, many analysts say.

"I would change the way people [in the mortgage industry] get compensated," for example, says Cohan, the management-consultant and venture capitalist.

Instead of paying commissions up front, which gives brokers and some lenders' representatives incentive to

Greg Giniel's house in Arizona's Queen Creek housing development in is in foreclosure, but he hopes to buy it back in November. Many borrowers got in trouble because they were saddled with high-risk, high-interest "subprime" mortgages, which are usually offered to people with bad credit histories. However, subprimes were also pushed on many people with good credit.

push buyers into mortgages whether they can afford them or not, "I'd put half the commission in escrow," Cohan says. If the mortgage "maintained value for 10 years, then brokers would get the money." But if the mortgage "collapsed, then the money would go to pay the cost of their mistakes."

"Reducing the incentive for volume" by decreeing that commissions can't be based on the number of deals a broker or salesperson arranges would help limit bad mortgages, says Syracuse University's Phillips.

"You need to regulate and supervise the mortgage brokers," says Phillips. To do that, federal laws would have to be reinterpreted or rewritten to allow regulation of brokers, she says. "Right now, they're in the cracks" and unregulated.

Risky loans proliferate partly because current disclosure rules don't require lenders to give borrowers clear, understandable information about exactly what their mortgage provisions mean, says the University of New Haven's Rainish. Today's rules about what lenders must tell borrowers "were made before anybody conceived of the current market," with its proliferation of complex mortgages, he says.

Subprime Loans Can Have Abusive Terms

A high percentage of subprime loans carry prepayment penalties and adjustable interest rates that are due to reset in two to three years. More than a third of the loans were issued based on little or no documentation of the borrower's income.

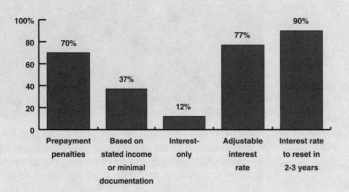

High-Risk Characteristics of Abusive Subprime Loan

Source: Testimony of Michael D. Calhoun, President, Center for Responsible Lending, before the Senate Banking Subcommittee on Housing, Transportation and Community Development, June 26, 2007

"Borrowers need a one-page summary that explains exactly what their mortgage entails," says Cohan. "Nobody reads these 65-page things" that current disclosure rules require, he says.

Should the government "bail out" borrowers caught in the mortgage meltdown?

Some analysts are encouraging states and the federal government to loosen the rules governing government-guaranteed mortgage programs to include homeowners in default and provide loan funds to help homeowners refinance. The Bush administration, congressional Democrats and several state governments back at least limited bailout plans, but some economists say any bailout encourages "bad behavior" to continue.

"Bailouts are terrible because they create moral hazard" — the tendency of people to make more bad choices in the future because they didn't have to face consequences of earlier choices, says Goodfriend of Carnegie Mellon University and the Richmond Federal Reserve Bank.

Even if bailouts are labeled as being for homeowners, it's lenders — many of whom engaged in risky and even predatory practices — who largely will benefit, some analysts say.

In August, President Bush announced a plan to open up Federal Housing Administration loans to some people struggling in the mortgage crisis. But, while the president "claims the bailout is for deserving homeowners, the thinly veiled policy changes are obviously meant to ensure that lenders are not defaulted on," commented the investment Web site eFinanceDirectory.com.[15]

Investors who carelessly speculated in high-risk securities would also be winners if fewer mortgages go into default, and the government should not prop them up, some financial analysts say.

"A borrower bailout and an investor bailout are synonymous," said Paul Jackson, a real-estate analyst for the mortgage blog Housing Wire. Furthermore, allowing people who can't afford their mortgages to get new ones for the same properties doesn't fix the fundamental problem — "millions of borrowers who simply can't afford a mortgage on the property they're now in," he said.[16]

Those who hope for a quick and simple bailout will be disappointed, says Illinois real-estate developer Sheridan. Because housing values won't quickly rebound, "federal legislation to help buyers hold on would have to be in place for a long time," he says.

Nevertheless, "there's a natural tendency by Congress and the executive branch to throw money at problems," so bailouts are likely inevitable, says American University's Losey. "But only the people who would qualify for loans anyway should have the opportunity to row their way out," he says.

"People are going to be hurt, but that doesn't mean we should subsidize them for buying a home they couldn't afford," Losey says. "There's no reason to say, 'Now we'll let you stay in that home.'"

Thirty percent or more of buyers in the recent, hot real-estate market "were speculators — non-occupying buyers" who bought homes with easy-to-get mortgages, then tried to "flip" them for a profit as prices rose, says Rainish, at the University of New Haven. Speculators "should not be bailed out," he says. If the government "is going to do a bailout, they need to be sure that only home-occupying buyers get assistance."

"We should not be bailing out people who invested in real estate, but it would be easy enough to separate speculators from owners," says Sheridan. "Just find out who's living in the house. Send them a letter. Show me the bills that come there."

Nevertheless, the sheer size of the foreclosure mess probably requires action, especially since government has stepped into similar crises as rescuer, says Rainish. "The government is trying to come up with a way for credit institutions to refinance these loans, but the question is how far they're willing to go," he says. "They spent $150 billion on the savings & loan crisis" of the late 1980s.[17] "And there's not much reason they can't do something similar to mitigate today's level of foreclosure," he says.

"You will have to say to some people, 'No matter how we restructure the financing, you can't afford the house,'" Rainish says. "But others can handle a restructured loan."

However, he adds, "You can't disentangle helping borrowers and lenders." But he argues that "it's not a bad idea to help the lenders. If lenders are going to come back in the game ever again, you have to help them. Otherwise, you won't have a market."

Left out of the Bush bailout are lower-income people, especially in minority neighborhoods, many of whom were deceived by predatory lenders into taking on more expensive loans than they realized, says Syracuse University's Phillips. "The irony of the proposal is that it only goes to upper-income people with good credit," she says. "I don't think we should leave out the population targeted for predatory loans," she says.

Community-advocacy groups working in neighborhoods hit by predatory lending "are doing a pretty good job helping people find a way to make the payments," says Phillips. A group she works with in Syracuse has helped many people stay in their homes, she says.

Number of Foreclosures to Double

The failure rate of recent subprime loans is expected to double, affecting 2.2 million borrowers. As housing prices decline, fewer delinquent borrowers have the equity needed to refinance their loan or sell their home to avoid foreclosure.

Chance of foreclosure for loan made in 2005 and 2006:
20 percent (vs. 10% for loans made in 2002)

Cost of foreclosures to borrowers:
Up to $164 billion

Number of foreclosed or soon-to-be-foreclosed loans:
2.2 million

Source: "Losing Ground: Foreclosures in the Subprime market and Their Cost to Homeowners," Center for Responsible Lending, December 2006

Sen. Charles E. Schumer, D-N.Y., has proposed legislation giving $300 million to community groups that specialize in foreclosure prevention. "This seems like a cost-effective investment to me," said Schumer. "It will save billions in spillover foreclosure costs."[18]

It wouldn't be difficult to provide assistance only to people saddled with predatory loans because the details of those abusive loans are a dead giveaway, says Phillips. "Looking at the loan agreement, in predatory loans you will see substantial charges [not found in other mortgages], and the fees will be high. There will be restrictions on refinancing."

Will the mortgage crisis trigger a larger financial crisis in the United States and elsewhere?

Most everyone agrees that people holding subprime mortgages — mostly low-income borrowers with poor credit — are defaulting and losing their homes. How far subprime fallout will spread in the economy, however, is sharply debated.

"The real bears in this market believe housing will lead the economy into recession," said John Burns, a real-estate consultant in Irvine, Calif. "Thus far, these bears are wrong. The housing market peaked in June 2005 and, two years into the downturn, economic growth is still positive. Unemployment remains very low . . . and consumers have started ramping up their credit-card debt again."[19]

Furthermore, the housing market itself is in good shape, according to Lawrence Yun, senior economist at the National Association of Realtors. "Although sales are off from an unsustainable peak in 2005, there is a historically high level of home sales . . . this year," he said. "One out of 15 American households is buying a home."[20]

"The speculative excesses have been removed from the market, and home sales are returning to fundamentally healthy levels, while prices remain near record highs, reflecting favorable mortgage rates and positive job gains," Yun said.

"Housing is only about 5 percent of the economy," said columnist Ben Stein at Yahoo! Finance. "If it falls by 15 percent, that would represent a fall-off [in the total economy] of about 0.75 percent. That's not trivial, but it's also not the stuff of which recessions are made."[21]

Eight out of the 10 U.S. recessions since World War II "were preceded by sustained and substantial problems in housing, and there was a more minor problem in housing prior to the 2001 recession," points out Edward E. Leamer, professor of management, economics and statistics at the University of California, Los Angeles.[22]

Nevertheless, "this time troubles in housing will stay in housing," Leamer said. "An official recession cannot occur without job loss, but . . . outside of manufacturing and construction there is little or no job loss. . . . Though this is largely uncharted territory, it doesn't look like manufacturing is positioned to shed enough jobs to generate a recession."[23]

But other analysts are less hopeful.

Some large financial entities, such as hedge funds and institutional investors like pension funds, bought risky packages of subprime mortgages, which are now defaulting at high rates. Worse, some have borrowed a lot of money against these securities, which they can't pay back, spreading the financial pain farther, says financial consultant Cohan. Just how far isn't clear because "we have an unknown amount of money that's been borrowed against these securities, and nobody is willing to mark the [value] truthfully," Cohan says.

The mortgage meltdown is a replay of similar events in the 1970s and '80s, says home-building consultant Schultz, However, "the results are bigger this time because prices were higher."

Adjustable-rate loans will reset to higher interest rates over the next two years, "so during that time people will be wondering, 'How do I move from my home? Can I take such a big loss?' " says the University of New Haven's Rainish. "The resulting uncertainty will freeze up the whole system, and the economy could go into shock."

Retirement funds and other investors who buy mortgage-backed securities "now don't know how to value part of their portfolio," Rainish says. "How do you manage your portfolio if you can't put a value on it? . . . Some of them will go under. If you want to sell these securities, you'll have to sell them at 10 or 15 percent below their real value."

Harvard Professor of Economics Martin Feldstein, a former chairman of the Council of Economic Advisers, said, "If house prices now decline" to traditional levels, "there will be serious losses of household wealth and resulting declines in consumer spending. Since housing wealth is now about $21 trillion, even a 20-percent . . . decline would cut wealth by some $4 trillion and might cut consumer spending by $200 billion or about 1.5 percent of GDP. The multiplier consequences of this could easily push the economy into recession."[24]

BACKGROUND

Losing Homes

The beloved 1946 movie "It's a Wonderful Life," starring Jimmy Stewart and Donna Reed, revolves around the struggle of a small-town banker to help workers hold onto their homes in hard times. The movie provides the traditional image most Americans have of the mortgage business — "there's an S&L [savings & loan] and a borrower, and they know each other," says management consultant and venture-capitalist Cohan.

Today, that picture is way out of date, says Cohan. "There are many, many more players than there used to be," and what happens to mortgages in one U.S. town "has ripples that spread out into the national and even international economy," he says. Moreover, mortgage debt is a much larger piece of each home-owning American's financial picture than in the past.[25]

Before the Great Depression of the 1930s, local savings institutions like banks made mortgage loans, and a mortgage lasted for five to 10 years, after which the outstanding principal had to be paid, or the loan had to be refinanced.

During the Depression, however, as employment and house values plummeted, lenders worried about losing money and refused to refinance mortgages. As a result, lenders repossessed many homes when owners failed to make the big final payment. At the height of the Depression, almost 10 percent of homes were in foreclosure.

The federal government began a series of interventions that gradually changed the way home loans are made. The first such program — the Home Owners' Loan Corporation (HOLC), established in 1933 — bought defaulted mortgages from banks and other lending institutions and returned the houses to owners who'd been foreclosed upon, with new mortgages.

The new HOLC loans lasted 20 years and had fixed interest rates. The new mortgages also were fully amortizing — that is, borrowers paid off both principal and interest for the life of the loan and didn't face a large "balloon" payment of the remaining principal when the 20 years was up.

HOLC was disbanded in 1936. But Congress continued to enact laws to ease access to homeownership over the next several decades.

Because the government didn't want to be in the business of holding the HOLC mortgages, in 1936 Congress created the Federal Housing Administration (FHA) to sell mortgage insurance. To encourage private investors to buy packages of government-originated HOLC loans, borrowers paid premiums into an FHA insurance pool that would protect investors from losses if homeowners defaulted.

Beginning in 1938, Congress created several entities authorized to invest in packages of mortgages in order to free up money at traditional lending institutions, such as banks, so they could offer more mortgages. The Federal National Mortgage Association (known as Fannie Mae) opened in 1938, and the Federal Home Loan Mortgage Corporation (Freddie Mac) was created in 1970 to provide competition for Fannie Mae. Over the years, Fannie's and Freddie's mandate expanded from purchasing government-originated loans to purchasing mortgages from private institutions.

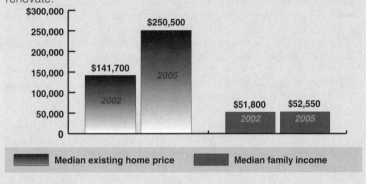

Florida Housing Prices Outraced Income Gains

Reflecting a nationwide trend, the median sales price of a single-family home in Florida increased 77 percent from 2002 to 2005 while incomes remained flat. As the cost of owning a home skyrocketed, more people turned to risky adjustable-rate or interest-only mortgages; many took on second mortgages to pay other bills or renovate.

Median existing home price ■   Median family income ■

Source: Florida Association of Realtors

U.S. home ownership — and the mortgage debt that goes with it — has grown over the years. In 1949, total mortgage debt equaled only 20 percent of total household income in the United States. By 2001, mortgage debt equaled 73 percent of income.

Selling Mortgages

While Fannie Mae and other government-initiated programs spurred home ownership, today's commercial mortgage market wasn't created until the 1990s, when more private investors became interested in buying up packages of home mortgages that were sold as financial assets — "securitized." The influx of private money into the housing market helped trigger today's foreclosure problems for subprime loans.

For decades, most private investors were reluctant to invest in packaged mortgages — mortgage-backed securities — "because they would have been bearing the full risk" should homeowners default, as a few inevitably will, says Jay Hartzell, an associate professor of real-estate finance at the University of Texas, Austin.

During the 1990s, however, financial institutions became more adept at "structuring" the securities: slicing up a single mortgage package — totaling hundreds or thousands of loans — into several investment vehicles, or tranches, with a range of risk.

CHRONOLOGY

1930s-1970s *After thousands of Americans lose their houses during the Great Depression, the federal government establishes programs to support home ownership.*

1933 Federal Home Owners Loan Corporation (HOLC) repurchases foreclosed homes, reinstates former mortgages.

1936 Federal Housing Administration (FHA) is created to insure HOLC mortgages so that investors will buy them.

1938 Federal National Mortgage Association — Fannie Mae — is founded as a "government-sponsored enterprise" to invest in mortgages, freeing up funds for lenders to make more home loans.

1944 Veterans' Bill of Rights creates a home-loan program for veterans.

1968 Truth in Lending Act passes, requiring lenders to informer borrowers about key terms in their loans. . . . Fannie Mae becomes a private, shareholder-owned company.

1970 Freddie Mac (Federal Home Loan Mortgage Corporation) joins Fannie Mae as a "secondary mortgage market," freeing up lenders' cash to offer more loans.

1974 Congress enacts Equal Credit Opportunity Act to stem lending discrimination against minority borrowers and others. . . . Real Estate Settlement Procedures Act requires lenders to give "good-faith estimates" of mortgage closing costs.

1980s-1990s *Adjustable-rate, interest-only and low down-payment mortgages become popular, spurring private investors to buy mortgage-backed securities. . . . Loans purchased by FHA, Fannie Mae and Freddie Mac decrease as a proportion of housing market.*

1989 First Bush administration and Congress act to bail out the savings and loan industry after S&Ls around the country make bad investments and collapse.

1992 Federal Reserve Bank of Boston concludes that low-income and minority neighborhoods face abusive lending practices and bias from borrowers.

2000s *House prices rise faster than inflation or incomes, and many homeowners take on second mortgages to pay other bills. Investors pour cash into the housing market, leading lenders to offer subprime mortgages, some of which don't document borrowers' incomes. Risky lending and soaring prices create a home-foreclosure crisis.*

2003 New mortgages are written worth $4 trillion.

2004 Federal Reserve Bank raises interest rates, causing a 26 percent drop in new home loans.

2005 Federal Reserve Chairman Alan Greenspan says that "without calling the overall national issue a [housing] bubble, it's pretty clear that it's an unsustainable underlying pattern." . . . Average house price grows more than three times faster than disposable income. . . . Delinquent payments and foreclosures rise. . . . House prices increase 49 percent over 2004 in Las Vegas; 43 percent in Phoenix. . . . Subprime loans make up 20 percent of new mortgages, up from 8 percent in 2003. . . . Forty percent of existing mortgages are refinanced.

2006 New Fed Chairman Ben S. Bernanke says housing market will "cool but not change very sharply." . . . New home construction drops. . . . Mortgage lender Ownit Mortgage Solutions files for bankruptcy. . . . Housing-finance giant Fannie Mae pays $400-million fine on accounting-fraud charges. . . . Risky new mortgages, like interest-only loans and loans that don't require documentation of the borrowers' income account for 13 percent of new mortgages, up from 2 percent in 2003.

2007 Mortgage lenders including New Century Financial, the second-largest subprime lender, file for bankruptcy. . . . Standard & Poor's and other securities-rating agencies downgrade securities backed by subprime mortgages. . . . Mortgage-market problems cause earnings to fall at major investment banks like Bear Stearns and Goldman Sachs; Merrill Lynch posts an $8-billion loss in the third quarter. . . . IDK, a German bank, slashes its earnings targets due to heavy losses on U.S. subprime investments. . . . In May, foreclosure filings are up 90 percent from May 2006.

"You take the same loan package, and you say the first 10 percent of the [mortgage] payments go to investors in this security — and it becomes the triple-A-rated, safest security in which the investors will always get paid," regardless of how many borrowers default, explains Rainish of the University of New Haven. That top-level security provides the lowest dollar payouts, but the payment is guaranteed, no matter what the level of default on the loans as a whole.

Then successive layers of security risk are carved out — each with a lesser guarantee of being paid in full but with a higher payout if they do, he says.

"Once people are able to buy the amount of the risk they want, more become willing to invest," says Hartzell.

"Nobody who was risk-averse" would buy mortgage-backed securities before the risk was segmented, explains Rainish. Once selling mortgage packages with different risk levels became widespread practice, however, "we have all this money flowing in" to housing lenders, he says. "We've created a money machine."

But the machine had flaws, says Rainish. Investors didn't really know how risky a buy they were making, a fact that has already led some investment funds to fail and now threatens further instability in financial markets. Bad mortgage loans, which in the past would have affected only a local bank or S&L, now have potential repercussions around the world.

"This is what happened [last summer] with two of [investment bank] Bear Stearns' hedge funds, which placed highly leveraged bets on packages of subprime-mortgage derivative products," says the British financial Web site Market Oracle. "When the value and creditworthiness of these bond packages . . . was cut due to the subprime defaults . . . the effect . . . was to virtually wipe out the total value of the funds that had been rated as low risk."[26]

Security risk was determined based on historical models predicting that between 5 and 10 percent of the mortgages would default, says Rainish. "But fraud and the lack of adequate underwriting" — documenting borrowers' finances and income to be sure they could make the payments — "changed the results," he says. "Investors did not anticipate that the underwriting standards would be changed to the degree they have been."

Determining risk involves seeing how many mortgages have defaulted in the past, then adding any important new factors into your calculation, says Yildiray Yildirim, an associate professor of finance at Syracuse. As the mortgage market heated up, "they didn't use the correct models" to gauge risk, and "some hedge funds and others trading these securities don't even have" a predictive model, he says. "If they see something they think will make money, they go after it."

Among the overlooked factors was how many subprime borrowers — most of whom have poor credit and low incomes — default on their loans after low "teaser" interest rates on their ARMs expired, Yildirim says.

Insecure Securities

Current accounting standards also encouraged non-bank lenders to write unusually risky mortgages, making it harder for investors to discern the true value of the mortgage-backed securities, says John D. Rossi, associate professor of accounting at Moravian College in Bethlehem, Pa.

A mortgage is essentially a liability for a lender until it's paid off in full, and traditionally it would be listed as such on lenders' account books, where auditors and potential creditors could use it to judge organizations' financial health. However, once a non-bank mortgage lender has "sold" mortgages to investors, current rules allow the lender to erase them from its books, even if the securities were sold on the promise that the lender would absorb some losses, should the mortgages default, Rossi explains.

Being able to take loans off their books increased the likelihood that lenders would engage in shoddier underwriting and make riskier loans, says Rossi. "Most likely it made them a lot less diligent," he says.

Securities-ratings agencies, like Standard & Poor's and Moody's Investors Service, rate securities based on risk. But the rating system broke down in the past few years, especially for mortgage-backed securities, many financial analysts say.

Based on the history of mortgage-backed securities, ratings agencies were listing subprime mortgage-backed securities as "A" grade — safe investments — when they were actually "B" grade — high risk, says Rainish. "The ratings agencies have been blindsided as much as others. They were pricing in a different world," he says.

Other analysts say ratings agencies and investors bear much of the blame for their woes.

Elderly, Rural and Minority Borrowers Are Easy Targets

Lenders add extra fees, omit key information.

Some mortgage lenders have taken advantage of the housing boom to saddle borrowers with loans they can't afford, especially in minority neighborhoods.

It's easy to take advantage of people when it comes to mortgages, says Robert Schultz, a Boca Raton, Fla., home-building consultant. Some lenders have pushed loans that were too good to be true, taking advantage of many borrowers' lack of financial savvy, "much like the credit-card industry trolls through college campuses and preys on kids' taste for instant gratification and the fact that they're not skilled in the ways of finance," says Schultz.

Higher interest "subprime" mortgages are generally offered to borrowers with poor credit. High interest rates on such loans protect lenders against the much higher probability that people with bad credit histories will default. But some lenders not only deceive borrowers about the true nature of the loans they're getting but also add in extra fees. Furthermore, in minority and rural communities, borrowers often are targeted for extremely expensive loans even though their incomes and credit histories would qualify them for lower-cost mortgages.

Some mortgage brokers have steered people into loans they clearly couldn't afford simply "because [the brokers] get the fees up front," says Sandra Phillips, an assistant professor of finance at Syracuse University. "Brokers got credit for volume, so the more you did, the more you got paid by banks."

In today's complex mortgage market, it's easy to slip costly loan provisions past borrowers, says Meghan Burns, co-founder of OfferAngel, a Scottsdale, Ariz., company that reviews and clarifies the terms of a mortgage offer for consumers. Federal rules about what lenders must disclose to borrowers "came out years ago, but meanwhile about 300 mortgage products have come out that weren't dreamed of" when the disclosure rules were written, says Burns.

"A house loan is much more complicated than a car loan, for example," and the disclosure rules make it easy for lenders to simply slip in some hair-raising provisions, she says. For example, lenders aren't required to flatly state in writing whether a mortgage carries a prepayment penalty — which socks the borrower with a substantial fee if they try to sell or refinance a property before a specified number of years have elapsed, says Burns.

Some brokers falsify borrower information on loan applications, sometimes with the borrowers' consent, sometimes without it, says real-estate developer Robert Sheridan, of River Forest, Ill. Lenders reassured borrowers that "we'll help you cook the books" to qualify for a loan, "and if people said they were worried about taking out too big a loan, they said, 'Don't worry! You can refinance!'" says Sheridan. But the reassurance about refinancing often wasn't true, he says. Prepayment penalties prevent borrowers from refinancing, and refinancing doesn't work if home prices don't rise, he says.

"More than ever, I'm seeing junk fees — unnecessary charges that lenders add to borrowers' bills to pad their own profits — and bigger junk fees than ever before," says Carolyn Warren, author of *Mortgage Ripoffs and Money*

"Wall Street and rating agencies, rather than state regulators or even lenders, largely decide what types of borrowers obtain subprime loans and how the loan products . . . are designed," Kurt Eggert, a professor at Chapman University School of Law in Orange, Calif., told the Senate Subcommittee on Securities, Insurance and Investments in April. But "unlike government agencies, ratings agencies work . . . in their own financial self-interest and . . . at the behest of investors and do not have the mandate to ensure consumer protection," he said.[27]

"In the end, Wall Street creates a demand for particular mortgages; underwriting criteria for these mortgages [are] set to meet this demand and [the] underwriting criteria, not the mortgage originator, [dictate] whether a consumer qualifies for this particular loan product," said

Savers. "A document-preparation fee! It's ridiculous," Warren says. "As if, otherwise, they weren't going to prepare documents at the end! It's like a restaurant charging you for a napkin. When I see a $695 processing fee, that's price gouging."

In addition, "a whole group of people inappropriately has been steered to more expensive loans" than they actually qualified for, says Corey Stone, CEO of Pay Rent, Build Credit, an Annapolis, Md., company that helps people rehabilitate bad credit histories.

Most people who've been steered to the worst loans are the nation's most vulnerable people — elderly, rural and minority residents who have less access to traditional financial institutions like banks than other Americans.

"The accumulated home equity and limited incomes of older homeowners have made them a primary target for predatory lending," said Jean Constantine-Davis, senior attorney for the AARP Foundation, a research group operated by the large seniors' lobby AARP. Predatory lenders often target elderly homeowners with pitches to refinance their homes to get extra cash to pay bills, she said.[1]

"One gentlemen, an 86-year-old stroke victim in a wheelchair, had a tax return that described him as a computer programmer who made $30,000 a year," said Constantine-Davis. Brokers and lenders had worked together to fabricate his and other tax returns to make it appear that elderly people "could afford mortgages whose monthly payments, in some cases, exceeded their incomes. Because our clients had owned their homes for decades, they had equity, and that was all the lender cared about."

Rural residents, who have limited access to banks, are among those heavily targeted by predatory lenders, according to the University of New Hampshire's Carsey Institute. In 2002, for example, rural borrowers were 20 percent more likely than urban residents to have mortgages that would sock them with large prepayment penalties if they paid off the loans or tried to refinance them.[2]

Minority borrowers are the most likely to have mortgages with oppressive terms, and many minority borrowers are pushed into expensive, subprime loans even though their incomes and credit histories qualify them for better interest rates.

In a study based on 2005 data, both African-Americans and Hispanics of all income levels were at least twice as likely to have high-cost loans as whites.[3]

In 2005, 52 percent of mortgages to blacks, 40 percent of mortgages to Hispanics, and only 19 percent of loans to whites were high-cost loans, said the Rev. Jesse L. Jackson.[4]

In New York City, 44 percent of mortgages in middle-income, predominantly black neighborhoods were subprime, compared to only 15 percent of the loans in economically comparable white neighborhoods, according to a 2002 study conducted for Sen. Charles E. Schumer, D-N.Y. "In other words, a significant proportion of black residents in New York City are being unnecessarily channeled into more expensive financing," said the report.[5]

This past summer the National Association for the Advancement of Colored People (NAACP) filed a class-action suit against more than a dozen mortgage companies — including Ameriquest, H&R Block's Option One, and Bear Stearns investment bank's Encore Credit — alleging "systematic, institutionalized racism in making home-mortgage loans."[6]

---

[1] Jean Constantine-Davis, testimony before the Senate Committee on Banking, Housing and Urban Affairs, Feb. 7, 2007.

[2] "Subprime and Predatory Lending in Rural America," Policy Brief No. 4, Carsey Institute, University of New Hampshire, fall 2006.

[3] "NAACP Subprime Discrimination Suit," *Mortgage News Daily*, July 16, 2007, www.mortgagenewsdaily.com.

[4] Testimony before Senate Committee on Banking, Housing and Urban Affairs, Feb. 7, 2007.

[5] "Capital Access 2002: Lending Patterns in Black and White Neighborhoods Tell a Tale of Two Cities, www.senate.gov/~schumer/SchumerWebsite/pressroom/special_reports/cap%20access%202002.pdf.

[6] "NAACP Subprime Discrimination Suit," *op. cit.*

Harry Dinham, president of the National Association of Mortgage Brokers.[28]

After lenders package mortgages into securities, ratings agencies "put a piece of gold wrapping paper around them," says venture capitalist Cohan. The agencies have a conflict of interest because "the investment banks shop the packages around and give the fee to the [agency] that gives the best rating," he says.

"I would be amazed if there weren't massive litigation" by investors against the ratings agencies down the line, says Illinois real-estate developer Sheridan. "They were advising clients how to put lipstick on the pig," and, "at a minimum, they sure didn't ring the fire alarm bell very quickly."

Ratings agencies reject such accusations.

The "issuer-pays business model" does have "potential conflicts of interest," acknowledged Michael

Home Values Always Go Up, Right?

Millions of Americans are discovering otherwise.

Between 1890 and 1997, inflation-adjusted house prices in the United States stayed roughly flat. But since around 1998, they've climbed each year, rising about 6 percent annually above inflation, according to Yale University Professor of economics and finance Robert J. Shiller.[1]

This unprecedented housing boom has helped create an urban myth — that home prices always rise, say economists. That idea is in for a severe test, however, as a wave of defaults on home mortgages builds, and the housing market undergoes huge changes.

Over the past several years, many Americans have used novel loan types — such as adjustable-rate mortgages (ARMs) and interest-only mortgages — to buy "more house" than they would have thought they could afford. Such loans have artificially low payments for the first several months or years, and borrowers gamble that, when it comes time for payments to rise, they can refinance into a different loan on the strength of their now much higher home value or sell the house for a profit.

Office manager Chaundra Carnes and her husband Michael, a winery production manager, purchased a $950,000 house just north of San Francisco in 2005 with a $700,000 interest-only mortgage. In the past, the couple's combined $100,000-a-year salary would have been considered far too low to afford the house, but their interest-only loan has low payments and they figured that, before higher payments came due, they'd be able to refinance or sell the house at a profit, as they had with three previous homes.[2]

"The only risk is if housing values go down," Chaundra said at the time. "And I guess that's a risk we're willing to take. And I think a lot of other people are too. So we're not alone."[3]

Today, however, the downside of that risk is around the corner, financial analysts say.

U.S. home prices peaked in the first quarter of 2006 and have since fallen 3.4 percent, said Shiller. Although that drop doesn't seem severe, "when there are declines, they may be muted at first" because "home sellers tend to hold out for high prices when prices are falling," Shiller said. "The 17 percent decline in the volume of U.S. existing home sales since the peak in volume of sales in 2005 is evidence that this is happening now."

It should have been clear that the recent, drastic run-up in house prices couldn't continue forever, because people don't have unlimited funds to spend on housing, even though easy mortgage terms made it seem they did, say some real-estate experts.

"The mismatch between income gains and higher real-estate values in some cities is particularly striking," said Jonathan Miller, CEO of the Manhattan-based real-estate appraisal firm Miller Samuel. "How can someone earning $70,000 a year afford a $500,000 home? They can't over the long run."[4]

The price boom began in metropolitan areas of California, the Northeast, and Florida, then spread inland, said Sheila C. Bair, chairman of the Federal Deposit Insurance Corporation. But "while home prices were effectively doubling in . . . boom markets, median incomes grew much more slowly, severely reducing the affordability of

Kanef, managing director of Moody's Investors Service Group, to the House Subcommittee on Capital Markets, Insurance, and Government-Sponsored Enterprises on Sept. 27. However, "we believe we have successfully managed" the conflicts by not paying analysts based on revenue earned by companies they rate, posting ratings methodologies on a public Web site, and having a separate analysis team monitor all rated securities on an ongoing basis."[29]

Easy Money

More private investors willing to invest in mortgage-backed securities gave lenders an incentive to make more loans. Easy money — and new 1990s technology that allowed financial institutions to automate credit checks and vary interest rates in real time — led lenders to create mortgages that made home ownership seem more affordable.

home ownership, despite the benefit of historically low interest rates," she said.[5]

But while recent prices may not be strictly "affordable" for the average American, easy mortgage terms blinded many to that reality and led to real-estate bidding wars that drove up prices all over. Good old-fashioned optimism, plus greed, played a role.

For most people who get into trouble, "it's not so much that they shouldn't have bought a house but that they shouldn't have bought such an expensive house," says Seattle-based Carolyn Warren, author of *Mortgage Ripoffs and Money Savers*. "Instead of tailoring their house demands to their budget, they fell in love with a house and then had to take a teaser rate to afford it, and then hope," she says.

Real-estate speculators also helped to drive up prices, says home-building consultant Robert Schultz, of Boca Raton, Fla. In earlier housing booms, flipping — buying a house in order to quickly sell it for a higher price — was relatively rare, says Schultz. But in the 2000s boom, flipping ran rampant. "The loans were so much easier to get this time," says Schultz.

"The number of pure speculators" was much higher than reported: "30 or 40 percent is my gut feeling," says real-estate developer Robert Sheridan, of River Forest, Ill.

With so many bidders in the game, it's no wonder that prices were driven sky-high, Schultz and Sheridan say.

The fact that house and condo prices have soared compared to the rest of the economy has been hidden by the way the government reports statistics, says University of Denver Professor of Law Robert Hardaway. "There was a purposeful 1983 decision to take house prices out" of the *Consumer Price Index* (CPI), he says.

"The decision was rationalized this way: People don't buy houses every year, so the cost of houses shouldn't be factored into the annual rise of the cost of living," Hardaway says. "But they do buy every six or seven years," he says.

At the same time, with speculators buying up houses they didn't plan to live in, rental properties flooded the market, driving rents down — and rents do get counted in the CPI, Hardaway says. "This makes it seem as if the price of living is rising even more slowly, but this is fraudulent. In fact, the real inflation rate is 15 percent when you put in housing."

Perhaps the most pernicious effect of skyrocketing prices was that it increased the temptation to borrow against homes' value to finance other wants. But if prices fall, a homeowner can end up unable to move without taking a huge loss and paying interest on their original loan many times over.

"Don't use your house as a piggybank for financing inessential things," says Warren. "You need to preserve your precious home equity or you'll end up like the 70-year-old who said to me, 'My bills are killing me! Can I do a debt consolidation?' He had [borrowed so many times on his house that he had] a mortgage of $350,000 even though he'd bought his house 30 years ago for $40,000."

The bottom line on home values is this, says Robert Losey, chairman of the Department of Finance at American University in Washington, D.C., where home prices have skyrocketed: "What goes up doesn't have to come down, but it usually does."

[1] Robert J. Shiller, "Understanding Recent Trends in House Prices and Home Ownership," paper presented to Federal Reserve Bank of Kansas City symposium, Jackson Hole, Wyo., September 2007.

[2] Quoted on "NOW," Public Broadcasting Service, Aug. 26, 2005, www.pbs.org/now/transcript/transcriptNOW134_full.html.

[3] *Ibid.*

[4] Jonathan J. Miller, "Unraveling the Pyramid of Bad Practices," Soapbox blog, Dec. 19, 2005, http://soapbox.millersamuel.com/?p=119.

[5] Testimony before House Financial Services Committee, Sept. 5, 2007.

Investors' interest in mortgage-backed securities increased after the 1990s technology boom went bust, says Ashton, the assistant professor of urban planning and policy at the University of Illinois. With investors wary of stocks and lenders "figuring out ways to help more and more people afford homes, suddenly the subprime mortgage market looked like a good place to park your capital," he says.

Non-U.S. investment also has flowed into housing. In the developing economies of China and India, "people

save a lot of income, they're unsure about their future" and that money needs to be invested, says economist Goodfriend. Oil-producing countries flush with cash from rising oil prices have provided another pot of housing investment, he says.

Finally, to keep the overall economy moving, Federal Reserve Bank Chairman Alan Greenspan kept interest rates at historically low levels for three years, until June 2004, when he began raising them again. Although the

How to Avoid Mortgage Troubles

Do's and don'ts for would-be homeowners.

Using common sense and being skeptical of hype can help you avoid mortgage trouble, experts say. Among the housing do's and don'ts:

- **Don't be in a hurry to buy.** "If you're going to move in two or three years, you should rent," says Robert Losey, chairman of the Department of Finance at American University in Washington, D.C. Switching houses carries "quite substantial transition costs" — as much as 3 to 4 percent of a home's value, he says.
- **Don't tap into home equity for non-essential purposes.** Second mortgages can mean trouble if home prices fall or you need to move. "You should think of your home as the place you live in, not something you should make money on," says Margaret Mann, head of the restructuring and insolvency practice at Heller Ehrman, a San Francisco law firm.
- **Shop for a house based on what you can afford.** "If buyers would tailor their desires to their budgets," home prices wouldn't rise sky high and lenders wouldn't offer dangerous mortgages like adjustable-rate and interest-only loans, says Carolyn Warren, author of *Mortgage Ripoffs and Money Savers*. Too often, "a person gets

preapproved by a lender for $350,000, but the real-estate agent comes back and asks to get them approved for $399,000," saying "they really want this sunken Jacuzzi," says Warren. That means a riskier loan and a skyward jump in local home prices, she says.
- **Remember that a lender's "good faith estimate" is just that, an estimate**, says Meghan Burns, co-founder of OfferAngel, a Scottsdale, Ariz., company that checks out mortgages for prospective home buyers. "The borrower takes it as gospel, thinking the estimate is a contract, but it's not," she says. "If you have somebody who's trying to lure you in" to a bad loan, "that's the bait in the bait-and-switch."
- **Watch for the signs** of predatory lenders, such as encouraging borrowers to lie about their income or assets to get a bigger loan; charging fees for unnecessary services; pressuring borrowers to accept higher-risk mortgages like interest-only loans; pressuring people in need of cash to refinance their homes; and using high-pressure sales tactics.[1]

---

[1] U.S. Department of Housing and Urban Development, www.hud.gov/offices/hsg/sfh/buying/loanfraud.cfm.

Fed sets interest rates only for bank-to-bank money transfers, other lenders take their cue from the Fed rate, and mortgage interest also hit historic lows.

In the 1970s and '80s, interest rates in double digits were the norm, soaring to over 20 percent in 1980. In the 1990s, interest on a 30-year, fixed-rate mortgage hovered between 7 percent and 9 percent. Beginning in 2003, however, rates dropped below 6 percent and have hovered at around 6 percent since, according to the mortgage-information Web site Lender 411.[30]

The Federal Reserve "wanted to prevent inflation, but in doing that they made homeownership dirt cheap," says the University of New Haven's Rainish.

Low interest rates created a surge in mortgage demand between 2001 and 2003, especially for refinancings that allowed homeowners to lower their interest payments and tap into extra cash at the same time, said Emory W. Rushton, senior deputy comptroller and chief national

bank examiner in the U.S. Office of the Comptroller of the Currency.

Surging demand prompted "lenders to expand their operations to boost capacity" and "attracted new market participants, often lenders with little business experience or financial strength," and a flood of new, risky mortgages ensued, Rushton told the Senate Banking Committee in March.[31]

As a result, "Lots of people in the United States who have no money — they are called subprime borrowers — borrowed 100 percent of the value of a house right at the top of a housing market which has since fallen sharply," wrote Paul Tustain, founder of a British investment-information Web site, BullionVault.com. With higher interest and a lower home value, many of these people can't make their new payments or refinance their houses.[32]

"The whole system allowed the frailty of human nature to triumph," says home-building consultant Schultz. "It took away all the restraints."

CURRENT SITUATION

Widespread Pain

Beginning in late 2006 and continuing this year, the wheels came off the mortgage bus. The number of people defaulting — falling behind — on payments, then losing homes to foreclosure, is rising sharply. Some lenders have gone bankrupt, and some recent investors in mortgage-backed securities have seen their investments quickly become worthless.

The financial industry and its regulators "got complacent" as mortgage loans got riskier and riskier, says the University of New Haven's Rainish. "It wasn't until sometime in 2006 that some of this stuff was starting to smell. Prior to that, nobody really got the gist of the excess that was taking place. But in the latter half of 2006, the most recent securities that were sold defaulted almost immediately," he says.

Midwestern states like Ohio are "national leaders in foreclosures," says the University of Chicago's Ashton. These areas have been in economic hard times for years, as the auto and steel industries waned, says Rainish. "You're seeing an implosion of income" at the same time as cash-flush lenders offered risky loans, he says. "People wanted to fix up, so they refinanced" with ARMs. "Then there was reset [of interest to higher rates], and they lost their equity."

The presence of foreclosed homes in a neighborhood affects everybody there, Rainish says. "Nobody can sell a home, even when they need to. You freeze the whole market. On a personal level, it's tragic."

"Even though we talk about people walking away from homes" and in some cases losing only a little cash since they made small — or no — down payments, "the foreclosure keeps you from buying a home later, and there are legal and moving costs associated with foreclosure, too," says Ashton.

While Chicago is not one of the hardest-hit areas, "there were still a lot of subprime loans for moderate-to-middle-income households in African-American neighborhoods," Ashton says. "It may be years — if ever — before they can get back into a home."

In Florida, Nevada, parts of California and some other sought-after locales, "flippers" — real-estate speculators — are big players in the ongoing crisis, says Ashton. "We've got flippers and speculators simply walking away" from properties, since the loan cost them little in the first place, Ashton says. That leaves lenders holding the bag, he says.

Some banks are ending up as owners of condos whose developers couldn't sell the majority of units before housing sales slowed, says Sheridan.

Banks aren't permitted to permanently manage residential properties, so they must sell them, he says. Meanwhile, "residents who've already bought in are locked into a property that isn't being cared for, whose value is deteriorating and which is likely to become a rental property," which is not what they plunked their money down for, says Sheridan. "The homeowner is not in a happy situation."

The selling and reselling of mortgage-loan packages to ever-more-distant investors may make it harder for some people facing foreclosure to work out a payment plan to keep their homes.

"How do you do a workout when nobody knows who owns what?" says Rainish. In the past, mortgages sold to a secondary market were in a big portfolio with Fannie Mae or Freddie Mac, organizations that are in the business of helping people stay in their houses. "Now the mortgages are owned by investment funds, by foreigners; they've been sold and resold," he says. "How are they going to deal with the workout? We don't know."

Nevertheless, "there still will be in almost every case a local institution that is the servicer" of the loan, says American University's Losey. "They don't have the same vested interest in working it out" as they did when local lenders held onto mortgages. Nevertheless, "I don't know that this means there will be that many more defaults or not," he says. "There should still be pressure from the institutions that own the securities to work out a logical deal."

Interest-Rate Cut

Debate rages over whether the government should bail out homeowners and whether strict new rules for mortgage lending should be created.

The first major action at the national level came from the Federal Reserve Board.[33]

In August and then again in September and late October, new Fed Chairman Ben S. Bernanke dropped key interest rates that make it easier for banks to lend money.[34] The moves came after the world's banks and other financial institutions began tightening credit, spooked by billion-dollar losses suffered by some banks and investment funds that had found their newly purchased mortgage-backed securities to be worthless. Banks became

AT ISSUE

Should the federal government impose stricter rules on the mortgage industry?

YES
Sen. Christopher J. Dodd, D-Conn.
*Chairman, Senate Committee on Banking,
Housing and Urban Affairs*

From a statement to the committee, Oct. 3, 2007

Today we are facing a serious meltdown in the subprime mortgage market. This crisis is the equivalent of a slow-motion, 50-state Katrina, taking people's homes one by one, devastating their lives and destroying their communities. As a result, 2.2 million families are in danger of losing their homes to foreclosures at a cost of over $160 billion in hard-earned home equity that should have been available to finance college educations, pay health-care expenses or [act] as a cushion against uncertainty.

President Bush and his administration need to get fully engaged. They need to press subprime servicers and lenders to modify loans into long-term, affordable mortgages. Where modifications are not possible, the administration must work with Fannie Mae and Freddie Mac to refinance troubled borrowers on fair and affordable terms.

In April, I convened a Homeownership Preservation Summit where a number of the largest subprime lenders and servicers pledged to do these modifications. Unfortunately, a recent report tells us that just 1 percent of subprime adjustable-rate mortgages have been modified. This is wholly inadequate, and the administration must work with us to press the lenders and servicers to live up to their obligation.

While we are focused today on how we can rescue homeowners that have been victimized by predatory practices, we are also mindful that we need to prevent these kinds of abuses in the future.

The federal regulators — the cops on the beat — must be far more aggressive in policing the markets. The Federal Reserve [Board] noted as early as 2003 that problems were developing. Yet, not until it came under intense pressure from the Congress did the Federal Reserve agree to meet its obligation under the Homeownership and Equity Protection Act to prohibit unfair or deceptive mortgage practices. The board has the power to put an end to many of the practices that have gotten us into this mess today. They ought to exercise that power, and they ought to do it comprehensively and quickly.

In addition, a number of us have introduced or outlined anti-predatory-lending legislation. Let me say, the measure of any legislation must be that it creates high lending standards for the subprime market, and it must include remedies and penalties sufficient to ensure those standards are adequately enforced. Today's crisis is a market failure. Legislation must reengineer that market so that it works to create long-term, sustainable and affordable homeownership.

NO
Rep. Tom Price, R-Ga.
*Member, House Committee
on Financial Services*

From a statement to the committee, Sept. 5, 2007

As anyone paying attention can tell you, we're seeing a dramatic increase in the actual number of foreclosures. To put the current "crisis" in perspective, according to the Mortgage Bankers Association in the first quarter of 2007 there are about 44 million mortgages in the U.S. and less than 14 percent of them are subprime. And only about 13 percent of those subprime mortgages are late on payments, with the majority of late payers working through their problems with the banks.

With approximately 561,857 mortgages in foreclosure — up from roughly 517,434 from the fourth quarter of 2006 — the subprime "meltdown" has given us an increase of 44,423 foreclosures. This still represents a small percentage of the number of home mortgages.

One of the main reasons we have seen a rise in foreclosures is that during the housing boom of the last few years, consumers with a higher credit risk qualified for mortgages. Now that those riskier loans are resetting to higher interest rates — a trend that will continue until April of 2008 — a credit crunch is occurring for home buyers. It will take time to determine which of the mortgage-backed securities contain "bad" loans and which don't, partially because the entire securitization process is relatively new and hasn't faced a challenge of this size.

A comprehensive consumer-advocacy-driven predatory-lending bill is not the answer. It is tantamount to fighting the last war and will only make the markets more skittish, as they have to react to new underwriting standards and liability issues, making the situation worse, not better. This would harm all consumers!

By the time a new "anti-predatory-lending" law goes into effect in the marketplace, this problem will already have changed, and we will be left with strict, national underwriting standards that will prohibit various loan products and banish a number of consumers to the rental market forever. This is not a goal that is responsible.

The American economy has more than enough liquidity and is plenty strong enough to weather this bump in the road. Congress should stay out of the way while the market corrects itself or it will only make matters worse. We saw last week just how strong the market is when the Commerce Department reported that the gross domestic product — the broadest measure of economic health — expanded at an annual rate of 4 percent in the April-June quarter, significantly higher than the 3.4-percent rate the government had initially estimated.

reluctant to loan to anyone, including other banks, because no one knows which institutions are holding the riskiest mortgage-backed securities.

But "the Federal Reserve's solution to the bubble" of rising house prices driven by easy money "is to keep the bubble going as long as possible," says Hardaway of the University of Denver, a critic of the move.

"It's like 17th-century Tulipmania in Holland," when high demand for the showy flowers led hundreds of frenzied speculators into the market, hoping to make a killing, Hardaway says. After prices for single bulbs rose to hundreds of dollars, the mania abruptly stopped as bidders worried that prices could not get any higher. Almost overnight, the price collapsed, bankrupting many middle-class people.[35]

"The Fed's policy is just like Holland: 'Let the mania continue, because if it stops, nobody else will be able to buy tulips,'" says Hardaway. "Better to let the bubble burst now," he argues. "That would flush out all excesses, like the 4-to-5-percent teaser [interest] rate, which is offered to people knowing they won't be able to afford it when it triples."

Others say the rate cut won't solve the problem but could keep it from worsening. "There's sludge in the system" as investors back away from securitized higher-risk mortgages, and "the Fed is reliquifying the system so banks can carry some new debt," says Rainish.

Government Role

Congress, the Bush administration, and several states are contemplating or have already acted to aid struggling homeowners and keep the housing market afloat.

Massachusetts, New York, Ohio, Pennsylvania, New Jersey and Maryland will build loan funds to help homeowners refinance. Ohio, and Pennsylvania will sell bonds to raise funds, for example.[36]

The federal Office of Federal Housing Enterprise Oversight (OFHEO) gave the green light Sept. 19 for Fannie Mae and Freddie Mac to increase the amount of mortgage loans they invest in by 2 percent annually, as private investors pull back.

The move was a big deal, given recent concerns about financial fraud at the two mortgage giants. In May 2006, OFHEO capped the size of Fannie Mae's portfolio after investigators said some Fannie Mae executives — since

Auctioneer Travis Toth, right, accepts bids for a foreclosed home on the steps of the Los Angeles County courthouse in Norwalk, Calif., on March 16, 2007. To help struggling homeowners stay put, the nation's biggest mortgage lender, Countrywide Financial Corp., is restructuring about 82,000 mortgages to make them more affordable.

departed — had manipulated accounts to show higher earnings to get bonuses. Fannie Mae paid a $400-million fine in 2006. And in September Freddie Mac paid a $50-million fine to settle its own charges of accounting fraud.[37] Nevertheless, the Fannie Mae and Freddie Mac upticks aren't considered large enough to jumpstart the slowing housing market.

Alternative legislation introduced in October by Sen. Schumer and House Financial Services Committee Chairman Rep. Barney Frank, D-Mass., would do more and also would assist current owners trying to hold onto homes. It would raise investment caps for both Fannie Mae and Freddie Mac by 10 percent for six months and direct 85 percent of the money to refinancing subprime mortgages, mostly for low-income borrowers.[38]

Critics of the bill, including the Bush administration, argue that it would be a costly distraction from what they see as a need to reform Fannie and Freddie.

"Frank must know that a temporary increase in the portfolio limits . . . will reduce the pressure for comprehensive reform," said Peter J. Wallison, a resident fellow at the free-market-oriented American Enterprise Institute think tank.[39]

The administration supports another Democratic initiative — eliminating the tax that kicks in for a homeowner when a lender forgives some mortgage debt after a house is sold or a loan is restructured.

"Say you take out a $310,000 mortgage to buy a house and then you find you can't keep up the payments and the house gets sold for $250,000," says developer Sheridan. "The bank may, out of a sense of compassion, and because they can't collect the $60,000 shortfall anyway, simply write it off." That sounds like good news for the strapped consumer, but under current law that money becomes taxable income at tax rates as high as 30 or 40 percent, he says. "That's a $15,000 bill you won't have the money to pay."

Congressional Democrats and the White House have recommended eliminating the tax. Democrats would end the tax permanently and cut tax breaks for sales of some vacation and rental properties to pay it. The White House wants a temporary elimination and would retain the other tax breaks.[40]

President Bush also has announced a new Federal Housing Administration program, FHASecure, to offer FHA-insured loans to creditworthy borrowers who are delinquent on their mortgages. Delinquent borrowers were ineligible in the past.[41]

Congress also is debating new consumer protections. In September the House Financial Services Committee approved a bill giving several additional federal agencies a watchdog role over mortgage lending.[42] Several states, including Massachusetts, Maine, Minnesota and North Carolina, now require mortgage brokers to scrutinize would-be borrowers more carefully to ensure they can afford their loans.[43]

OUTLOOK

Hitting Bottom

One thing about fallout from the mortgage crisis is not in doubt: Washington will tighten some rules, says American University's Losey. "Congress reacts to crises," he says.

But the changes will come against a backdrop of stark financial pain and an end to giddy times in which people believed that house values would rise forever.

It will be two years or more before all existing ARMs reset, and only then will the extent of home losses be known, says the University of New Haven's Rainish. "For the subprime mortgage holders, the American dream will be crushed," he says. "Even many who have been making full payments won't be able to refinance because of prepayment penalties" in many subprime mortgages.

He predicts the housing market will be slow for the next two to three years. "The investment community will take a $100-$200 billion haircut, and many people will be hurt. Consumption growth will be slowed."

To emerge from the other side of this crisis, we need house prices to contract 20 percent or even as much as 40 percent, says the University of Chicago's Ashton.

"That's not a painless process," as many homeowners may end up owing more than their houses are worth, Ashton says. Owners with ARMs as their first or second mortgages must either make huge monthly mortgage payments when rates reset or try to refinance. But most won't be able to get a new loan for the full amount of their debt, since falling prices will slash their equity.

"We may hit bottom [on home prices] in early 2009, and maybe 2010 in some markets," says Sheridan. "There'll be a long period of prices staying down."

Most if not all subprime borrowers would have been unable to seek loans except under the conditions of the past few years, "so now that whole demand has gone away," possibly permanently, says Margaret Mann, head of the restructuring and insolvency practice at San Francisco-based law firm Heller Ehrman.

"Builders have almost stopped building," and a glut of housing inventory sits in some markets, says Florida home-building consultant Schultz. In South Florida, for example, three to four years' worth of condo inventory already sits empty, he says. "I doubt that the demand will ever be back to the level of 2007. A lot of regional and national builders will have to scale back."

Commercial real estate could be next to go bust. New, empty office buildings with large construction debts and vacant retail malls are being reported around the country, according to Michael Shedlock, an investment consultant for SitkaPacific Capital Management, in Prairie Grove, Ill.

"Here we are, right near the tip top in commercial real-estate insanity where no price was too high to pay for a building on the silly belief that property values would continually rise," said Shedlock. "Given how rapidly investor psychology is changing in this sector, it won't take much now to send it over the edge."[44]

Furthermore, many analysts say it's only a matter of time before a new boom of risky loans and investments occurs again, followed by inevitable bust.

"People's memories are usually good for five to 10 years," says Hardaway at the University of Denver. "For that period of time, maybe they'll remember they should look at the collateral."

NOTES

1. Delores King, testimony before Senate Committee on Banking, Housing and Urban Affairs, February 2007.

2. Eric Stein, testimony before House Judiciary Subcommittee on Commercial and Administrative Law, Sept. 25, 2007.

3. "What's Ahead for Financial Markets?" Knowledge@Wharton electronic newsletter, Oct. 3, 2007, http://knowledge.wharton.upenn.edu.

4. David Cho, "Huge Mortgage Lender Files for Bankruptcy," *The Washington Post*, April 3, 2007, p. A1.

5. "Subprime Mess Hits Wall Street Again," *Mortgage News Daily*, www.mortgagenewsdaily.com, June 25, 2007.

6. Doug Noland, "Structured Finance Under Duress," *Asia Times online*, Oct. 30, 2007, www.atimes.com/atimes/Global_Economy/IJ30Dj02.html.

7. Robert J. Shiller, "Understanding Recent Trends in House Prices and Home Ownership," paper presented at the Jackson Hole symposium of the Federal Reserve Bank of Kansas City, September 2007.

8. Martin Eakes, testimony before Senate Committee on Banking, Housing and Urban Affairs, Feb. 7, 2007.

9. For background see J.W. Elphinstone, "Mortgage Bailouts Run Into Opposition," The Associated Press, *The Salt Lake Tribune online*, Sept. 29, 2007, www.sltrib.com/realestate/ci_7038862.

10. Les Christie, "Countrywide Wins Over Critics," CNNMoney.com, Oct. 24, 2007, http://money.cnn.com/2007/10/24/real_estate/Countrywide_plan_wins_support/index.htm?postversion=2007102416.

11. For background, see "Interagency Guidance on Nontraditional Mortgage Product Risks," Office of Thrift Supervision, Department of the Treasury, October 2006, www.ots.treas.gov/docs/2/25244.pdf.

12. Douglas G. Duncan, testimony before Senate Committee on Banking, Housing and Urban Affairs, Feb. 7, 2007.

13. Sandor Samuels, testimony before Senate Committee on Banking, Housing and Urban Affairs, March 22, 2007.

14. "Home Ownership Rates," Danter Co., www.danter.com/statistics/hometown.htm.

15. "Why Bush's Mortgage Bailout Plan Is a Bad Idea," *eFinanceDirectory.com*, Sept. 4, 2007.

16. "Mortgage Fallout: Interview With Housing Wire," *eFinanceDirectory.com*, Sept. 6, 2007.

17. For background see "Behind the S&L Crisis," *Editorial Research Reports*, 1988, Vol. II, *CQ Researcher online*; and "S&L Bailout: Assessing the Impact," *Editorial Research Reports*, 1990, *CQ Researcher online*..

18. "Schumer, Others Propose First Major Legislation to Deal with Subprime Crisis as Weakening Housing Market Threatens Economy," press release, office of Sen. Charles Schumer, May 3, 2007, http://schumer.senate.gov.

19. "The Truly Bearish Case Isn't Playing Out," John Burns Real-Estate Consulting Web site, July 2007, www.realestateconsulting.com.

20. "Improvement in Mortgage Market Bodes Well for Housing in 2008," press release, National Association of Realtors, Oct. 10, 2007.

21. Ben Stein, "How Speculators Exploit Market Fears," Yahoo! Finance, Aug. 2, 2007, http://finance.yahoo.com.

22. Edward E. Leamer, "Housing and the Business Cycle," paper presented at the Jackson Hole symposium of the Federal Reserve Bank of Kansas City, September 2007.

23. *Ibid.*

24. Martin Feldstein, "Housing, Housing Finance, and Monetary Policy," remarks presented at the Jackson Hole symposium of the Federal Reserve Bank of Kansas City, September 2007.

25. For background see Richard K. Green and Susan M. Wachter, "The American Mortgage in Historical and International Context," *Journal of Economic Perspectives*, fall 2005, pp. 92-114.

26. Nadeem Walayat, "Hedge Fund Subprime Credit Crunch to Impact Interest Rates," The Market Oracle: Financial Markets Forecasting and Analysis, July 31, 2007, www.marketoracle.co.uk.

27. Kurt Eggert, testimony before Senate Subcommittee on Securities, Insurance and Investments, April 17, 2007.

28. Quoted in *Ibid.*

29. Michael Kanef, testimony before House Subcommittee on Capital Markets, Insurance, and Government Sponsored Enterprises, Sept. 27, 2007.

30. Mortgage Rates: A Historical Look at Mortgage Interest Rates, Lender 411, www.lender411.com/mortgage-articles/index_desc.php?art _id=37.

31. Emory W. Rushton, testimony before U.S. Senate Committee on Banking, Housing, and Urban Affairs, March 22, 2007.

32. Paul Tustain, "Bear Stearns and MBS Hedge Funds: What Are the Real Risks Today?" Financial Sense University, June 23, 2007, www.financialsense.com/fsu/editorials/tustain/2007/0623.html.

33. For background see David Masci, "The Federal Reserve," *CQ Researcher*, Sept. 1, 2000, pp. 673-688.

34. For background see Martin Crutsinger, "Fed Approves Cut in Discount Loan Rate," The Associated Press, Yahoo! Finance Web site, Aug. 17, 2007, http://biz.yahoo.com/ap/070817/fed_interest_rates.html.

35. For background see "Tulip Mania," *Encyclopaedia Britannica online*, 2007.

36. For background see "$500 Million-Dollar Bailout Extended to U.S. Mortgage Borrowers," eFinance-Directory Web site, July 24, 2007, http://efinance-directory.com.

37. For background see Kathleen Day, "Study Finds 'Extensive' Fraud at Fannie Mae," *The Washington Post*, May 24, 2006, p. A1.

38. For background see Benton Ives, "Short-Term Foreclosure Fix Could Cloud Long-Term Regulatory Overhaul," *CQ Today*, Oct. 15, 2007, www.cq.com.

39. Quoted in *ibid*.

40. For background see Richard Rubin, "Tax Relief Plan for Struggling Homeowners Would Exclude the Wealthy," *CQ Today*, Oct. 2, 2007, www.cq.com.

41. For background, see "Fact Sheet: New Steps to Help Homeowners Avoid Foreclosure," White House Web site, Aug. 31, 2007, www.whitehouse.gov/news/releases/2007/08/20070831-4.html.

42. For background, see Michael R. Crittenden, "Measure Outlines Expansion of Financial Protections for Consumers," *CQ Today*, Sept. 18, 2007, www.cq.com.

43. Amy Scott, "States Crack Down on Mortgage Market," Marketplace, National Public Radio, Oct. 19, 2007.

44. Michael Shedlock, "Commercial Real Estate Abyss," Mish's Global Economic Trend Analysis blog, Sept. 13, 2007, http://globaleconomicanalysis.blogspot.com.

BIBLIOGRAPHY

Books

Gramlich, Edward M., and Robert D. Reischauer, *Subprime Mortgages: America's Latest Boom and Bust*, Urban Institute Press, 2007.
Two experts recount the history of the subprime-mortgage market and suggest reforms. Gramlich once chaired the Federal Reserve's Consumer and Community Affairs Committee; Reischauer is president of the Urban Institute.

Schwartz, Alex F., *Housing Policy in the United States: An Introduction*, Routledge, 2006.
An associate professor of housing policy at New School University describes the housing-finance system.

Articles

Morgenson, Gretchen, "Can These Mortgages Be Saved?" *The New York Times*, Sept. 30, 2007, Sec. 3, p. 1.
Many borrowers in trouble say mortgage lenders aren't helping them to keep their homes.

Rokakis, Jim, "The Shadow of Debt," *The Washington Post*, Sept. 30, 2007, p. B1.
A once-tranquil Cleveland neighborhood becomes crime-infested after predatory lending leads to massive foreclosures.

Smith, David, "HUD Homes Go Cheap," *Journal & Courier* [Lafayette, Indiana], September 16, 2007, http://m.jconline.com.

The Department of Housing and Urban Development has bought so many foreclosed Indiana properties it is now the state's largest home seller.

Wargo, Brian, "Cancellations of New-Home Purchases Climb," *In Business Las Vegas*, Sept. 21-27, 2007, edition, www.inbusinesslasvegas.com.
Many Nevada homebuyers are canceling sales. Meanwhile, the National Association of Hispanic Real Estate Professionals is trying to protect Latinos from predatory lending.

Reports and Studies

"Ask Yourself Why . . . Mortgage Foreclosure Rates Are So High," *Common Cause*, 2007.
A citizens' group argues that $210 million in campaign funds and lobbying costs spent by the mortgage-lending industry has made Congress unwilling to curb industry practices.

"Mortgage Liquidity Du Jour: Underestimated No More," *Credit Suisse*, March 2007.
A large investment bank concludes dangers lurk in all sectors of the mortgage market, not just subprime loans.

Subprime and Predatory Lending in Rural America, Policy Brief No. 4, **Carsey Institute,** *University of New Hampshire,* **fall 2006.**
Affordable housing groups say many rural residents fall prey to predatory lenders, partly because they have little access to mainstream banks.

Essene, Ren S., and William Apgar, "Understanding Mortgage-Market Behavior: Creating Good Mortgage Options for All Americans," *Joint Center for Housing Studies, Harvard University*, April 2007.
Researchers conclude many consumers can't accurately evaluate the many mortgages that have sprung up.

Larson, Michael D., "How Federal Regulators, Lenders, and Wall Street Created America's Housing Crisis," *Weiss Research*, July 2007.
A financial analyst describes what house prices, foreclosures and other data reveal about the housing crisis and argues federal regulators underestimated the problems.

Murphy, Edward Vincent, "Alternative Mortgages: Risks to Consumers and Lenders in the Current Housing Cycle," *Congressional Research Service*, Dec. 27, 2006.
A CRS analyst describes how alternative mortgages have trapped some homeowners.

Schloemer, Ellen, et al., "Losing Ground: Foreclosures in the Subprime Market and Their Cost to Homeowners," *Center for Responsible Lending*, December 2006.
Analysts predict 2.2 million subprime borrowers will lose their houses in the current crisis.

Helpful Web Sites

How to avoid predatory lenders: **www.hud.gov/offices/hsg/sfh/buying/loanfraud.cfm.**

How to calculate how much house you can afford, whether to buy or rent: **www.hud.gov/buying/index.cfm.**

What you should know about mortgage brokers: **http://homebuying.about.com/od/findingalender/qt/0407LoanOffRep.htm.**

Definitions of terms connected with home buying: **www.statefarm.com/bank/sr_center/morgloss.asp.**

Explanations of mortgage terms and advice about various types of loans: **http://michaelbluejay.com/house/loan.html.**

For More Information

Carsey Institute, University of New Hampshire, 73 Main St., Huddleston Hall, Durham, NH 03824; (603) 862-2821; http://carseyinstitute.unh.edu. Researches housing and other economic issues in rural America.

Center for Responsible Lending, 302 West Main St., Durham, NC 27701; (919) 313-8500; www.responsible lending.org. Provides information on predatory lending and other abusive practices.

Fannie Mae, 3900 Wisconsin Ave., N.W., Washington, DC 20016; (202) 752-7000; www.fanniemae.com/index .jhtml. The government-sponsored, shareholder-owned corporation buys mortgages in the secondary market to provide capital for the mortgage industry.

Freddie Mac, 8200 Jones Branch Dr., McLean, VA 22102-3110; (703) 903-2000; www.freddiemac.com/index.html. The government-sponsored company supports the mortgage market.

Housing, Housing Finance, and Monetary Policy, 2007 Symposium of the Federal Reserve Bank of Kansas City, http://www.kc.frb.org/home/subwebnav.cfm?level=3&theI D=10982&SubWeb=10658. The symposium on the mortgage crisis features papers presented by leading economists, including Federal Reserve Chairman Ben S. Bernanke.

Joint Center for Housing Studies, Harvard University, 1033 Massachusetts Ave., 5th Floor, Cambridge, MA 02138; (617) 495-7908; www.jchs.harvard.edu/index.htm. Provides information and research on U.S. housing issues.

Mortgage Professor's Web Site, www.mtgprofessor.com/. The University of Pennsylvania's Wharton School of Business provides financial education and policy analysis.

National Association of Mortgage Brokers, 7900 Westpark Dr., Suite T309, McLean, VA 22102; (703) 342-5900; www.namb.org/namb/Default.asp. Provides information on the mortgage industry, including legislative proposals.

National Association of Realtors, 500 New Jersey Ave., N.W., Washington, DC 20001-2020; (800) 874-6500; www.realtor.org. Provides and analyzes its own data on housing-market trends.

National Mortgage News Online, www.nationalmortgage news.com/. The independent news outlet covers mortgage-related news.

Office of Federal Housing Enterprise Oversight, 1700 G St., N.W., 4th Floor, Washington, DC 20552; (202) 414-3800; www.ofheo.gov. Oversees Fannie and Freddie and provides data and research on housing.

U.S. Department of Housing and Urban Development, 451 7th St., S.W., Washington, DC 20410; (202) 708-1112; www.hud.gov/. Provides information about mortgages, home buying and related federal programs.

4

Gender Pay Gap

Are Women Paid Fairly in the Workplace?

Thomas J. Billitteri

A suit filed by Betty Dukes, right, and other female Wal-Mart employees accuses the retail giant of sex discrimination in pay, promotions and job assignments in violation of the Civil Rights Act of 1964. The case, covering perhaps 1.6 million current and former Wal-Mart employees, is the biggest class-action lawsuit against a private employer in U.S. history.

AP Photo/Noah Berger

From *CQ Researcher*, March 14, 2008.

"An insult to my dignity" is the way Lilly Ledbetter described it.[1] For 19 years, she worked at the Goodyear Tire plant in Gadsden, Ala., one of a handful of women among the roughly 80 people who held the same supervisory position she did. Over the years, unbeknownst to her, the company's pay-raise decisions created a growing gap between her wages and those of her male colleagues. When she left Goodyear, she was earning $3,727 a month. The lowest-paid man doing the same work got $4,286. The highest-paid male made 40 percent more than she did.[2]

Ledbetter sued in 1998, and a jury awarded her back pay and more than $3 million in damages. But in the end, she lost her case in the U.S. Supreme Court.[3]

A conservative majority led by Justice Samuel A. Alito Jr. ruled that under the nation's main anti-discrimination law she should have filed a formal complaint with the federal government within 180 days of the first time Goodyear discriminated against her in pay. Never mind, the court said, that Ledbetter didn't learn about the pay disparity for years.

"The Supreme Court said that this didn't count as illegal discrimination," she said after the ruling, "but it sure feels like discrimination when you are on the receiving end of that smaller paycheck and trying to support your family with less money than the men are getting for doing the same job."[4]

The *Ledbetter* decision has added fuel to a long-burning debate over sex discrimination in women's wages and whether new laws are needed to narrow the disparity in men's and women's pay.

Women Closing the Pay Gap . . . Slowly

More than 40 years after women began demanding equal rights and opportunities, they still earn 77 percent of what men earn. The pay gap has been closing, however, because women's earnings have been rising faster than men's.

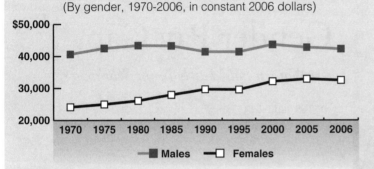

Median Annual Earnings of Full-time, Year-round Workers
(By gender, 1970-2006, in constant 2006 dollars)

■ Males □ Females

Source: Carmen DeNavas-Walt, et. al., "Income, Poverty, and Health Insurance Coverage in the United States: 2006," U.S. Census Bureau, August 2007

a wage gap exists between men and women. In 2006 full-time female workers earned 81 percent of men's weekly earnings, according to the latest U.S. Labor Department data, with the wage gap broader for older workers and narrower for younger ones. Separate U.S. Census Bureau data put the gap at about 77 percent of men's median full-time, year-round earnings.[6]

The fundamental issues are why the gap exists, how much of it stems from discrimination and what should be done about it.

Some contend the disparity can largely be explained by occupational differences between women and men, variations in work experience, number of hours worked each year and other such things.

June O'Neill, an economics professor at the City University of New York's Baruch College and former director of the Congressional Budget Office in the Clinton administration, says that the most important factors affecting the pay gap stem from differences in the roles of women and men in family life. When the wages of men and women who share similar work experience and life situations are measured, the wage gap largely disappears, she says. Reasons that the earnings disparity may appear bigger in some research, she says, include the fact that many studies do not control for differences in years of work experience, the extent of part-time work and differences in training and occupational choices. O'Neill notes that Labor Department data show median weekly earnings of female part-time workers exceed those of male part-timers. She also says the wage gap has been narrowing over time as women's work experience, education and other job-related skills have been converging with those of men.

"Large amounts of discrimination? No," she says. "Individual women may experience discrimination, and it's good to have laws that deal with it," she adds. "But those cases don't change the overall picture. The vast majority of employers don't harbor prejudice against women."

"A significant wage gap is still with us, and that gap constitutes nothing less than an ongoing assault on women's economic freedom," declared U.S. Rep. Rosa L. DeLauro, D-Conn., at a congressional hearing on a pay-equity bill she is sponsoring, one of several proposed on Capitol Hill.

But that view is hardly universal. "Men and women generally have equal pay for equal work now — if they have the same jobs, responsibilities and skills," testified Diana Furchtgott-Roth, a senior fellow at the Hudson Institute, a conservative think tank, and former chief economist at the Labor Department in the George W. Bush administration.[5]

The wrangle over wages is playing out not just in Washington but in cities and towns across America. In the biggest sex-discrimination lawsuit in U.S. history, a group of female Wal-Mart employees has charged the retail giant with bias in pay and promotions. The case could affect perhaps 1.6 million women employees of Wal-Mart and result in billions of dollars in back pay and damages. (*See sidebar, p. 86.*)

The enormously complex gender-pay debate encompasses economics, demographics, law, social justice, culture, history and sometimes raw emotion. Few dispute that

Yet others argue that beneath such factors as occupation and number of hours worked lies evidence of significant discrimination — covert if not overt.

"Women do not realize the enormous price that they pay for gender wage discrimination because they do not see big bites taken out of their paychecks at any one time," Evelyn F. Murphy, president of The Wage Project, a non-profit organization that works on eliminating the gender wage gap and author of *Getting Even: Why Women Don't Get Paid Like Men and What To Do About It*, told a congressional panel last year.[7]

In her book, she told the hearing, she wrote of employers "who had to pay women employees or former employees to settle claims of gender discrimination, or judges and juries ordered them to pay up. The behavior of these employers vividly [illustrates] the commonplace forms of today's wage discrimination: barriers to hiring and promoting qualified women; arbitrary financial penalties imposed on pregnant women; sexual harassment by bosses and co-workers; failure to pay women and men the same amount of money for doing the same jobs," and "everyday discrimination" marked by "the biases and stereotypes which influence [managers'] decisions about women."

Women's advocates point to a 2003 General Accounting Office (GAO) study concluding that while "work patterns" were key in accounting for the wage gap, the GAO could not explain all the differences in earnings between men and women. "When we account for differences between male and female work patterns as well as other key factors, women earned, on average, 80 percent of what men earned in 2000. . . . We cannot determine whether this remaining difference is due to discrimination or other factors," the GAO report said.[8]

The study said that in the view of certain experts some women trade promotions or higher pay for job flexibility that allows them to balance work and family responsibilities.

Women's advocates point out that many women have little choice but to work in jobs that offer flexibility but pay less because they typically shoulder the bulk of family caregiving duties. And, they argue further, expectations within companies and society — typically subtle, but sometimes not — often channel women away from male-dominated jobs into female-dominated ones that pay less.

"People who argue that [wage discrimination] is small will say a lot of it is due to women's choices," such as the choice to stay home with the children, work part time or enter lower-paying fields, says Reeve Vanneman, a sociology professor at the University of Maryland, College Park, who studies gender inequality. But, he says, it's misleading to explain most of the wage gap in that way, especially when mid-career and older female workers are concerned.

"Why do women make those choices? Part of the reason is because they are discriminated against in the job. They see men getting rewarded more and promoted more than they are."

Women face unequal work not just on the job but at home, too, Vanneman says, with husbands not picking up their share.

Part of the wage gap stems from weak government enforcement, some argue. A U.S. inspector general's report stated last fall that the Equal Employment Opportunity Commission, which enforces federal employment-discrimination laws, is "challenged in accomplishing its mission" because of "a reduced workforce and an increasing backlog of pending cases." The agency has experienced a "significant loss of its workforce, mostly to attrition and buyouts . . . offered to free up resources," the report said.[9]

The news on gender discrimination in pay is not all bad. The wage gap has narrowed considerably in recent decades. For example, Labor Department data show that for 35- to 44-year-olds, the earnings ratio of women to men rose from 58 percent in 1979 to 77 percent in 2006. For 45- to 54-year-olds, it went from 57 percent to 74 percent.[10] Among the youngest workers, ages 16 to 24, only about 5 percentage points separated median weekly wages of men and women in 2006.[11]

Still, many experts say the progress of the 1980s and early '90s has slowed or stalled in recent years, with the wage gap stuck in the range of 20 to 24 percent, although it is not entirely clear why. Some argue that entrenched wage discrimination remains a major culprit.

In a study of college graduates last year, the American Association of University Women Educational Foundation found that one year out of college, women working full time earn only 80 percent as much as their male colleagues, and 10 years after graduation the gap widens to 69 percent. Even after controlling for hours worked, training and education and other factors, the portion of the pay gap that remains unexplained is 5 percent one year after graduation and 12 percent a decade afterward, the study found.[12] (*See graph, right.*)

"These unexplained gaps are evidence of discrimination," the study concluded.

Employer advocates challenge such conclusions, though. Michael Eastman, executive director of labor policy at the U.S. Chamber of Commerce, questions the assumption "that whatever gap is not explained must be due to discrimination. An unexplained gap is simply that — it's unexplained."

Election-year politics and the recent shift toward Democratic control of Congress — along with the Supreme Court's decision in the *Ledbetter* case — have helped to reinvigorate the pay debate. Proposed gender-pay bills have strong support from women's-rights groups and some economists, who argue that the Equal Pay Act and Title VII of the Civil Rights Act of 1964 — the main avenues for attacking wage discrimination — fall short.

Presidential contender Sen. Hillary Rodham Clinton, D-N.Y., is sponsoring the Senate version of the DeLauro bill; another presidential hopeful, Sen. Barack Obama, D-Ill., is one of the 22 co-sponsors, although he didn't sign on to it until more than a month after she introduced it. Among other things, the measure would raise penalties under the Equal Pay Act, which bars paying men and women differently for doing the same job.[13]

Gap Widens for College Graduates

College-educated women earn only 80 percent of what their male counterparts earn a year after graduation, when both male and female employees have the same level of work experience and (usually) no child-care obligations — factors often used to explain gender pay differences. The gap widens to 69 percent by 10 years after graduation.

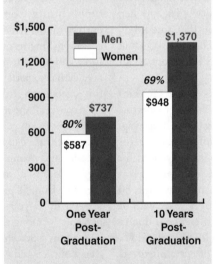

Gap in Average Weekly Earnings for Bachelor's Degree Recipients
(For full-time workers)

Source: "Beyond the Pay Gap," American Association of University Women, based on data from the "2003 Baccalaureate and Beyond Longitudinal Study," National Center for Education Statistics, U.S. Department of Education

Obama is co-sponsoring a more controversial bill, introduced in the Senate by Sen. Tom Harkin, D-Iowa, that advocates the notion of comparable worth; the idea, generally speaking, suggests that a female-dominated occupation such as social work may merit wages that are comparable to those of a male-dominated job such as a probation officer.[14] The Harkin measure would bar wage discrimination in certain cases where the work is deemed comparable in skill, effort, responsibility and working conditions, even if the job titles or duties are different. (*See sidebar, p. 84.*)

A third effort would undo the Supreme Court's ruling in the *Ledbetter* case.[15] A bill passed the House last summer, and advocates are hoping the Senate version — sponsored by Sen. Edward M. Kennedy, D-Mass., and co-sponsored by Clinton and Obama — moves forward soon. But the Bush administration has threatened a veto, and business interests are vehemently opposed.

As the debate over wage disparities continues, these are some of the questions being discussed:

Is discrimination a major cause of the wage gap?

When economist David Neumark studied sex discrimination in restaurant hiring in the mid-1990s, he discovered something intriguing: In expensive restaurants, where waiters and waitresses can earn more than they can at low-price places, the chances of a woman getting a wait-staff job offer were 40 percentage points lower than those of a man with similar experience.[16]

The study is a telling bit of evidence that the wage gap is real and that discrimination plays a significant part in it, says Vicky Lovell, director of employment and work/life programs at the Institute for Women's Policy Research, an advocacy group in Washington. She estimates that perhaps a third of the wage gap stems from discrimination — mostly "covert" bias that occurs when people make false assumptions about the ability or career commitment of working women.

Lovell has little patience with those who say the wage gap stems from non-discriminatory reasons that simply haven't yet been identified. "That's just specious," she says. "If we can't explain why women on average get paid less, what is the alternative explanation?"

The role of discrimination lies at the heart of the pay-gap debate. Researchers fall into different camps.

Some see little evidence that bias plays a big part in the gap. When adjusted for work experience, education, time in the labor force and other variables, wages of men and women are largely comparable, they contend.

"This so-called wage gap is not necessarily due to discrimination," the Hudson Institute's Furchtgott-Roth said in congressional testimony. "Decisions about field of study, occupation and time in the work force can lead to lower compensation, both for men and women."[17]

What's more, "some jobs command more than others because people are willing to pay more for them," she said. "Many jobs are dirty and dangerous. . . . Other highly paid occupations have long, inflexible hours. . . . Women are not excluded from these or other jobs but often select professions with a more pleasant environment and potentially more flexible schedules, such as teaching and office work. Many of these jobs pay less."

Warren Farrell, who in the 1970s served on the board of the New York City chapter of the National Organization for Women, argues in his 2005 book — *Why Men Earn*

More: The Startling Truth Behind the Pay Gap — and What Women Can Do About It — that women pay an economic price by seeking careers that are more fulfilling, flexible and safe. With a stated goal of helping women gain higher pay, Farrell offers 25 "differences in the way women and men behave in the workplace." Those who earn more, he says, work longer hours, are more willing to relocate, require less security and produce more, among other things.

O'Neill, of Baruch College, points out that women are much more likely to go into occupations that will allow them to work part time, and typically "that doesn't pay as well."

She studies data that track the work histories of women and men over a long period of time. "Women have just not worked as many weeks and hours over their lives as men," she says. "When you adjust for that, you explain most of the [pay] difference. . . . You're still left with a difference, but then there are other things that become harder to measure."

The AAUW study found that even women who make the same choices as men in terms of fields of study and occupation earn less than their male counterparts. A typical college-educated woman working full time earns $46,000 a year compared to $62,000

Wage Disparities Highest Among Asians

The median weekly earnings for women are lower than men's across all ethnic groups. The largest disparity is among Asians, where men earn $183 more on average per week than their female counterparts. The average difference for all groups is $143.

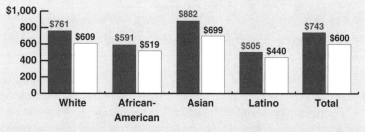

Median Weekly Earnings of Full-Time Workers
(by gender and ethnicity, 2006)

White: Men $761, Women $609
African-American: Men $591, Women $519
Asian: Men $882, Women $699
Latino: Men $505, Women $440
Total: Men $743, Women $600

Source: "Highlights of Women's Earnings in 2006," Bureau of Labor Statistics, September 2007

■ Men □ Women

Pay Gap Exists Despite Women's Choices

Those who discount the seriousness of gender pay bias often blame differences in men's and women's salaries on women's choices to study "softer" sciences or to have children. But a recent study shows that the pay gap persists even when women choose not to have children and when they choose male-dominated fields of study and occupation — such as business, engineering, mathematics and medicine. The pay gap is greatest in the biology, health and mathematics fields. Women out-earn men only in the history professions.

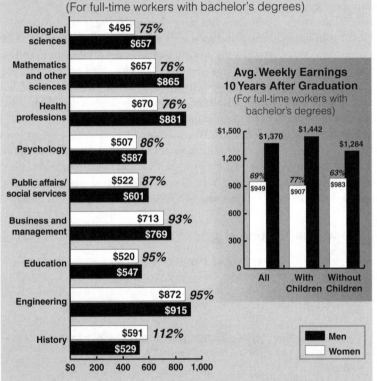

Avg. Weekly Earnings One Year After Graduation
(For full-time workers with bachelor's degrees)

	Women	%	Men
Biological sciences	$495	75%	$657
Mathematics and other sciences	$657	76%	$865
Health professions	$670	76%	$881
Psychology	$507	86%	$587
Public affairs/ social services	$522	87%	$601
Business and management	$713	93%	$769
Education	$520	95%	$547
Engineering	$872	95%	$915
History	$591	112%	$529

$0   200   400   600   800   1,000

Avg. Weekly Earnings 10 Years After Graduation
(For full-time workers with bachelor's degrees)

	All	With Children	Without Children
Men	$1,370	$1,442	$1,284
Women	$949 (69%)	$907 (77%)	$983 (63%)

■ Men
□ Women

Source: "Behind the Pay Gap," American Association of University Women, 2007

5 percent one year after graduation and 12 percent 10 years after graduation. These unexplained gaps are evidence of discrimination, which remains a serious problem for women in the work force."[18]

"This research asked a basic but important question: If a woman made the same choices as a man, would she earn the same pay? The answer is no," Catherine Hill, director of research at the AAUW, told a House Committee on Education and Labor hearing last year.

Speaking more generally about pay inequity, Linda Meric, national director of 9to5, National Association of Working Women, a Milwaukee-based advocacy group, says that "when you control for all the other so-called factors" that might explain the wage gap, "there is still a gap."

"And many of those so-called factors are not independent of discrimination and stereotypes of women. One is time in the work force. If there aren't policies that allow women to get jobs and maintain and advance in employment at the same time they are meeting their responsibility in terms of family caregiving, that's not an independent factor. It's something that influences the pay gap significantly."

Heather Boushey, senior economist at the Center for Economic and Policy Research, a Washington think tank, noted that time away from the workforce strongly affects lifetime earnings. She said it is a myth that women choose lower-paying occupations because they provide the flexibility to better manage work and family. "The empirical evidence shows that mothers are actually less likely to be employed in jobs that provide them with greater flexibility."[19]

Echoing that sentiment, Beth Shulman, co-director of the Fairness Initiative on Low Wage Work, a public policy advocacy group also in Washington, says, "We have kind of an Ozzie and Harriet workplace, with a full-time worker

for college-educated male workers — a difference of $16,000.

"The pay gap between female and male college graduates cannot be fully accounted for by factors known to affect wages, such as experience (including work hours), training, education and personal characteristics," the AAUW study says. "In this analysis the portion of the pay gap that remains unexplained after all other factors are taken into account is

and the wife at home," but "70 percent of women with children are in the workplace." She adds, "Our structures haven't kept up with that. So women who are primary caregivers get punished."

Shulman, author of *The Betrayal of Work: How Low-Wage Jobs Fail 30 Million Americans*, says that while overt gender discrimination exists in the job market, an equally important contributor to the wage gap is the lack of flexibility for low-income working women with families. For example, she says, female factory employees with family responsibilities often find it difficult to accept better-paying manufacturing jobs because such jobs often require mandatory overtime.

Shulman also says that three-fourths of women in low-wage jobs don't have paid sick days. So when a child is sick or an elderly parent needs help, women may be forced to leave the workforce and then re-enter it — something that has a huge effect on wages over time.

"Low-wage workers get kind of ghettoized into these part-time jobs that have poor wages, poor benefits and less government protection," Shulman says.

In a 1998 study, Cornell University economists Francine Blau and Lawrence Kahn found that 40 percent of the pay gap is unexplained after adjusting for gender differences in experience, education, occupation and industry. Blau cautions that such an estimate is conservative, because variables such as women's choices of occupation or industry and even their education and work experience can themselves be affected by discrimination. On the other hand, she acknowledges that some of the unexplained differences may be due to unmeasured productivity characteristics that increase men's earnings relative to women's earnings.

Applying that 40 percent figure to current government wage-gap data would suggest that 8 to 9 cents of each dollar in wage disparity is unexplained, with an unknown portion of that amount caused by discrimination.

Martha Burk, who directs the Corporate Accountability Project for the National Council of Women's Organizations, a coalition of more than 200 women's groups, says some of the pay gap stems from "historical discrimination" rooted in a time when employers could legally exclude women from certain jobs and pay them less for the kinds of jobs they typically did hold, such as teaching and clerical work.

Burk, who led the fight to open the Augusta (Ga.) National Golf Club to women, says those female-dominated jobs "were systematically devalued, and that has carried through to modern times."

Are new laws needed to close the gender pay gap?

When President John F. Kennedy signed the Equal Pay Act in 1963, he called it "a first step."[20]

Over the decades, the pay gap has narrowed significantly, but the push for new laws to curb gender-pay inequity goes on, fueled in part by the view among women's advocates that progress toward wage equity has slowed or stalled in recent years.

"The best way is for corporations to behave as socially responsible corporate citizens [and] examine their wage practices," says Lovell of Women's Policy Research. "But that is not going to happen. I don't see any reason to think the private sector is going to address this issue on its own. A few will to the extent they can within their own workforces. But if corporations individually or within industry groups aren't going to make this a priority, then that's why we have a government."

Opponents of new laws have sharply different views, though.

Roger Clegg, president and general counsel of the Center for Equal Opportunity, a conservative think tank in Falls Church, Va., says some gender discrimination will always exist but that existing laws can address it. Besides, Clegg says, the amount of gender discrimination that remains in the American work force "is greatly exaggerated by the groups pushing for legislation."

Much of the support for new laws rests on the view that some jobs pay poorly because females historically have dominated them. Jocelyn Samuels, vice president for Education and Employment at the National Women's Law Center, a Washington advocacy group, told a congressional hearing last year that 95 percent of child-care workers are female while the same proportion of mechanical engineers are male.

Moreover, she said, wages in fields dominated by women "have traditionally been depressed and continue to reflect the artificially suppressed pay scales that were historically applied to so-called 'women's work.' " Maids and housecleaners — 87 percent of whom are women — make roughly $3,000 per year less than janitors and building cleaners, 72 percent of whom are men, she said. "Current law simply does not provide the tools to address this continuing devaluation of traditionally female fields."[21]

AP Photo/Ron Edmonds

U.S. Rep. Rosa L. DeLauro, D-Conn., is sponsoring one of several pay-equity bills in Congress. Presidential contender Sen. Hillary Rodham Clinton, D-N.Y., is sponsoring the Senate version of DeLauro's bill; Sen. Barack Obama, D-Ill., is one of the 22 co-sponsors. "A significant wage gap is still with us, and that gap constitutes nothing less than an ongoing assault on women's economic freedom," DeLauro says.

To attack that situation, some advocates back the comparable-worth theory, arguing that women should be paid commensurate with men for jobs of equivalent value to a company, even if the work is different. But critics argue that such an approach violates the free-market principles of supply and demand for labor and that it could hurt both the economy and the cause of women.

"The comparable-worth approach has the government setting wages rather than the free market, and a great lesson of the 20th century is that centrally planned economies and centrally planned wage and price systems do not work," Clegg says.

Carrie Lukas, vice president for policy and economics at the Independent Women's Forum, a conservative group in Washington that backs limited government, contends that "government attempts to 'solve' the problem of the wage gap may in fact exacerbate some of the challenges women face, particularly in balancing work and family."

In an opinion column last year, she criticized the Clinton/DeLauro bill, which calls for guidelines to help companies voluntarily "compare wages paid for different jobs . . . with the goal of eliminating unfair pay disparities between occupations traditionally dominated by men or women." Lukas wrote that the bill would "give Washington bureaucrats more power to oversee how wages are determined, which might prompt businesses to make employment options more rigid." Flexible job structures would become less common, she argued. Why, Lukas wondered, "would companies offer employees a variety of work situations and compensation packages if doing so puts them at risk of being sued?"[22]

Not only might women suffer from new laws, but so would employers, some argue. Washington lawyer Barbara Berish Brown, vice-chair of the American Bar Association's Labor and Employment Law Section, said in a hearing on the Clinton/DeLauro bill that she is "unequivocally committed" to erasing gender-pay bias, but that existing laws suffice.

"All that the proposed changes will do is encourage more employment-related litigation, which is already drowning the federal court docket, and make it much more difficult, if not impossible, for employers, particularly small businesses, to prove the legitimate, nondiscriminatory reasons that explain differences between the salaries of male and female employees," she said.[23]

But longtime activists such as Burk, author of *Cult of Power: Sex Discrimination in Corporate America and What Can Be Done About It*, say existing laws are not effective enough to stamp out wage bias. "It has always been the view of conservatives that if you pay women equally, it's going to destroy capitalism," she says. "So far capitalism has survived quite well."

Is equity possible after the Supreme Court's Ledbetter ruling?

After the Supreme Court ruled in the Goodyear pay-discrimination case, Eleanor Smeal, president of the Feminist Majority, urged congressional action to reverse the decision. "We cannot stand by and watch a Bush-stacked court destroy in less than a year Title VII — the bedrock of women's rights and civil rights protection in wage-discrimination cases," she said.[24]

Yet, such outrage at the Supreme Court is matched by praise from business advocates. "We think the court got it exactly right," says Eastman, the U.S. Chamber of Commerce labor policy official.

In the 5-4 ruling, the court said workers can't sue under Title VII of the Civil Rights Act, the main federal anti-discrimination law, unless they file a formal complaint with the EEOC within 180 days of a discriminatory act. And in Ledbetter's case, the clock didn't start each time a new paycheck was issued. The 180-day timeline applies whether or not the employee immediately spots the discrimination.

Critics argue that because pay decisions are seldom broadcast throughout a company, the ruling makes it difficult — if not impossible — for an employee to detect bias until it may have gone on for years. "The ruling essentially says 'tough luck' to employees who don't immediately challenge their employer's discriminatory acts, even if the discrimination continues to the present time," said Marcia Greenberg, co-president of the National Women's Law Center.[25]

"With this misguided decision, the court ignores the realities of the 21st-century workplace," Margot Dorfman, chief executive officer of the U.S. Women's Chamber of Commerce, told a congressional panel this year. "The confidential nature of employee salary information complicates workers' abilities to recognize and report discriminatory treatment."[26]

Lovell, of the Institute for Women's Policy Research, says the Ledbetter ruling "seems to reflect a complete lack of understanding of the labor market and a complete lack of concern for individuals who are at any kind of disadvantage in the labor market." Workers wouldn't necessarily know right away that they were being discriminated against, she says. When Congress passed Title VII, it "was trying to establish an avenue for people who are discriminated against to pursue their claims . . ., not trying to make it impossible."

In a strongly worded dissent to the Ledbetter ruling, Justice Ruth Bader Ginsburg noted that pay disparities often occur in small increments, evidence of bias may develop over time, and wage information is typically hidden from employees. At the end of her dissent she wrote that "the ball is in Congress' court" to correct the Supreme Court's "parsimonious reading of Title VII" in the Ledbetter decision, just as Congress dealt with a spate of earlier Supreme Court decisions with passage of the 1991 Civil Rights Act.

Business groups have stood firm in the face of such impassioned views, though.

An exchange between Eastman of the U.S. Chamber of Commerce and law professor Deborah Brake last fall on the National Public Radio show "Justice Talking" helped underscore how polarizing the Ledbetter decision has been between advocates for women and for employers.[27]

Brake, a professor at the University of Pittsburgh School of Law who once litigated sex-discrimination cases for the National Women's Law Center, said she thought it was questionable whether the ruling was even good for employers.

"What an employee is supposed to do, let's say from the moment in time that they are hired, is search around the workplace and make sure that they're not being paid less if it's a woman than her male colleagues," she said on the radio program.

"If she has the slightest inkling or suspicion that she might be paid less than her male colleagues, she'd better immediately file a pay-discrimination claim. At every raise decision she better be sniffing around to make sure that her raise wasn't less than that of her male colleagues. And if she hears that someone got a higher raise than her who was a male, to preserve her rights under [the Ledbetter ruling] she'd better immediately file an EEOC claim. I don't think that is in the best interest, long-term, of employer or employees."

Eastman, though, said Title VII "has a strong incentive for employees to file claims quickly so that matters are resolved while all the facts and evidence are fresh and in people's minds. And it is very difficult for employers to defend themselves from allegations made many, many years down the line."

Brake said it wasn't the 180-day limit that bothered her. "What I'm objecting to is a ruling that starts the clock running before any employee has enough reason or incentive to even think about filing a discrimination claim," she said.

BACKGROUND

Early Wage Gap

From the republic's beginning, women have played an integral role in American economic growth and prosperity, yet a wage gap has always been present.

CHRONOLOGY

1900-1940 *Women make economic gains but face discrimination.*

1914 Start of World War I marks a period of advancement in the status of women, who go to work in traditionally male jobs.

1919 Women gain the right to vote through the 19th Amendment.

1923 The Equal Rights Amendment is introduced, but it falls three states short of ratification.

1930 Half of single women are in the labor force, and the labor-participation rate among married women approaches 12 percent.

1938 Fair Labor Standards Act establishes rules for a minimum wage, overtime pay and child labor.

1940-1960 *Women make major contribution to wartime manufacturing efforts but don't gain wage equality with men.*

1942 National War Labor Board urges employers to equalize pay between men and women in defense jobs.

1945 Congress fails to approve Women's Equal Pay Act.

1955 Census Bureau begins calculating female-to-male earnings ratio.

1960-1980 *Major anti-discrimination laws helps women to fight pay bias.*

1963 Equal Pay Act bans gender pay discrimination in equal jobs.

1963 *The Feminine Mystique* by Betty Friedan challenges idea that women can find happiness only through marriage.

1964 Title VII of the Civil Rights Act bans job discrimination on the basis of race, color, religion, national origin and sex.

1965 Equal Employment Opportunity Commission founded.

1966 National Organization For Women is formed.

1973 Supreme Court's Roe v. Wade ruling overturns laws barring abortion, energizes the women's movement.

1979 National Committee on Pay Equity is formed.

1980-2000 *Gender pay gap continues to narrow, but progress toward wage equality shows signs of slowing in the 1990s.*

1981 Supreme Court ruling in County of Washington v. Gunther allows female jail guards to sue for sex discrimination but declines to authorize suits based on theory of comparable worth.

1993 Family and Medical Leave Act requires employers to grant unpaid leave for medical emergencies, birth and care of newborns and other family-related circumstances.

2001-Present *States expand laws to help working families, while several major corporations face gender-bias accusations.*

2001 Wal-Mart employees file for sex-discrimination claim against the retailer, to become the largest class-action lawsuit against a private employer in U.S. history.

2004 California grants up to six weeks partial pay for new parents.

2004 Equal Employment Opportunity Commission and Morgan Stanley announce $54 million settlement of sex-discrimination suit. . . . Wachovia Corp. agrees to pay $5.5 million in a pay-discrimination case involving more than 2,000 current and former female employees.

2007 San Francisco requires employers to provide paid sick leave to all employees, including temporary and part-time workers.

2007 In *Ledbetter v. Goodyear*, Supreme Court rules that a female worker's pay-discrimination claim was invalid because it was filed after a 180-day deadline.

During the Industrial Revolution of the 19th century, as the nation's productivity and wealth exploded, young, single women moved from farm to city and took jobs as mill workers, teachers and domestic servants.

The factory work wasn't easy, and owners exploited women and girls as cheap sources of labor. In 1830, females often worked 12 hours a day in "boarding-house mills" — factories with housing provided by mill owners. They earned perhaps $2.50 a week. "Minor infractions such as a few minutes' lateness were punished severely," historian Richard B. Morris noted, and "one-sided contracts gave them no power over conditions and no rewards for work."[28]

Still, young women flocked to manufacturing jobs in the cities. In Massachusetts, among the earliest states to industrialize, a third of all women ages 10 to 29 worked in industry in 1850, according to Harvard University economist Claudia Goldin.[29]

As demand for goods grew along with the nation's population, the wages of women working full time in manufacturing rose slowly as a percentage of men's pay. The wage gap narrowed from about 30 percent of men's earnings in 1820 to 56 percent nationwide in 1885, according to Goldin.[30]

But progress came more slowly, if at all, in ensuing years and decades.

In manufacturing, Goldin noted in a 1990 book on the economic history of American women, "The ratio of female to male wages . . . continued to rise slowly across most of the nineteenth century but reached a plateau before 1900."[31]

As the 20th century dawned, some women's advocates pushed for equal pay for equal work between the sexes. But others questioned the equal-pay idea. In 1891, the British economist Sidney Webb pointed to "the impossibility of discovering any but a very few instances in which men and women do precisely similar work, in the same place and at the same epoch."[32]

By the turn of the 20th century, women's jobs had started growing more diverse. Women found work not only in domestic service and manufacturing but also in teaching, sales and clerical positions. Still, only 21 percent of American women worked outside the home in 1900, and most left the labor force upon or right after marriage.[33]

Women seeking to move up in the business world faced huge cultural hurdles. In 1900 *Ladies' Home Journal* told its readers: "Although the statement may seem a hard one, and will unquestionably be controverted, it nevertheless is a plain, simple fact that women have shown themselves naturally incompetent to fill a great many of the business positions which they have sought to occupy. . . . The fact is that no one woman in a hundred can stand the physical strain of the keen pace which competition has forced upon every line of business today."[34]

Women's labor participation gradually rose in the early decades of the 20th century, fueled in part by World War I, which ended in 1918. By 1920, almost a quarter of all U.S. women were in the labor force, and 46 percent of single women worked.[35]

World War I advanced women's status, historian Michael McGerr noted. "Although the number of employed women grew only modestly during the 1910s, the wartime departure of men for military service opened up jobs traditionally denied to women in offices, transportation and industry. Leaving jobs as domestic servants, seamstresses and laundresses, women became clerks, telephone operators, streetcar conductors, drill press operators and munitions makers. Women's new prominence in the work force led in turn to the creation of a Women's Bureau in the Department of Labor."[36]

In 1920 women gained the right to vote with adoption of the 19th Amendment. Soon afterward, Quaker activist Alice Paul introduced the first version of today's Equal Rights Amendment. In 1982 the amendment fell three states short of ratification, and its passage remains controversial today.[37] (*See "At Issue," p. 90.*)

During the Great Depression of the 1930s, the proportion of single women who were working stayed more or less flat. But the percentage of married women who worked rose to almost 14 percent by 1940 — a jump of more than 50 percent over the 1920 rate.[38] World War II brought millions more women into the labor force, as females — characterized by the iconic image of Rosie the Riveter — took jobs in defense plants doing work traditionally performed by men.

Equal-Pay Initiatives

As women proved their mettle behind the drill press and rivet gun, advocates continued to push for equal pay. In 1942 President Franklin D. Roosevelt had the National War Labor Board urge employers to equalize wage rates between men and women "for comparable quality and quantity of work on the same or similar operations."[39]

Debating the Comparable-Worth Doctrine

Would the approach help close the gender gap?

Imagine a company whose employees include a man who supervises telephone linemen and a woman who supervises clerical employees. They oversee the same number of workers, report to the same number of bosses, work the same hours and their jobs have been deemed of equal value to the company. Should their paychecks be the same?

Should the man get extra points for having to work outside in the cold? Should the woman get extra points for having a college degree or more years of experience?

Or, as some argue, should competitive market forces and the laws of supply and demand determine how much the man and woman earn?

Such questions lie at the heart of the debate over "comparable worth." The doctrine argues that when jobs require similar levels of skill, effort, responsibility and working conditions, the pay should be the same — even if the duties are entirely different.

Advocates of comparable worth say the market historically has undervalued jobs traditionally held by women — such as social work, secretarial work and teaching — and that such inequity has been a major contributor to the gender pay gap. If comparable worth were taken into account, they argue, it would even out wage inequality between those working in jobs dominated by women and those traditionally held by men when an impartial evaluation deems the jobs are of equal value to an employer.

Advocates also say neither the Equal Pay Act of 1963 — which bars unequal pay for the same job — nor Title VII of

the Civil Rights Act of 1964, which bans discrimination based on race, color, gender, religion and national origin in hiring and promotion, do what the comparable-worth doctrine would do: Root out bias against entire occupations traditionally dominated by females.[1]

Although women began entering non-traditional fields decades ago, Labor Department data show that certain occupations still are filled mostly by females. For example, in 2006, 89 percent of paralegals and legal assistants were women, while only 33 percent of lawyers were women. And only 7 percent of machinists were women, while 84 percent of special-education teachers were female.[2]

"There's a lot of [job] segregation, and the closer you look, the more segregation you find," says Philip Cohen, a sociologist at the University of North Carolina who studies gender inequality. "Under current law, it's very difficult to bring legal action successfully and say the pay gap between men and women is discrimination, because the employer can say 'they're doing different jobs.' "

But critics say comparable worth would disrupt the traditional market-based system of determining wages based on the laws of supply and demand. "You would have people moving into occupations where there was really no shortage" of workers, says June O'Neill, an economist at the City University of New York's Baruch College. "You would have gluts in some [job categories] and shortages in others."

In 2000 testimony before a congressional panel, O'Neill outlined what she saw as the dangers of adopting a

In the closing months of the war, the first bill aimed at barring gender pay discrimination came to the floor of Congress. The Women's Equal Pay Act of 1945 went nowhere, though.[40]

By 1960, more than a third of women were working, and among single, white women ages 25 to 34, the labor participation rate was a then-record 82 percent.[41] But most women continued to work in low-paying clerical, service and manufacturing jobs, and the wage gap between males and females was wide. By 1963, women made only 59 cents for every dollar in median year-round earnings

paid to men.[42] Women who tried to break into so-called "men's" occupations faced huge resistance.

That year, after decades of struggle by women's advocates for federal legislation on gender pay equity, Congress passed the Equal Pay Act as an amendment to the Fair Labor Standards Act of 1938. In signing the act, President Kennedy said the law "affirms our determination that when women enter the labor force they will find equality in their pay envelopes."[43]

The measure, as finally adopted, stopped short of ensuring the elusive comparable-worth standard that

comparable-worth approach. Because there is no uniform way to rank occupations by worth, she says, such a policy would "lead to politically administered wages that would depart from a market system of wage determination." Pay in traditionally female occupations would likely rise — appointing people favorable to the comparable-worth idea "would all but guarantee that result," she said. But that higher pay would raise costs for employers, leading them to put many women out of work, she suggested. "The ironic result is that fewer workers would be employed in traditionally female jobs."

Not only that, but some employers would respond to the higher wage levels by providing fewer non-monetary benefits, such as favorable working hours, that help accommodate women with responsibilities at home, O'Neill said. "Apart from the inefficiency and inequality it would breed," she concluded, "I find comparable worth to be a truly demeaning policy for women. It conveys the message that some cannot compete in non-traditional jobs and can only be helped through the patronage of a job evaluator."

Critics also say that comparable worth would put the government into the role of setting wages for private business, an idea that is anathema to business interests.

"Who determines what is equal value?" asks Michael Eastman, executive director of labor policy at the U.S. Chamber of Commerce. "Equal value to society? Who's setting wages then? Is the government coming up with

Martha Burk directs the Corporate Accountability Project for the National Council of Women's Organizations.

guidelines? For example, are truckers equal to nurses, and who's making that comparison? We've never had the government setting private-sector wage rates like that."

Supporters of comparable worth brush off such concerns. Martha Burk, a longtime women's activist, notes that a bill proposed by Sen. Tom Harkin, D-Iowa, would require companies to disclose how they pay women and men by job categories, a practice that alone would lead to more equitable wages. "What you have is a government solution that is not telling anybody what to pay their employees," she says. It would only "increase the transparency so the company can solve its own problem if it has one."

As to the notion that comparable worth amounts to government intrusion in the private market, Burk says, "Free marketers think anything short of totally unregulated capitalism is interfering in the free market."

"It may be that markets are efficient from the point of view of employers," adds Vicky Lovell, director of employment and work/life programs at the Institute for Women's Policy Research in Washington. "But I don't think they're efficient from the point of view of workers."

[1] For background, see June O'Neill, "Comparable Worth," *The Concise Encyclopedia of Economics*, The Library of Economics and Liberty, www.econlib.org.

[2] "Women in the Labor Force: A Databook," U.S. Department of Labor, Report 1002, September 2007, Table 11, pp. 28-34.

women's advocates had so long sought. Instead, the bill made it illegal to discriminate in pay and benefits on the basis of sex when men and women performed the same job at the same employer.

Under the law, for example, a company couldn't pay a full-time female store clerk less per hour than a male one for doing the same job in stores located in the same city. But the law was silent on situations in which, say, the work of a female secretarial supervisor was deemed to be of comparable worth to that of a male who supervised the same company's truck drivers.

While the Equal Pay Act marked progress, it was far from an airtight guarantee of "equality in . . . pay envelopes." For example, the law initially did not cover executive, administrative or professional jobs; that exemption was lifted in 1972. Yet, one study argues that courts have interpreted the act so narrowly that white-collar female workers have had trouble winning claims through its provisions.[44]

Perhaps more significantly, the law gives companies several defenses for pay disparities: when wage differences stem from seniority or merit systems, are based on

Did Wal-Mart Favor Male Workers?

Women's suit seeks billions in damages.

Dedra Farmer, the daughter of an auto mechanic, worked in the Tire Lube Express Division of Wal-Mart Stores, the only female in her district who held a salaried manager position in that division. During her 13 years with the retail giant, she told a congressional panel last year, she saw evidence that women — herself among them — earned less than men holding the same jobs.

Farmer said she complained to Wal-Mart's CEO through e-mails, expressed her concern at a store meeting and was assured by the store manager that she'd get a response. "The response I received was a pink slip," she said.[1]

Farmer has joined a class-action lawsuit accusing Wal-Mart of sex discrimination in pay and promotions. The case, which could cover perhaps 1.6 million current and former female employees and result in billions of dollars in damages, is the biggest workplace discrimination lawsuit in the nation's history.

Filed in 2001 by Betty Dukes and five other Wal-Mart employees, the case has gone through a series of legal maneuverings, most recently in December, when a three-judge panel of the U.S. 9th Circuit Court of Appeals reaffirmed its certification as a class-action lawsuit but left the door open for Wal-Mart to ask for a rehearing on that status. If the appeals court does not reconsider the class-action designation, the company reportedly will petition the Supreme Court.[2]

The stakes in the case are high. Goldman Sachs Group last year estimated potential damages at between $1.5 billion and $3.5 billion if the retailer loses, and punitive damages could raise the figure to between $13.5 billion and $31.5 billion.[3]

The company's lawyers have asserted that a class-action suit is an inappropriate vehicle to use because Wal-Mart's employment policies are decentralized, and individual store managers and district managers make pay and promotion decisions.[4]

Theodore J. Boutrous Jr., a lawyer for Wal-Mart, has said that decisions by thousands of managers at 3,400 Wal-Mart stores during six years were "highly individualized and cannot be tried in one fell swoop in a nationwide class action."[5] He has also said the company has a "strong diversity policy and anti-discrimination policy."[6]

But Brad Seligman, executive director of the Impact Fund, a nonprofit group in Berkeley, Calif., representing the plaintiffs, said, "No amount of PR or spin is going to allow Wal-Mart to avoid facing its legacy of discrimination."[7]

A statistician hired by the plaintiffs said it took women an average of 4.38 years from the date of hire to be promoted to assistant manager, while it took men 2.86 years. Moreover, it took an average of 10.12 years for women to become managers compared with 8.64 for men.[8]

The statistician, Richard Drogin, of California State University at East Bay, also found that female managers made an average annual salary of $89,280, while men in the same position earned an average of $105,682. Female hourly workers earned 6.7 percent less than men in comparable positions.[9]

quantity or quality of production, or stem from "any other factor other than sex."

That last provision, critics say, can sometimes allow business practices that may seem gender-neutral on the surface but discriminate nonetheless.

The Equal Pay Act took effect in 1964, and that same year Congress passed Title VII of the Civil Rights Act of 1964, a broad measure that prohibits employment discrimination on the basis of race, color, religion, national origin and sex, and covers hiring, firing and promotion as well as pay. A measure called the Bennett Amendment, sponsored by Rep. Wallace F. Bennett, a Utah Republican,

sought to bring Title VII and the Equal Pay Act in line with each other.

In ensuing years, the overlap of the Equal Pay Act and Title VII created confusion but also helped to animate the battle against wage discrimination. Part of the conflict over pay equity played out in the courts in the 1970s and '80s.

Key Court Rulings

In a case that initially raised hopes for the theory of comparable worth, the U.S. Supreme Court ruled 5-4 to

Appellate Judge Andrew J. Kleinfeld has dissented in the case, arguing that certifying the suit as a class action deprived the retailer of its right to defend against individual cases alleging bias. In addition, he argued that female employees who were discriminated against would be hurt by class-action status, because women "who were fired or not promoted for good reasons" would also share in any award if Wal-Mart lost the case.[10]

Business lobbies also have urged that the class-action certification be reversed. An official of the U.S. Chamber of Commerce, which filed a "friend of the court" (*amicus curiae*) brief in the case, warned of "potentially limitless claims" against companies "with limited ability to defend against them." He added: "The potential financial exposure to an employer facing a class action of this size creates tremendous pressure to settle regardless of the case's merit."[11]

But women's advocates argue that a class-action approach is appropriate. It "provides the only practical means for most women in low-wage jobs to redress discrimination in pay because of such workers' often tenuous economic status," stated an *amicus* letter written to the appeals court on behalf of the U.S. Women's Chamber of Commerce.[12]

Added Margot Dorfman, chief executive officer of the group: "A woman with family responsibilities often isn't in a

A Wal-Mart store manager reads the store's weekly sales results to other workers. Male hourly workers at Wal-Mart earn 6.7 percent more than women in comparable positions, a pay-equity study contends.

position to quit her job or risk antagonizing her employer with a challenge to a bad workplace practice."[13]

[1] Statement of Dedra Farmer before House Committee on Education and Labor, April 24, 2007.

[2] Amy Joyce, "Wal-Mart Loses Bid to Block Group Bias Suit," *The Washington Post*, Feb. 7, 2007, p. 1D.

[3] Details of the Goldman Sachs analysis are from Steve Painter, "Judges modify sex-bias decision; Wal-Mart appeal likely to see delay," *Arkansas Democrat-Gazette*, Dec. 12, 2007.

[4] Steven Greenhouse and Constance L. Hays, "Wal-Mart Sex-Bias Suit Given Class-Action Status," *The New York Times*, June 23, 2004.

[5] Joyce, *op. cit.*

[6] Quoted in Bob Egelko, "Wal-Mart sex discrimination suit advances; Appeals court OKs class action status for 2 million women," *San Francisco Chronicle*, Feb. 7, 2007, p. B1.

[7] Joyce, *op. cit.*

[8] *Ibid.*

[9] *Ibid.*

[10] Painter, *op. cit.*

[11] "U.S. Chamber Files Brief in Wal-Mart Class Action," press release, U.S. Chamber of Commerce, Dec. 13, 2004, www.uschamber.com/press/releases/2004/december/04-159.htm.

[12] Mark E. Burton Jr., Hersh & Hersh, San Francisco, et al., letter submitted to 9th U.S. Circuit Court of Appeals, March 27, 2007, www.uswcc.org/amicus.pdf.

[13] PR Newswire, "U.S. Women's Chamber of Commerce Joins Fight in Landmark Women's Class Action Suit Against Wal-Mart," March 28, 2007.

allow female jail guards to sue for sex discrimination. The women, called "matrons," earned 30 percent less than male guards, called "deputy sheriffs."[45] The women argued that while they had fewer prisoners to guard and more clerical duties than the male guards, their work was comparable. An outside job evaluation showed that the women did 95 percent of what the men were doing, but received $200 less a month than the men.[46]

Prior to the Supreme Court's ruling, *The Washington Post* noted at the time, "the only sure grounds for a pay discrimination claim by a woman under federal law was 'unequal pay for equal work' — an allegation that she

was paid less than a man holding an identical job. The jail matrons and women's rights lawyers said that lower pay for a comparable, if not equal, job could also be the basis for a sex-discrimination charge."

Justice William J. Brennan wrote that a claim of wage discrimination under Title VII did not have to meet the equal work standards of the Equal Pay Act. Thus, noted Clare Cushman, director of publications at the Supreme Court Historical Society, "a woman employee could sue her employer for gender-based pay discrimination even if her company did not employ a man to work the same job for higher pay."[47]

Still, Cushman wrote, while the court "opened the door slightly for women working in jobs not strictly equal to their male counterparts, it also specifically declined to authorize suits based on the theory of comparable worth."

In 1985 that theory suffered a blow that continues to resonate today, partly because of the personalities who were involved. In *AFSCME v. the State of Washington*, the 9th U.S. Circuit Court of Appeals overturned a lower court's ruling ordering Washington to pay more than $800 million in back wages to some 15,000 state workers, most of them women.[48]

The case turned on the question of whether employers were required to pay men and women the same amounts for jobs of comparable worth, rather than equal wages for the same jobs. It eventually ended in a draw when the state negotiated a settlement with AFSCME (American Federation of State, County and Municipal Employees union).[49]

Judge Anthony M. Kennedy, who now sits on the U.S. Supreme Court and presumably could help decide a comparable-worth case should one arise before the justices, wrote the appellate court's decision. Kennedy wrote: "Neither law nor logic deems the free-market system a suspect enterprise." During this same period, two other personalities who now sit on the high court also expressed negative views on comparable worth. As a lawyer in the Reagan administration, John Roberts, now chief justice, described it as "a radical redistributive concept."[50] And the EEOC, then under Chairman Clarence Thomas, rejected comparable worth as a means of determining job discrimination. "We found that sole reliance on a comparison of the intrinsic value of dissimilar jobs — which command different wages in the market — does not prove a violation of Tile VII," Thomas stated.[51]

The views of Thomas and Roberts reflected the conservative policies of the Reagan administration during the 1980s. Yet despite the political tenor of that era, women made major strides toward workplace equality. From 1980 to 1992, the wage gap in median weekly earnings of full-time female wage and salary workers narrowed from 64 percent to 76 percent after adjusting for inflation. But it shrank only from 77 percent to 81 percent from 1993 — the year that Democratic President Bill Clinton took office and the Family and Medical Leave Act was enacted — to 2006.[52]

Measuring Progress

Experts debate whether and to what degree women's gains may have slowed or stopped in recent years. Some point to huge political gains in this decade, including Sen. Clinton's role in the presidential race and the rise of Rep. Nancy Pelosi, D-Calif., to speaker of the House. Others cite such evidence as a recent study showing that female corporate directors, though a small minority in boardrooms, out-earn male directors.[53]

But many scholars believe women's gains have indeed slowed.

Vanneman, the University of Maryland sociologist, has carefully charted a number of trends linked to the so-called gender revolution, and on his Web site he notes that he and several colleagues are studying the pace of women's progress.

"For much of the last quarter of the 20th century, women gradually reduced gender inequalities on many fronts," he wrote, citing such trends as women entering the labor force in growing numbers, the opening of previously male-dominated jobs to women, the narrowing wage gap, women's role in politics and a growing openness in public opinion about the participation of women in public and community life.

But, he added, "all this changed in the early to mid-1990s." A "flattening of the gender trend lines" is seen in nearly all parts of society, he added: working-class and middle-class, black, white, Asian and Hispanic, mothers with young children and those with older ones, and so on. "All groups experienced major gender setbacks during the 1990s. The breadth of this reversal suggests something fundamental has happened to the U.S. gender structure."

In an interview, Vanneman says he has no theories as to what accounts for that reversal — only hunches — as he continues to study the phenomenon. One hunch is that the flattening started happening in the 1980s but didn't show up in a big way until the 1990s. He also says he suspects the reversal in women's progress gathered momentum in the 1990s as the "culture of parenting" changed. Americans, he says, became less accepting of women trying to balance busy careers with the pressures of motherhood, a shift that has put women in more of a bind than they felt in previous periods. As a result, many women have backed away from high-paying careers and devoted more time to family, he says.

"There's been tremendous growth in expectations of what it means to be a good parent," Vanneman says.

Cornell University economist Blau agrees that progress in women's wages slowed in recent years, though she sees some evidence that the picture has brightened a bit.

One reason for the slowdown in the 1990s, she says, may have been that the increase in demand for white-collar and service workers shifted into a lower gear compared to the 1980s, when many women benefited from a surge in hiring for white-collar jobs, including ones that required computer skills, while blue-collar jobs dominated by men began to wane.

In addition, Blau says that during the eighties, as many women began to stay in the workforce even after marriage and childbirth, employers' view of the value of female workers improved. That, she says, helped narrow the wage gap at a faster pace than in earlier decades.

Blau also sees evidence that men were doing more at home in the 1980s than ever before. That trend didn't go away in the past decade, she says, but it hasn't grown much either.

CURRENT SITUATION

Prospects in Congress

As concerns over the progress of gender equity grow, women's advocates are hoping that the Democrat-controlled Congress will pass new laws this year. But proposed legislation is likely to face stiff opposition.

Reversing the Supreme Court's *Ledbetter* decision seems to have the best chance of making it through Congress. The House passed the Ledbetter Fair Pay Act last July 31 by a 225-199 vote, largely along party lines.[54] A companion bill in the Senate, called the Lilly Ledbetter Fair Pay Restoration Act, had garnered 37 co-sponsors as of early March. Momentum continued this year with a Senate hearing.

In introducing the Senate version of the bill last July, Sen. Kennedy said it "simply restores the status quo" that existed before the *Ledbetter* decision "so that victims of ongoing pay discrimination have a reasonable time to file their claims."[55]

But employer advocates such as the U.S. Chamber of Commerce dispute such descriptions. Pointing to the House version that passed last summer, chamber officials said it would broaden existing law to apply to unintentional as well as intentional discrimination and would lead to an "explosion of litigation second-guessing legitimate employment and personnel decisions."[56]

The Bush administration has threatened a veto, saying last year that if the House bill came to the president, "his senior advisers would recommend that he veto" it.[57]

The measure would "impede justice" by allowing employees to sue over pay or other employment-related discrimination "years or even decades after the alleged discrimination occurred," the administration said. Moreover, the House bill "far exceeds the stated purpose of undoing the court's decision" by "extending the expanded statute of limitations to any 'other practice' that remotely affects an individual's wages, benefits, or other compensation in the future."

Eric Dreiband, a former EEOC general counsel in the Bush administration, told this year's hearing on the Senate bill that the measure would subject state and local governments, unions, employers and others to potentially unlimited penalties and could expose pension funds to "potentially staggering liability."[58]

Still, women's advocates remain sanguine about the measure's prospects. "My hope is that the bill will move expeditiously [this] spring" in the Senate and that "the president will reconsider and recognize how important this fix to the law is," says Samuels of the National Women's Law Center.

The other two main bills on gender pay equity could have rougher sledding.

Sen. Clinton's Paycheck Fairness Act is similar to a bill by the same name proposed during her husband's presidential administration. As of early March, the bill had garnered 22 co-sponsors in the Senate and 226 in the House.

Among other things, it would strengthen penalties on employers who violate the Equal Pay Act, make it harder for companies to use the law's defense for wage differences based on factors "other than sex," and bar employers from retaliating against workers who share wage information with each other. It also calls for the Labor Department to draw up guidelines aimed at helping employers voluntarily evaluate job categories and compare wages paid for different jobs with the aim of eliminating unfair wage differences between male- and female-dominated occupations.

The bill has drawn enthusiastic support from some women's advocates, but it also has opponents. Washington lawyer Brown said the goal of the provision on voluntary guidelines was "nothing more than the discredited 'comparable-worth' theory in new clothing."[59]

The Fair Pay Act, proposed by Sen. Harkin and Del. Eleanor Holmes Norton, D-D.C., a former EEOC chair, steps even closer to embracing the comparable-worth theory and thus, many observers believe, is likely to face stiff headwinds. The main ideas have circulated in Congress for years.

Is the Equal Rights Amendment to the Constitution still needed?

YES
Idella Moore
Executive Officer, 4ERA

Written for *CQ Researcher*, February 2008

We still need the Equal Rights Amendment (ERA) because sex discrimination is still a problem in our country. Like race or religious discrimination, gender discrimination is intended to render its victims economically, socially, legally and politically disadvantaged. But unlike racism and religious intolerance — whose practice against certain groups is localized within countries or regions — sex discrimination is universal. Why, then, in our court system are race and religious discrimination considered more serious offenses?

Today, American women — of all races and religions — are still fighting to achieve equal opportunity, pay, status and recognition in all realms of our society. At this moment, the largest class-action lawsuit in the history of this country is being argued on behalf of 1.6 million women who were discriminated against purely because of their gender. If the ERA had been ratified back in the 1970s, by now these types of lawsuits would be extinct.

We still need the ERA because ratification of the amendment will elevate "sex" to, in legal terms, a so-called suspect class. A suspect class has the advantage in discrimination cases. Gender, as yet, is not afforded that advantage. As we've seen with race, suspect class status increased the chance of favorable outcomes in discrimination cases. This, in turn, served as a deterrent. Consequently, in our society racism is now socially unacceptable. Sex discrimination, however, is not.

We still need the ERA because the continuing struggle for legal equality for women should be seen as a shameful and embarrassing condition of our society. Yet today lawmakers — sworn to represent all their constituents — proudly voice their objections to granting legal equality to women and without any fear of consequences to their political careers. How different our reactions would be if they were espousing racism.

The Equal Rights Amendment will perfect our Constitution by explicitly guaranteeing that the privileges, laws and responsibilities it contains apply equally to men and women. As it stands today the Constitution is sometimes interpreted that way, but women, as a universally and historically disadvantaged group, cannot rely on such interpretations. We have seen these "interpretations" vary and change, often due to the whims of the political climate. Therefore, without the ERA any gains women make will always be tenuous.

I see the Equal Rights Amendment, too, as a pledge to ourselves and posterity that we recognize that sexism exists and that we as a country are determined to continue perfecting our democracy by proudly and unequivocally guaranteeing that one's gender will no longer be a detriment to achieving the American dream.

NO
Phyllis Schlafly
President, Eagle Forum

Written for *CQ Researcher*, February 2008

The Equal Rights Amendment (ERA) was fiercely debated across America for 10 years (1972-1982) and was rejected. ERA has been reintroduced into the current Congress under a slightly different name, but it's the same old amendment with the same bad effects.

The principal reason ERA failed is that although it was marketed as a benefit to women, its advocates were never able to prove it would provide any benefit whatsoever to women. ERA would put "sex" (not women) in the Constitution and just make all our laws sex-neutral.

ERA advocates used their massive access to a friendly media to suggest that ERA would raise women's wages. But ERA would have no effect on wages because our employment laws are already sex-neutral. The equal-pay-for-equal-work law was passed in 1963, and the Equal Employment Opportunity Act — with all its enforcement mechanisms — was passed in 1972.

Supreme Court Justice Ruth Bader Ginsburg's book *Sex Bias in the U.S. Code* spells out the changes ERA would require, and it proves ERA would take away benefits from women. For example, the book states that the "equality principle" would eliminate the concept of "dependent women." This would deprive wives and widows of their Social Security dependent-wife benefits, on which millions of mothers and grandmothers depend.

Looking at the experience of states that have put ERA language into their constitutions, we see that ERA would most probably require taxpayer funding of abortions. The feminists aggressively litigate this issue. Their most prominent victory was in the New Mexico Supreme Court, which accepted the notion that since only women undergo abortions, the denial of taxpayer funding is sex discrimination.

ERA would also give the courts the power to legalize same-sex marriages. Courts in four states have ruled that the ERA's ban on gender discrimination requires marriage licenses to be given to same-sex couples. In Maryland and Washington, those decisions were overturned by a higher court by only a one-vote margin. The ERA would empower the judges to rule either way.

If all laws are made sex-neutral, the military draft-registration law would have to include women. We don't have a draft today, but we do have registration, and those who fail to register immediately lose their college grants and loans and will never be able to get a federal job.

As Harkin describes it, the bill requires employers to provide equal pay for jobs that are comparable in skill, effort, responsibility and working conditions, regardless of sex, race or national origin, and it bars companies from reducing other employees' wages to achieve pay equity.[60]

Again, advocates such as Samuels are hopeful Congress will pass both the Paycheck Fairness and Fair Pay Act and that the president won't veto them if they do make it to his desk. "The hope would be that the level of support for these bills both in Congress and among the public is so substantial, and they so clearly are a necessary step toward ensuring true equality of wages, that the president would understand the necessity for them and sign them," she says.

But business opposition is likely to be strong. Eastman at the U.S. Chamber of Commerce lists a variety of complaints about both bills, such as their provisions for punitive damages and their allowances for class-action suits against employers. "The case has not been made that these bills are justified," he says.

State Action

While women's advocates hold out hope for congressional action, they also are turning their attention to the states in hopes of pressing legislatures to stiffen laws on pay equity and make local economies friendlier to gender issues. As of April 2007, all but 11 states and the District of Columbia had laws on equal pay.[61]

Minnesota has had a system of comparable worth, or "pay equity," for public employees since the 1980s, and last year proposals were made to expand the system to private employers that do business with the state. The Minnesota program gave smaller raises to public workers in male-dominated jobs and bigger raises to those in female-dominated ones, according to a former staff member of the Minnesota Commission on the Economic Status of Women. The system shrank the pay gap from 72 percent to nearly equal pay.[62]

A report by the Institute for Women's Policy Research said in 2006 that while women's wages had risen in all states in inflation-adjusted terms since 1989, "in no state does the typical full-time woman worker earn as much as the typical man." It would take 50 years "at the present rate of progress" for women to achieve wage parity with men nationwide, it said.[63]

Some advocates are unwilling to wait that long. In Colorado, for example, a Pay Equity Commission appointed by Donald J. Mares, executive director of the state Department of Labor and Employment, worked since last June to formulate policy recommendations to curb gender and racial pay inequities in the private and public sectors. The 12-member commission includes policy analysts, business and labor union representatives, academics and advocates for women and minorities.[64]

Meric, the 9to5 director and a Colorado resident, said her group was instrumental in getting the state to appoint the commission. Although the panel has no authority to force employers to alter pay practices, Meric hopes the commission's work leads to change. One key recommendation, she says, is that employers do more to create flexible policies so that workers — especially women with caregiving responsibilities — aren't penalized for meeting both work and family responsibilities.

Mares told the Colorado Women's Legislative Breakfast in February that another recommendation calls for making the commission permanent, so it can continue to monitor gender pay equity in the state and help educate businesses on good practices.

In Colorado, he said, the average woman makes 79 cents for every dollar earned by the average man. "Every day you as a community walk in the door," he told the gathering of women, "your pay is being discounted. That's not good."[65]

Better negotiating skills could help narrow the gender wage gap, in the view of women's advocates. The Clinton/DeLauro bill calls for grants to help women and girls "strengthen their negotiation skills to allow the girls and women to obtain higher salaries and the best compensation packages possible for themselves."

It's a talent that many women don't exercise, says Linda Babcock, an economist at Carnegie Mellon University in Pittsburgh and co-author of the recent book *Women Don't Ask: Negotiation and the Gender Divide.* Babcock found in a study of Carnegie Mellon students graduating with master's degrees in public policy that only 12.5 percent of females tried to negotiate for better pay when they received a job offer, while 51.5 percent of males did. Afterward, the females earned 8.5 percent less than the males.

Babcock sees several reasons why women are not inclined to negotiate more, including that they have been socialized by American culture to be less assertive than men. And, she says, women who do try to bargain for better wages often are subjected to "backlash" by employers and peers.

Not that women are incapable of negotiating, Babcock stresses. While they may not always stand up for themselves in seeking higher wages, women outperform men when negotiating on behalf of somebody else, she has found.

"It's really striking," she says. "If we were missing some gene, we wouldn't really be able to turn it on on behalf of somebody else."

OUTLOOK

Pressure for Change

Some women's advocates are not especially sanguine about the possibility of big strides on the gender-wage front, at least in the near future.

"I don't think five years is long enough [for there] to be much change, particularly if we don't see much concerted effort among employers," says Lovell of the Institute for Women's Policy Research.

Big change would require a "push from the federal government" or "some dramatic effort on the part of socially conscious employers," she says. "That hasn't happened before, and I don't think it will in the next few years."

Still, observers believe that social and political shifts will produce new pressure for changes in the way employers deal with wage equity.

Meric says 9to5's "long-term agenda" is to have the theory of comparable worth enshrined in law as well as to have "guaranteed minimum labor standards" for all workers that include paid sick leave and expanded coverage under the Family and Medical Leave Act. In Colorado, she hopes the recommendations outlined by the Pay Equity Commission will serve as a model for other states and "move us closer" to that long-term goal. "Basic protections should apply to workers wherever they live in the United States."

"In the last five or 10 years we have seen progress stall in [achieving] gender equality," says Philip Cohen, a sociologist at the University of North Carolina at Chapel Hill who studies gender inequity. But in coming years, he says he is inclined to think that college-educated women will exert increasing pressure on federal and state lawmakers and employers to make policy changes that can narrow the wage gap.

"If you look back to feminism in the '60s," Cohen says, "a lot of women had college degrees but weren't able to take advantage of their skills in the marketplace, and that became the 'feminine mystique' " explored in Betty Friedan's groundbreaking 1963 book.

Today, "Women are outnumbering men in college graduation rates, and I think we are going to see more and more women looking around for better opportunities. If they don't see gender equality resulting, they're going to be very dissatisfied."

And that dissatisfaction, Cohen says, could well show up in the political arena.

Samuels of the National Women's Law Center hopes the debate in Congress and fallout from the Supreme Court's *Ledbetter* decision will spur further gains in wage equity for women.

"Unfortunately, over the course of the last several years things have pretty much stagnated," she says. "I do hope that the recent public attention paid to wage disparity will cause employers to take a look at their pay scales and try to do the right thing."

NOTES

1. Testimony of Lilly Ledbetter before the Committee on Education and Labor, U.S. House of Representatives, on the Amendment of Title VII, June 12, 2007.

2. Testimony of Lilly Ledbetter before Senate Committee on Health, Education, Labor and Pensions, Jan. 24, 2008.

3. *Ledbetter v. Goodyear Tire & Rubber Co. Inc.*, 550 U.S. __ (May 29, 2007).

4. Ledbetter testimony, *op. cit.*, June 12, 2007.

5. Diana Furchtgott-Roth, testimony on the Paycheck Fairness Act before House Committee on Education and Labor, April 24, 2007.

6. "Highlights of Women's Earnings in 2006," U.S. Department of Labor, September 2007, Table 1, p. 7. Data are for median usual weekly earnings of full-time wage and salary workers ages 16 and older. For the Census Bureau data, see www.census.gov/ compendia/statab/tables/08s0628.pdf. The Census Bureau data represent median full-time, year-round earnings for male and female workers 15 years old and older as of March 2006.

7. Testimony before Senate Committee on Health, Education, Labor and Pensions, April 12, 2007.

8. "Women's Earnings: Work Patterns Partially Explain Difference between Men's and Women's

Earnings," U.S. General Accounting Office, October 2003.

9. U.S. Equal Employment Opportunity Commission, Office of Inspector General, "Semiannual Report to Congress," April 1, 2007-Sept. 30, 2007, Oct. 30, 2007, p. 7.

10. "Highlights of Women's Earnings," *op. cit.*, p. 1.

11. *Ibid.*, Table 1, p. 7.

12. Judy Goldberg Dey and Catherine Hill, "Behind the Pay Gap," American Association of University Women Educational Foundation, 2007.

13. Paycheck Fairness Act, HR 1338, S 766.

14. Fair Pay Act, S 1087 and HR 2019, sponsored in the House of Representatives by Del. Eleanor Holmes Norton, D-D.C.

15. Lilly Ledbetter Fair Pay Act, HR 2831 and Fair Pay Restoration Act, S 1843.

16. David Neumark, with the assistance of Roy J. Bank and Kyle D. Van Nort, "Sex Discrimination in Restaurant Hiring: An Audit Study," *The Quarterly Journal of Economics*, August 1996.

17. Furchtgott-Roth testimony, *op. cit.*

18. Dey and Hill, *op. cit.*

19. Testimony of Heather Boushey before House Committee on Education and Labor, April 24, 2007, p. 4.

20. John F. Kennedy, Remarks Upon Signing the Equal Pay Act, June 10, 1963, quoted in John T. Woolley and Gerhard Peters, *The American Presidency Project* [online], Santa Barbara, Calif., University of California (hosted), Gerhard Peters (database), www .presidency.ucsb.edu/ws/?pid=9267.

21. Testimony of Jocelyn Samuels before Senate Committee on Health, Education, Labor and Pensions, "Closing the Gap: Equal Pay for Women Workers," April 12, 2007, p. 6.

22. Carrie Lukas, "A Bargain At 77 Cents To a Dollar," *The Washington Post*, April 3, 2007, p. 23A.

23. Testimony of Barbara Berish Brown before Senate Committee on Health, Education, Labor and Pensions, April 12, 2007.

24. Quoted in Justine Andronici, "Court Gives OK To Unequal Pay," *Ms. Magazine*, summer 2007, accessed at www.msmagazine.com/summer2007/ledbetter.asp.

25. Quoted in Michael Doyle, "Justices Put Bias Lawsuits on Tight Schedule," *Kansas City Star*, May 30, 2007, p. 1A.

26. Testimony of Margot Dorfman before Senate Committee on Health, Education, Labor and Pensions on the "The Fair Pay Restoration Act: Ensuring Reasonable Rules in Pay Discrimination Cases," Jan. 24, 2008, pp. 2-3.

27. "Employment Discrimination: Post-Ledbetter Discrimination," "Justice Talking," National Public Radio, Oct. 22, 2007, accessed at www.justicetalking .org/transcripts/071022_EqualPay_transcript.pdf.

28. Richard B. Morris, ed., "The U.S. Department of Labor Bicentennial History of the American Work," U.S. Department of Labor, 1976, p. 67.

29. Claudia Goldin, *Understanding the Gender Gap: An Economic History of American Women* (1990), p. 50.

30. *Ibid.*, Figure 3.1, p. 62, and text pp. 63, 66.

31. *Ibid.*, p. 67.

32. Quoted in *ibid.*, p. 209.

33. *Ibid.*, Table 2.1, p. 17, citing U.S. Census data.

34. "Setting a New Course," *CQ Researcher*, May 10, 1985, citing Julie A. Matthaei, *An Economic History of Women in America* (1982), p. 222.

35. Goldin, *op. cit.*, p. 17.

36. Michael McGerr, *A Fierce Discontent: The Rise and Fall of the Progressive Movement in America, 1870-1920* (2003), pp. 295-296.

37. For background, see Richard Boeckel, "Sex Equality and Protective Laws," *Editorial Research Reports*, July 13, 1926; and Richard Boeckel, "The Woman's Vote in National Elections," *Editorial Research Reports*, May 31, 1927, both available at *CQ Researcher Plus Archive*, www.cqpress.com.

38. *Ibid.*

39. American Association of University Women, "A Brief History of the Wage Gap, Pay Inequity, and the Equal Pay Act," www.aauw.org/advocacy/laf/ lafnetwork/library/payequity_hist.cfm. For background, see K. R. Lee, "Women in War Work," *Editorial Research Reports*, Jan. 26, 1942, available at *CQ Researcher Plus Archive*, www.cqpress.com.

40. *Ibid.*

41. Goldin, *op. cit.*, Table 2.2, p. 18.

42. *Ibid.*, Table 3.1, p. 60.

43. John F. Kennedy, *op. cit.*

44. Juliene James, "The Equal Pay Act in the Courts: A De Facto White-Collar Exemption," *New York University Law Review*, Vol. 79, November 2004, p. 1875.

45. Clare Cushman, *Supreme Court Decisions and Women's Rights*, CQ Press (2000), p. 146. The case is *County of Washington v. Gunther* (1981). For background, see Sandra Stencel, "Equal Pay Fight," *Editorial Research Reports*, March 20, 1981, and R. Thompson, "Women's Economic Equity," *Editorial Research Reports*, May 10, 1985, both available at *CQ Researcher Plus Archive*, www.cqpress.com.

46. Deborah Churchman, "Comparable Worth: The Equal-Pay Issue of the '80s," *The Christian Science Monitor*, July 22, 1982, p. 15.

47. Cushman, *op. cit.*

48. James Warren, "Fight for Pay Equity Produces Results, But Not Parity," *Chicago Tribune*, Sept. 8, 1985, p. 13.

49. Judy Mann, "New Victory in Women's Pay," *The Washington Post*, Aug. 27, 1986, p. 3B.

50. Linda Greenhouse, "Judge Roberts, the Committee Is Interested in Your View On . . . ," *The New York Times*, Sept. 11, 2005, p. 1A.

51. "Women Dealt Setback on 'Comparable Worth,' " *Chicago Tribune*, June 18, 1985, p. 1.

52. "Highlights of Women's Earnings in 2006," *op. cit.*, Table 13, p. 28.

53. Martha Graybow, "Female U.S. corporate directors out-earn men: study," Reuters, Nov. 7, 2007. The study of more than 25,000 directors at more than 3,200 U.S. companies was done by the Corporate Library. It found that female directors earned median compensation of $120,000 compared with $104,375 for male board members.

54. Libby George, "House Democrats Prevail in Effort to Clarify Law on Wage Discrimination," *CQ Weekly*, Aug. 6, 2007, p. 2381.

55. Sen. Edward Kennedy, statement on S 1843, "Statements on Introduced Bills and Joint Resolutions," Senate, July 20, 2007, accessed at www.thomas.gov.

56. U.S. Chamber of Commerce, "Letter Opposing HR 2831, the Ledbetter Fair Pay Act," July 27, 2007, accessed at www.uschamber.com/issues/letters/2007/070727_ledbetter.htm.

57. "Statement of Administration Policy: HR 2831, Lilly Ledbetter Fair Pay Act of 2007," Executive Office of the President, Office of Management and Budget, July 27, 2007, accessed at www.whitehouse.gov/omb/legislative/sap/110-1/hr2831sap-r.pdf.

58. Statement of Eric S. Dreiband before Senate Committee on Health, Education, Labor and Pensions, Jan. 24, 2008, pp. 11-13.

59. Barbara Berish Brown testimony, *op. cit.*

60. Statement of Sen. Tom Harkin at the Health, Education, Labor and Pensions Committee Hearing on Equal Pay for Women Workers, April 12, 2007, accessed at www.harkin.senate.gov/pr/p.cfm?i=272330.

61. National Conference of State Legislatures, "State Laws on Equal Pay," April 2007.

62. H.J. Cummins, "Legislature will look at closing the gender gap," *Star Tribune*, April 23, 2007, p. 1D.

63. Heidi Hartmann, Olga Sorokina and Erica Williams, "The Best and Worst State Economies for Women," Institute for Women's Policy Research, December 2006.

64. "Pay Equity Commission holds first meeting," *Denver Business Journal*, June 26, 2007.

65. Remarks of Donald Mares, Colorado Women's Legislative Breakfast, Feb. 12, 2008, accessed at www.youtube.com/watch?v=UIO0mlHb6b8&feature=related.

BIBLIOGRAPHY

Books

Cushman, Clare, *Supreme Court Decisions and Women's Rights*, CQ Press, 2000.
In clear prose, the director of publications for the Supreme Court Historical Society covers the waterfront of Supreme Court cases and issues involving women's rights, including those related to pay equity and discrimination in the workplace.

Farrell, Warren, *Why Men Earn More,* **AMACOM,** 2005.

The only man elected three times to the board of directors of the National Organization for Women's New York chapter argues that the pay gap can no longer be ascribed to discrimination, and he seeks "to give women ways of earning more rather than suing more."

Goldin, Claudia, *Understanding the Gender Gap: An Economic History of American Women,* **Oxford University Press,** 1990.

A Harvard University economics professor traces the evolution of female workers and gender differences in occupations and earnings from the early days of the republic to the modern era.

Murphy, Evelyn, with E.J. Graff, *Getting Even: Why Women Don't Get Paid Like Men — and What to Do About It,* **Touchstone,** 2005.

The former Massachusetts lieutenant governor writes in this anecdote-filled book that the "gender wage gap is unfair" and "it's not going away on its own."

Articles

Hymowitz, Carol, "On Diversity, America Isn't Putting Its Money Where Its Mouth Is," *The Wall Street Journal,* **Feb. 25, 2008.**

Progress for women and minorities in business has stalled or moved backward at many of the nation's largest companies, and the inequality shapes perceptions about who can or should fill leadership roles.

Murphy, Cait, "Obama flunks Econ 101," *Fortune, CNNMoney.com,* **June 6, 2007, http://money.cnn .com/2007/06/04/magazines/fortune/muphy_ payact.fortune/index.htm.**

The presidential candidate is "flirting with a very bad idea" by co-sponsoring the Fair Pay Act, "a bill that would bureaucratize most of the labor market," Murphy argues.

Parloff, Roger, and Susan M. Kaufman, "The War Over Unconscious Bias," *Fortune,* **Oct. 15, 2007.**

Wal-Mart and other companies are facing accusations of gender pay bias and other forms of job discrimination, "but the biggest problem isn't their policies, it's their managers' unwitting preferences."

Reports and Studies

Dey, Judy Goldberg, and Catherine Hill, "Behind the Pay Gap," *American Association of University Women Educational Foundation,* **April 2007, www.aauw.org/ research/upload/behindPayGap.pdf.**

A study of college graduates concludes that one year out of college women working full time earn only 80 percent as much as their male colleagues and that a decade after graduation the proportion falls to 69 percent.

Foust-Cummings, Heather, Laura Sabattini and Nancy Carter, "Women in Technology: Maximizing Talent, Minimizing Barriers," *Catalyst,* **2008, www .catalyst.org/files/full/2008%20Women%20in%20 High%20Tech.pdf.**

Technology companies are making progress at creating more diverse work environments, but women in the high-technology field still face barriers to advancement, such as a lack of role models, mentors and access to networks.

Hartmann, Heidi, Olga Sorokina and Erica Williams, et al., "The Best and Worst State Economies for Women," *Institute for Women's Policy Research,* **IWPR No. R334, December 2006, www.iwpr.org/ pdf/R334_BWState Economies2006.pdf.**

The advocacy group concludes that women's wages have risen in all states since 1989 after adjusting for inflation, but that in "no state does the typical full-time woman worker earn as much as the typical man."

U.S. General Accounting Office, "Women's Earnings: Work Patterns Partially Explain Difference between Men's and Women's Earnings," **October 2003, www .gao.gov/new.items/d0435.pdf.**

This statistical study concludes that "work patterns are key" among the factors that account for earnings differences between men and women, but that some differences remain unexplained.

U.S. Department of Labor, U.S. Bureau of Labor Statistics, "Highlights of Women's Earnings in 2006," **Report 1002, September 2007, www.bls.gov/cps/ cpswom2006.pdf.**

Among this report's conclusions: The earnings gap between men and women narrowed for most major age groups between 1979 and 2006 and was largest among those ages 45 to 64, with women earning about 73 percent as much as men in that age range.

For More Information

Eagle Forum, PO Box 618, Alton, IL 62002; (618) 462-5415; www.eagleforum.org. Conservative social-policy organization opposed to ratification of the Equal Rights Amendment.

4ERA, 4355J Cobb Parkway, #233, Atlanta, GA 30339; (678) 793-6965; www.4era.org. Single-issue organization advocating ratification of the Equal Rights Amendment.

Institute for Women's Policy Research, 1707 L St., N.W., Suite 750, Washington, DC 20036; (202) 785-5100; www.iwpr.org. Research organization that focuses on gender pay as well as other issues affecting women, including poverty and education.

National Committee on Pay Equity, c/o AFT, 555 New Jersey Ave., N.W., Washington, DC 20001-2029; (703) 920-2010; www.pay-equity.org. Coalition of women's and civil rights organizations, labor unions, religious, professional, legal and educational associations and others focused on pay-equity issues.

National Women's Law Center, 11 Dupont Circle, N.W., Suite 800, Washington, DC 20036; (202) 588-5180; www.nwlc.org. Advocacy group that focuses on employment, health, education and economic-security issues affecting women and girls.

9to5, National Association of Working Women, 207 E. Buffalo St., #211, Milwaukee, WI 53202; (414) 274-0925; www.9to5.org. Grassroots organization focusing on economic-justice issues for women.

U.S. Chamber of Commerce, 1615 H St., N.W., Washington, DC 20062-2000; (202) 659-6000; www.uschamber.com. Represents business interests before Congress, government agencies and the courts.

Women's Rights

Are Violence and Discrimination Against Women Declining?

Karen Foerstel

Iraqi teenager Du'a Khalil Aswad lies mortally wounded after her "honor killing" by a mob in the Kurdish region of Iraq. No one has been prosecuted for the April 2007 murder, even though a cell-phone video of the incident was posted on the Internet. Aswad's male relatives are believed to have arranged her ritualistic execution because she had dated a boy from outside her religious sect. The United Nations estimates that 5,000 women and girls are murdered in honor killings around the globe each year.

AFP/Getty Images

S he was 17 years old. The blurry video shows her lying in a dusty road, blood streaming down her face, as several men kick and throw rocks at her. At one point she struggles to sit up, but a man kicks her in the face forcing her back to the ground. Another slams a large, concrete block down onto her head. Scores of onlookers cheer as the blood streams from her battered head.[1]

The April 7, 2007, video was taken in the Kurdish area of northern Iraq on a mobile phone. It shows what appear to be several uniformed police officers standing on the edge of the crowd, watching while others film the violent assault on their phones.

The brutal, public murder of Du'a Khalil Aswad reportedly was organized as an "honor killing" by members of her family — and her uncles and a brother allegedly were among those in the mob who beat her to death. Her crime? She offended her community by falling in love with a man outside her religious sect.[2]

According to the United Nations, an estimated 5,000 women and girls are murdered in honor killings each year, but it was only when the video of Aswad's murder was posted on the Internet that the global media took notice.[3]

Such killings don't only happen in remote villages in developing countries. Police in the United Kingdom estimate that up to 17,000 women are subjected to some kind of "honor"-related violence each year, ranging from forced marriages and physical attacks to murder.[4]

But honor killings are only one type of what the international community calls "gender based violence" (GBV). "It is universal," says Taina Bien-Aimé, executive director of the New York-based

From *CQ Researcher*, May 2008.

Only Four Countries Offer Total Equality for Women

Costa Rica, Cuba, Sweden and Norway receive the highest score (9 points) in an annual survey of women's economic, political and social rights. Out of the world's 193 countries, only 26 score 7 points or better, while 28 — predominantly Islamic or Pacific Island countries — score 3 or less. The United States rates 7 points: a perfect 3 on economic rights but only 2 each for political and social rights. To receive 3 points for political rights, women must hold at least 30 percent of the seats in the national legislature. Women hold only 16.6 percent of the seats in the U.S. Congress. The U.S. score of 2 on social rights reflects what the report's authors call "high societal discrimination against women's reproductive rights."

Status of Women's Rights Around the Globe

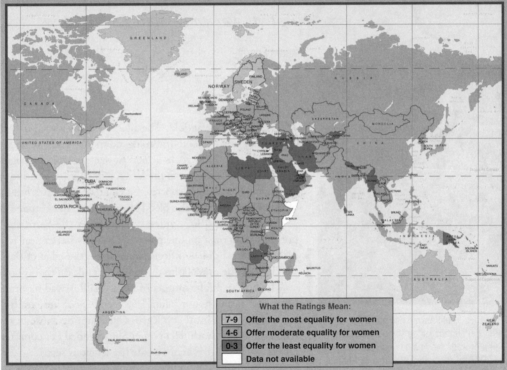

What the Ratings Mean:
- **7-9** Offer the most equality for women
- **4-6** Offer moderate equality for women
- **0-3** Offer the least equality for women
- Data not available

Source: Cingranelli-Richards Human Rights Dataset, http://ciri.binghamton.edu/, based on Amnesty International's annual reports and U.S. State Department annual Country Reports on Human Rights. The database is co-directed by David Louis Cingranelli, a political science professor at Binghamton University, SUNY, and David L. Richards, an assistant political science professor at the University of Memphis.

women's-rights group Equality Now. "There is not one country in the world where violence against women doesn't exist."

Thousands of women are murdered or attacked around the world each day, frequently with impunity. In Guatemala, where an estimated 3,000 women have been killed over the past seven years, most involving some kind of misogynistic violence, only 1 percent of the perpetrators were convicted.[5] In India, the United Nations estimates that five women are burned to death each day by husbands upset that they did not receive sufficient dowries from their brides.[6] In Asia, nearly 163 million females are "missing" from the population — the result of sex-selective abortions, infanticide or neglect.

And since the 1990s some African countries have seen dramatic upsurges in rapes of very young girls by men who believe having sex with a virgin will protect or cure them from HIV-AIDS. After a 70-year-old man allegedly raped a 3-year-old girl in northern Nigeria's commercial hub city of Kano, Deputy Police Chief Suleiman Abba told reporters in January, "Child rape is becoming rampant in Kano." In the last six months of 2007, he said, 54 cases of child rape had been reported. "In some cases the victims are gang-raped."[7]

Epidemics of sexual violence commonly break out in countries torn apart by war, when perpetrators appear to have no fear of prosecution. Today, in Africa, for instance, UNICEF says there is now a "license to rape" in eastern regions of the Democratic Republic of the Congo, where some human-rights experts estimate that up to a quarter of a million women have been raped and often sexually mutilated with knives, branches or machetes.[8] Several of the Congolese rapists remorselessly bragged to an American filmmaker recently about how many women they had gang-raped.[9]

"The sexual violence in Congo is the worst in the world," said John Holmes, the United Nations under secretary general for humanitarian affairs. "The sheer numbers, the wholesale brutality, the culture of impunity — it's appalling."[10]

In some cultures, the female victims themselves are punished. A report by the Human Rights Commission of Pakistan found that a woman is gang-raped every eight hours in that country. Yet, until recently, rape cases could not be prosecuted in Pakistan unless four Muslim men "all of a pious and trustworthy nature" were willing to testify that they witnessed the attack. Without their testimony the victim could be prosecuted for fornication and alleging a false crime, punishable by stoning, lashings or prison.[11] When the law was softened in 2006 to allow judges to decide whether to try rape cases in Islamic courts or criminal courts, where such witnesses are not required, thousands took to the streets to protest the change.[12]

Honor killings are up 400 percent in Pakistan over the last two years, and Pakistani women also live in fear of being blinded or disfigured by "acid attacks" — a common practice in Pakistan and a handful of other countries — in which attackers, usually spurned suitors, throw acid on a woman's face and body.

Women's Suffering Is Widespread

More than two decades after the U.N. Decade for Women and 29 years after the U.N. adopted the Convention on the Elimination of All Forms of Discrimination against Women (CEDAW), gender discrimination remains pervasive throughout the world, with widespread negative consequences for society.

According to recent studies on the status of women today:

- Violence against women is pervasive. It impoverishes women, their families, communities and nations by lowering economic productivity and draining resources. It also harms families across generations and reinforces other violence in societies.

- Domestic violence is the most common form of violence against women, with rates ranging from 8 percent in Albania to 49 percent in Ethiopia and Zambia. Domestic violence and rape account for 5 percent of the disease burden for women ages 15 to 44 in developing countries and 19 percent in developed countries.

- Femicide — the murder of women — often involves sexual violence. From 40 to 70 percent of women murdered in Australia, Canada, Israel, South Africa and the United States are killed by husbands or boyfriends. Hundreds of women were abducted, raped and murdered in and around Juárez, Mexico, over the past 15 years, but the crimes have never been solved.

- At least 160 million females, mostly in India and China, are "missing" from the population — the result of sex-selective abortions.

- Rape is being used as a genocidal tool. Hundreds of thousands of women have been raped and sexually mutilated in the ongoing conflict in Eastern Congo. An estimated 250,000 to 500,000 women were raped during the 1994 genocide in Rwanda; up to 50,000 women were raped during the Bosnian conflict in the 1990s. Victims are often left unable to have children and are deserted by their husbands and shunned by their families, plunging the women and their children into poverty.

- Some 130 million girls have been genitally mutilated, mostly in Africa and Yemen, but also in immigrant communities in the West.

- Child rape has been on the increase in the past decade in some African countries, where some men believe having sex with a virgin will protect or cure them from HIV-AIDS. A study at the Red Cross children's hospital in Cape Town, South Africa, found that 3-year-old girls were more likely to be raped than any other age group.

- Two million girls between the ages of 5 and 15 are forced into the commercial sex market each year, many of them trafficked across international borders.

- Sexual harassment is pervasive. From 40 to 50 percent of women in the European Union reported some form of sexual harassment at work; 50 percent of schoolgirls surveyed in Malawi reported sexual harassment at school.

- Women and girls constitute 70 percent of those living on less than a dollar a day and 64 percent of the world's illiterate.

- Women work two-thirds of the total hours worked by men and women but earn only 10 percent of the income.

- Half of the world's food is produced by women, but women own only 1 percent of the world's land.

- More than 1,300 women die each day during pregnancy and childbirth — 99 percent of them in developing countries.

Sources: "Ending violence against women: From words to action," United Nations, October, 2006,
www.un.org/womenwatch/daw/public/VAW_Study/VAW studyE.pdf;
www.womankind.org.uk; www.unfp.org; www.oxfam.org.uk; www.ipu.org;
www.unicef.org; www.infant-trust.org.uk; "State of the World Population 2000;"
http://npr.org; http://asiapacific.amnesty.org; http://news.bbc.co.uk

Negative Attitudes Toward Women Are Pervasive

Negative attitudes about women are widespread around the globe, among women as well as men. Rural women are more likely than city women to condone domestic abuse if they think it was provoked by a wife's behavior.

	Percentage of women in selected countries who agree that a man has good reason to beat his wife if:						Women who agree with:	
	Wife does not complete housework	Wife disobeys her husband	Wife refuses sex	Wife asks about other women	Husband suspects infidelity	Wife is unfaithful	One or more of the reasons mentioned	None of the reasons mentioned
Location								
Bangladesh city	13.8	23.3	9.0	6.6	10.6	51.5	53.3	46.7
Bangladesh province	25.1	38.7	23.3	14.9	24.6	77.6	79.3	20.7
Brazil city	0.8	1.4	0.3	0.3	2.0	8.8	9.4	90.6
Brazil province	4.5	10.9	4.7	2.9	14.1	29.1	33.7	66.3
Ethiopia province	65.8	77.7	45.6	32.2	43.8	79.5	91.1	8.9
Japan city	1.3	1.5	0.4	0.9	2.8	18.5	19.0	81.0
Namibia city	9.7	12.5	3.5	4.3	6.1	9.2	20.5	79.5
Peru city	4.9	7.5	1.7	2.3	13.5	29.7	33.7	66.3
Peru province	43.6	46.2	25.8	26.7	37.9	71.3	78.4	21.6
Samoa	12.1	19.6	7.4	10.1	26.0	69.8	73.3	26.7
Serbia and Montenegro city	0.6	0.97	0.6	0.3	0.9	5.7	6.2	93.8
Thailand city	2.0	0.8	2.8	1.8	5.6	42.9	44.7	55.3
Thailand province	11.9	25.3	7.3	4.4	12.5	64.5	69.5	30.5
Tanzania city	24.1	45.6	31.1	13.8	22.9	51.5	62.5	37.5
Tanzania province	29.1	49.7	41.7	19.8	27.2	55.5	68.2	31.8

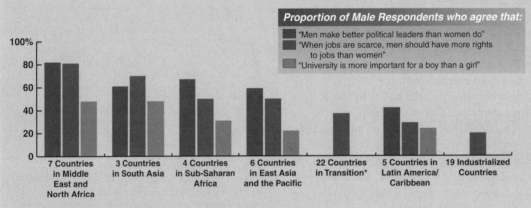

Proportion of Male Respondents who agree that:
- "Men make better political leaders than women do"
- "When jobs are scarce, men should have more rights to jobs than women"
- "University is more important for a boy than a girl"

7 Countries in Middle East and North Africa · *3 Countries in South Asia* · *4 Countries in Sub-Saharan Africa* · *6 Countries in East Asia and the Pacific* · *22 Countries in Transition** · *5 Countries in Latin America/ Caribbean* · *19 Industrialized Countries*

* Countries in transition are generally those that were once part of the Soviet Union.

Sources: World Health Organization, www.who.int/gender/violence/who_multicountry_study/Chapter3-Chapter4.pdf; "World Values Survey," www.worldvaluessruvey.org

But statistics on murder and violence are only a part of the disturbing figures on the status of women around the globe. Others include:

- Some 130 million women have undergone female genital mutilation, and another 2 million are at risk every year, primarily in Africa and Yemen.
- Women and girls make up 70 percent of the world's poor and two-thirds of its illiterate.
- Women work two-thirds of the total hours worked by men but earn only 10 percent of the income.
- Women produce more than half of the world's food but own less than 1 percent of the world's property.
- More than 500,000 women die during pregnancy and childbirth every year — 99 percent of them in developing countries.
- Two million girls between the ages of 5 and 15 are forced into the commercial sex market each year.[13]
- Globally, 10 million more girls than boys do not attend school.[14]

Despite these alarming numbers, women have made historic progress in some areas. The number of girls receiving an education has increased in the past decade. Today 57 percent of children not attending school are girls, compared to two-thirds in the 1990s.[15]

And women have made significant gains in the political arena. As of March, 2008, 14 women are serving as elected heads of state or government, and women now hold 17.8 percent of the world's parliamentary seats — more than ever before.[16] And just three months after the brutal killing of Aswad in Iraq, India swore in its first female president, Pratibha Patil, who vows to eliminate that country's practice of aborting female fetuses because girls are not as valued as boys in India. (*See "At Issue," p. 119.*)[17]

Last October, Argentina elected its first female president, Cristina Fernández de Kirchner,* the second woman in two years to be elected president in South America. Michelle Bachelet, a single mother, won the presidency in Chile in 2006.[18] During her inaugural speech Kirchner

admitted, "Perhaps it'll be harder for me, because I'm a woman. It will always be harder for us."[19]

Indeed, while more women than ever now lead national governments, they hold only 4.4 percent of the world's 342 presidential and prime ministerial positions. And in no country do they hold 50 percent or more of the national legislative seats.[20]

"Women make up half the world's population, but they are not represented" at that level, says Swanee Hunt, former U.S. ambassador to Austria and founding director of the Women and Public Policy Program at Harvard's Kennedy School of Government.

While this is "obviously a fairness issue," she says it also affects the kinds of public policies governments pursue. When women comprise higher percentages of officeholders, studies show "distinct differences in legislative outputs," Hunt explains. "There's less funding of bombs and bullets and more on human security — not just how to defend territory but also on hospitals and general well-being."

Today's historic numbers of women parliamentarians have resulted partly from gender quotas imposed in nearly 100 countries, which require a certain percentage of women candidates or officeholders.[21]

During the U.N.'s historic Fourth World Conference on Women — held in Beijing in 1995 — 189 governments adopted, among other things, a goal of 30 percent female representation in national legislatures around the world.[22] But today, only 20 countries have reached that goal, and quotas are often attacked as limiting voters' choices and giving women unfair advantages.[23]

Along with increasing female political participation, the 5,000 government representatives at the Beijing conference — one of the largest gatherings in U.N. history — called for improved health care for women, an end to violence against women, equal access to education for girls, promotion of economic independence and other steps to improve the condition of women around the world.[24]

"Let Beijing be the platform from which our global crusade will be carried forward," Gertrude Mongella, U.N. secretary general for the conference, said during closing ceremonies. "The world will hold us accountable for the implementation of the good intentions and decisions arrived at in Beijing."[25]

---

* Isabel Martínez Perón assumed the presidency of Argentina on the death of her husband, Juan Perón, in 1974 and served until she was deposed in a coup d'etat in 1976; but she was never elected.

AP Photo/Bernat Armangue

Spain's visibly pregnant new Defense minister, Carme Chacón, reviews troops in Madrid on April 14, 2008. She is the first woman ever to head Spain's armed forces. Women hold nine out of 17 cabinet posts in Spain's socialist government, a reflection of women's entrance into the halls of power around the world.

But more than 10 years later, much of the Beijing Platform still has not been achieved. And many question whether women are any better off today than they were in 1995.

"The picture's mixed," says June Zeitlin, executive director of the Women's Environment & Development Organization (WEDO). "In terms of violence against women, there is far more recognition of what is going on today. There has been some progress with education and girls. But the impact of globalization has exacerbated differences between men and women. The poor have gotten poorer — and they are mostly women."

Liberalized international trade has been a two-edged sword in other ways as well. Corporations have been able to expand their global reach, opening new businesses and factories in developing countries and offering women unprecedented employment and economic opportunities. But the jobs often pay low wages and involve work in dangerous conditions because poor countries anxious to attract foreign investors often are willing to ignore safety and labor protections.[26] And increasingly porous international borders have led to growing numbers of women and girls being forced or sold into prostitution or sexual slavery abroad, often under the pretense that they will be given legitimate jobs overseas.[27]

Numerous international agreements in recent years have pledged to provide women with the same opportunities and protections as men, including the U.N.'s Millennium Development Goals (MDGs) and the Convention on the Elimination of All Forms of Discrimination Against Women (CEDAW). But the MDGs' deadlines for improving the conditions for women have either been missed already or are on track to fail in the coming years.[28] And more than 70 of the 185 countries that ratified CEDAW have filed "reservations," meaning they exempt themselves from certain parts.[29] In fact, there are more reservations against CEDAW than against any other international human-rights treaty in history.[30] The United States remains the only developed country in the world not to have ratified it.[31]

"There has certainly been progress in terms of the rhetoric. But there are still challenges in the disparities in education, disparities in income, disparities in health," says Carla Koppell, director of the Cambridge, Mass.-based Initiative for Inclusive Security, which advocates for greater numbers of women in peace negotiations.

"But women are not just victims," she continues. "They have a very unique and important role to play in solving the problems of the developing world. We need to charge policy makers to match the rhetoric and make it a reality. There is a really wonderful opportunity to use the momentum that does exist. I really think we can."

Amidst the successes and failures surrounding women's issues, here are some of the questions analysts are beginning to ask:

Has globalization been good for women?

Over the last 20 years, trade liberalization has led to a massive increase of goods being produced and exported from developing countries, creating millions of manufacturing jobs and bringing many women into the paid workforce for the first time.

"Women employed in export-oriented manufacturing typically earn more than they would have in traditional sectors," according to a World Bank report. "Further, cash income earned by women may improve their status and bargaining power in the family."[32] The report cited a study of 50 families in Mexico that found "a significant proportion of the women reported an improvement in their 'quality of life,' due mainly to their income from working outside their homes, including in (export-oriented) factory jobs."

But because women in developing nations are generally less educated than men and have little bargaining power, most of these jobs are temporary or part-time, offering no health-care benefits, overtime or sick leave.

Women comprise 85 percent of the factory jobs in the garment industry in Bangladesh and 90 percent in Cambodia. In the cut flower industry, women hold 65 percent of the jobs in Colombia and 87 percent in Zimbabwe. In the fruit industry, women constitute 69 percent of temporary and seasonal workers in South Africa and 52 percent in Chile.[33]

Frequently, women in these jobs have no formal contract with their employers, making them even more vulnerable to poor safety conditions and abuse. One study found that only 46 percent of women garment workers in Bangladesh had an official letter of employment.[34]

"Women are a workforce vital to the global economy, but the jobs women are in often aren't covered by labor protections," says Thalia Kidder, a policy adviser on gender and sustainable livelihoods with U.K.-based Oxfam, a confederation of 12 international aid organizations. Women lack protection because they mostly work as domestics, in home-based businesses and as part-time workers. "In the global economy, many companies look to hire the most powerless people because they cannot demand high wages. There are not a lot of trade treaties that address labor rights."

In addition to recommending that countries embrace free trade, Western institutions like the International Monetary Fund and the World Bank during the 1990s recommended that developing countries adopt so-called structural adjustment economic reforms in order to qualify for certain loans and financial support. Besides opening borders to free trade, the neo-liberal economic regime known as the Washington Consensus advocated privatizing state-owned businesses, balancing budgets and attracting foreign investment.

But according to some studies, those reforms ended up adversely affecting women. For instance, companies in Ecuador were encouraged to make jobs more "flexible" by replacing long-term contracts with temporary, seasonal and hourly positions — while restricting collective bargaining rights.[35] And countries streamlined and privatized government programs such as health care and education, services women depend on most.

Globalization also has led to a shift toward cash crops grown for export, which hurts women farmers, who produce 60 to 80 percent of the food for household consumption in developing countries.[36] Small women farmers are being pushed off their land so crops for exports can be grown, limiting their abilities to produce food for themselves and their families.

While economic globalization has yet to create the economic support needed to help women out of poverty, women's advocates say females have benefited from the broadening of communications between countries prompted by globalization. "It has certainly improved access to communications and helped human-rights campaigns," says Zeitlin of WEDO. "Less can be done in secret. If there is a woman who is condemned to be stoned to death somewhere, you can almost immediately mobilize a global campaign against it."

Homa Hoodfar, a professor of social anthropology at Concordia University in Montreal, Canada, and a founder of the group Women Living Under Muslim Laws, says women in some of the world's most remote towns and villages regularly e-mail her organization. "Globalization has made the world much smaller," she says. "Women are getting information on TV and the Internet. The fact that domestic violence has become a global issue [shows globalization] provides resources for those objecting locally."

But open borders also have enabled the trafficking of millions of women around the world. An estimated 800,000 people are trafficked across international borders each year — 80 percent of them women and girls — and most are forced into the commercial sex trade. Millions more are trafficked within their own countries.[37] Globalization has sparked a massive migration of women in search of better jobs and lives. About 90 million women — half of the world's migrants and more than ever in history — reside outside their home countries. These migrant women — often unable to speak the local language and without any family connections — are especially susceptible to traffickers who lure them with promises of jobs abroad.[38]

And those who do not get trapped in the sex trade often end up in low-paying or abusive jobs in foreign factories or as domestic maids working under slave-like conditions.

Female Peacekeepers Fill Vital Roles

Women bring a different approach to conflict resolution.

The first all-female United Nations peacekeeping force left Liberia in January after a year's mission in the West African country, which is rebuilding itself after 14 years of civil war. Comprised of more than 100 women from India, the force was immediately replaced by a second female team.

"If anyone questioned the ability of women to do tough jobs, then those doubters have been [proven] wrong," said U.N. Special Representative for Liberia Ellen Margrethe Løj, adding that the female peacekeepers inspired many Liberian women to join the national police force.[1]

Women make up half of the world's refugees and have systematically been targeted for rape and sexual abuse during times of war, from the 200,000 "comfort women" who were kept as sex slaves for Japanese soldiers during World War II[2] to the estimated quarter-million women reportedly raped and sexually assaulted during the current conflict in the Democratic Republic of the Congo.[3] But women account for only 5 percent of the world's security-sector jobs, and in many countries they are excluded altogether.[4]

In 2000, the U.N. Security Council unanimously adopted Resolution 1325 calling on governments — and the U.N. itself — to include women in peace building by adopting a variety of measures, including appointing more women as special envoys, involving women in peace negotiations, integrating gender-based policies in peacekeeping missions and increasing the number of women at all decision-making levels.[5]

But while Resolution 1325 was a critical step in bringing women into the peace process, women's groups say more women should be sent on field missions and more data collected on how conflict affects women around the world.[6]

"Women are often viewed as victims, but another way to view them is as the maintainers of society," says Carla Koppell, director of the Cambridge, Mass.-based Initiative for Inclusive Security, which promotes greater numbers of women in peacekeeping and conflict resolution. "There must be a conscious decision to include women. It's a detriment to promote peace without including women."

Women often comprise the majority of post-conflict survivor populations, especially when large numbers of men have either fled or been killed. In the wake of the 1994 Rwandan genocide, for example, women made up 70 percent of the remaining population.

And female peacekeepers and security forces can fill vital roles men often cannot, such as searching Islamic women wearing burkas or working with rape victims who may be reluctant to report the crimes to male soldiers.

But some experts say the real problem is not migration and globalization but the lack of labor protection. "Nothing is black and white," says Marianne Mollmann, advocacy director for the Women's Rights Division of Human Rights Watch. "Globalization has created different employment opportunities for women. Migration flows have made women vulnerable. But it's a knee-jerk reaction to say that women shouldn't migrate. You can't prevent migration. So where do we need to go?" She suggests including these workers in general labor-law protections that cover all workers.

Mollmann said countries can and should hammer out agreements providing labor and wage protections for domestic workers migrating across borders. With such protections, she said, women could benefit from the jobs and incomes promised by increased migration and globalization.

Should governments impose electoral quotas for women?

In 2003, as Rwanda struggled to rebuild itself after the genocide that killed at least 800,000 Hutus and Tutsis, the country adopted an historic new constitution that, among other things, required that women hold at least 30 percent of posts "in all decision-making organs."[39]

Today — ironically, just across Lake Kivu from the horrors occurring in Eastern Congo — Rwanda's lower house of parliament now leads the world in female representation, with 48.8 percent of the seats held by women.[40]

"Women bring different experiences and issues to the table," says Koppell. "I've seen it personally in the Darfur and Uganda peace negotiations. Their priorities were quite different. Men were concerned about power- and wealth-sharing. Those are valid, but you get an entirely different dimension from women. Women talked about security on the ground, security of families, security of communities."

In war-torn countries, women have been found to draw on their experiences as mothers to find nonviolent and flexible ways to solve conflict.[7] During peace negotiations in Northern Ireland, for example, male negotiators repeatedly walked out of sessions, leaving a small number of women at the table. The women, left to their own, found areas of common ground and were able to keep discussions moving forward.[8]

"The most important thing is introducing the definition of security from a woman's perspective," said Orzala Ashraf, founder of Kabul-based Humanitarian Assistance for the Women and Children of Afghanistan. "It is not a man in a uniform standing next to a tank armed with a gun. Women have a broader term — human security — the ability to go to school, receive health care, work and have access to

The first all-female United Nations peacekeeping force practices martial arts in New Delhi as it prepares to be deployed to Liberia in 2006.

AP Photo/Mustafa Quraishi

justice. Only by improving these areas can threats from insurgents, Taliban, drug lords and warlords be countered."[9]

---

[1] "Liberia: UN envoy welcomes new batch of female Indian police officers," U.N. News Centre, Feb. 8, 2008, www.un.org/apps/news/story.asp?NewsID=25557&Cr=liberia&Cr1=.

[2] "Japan: Comfort Women," European Speaking Tour press release, Amnesty International, Oct. 31, 2007.

[3] "Film Documents Rape of Women in Congo," "All Things Considered," National Public Radio, April 8, 2008, www.npr.org/templates/story/story.php?story Id=89476111.

[4] "Ninth Annual Colloquium and Policy Forum," Hunt Alternatives Fund, Jan. 22, 2008, www.huntalternatives.org/pages/7650_ninth_annual_colloquium_and_policy_forum.cfm. Also see Elizabeth Eldridge, "Women cite utility in peace efforts," *The Washington Times*, Jan. 25, 2008, p. A1.

[5] "Inclusive Security, Sustainable Peace: A Toolkit for Advocacy and Action," International Alert and Women Waging Peace, 2004, p. 15, www.huntalternatives.org/download/35_introduction.pdf.

[6] *Ibid.*, p. 17.

[7] Jolynn Shoemaker and Camille Pampell Conaway, "Conflict Prevention and Transformation: Women's Vital Contributions," Inclusive Security: Women Waging Peace and the United Nations Foundation, Feb. 23, 2005, p. 7.

[8] The Initiative for Inclusive Security, www.huntalternatives.org/pages/460_ the_vital_role_of_women_in_peace_building.cfm.

[9] Eldridge, *op. cit.*

Before the civil war, Rwandan women never held more than 18 percent of parliament. But after the genocide, the country's population was 70 percent female. Women immediately stepped in to fill the vacuum, becoming the heads of households, community leaders and business owners. Their increased presence in leadership positions eventually led to the new constitutional quotas.[41]

"We see so many post-conflict countries going from military regimes to democracy that are starting from scratch with new constitutions," says Drude Dahlerup, a professor of political science at Sweden's Stockholm University who studies the use of gender quotas. "Today, starting from scratch means including women. It's seen as a sign of modernization and democratization."

Both Iraq and Afghanistan included electoral quotas for women in their new constitutions, and the number of women in political office in sub-Saharan Africa has increased faster than in any other region of the world, primarily through the use of quotas.[42]

But many point out that simply increasing the numbers of women in elected office will not necessarily expand women's rights. "It depends on which women and which positions they represent," says Wendy Harcourt, chair of Women in Development Europe (WIDE), a feminist network in Europe, and editor of *Development*, the journal of the Society for International Development, a global network of individuals and institutions working on development issues. "It's positive, but I don't see yet what it means [in terms of addressing] broader gender issues."

Few Women Head World Governments

Fourteen women currently serve as elected heads of state or government including five who serve as both. Mary McAleese, elected president of Ireland in 1997, is the world's longest-serving head of state. Helen Clark of New Zealand has served as prime minister since 1999, making her the longest-serving female head of government. The world's first elected female head of state was Sirimavo Bandaranaike of Sri Lanka, in 1960.

Current Female Elected Heads of State and Government

Heads of both state and government:

 Gloria Macapagal-Arroyo — President, the Philippines, since 2001; former secretary of Defense (2002) and secretary of Foreign Affairs (2003 and 2006-2007).

 Ellen Johnson-Sirleaf — President, Liberia, since 2006; held finance positions with the government and World Bank.

 Michelle Bachelet Jeria — President, Chile, since 2006; former minister of Health (2000-2002) and minister of Defense (2002-2004).

 Cristina E. Fernández — President, Argentina, since 2007; succeeded her husband, Nestor de Kirchner, as president; former president, Senate Committee on Constitutional Affairs.

 Rosa Zafferani — Captain Regent, San Marino, since April 2008; secretary of State of Public Education, University and Cultural Institutions (2004 to 2008); served as captain regent in 1999; San Marino elects two captains regent every six months, who serve as co-heads of both state and government.

Heads of Government:

 Helen Clark — Prime Minister, New Zealand, since 1999; held government posts in foreign affairs, defense, housing and labor.

 Luísa Días Diogo — Prime Minister, Mozambique, since 2004; held several finance posts in Mozambique and the World Bank.

Angela Merkel — Chancellor, Germany, since 2005; parliamentary leader of Christian Democratic Union Party (2002-2005).

Yuliya Tymoshenko — Prime Minister, Ukraine, since 2007; chief of government (2005) and designate prime minister (2006).

Zinaida Grecianîi — Prime Minister, Moldova, since March 2008; vice prime minister (2005-2008).

Heads of State:

 Mary McAleese — President, Ireland, since 1997; former director of a television station and Northern Ireland Electricity.

 Tarja Halonen — President, Finland, since 2000; former minister of foreign affairs (1995-2000).

 Pratibha Patil — President, India, since 2007; former governor of Rajasthan state (2004-2007).

Borjana Kristo — President, Bosnia and Herzegovina, since 2007; minister of Justice of Bosniak-Croat Federation, an entity in Bosnia and Herzegovina (2003-2007).

Source: www.guide2womenleaders.com

While Afghanistan has mandated that women hold at least 27 percent of the government's lower house seats and at least 17 percent of the upper house, their increased representation appears to have done little to improve women's rights.[43] Earlier this year, a student journalist was condemned to die under Afghanistan's strict Islamic sharia law after he distributed articles from the Internet on women's rights.[44] And non-governmental groups in Afghanistan report that Afghan women and girls have begun killing themselves in record numbers, burning themselves alive in order to escape widespread domestic abuse or forced marriages.[45]

Having gender quotas alone doesn't necessarily ensure that women's rights will be broadened, says Hoodfar of Concordia University. It depends on the type of quota a government implements, she argues, pointing out that in Jordan, for example, the government has set aside parliamentary seats for the six women who garner the most votes of any other female candidates in their districts — even if they do not win more votes than male candidates.[46] Many small, conservative tribes that cannot garner enough votes for a male in a countrywide victory are now nominating their sisters and wives in the hope that the lower number of votes needed to elect a woman will get them one of the reserved seats. As a result, many of the women moving into the reserved seats are extremely conservative and actively oppose providing women greater rights and freedoms.

And another kind of quota has been used against women in her home country of Iran, Hoodfar points out. Currently, 64 percent of university students in Iran are women. But the government recently mandated that at least 40 percent of university enrollees be male, forcing many female students out of school, Hoodfar said.

"Before, women didn't want to use quotas for politics because of concern the government may try to use it against women," she says. "But women are beginning to look into it and talk about maybe developing a good system."

Quotas can be enacted by constitutional requirements, such as those enacted in Rwanda, by statute or voluntarily by political parties. Quotas also can vary in their requirements: They can mandate the number of women each party must nominate, how many women must appear on the ballot (and the order in which they appear, so women are not relegated to the bottom of the list), or the number of women who must hold government office. About 40 countries now use gender quotas in national parliamentary elections, while another 50 have major political parties that voluntarily use quotas to determine candidates.

Aside from questions about the effectiveness of quotas, others worry about the fairness of establishing quotas based on gender. "That's something feminists have traditionally opposed," says Harcourt.

"It's true, but it's also not fair the way it is now," says former Ambassador Hunt. "We are where we are today through all kinds of social structures that are not fair. Quotas are the lesser of two evils."

Women Still Far from Reaching Political Parity

Although they have made strides in the past decade, women hold only a small minority of the world's leadership and legislative posts (right). Nordic parliaments have the highest rates of female representation — 41.4 percent — compared with only 9 percent in Arab countries (below). However, Arab legislatures have nearly tripled their female representation since 1997, and some countries in Africa have dramatically increased theirs as well: Rwanda, at 48.8 percent, now has the world's highest percentage of women in parliament of any country. The U.S. Congress ranks 70th in the world, with 89 women serving in the 535-member body — or 16.6 percent.

Women in Government

| | 1997 | 2008 |

Elected to Parliament: 11.7% (1997), 17.8% (2008)
Serving as Ministers*: N/A (1997), 20.6% (2008)
Elected Heads of Government/State: 5.8% (1997), 7.3% (2008)

Women in Parliament
(Percentage by region, 1997 and 2008)

Nordic countries: 36%, 41.4%
Americas (including U.S.): 13%, 21.3%
Europe, non-Nordic countries: 14%, 18.8%
Sub-Saharan Africa: 10%, 17.8%
Asia: 13%, 16.7%
United States: 11.2%, 16.6%
Pacific Countries: 10%, 15%
Arab States: 3%, 9.1%

* Includes deputy prime ministers, ministers and prime ministers who hold ministerial portfolios.

Sources: Interparliamentarian Union, www.ipu.org/wmn-e/world.htm; State of the World's Children 2007, UNICEF, www.unicef.org/sowc07/; "Worldwide Guide to Women in Leadership" database, www.un.org/womenwatch/daw/csw/41sess.htm.

Stockholm University's Dahlerup says quotas are not "discrimination against men but compensation for discrimination against women." Yet quotas are not a panacea for women in politics, she contends. "It's a mistake to think this is a kind of tool that will solve all problems. It doesn't solve problems about financing campaigns, caring for families while being in politics or removing patriarchal attitudes. It would be nice if it wasn't necessary, and hopefully sometime in the future it won't be."

Until that time, however, quotas are a "necessary evil," she says.

AP Photo/Rajesh Kumar Singh

National Geographic/Getty Images/Melvyn Goldstein

Women's Work: From Hauling and Churning . . .

Women's work is often back-breaking and monotonous, such as hauling firewood in the western Indian state of Maharashtra (top) and churning yogurt into butter beside Lake Motsobunnyi in Tibet (bottom). Women labor two-thirds of the total hours worked around the globe each year but earn only 10 percent of the income.

Do international treaties improve women's rights?

In recent decades, a variety of international agreements have been signed by countries pledging to improve women's lives, from the 1979 Convention for the Elimination of All Forms of Discrimination Against Women to the Beijing Platform of 1995 to the Millennium Development Goals (MDGs) adopted in 2000. The agreements aimed to provide women with greater access to health, political representation, economic stability and social status. They also focused attention on some of the biggest obstacles facing women.

But despite the fanfare surrounding the launch of those agreements, many experts on women's issues say on-the-ground action has yet to match the rhetoric. "The report is mixed," says Haleh Afshar, a professor of politics and women's studies at the University of York in the United Kingdom and a nonpartisan, appointed member of the House of Lords, known as a crossbench peer. "The biggest problem with Beijing is all these things were stated, but none were funded. Unfortunately, I don't see any money. You don't get the pay, you don't get the job done."

The Beijing Platform for Action, among other things, called on governments to "adjust budgets to ensure equality of access to public sector expenditures" and even to "reduce, as appropriate, excessive military expenditure" in order to achieve the Platform goals.

But adequate funding has yet to be provided, say women's groups.[47] In a report entitled "Beijing Betrayed," the Women's Environment & Development Organization says female HIV cases outnumber male cases in many parts of the world, gender-related violence remains a pandemic and women still make up the majority of the world's poor — despite pledges in Beijing to reverse these trends.[48]

And funding is not the only obstacle. A 2004 U.N. survey revealed that while many countries have enacted laws in recent years to help protect women from violence and discrimination, long-standing social and cultural traditions block progress. "While constitutions provided for equality between women and men on the one hand, [several countries] recognized and gave precedent to customary law and practice in a number of areas . . . resulting in discrimination against women," the report said. "Several countries noted that statutory, customary and religious law coexist, especially in regard to family, personal status and inheritance and land rights. This perpetuated discrimination against women."[49]

While she worries about the lack of progress on the Beijing Platform, WEDO Executive Director Zeitlin says international agreements are nevertheless critical in raising global awareness on women's issues. "They have a major impact on setting norms and standards," she says. "In many countries, norms and standards are very important in setting goals for women to advocate for. We complain about lack of implementation, but if we didn't have the norms and standards we couldn't complain about a lack of implementation."

Like the Beijing Platform, the MDGs have been criticized for not achieving more. While the U.N. says promoting women's rights is essential to achieving the millenium goals — which aim to improve the lives of all the world's populations by 2015 — only two of the eight specifically address women's issues.[50]

One of the goals calls for countries to "Promote gender equality and empower women." But it sets only one measurable target: "Eliminate gender disparity in primary and secondary education, preferably by 2005, and in all levels of education" by 2015.[51] Some 62 countries failed to reach the 2005 deadline, and many are likely to miss the 2015 deadline as well.[52]

Another MDG calls for a 75 percent reduction in maternal mortality compared to 1990 levels. But according to the human-rights group ActionAid, this goal is the "most off track of all the MDGs." Rates are declining at less than 1 percent a year, and in some countries — such as Sierra Leone, Pakistan and Guatemala — maternal mortality has increased since 1990. If that trend continues, no region in the developing world is expected to reach the goal by 2015.[53]

Activist Peggy Antrobus of Development Alternatives with Women for a New Era (DAWN) — a network of feminists from the Southern Hemisphere, based currently in Calabar, Cross River State, Nigeria — has lambasted the MDGs, quipping that the acronym stands for the "Most Distracting Gimmick."[54] Many feminists argue that the goals are too broad to have any real impact and that the MDGs should have given more attention to women's issues.

But other women say international agreements — and the public debate surrounding them — are vital in promoting gender equality. "It's easy to get disheartened, but Beijing is still the blueprint of where we need to be," says Mollmann of Human Rights Watch. "They are part of a political process, the creation of an international culture. If systematically everyone says [discrimination against women] is a bad thing, states don't want to be hauled out as systematic violators."

In particular, Mollmann said, CEDAW has made real progress in overcoming discrimination against women. Unlike the Beijing Platform and the MDGs, CEDAW legally obliges countries to comply. Each of the 185 ratifying countries must submit regular reports to the U.N. outlining their progress under the convention. Several

AP Photo/Sergei Grits

AFP/Getty Images/Ali Burafi

. . . to Gathering and Herding

While many women have gotten factory jobs thanks to globalization of trade, women still comprise 70 percent of the planet's inhabitants living on less than a dollar a day. Women perform a variety of tasks around the world, ranging from gathering flax in Belarus (top) to shepherding goats in central Argentina (bottom).

countries — including Brazil, Uganda, South Africa and Australia — also have incorporated CEDAW provisions into their constitutions and legal systems.[55]

Still, dozens of ratifying countries have filed official "reservations" against the convention, including Bahrain, Egypt, Kuwait, Morocco and the United Arab Emirates, all of whom say they will comply only within the bounds of Islamic sharia law.[56] And the United States has refused to ratify CEDAW, with or without reservations, largely because of conservatives who say it would, among other things, promote abortion and require the government to pay for such things as child care and maternity leave.

Indian women harvest wheat near Bhopal. Women produce half of the food used domestically worldwide and 60 to 80 percent of the household food grown in developing countries.

BACKGROUND

'Structural Defects'

Numerous prehistoric relics suggest that at one time matriarchal societies existed on Earth in which women were in the upper echelons of power. Because early societies did not understand the connection between sexual relations and conception, they believed women were solely responsible for reproduction — which led to the worship of female goddesses.[57]

In more modern times, however, women have generally faced prejudice and discrimination at the hands of a patriarchal society. In about the eighth century B.C. creation stories emerged describing the fall of man due to the weakness of women. The Greeks recounted the story of Pandora who, through her opening of a sealed jar, unleashed death and pain on all of mankind. Meanwhile, similar tales in Judea eventually were recounted in Genesis, with Eve as the culprit.[58]

In ancient Greece, women were treated as children and denied basic rights. They could not leave their houses unchaperoned, were prohibited from being educated or buying or selling land. A father could sell his unmarried daughter into slavery if she lost her virginity before marriage. If a woman was raped, she was outcast and forbidden from participating in public ceremonies or wearing jewelry.[59]

The status of women in early Rome was not much better, although over time women began to assert their

voices and slowly gained greater freedoms. Eventually, they were able to own property and divorce their husbands. But early Christian leaders later denounced the legal and social freedom enjoyed by Roman women as a sign of moral decay. In the view of the early church, women were dependent on and subordinate to men.

In the 13th century, the Catholic priest and theologian St. Thomas Aquinas helped set the tone for the subjugation of women in Western society. He said women were created solely to be "man's helpmate" and advocated that men should make use of "a necessary object, woman, who is needed to preserve the species or to provide food and drink."[60]

From the 14th to 17th centuries, misogyny and oppression of women took a step further. As European societies struggled against the Black Plague, the 100 Years War and turmoil between Catholics and Reformers, religious leaders began to blame tragedies, illnesses and other problems on witches. As witch hysteria spread across Europe — instituted by both the religious and non-religious — an estimated 30,000 to 60,000 people were executed for allegedly practicing witchcraft. About 80 percent were females, some as young as 8 years old.[61]

"All wickedness is but little to the wickedness of a woman," Catholic inquisitors wrote in the 1480s. "What else is woman but a foe to friendship, an unescapable punishment, a necessary evil, a natural temptation, a desirable calamity. . . . Women are . . . instruments of Satan, . . . a structural defect rooted in the original creation."[62]

Push for Protections

The Age of Enlightenment and the Industrial Revolution in the 18th and 19th centuries opened up job opportunities for women, released them from domestic confines and provided them with new social freedoms.

In 1792 Mary Wollstonecraft published *A Vindication of the Rights of Women*, which has been hailed as "the feminist declaration of independence." Although the book had been heavily influenced by the French Revolution's notions of equality and universal brotherhood, French revolutionary leaders, ironically, were not sympathetic to feminist causes.[63] In 1789 they had refused to accept a Declaration of the Rights of Women when it was presented at the National Assembly. And Jean Jacques Rousseau, one of the philosophical founders of the revolution, had written in 1762:

"The whole education of women ought to be relative to men. To please them, to be useful to them, to make themselves loved and honored by them, to educate them when young, to care for them when grown, to counsel them, to make life sweet and agreeable to them — these are the duties of women at all times, and what should be taught them from their infancy."[64]

As more and more women began taking jobs outside the home during the 19th century, governments began to pass laws to "protect" them in the workforce and expand their legal rights. The British Mines Act of 1842, for instance, prohibited women from working underground.[65] In 1867, John Stuart Mill, a supporter of women's rights and author of the book *Subjection of Women*, introduced language in the British House of Commons calling for women to be granted the right to vote. It failed.[66]

But by that time governments around the globe had begun enacting laws giving women rights they had been denied for centuries. As a result of the Married Women's Property Act of 1870 and a series of other measures, wives in Britain were finally allowed to own property. In 1893, New Zealand became the first nation to grant full suffrage rights to women, followed over the next two decades by Finland, Norway, Denmark and Iceland. The United States granted women suffrage in 1920.[67]

One of the first international labor conventions, formulated at Berne, Switzerland, in 1906, applied exclusively to women — prohibiting night work for women in industrial occupations. Twelve nations signed on to it. During the second Berne conference in 1913, language was proposed limiting the number of hours women and children could work in industrial jobs, but the outbreak of World War I prevented it from being enacted.[68] In 1924 the U.S. Supreme Court upheld a night-work law for women.[69]

In 1946, public attention to women's issues received a major boost when the United Nations created the Commission on the Status of Women to address urgent problems facing women around the world.[70] During the 1950s, the U.N. adopted several conventions aimed at improving women's lives, including the Convention on the Political Rights of Women, adopted in 1952 to ensure women the right to vote, which has been ratified by 120 countries, and the Convention on the Nationality of Married Women, approved in 1957 to ensure that marriage to an alien does not automatically affect the

nationality of the woman.[71] That convention has been ratified by only 73 countries; the United States is not among them.[72]

In 1951 The International Labor Organization (ILO), an agency of the United Nations, adopted the Convention on Equal Remuneration for Men and Women Workers for Work of Equal Value, to promote equal pay for equal work. It has since been ratified by 164 countries, but again, not by the United States.[73] Seven years later, the ILO adopted the Convention on Discrimination in Employment and Occupation to ensure equal opportunity and treatment in employment. It is currently ratified by 166 countries, but not the United States.[74] U.S. opponents to the conventions claim there is no real pay gap between men and women performing the same jobs and that the conventions would impose "comparable worth" requirements, forcing companies to pay equal wages to men and women even if the jobs they performed were different.[75]

In 1965, the Commission on the Status of Women began drafting international standards articulating equal rights for men and women. Two years later, the panel completed the Declaration on the Elimination of Discrimination Against Women, which was adopted by the General Assembly but carried no enforcement power.

The commission later began to discuss language that would hold countries responsible for enforcing the declaration. At the U.N.'s first World Conference on Women in Mexico City in 1975, women from around the world called for creation of such a treaty, and the commission soon began drafting the text.[76]

Women's 'Bill of Rights'

Finally in 1979, after many years of often rancorous debate, the Convention on the Elimination of All Forms of Discrimination Against Women (CEDAW) was adopted by the General Assembly — 130 to none, with 10 abstentions. After the vote, however, several countries said their "yes" votes did not commit the support of their governments. Brazil's U.N. representative told the assembly, "The signatures and ratifications necessary to make this effective will not come easily."[77]

Despite the prediction, it took less than two years for CEDAW to receive the required number of ratifications to enter it into force — faster than any human-rights convention had ever done before.[78]

CHRONOLOGY

1700s-1800s *Age of Enlightenment and Industrial Revolution lead to greater freedoms for women.*

1792 Mary Wollstonecraft publishes *A Vindication of the Rights of Women*, later hailed as "the feminist declaration of independence."

1893 New Zealand becomes first nation to grant women full suffrage.

1920 Tennessee is the 36th state to ratify the 19th Amendment, giving American women the right to vote.

1940s-1980s *International conventions endorse equal rights for women. Global conferences highlight need to improve women's rights.*

1946 U.N. creates Commission on the Status of Women.

1951 U.N. International Labor Organization adopts convention promoting equal pay for equal work, which has been ratified by 164 countries; the United States is not among them.

1952 U.N. adopts convention calling for full women's suffrage.

1960 Sri Lanka elects the world's first female prime minister.

1974 Maria Estela Martínez de Perón of Argentina becomes the world's first woman president, replacing her ailing husband.

1975 U.N. holds first World Conference on Women, in Mexico City, followed by similar conferences every five years. U.N. launches the Decade for Women.

1979 U.N. adopts Convention on the Elimination of All Forms of Discrimination against Women (CEDAW), dubbed the "international bill of rights for women."

1981 CEDAW is ratified — faster than any other human-rights convention.

1990s *Women's rights win historic legal recognition.*

1993 U.N. World Conference on Human Rights in Vienna, Austria, calls for ending all violence, sexual harassment and trafficking of women.

1995 Fourth World Conference on Women in Beijing draws 30,000 people, making it the largest in U.N. history. Beijing Platform outlining steps to grant women equal rights is signed by 189 governments.

1996 International Criminal Tribunal convicts eight Bosnian Serb police and military officers for rape during the Bosnian conflict — the first time sexual assault is prosecuted as a war crime.

1998 International Criminal Tribunal for Rwanda recognizes rape and other forms of sexual violence as genocide.

2000s *Women make political gains, but sexual violence against women increases.*

2000 U.N. calls on governments to include women in peace negotiations.

2006 Ellen Johnson Sirleaf of Liberia, Michelle Bachelet of Chile and Portia Simpson Miller of Jamaica become their countries' first elected female heads of state. . . . Women in Kuwait are allowed to run for parliament, winning two seats.

2007 A woman in Saudi Arabia who was sentenced to 200 lashes after being gang-raped by seven men is pardoned by King Abdullah. Her rapists received sentences ranging from 10 months to five years in prison, and 80 to 1,000 lashes. . . . After failing to recognize any gender-based crimes in its first case involving the Democratic Republic of the Congo, the International Criminal Court hands down charges of "sexual slavery" in its second case involving war crimes in Congo. More than 250,000 women are estimated to have been raped and sexually abused during the country's war.

2008 Turkey lifts 80-year-old ban on women's headscarves in public universities, signaling a drift toward religious fundamentalism. . . . Former housing minister Carme Chacón — 37 and pregnant — is named defense minister of Spain, bringing to nine the number of female cabinet ministers in the Socialist government. . . . Sen. Hillary Rodham Clinton becomes the first U.S. woman to be in a tight race for a major party's presidential nomination.

Often described as an international bill of rights for women, CEDAW defines discrimination against women as "any distinction, exclusion or restriction made on the basis of sex which has the effect or purpose of impairing or nullifying the recognition, enjoyment or exercise by women, irrespective of their marital status, on a basis of equality of men and women, of human rights and fundamental freedoms in the political, economic, social, cultural, civil or any other field."

Ratifying countries are legally bound to end discrimination against women by incorporating sexual equality into their legal systems, abolishing discriminatory laws against women, taking steps to end trafficking of women and ensuring women equal access to political and public life. Countries must also submit reports at least every four years outlining the steps they have taken to comply with the convention.[79]

CEDAW also grants women reproductive choice — one of the main reasons the United States has not ratified it. The convention requires signatories to guarantee women's rights "to decide freely and responsibly on the number and spacing of their children and to have access to the information, education and means to enable them to exercise these rights."[80]

While CEDAW is seen as a significant tool to stop violence against women, it actually does not directly mention violence. To rectify this, the CEDAW committee charged with monitoring countries' compliance in 1992 specified gender-based violence as a form of discrimination prohibited under the convention.[81]

In 1993 the U.N. took further steps to combat violence against women during the World Conference on Human Rights in Vienna, Austria. The conference called on countries to stop all forms of violence, sexual harassment, exploitation and trafficking of women. It also declared that "violations of the human rights of women in situations of armed conflicts are violations of the fundamental principles of international human rights and humanitarian law."[82]

Shortly afterwards, as fighting broke out in the former Yugoslavia and Rwanda, new legal precedents were set to protect women against violence — and particularly rape — during war. In 1996, the International Criminal Tribunal in the Hague, Netherlands, indicted eight Bosnian Serb police officers in connection with the mass rape of Muslim women during the Bosnian war, marking the first time sexual assault had ever been prosecuted as a war crime.[83]

Two years later, the U.N.'s International Criminal Tribunal for Rwanda convicted a former Rwandan mayor for genocide, crimes against humanity, rape and sexual violence — the first time rape and sexual violence were recognized as acts of genocide.[84]

"Rape is a serious war crime like any other," said Regan Ralph, then executive director of Human Rights Watch's Women's Rights Division, shortly after the conviction. "That's always been true on paper, but now international courts are finally acting on it."[85]

Today, the International Criminal Court has filed charges against several Sudanese officials for rape and other crimes committed in the Darfur region.[86] But others are demanding that the court also prosecute those responsible for the rapes in the Eastern Congo, where women are being targeted as a means of destroying communities in the war-torn country.[87]

Beijing and Beyond

The U.N. World Conference on Women in Mexico City in 1975 produced a 44-page plan of action calling for a decade of special measures to give women equal status and opportunities in law, education, employment, politics and society.[88] The conference also kicked off the U.N.'s Decade for Women and led to creation of the U.N. Development Fund for Women (UNIFEM).[89]

Five years later, the U.N. held its second World Conference on Women in Copenhagen and then celebrated the end of the Decade for Women with the third World Conference in Nairobi in 1985. More than 10,000 representatives from government agencies and NGOs attended the Nairobi event, believed to be the largest gathering on women's issues at the time.[90]

Upon reviewing the progress made on women's issues during the previous 10 years, the U.N. representatives in Nairobi concluded that advances had been extremely limited due to failing economies in developing countries, particularly those in Africa struggling against drought, famine and crippling debt. The conference developed a set of steps needed to improve the status of women during the final 15 years of the 20th century.[91]

Ten years later, women gathered in Beijing in 1995 for the Fourth World Conference, vowing to turn the rhetoric of the earlier women's conferences into action. Delegates from 189 governments and 2,600

Women Suffer Most in Natural Disasters

Climate change will make matters worse.

In natural disasters, women suffer death, disease and hunger at higher rates then men. During the devastating 2004 tsunami in Asia, 70 to 80 percent of the dead were women.[1] During cyclone-triggered flooding in Bangladesh that killed 140,000 people in 1991, nearly five times more women between the ages of 20 and 44 died than men.[2]

Gender discrimination, cultural biases and lack of awareness of women's needs are part of the problem. For instance, during the 1991 cyclone, Bangladeshi women and their children died in higher numbers because they waited at home for their husbands to return and make evacuation decisions.[3] In addition, flood warnings were conveyed by men to men in public spaces but were rarely communicated to women and children at home.[4]

And during the tsunami, many Indonesian women died because they stayed behind to look for children and other family members. Women clinging to children in floodwaters also tired more quickly and drowned, since most women in the region were never taught to swim or climb trees.[5] In Sri Lanka, many women died because the tsunami hit early on a Sunday morning when they were inside preparing breakfast for their families. Men were generally outside where they had earlier warning of the oncoming floods so they were better able to escape.[6]

Experts now predict global climate change — which is expected to increase the number of natural disasters around the world — will put women in far greater danger than men because natural disasters generally have a disproportionate impact on the world's poor. Since women comprise 70 percent of those living on less than $1 a day, they will be hardest hit by climate changes, according to the Intergovernmental Panel on Climate Change.[7]

"Climate change is not gender-neutral," said Gro Harlem Brundtland, former prime minister of Norway and now special envoy to the U.N. secretary-general on climate change. "[Women are] more dependent for their livelihood on natural resources that are threatened by climate change.... With changes in climate, traditional food sources become more unpredictable and scarce. This exposes women to loss of harvests, often their sole sources of food and income."[8]

Women produce 60 to 80 percent of the food for household consumption in developing countries.[9] As drought, flooding and desertification increase, experts say women and their families will be pushed further into poverty and famine.

Women also suffer more hardship in the aftermath of natural disasters, and their needs are often ignored during relief efforts.

In many Third World countries, for instance, women have no property rights, so when a husband dies during a natural disaster his family frequently confiscates the land from his widow, leaving her homeless and destitute.[10] And because men usually dominate emergency relief and response agencies, women's specific needs, such as contraceptives and sanitary napkins, are often overlooked. After floods in Bangladesh in 1998, adolescent girls reported high rates of rashes and urinary tract infections because they had

NGOs attended. More than 30,000 women and men gathered at a parallel forum organized by NGOs, also in Beijing.[92]

The so-called Beijing Platform that emerged from the conference addressed 12 critical areas facing women, from poverty to inequality in education to inadequate health care to violence. It brought unprecedented attention to women's issues and is still considered by many as the blueprint for true gender equality.

The Beijing Conference also came at the center of a decade that produced historic political gains for women around the world — gains that have continued, albeit at a slow pace, into the new century. The 1990s saw more women entering top political positions than ever before. A record 10 countries elected or appointed women as presidents between 1990 and 2000, including Haiti, Nicaragua, Switzerland and Latvia. Another 17 countries chose women prime ministers.[93]

In 2006 Ellen Johnson Sirleaf of Liberia became Africa's first elected woman president.[94] That same year, Chile elected its first female president, Michelle Bachelet, and Jamaica elected Portia Simpson Miller as its

no clean water, could not wash their menstrual rags properly in private and had no place to hang them to dry.[11]

"In terms of reconstruction, people are not talking about women's needs versus men's needs," says June Zeitlin, executive director of the Women's Environment and Development Organization, a New York City-based international organization that works for women's equality in global policy. "There is a lack of attention to health care after disasters, issues about bearing children, contraception, rape and vulnerability, menstrual needs — things a male programmer is not thinking about. There is broad recognition that disasters have a disproportionate impact on women. But it stops there. They see women as victims, but they don't see women as agents of change."

Women must be brought into discussions on climate change and emergency relief, say Zeitlin and others. Interestingly, she points out, while women are disproportionately affected by environmental changes, they do more than men to protect the environment. Studies show women emit less climate-changing carbon dioxide than men because they recycle more, use resources more efficiently and drive less than men.[12]

"Women's involvement in climate-change decision-making is a human right," said Gerd Johnson-Latham, deputy director of the Swedish Ministry for Foreign Affairs. "If we get more women in decision-making positions, we

The smell of death hangs over Banda Aceh, Indonesia, which was virtually destroyed by a tsunami on Dec. 28, 2004. From 70 to 80 percent of the victims were women.

will have different priorities, and less risk of climate change."[13]

[1] "Tsunami death toll," CNN, Feb. 22, 2005. Also see "Report of High-level Roundtable: How a Changing Climate Impacts Women," Council of Women World Leaders, Women's Environment and Development Organization and Heinrich Boll Foundation, Sept. 21, 2007, p. 21, www.wedo.org/files/Roundtable%20Final%20Report%206%20Nov.pdf.

[2] *Ibid.*

[3] "Cyclone Jelawat bears down on Japan's Okinawa island," CNN.com, Aug. 7, 2000, http://archives.cnn.com/2000/ASIANOW/east/08/07/asia.weather/index.html.

[4] "Gender and Health in Disasters," World Health Organization, July 2002, www.who.int/gender/other_health/en/genderdisasters.pdf.

[5] "The tsunami's impact on women," Oxfam briefing note, March 5, 2005, p. 2, www.oxfam.org/en/files/bn050326_tsunami_women/download.

[6] "Report of High-level Roundtable," *op. cit.*, p. 5.

[7] "Gender Equality" fact sheet, Oxfam, www.oxfam.org.uk/resources/issues/gender/introduction.html. Also see *ibid.*

[8] *Ibid.*, p. 4.

[9] "Five years down the road from Beijing: Assessing progress," *News and Highlights*, Food and Agriculture Organization, June 2, 2000, www.fao.org/News/2000/000602-e.htm.

[10] "Gender and Health in Disasters," *op. cit.*

[11] *Ibid.*

[12] "Women and the Environment," U.N. Environment Program, 2004, p. 17, www.unep.org/Documents.Multilingual/Default.asp?DocumentID=468&ArticleID=4488&l=en. Also see "Report of High-level Roundtable," *op. cit.*, p. 7.

[13] *Ibid.*

first female prime minister.[95] Also that year, women ran for election in Kuwait for the first time. In Bahrain, a woman was elected to the lower house of parliament for the first time.[96] And in 2007, Fernández de Kirchner became the first woman to be elected president of Argentina.

Earlier, a World Bank report had found that government corruption declines as more women are elected into office. The report also cited numerous studies that found women are more likely to exhibit "helping" behavior, vote based on social issues, score higher on

"integrity tests," take stronger stances on ethical behavior and behave more generously when faced with economic decisions.[97]

"Increasing the presence of women in government may be valued for its own sake, for reasons of gender equality," the report concluded. "However, our results suggest that there may be extremely important spinoffs stemming from increasing female representation: If women are less likely than men to behave opportunistically, then bringing more women into government may have significant benefits for society in general."[98]

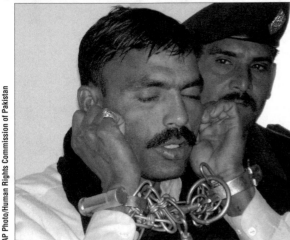

Honor Killings on the Rise

Women in Multan, Pakistan, demonstrate against "honor killings" in 2003 (top). Although Pakistan outlawed such killings years ago, its Human Rights Commission says 1,205 women were killed in the name of family honor in 2007 — a fourfold jump in two years. Nazir Ahmed Sheikh, a Punjabi laborer (bottom), unrepentantly told police in December 2005 how he slit the throats of his four daughters one night as they slept in order to salvage the family's honor. The eldest had married a man of her choice, and Ahmed feared the younger daughters would follow her example.

CURRENT SITUATION
Rise of Fundamentalism

Despite landmark political gains by women since the late 1990s, violence and repression of women continue to be daily occurrences — often linked to the global growth of religious fundamentalism.

In 2007, a 21-year-old woman in Saudi Arabia was sentenced to 200 lashes and ordered jailed for six months after being raped 14 times by a gang of seven men. The Saudi court sentenced the woman — who was 19 at the time of the attack — because she was alone in a car with her former boyfriend when the attack occurred. Under Saudi Arabia's strict Islamic law, it is a crime for a woman to meet in private with a man who is not her husband or relative.[99]

After public outcry from around the world, King Abdullah pardoned the woman in December. A government spokesperson, however, said the king fully supported the verdict but issued the pardon in the "interests of the people."[100]

Another Saudi woman still faces beheading after she was condemned to death for "witchcraft." Among her accusers is a man who claimed she rendered him impotent with her sorcery. Despite international protest, the king has yet to say if he will pardon her.[101]

In Iraq, the rise of religious fundamentalism since the U.S. invasion has led to a jump in the number of women being killed or beaten in so-called honor crimes. Honor killings typically occur when a woman is suspected of unsanctioned sexual behavior — which can range from flirting to "allowing" herself to be raped. Her relatives believe they must murder her to end the family's shame. In the Kurdish region of Iraq, the stoning death of 17-year-old Aswad is not an anomaly. A U.N. mission in October 2007 found that 255 women had been killed in Iraqi Kurdistan in the first six months of 2007 alone — most thought to have been murdered by their communities or families for allegedly committing adultery or entering into a relationship not sanctioned by their families.[102]

The rise of fundamentalism is also sparking a growing debate on the issue of women wearing head scarves, both in Iraq and across the Muslim world. Last August Turkey elected a conservative Muslim president whose wife wears a head scarf, signaling the emergence of a new ruling elite that is more willing to publicly display religious beliefs.[103] Then in February, Turkey's parliament voted to ease an

80-year ban on women wearing head scarves in universities, although a ban on head scarves in other public buildings remains in effect.

"This decision will bring further pressure on women," Nesrin Baytok, a member of parliament, said during debate over the ban. "It will ultimately bring us Hezbollah terror, al Qaeda terror and fundamentalism."[104]

But others said lifting the ban was actually a victory for women. Fatma Benli, a Turkish women's-rights activist and lawyer, said the ban on head scarves in public buildings has forced her to send law partners to argue her cases because she is prohibited from entering court wearing her head scarf. It also discourages religiously conservative women from becoming doctors, lawyers or teachers, she says.[105]

Many women activists are quick to say that it is unfair to condemn Islam for the growing abuse against women. "The problem women have with religion is not the religion but the ways men have interpreted it," says Afshar of the University of York. "What is highly negative is sharia law, which is made by men. Because it's human-made, women can unmake it. The battle now is fighting against unjust laws such as stoning."

She says abuses such as forced marriages and honor killings — usually linked in the Western media to Islamic law — actually go directly against the teachings of the *Koran*. And while the United Nations estimates that some 5,000 women and girls are victims of honor killings each year, millions more are abused and killed in violence unrelated to Islam. Between 10 and 50 percent of all women around the world have been physically abused by an intimate partner in their lifetime, studies show.[106]

"What about the rate of spousal or partner killings in the U.K. or the U.S. that are not called 'honor killings'?" asks Concordia University's Hoodfar. "Then it's only occasional 'crazy people' [committing violence]. But when it's present in Pakistan, Iran or Senegal, these are uncivilized people doing 'honor killings.' "

And Islamic fundamentalism is not the only brand of fundamentalism on the rise. Christian fundamentalism is also growing rapidly. A 2006 Pew Forum on Religion and Public Life poll found that nearly one-third of all Americans feel the Bible should be the basis of law across the United States.[107] Many women's-rights activists say Christian fundamentalism threatens women's rights, particularly with regard to reproductive issues. They also condemn the Vatican's opposition to the use of condoms, pointing

Getty Images/Paula Bronstein

Pakistani acid attack survivors Saira Liaqat, right, and Sabra Sultana are among hundreds, and perhaps thousands, of women who are blinded and disfigured after being attacked with acid each year in Pakistan, Bangladesh, India, Cambodia, Malaysia, Uganda and other areas of Africa. Liaqat was attacked at age 18 during an argument over an arranged marriage. Sabra was 15 when she was burned after being married off to an older man who became unsatisfied with the relationship. Only a small percentage of the attacks — often perpetrated by spurned suitors while the women are asleep in their own beds — are prosecuted.

out that it prevents women from protecting themselves against HIV.

"If you look at all your religions, none will say it's a good thing to beat up or kill someone. They are all based on human dignity," says Mollmann of Human Rights Watch. "[Bad things] are carried out in the name of religion, but the actual belief system is not killing and maiming women."

In response to the growing number of honor-based killings, attacks and forced marriages in the U.K., Britain's Association of Chief Police Officers has created an honor-based violence unit, and the U.K.'s Home Office is drafting an action plan to improve the response of police and other agencies to such violence. Legislation going into effect later this year will also give U.K. courts greater guidance on dealing with forced marriages.[108]

Evolving Gender Policies

This past February, the U.N. Convention on the Elimination of All Forms of Discrimination Against Women issued a report criticizing Saudi Arabia for its repression of women. Among other things, the report attacked Saudi Arabia's ban on women drivers and its

AP Photo/Light Press/Alex de Jesus

Female farmworkers in Nova Lima, Brazil, protest against the impact of big corporations on the poor in March 2006, reflecting the increasing political activism of women around the globe.

system of male guardianship that denies women equal inheritance, child custody and divorce rights.[109] The criticism came during the panel's regular review of countries that have ratified CEDAW. Each government must submit reports every four years outlining steps taken to comply with the convention.

The United States is one of only eight countries — among them Iran, Sudan and Somalia — that have refused to ratify CEDAW.[110] Last year, 108 members of the U.S. House of Representatives signed on to a resolution calling for the Senate to ratify CEDAW, but it still has not voted on the measure.[111] During a U.N. vote last November on a resolution encouraging governments to meet their obligations under CEDAW, the United States was the lone nay vote against 173 yea votes.[112]

American opponents of CEDAW — largely pro-life Christians and Republicans — say it would enshrine the right to abortion in *Roe v. Wade* and be prohibitively expensive, potentially requiring the U.S. government to provide paid maternity leave and other child-care services to all women.[113] They also oppose requirements that the government modify "social and cultural patterns" to eliminate sexual prejudice and to delete any traces of gender stereotypes in textbooks — such as references to women's lives being primarily in the domestic sector.[114] Many Republicans in Congress also have argued that CEDAW would give too much control over U.S. laws to the United Nations and that it could even require the legalization of prostitution and the abolition of Mother's Day.[115]

The last time the Senate took action on CEDAW was in 2002, when the Senate Foreign Relations Committee, chaired by Democratic Sen. Joseph Biden of Delaware, voted to send the convention to the Senate floor for ratification. The full Senate, however, never took action. A Biden spokesperson says the senator "remains committed" to the treaty and is "looking for an opportune time" to bring it forward again. But Senate ratification requires 67 votes, and there do not appear to be that many votes for approval.

CEDAW proponents say the failure to ratify not only hurts women but also harms the U.S. image abroad. On this issue, "the United States is in the company of Sudan and the Vatican," says Bien-Aimé of Equality Now.

Meanwhile, several countries are enacting laws to comply with CEDAW and improve the status of women. In December, Turkmenistan passed its first national law guaranteeing women equal rights, even though its constitution had addressed women's equality.[116] A royal decree in Saudi Arabia in January ordered an end to a long-time ban on women checking into hotels or renting apartments without male guardians. Hotels can now book rooms to women who show identification, but the hotels must register the women's details with the police.[117] The Saudi government has also said it will lift the ban on women driving by the end of the year.[118]

And in an effort to improve relations with women in Afghanistan, the Canadian military, which has troops stationed in the region, has begun studying the role women play in Afghan society, how they are affected by military operations and how they can assist peacekeeping efforts. "Behind all of these men are women who can help eradicate the problems of the population," said Capt. Michel Larocque, who is working with the study. "Illiteracy, poverty, these things can be improved through women."[119]

In February, during the 52nd session of the Commission on the Status of Women, the United Nations kicked off a new seven-year campaign aimed at ending violence against women. The campaign will work with international agencies, governments and individuals to increase funding for anti-violence campaigns and pressure policy makers around the world to enact legislation to eliminate violence against women.[120]

But women's groups want increased U.N. spending on women's programs and the creation of a single unified

AT ISSUE

Should sex-selective abortions be outlawed?

YES

Nicholas Eberstadt
Henry Wendt Chair in Political Economy,
American Enterprise Institute Member,
President's Council on Bioethics

Written for *CQ Global Researcher*, April 2008

The practice of sex-selective abortion to permit parents to destroy unwanted female fetuses has become so widespread in the modern world that it is disfiguring the profile of entire countries — transforming (and indeed deforming) the whole human species.

This abomination is now rampant in China, where the latest census reports six boys for every five girls. But it is also prevalent in the Far East, South Korea, Hong Kong, Taiwan and Vietnam, all of which report biologically impossible "sex ratios at birth" (well above the 103-106 baby boys for every 100 girls ordinarily observed in human populations). In the Caucasus, gruesome imbalances exist now in Armenia, Georgia and Azerbaijan; and in India, the state of Punjab tallies 126 little boys for every 100 girls. Even in the United States, the boy-girl sex ratio at birth for Asian-Americans is now several unnatural percentage points above the national average. So sex-selective abortion is taking place under America's nose.

How can we rid the world of this barbaric form of sexism? Simply outlawing sex-selective abortions will be little more than a symbolic gesture, as South Korea's experience has shown: Its sex ratio at birth continued a steady climb for a full decade after just such a national law was passed. As long as abortion is basically available on demand, any legislation to abolish sex-selective abortion will have no impact.

What about more general restrictions on abortion, then? Poll data consistently demonstrate that most Americans do not favor the post-*Roe* regimen of unconditional abortion. But a return to the pre-*Roe* status quo, where each state made its own abortion laws, would probably have very little effect on sex-selective abortion in our country. After all, the ethnic communities most tempted by it are concentrated in states where abortion rights would likely be strongest, such as California and New York.

In the final analysis, the extirpation of this scourge will require nothing less than a struggle for the conscience of nations. Here again, South Korea may be illustrative: Its gender imbalances began to decline when the public was shocked into facing this stain on their society by a spontaneous, homegrown civil rights movement.

To eradicate sex-selective abortion, we must convince the world that destroying female fetuses is horribly wrong. We need something akin to the abolitionist movement: a moral campaign waged globally, with victories declared one conscience at a time.

NO

Marianne Mollmann
Advocacy Director, Women's Rights Division,
Human Rights Watch

Written for *CQ Global Researcher*, April 2008

Medical technology today allows parents to test early in pregnancy for fetal abnormalities, hereditary illnesses and even the sex of the fetus, raising horrifying questions about eugenics and population control. In some countries, a growing number of women apparently are terminating pregnancies when they learn the fetus is female. The resulting sex imbalance in countries like China and India is not only disturbing but also leads to further injustices, such as the abduction of girls for forced marriages.

One response has been to criminalize sex-selective abortions. While it is tempting to hope that this could safeguard the gender balance of future generations, criminalization of abortion for whatever reason has led in the past only to underground and unsafe practices. Thus, the criminalization of sex-selective abortion would put the full burden of righting a fundamental wrong — the devaluing of women's lives — on women.

Many women who choose to abort a female fetus face violence and exclusion if they don't produce a boy. Some see the financial burden of raising a girl as detrimental to the survival of the rest of their family. These considerations will not be lessened by banning sex-selective abortion. Unless one addresses the motivation for the practice, it will continue — underground.

So what is the motivation for aborting female fetuses? At the most basic level, it is a financial decision. In no country in the world does women's earning power equal men's. In marginalized communities in developing countries, this is directly linked to survival: Boys may provide more income than girls.

Severe gaps between women's and men's earning power are generally accompanied by severe forms of gender-based discrimination and rigid gender roles. For example, in China, boys are expected to stay in their parental home as they grow up, adding their manpower (and that of a later wife) to the family home. Girls, on the other hand, are expected to join the husbands' parental home. Thus, raising a girl is a net loss, especially if you are only allowed one child.

The solution is to remove the motivation behind sex-selective abortion by advancing women's rights and their economic and social equality. Choosing the blunt instrument of criminal law over promoting the value of women's lives and rights will only serve to place further burdens on marginalized and often vulnerable women.

agency addressing women's issues, led by an under-secretary general.[121] Currently, four different U.N. agencies address women's issues: the United Nations Development Fund for Women, the International Research and Training Institute for the Advancement of Women (INSTRAW), the Secretary-General's Special Advisor on Gender Issues (OSAGI) and the Division for the Advancement of Women. In 2006, the four agencies received only $65 million — a fraction of the more than $2 billion budget that the U.N.'s children's fund (UNICEF) received that year.[122]

"The four entities that focus on women's rights at the U.N. are greatly under-resourced," says Zeitlin of the Women's Environment & Development Organization. "If the rhetoric everyone is using is true — that investing in women is investing in development — it's a matter of putting your money where your mouth is."

Political Prospects

While the number of women leading world governments is still miniscule compared to their male counterparts, women are achieving political gains that just a few years ago would have been unthinkable.

While for the first time in U.S. history a woman is in a tight race for a major party's nomination as its candidate for president, South America — with two sitting female heads of state — leads the world in woman-led governments. In Brazil, Dilma Rousseff, the female chief of staff to President Luiz Inacio Lula da Silva, is the top contender to take over the presidency when da Silva's term ends in 2010.[123] In Paraguay, Blanca Ovelar was this year's presidential nominee for the country's ruling conservative Colorado Party, but she was defeated on April 20.[124]

And in Europe, Carme Chacón was named defense minister of Spain this past April. She was not only the first woman ever to head the country's armed forces but also was pregnant at the time of her appointment. In all, nine of Spain's 17 cabinet ministers are women.

In March, Pakistan's National Assembly overwhelmingly elected its first female speaker, Fahmida Mirza.[125] And in India, where Patil has become the first woman president, the two major political parties this year pledged to set aside one-third of their parliamentary nominations for women. But many fear the parties will either not keep their pledges or will run women only in contests they are unlikely to win.[126]

There was also disappointment in Iran, where nearly 600 of the 7,000 candidates running for parliament in March were women.[127] Only three won seats in the 290-member house, and they were conservatives who are not expected to promote women's rights. Several of the tallies are being contested. Twelve other women won enough votes to face run-off elections on April 25; five won.[128]

But in some countries, women running for office face more than just tough campaigns. They are specifically targeted for violence. In Kenya, the greatest campaign expense for female candidates is the round-the-clock security required to protect them against rape, according to Phoebe Asiyo, who served in the Kenyan parliament for more than two decades.[129] During the three months before Kenya's elections last December, an emergency helpdesk established by the Education Centre for Women in Democracy, a nongovernmental organization (NGO) in Nairobi, received 258 reports of attacks against female candidates.[130]

The helpdesk reported the attacks to police, worked with the press to ensure the cases were documented and helped victims obtain medical and emotional support. Attacks included rape, stabbings, threats and physical assaults.[131]

"Women are being attacked because they are women and because it is seen as though they are not fit to bear flags of the popular parties," according to the center's Web site. "Women are also viewed as guilty for invading 'the male territory' and without a license to do so!"[132]

"All women candidates feel threatened," said Nazlin Umar, the sole female presidential candidate last year. "When a case of violence against a woman is reported, we women on the ground think we are next. I think if the government assigned all women candidates with guns...we will at least have an item to protect ourselves when we face danger."[133]

Impunity for Violence

Some African feminists blame women themselves, as well as men, for not doing enough to end traditional attitudes that perpetuate violence against women.

"Women are also to blame for the violence because they are the gatekeepers of patriarchy, because whether educated or not they have different standards for their sons and husbands [than for] their daughters," said Njoki Wainaina, founder of the African Women Development

Communication Network (FEMNET). "How do you start telling a boy whose mother trained him only disrespect for girls to honor women in adulthood?"[134]

Indeed, violence against women is widely accepted in many regions of the world and often goes unpunished. A study by the World Health Organization found that 80 percent of women surveyed in rural Egypt believe that a man is justified in beating a woman if she refuses to have sex with him. In Ghana, more women than men — 50 percent compared to 43 percent — felt that a man was justified in beating his wife if she used contraception without his consent.[135] (*See survey results, p. 100.*)

Such attitudes have led to many crimes against women going unpunished, and not just violence committed during wartime. In Guatemala, no one knows why an estimated 3,000 women have been killed over the past seven years — many of them beheaded, sexually mutilated or raped — but theories range from domestic violence to gang activity.[136] Meanwhile, the government in 2006 overturned a law allowing rapists to escape charges if they offered to marry their victims. But Guatemalan law still does not prescribe prison sentences for domestic abuse and prohibits abusers from being charged with assault unless the bruises are still visible after 10 days.[137]

In the Mexican cities of Chihuahua and Juárez, more than 400 women have been murdered over the past 14 years, with many of the bodies mutilated and dumped in the desert. But the crimes are still unsolved, and many human-rights groups, including Amnesty International, blame indifference by Mexican authorities. Now the country's 14-year statute of limitations on murder is forcing prosecutors to close many of the unsolved cases.[138]

Feminists around the world have been working to end dismissive cultural attitudes about domestic violence and other forms of violence against women, such as forced marriage, dowry-related violence, marital rape, sexual harassment and forced abortion, sterilization and prostitution. But it's often an uphill battle.

After a Kenyan police officer beat his wife so badly she was paralyzed and brain damaged — and eventually died — media coverage of the murder spurred a nationwide debate on domestic violence. But it took five years of protests, demonstrations and lobbying by both women's advocates and outraged men to get a family protection bill enacted criminalizing domestic violence. And the bill passed only after legislators removed a provision outlawing

marital rape. Similar laws have languished for decades in other African legislatures.[139]

But in Rwanda, where nearly 49 percent of the elected representatives in the lower house are female, gender desks have been established at local police stations, staffed mostly by women trained to help victims of sexual and other violence. In 2006, as a result of improved reporting, investigation and response to rape cases, police referred 1,777 cases for prosecution and convicted 803 men. "What we need now is to expand this approach to more countries," said UNIFEM's director for Central Africa Josephine Odera.[140]

Besides criticizing governments for failing to prosecute gender-based violence, many women's groups also criticize the International Criminal Court (ICC) for not doing enough to bring abusers to justice.

"We have yet to see the investigative approach needed to ensure the prosecution of gender-based crimes," said Brigid Inder, executive director of Women's Initiatives for Gender Justice, a Hague-based group that promotes and monitors women's rights in the international court.[141] Inder's group released a study last November showing that of the 500 victims seeking to participate in ICC proceedings, only 38 percent were women. When the court handed down its first indictments for war crimes in the Democratic Republic of the Congo last year, no charges involving gender-based crimes were brought despite estimates that more than 250,000 women have been raped and sexually abused in the country. After an outcry from women's groups around the world, the ICC included "sexual slavery" among the charges handed down in its second case involving war crimes in Congo.[142]

The Gender Justice report also criticized the court for failing to reach out to female victims. It said the ICC has held only one consultation with women in the last four years (focusing on the Darfur conflict in Sudan) and has failed to develop any strategies to reach out to women victims in Congo.[143]

OUTLOOK
Economic Integration

Women's organizations do not expect — or want — another international conference on the scale of Beijing. Instead, they say, the resources needed to launch such a

Seaweed farmer Asia Mohammed Makungu in Zanzibar, Tanzania, grows the sea plants for export to European companies that produce food and cosmetics. Globalized trade has helped women entrepreneurs in many developing countries improve their lives, but critics say it also has created many low-wage, dangerous jobs for women in poor countries that ignore safety and labor protections in order to attract foreign investors.

conference would be better used to improve U.N. oversight of women's issues and to implement the promises made at Beijing.

They also fear that the growth of religious fundamentalism and neo-liberal economic policies around the globe have created a political atmosphere that could actually set back women's progress.

"If a Beijing conference happened now, we would not get the type of language or the scope we got 10 years ago," says Bien-Aimé of Equity Now. "There is a conservative movement, a growth in fundamentalists governments — and not just in Muslim countries. We would be very concerned about opening up debate on the principles that have already been established."

Dahlerup of Stockholm University agrees. "It was easier in the 1990s. Many people are afraid of having big conferences now, because there may be a backlash because fundamentalism is so strong," she says. "Neo-liberal trends are also moving the discourse about women toward economics — women have to benefit for the sake of the economic good. That could be very good, but it's a more narrow discourse when every issue needs to be adapted into the economic discourse of a cost-benefit analysis."

For women to continue making gains, most groups say, gender can no longer be treated separately from

broader economic, environmental, health or other political issues. While efforts to improve the status of women have historically been addressed in gender-specific legislation or international treaties, women's groups now say women's well-being must now be considered an integral part of all policies.

Women's groups are working to ensure that gender is incorporated into two major international conferences coming up this fall. In September, the Third High-Level Forum on Aid Effectiveness will be hosted in Accra, Ghana, bringing together governments, financial institutions, civil society organizations and others to assess whether assistance provided to poor nations is being put to good use. World leaders will also gather in November in Doha, Qatar, for the International Conference on Financing for Development to discuss how trade, debt relief and financial aid can promote global development.

"Women's groups are pushing for gender to be on the agenda for both conferences," says Zeitlin of WEDO. "It's important because . . . world leaders need to realize that it really does make a difference to invest in women. When it comes to women's rights it's all micro, but the big decisions are made on the macro level."

Despite decades of economic-development strategies promoted by Western nations and global financial institutions such as the World Bank, women in many regions are getting poorer. In Malawi, for example, the percentage of women living in poverty increased by 5 percent between 1995 and 2003.[144] Women and girls make up 70 percent of the world's poorest people, and their wages rise more slowly than men's. They also have fewer property rights around the world.[145] With the growing global food shortage, women — who are the primary family caregivers and produce the majority of crops for home consumption in developing countries — will be especially hard hit.

To help women escape poverty, gain legal rights and improve their social status, developed nations must rethink their broader strategies of engagement with developing countries. And, conversely, female activists say, any efforts aimed at eradicating poverty around the world must specifically address women's issues.

In Africa, for instance, activists have successfully demanded that women's economic and security concerns be addressed as part of the continent-wide development plan known as the New Partnership for Africa's Development (NEPAD). As a result, countries participating in NEPAD's peer review process must now show they are taking measures to promote and protect women's rights. But, according to Augustin Wambo, an agricultural specialist at the NEPAD secretariat, lawmakers now need to back up their pledges with "resources from national budgets" and the "necessary policies and means to support women."[146]

"We have made a lot of progress and will continue making progress," says Zeitlin. "But women's progress doesn't happen in isolation to what's happening in the rest of the world. The environment, the global economy, war, peace — they will all have a major impact on women. Women all over world will not stop making demands and fighting for their rights."

NOTES

1. http://ballyblog.wordpress.com/2007/05/04/warning-uncensored-video-iraqis-stone-girl-to-death-over-loving-wrong-boy/.

2. Abdulhamid Zebari, "Video of Iraqi girl's stoning shown on Internet," Agence France Presse, May 5, 2007.

3. *State of the World Population 2000*, United Nations Population Fund, Sept. 20, 2000, Chapter 3, "Ending Violence against Women and Girls," www.unfpa.org/swp/2000/english/ch03.html.

4. Brian Brady, "A Question of Honour," *The Independent on Sunday*, Feb. 10, 2008, p. 8, www.independent.co.uk/news/uk/home-news/a-question-of-honour-police-say-17000-women-are-victims-every-year-780522.html.

5. Correspondance with Karen Musalo, Clinical Professor of Law and Director of the Center for Gender & Refugee Studies at the University of California Hastings School of Law, April 11, 2008.

6. "Broken Bodies, Broken Dreams: Violence Against Women Exposed," United Nations, July 2006, http://brokendreams.wordpress.com/2006/12/17/dowry-crimes-and-bride-price-abuse/.

7. Various sources: www.womankind.org.uk, www.unfpa.org/gender/docs/studies/summaries/reg_exe_summary.pdf, www.oxfam.org.uk. Also see "Child rape in Kano on the increase," IRIN Humanitarian News and Analysis, United Nations, www.irinnews.org/report.aspx?ReportId=76087.

8. "UNICEF slams 'licence to rape' in African crisis," Agence France-Press, Feb. 12, 2008.

9. "Film Documents Rape of Women in Congo," "All Things Considered," National Public Radio, April 8, 2008, www.npr.org/templates/story/story.php?storyId=89476111.

10. Jeffrey Gettleman, "Rape Epidemic Raises Trauma Of Congo War," *The New York Times*, Oct. 7, 2007, p. A1.

11. Dan McDougall, "Fareeda's fate: rape, prison and 25 lashes," *The Observer*, Sept. 17, 2006, www.guardian.co.uk/world/2006/sep/17/pakistan.theobserver.

12. Zarar Khan, "Thousands rally in Pakistan to demand government withdraw rape law changes," The Associated Press, Dec. 10, 2006.

13. *State of the World Population 2000, op. cit.*

14. Laura Turquet, Patrick Watt, Tom Sharman, "Hit or Miss?" ActionAid, March 7, 2008, p. 10.

15. *Ibid.*, p. 12.

16. "Women in Politics: 2008" map, International Parliamentary Union and United Nations Division for the Advancement of Women, February 2008, www.ipu.org/pdf/publications/wmnmap08_en.pdf.

17. Gavin Rabinowitz, "India's first female president sworn in, promises to empower women," The Associated Press, July 25, 2007. Note: India's first female prime minister was Indira Ghandi in 1966.

18. Monte Reel, "South America Ushers In The Era of La Presidenta; Women Could Soon Lead a Majority of Continent's Population," *The Washington Post*, Oct. 31, 2007, p. A12. For background, see Roland Flamini, "The New Latin America," *CQ Global Researcher*, March 2008, pp. 57-84.

19. Marcela Valente, "Cristina Fernandes Dons Presidential Sash," Inter Press Service, Dec. 10, 2007.

20. "Women in Politics: 2008" map, *op. cit.*

21. *Ibid.*; Global Database of Quotas for Women, International Institute for Democracy and Electoral Assistance and Stockholm University, www.quotaproject.org/country.cfm?SortOrder =Country.

22. "Beijing Betrayed," Women's Environment and Development Organization, March 2005, p. 10, www.wedo.org/files/gmr_pdfs/gmr2005.pdf.

23. "Women in Politics: 2008" map, *op. cit.*

24. Gertrude Mongella, address by the Secretary-General of the 4th World Conference on Women, Sept. 4, 1995, www.un.org/esa/gopher-data/conf/fwcw/conf/una/950904201423.txt. Also see Steven Mufson, "Women's Forum Sets Accord; Dispute on Sexual Freedom Resolved," *The Washington Post*, Sept. 15, 1995, p. A1.

25. "Closing statement," Gertrude Mongella, U.N. Division for the Advancement of Women, Fourth World Conference on Women, www.un.org/esa/gopher-data/conf/fwcw/conf/una/closing.txt.

26. "Trading Away Our Rights," Oxfam International, 2004, p. 9, www.oxfam.org.uk/resources/policy/trade/downloads/trading_rights.pdf.

27. "Trafficking in Persons Report," U.S. Department of State, June 2007, p. 7, www.state.gov/g/tip/rls/tiprpt/2007/.

28. Turquet, *et al.*, *op. cit.*, p. 4.

29. United Nations Division for the Advancement of Women, www.un.org/womenwatch/daw/cedaw/.

30. Geraldine Terry, *Women's Rights* (2007), p. 30.

31. United Nations Division for the Advancement of Women, www.un.org/womenwatch/daw/cedaw/.

32. "The impact of international trade on gender equality," The World Bank PREM notes, May 2004, http://siteresources.worldbank.org/INTGENDER/Resources/premnote86.pdf.

33. Thalia Kidder and Kate Raworth, " 'Good Jobs' and hidden costs: women workers documenting the price of precarious employment," *Gender and Development*, July 2004, p. 13.

34. "Trading Away Our Rights," *op. cit.*

35. Martha Chen, *et al.*, "Progress of the World's Women 2005: Women, Work and Poverty," UNIFEM, p. 17, www.unifem.org/attachments/products/PoWW2005_eng.pdf.

36. Eric Neumayer and Indra de Soys, "Globalization, Women's Economic Rights and Forced Labor," London School of Economics and Norwegian University of Science and Technology, February 2007, p. 8, http://papers.ssrn.com/sol3/papers.cfm?abstract_id=813831. Also see "Five years down the road from Beijing — assessing progress," *News and Highlights*, Food and Agriculture Organization, June 2, 2000, www.fao.org/News/2000/000602-e.htm.

37. "Trafficking in Persons Report," *op. cit.*, p. 13.

38. "World Survey on the Role of Women in Development," United Nations, 2006, p. 1, www.un.org/womenwatch/daw/public/WorldSurvey2004-Women&Migration.pdf.

39. Julie Ballington and Azza Karam, eds., "Women in Parliament: Beyond the Numbers," International Institute for Democracy and Electoral Assistance, 2005, p. 155, www.idea.int/publications/wip2/upload/WiP_inlay.pdf.

40. "Women in Politics: 2008," *op. cit.*

41. Ballington and Karam, *op. cit.*, p. 158.

42. *Ibid.*, p. 161.

43. Global Database of Quotas for Women, *op. cit.*

44. Jerome Starkey, "Afghan government official says that student will not be executed," *The Independent*, Feb. 6, 2008, www.independent.co.uk/news/world/asia/afghan-government-official-says-that-student-will-not-be-executed-778686.html?r=RSS.

45. "Afghan women seek death by fire," BBC, Nov. 15, 2006, http://news.bbc.co.uk/1/hi/world/south_asia/6149144.stm.

46. Global Database for Quotas for Women, *op. cit.*

47. "Beijing Declaration," Fourth World Conference on Women, www.un.org/womenwatch/daw/beijing/beijingdeclaration.html.

48. "Beijing Betrayed," *op. cit.*, pp. 28, 15, 18.

49. "Review of the implementation of the Beijing Platform for Action and the outcome documents of the special session of the General Assembly entitled 'Women 2000: gender equality, development and peace for the twenty-first century,' " United Nations, Dec. 6, 2004, p. 74.

50. "Gender Equality and the Millennium Development Goals," fact sheet, www.mdgender.net/upload/tools/MDGender_leaflet.pdf.

51. *Ibid.*

52. Turquet, *et al.*, *op. cit.*, p. 16.

53. *Ibid.*, pp. 22-24.

54. Terry, *op. cit.*, p. 6.

55. "Inclusive Security, Sustainable Peace: A Toolkit for Advocacy and Action," International Alert and Women Waging Peace, 2004, p. 12, www.huntalternatives.org/download/35_introduction.pdf.

56. "Declarations, Reservations and Objections to CEDAW," www.un.org/womenwatch/daw/cedaw/reservations-country.htm.

57. Merlin Stone, *When God Was a Woman* (1976), pp. 18, 11.

58. Jack Holland, *Misogyny* (2006), p. 12.

59. *Ibid.*, pp. 21-23.

60. Holland, *op. cit.*, p. 112.

61. "Dispelling the myths about so-called witches" press release, Johns Hopkins University, Oct. 7, 2002, www.jhu.edu/news_info/news/home02/oct02/witch.html.

62. The quote is from the *Malleus maleficarum* (*The Hammer of Witches*), and was cited in "Case Study: The European Witch Hunts, c. 1450-1750," *Gendercide Watch*, www.gendercide.org/case_witch-hunts.html.

63. Holland, *op. cit.*, p. 179.

64. Cathy J. Cohen, Kathleen B. Jones and Joan C. Tronto, *Women Transforming Politics: An Alternative Reader* (1997), p. 530.

65. *Ibid.*

66. Holland, *op. cit*, p. 201.

67. "Men and Women in Politics: Democracy Still in the Making," IPU Study No. 28, 1997, http://archive.idea.int/women/parl/ch6_table8.htm.

68. "Sex, Equality and Protective Laws," *CQ Researcher*, July 13, 1926.

69. The case was *Radice v. People of State of New York*, 264 U. S. 292. For background, see F. Brewer, "Equal Rights Amendment," *Editorial Research Reports*, April 4, 1946, available at *CQ Researcher Plus Archive*, www.cqpress.com.

70. "Short History of the CEDAW Convention," U.N. Division for the Advancement of Women, www.un.org/womenwatch/daw/cedaw/history.htm.

71. U.N. Women's Watch, www.un.org/womenwatch/asp/user/list.asp-ParentID=11047.htm.

72. United Nations, http://untreaty.un.org/ENGLISH/bible/englishinternetbible/partI/chapterXVI/treaty2.asp.

73. International Labor Organization, www.ilo.org/public/english/support/lib/resource/subject/gender.htm.

74. *Ibid.*

75. For background, see "Gender Pay Gap," *CQ Researcher*, March 14, 2008, pp. 241-264.

76. "Short History of the CEDAW Convention" *op. cit.*

77. "International News," The Associated Press, Dec. 19, 1979.

78. "Short History of the CEDAW Convention" *op. cit.*

79. "Text of the Convention," U.N. Division for the Advancement of Women, www.un.org/womenwatch/daw/cedaw/cedaw.htm.

80. Convention on the Elimination of All Forms of Discrimination against Women, Article 16, www.un.org/womenwatch/daw/cedaw/text/econvention.htm.

81. General Recommendation made by the Committee on the Elimination of Discrimination against Women No. 19, 11th session, 1992, www.un.org/womenwatch/daw/cedaw/recommendations/recomm.htm#recom19.

82. See www.unhchr.ch/huridocda/huridoca.nsf/(Symbol)/A.CONF.157.23.En.

83. Marlise Simons, "For First Time, Court Defines Rape as War Crime," *The New York Times*, June 28, 1996, www.nytimes.com/specials/bosnia/context/0628warcrimes-tribunal.html.

84. Ann Simmons, "U.N. Tribunal Convicts Rwandan Ex-Mayor of Genocide in Slaughter," *Los Angeles Times*, Sept. 3, 1998, p. 20.

85. "Human Rights Watch Applauds Rwanda Rape Verdict," press release, Human Rights Watch, Sept. 2, 1998, http://hrw.org/english/docs/1998/09/02/rwanda1311.htm.

86. Frederic Bichon, "ICC vows to bring Darfur war criminals to justice," Agence France-Presse, Feb. 24, 2008.

87. Rebecca Feeley and Colin Thomas-Jensen, "Getting Serious about Ending Conflict and Sexual Violence in Congo," Enough Project, www.enoughproject.org/reports/congoserious.

88. "Women; Deceived Again?" *The Economist*, July 5, 1975.

89. "International Women's Day — March 8: Points of Interest and Links with UNIFEM," UNIFEM New Zealand Web site, www.unifem.org.nz/IWDPointsofinterest.htm.

90. Joseph Gambardello, "Reporter's Notebook: Women's Conference in Kenya," United Press International, July 13, 1985.

91. "Report of the World Conference to Review and Appraise the Achievements of the United Nations Decade for Women: Equality Development and Peace," United Nations, 1986, paragraph 8, www.un.org/womenwatch/confer/nfls/Nairobi1985report.txt.

92. U.N. Division for the Advancement of Women, www.un.org/womenwatch/daw/followup/background.htm.

93. "Women in Politics," Inter-Parliamentary Union, 2005, pp. 16-17, www.ipu.org/PDF/publications/wmn45-05_en.pdf.

94. "Liberian becomes Africa's first female president," Associated Press, Jan. 16, 2006, www.msnbc.msn.com/id/10865705/.

95. "Women in the Americas: Paths to Political Power," *op. cit.*, p. 2.

96. "The Millennium Development Goals Report 2007," United Nations, 2007, p. 12, www.un.org/millenniumgoals/pdf/mdg2007.pdf.

97. David Dollar, Raymond Fisman, Roberta Gatti, "Are Women Really the 'Fairer' Sex? Corruption and Women in Government," The World Bank, October 1999, p. 1, http://siteresources.worldbank.org/INTGENDER/Resources/wp4.pdf.

98. *Ibid.*

99. Vicky Baker, "Rape victim sentenced to 200 lashes and six months in jail; Saudi woman punished for being alone with a man," *The Guardian*, Nov. 17, 2007, www.guardian.co.uk/world/2007/nov/17/saudiarabia.international.

100. Katherine Zoepf, "Saudi King Pardons Rape Victim Sentenced to Be Lashed, Saudi Paper Reports," *The New York Times*, Dec. 18, 2007, www.nytimes.com/2007/12/18/world/middleeast/18saudi.html.

101. Sonia Verma, "King Abdullah urged to spare Saudi 'witchcraft' woman's life," *The Times* (Of London), Feb. 16, 2008.

102. Mark Lattimer, "Freedom lost," *The Guardian*, Dec. 13, 2007, p. 6.

103. For background, see Brian Beary, "Future of Turkey," *CQ Global Researcher*, December, 2007, pp. 295-322.

104. Tracy Clark-Flory, "Does freedom to veil hurt women?" *Salon.com*, Feb. 11, 2008.

105. Sabrina Tavernise, "Under a Scarf, a Turkish Lawyer Fighting to Wear It," *The New York Times*, Feb. 9, 2008, www.nytimes.com/2008/02/09/world/europe/09benli.html?pagewanted=1&sq=women&st=nyt&scp=96.

106. Terry, *op. cit.*, p. 122.

107. "Many Americans Uneasy with Mix of Religion and Politics," The Pew Forum on Religion and Public Life, Aug. 24, 2006, http://pewforum.org/docs/index.php?DocID=153.

108. Brady, *op. cit.*

109. "Concluding Observations of the Committee on the Elimination of Discrimination against Women: Saudi Arabia," Committee on the Elimination of Discrimination against Women, 40th Session, Jan. 14-Feb. 1, 2008, p. 3, www2.ohchr.org/english/bodies/cedaw/docs/co/CEDAW.C.SAU.CO.2.pdf.

110. Kambiz Fattahi, "Women's bill 'unites' Iran and US," BBC, July 31, 2007, http://news.bbc.co.uk/2/hi/middle_east/6922749.stm.

111. H. Res. 101, Rep. Lynn Woolsey, http://thomas.loc.gov/cgi-bin/bdquery/z?d110:h.res.00101.

112. "General Assembly Adopts Landmark Text Calling for Moratorium on Death Penalty," States News Service, Dec. 18, 2007, www.un.org/News/Press/docs//2007/ga10678.doc.htm.

113. Mary H. Cooper, "Women and Human Rights," *CQ Researcher*, April 30, 1999, p. 356.

114. Christina Hoff Sommers, "The Case against Ratifying the United Nations Convention on the Elimination of All Forms of Discrimination against Women," testimony before the Senate Foreign Relations Committee, June 13, 2002, www.aei.org/publications/filter.all,pubID.15557/pub_detail.asp.

115. "CEDAW: Pro-United Nations, Not Pro-Woman" press release, U.S. Senate Republican Policy Committee, Sept. 16, 2002, http://rpc.senate.gov/_files/FOREIGNje091602.pdf.

116. "Turkmenistan adopts gender equality law," BBC Worldwide Monitoring, Dec. 19, 2007.

117. Faiza Saleh Ambah, "Saudi Women See a Brighter Road on Rights," *The Washington Post*, Jan. 31, 2008, p. A15, www.washingtonpost.com/wp-dyn/content/article/2008/01/30/AR2008013003805.html.

118. Damien McElroy, "Saudi Arabia to lift ban on women drivers," *The Telegraph*, Jan. 1, 2008.

119. Stephanie Levitz, "Lifting the veils of Afghan women," *The Hamilton Spectator* (Ontario, Canada), Feb. 28, 2008, p. A11.

120. "U.N. Secretary-General Ban Ki-moon Launches Campaign to End Violence against Women," U.N. press release, Feb. 25, 2008, http://endviolence.un.org/press.shtml.

121. "Gender Equality Architecture and U.N. Reforms," the Center for Women's Global Leadership and the Women's Environment and Development Organization, July 17, 2006, www.wedo.org/files/Gender%20Equality%20Architecture%20and%20UN%20Reform0606.pdf.

122. Bojana Stoparic, "New-Improved Women's Agency Vies for U.N. Priority," Women's eNews, March 6, 2008, www.womensenews.org/article.cfm?aid=3517.

123. Reel, *op. cit.*

124. Eliana Raszewski and Bill Faries, "Lugo, Ex Bishop, Wins Paraguay Presidential Election," Bloomberg, April 20, 2008.

125. Zahid Hussain, "Pakistan gets its first woman Speaker," *The Times* (of London), March 20, p. 52.

126. Bhaskar Roy, "Finally, women set to get 33% quota," *Times of India*, Jan. 29, 2008.

127. Massoumeh Torfeh, "Iranian women crucial in Majlis election," BBC, Jan. 30, 2008, http://news.bbc.co.uk/1/hi/world/middle_east/7215272.stm.

128. "Iran women win few seats in parliament," Agence-France Presse, March 18, 2008.

129. Swanee Hunt, "Let Women Rule," *Foreign Affairs*, May-June 2007, p. 109.

130. Kwamboka Oyaro, "A Call to Arm Women Candidates With More Than Speeches," Inter Press Service, Dec. 21, 2007, http://ipsnews.net/news.asp?idnews=40569.

131. Education Centre for Women in Democracy, www.ecwd.org.

132. *Ibid.*

133. Oyaro, *op. cit.*

134. *Ibid.*

135. Mary Kimani, "Taking on violence against women in Africa," *AfricaRenewal*, U.N. Dept. of Public Information, July 2007, p. 4, www.un.org/ecosocdev/geninfo/afrec/vol21no2/212-violence-aganist-women.html.

136. Correspondence with Karen Musalo, Clinical Professor of Law and Director of the Center for Gender & Refugee Studies, University of California Hastings School of Law, April 11, 2008.

137. "Mexico and Guatemala: Stop the Killings of Women," Amnesty International USA Issue Brief, January 2007, www.amnestyusa.org/document.php?lang=e&id=engusa20070130001.

138. Manuel Roig-Franzia, "Waning Hopes in Juarez," *The Washington Post*, May 14, 2007, p. A10.

139. Kimani, *op. cit.*

140. *Ibid.*

141. "Justice slow for female war victims," *The Toronto Star*, March 3, 2008, www.thestar.com/News/GlobalVoices/article/308784p.

142. Speech by Brigid Inder on the Launch of the "Gender Report Card on the International Criminal Court," Dec. 12, 2007, www.iccwomen.org/news/docs/Launch_GRC_2007.pdf

143. "Gender Report Card on the International Criminal Court," Women's Initiatives for Gender Justice,

November 2007, p. 32, www.iccwomen.org/publications/resources/docs/GENDER_04-01-2008_FINAL_TO_PRINT.pdf.

144. Turquet, *et al.*, *op. cit.*, p. 8.

145. Oxfam Gender Equality Fact Sheet, www.oxfam.org.uk/resources/issues/gender/introduction.html.

146. Itai Madamombe, "Women push onto Africa's agenda," *AfricaRenewal*, U.N. Dept. of Public Information, July 2007, pp. 8-9.

BIBLIOGRAPHY

Books

Holland, Jack, *Misogyny: The World's Oldest Prejudice, Constable & Robinson*, 2006.
The late Irish journalist provides vivid details and anecdotes about women's oppression throughout history.

Stone, Merlin, *When God Was a Woman, Harcourt Brace Jovanovich*, 1976.
The book contends that before the rise of Judeo-Christian patriarchies women headed the first societies and religions.

Terry, Geraldine, *Women's Rights, Pluto Press*, 2007.
A feminist who has worked for Oxfam and other non-governmental organizations outlines major issues facing women today — from violence to globalization to AIDS.

***Women and the Environment, UNEP*, 2004.**
The United Nations Environment Programme shows the integral link between women in the developing world and the changing environment.

Articles

Brady, Brian, "A Question of Honour," *The Independent on Sunday*, Feb. 10, 2008, p. 8.
"Honor killings" and related violence against women are on the rise in the United Kingdom.

Kidder, Thalia, and Kate Raworth, " 'Good Jobs' and hidden costs: women workers documenting the price of precarious employment," *Gender and Development*, Vol. 12, No. 2, p. 12, July 2004.
Two trade and gender experts describe the precarious working conditions and job security experienced by food and garment workers.

Reports and Studies

"Beijing Betrayed," *Women's Environment and Development Organization*, March 2005, www.wedo.org/files/gmr_pdfs/gmr2005.pdf.
A women's-rights organization reviews the progress and shortcomings of governments in implementing the commitments made during the Fifth World Congress on Women in Beijing in 1995.

"The Millennium Development Goals Report 2007," *United Nations*, 2007, www.un.org/millenniumgoals/pdf/mdg2007.pdf.
International organizations demonstrate the progress governments have made — or not — in reaching the Millennium Development Goals.

"Trafficking in Persons Report," *U.S. Department of State*, June 2007, www.state.gov/documents/organization/82902.pdf.
This seventh annual report discusses the growing problems of human trafficking around the world.

"The tsunami's impact on women," *Oxfam briefing note*, March 5, 2005, www.oxfam.org/en/files/bn050326_tsunami_women/download.
Looking at how the 2004 tsunami affected women in Indonesia, India and Sri Lanka, Oxfam International suggests how governments can better address women's issues during future natural disasters.

"Women in Politics," *Inter-Parliamentary Union*, 2005, www.ipu.org/PDF/publications/wmn45-05_en.pdf.
The report provides detailed databases of the history of female political representation in governments around the world.

Ballington, Julie, and Azza Karam, "Women in Parliament: Beyond the Numbers," *International Institute for Democracy and Electoral Assistance*, 2005, www.idea.int/publications/wip2/upload/WiP_inlay.pdf.
The handbook provides female politicians and candidates information and case studies on how women have overcome obstacles to elected office.

Chen, Martha, Joann Vanek, Francie Lund, James Heintz, Renana Jhabvala and Christine Bonner, "Women, Work and Poverty," *UNIFEM*, 2005, www.unifem.org/attachments/products/PoWW2005_eng.pdf.
The report argues that greater work protection and security is needed to promote women's rights and reduce global poverty.

Larserud, Stina, and Rita Taphorn, "Designing for Equality," *International Institute for Democracy and Electoral Assistance*, 2007, www.idea.int/publications/designing_for_equality/upload/Idea_Design_low.pdf.

The report describes the impact that gender quota systems have on women's representation in elected office.

Raworth, Kate, and Claire Harvey, "Trading Away Our Rights," *Oxfam International*, 2004, www.oxfam.org.uk/resources/policy/trade/downloads/trading_rights.pdf.
Through exhaustive statistics, case studies and interviews, the report paints a grim picture of how trade globalization is affecting women.

Turquet, Laura, Patrick Watt and Tom Sharman, "Hit or Miss?" *ActionAid*, March 7, 2008.
The report reviews how governments are doing in achieving the U.N.'s Millennium Development Goals.

For More Information

Equality Now, P.O. Box 20646, Columbus Circle Station, New York, NY 10023; www.equalitynow.org. An international organization working to protect women against violence and promote women's human rights.

Global Database of Quotas for Women; www.quotaproject.org. A joint project of the International Institute for Democracy and Electoral Assistance and Stockholm University providing country-by-country data on electoral quotas for women.

Human Rights Watch, 350 Fifth Ave., 34th floor, New York, NY 10118-3299; (212) 290-4700; www.hrw.org. Investigates and exposes human-rights abuses around the world.

Hunt Alternatives Fund, 625 Mount Auburn St., Cambridge, MA 02138; (617) 995-1900; www.huntalternatives.org. A private foundation that provides grants and technical assistance to promote positive social change; its Initiative for Inclusive Security promotes women in peacekeeping.

Inter-Parliamentary Union, 5, Chemin du Pommier, Case Postale 330, CH-1218 Le Grand-Saconnex, Geneva, Switzerland; +(4122) 919 41 50; www.ipu.org. An organization of parliaments of sovereign states that

maintains an extensive database on women serving in parliaments.

Oxfam International, 1100 15th St., N.W., Suite 600, Washington, DC 20005; (202) 496-1170; www.oxfam.org. Confederation of 13 independent nongovernmental organizations working to fight poverty and related social injustice.

U.N. Development Fund for Women (UNIFEM), 304 East 45th St., 15th Floor, New York, NY 10017; (212) 906-6400; www.unifem.org. Provides financial aid and technical support for empowering women and promoting gender equality.

U.N. Division for the Advancement of Women (DAW), 2 UN Plaza, DC2-12th Floor, New York, NY 10017; www.un.org/womenwatch/daw. Formulates policy on gender equality, implements international agreements on women's issues and promotes gender mainstreaming in government activities.

Women's Environment & Development Organization (WEDO), 355 Lexington Ave., 3rd Floor, New York, NY 10017; (212) 973-0325; www.wedo.org. An international organization that works to promote women's equality in global policy.

Reproductive Ethics

*Should Fertility Medicine
Be Regulated More Tightly?*

Marcia Clemmitt

6

Wendy Kramer of Nederland, Colo., and her son Ryan — who was conceived through donor insemination — founded and run the Donor Sibling Registry to help donor-conceived children locate siblings and learn about their genetic lineage. Ryan has learned of six half-sisters to date. As of February, more than 6,200 siblings have been connected via the online registry, which was launched in 2000.

From *CQ Researcher*,
May 15, 2009.

fter 33-year-old Nadya Suleman, a mother of six, gave birth to octuplets on Jan. 26, the California fertility specialist who treated her was summoned to appear before the Medical Board of California. The board — which can revoke physicians' licenses for egregious misconduct — is investigating whether Michael Kamrava, head of the West Coast IVF Clinic in Beverly Hills, violated accepted standards of medical practice when he implanted at least six embryos in Suleman during in vitro fertilization (IVF) treatment in 2008, leading to the multiple birth.[1]

Suleman has told reporters that all 14 of her children were conceived using IVF — a high-tech treatment in which eggs are fertilized in the laboratory, then implanted into a woman's uterus for gestation — and that six embryos were implanted in each of her six pregnancies, although she's had only two multiple births: the octuplets and a set of twins. But professional guidelines from the American Society for Reproductive Medicine recommend implanting only one or two embryos in younger women, such as Suleman, because of the high risk multiple births pose to children and mothers.

Multiple-birth babies, including twins, have a significantly higher risk for developing severe, debilitating disabilities such as chronic lung diseases or cerebral palsy, which occurs six times more often among twins and 20 times more often in triplets than it does in single babies.[2]

The cost to the health-care system of multiple births is enormous. "The cost of caring for the octuplets would probably cover more than a year of providing IVF for everyone in L.A. County who needed it," says David L. Keefe, professor of obstetrics and gynecology at the University of South Florida, in Tampa. "The

Most States Don't Require Infertility Coverage

Only 12 states require all state-regulated health insurance plans to cover infertility diagnosis and treatment. Two states — California and Texas — require only that every insurer offer at least one plan with fertility coverage.

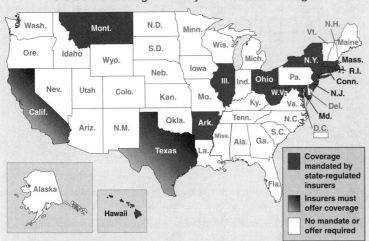

States Mandating Infertility Insurance Coverage

Coverage mandated by state-regulated insurers

Insurers must offer coverage

No mandate or offer required

Source: InterNational Council on Infertility Information Dissemination

likelihood that some of those kids will get cerebral palsy means they'll need a lifetime of care."

The high-profile Suleman case has spurred calls for government regulation of fertility medicine — sometimes called assisted reproductive technologies, or ART. (*See box, p. 147.*) Like U.S. medicine generally, ART is not regulated by the federal government and only lightly supervised by state agencies. Since 1978 — when the world's first IVF baby, Louise Brown, was born in England — more than 3 million ART babies have been born worldwide, and some experts and ethicists fear the field's rapid expansion leaves too much room for abuses.[3]

Others argue that lack of insurance coverage for IVF is the biggest problem with ART in the United States. Fertility treatments can cost more than $12,000 per cycle, pushing cash-strapped would-be parents to opt for the higher-risk, multiple-embryo implantation to increase their chances of a pregnancy.

By contrast, in most European countries — where IVF procedures are paid for through universal health-care systems — doctors generally implant only one fertilized embryo at a time. In Sweden and Finland, for instance,

where the procedure is covered by insurance, doctors perform single-embryo implantations 70 percent and 60 percent of the time, respectively, compared to only 3.3 percent of the time in the United States.[4] (*See graph, p. 138.*)

In fact, some European governments prohibit multiple-embryo transfers for women under 36 and limit older women to no more than two embryos per cycle. As a result, "Triplets have virtually disappeared in Europe," a Danish doctor told European colleagues at a 2006 fertility conference.[5]

Self-regulation of ART in the United States clearly isn't working, said Marcy Darnovsky, associate executive director of the Oakland, Calif.-based Center for Genetics and Society, which advocates for responsible use of genetic technologies. According to the federal Centers for Disease Control and Prevention (CDC), to which ART clinics must report data, 80 percent of programs do not strictly follow American Society for Reproductive Medicine guidelines, making government regulation "long overdue," she said.[6]

"In reproductive matters, individuals are making decisions [that affect] not just themselves, but . . . others as well," which makes regulation appropriate, said Johns Hopkins University scholars Franco Furger and Francis Fukuyama. Reproductive medicine is headed toward giving prospective parents "a range of . . . techniques to make specific choices about a baby's health and sex and eventually about other attributes," said Furger, a research professor, and Fukuyama, a professor of international political economy, both at the Paul H. Nitze School of Advanced International Studies in Washington, D.C. "It would be misguided to take a wait-and-see attitude."[7]

Industrialized countries that pay for IVF through their universal health-care systems strictly regulate which services may be provided, says Susannah Baruch, director for law and policy at the Genetics & Public Policy Center, a think tank at John Hopkins funded by the Pew Charitable Trusts. The services typically include pre-implantation genetic diagnosis (PGD) — genetic testing of embryos. While PGD to detect serious genetic illnesses is conducted routinely, many countries strictly limit other PGD uses, such as selecting a child's gender, because they aren't considered in the public interest, she says.

However, in the United States — even though U.S. reproductive-medicine experts roundly criticize Kamrava's implantation of multiple embryos in the Suleman case — many ART experts also argue that government regulation of the industry is not necessarily a solution.

Suleman's case is much more of an outlier today than it would have been 15 years ago, when it wasn't unusual to have six embryos transferred, says Josephine Johnston, a research scholar at the Hastings Center for bioethics research in Garrison, N.Y. "I would have bet money that it was not IVF" that led to the octuplet birth, she says, but the use of ovary-stimulating drugs — a much cheaper, far less controllable method of assisted reproductive technology.

Multiple-embryo implantation is being phased out as ART technologies improve, Johnston says, and six-embryo implantation is "so far outside the guidelines it's amazing that a physician would do it."

Such hair-raising cases are virtually always outliers and shouldn't be used to hastily enact laws, some analysts say.

For example, ever since artificial insemination was introduced sperm banks have promised would-be parents a genetic lineage of intelligence, athleticism and good looks for babies born from donor sperm, says R. Alta Charo, a professor of law and bioethics at the University of Wisconsin Law School. But "it hasn't undermined Western culture as we know it," she says. "So why do we think that people are very likely to go through much more onerous PGD to choose traits?" Very few will try to use it to enhance their baby's intelligence or appearance, so there would be little point in prohibiting such behavior, she says.

Majority of ART Pregnancies Result in a Live Birth

About 82 percent of the U.S. pregnancies resulting from assisted reproductive technology (ART) in 2006 resulted in live births. More than half were a single-child birth, and a quarter were multiple-infant births. Nearly three-quarters of U.S. ART procedures use fresh, non-donor sperm or eggs.

Outcomes of Pregnancies Resulting From ART Cycles Using Fresh, Non-donor Eggs or Embryos, 2006

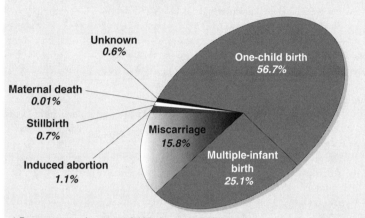

*Percentages do not total 100 due to rounding.

Source: "Assisted Reproductive Technology Success Rates 2006," Centers for Disease Control and Prevention, 2008

A recent study by New York University's Langone Medical Center supports Charo's view somewhat. Of 999 patients who completed a survey on traits they thought warranted use of PGD screening, solid majorities named potential conditions such as mental retardation, blindness, deafness, heart disease and cancer. Only 10 percent said they might use PGD to choose a child with exceptional athletic ability and 12.6 percent, high intelligence.[8]

"People are after different things" in calling for ART regulation, making legislation difficult, Charo says. Some may want limits on the number of embryos implanted per cycle, but most are calling for rules to enforce "personal morality," such as whether gay couples should become parents or whether lower-income mothers should be allowed to have very large families, Charo says.

As Technology Advances, Questions Emerge

Multiple births threaten poor families.

Ghazala Khamis and her husband, a farmworker, had three daughters, but they longed for a son. Last year, the 27-year-old Egyptian woman gave birth to healthy septuplets, four boys and three girls, by Caesarian section near the end of her eighth month of pregnancy. Before the septuplets, she had not conceived for five years.[1]

Khamis conceived the septuplets using one of the oldest fertility technologies, introduced in the 1950s and '60s — fertility drugs that stimulate women's ovaries to produce multiple eggs. While effective for many, the drugs — which are becoming cheap and widely available around the world — are also among the most dangerous and unpredictable treatments, often leading to multiple births, and as they spread into poor communities the consequences can be dire.

"I'm really scared," Khamis said, soon after her delivery. "We live in a mud hut with only two rooms. I don't know how we're going to afford 10 children."[2]

The positive side of the medications' increased availability is that poor people have the greatest risk of infertility and, until recently, had literally no access to help. "The less money you have, the more likely you are to have difficulty conceiving," wrote Liza Mundy, author of a 2007 book on fertility medicine, *Everything Conceivable.* "Much infertility has always been caused by infections that can damage reproductive passageways," and "the lower your tax bracket, the less likely you are to have received the fairly simple medical treatment that can stave off these consequences."[3]

But the spread of the hard-to-control drugs, coupled with many families' desire for sons, can create tragedies in poor communities, especially in the developing world. Khamis' delivery ultimately went well, but because Egypt doesn't have enough respirators for newborns, doctors held back from performing the Caesarian section until long after Western doctors would have removed the children. "We were simply blessed by God that no complication happened," Khamis' physician, Mahmoud Meleis, said. "If there had been a complication, Ghazala would have died."[4]

As older fertility technologies spread, newer ones are being created, sometimes solving problems but sometimes creating new ones.

A fledgling technique — freezing women's eggs, rather than embryos, for later use — could eventually help solve two problems with fertility treatments, says John Jain, head of an IVF clinic in Santa Monica, Calif., and an early U.S. adopter of egg freezing, which began in 2005 in Italy. First, freezing eggs can offset the fertility problems often caused by the upward creep in the age at which people start families. Second, freezing eggs causes fewer moral and religious qualms than freezing embryos,

"I have patients flying in because I will freeze eggs rather than embryos," thus allowing women to bank their own eggs against future infertility, whatever its cause, such as cancer treatment or aging, he says. "The pregnancy rate from frozen eggs is as good as from frozen embryos."

"We must then ask why we would regulate these [reproductive] personal choices differently from other personal choices."

ART-related law would likely be based on the unusual cases that make headlines, "and bad cases make bad policy," she says.

Opposition to regulation might drop considerably if insurance covered IVF and other artificial reproduction procedures, but today only 12 states require such coverage. (*See map, p. 132.*)

For instance, limitations on multiple-embryo implantations might be acceptable if insurance covered several single-embryo implantations for all patients who have experienced six months of proven infertility, suggests

Ronald M. Green, a professor of ethics and human values at Dartmouth College.

Because of the high cost of IVF treatments, the lack of insurance coverage has deprived "the vast majority of the middle class" in America, as well as the poor, from the modern ART "revolution," says Keefe at the University of South Florida. "Once you have the middle class covered, then I have no trouble saying, 'We're not going to pay' " for multiple-embryo implantation.

Furthermore, the procedure doesn't have to cost $12,000 per cycle, as evidenced by the lower amounts accepted by IVF clinics when insurance companies that are required to cover the procedure negotiate lower fees, he says. "It's a lot cheaper [for society] to pay for IVF at

But others warn that egg freezing hasn't been fully tested.

"The biggest misconception coming down the pike is freezing eggs,'" says David L, Rosenfeld, director of the Center for Human Reproduction at the North Shore-Long Island Jewish Health System in Manhasset, N.Y. "It's experimental, and right now the public expectations are unreal." Currently it's unknown how long frozen eggs can be stored — whether they'll be like embryos and sperm, which can be stored long term without apparent harm, or more fragile. "The technology will improve, but expectations are running way ahead of that," he says.

Like all reproductive technology, egg freezing could still raise ethics issues. In April 2007, a Canadian woman triggered a bioethical debate when she froze some of her own eggs so that her 7-year-old daughter, who has a genetic disorder that causes infertility, could use them as an adult.

A daughter potentially giving birth to her mother's child is unusual enough so that "we have to look very carefully into what we're doing here," said Margaret Somerville, an ethicist at McGill University in Toronto.

But other ethicists aren't troubled a bit. "It's hard for me to see what difference it'd make to the child that one of her gametes came from her grandmother [rather] than her mother," said Wayne Summer, a University of Toronto philosophy professor.[5]

Meanwhile, a new sperm-donation technique is drastically changing fertility medicine. Intra-cytoplasmic sperm injection, or ICSI, allows even a single, weak sperm to fertilize an egg. ICSI is quickly displacing sperm donation, once widely used by heterosexual infertility patients but increasingly used only by single women and lesbian couples.

ICSI now allows many men to become fathers who previously could not have conceived, and it's spread like wildfire in the past decade. In Europe in 2005 — the most recent year for which data has been analyzed — the technique was used in 63.3 percent of all assisted-reproduction cases, up from 34.7 percent in 1997, when European data collection began.[6]

Using ICSI and other techniques, "you're probably helping people have a child that Mother Nature wouldn't have allowed for," and that has both risks and benefits, says Angeline Beltsos, medical director of the Chicago-based Fertility Centers of Illinois.

Indeed, evidence is growing that sons conceived through ICSI inherit their father's infertility, raising questions about consequences generations down the road.

"We may have tens of thousands of boys born with infertility," said Tommaso Falcone, head of obstetrics and gynecology at the Cleveland Clinic.[7]

---

[1] For background, see Hadeel Al-Shalchi, "Egypt Septuplets Stir Debate on Fertility Drugs," The Associated Press, ABC News Web site, Aug. 26, 2008, http://abcnews.go.com/print?id=5661108.

[2] Quoted in *ibid.*

[3] Liza Mundy, *Everything Conceivable* (2007), p. xiv.

[4] Quoted in Al-Shalchi, *op. cit.*

[5] Quoted in "Assisted Human Reproduction: Regulating and Treating Conception Problems," CBC News Web site, Feb. 5, 2009, www.cbc.ca.

[6] "Fertility Treatments: Researcher Says that ICSI May Be Over-used in Some Countries," *Science Daily* Web site, July 9, 2008, www.sciencedaily.com.

[7] Quoted in JoNel Aleccia, "Pass It On: Sons of Infertile Men May Be Next," MSNBC.com, Sept. 27, 2008, www.msnbc.msn.com.

$3,000 or $4,000 per procedure and deliver only singletons," thus avoiding the harrowing medical problems and high costs associated with multiple births, he says.

Mandating coverage not only reduces the number of multiple births but also increases access for the middle class. "I practiced in Massachusetts and Rhode Island [which require coverage], where sheet-metal workers and heiresses from Newport" mingled at IVF clinics because insurance picked up the tab, Keefe says.

However, not all fertility doctors would opt into a fully insured system, says Dawn Gannon, director of professional outreach for RESOLVE, the National Infertility Association, which advocates that insurance

companies treat infertility like any other medical condition. For example, when New Jersey mandated coverage, in 2001, "some clinics didn't take insurance at all, and some started taking it and then stopped," she says, because "they got less money per procedure."

If the United States enacts universal health-care coverage, advocates for the infertile hope ART will be covered as it is in other industrialized countries.

But universal coverage would still leave thorny issues unsettled, such as whether taxpayer subsidies should support ART for unmarried women or women over 40. For older women, the debate centers on whether it is appropriate for health insurance to subsidize an infertility problem that is the result of natural aging and not the

Most ART Cycles Don't End in Deliveries

Approximately 100,000 assisted reproductive technology (ART) cycles were performed in 2006 using fresh, non-donor eggs or embryos. Of that amount, less than 35,000 resulted in pregnancies. Only about 28,000 actually resulted in live-birth deliveries.

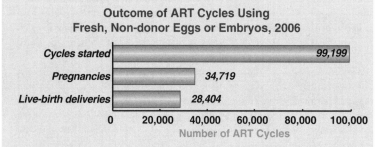

Outcome of ART Cycles Using Fresh, Non-donor Eggs or Embryos, 2006

Source: "Assisted Reproductive Technology Success Rates 2006," Centers for Disease Control and Prevention, 2008

Should fertility medicine be regulated more vigorously?

Should a mother of six with limited income be allowed to give birth to eight additional children through IVF? If a man donates sperm that results in hundreds of babies — technically making them all half brothers and sisters — should the offspring be given the identity of their biological father so they won't end up dating or marrying a half-sibling? Is a father whose child was the product of donated egg and sperm liable for child support if the couple divorces?

These are just a handful of the sticky ethical questions that have emerged from the brave, new world of sperm and egg donation.[10]

Of course, outlier cases like that of the California octuplets quickly spur vociferous calls for government limits on in vitro fertilization. And others say the well-being of patients demands at least some rules. Finally, since many ART-related questions wind up in court, judges say they need more legislative guidance than the current case-by-case approach being used to settle IVF cases.

"No matter what one thinks of artificial insemination, and — as now appears in the not-too-distant future, cloning and even gene splicing — courts are still going to be faced with the problem of determining legal parentage," declared a unanimous California Court of Appeals ruling in the 1998 case *Buzzanca v. Buzzanca.* "Courts can continue to make decisions on an ad hoc basis . . . or the legislature can act to improve a broader order which . . . would bring some predictability to those who seek to make use of artificial reproductive techniques," said the justices in a case involving a divorcing husband who claimed no financial responsibility for his daughter, conceived from donor egg and sperm and borne by a surrogate mother.[11]

Creating a federal-government registry of information on egg and sperm donors would give adults born from donated gametes (sperms or eggs) access to their

result of a medical condition. Also, pregnancy is riskier for both the older mother and the child.

Earlier in IVF's history, many clinicians routinely refused ART to single women, older women, lesbians and, in some cases, poor people. A 1993 survey of Finnish ART clinics found that many doctors "preferred not to treat either lesbian or single women," arguing that they "wanted to protect children from having inappropriate parents, primarily 'bad mothers,'" according to Maili Malin, a medical sociologist at Finland's National Institute of Public Health. A single woman's marital status and "wish to have a child" were both "considered indications of . . . questionable mental health."[9]

Whatever the outcome, the coverage debate will generate intense emotion. "So much of your life feels out of control when you want a child but find that you can't have one," says Jan Elman Stout, a clinical psychologist in Chicago. "This is often the very first challenge that people encounter in their lives that, no matter how hard they work at it, it may not work out for them."

As ethicists, lawmakers and physicians debate how best to provide access and oversight for reproductive medicine, here are some of the questions being asked:

genetic history in order to prevent half-siblings from marrying each other. It would also allow limits on the numbers of children created through one person's donations, said Naomi Cahn, a research professor at the George Washington University Law School. In England, no more than 10 children can be created from a single donor's sperm.[12]

The federal government should exercise more aggressively the authority it already has to oversee the safety and efficacy of some ART technologies, say some experts.

For instance, inserting one woman's egg into another woman's body is arguably a type of tissue transplant — a procedure over which the Food and Drug Administration (FDA) has jurisdiction but has been lax in regulating, says the University of Wisconsin's Charo. "That's an appropriate place to step in to ask whether we have assurance of safety for the stuff that's being developed," she says.

The FDA has a role in determining whether genetic tests are safe and whether they work or are medically useful, says Baruch of the Genetics & Public Policy Center. For instance, many labs manufacture genetic tests that they don't market to other companies — called "home-brew" tests — but the FDA "has chosen not to regulate them," she says. "We believe that they have the authority" and would like to see them do it.

Genetic testing of embryos — pre-implantation genetic diagnosis or PGD, which requires permanent removal of one cell from an eight-cell embryo — is much more technically difficult than other forms of genetic testing but gets less government scrutiny, according to Baruch's organization. And, the center points out, even the general quality standards for laboratories under the federal Clinical Laboratory Improvement Amendments of 1988 are not being applied to PGD labs.[13]

But aside from testing the safety and efficacy of medical products and drugs, the U.S. government does not, in general, regulate the practice of medicine, says Wisconsin's Charo. "That being the case, the issue of regulating fertility clinics actually becomes, 'Should they be regulated differently from the rest of medicine?' " she says. "It would be difficult to make that case."

"Muddling through" without regulation "is a respectable policy option, especially for a pragmatic people faced with irreconcilable moral quandaries" such as those often posed by ART, said John A. Robertson, a professor at the University of Texas College of Law in Austin. "This non-system 'system' has served well to date — even if not all the time and never perfectly — both in other contexts and for assisted reproduction." The current system can deal with even thorny issues, he adds, such as questions surrounding the "genetic screening of embryos…and the other edge technologies looming ahead."[14]

Furthermore, he pointed out, the President's Council on Bioethics appointed by George W. Bush examined the ART field for more than a year and found that the biggest problems were "on the margins, not at the core." The panel recommended only "tinker[ing] with ways to get more data" and making professional self-regulation more effective.[15]

National Infertility Association Executive Director Barbara L. Collura also advocates caution in regulating ART. While limiting the number of embryos implanted per cycle may seem like a no-brainer, she says, such a rule could be prohibitively difficult because of the wide variety of medical conditions that could occur. For example, she argues, while the American Society for Reproductive Medicine strongly recommends transferring only one — or at most two — embryos at a time, if a woman has already had three or four cycles of IVF and her embryo quality is poor, a doctor could easily justify implanting multiple embryos. "How do you put that into a law?" she asks.

And some fertility doctors argue that they're already more regulated than most other U.S. physicians. "FDA put in tons of rules a few years ago . . . [that] added hundreds of dollars to the cost," says John Jain, who heads a fertility clinic in Santa Monica, Calif. The guidelines, which mainly dealt with disease-testing of donated gametes, involved "viruses I've never seen in my life." He fears that other regulations "will add to the already exorbitant cost."

David L. Rosenfeld, director of the Center for Human Reproduction at the North Shore-Long Island Jewish Health System in Manhasset, N.Y., makes the same point. "We're already highly scrutinized," he says. Thanks to the CDC's fertility-clinic database, he adds, reproductive-medicine specialists are "the only physicians in the country whose numbers are published nationally."

Sanctions for outlier physicians already exist at state licensing boards such as the one scrutinizing Suleman's

Single-Embryo Use Is Rare in U.S.

In countries where insurance pays for IVF procedures, doctors generally implant single embryos in women. By contrast, single-embryo implantation is rare in the United States, where the procedure is not usually covered by insurance, which forces women to have multiple implantations.

Percent of IVF Cycles Involving Single-Embryo Transfers

Source: BBC News, June 26, 2008, http://news.bbc.co.uk/2/hi/health/7475392.stm

doctor, says Jain. "As a physician, how far do I need to be policed? If there are poor outcomes, a level of public scrutiny" emerges — as it has in the octuplets' case — which helps rein in doctors inclined to go too far, he says.

Finally, some doctors contend that having light government oversight allows U.S. medicine to advance rapidly.

"We are probably leaders in the field of reproductive medicine because we can advance without government interference," says Angeline Beltsos, medical director of the Chicago-based Fertility Centers of Illinois. "Creating guidelines is critical, but legislating is dangerous."

Should parents be allowed to choose their babies' characteristics, such as gender?

When pre-implantation genetic diagnosis is used in combination with in vitro fertilization, parents can select specific embryos for their characteristics, raising a variety of ethical questions.[16]

Today, PGD — which removes one cell from an eight-cell embryo — can generally test for only one trait. But soon "we're going to be able to look for many markers at once," opening the door to choosing various characteristics, explains Baruch of the Genetics & Public Policy Center. For instance, eventually hair and eye color will be on the list, "and that'll give people pause."

Many analysts see no problem with allowing parents to opt for PGD, since it seems unlikely that many would go through the rigors of IVF just for the chance to choose a child's gender or appearance.

"We've exercised the ability to choose characteristics for a long time, by deciding who we'll marry or by carefully choosing" a sperm donor for artificial insemination, yet history shows that few people put much effort into choosing traits that might produce a "superior" human, the University of Wisconsin's Charo says. "I'm the only person sent by Congress on taxpayer money to see" the so-called Nobel Prize-winner sperm bank, the Repository for Germinal Excellence, in Southern California, and "I found that nobody ever used that sperm."

Some bioethics experts say there's nothing necessarily wrong with choosing a baby's gender. "I'm the mother of four boys and . . . my sons are marvelous, but at the same time, I certainly would have liked to have had a girl," said University of Chicago professor of medicine Janet D. Rowley during a 2003 deliberation by the President's Council on Bioethics. "This is an area we should leave alone . . . unregulated."[17]

Sex selection to achieve what some call "gender balance" in a family is probably acceptable, says Robertson of the University of Texas. "I have a hard time finding sexism or bias" in a family with three daughters using PGD to have a son, he says.

Meanwhile, Robertson says selecting out genes for non-medical conditions or attributes like looks, personality and abilities probably won't be possible anytime soon. "Most conditions aren't controlled by a single gene," he explains, and scientists don't know which genes make the difference for potentially desirable traits like athleticism or intelligence. Even for single-gene traits, like "fast-twitch muscles" that help some athletes, "the idea of going through IVF when your child won't necessarily become a top athlete anyway seems outlandish," he says. "I think the fears of designer babies are overblown."

Likewise, Paul Miller, a former commissioner of the Equal Employment Opportunity Commission, thinks fears are probably unfounded that allowing parents to select against characteristics like shortness or baldness would increase stigmatization of those traits. "There have been opportunities to terminate fetuses with Down's syndrome . . . for a generation," Miller said, "and yet I don't believe that individuals . . . with Down's syndrome are any more or less excluded or that . . . society has the sense that [such] a child . . . should have been prevented."[18]

But others say there's more interest among the public in choosing traits like gender than had been expected and that it's worrisome.

"Looking to the future, some observers view PGD, or any technology that allows parents to choose the characteristics of their children, as having the potential to fundamentally alter the way we view human reproduction and our offspring," noted researchers from the Genetics & Public Policy Center think tank. Rather than viewing "reproduction as a mysterious process that results in the miraculous gift of a child," children may become viewed as a commodity, created by a "series of meticulous, technology-driven" parental choices, said a center report.[19]

Potentially, wealthier people could increase their social advantage because they could afford to create babies with "genes selected to increase their chances of having good looks, musical talent . . . or whatever," thus worsening social inequalities, said the report. In addition, if trait selection becomes common, children born with genetic traits such as hereditary deafness or small stature could face increased social stigma, and parents could face pressure to use PGD to avoid having such children, center analysts speculated.[20]

While Baruch finds it difficult to believe anybody would go through IVF and PGD just to choose their child's gender, recent data indicate that there has been an unexpected uptick in interest in sex selection. "I have heard directly from IVF clinics who were surprised to have people come in primarily for sex selection," she says. Nevertheless, "we need to see better numbers before we call for regulation."

Researchers are finding evidence that some Asian immigrant families, for instance, are using ART to have sons. In some Asian countries, boys are so highly valued over girls that many families have selectively aborted or even murdered girl babies, leading to whole generations in which boys greatly outnumber girls.[21]

Separate research from scholars at Columbia University and the University of Texas concludes that some Asian families in the United States have used and are using whatever technology is available to produce sons, especially for second, third and subsequent children. In the 1990s, the chosen technique was most likely gender-selective abortion, but today more families appear to be using PGD as well.[22]

The researchers found that during the 1990s Chinese, Indian and Korean families' first children mirrored the gender balance in non-Asian families, but their subsequent children included significantly higher proportions of sons. Among Indian families in Santa Clara County, Calif., for example, University of Texas economist Jason Abrevaya found a 58-percent likelihood that a third child would be a son — significantly higher than the natural 51-percent chance of having a boy.[23]

In 2004, at least 70 percent of the parents using the Fertility Institute of Los Angeles wanted to choose their child's gender — far more than those who wanted the clinic's services to test for genetic diseases, reported Deborah L. Spar, a professor of business administration at Harvard Business School.[24] The clinic's medical director, Jeffrey Steinberg, generated some controversy in February when *The Wall Street Journal* reported that his clinic would now offer not only gender selection but selection for physical traits like eye and hair color, which he dubbed "cosmetic medicine."[25]

From some religious perspectives, PGD is immoral for any purpose, including ensuring a child will be free of a deadly genetic disease, wrote Marilyn E. Coors, associate professor of bioethics and genetics at the University of Colorado at Denver. In Catholic teaching, she wrote, PGD is "intrinsically immoral, because it involves the creation and destruction of human lives, replaces the conjugal act and involves third-party intervention in conception."[26]

Some ethicists warn that trait selection of any kind "treats the children . . . as 'products' as we try to mix the right characteristics," said Toby L. Schonfeld, assistant professor of medical ethics at the University of Nebraska Medical Center. "The increased pressure on these children to fulfill the goals of the parents . . . seems to minimize their autonomy and even exploit them."[27]

The proper use of PGD is for curing or averting disease, and "sex is not a disease," said PGD pioneer Mark Hughes, founder of the Genesis Genetics Institute in Detroit, Mich., explaining why he opposes gender selection.[28]

"I . . . fear . . . that clinics offering trait selection to satisfy the whims of parents will turn people against a procedure that can save lives," said Allen Goldberg, a marketing executive from Washington, D.C., whose 7-year-old son Henry died in 2002 of a rare genetic disease, Fanconi anemia. In the late 1990s, Goldberg and his wife tried unsuccessfully to use PGD to conceive a disease-free sibling who could donate umbilical-cord blood to Henry; other families have used the approach successfully.

However, some ethicists also condemn this use of PGD, arguing that the trait-selected newborn is being unfairly used as a tool to serve the medical needs of its sibling.[29]

Should doctors be able to refuse ART services to gay, older or single people?

The University of South Florida's Keefe says that a gay, male couple came into his clinic in Tampa and were at their wits' end. They had been to several assisted reproductive technology (ART) clinics seeking services, only to be turned away because center officials said they didn't want to be known as a clinic that welcomed gay families.

"These were taxpaying Americans who were very loving to each other, and they'd been bounced from one place to another," says Keefe, who helped the couple conceive a child using donor eggs and a surrogate.

Indeed, some doctors refuse to provide IVF to would-be parents because of their single, gay or elder status, usually citing religious or ethical reasons — or, in the case of older parents — concern about the long-term welfare of the child.

Some ethicists say clinics must first consider the welfare of the children in choosing whom to treat, and questions of religion and conscience figure strongly in such decisions.

In a 2007 report, the ethics committee of the American College of Obstetricians and Gynecologists described a California physician who refused to perform artificial insemination for a lesbian couple, "prompted by religious beliefs and disapproval of lesbians having children." In reproductive medicine, the report said, "health-care providers may find that providing indicated, even standard, care would present for them a personal moral problem — a conflict of conscience." The committee upheld doctors' right to refuse care on those grounds, but said doctors who refuse service must refer patients to other providers.[30]

Because the desire to raise children is not a medical need, physicians may ethically refuse to help people seeking IVF services, argued Julien S. Murphy, a professor of philosophy at the University of Southern Maine. In general, "it is assumed that physicians have a duty to treat 'medical conditions,'" she wrote, "but addressing the fulfillment of reproductive possibilities" opened up by new technology "is an optional matter."[31]

A 2005 survey of fertility doctors found that only 44 percent believed doctors do not have the right to decide who is fit to procreate, according to *Everything Conceivable* author Mundy. Nearly half the physicians surveyed said they'd refuse services to a gay couple, 40 percent said they'd refuse service to a couple on welfare who wanted to pay with Social Security disability checks and 20 percent said they would turn away a single woman.[32]

Such ethical debates are not limited to the United States. Arguing for a ban on ART for single or lesbian women, a member of the Danish Parliament stated that such women have "completely, freely chosen to live" in a manner that "cannot naturally produce children," making providing ART to them "completely against nature, artificial and absurd."[33]

Many English fertility clinics will not serve single women, said Clare Murray, a psychologist at City University London. "Clinics treat lesbian couples at the drop of a hat, but still won't treat single women. They're the pariahs of the assisted-reproduction field."[34]

And University of Pennsylvania bioethicist Arthur L. Caplan argues that physicians have every right — and perhaps a moral duty — to refuse ART for people who are too old. He was commenting on the 2005 Caesarian-section birth of a daughter to 66-year-old Adriana Iliescu, an unmarried professor in Bucharest, Romania.

Such pregnancies are medically risky, Caplan noted. For instance, in Iliescu's IVF treatments, she initially had a miscarriage, then a stillbirth and, finally, a live child

CHRONOLOGY

1980s-1990s *First U.S. in vitro fertilization (IVF) clinics open, with early success rates around 5 percent. Concerns grow about fate of frozen IVF embryos.*

1981 Elizabeth Jordan Carr is first U.S. IVF baby, the 15th worldwide.

1982 The Sperm Bank of California opens in Berkeley to serve lesbians and single women; the next year it launches first U.S. program allowing donors to release their identities to offspring.

1984 Sweden is first nation to give grown offspring access to sperm donors' identities.

1985 Maryland requires all insurance plans to cover IVF.

1987 Massachusetts and Hawaii require all insurance plans to cover IVF. . . . Texas requires all insurers to offer a plan that covers IVF.

1989 Rhode Island requires all insurance plans to cover IVF. . . . Connecticut requires all insurers except HMOs to offer a plan covering IVF.

1991 Illinois requires all insurance plans to cover IVF.

1992 Congress requires all fertility clinics to report success rates annually.

1993 Richard Paulson, a University of Southern California fertility scientist, demonstrates that women in their 50s can become pregnant with donated eggs. . . . Canada's Royal Commission on New Reproductive Technologies says fertility doctors aren't following professional standards and that stronger laws are needed.

1995 Congress passes Dickey-Wicker amendment, banning government funding of research that may harm a human embryo. Subsequently, it is passed annually in spending bills for the Department of Health and Human Services.

1997 Californian Arceli Keh becomes a first-time mother at 63, after falsely telling IVF doctor Paulson she is in her 50s. . . . Denmark, widely considered a gay-friendly nation, limits government-provided artificial-insemination services to women in relationships with men, effectively shutting out lesbians and single women.

2000s *Fertility treatments become more widely available worldwide.*

2001 American Society for Reproductive Medicine (ASRM) enrages some feminist groups with public-service announcements that list a woman's advancing age as among the top threats to fertility. . . . New Jersey requires all insurance plans to cover IVF.

2003 Norway revises its reproductive-medicine laws, ending anonymity for sperm donors but retaining a ban on egg donation.

2004 Canada bans sale of human eggs and sperm and sex selection of children. . . . ASRM recommends that parents inform IVF children they were born from donated eggs or sperm.

2005 Sperm donors in the United Kingdom must release identifying information to grown offspring. . . . Food and Drug Administration requires sperm banks to test for HIV and other communicable diseases.

2006 Canada establishes Assisted Human Reproduction Agency to regulate reproductive medicine.

2008 An impoverished 27-year-old Egyptian mother of three delivers septuplets after taking inexpensive fertility drugs now available worldwide, including in countries lacking health-care facilities to manage multiple births. . . . Colorado voters reject a referendum to amend the state constitution to consider a human embryo a legal "person."

2009 A 33-year-old California woman, Nadya Suleman, has octuplets after requesting that her doctor implant six frozen embryos created by IVF. . . . Reproductive tourism to Italy, one of the few European countries that don't regulate IVF, is up 75 percent since 2003. . . . England's reproductive-medicine regulatory agency says it will inform donor-conceived children at age 16 whether they're genetically related to a person they plan to be sexually intimate with. . . . Georgia legislature considers but doesn't enact law granting personhood to embryos. . . . California and Missouri legislatures consider legislation to regulate fertility clinics.

Searching the Web for Biological Parents

The era of anonymous egg and sperm donors may be ending.

The 15-year-old American boy had been conceived by his mother using an anonymous sperm donor. But the youth wanted to know the identity of his biological father, and in 2005 he made news and perhaps history by tracking down the donor online.

"This is the first time that I know of it being done," said Bryan Sykes, a geneticist at the University of Oxford in the United Kingdom.[1]

The case raises the question of whether the anonymity long promised to many egg and sperm donors is realistic in the 21st century.

Indeed, as happened over the past few decades with adoption, egg and sperm donation is gradually becoming an open process, analysts say.

"We're moving toward giving donors the opportunity to be contacted or identified," as more donation-organizations offer this option and online donor registries are established, says John A. Robertson, a professor at the University of Texas College of Law at Austin. "As a psychological matter, there's wide agreement that it's good to disclose, but you won't see anything in the United States as draconian as in England, where you can't be anonymous."

The American teenager sent his own DNA to an online genealogy Web site for testing and then was able to contact two men with closely matching DNA who were likely relatives. Using their surnames, plus information his mother had received about the donor's date and place of birth, he paid another online site for a list of everyone born in that place on that day. In less than two weeks, he had made contact with the donor.[2]

The incident reveals the "hunger for . . . connection and an understanding of this invisible part of themselves" that many donor offspring experience, according to Wendy Kramer, a Colorado mother who launched a voluntary Internet registry for donors, donor-conceived children and their families.[3]

"This boy did wonder why it was always assumed that the rights of a donor to remain anonymous trumped a child's right to know his genetic heritage" since he "had not entered into . . . anonymity agreements with anyone," wrote Kramer, who started the Donor Sibling Registry with her donor-conceived son Ryan about nine years ago. "Will every kid who swabs his cheek find his donor? Probably not. But we can expect this to happen with greater frequency as DNA data banks swell."[4]

The move away from anonymity and toward establishing a registry is spurred by more than young people's curiosity, says Jan Elman Stout, a clinical psychologist in Chicago.

born prematurely from a "life-threatening emergency C-section." Furthermore, he pointed out, when the daughter enters high school, Iliescu will be 80, too old to raise a teenager to adulthood.

Caplan said he would refuse ART to single people over 65 or to a couple with one member who is 65 or older, making their total age higher than 130, and to any woman age 55 or older who could not pass "a rigorous physical examination."[35]

But other physicians say that — aside from screening out patients with severe mental disorders — deciding who may have children should not be up to the doctor. "How does that become my responsibility?" says Beltsos, of the Fertility Centers of Illinois. The case of octuplet-mother Suleman is "a tough one, but just because I might think it's inappropriate or irresponsible to have 14 kids,

does that mean I can decide for someone else? Where does the line get drawn?"

As for worrying about the welfare of the child, the Hastings Center's Johnston says that IVF clinics deal with people who fervently want children. "This is not the population where the real child-welfare problem is," she says. "We take wanting a child as kind of placeholder for doing a pretty good job with the child," so she says she probably wouldn't support clinics adding child-welfare considerations to their protocols for accepting ART patients.

In August 2008, the California Supreme Court ruled that denying ART services to a lesbian constitutes unlawful discrimination under a law requiring businesses to guarantee all persons "full and equal accommodations."[36]

In *North Coast Women's Care Medical Group, Inc. v. Superior Court* the court ruled in favor of Guadalupe

As the number of children born from donor sperm has increased, so has the likelihood that children from the same donor might unknowingly fall in love, have sexual relations or marry.

That possibility is particularly strong in smaller nations, which are acting to head off the problem. Beginning this October, for example, teens 16 and older in the United Kingdom who plan to become sexually intimate can contact the government's reproductive-medicine agency to find out whether they are genetically related to their partners.[5]

Statisticians say the United States is below the threshold where there's much chance sperm donors' children will meet and marry, "but I'm not sure the reporting of successful births is reliable enough" to be certain, says Stout. Some U.S. mental-health professionals are championing establishment of a centralized donor registry, but there's pushback both from patients and doctors, who worry that an end to anonymity will mean many fewer men will donate sperm, she says.

Laws in several countries ending donor anonymity are too new to draw firm conclusions.

When two Australian states abolished anonymity, donations fell off drastically. Western Australia, with a population of 1.4 million people, ended up with only 35 available sperm donors. Some Australian clinics offered all-expense-paid tours of their country — complete with free visits to dance clubs and other night spots — to Canadian college students, in return for sperm donations.[6]

But widespread concern that laws abolishing donor anonymity will cut the number of donors permanently may not be justified, according to Ken Daniels, a professor of social work at the University of Canterbury in Christchurch, New Zealand. For the most part, surveys showing that donors are super-leery of being identified have only polled people who had donated before disclosure laws had taken effect and could be expected to be biased against it, he said.[7]

Under new non-anonymity laws, a new and different group of potential donors — possibly older, married people with children — may come forward, inspired by their own parenthood to help others conceive, Daniels predicts. He recounts a conversation with a donor who said that, as a young man, he donated for the money, but "having his own children has made him aware of the child's perspective and the possible need for information."[8]

[1] Quoted in Alison Motluk, "Anonymous Sperm Donor Traced on Internet," *New Scientist online*, Nov. 5, 2005, www.newscientist.com.

[2] *Ibid.*

[3] Wendy Kramer, "DNA and the Exploding Myth of Donor Anonymity," Donor Sibling Registry Web site, www.donorsiblingregistry.com.

[4] *Ibid.*

[5] *The HFEA Register*, Human Fertilisation and Embryology Authority Web site, www.hfea.gov.uk/.

[6] Liza Mundy, *Everything Conceivable* (2007), p. 187.

[7] Ken Daniels, "Donor Gametes: Anonymous or Identified," *Best Practice & Research: Clinical Obstetrics and Gynecology*, February 2007, pp. 113-128.

[8] Quoted in *ibid.*, p. 119.

Benitez, a lesbian in a long-term relationship who sued the facility after two physicians refused to artificially inseminate her and referred her to another clinic. The doctors argued that their rights to religious liberty would be violated if they were required to provide ART to all comers. But the court said the state's civil rights law trumps the religious-liberty claim and requires the clinic to either offer ART to no one or have at least one physician on staff who will provide it to all clients.[37]

An American Society for Reproductive Medicine ethics committee declared in 2006 that, "as a matter of ethics, we believe the ethical duty to treat persons with equal respect requires that fertility programs treat single persons and gay and lesbian couples equally with married couples in determining which services to provide."[38]

BACKGROUND

Stigma and Silence

Throughout history, many childless couples have struggled to have a child to call their own.[39]

The biblical book of *Genesis* describes how Sarah, the infertile wife of Israelite patriarch Abraham, was so distraught over the couple's childlessness that she offered her maid Hagar as a surrogate mother with whom Abraham conceived a child, his son Ishmael.[40]

In England, King Henry VIII married wife after wife, primarily in order to satisfy his desire for a male heir. That 16th-century saga not only demonstrates how fierce the desire for children can be but also how the concept of fertility is intertwined with male virility. "The wives of Henry VIII knew all too well how women tend to be

Sixty Percent of ART Users Are Over 35

About 60 percent of women who turned to assisted reproductive technology (ART) in 2006 were over age 35. Women's fertility begins to drop off around age 24 and declines steeply after 35.

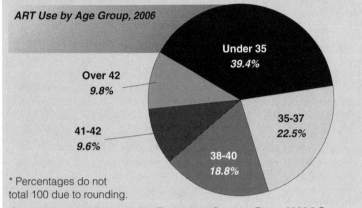

ART Use by Age Group, 2006

- Under 35 **39.4%**
- 35-37 *22.5%*
- 38-40 *18.8%*
- 41-42 **9.6%**
- Over 42 **9.8%**

* Percentages do not total 100 due to rounding.

Source: "Assisted Reproductive Technology Success Rates 2006," Centers for Disease Control and Prevention, 2008

blamed for male-factor [fertility] issues," since several ended up divorced, with their marriages involuntarily annulled or even beheaded in Henry's quest for sons, observed *Everything Conceivable* author Mundy.[41]

Ironically, the "father of our country," U.S. President George Washington, was most likely infertile. But he blamed his wife Martha when he could not father children, "despite the rather glaring evidence of her fertility, provided by four children from a recent prior marriage," wrote Mundy.[42]

Bemoaning his childless state at age 54, Washington wrote that "if Mrs. Washington should survive me, there is a moral certainty of my dying without issue." Furthermore, he wrote, "should I be longest lived, the matter...is hardly less certain for . . . I shall never marry a girl; and it is not probable that I should have children by a woman of an age suitable to my own."[43]

Despite clear evidence of Washington's infertility, it is hardly ever mentioned in historical accounts of his life, said John K. Amory, associate professor of medicine at the University of Washington School of Medicine in Seattle.

The silence probably results from a "frequent erroneous assumption that infertility is mostly female in origin," Amory wrote, and fear that discussion of Washington's infertility "would diminish him in some way," even though

infertility has nothing to do with one's other characteristics and occurs "without regard to [one's] historical stature."[44]

Stigma and silence may also help keep fertility treatment out of the mainstream of American medicine, some analysts say. Unlike most medical specialties, except plastic surgery, fertility medicine is largely provided on a cash-pay basis because it is not covered by insurance.

By definition, "infertility is an illness" — an "impairment of normal biological functioning that causes great distress," says Dartmouth's Green. "Nevertheless, we don't think of it that way because it affects only a few people. I teach an ART course to undergraduates, and they often don't get it, because at their age the big problem for most is keeping their fertility in check. But when you are ready to have a child, it becomes a grave, grave matter." The "mental suffering is as bad as that for cancer."

Nevertheless, it's been difficult to assemble a strong advocacy community around expanding IVF insurance coverage because "there's still a lot of public stigma," says Collura of the National Infertility Association. "We're where breast cancer was 25 years ago."

Breast-cancer and AIDS patients eventually "came out" and forced the public to confront those diseases, but igniting such a movement may be even harder for infertility, she says. "It's such a personal, private thing, so emotionally painful; and because people are private about it, we don't realize the extent of it."

But even with public recognition of how many people infertility affects, some experts doubt the U.S. health-care system — in which more than 45 million people lack coverage entirely — can afford to add more services, especially one as costly as IVF.[45]

ART "can be quite expensive," notes the National Conference on State Legislatures (NCSL). "On average each cycle of IVF costs $8,158 plus an average of $4,000 for medications — and debate exists about whether insurance plans should be required to cover them." Estimates of the monthly cost to mandate IVF coverage range from

Insurance Coverage Affects Fertility Decisions

More people use IVF when insurance covers the procedure.

With more and more patients turning to alternative means of reproduction over the past two decades, 14 states have enacted legislation offering at least some insurance coverage to help people have the families they long for.

Most of these states require all insurers under state regulation to include at least some infertility coverage in all insurance plans they sell, while two states, California and Texas, only require all insurers to "offer" everyone coverage — that is, insurers must offer at least one plan that covers infertility treatments.

While the laws may be similar, the actual coverage provided is anything but. States run the gamut from covering only screening tests to ascertain whether a couple is infertile to full coverage of multiple in vitro fertilization (IVF) treatments. Each state also limits who can access infertility treatment. For example, a state might limit the medical condition of infertility to apply only to a married couple who have tried unsuccessfully for a specified amount of time to conceive. In that state, an unmarried woman would not be eligible for any treatment coverage.

Insurance mandates definitely improve access. In Europe, for example, where IVF often is funded by government-financed health coverage, up to 4 percent of children are born following some kind of fertility procedure, compared to only about 1 percent in the United States.[1]

Increasing access by helping people pay for infertility treatments matters because "the less money you have, the more likely you are to have difficulty conceiving," wrote reporter Liza Mundy, author of the 2007 book Everything Conceivable. "Much infertility has always been caused by infections that can damage reproductive passageways," and "the lower your tax bracket, the less likely you are to have received the fairly simple medical treatment that can stave off these consequences."[2]

Insurance coverage — or the lack of it — "greatly impacts the decisions that doctors and patients make," says Angeline Beltsos, medical director of the Chicago-based Fertility Centers of Illinois. Illinois will pay for four IVF tries for a first baby for an infertile woman, regardless of her age.

In a state without an insurance mandate, a couple with a one-in-five chance of conceiving through IVF is highly likely to look at the average $12,000 price tag for one IVF cycle and simply give up, trying donor eggs, adoption or cheaper drug or surgical interventions instead, Beltsos says. "But here in our state you get a very different approach. Here, people say, 'OK, let's try IVF before we try donor eggs.' " Even some "younger couples who probably could get pregnant without IVF" opt for it because it costs them little.

And few Illinois patients try lower-tech drug or surgical procedures — which also may not work — Beltsos says. "They just go into IVF" instead, and "don't waste years and years with things that may not work very well, ultimately ending up in IVF only when they're so old" that simple, age-related fertility decline may doom IVF to failure, she says.

Once IVF treatment begins, patients in insured states again behave differently, Beltsos says. For example, "no insurance covers the $200 to $1,000 cost of freezing extra embryos," so people with IVF coverage are more likely to say "go ahead and destroy" the extras, she says. "But if you had paid for that cycle, they'd be begging to have the embryos frozen" since doing so "would significantly reduce the cost" of subsequent cycles, she says.

— Additional reporting by Vyomika Jairam

---

[1] Liza Mundy, *Everything Conceivable* (2007), pp. 3-4.

[2] *Ibid.*, p. xiv.

$.20 to $2.00 per insurance-plan member, according to the NCSL.[46]

"Not having these treatments covered is unfortunate, but it is not unfair," because, "in fact, people don't have the [legal] right to any health care in this country except emergency care," said George J. Annas, professor of health law and bioethics at the Boston University School of Public Health. "To mandate [ART coverage], given the growing numbers of uninsured people, makes no legal, economic or health-care sense."[47]

Moreover, notes the NCSL, the use of ART over the years has raised overall health-care costs by contributing to an increase in multiple births, which have a higher rate of prematurity than single births. By 2004, for example, the

AP Photo/Gary Kazanjian

The online Donor Sibling Registry makes a unique family reunion possible in Fresno, Calif., for three mothers and their children. The children were all conceived after their mothers were artificially inseminated by sperm from the same donor and thus are half-siblings. From left: Dawn Warthen and Allyson, Michelle Jorgenson and Cheyenne, and Jenafer Elin and Joshua.

percentage of babies considered to have low birth weight had risen to 8.1 percent, the highest level since the early 1970s, driven largely by ART-caused multiple births.[48]

Advocates of insurance coverage argue that it might eventually lower health-system costs, because there would be fewer high-risk multiple births if parents-to-be could opt for several single-embryo procedures rather than one multiple-embryo implantation. "The rate of triplets in insurance-mandate states is much lower," says Keefe, of the University of South Florida.

"In states where infertility treatments are not paid for, physicians run up expensive tabs for services that aren't needed, like surgery to reconnect scarred fallopian tubes," argues Green. Fertility doctors in those states may also spend too much time trying to diagnose the condition — because the diagnostics are often paid for by insurance — when it would have been cheaper just to try IVF immediately, he adds.

Since the 1980s, 14 states — Arkansas, California, Connecticut, Hawaii, Illinois, Maryland, Massachusetts, Montana, New Jersey, New York, Ohio, Rhode Island, Texas and West Virginia — have required insurers to either cover or offer at least one plan that covers some ART, although not necessarily IVF, according to the NCSL. (*See map, p. 132, and sidebar, p. 145.*)

Two of the states, California and New York, explicitly exclude IVF from the coverage mandate while covering other services such as diagnosis of infertility problems.[49] However, in 2002, New York authorized a demonstration program — still ongoing — to test the effects of IVF coverage by picking up a share of the costs for some patients, with the subsidy prorated by income.[50]

Fertility Industry

Physicians see advantages and disadvantages in fertility medicine's "cash-only" status.

"There are very few fields" in medicine as lucrative, says Jain of the Santa Monica Fertility Specialists.

As a result, when it comes to technical innovation, "I don't think there's a field that's evolved as rapidly as ours in the last 20 years," says Rosenfeld of New York's North Shore-Long Island Jewish Health System. With no public insurers and few private insurers involved, "we don't have any oversight — only our peers — so there's a lot more room for freelancing, for entrepreneurialism," Jain says.

Entrepreneurialism can lead to innovation but can also in many cases "be a euphemism for exploitation," Jain says. For example, "some will overrecommend IVF because it's so lucrative," rather than saving IVF as a last resort and taking patients through less-extreme procedures first, according to Jain.

The CDC keeps a database of fertility-clinic data as an oversight tool, in lieu of stronger policing, but when that information is combined with the highly competitive nature of the business, it can backfire, says Rosenfeld.

"How do people decide which clinic to choose?" he asks. They go online to the database, Rosenfeld says, and find that one clinic, for example, has a 46-percent success rate and another, 48 percent. But they don't realize that a clinic with a higher success rate might accept only patients with a higher probability of conceiving, so the data reporting process provides an incentive for physicians to "do things they might not otherwise do," such as rejecting patients with a low likelihood of conception or using the data as a marketing tool, without including caveats about what it actually means, he says.

The University of South Florida's Keefe headed an American Society for Reproductive Medicine committee on the CDC registry and "wanted to put a "Click to see [patient] inclusion criteria' " button on each clinic's statistics to help patients understand them better, he recalls. "But everybody said, 'That would be too confusing,' " so it didn't happen.

The profit motive extends to egg donation, according to author Mundy. In the early days of IVF, many donors were women who'd finished childbearing and wanted to help others, and "women helping women" was the byword of the then-nonprofit organizations that arranged for donation, she said. Today, most donors are young women in need of cash and, because some donors "are paid a lot" — based on physical and intellectual characteristics, such as an Ivy League diploma — private commercial agencies have gotten more aggressive in procuring eggs, she said.[51]

The profit motive in egg donation may be dangerous both to donors and potential offspring, Tucson, Ariz.-based physician Jennifer Schneider told a congressional briefing in November 2007. Schneider's college-age daughter Jessica donated eggs to supplement her income and, six years later, at age 29, died of colon cancer, a condition that her mother suspects could have been related to the donation process, in which women take fertility drugs to stimulate multiple egg production.[52]

Unfortunately, "I'm here to tell you that hardly anything is known" about an egg-donation-colon-cancer link — also present in several other cases of unusual colon cancers in young women — "because once a young woman walks out of an IVF clinic, she is of no interest to anyone," Schneider told lawmakers.

Egg brokers "make enormous sums" of money and want to maximize the number of eggs they have, giving them "every reason to avoid follow-up of egg donors and studies of their possible long-term risks," she said. When she called Jessica's broker to warn that children born of her eggs should be tested, since the cancer may be genetic, Schneider was told that the records had already been destroyed, and offspring could not be tracked.[53]

Research Stinted

Fertility research has not been funded through the traditional routes, such as the National Institutes of Health (NIH), says fertility specialist Jain. Although the NIH funds most medical research in America, fertility medicine

---

Using Assisted Reproductive Technology
The ART birth cycle from beginning to end

Here are the steps toward pregnancy and live birth using assisted reproductive technology (ART) and fresh, non-donor eggs or embryos:

1. **Cycle starts:** Woman starts taking medication to stimulate the ovaries to develop eggs or, if no drugs are given, the woman begins having her ovaries monitored for natural egg production.

2. **Egg retrieval:** If eggs are produced, a surgical procedure is used to collect them from the ovaries.

3. **Egg and sperm combine:** In vitro fertilization combines egg and sperm in the laboratory. If fertilization is successful, one or more of the resulting embryos are transferred, most often into the uterus through the cervix.

4. **Pregnancy:** If one or more embryos implant within the uterus, the cycle may progress to pregnancy.

5. **Birth:** The pregnancy may progress to the delivery of one or more live-born infants.

---

gets little NIH attention because the field operates largely without public and private insurance and because legislators have religion- and morality-based qualms about research using human embryos.

"IVF has had a 30-year life span," says Jain. "It came out of Ph.Ds who worked in zoos," conducting embryo research on animals. "But there's an absence of NIH funding for the basic science in human embryology. The field has had to sponsor its own studies."

After 30 years of IVF, there have been no multi-center studies — large-scale research coordinated at several clinical sites — the gold standard of medicine, says Dartmouth's Green. In the early 1990s, the National Institute on Child Health and Development (NICHD) tried to get research going, he says, after an advisory panel that he served on recommended increased federal funding.

But in 1995, Congress not only rejected NICHD's pitch but banned federal funding of any "research in which a human embryo or embryos are destroyed, discarded or knowingly subjected to risk of injury or death." Congress has included the ban as a part of annual appropriations legislation ever since then.[54]

While discussions of the ban usually focus on its effect on stem-cell research, it also significantly limits what scientists know about infertility and the early stages of human development. "We know very little about what is a good and what's a bad embryo," says Collura of the National Infertility Association. As a result, one of the top questions for any embryologist is which among a group of embryos are most likely to produce a full-term baby. "But if you have 10 different embryologists in a room, you'll get 10 different answers."

Knowing the answer would help reduce multiple births. "If you want singletons, it's important to know which embryos are the right ones to transfer," she says.

CURRENT SITUATION

Regulating IVF

In the wake of the octuplets' birth, a California legislator introduced a proposal that the state regulate fertility clinics,[55] and the Georgia legislature considered limiting the number of eggs that may be fertilized and embryos implanted during IVF.[56]

In the past year, a spate of state proposals have addressed fertility medicine, many by granting legal "personhood" to embryos, about 500,000 of which now sit frozen in fertility clinics around the country, their ultimate fate undecided since many of the families who created them are now finished with childbearing.[57] No bill has yet gained much traction, however.

The California bill, which would bring fertility clinics under the jurisdiction of the Medical Board of California and set accreditation standards, is one of a handful that would increase government oversight of fertility clinics. Missouri's House Bill 810, for instance, would require doctors to follow American Society for Reproductive Medicine (ASRM) guidelines on embryo implantation or face sanctions.[58]

"The people of this state don't need to be paying millions of dollars for some woman who has eight babies at once," said the bill's sponsor, Republican Missouri state Rep. Bob Schaaf.[59]

ASRM supports Schaaf's proposal. "We are very supportive of the bill," said Sean Tipton, ASRM director of public affairs, "because it defers to medical knowledge and experience and protects both women and unborn children."[60]

Legislative efforts to grant "personhood" to embryos — such as Colorado's proposed constitutional Amendment 48 defeated by voters last November — are heavily criticized by the reproductive-medicine community but win plaudits from right-to-life groups.

After fierce legislative wrangling and numerous language changes, Georgia's Senate-passed personhood bill was not brought to the House floor before the 2009 legislative session ended in March. The Georgia Right to Life group praised the bill for its attempt to limit the number of embryos created.

"The human embryo is one of us, fully human with great potential," and "we do not . . . need to sacrifice human life for money and economic development or the remote possibility of a medical cure for someone else," said Daniel Becker, the group's president.[61]

But ASRM's Tipton said the measure would hurt infertile people by presuming "that politicians know what is best . . . and not physicians."[62]

"Some of the people writing legislation don't understand ART," says Collura of the National Infertility Association. For example, some Georgia lawmakers backed language allowing doctors to fertilize only two eggs per IVF cycle. That's unworkable, she says, because currently IVF is a process in which as many eggs as possible are fertilized in order to improve the chances that some embryos will be viable.

Those who would ban processes like embryo freezing don't realize how many people would be hurt, including cancer patients who can bear children after their ovaries are surgically removed only if their embryos are frozen before the treatment, she says.

Social Changes

Powerful social trends make it likely that usage of advanced assisted reproductive technology will increase.

The delay in childbearing until women are older, for instance, has increased the incidence of infertility. Human biology "is not built for a society where [women] first go to medical school" before bearing children, says Dartmouth's Green, so "we are seeing increasing infertility."

In addition, some large-scale recent studies have suggested — though not proven — that men's sperm counts have been declining for a half-century or so, mainly in industrialized countries. For example, a large 2000 study by Shanna Swan, professor of obstetrics, gynecology and environmental medicine at the University of Rochester's School of Medicine and Dentistry in New York state, suggested that sperm counts were dropping by about

Should egg and sperm donors be paid?

YES
Josephine Johnston
Director of Research Operations
The Hastings Center

Written for *CQ Researcher*, May 2009

Modest payments for gametes are fair, necessary for some kinds of fertility treatment and show respect for the autonomy and dignity of donors. Egg donors should receive more than sperm donors given the invasive and sometimes painful procedures they endure.

Sperm donation isn't as quick or pleasurable as one might assume, but it isn't terribly arduous either. Eggs are another story. Egg donors are medically assessed before beginning the daily routine of mixing and injecting themselves in the stomach or thigh with hormones to suppress and then dramatically increase egg production. They visit the fertility clinic regularly over the month-long process for blood tests and ultrasounds to monitor egg development. They then undergo minor surgery to remove the eggs, followed by a day of bed rest. The hormones and the surgery carry physical risks and often result in discomfort or pain. The drugs can cause emotions to fluctuate, and some anxiety often accompanies the process (how will her body respond to the drugs, what does an unsuccessful attempt imply about her own fertility?).

In the United States, sperm donors are usually paid (not much, but they can donate every five days). Egg donors receive far more, from $2,000 to tens of thousands of dollars. Technically, the money is for time and effort, not the gametes produced. Whether or not you buy that distinction, egg donation in particular can provide significant income.

I share the concern that $10,000 or $50,000 could easily persuade someone to undergo procedures without proper consideration of the risks. But the average egg donor receives just over $4,000 for the weeks she spends in and out of physician's offices, the daily self-administered injections and surgical retrieval of her eggs. Not to mention the discomfort, pain and apprehension. Would you do this for free? Few do.

While money for sperm rarely raises concern, many remain uneasy about paying egg donors. Is it because eggs, even if plentiful, are more difficult to remove and (perhaps) limited in number? If it's the risks, isn't doing it for free just as dangerous? Or does the unease represent an unexamined desire to control women's bodies, particularly their reproductive capacity, and a mistrust of their ability to make medical and reproductive decisions?

This society allows young women to make the same life-changing choices as any other adult. If few will donate their eggs for free, we should trust that they can make an ethical decision to do so for pay.

NO
Scott B. Rae
Professor of Christian Ethics
Talbot School of Theology
Biola University

Written for *CQ Researcher*, May 2009

Paying sperm and egg donors should be discouraged. Egg selling involves often unrecognized health risks to the donor. The egg-harvesting process is highly invasive. Women run a short-term risk of ovarian hyperstimulation syndrome (OHSS). OHSS can cause potentially serious long-term thrombosis, liver and renal problems and respiratory distress — and in rare instances, death. Over time, donors risk future infertility and, potentially, development of cancers related to the synthetic hormones used to hyperstimulate the ovaries. Bear in mind, the egg donor is an otherwise healthy woman, not an infertile "patient" who chooses to assume these risks for the benefit of a baby.

Granted, sperm "donors" are not paid that much, and sperm "donation" does not entail risks to donors, but other concerns still apply.

Paying "donors" may undermine a child's right to know his or her biological parents. Most donors do not want to be identified, and in countries where the law requires identification, not surprisingly, the number of donors has diminished quickly. The Donor Sibling Registry has thousands of children still looking for their other biological parent. And, while they may not find their fathers, they often connect with many (10 or more) half-siblings, with uncertain consequences. One site (donorsibling.com) has traced over 100 children back to a single donor.

An apparent interest in eugenics has moved society toward "designer children," another issue potentially exacerbated by donor payments. One advertisement for an egg donor offered $75,000 if the donor was 5'10" or above, blond, blue-eyed, athletic and scored above 1400 on her SAT exams. In a culture that values diversity, producing designer children risks reinforcing damaging stereotypes.

Another concern comes with new types of families that are being intentionally preplanned. "Single mothers by choice" are increasingly common, yet a growing body of empirical evidence shows the importance of fathers to children's well-being. That is not to say that single-parent families that result from widowhood or divorce can't adequately raise children. But those situations are different from preplanned single-parent families.

Increasing the number of gamete donors by offering payment could also lead to a decrease in traditional adoptions or adoptions of existing embryos. I often suggest adoption of embryos to couples contemplating using donor eggs, because it provides the experience of pregnancy and birth but avoids using a "pro-creative pinch-hitter."

1.5 percent a year in the United States and 3 percent annually in Europe and Australia. Rural areas seemed to have the lower counts, perhaps due to agricultural chemicals.[63]

Increasing the pressure on those hoping to start a family, the number of infants available for adoption in the United States has dropped steadily for decades. Before 1973, for example, nearly 20 percent of never-married, white, pregnant women relinquished the babies to adoption. By the mid-1990s, the percentage had plummeted to 1.7 percent — a "dramatic decline" that shows no signs of a turnaround, according to the Department of Health and Human Services.[64]

During the 1990s, international adoptions by Americans skyrocketed, partly compensating for the declining availability of U.S. infants, but recently some countries have clamped down on such adoptions out of fear of baby selling.[65]

Meanwhile, most people remain unaware of how quickly the average woman's fertility declines after age 30 and how many women and men have other medical issues that decrease fertility.

Celebrity births to women over age 40 and even over 50 — hyped in the media with no mention that virtually all resulted from IVF and, in many cases, donor eggs — contribute to a false public impression, said author Mundy. "A parade of high-profile women . . . have made 40-something motherhood seem almost natural," she wrote, citing actresses Jane Seymour, who had a baby at 44; Susan Sarandon, 46; Geena Davis, twins at 47; Holly Hunter, twins at 47; and the late playwright Wendy Wasserstein, who had a premature daughter at 48.[66]

"They're perpetuating a false impression" that fertility wanes less quickly than it does, says psychologist Stout. "They're also perpetuating a cultural notion that all of this is secret," thus helping maintain the social stigma that surrounds ART, she says. "The more we open up, the better."

OUTLOOK
Health-care Reform

Congress and the Obama administration plan to propose massive health-care reform. If the United States moves to a health-care system with guaranteed coverage for all,

intense debate will surround the question of which services should be covered.

Coverage for a procedure can easily be nixed if enough people say, "I'm a taxpayer and I object to that," since everyone would be subsidizing the system, says Wisconsin's Charo. Although all other industrialized countries have universal health care, and most pay for a very broad range of ART services, including IVF, discussions in the United States would be difficult "because women's sexuality and childbirth resonate so strongly" with many religious groups here, she says.

Some countries, such as Australia, subsidize IVF partly to boost birthrates, a goal the government and much of the public support, says Washington-based health-care consultant Gleason, but even in such situations, payment for ART bumps up against the economic reality that there aren't enough dollars to go around.

Today "we use [services like IVF] only a tenth as much as France and Israel," for example, says Keefe of the University of South Florida. "There's a huge, unmet need."

Universal coverage would lead to more regulation, including holding clinics accountable for following medical guidelines, Keefe says. "You wouldn't give coverage for it just the way it's done now," he says.

Questions would be raised as to "whether you'd cover IVF generally and for what purposes you'd cover PGD," says Baruch at the Genetics & Public Policy Center. Another question, she says: Could people still pay privately for whatever additional services they want or would some procedures be banned altogether?

If universal coverage is provided, "we'll have to get used to drawing lines" regarding coverage, and not just for ART, says Dartmouth's Green. "In Great Britain, for example, nobody over age 65 gets dialysis," he says. When it comes to IVF, government might well say, "We won't pay after you've already had two children."

Whether universal coverage would help or hurt ART "would depend on how they restricted care," says Rosenfeld at the North Shore-Long Island Jewish Health System. "If they started restricting it like they do in Europe" — where some countries outlaw implantation of more than one or two embryos, for example — "it would be a problem."

Oregon and Massachusetts have both experimented with universal coverage — Oregon in the 1990s and Massachusetts currently — and ART fared differently in each of those states, Rosenfeld notes. In Massachusetts, a state law mandates IVF coverage, but when Oregon deliberated over which services to cut, given budget constraints, reproductive medicine "fell below the line and wasn't paid for," offering a sobering example of how universal coverage mandates can cut both ways, he says.

NOTES

1. "Medical Society Probes Octuplets' Conception," The Associated Press, MSNBC.com, Feb. 10, 2009, www.msnbc.msn.com/id/29123731.

2. Liza Mundy, *Everything Conceivable* (2007), p. 217.

3. For background, see "Three Million Babies Born Using Assisted Reproductive Technologies," *Medical News Today*, June 25, 2006, www.medicalnewstoday.com.

4. See Marcy Darnovsky, *Biopolitical Times blog*, Center for Genetics and Society, Feb. 27, 2009, www .biopoliticaltimes.org/article.php?id=4550.

5. See " 'One Egg' IVF Strategy Launched," BBC News, June 26, 2008, www.news.bbc.co.uk/2/hi/health/ 7475392.stm. Also see Mundy, *op. cit.*, p. 214.

6. Marcy Darnovsky, "Voluntary Isn't Working," *Modern Healthcare*, April 13, 2009, www.modern healthcare.com/apps/pbcs.dll/article?Date= 20090413&Category=SUB&ArtNo=304139998& SectionCat=&Template=printpicart.

7. Franco Furger and Francis Fukuyama, "A Proposal for Modernizing the Regulation of Human Biotechnologies," *Hastings Center Report*, July/August 2007, pp. 16-20.

8. "Consumers Desire More Genetic Testing, But not Designer Babies," *ScienceDaily*, Jan. 26, 2009, www .sciencedaily.com/releases/2009/01/090126100642.htm.

9. Maili Malin, "Good, Bad and Troublesome: Infertility Physicians' Perceptions of Women Patients," *European Journal of Women's Studies*, August 2003, pp. 301-319.

10. For background, see Brian Hansen, "Cloning Debate," *CQ Researcher*, Oct. 22, 2004, pp. 877-900.

11. *Buzzanca v. Buzzanca*, Cal. App. 4th 1410 (1998), quoted in Linda S. Maule and Karen Schmid, "Assisted Reproduction and the Courts: The Case of California," *Journal of Family Issues*, April 1, 2006, pp. 464-482.

12. Naomi Cahn, Necessary Subjects: The Need for a Mandatory National Donor Gamete Registry, April 2008, *DePaul Journal of Healthcare Law*, http://papers .ssrn.com/sol3/papers.cfm?abstract_id=1120389.

13. Audrey Huang and Susannah Baruch, "Oversight of PGD," issue brief, Genetics & Public Policy Center, July 2007, www.dnapolicy.org/policy.issue.php? action=detail&issuebrief_id=8.

14. John A. Robertson, "The Virtues of Muddling Through," *Hastings Center Report*, July/August 2007, pp. 26-28.

15. *Ibid.*

16. For background, see David Masci, "Designer Humans," *CQ Researcher*, May 18, 2001, pp. 425-440.

17. Transcript, discussion of staff working paper, "Ethical Aspects of Sex Control," President's Council on Bioethics, Jan. 16, 2003, http://bioethicsprint .bioethics.gov/transcripts/jan03/session4.html.

18. Quoted in "Reproductive Genetic Testing: Issues and Options for Policymakers," Genetics & Public Policy Center, 2004.

19. "Preimplantation Genetic Diagnosis: A Discussion of Challenges, Concerns, and Preliminary Policy Options Related to the Genetic Testing of Human Embryos," Genetics & Public Policy Center, January 2004, www.dnapolicy.org/pub.reports.php?action= detail&report_id=8.

20. *Ibid.*, p. 7.

21. For background, see Scott Baldauf, "India's 'Girl Deficit' Deepest Among Educated," *The Christian Science Monitor*, Jan. 13, 2006, www.csmonitor .com/2006/0113/p01s04-wosc.html, and "Female Deficit in Asia," conference proceedings, Committee for International Cooperation in National Research in Demography, December 2005, www.cicred.org/Eng/ Seminars/Details/Seminars/FDA/FDdraftpapers.htm.

22. Mike Swift, "It's a Boy! Asian Immigrants Use Medical Technology to Satisfy Age-old Desire: A Son," *San Jose* [California] *Mercury News*, Jan. 7, 2009.

23. *Ibid.*

24. Deborah L. Spar, *The Baby Business: How Money, Science, and Politics Drive the Commerce of Conception* (2006), p. 99.

25. For background, see Gautam Naik, "A Baby, Please. Blond, Freckles — Hold the Colic," *The Wall Street Journal*, Feb. 12, 2009, p. A10.

26. Marilyn E. Coors, "Genetic Enhancement: Custom Kids and Chimeras," United States Conference of Catholic Bishops, Secretariat for Pro-Life Activities, www.usccb .org/prolife/programs/rlp/coors05finaleng.pdf.

27. Toby L. Schonfeld, "Smart Men, Beautiful Women: Social Values and Gamete Commodification," *Bulletin of Science, Technology and Society*, June 2003, p. 168.

28. Quoted in Ronald M. Green, *Babies by Design* (2007), p. 45.

29. Allen Goldberg, *Dear Henry blog*, March 8, 2009, http://henrystrongingoldberg.blogspot.com.

30. "The Limits of Conscientious Refusal in Reproductive Medicine," American College of Obstetrics and Gynecology, Committee on Ethics, November 2007.

31. Julien S. Murphy, "Should Lesbians Count as Infertile Couples? Antilesbian Discrimination in Assisted Reproduction," in Anne Donchin and Laura Martha Purdy, eds., *Embodying Bioethics* (1999), p. 107.

32. Mundy, *op. cit.*, p. 202.

33. Quoted in Ingrid Lüttichau, " 'We Are Family': The Regulation of 'Female-Only' Reproduction," *Social and Legal Studies*, March 2004, pp. 81-101.

34. Quoted in Mundy, *op. cit.*, p. 160.

35. Arthur L. Caplan, "How Old Is Too Old to Have a Baby?" *The American Journal of Bioethics*, Bioethics. net, Jan. 24, 2005, www.bioethics.net.

36. For background, see Joanna Grossman, "The California Supreme Court Rules that Fertility Doctors Must Make Their Services Available to Lesbians, Despite Religious Objections," *FindLaw. com*, Sept. 2, 2008, http://writ.lp.findlaw.com.

37. *Ibid.*

38. "Access to Fertility Treatment by Gays, Lesbians, and Unmarried Persons," Ethics Committee of the American Society for Reproductive Medicine, Fertility and Sterility, November 2006, p. 1333.

39. For background, see Susan C. Phillips, "Reproductive Ethics," *CQ Researcher*, April 8, 1994, pp. 289-312; see also Mundy, *op. cit.*

40. *Genesis*, ch. 16.

41. Mundy, *op. cit.*, p. 72.

42. *Ibid.*

43. Quoted in John K. Amory, "George Washington's Infertility: Why Was the Father of Our Country Never a Father," *Fertility and Sterility*, March 2004, pp. 495-499.

44. *Ibid.*

45. For background, see Marcia Clemmitt, "Rising Health Costs," *CQ Researcher*, April 7, 2006, pp. 289-312; Marcia Clemmitt, "Universal Coverage," *CQ Researcher*, March 30, 2007, pp. 265-288.

46. "State Laws Related to Insurance Coverage for Infertility Treatment," National Conference of State Legislatures, www.ncsl.org/programs/health/50infert .htm.

47. Quoted in Esther B. Fein, "Calling Infertility a Disease, Couples Battle With Insurers," *The New York Times*, Feb. 22, 1998, www.nytimes.com/specials/ women/warchive/980222_2181.html.

48. "State Laws Related to Insurance Coverage for Infertility Treatment," *op. cit.*

49. *Ibid.*

50. "NYS Infertility Demonstration Program," New York State Department of Health, www.health.state .ny.us/community/reproductive_health/infertility.

51. Mundy, *op. cit.*, p. 59.

52. Jennifer Schneider, "It's Time for an Egg-Donor Registry and Long-term Follow-up," Nov. 14, 2007, www.geneticsandsociety.org.

53. *Ibid.*

54. For background, see Adriel Bettelheim, "Embryo Research," *CQ Researcher*, Dec. 17, 1999, pp. 1065-1088; Marcia Clemmitt, "Stem Cell Research," *CQ Researcher*, Sept. 1, 2006, pp. 697-720.

55. For background, Malcolm Maclachlan, " 'Octomom' Inspires Bill to Regulate Fertility Clinics," *Capitol Weekly*, March 5, 2009, www.capitolweekly.net/ article.php?xid=xt1wfvpujdxifs.

56. For background, see Betsy McKay, "In-Vitro Fertilization Limit Is Sought," *The Wall Street Journal online*, March 3, 2009, http://online.wsj.com/ article/SB123603828823714509.html.

57. For background, see Liza Mundy, "Souls on Ice: America's Embryo Glut and the Wasted Promise of Stem-Cell Research," *Mother Jones*, July/August 2006, p. 39, www.motherjones.com/politics/2006/07/souls-ice-americas-embryo-glut-and-wasted-promise-stem-cell-research.

58. For background, see Michael Bushnell, "Missouri House Bill Seeks Limits on Embryo Implants," *Columbia Missourian*, March 5, 2009, www.columbiamissourian.com.

59. *Ibid.*

60. *Ibid.*

61. "Georgia Takes Action: SB 169 to Protect Human Embryos," press release, Georgia Right to Life, Christian NewsWire, March 9, 2009, www.christiannewswire.com/index.php?module=releases&task=view&releaseID=9682.

62. Quoted in Bushnell, *op. cit.*

63. Mundy, *Everything Conceivable, op. cit.*, p. 69.

64. "Voluntary Relinquishment for Adoption," Child Welfare Information Gateway, 2005, www.childwelfare.gov/pubs/s_place.cfm.

65. "International Adoption Facts," Adoption Institute, www.adoptioninstitute.org/FactOverview/international.html.

66. Mundy, *Everything Conceivable, op. cit.*, p. 54.

BIBLIOGRAPHY

Books

Green, Ronald M., *Babies by Design,* **Yale University Press, 2007.**
A Dartmouth University ethicist lays out probable scenarios for the choices genetic technology will soon lay before parents and argues that such "directed human evolution" can operate for humanity's good.

Knowles, Lori P., and Gregory E. Kaebnick, eds., *Reprogenetics: Law, Policy, and Ethics,* **The Johns Hopkins University Press, 2007.**
Bioethicists from Canada's University of Alberta (Knowles) and the Hastings Center in New York assemble essays discussing international regulatory schemes for assisted reproductive technology (ART) and related issues.

Mundy, Liza, *Everything Conceivable: How the Science of Assisted Reproduction Is Changing Men, Women, and the World,* **Anchor, 2008.**
A science writer reports on the rapidly changing landscape of assisted reproduction, based on interviews with parents, gamete donors, doctors and scientists.

Spar, Debora L., *The Baby Business: How Money, Science, and Politics Drive the Commerce of Conception,* **Harvard Business School Press, 2006.**
A professor of business at Harvard describes the commercial workings of reproductive medicine and adoption in the United States, including gamete donation and fertility clinics, and discusses possibilities for regulating the field.

Articles

Al-Shalchi, Hadeel, "Egypt Septuplets Stir Debate on Fertility Drugs," *The Associated Press,* **Aug. 26, 2008, www.msnbc.msn.com/id/26408452.**
Cheap, unpredictable fertility drugs pose dilemmas in developing countries.

Hopkins, Jim, "Egg-Donor Business Booms on Campuses," *USA Today,* **March 15, 2006, p. A1.**
College women are the most sought-after donors in the growing market for human eggs.

Naik, Gautam, "A Baby, Please. Blond, Freckles — Hold the Colic," *The Wall Street Journal,* **Feb. 12, 2009, p. A10.**
Preimplantation genetic diagnosis (PGD) — the technique of testing three-day-old in vitro fertilization (IVF) embryos for genetic characteristics — is increasingly used for choosing children's traits, not just to screen for serious genetic diseases, as in the past.

Roan, Shari, "On the Cusp of Life, and of Law," *Los Angeles Times,* **Oct. 6, 2008.**
Some 500,000 embryos are preserved in freezers in the U.S., some destined for further IVF cycles but many belonging to mothers who've finished with childbearing and now struggle to decide whether to discard the leftover embryos.

Reports and Studies

"2006 Assisted Reproductive Technology Success Rates," *National Summary and Fertility Clinic Reports, Centers for Disease Control and Prevention/*

American Society for Reproductive Medicine, November 2008, www.cdc.gov/ART/ART2006.
The report analyzes practices and outcomes in U.S. fertility medicine in 2006, based on mandatory reporting by fertility clinics nationwide.

The Hastings Center Report, July-August 2007, Hastings Center, July 2007, Vol. 37, No. 4, www.thehastingscenter.org/Publications/HCR/Default.aspx?id=752.
Scholars discuss the potential for regulating ART from various legal and ethical perspectives.

"Old Lessons for a New World; Applying Adoption Research and Experience to Assisted Reproductive Technology," *Evan B. Donaldson Adoption Institute*, February 2009, www.adoptioninstitute.org.
A nonprofit advocacy group for improved adoption practices argues that reproductive medicine would benefit from adopting state regulation and establishing a national database of adoptees' records.

"Reproductive Genetic Testing: Issues and Options for Policymakers," *Genetics & Public Policy Center*, 2004, www.dnapolicy.org/images/reportpdfs/ReproGenTestIssuesOptions.pdf.
A nonprofit think tank lays out the pros and cons for policy questions, such as, Should governments ban or establish strict rules for reproductive genetic testing, and Should doctors increase the amount of genetic counseling they provide to prospective parents?

"Reproductive Genetic Testing: What America Thinks," *Genetics & Public Policy Center*, 2004, www.dnapolicy.org/images/reportpdfs/ReproGenTestAmericaThinks.pdf.
Americans are divided over the morality of genetic testing of embryos, but many agree that it's probably acceptable to use the technology to avoid giving birth to a child with a life-threatening childhood illness or to try to conceive a child who could donate tissue to a sick sibling.

For More Information

American Society for Reproductive Medicine, 1209 Montgomery Highway, Birmingham, AL 35216-2809; (205) 978-5000; www.asrm.org/. Publishes information on infertility medicine and legal and legislative developments related to assisted reproduction.

The Center for Bioethics and Human Dignity, Trinity International University, 2065 Half Day Road, Deerfield, IL 60015; (847) 317-8180; www.cbhd.org. Explores Christian viewpoints on assisted reproduction and other bioethics issues.

Center for Genetics and Society, 436 14th St., Suite 700, Oakland, CA 94612; (510) 625-0819; www.geneticsandsociety.org. Promotes responsible oversight of genetic technologies.

Centers for Disease Control and Prevention, Assisted Reproductive Technology, 1600 Clifton Rd., Atlanta, GA 30333; (404) 639-3311; www.cdc.gov/ART. Federal agency that provides information and data on assisted reproduction, including success rates for U.S. clinics.

Donor Sibling Registry, P.O. Box 1571, Nederland, CO 80466; www.donorsiblingregistry.com. Provides information on donor-gamete issues and a forum for donor-conceived children to locate genetic relatives.

Genetics & Public Policy Center, 1717 Massachusetts Ave., N.W., Suite 530, Washington, DC 20036; (202) 663-5971; www.dnapolicy.org. Research center connected to Johns Hopkins University that analyzes and proposes public policy on genetic technologies.

The Hastings Center, 21 Malcolm Gordon Rd., Garrison, NY 10524; (845) 424-4040; www.thehastingscenter.org. Researches and provides information on bioethics issues from various ethical perspectives.

Human Fertilisation and Embryology Authority, 21 Bloomsbury St., London, UK, WC1B 3HF; 020 7291 8200; www.hfea.gov.uk. The United Kingdom's oversight agency for assisted reproduction; sets standards of practice and provides information on assisted reproduction.

RESOLVE: The National Infertility Association, 1760 Old Meadow Rd., Suite 500, McLean, VA 22102; (703) 556-7172; www.resolve.org. Advocates for improved access to infertility services and provides support for patients.

7

Domestic Poverty

Is A New Approach Needed to Help the Poorest Americans?

Thomas J. Billitteri

AP Photo/Lynne Sladky

Hispanic day laborers negotiate with a potential employer in Homestead, Fla. As low-skilled immigrants, many living below the poverty line, move to the South and Midwest to work in meatpacking and other industries, debate intensifies over immigration's impact on native-born Americans at the bottom of the income scale. Newly released Census data for 2006 show that 36.5 million Americans — including nearly 13 million children — lived below the federal poverty line of $20,614 in income for a family of four.

From *CQ Researcher*,
September 7, 2007.

Marilyn Bezear, a 52-year-old single parent in Harlem who lost her husband to cancer, was living in run-down public housing and working two jobs last winter, cleaning offices and doing clerical work for a temp agency.

"Together, after taxes, I bring home up to $300 a week," she told a congressional panel in February. "With this I pay my rent, food, telephone and payments for the loan that I took out for my daughter to go to college." When the temp agency has no work, Bezear scrambles for ways to meet expenses, like working the late shift at a bowling alley and "getting home at 4:30 in the morning."

Bezear added: "I am just one of many who live through these struggles. . . . Wages, education, training and health care are a necessity. I hope my testimony did not fall on deaf ears."[1]

It's a hope that many of America's poorest citizens would no doubt echo. Despite a relatively stable economy, an overhaul of the welfare system a decade ago and billions spent on programs for the needy, poverty remains pervasive and intractable across the nation.

Conservatives say solutions must emphasize personal responsibility, higher marriage rates and fewer out-of-wedlock births, while liberals blame the negative effects of budget cuts for anti-poverty programs, tax cuts benefiting the wealthy and the need for more early-childhood-development programs. The Democratic Congress has made poverty a priority issue. And a number of presidential candidates are focusing either squarely on poverty or more generally on ideas to narrow the growing gap between the rich and poor.

Newly released Census data for 2006 show that 36.5 million Americans — about one in eight — lived below the federal poverty line of $20,614 in income for a family of four. More than a

South Is Most Impoverished Region

Almost all the Southern states have poverty levels exceeding the national average of 12.3 percent of residents living in poverty. Mississippi leads the nation with a poverty rate of 20.6 percent. New Hampshire has the lowest rate, 5.4 percent.

Percentage of People in Poverty by State, 2006

Legend:
- Less than 10%
- 10.0-12.2%
- 12.3-14.9%
- 15.0% and over

U.S. Total: 12.3%

Source: "Historical Poverty Tables," U.S. Census Bureau, 2007

- The gap between rich and poor is growing. In 2005, the average income of the top 1 percent of U.S. households rose $102,000 (adjusted for inflation), but the bottom 90 percent saw incomes rise $250, according to economists Thomas Piketty and Emmanuel Saez.[6] And the top 1 percent got the biggest share of national income since 1928.[7]

- The chance an average American family will see its income plummet at least 50 percent is roughly two-and-a-half times that of the 1970s.[8]

- At some time, most Americans will live at least one year below the poverty line, according to sociologists Mark R. Rank and Thomas A. Hirschl.[9]

Such trends have helped push poverty and broader issues of inequality and economic insecurity onto the

third of them are children, and 3.4 million are 65 and older. And while the nation's poverty rate declined for the first time this decade, from 12.6 percent in 2005 to 12.3 percent last year, the number of children without health insurance rose to 11.7 percent in 2006.[2]

Indeed, among "rich" nations, the United States ranked second — behind Mexico — in poverty at the turn of the 21st century.[3]

"An astonishing number of people are working as hard as they possibly can but are still in poverty or have incomes that are not much above the poverty line," said Peter Edelman, a law professor at Georgetown University who was co-chairman of a poverty task force this year for the Center for American Progress, a Washington think tank.[4]

A number of indicators underscore the depth and breadth of American poverty:

- Those in "deep," or severe, poverty, with incomes of half or less of the official poverty threshold, number over 15 million — more than the populations of New York City, Los Angeles and Chicago combined. Severe poverty hit a 32-year high in 2005, according to McClatchy Newspapers.[5]

national stage in ways not seen for decades. Two years ago, televised images of squalor in post-Katrina New Orleans refocused the nation's attention — at least temporarily — on poverty. More recently, the subprime mortgage debacle, higher gas prices and spiraling medical costs have edged millions of middle-class Americans closer to economic ruin. Meanwhile, Main Street angst is growing over globalization, which has contributed to the elimination of one-sixth of U.S. factory jobs in the past six years.[10]

Jacob S. Hacker, a political scientist at Yale University and author of the 2006 book *The Great Risk Shift: The Assault on American Jobs, Families, Health Care, and Retirement — And How You Can Fight Back*, says poverty is on the nation's radar for reasons that go beyond high-profile events like Katrina.

"Poverty is something the middle class cares about when it looks down and sees itself poised on the financial precipice," he says. The middle class is looking up, too, at those in the top income strata, and "there's a lot more discussion about [income] inequality." And finally, many middle-class Americans "have a deep concern about the fact that we're such a rich nation, and yet children and hardworking adults who moved into the labor market after welfare reform are struggling to get by."

While politicians in both major parties have spoken to concerns about middle-class vulnerability, Democrats have been focusing squarely on poverty and inequality, blending appeals for middle-class protections with rhetoric reminiscent of the 1960s "War on Poverty."

Since assuming control of Congress in January, Democrats have held several hearings on poverty, hunger and economic threats to the needy. Rep. Charles B. Rangel, D-N.Y., chairman of the powerful House Ways and Means Committee, declared this spring that "with the exception of getting the hell out of the Middle East, I can't think of anything more patriotic that we can do than eliminate poverty."[11]

In the 2008 presidential race, Sen. Hillary Clinton, D-N.Y., has accused the Bush administration of making the middle class and working families into "invisible Americans,"[12] while Sen. Barack Obama, D-Ill., alluding to his work as a community organizer in Chicago, has said poverty "is the cause that led me to a life of public service."[13] Former Sen. John Edwards, D-N.C., has staked his campaign on the poverty issue, calling it "the great moral issue of our time."[14]

Among other contenders, Mayor Michael Bloomberg of New York — who dropped his affiliation with the Republican Party in June — has been among the most outspoken on poverty. On Aug. 28, the billionaire founder of Bloomberg News, who is thought to be considering a third-party presidential bid, proposed a sharp expansion in the Earned Income Tax Credit (EITC), which provides tax relief to the working poor, and called on politicians of both parties to move beyond ideology to overcome poverty. Bloomberg proposed roughly doubling the number of Americans eligible to benefit from the EITC to 19.7 million people.[15]

"We are beginning to hear a chorus of voices urging action on poverty," Rep. Jim McDermott, D-Wash., chairman of the House Ways and Means Subcommittee on Income Security and Family Support, said in April.[16]

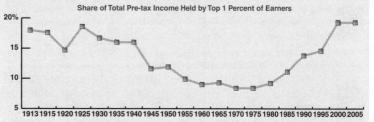

Gap Between Rich and Poor Widened

The top 1 percent of income households earned about 20 percent of the nation's total income in 2005, its highest share since 1929. From 2004 to 2005, the average income of such earners increased by $102,000, after adjusting for inflation. By contrast, the average income of the bottom 90 percent rose by $250.

Share of Total Pre-tax Income Held by Top 1 Percent of Earners

Source: Thomas Picketty and Emmanuel Saez, based on IRS data; in Aviva Aron-Dine, "New Data Show Income Concentration Jumped Again in 2005: Income Share of Top 1% Returned to Its 2000 Level, the Highest Since 1929," Center on Budget and Policy Priorities, March 29, 2007

Edelman, at the Center for American Progress, echoed the point. "There's a rising concern in the country about inequality," he said. "There's concern about giveaways to the really wealthy, and there's concern about economic insecurity. The poverty issue is embedded in that."[17]

Nevertheless, it remains unclear how far voters will go in supporting new programs for the poor. A mere 1 percent of respondents to a Gallup Poll in June ranked the "gap between rich and poor" as the most important economic problem, and only 5 percent named "poverty, hunger and homelessness" as the most important "noneconomic" problem.[18]

Likewise, Edwards has trailed his rivals for the Democratic nomination and even failed to capture much support from voters who are struggling financially. In a survey of independent voters, 40 percent of respondents in households earning less than $20,000 said they would not vote for Edwards if he were the Democratic nominee.[19]

The public's fickle interest in the poor has been evident in the two years following Hurricane Katrina, which produced some of the starkest and most widely disseminated images of urban poverty in American history.

"After Katrina, with its vivid images, a lot of people who have been working in the area of poverty reduction were excited. They said, 'now we have some visible images, now people will get excited, and we can push this anti-poverty platform,'" says Elsie L. Scott, president of the Congressional Black Caucus Foundation. "That lasted a month maybe, that excitement. Now

Democratic Candidates' Stands on Poverty

 Joseph Biden voted for the Fair Minimum Wage Act of 2007, which raised the minimum wage from $5.15 an hour to $7.25 an hour. Biden broke with his party to vote in favor of the Bankruptcy Abuse Prevention and Consumer Protection Act of 2005, which makes it harder for people to erase debt by declaring bankruptcy.

 Hillary Clinton accuses the Bush administration of turning the middle class into "invisible Americans," and says if she is elected president, "they will no longer be invisible." In 2002, Clinton was criticized by liberal groups for supporting an increase in the work requirement for welfare; she said that she supported the measure because it was tied to $8 billion in funding of day care for welfare recipients. She advocated for welfare reform under her husband's administration. As a senator, Clinton voted for an increase in the federal minimum wage.

 Christopher Dodd says that one of his policy priorities influenced by Catholic social teachings and the emphasis on the common good is "creating safety nets for the disadvantaged." As a senator, one of Dodd's priorities has been helping children, and he has authored numerous child care bills. Dodd has favored increases in the federal minimum wage.

 John Edwards has made reducing poverty the signature issue of his campaign, calling it "the great moral issue of our time." He has set a goal of ending poverty in 30 years by lifting one-third of the 37 million currently impoverished Americans above the poverty line each decade through a higher minimum wage, tax cuts for low-income workers, universal health care and housing vouchers for poor families.

 Mike Gravel says America's war on drugs must end because it "does nothing but savage our inner cities and put our children at risk." Gravel proposes to help end poverty by creating a progressive tax system in which consumers of new products would be taxed at a flat rate. This would encourage Americans to save, Gravel says. This proposed system would replace the income tax and Internal Revenue Service.

 Dennis Kucinich advocates ending the war in Iraq and using the money saved to fight domestic poverty, calling homelessness, joblessness and poverty "weapons of mass destruction." In July 2007, Kucinich said that he was in favor of reparations for slavery, saying, "The Bible says we shall and must be repairers of the breach. And a breach has occurred. . . . It's a breach that has resulted in inequality in opportunities for education, for health care, for housing, for employment."

 Barack Obama In the Illinois Senate, Obama helped author the state's earned income tax credit, which provided tax cuts for low-income families. Obama has supported bills to increase the minimum wage. In *The Audacity of Hope*, Obama describes what he calls America's "empathy deficit," writing that a "stronger sense of empathy would tilt the balance of our current politics in favor of those people who are struggling in this society."

 Bill Richardson As governor of New Mexico, Richardson took steps to combat poverty in the state, one of the nation's poorest. He eliminated the tax on food and offered tax breaks to companies paying above the prevailing wage. Richardson has backed a living wage in the state and created tax credits for the creation of new jobs.

Source: This information first appeared on www.pewforum.org. Reprinted with permission from the Pew Forum on Religion & Public Life and Pew Research Center.

that people in New Orleans have been dispersed around the country, people want to forget about it. They don't want to admit we have this kind of poverty in the United States."

Policy experts say it would be unfortunate if Middle America fails to recognize how much poverty undermines the nation's overall well-being. Childhood poverty alone saps the United States of $500 billion per year in crime and health costs and reduced productivity, according to Harry J. Holzer, a professor of public policy at Georgetown University.[20]

Rising poverty should be a concern even among those who don't see a moral obligation to aid the poor, experts warn. "The global competitiveness of the U.S. economy suffers if workers are too poor to obtain an education and modern job skills, the government loses tax revenue and spends more on public assistance because of poverty, and communities fall victim to urban decay, crime, and unrest," notes a recent study on severe poverty in the *American Journal of Preventive Medicine*.[21]

Yet, the American public has always had a tendency to blame the poor for their ills, some poverty experts lament. "There is a common perception that the problem with the poor folks in the United States is a problem with values," said Dalton Conley, chairman of the Department of Sociology at New York University. "It's not a values deficit at all; it's really a resource deficit."[22]

And that deficit can be steep. "Most Americans would be shocked to know that full-time male workers, at the median, earned no more in 2005 than they did in 1973" after taking inflation into account, says Sheldon H Danziger, a professor of public policy at the University of Michigan. And that wage stagnation came amid a boom in productivity in the 1990s, he adds.

"There's a tendency for people to blame the poor for their own circumstances," Danziger says. "And I don't think anybody would blame full-time male workers."

As Congress, policy experts and presidential candidates consider what to do about poverty, here are some of the questions they are asking:

Is extreme poverty growing?

In Savannah, Ga., not far from the lush parks and antebellum mansions of the city's fabled historic district, poverty runs wide and deep.

More than one-fifth of Savannah's residents live below the federal poverty line, and that's not the worst of it.* "We have six census tracts with over a 50-percent poverty rate," says Daniel Dodd, who directs a project that enlists Savannah's business community in helping the poor.

Savannah is hardly unique. At least one neighborhood of "concentrated" poverty — often defined as a place where at least 40 percent of residents live below the poverty line — exists in 46 of the nation's 50 biggest cities, according to Alan Berube, a fellow in the Metropolitan Policy Program of the Brookings Institution, a think tank in Washington.[23]

McClatchy Newspapers concluded this year that 43 percent of the nation's 37 million poor people live in severe poverty — sometimes called "extreme" or "deep" poverty. Severe poverty reflects those with incomes of less than half the federal poverty threshold — in other words, under $9,903 for a family of four and $5,080 for an individual in 2005.

Republican Candidates' Stands on Poverty

 Sam Brownback voted for the 1996 welfare reform bill that required more work for recipients and placed limits on the amount of time they could receive benefits. He says poverty can best be addressed by encouraging people to get married, get a job and not have children out of wedlock. He has promoted a "marriage development account program" to help married couples get training, buy a car, get an education or purchase a house. Brownback has voted against increasing the minimum wage.

 Rudolph Giuliani advocates requiring welfare recipients to work or engage in job training to receive benefits. New York City's welfare rolls were cut by more than half while Giuliani was mayor, and he touts his overhaul of the city's welfare system as one of his major successes. During his 2000 senate campaign, Giuliani indicated that he would support an increase in the minimum wage if studies showed it would not reduce the number of available jobs.

 Mike Huckabee says one of his priorities is to address poverty because it's "consistent with me being pro-life." He calls his desire to fight poverty a "faith position" rather than a political position. He says it is impossible to address poverty without "prioritizing stable homes and families."

 Duncan Hunter says tax cuts are the best tool for reducing poverty because they enable the poor to save and support their families. He advocates what he calls a "Fair Tax," which would replace the national income tax with a national retail sales tax. As part of his anti-poverty agenda, he supports tariffs on Chinese imports to help preserve American manufacturing jobs.

 John McCain voted for a 1996 welfare reform bill that required more work for recipients and placed limits on the amount of time they could receive benefits. Although McCain voted for a bill to increase the federal minimum wage in February 2007, he has historically voted against minimum wage increases, arguing that they can hurt small businesses.

 Ron Paul In May 2007, Paul asserted that "subsidies and welfare" only provide poor people with "crumbs," while "the military-industrial complex and the big banks" receive "the real big welfare," further impoverishing the middle class and the poor. Paul opposes foreign aid, writing that "the redistribution of wealth from rich to poor nations has done little or nothing to alleviate suffering abroad."

 W. Mitt Romney As Massachusetts governor, Romney proposed a plan requiring more people to work in order to receive state welfare benefits, bringing Massachusetts policy in line with federal welfare reforms. He supports increasing the minimum wage to match inflation but vetoed a bill to raise it in Massachusetts, saying it called for increases that were too extreme and too abrupt.

 Tom Tancredo The Colorado Congressman advocates moving from an income-based tax to a consumption-based tax, which he says would create an "explosion of job opportunities and economic growth" that would benefit all sectors of society, particularly the poor. He also supports repealing the 16th Amendment and establishing a flat, national sales tax to alleviate the burden on American companies and "put billions back into the economy."

 Fred Thompson In May the actor and former U.S. senator criticized programs that would "redistribute the income among our citizens" as "defeatist." A policy of lowering taxes, he said, would stimulate economic growth and "make the pie bigger." In 1999 he voted against an increase in the minimum wage. He also voted to reduce taxes on married couples in 2000. He has yet to officially declare his candidacy.

Source: This information first appeared on www.pewforum.org. Reprinted with permission from the Pew Forum on Religion & Public Life and Pew Research Center.

---

* Many people who study domestic poverty criticize the way the government measures poverty, arguing the standard federal poverty index does not accurately count the poor. Presidential candidate John Edwards is among those who call for reform of the poverty measure. His Web site states that it "excludes necessities like taxes, health care, child care and transportation" and "fails to count some forms of aid including tax credits, food stamps, Medicaid and subsidized housing. The National Academy of Sciences has recommended improvements that would increase the count of people in poverty by more than 1 million." See also, for example, Reid Cramer, "The Misleading Way We Count the Poor: Alternatives to Our Antiquated Poverty Measure Should Consider Assets," New America Foundation, September 2003, and Douglas J. Besharov, senior scholar, American Enterprise Institute, testimony before House Subcommittee on Income Security and Family Support, "Measuring Poverty in America," Aug. 1, 2007.

TANF Assistance on the Decline

The number of households receiving financial support through the Temporary Assistance for Needy Families (TANF) program has declined every fiscal year since 1996. A monthly average of just over 4 million households received TANF assistance in 2006, less than a third of the number of recipients 10 years earlier.

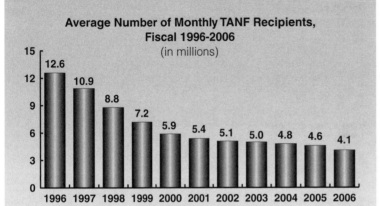

Average Number of Monthly TANF Recipients, Fiscal 1996-2006
(in millions)

Source: "2008 Budget in Brief," Department of Health and Human Services, 2007

"The number of severely poor Americans grew by 26 percent from 2000 to 2005," McClatchy reported. "That's 56 percent faster than the overall poverty population grew in the same period."

The rise in severe poverty extends beyond large urban counties to suburban and rural areas. "Severe poverty is worst near the Mexican border and in some areas of the South, where 6.5 million severely poor residents are struggling to find work as manufacturing jobs in the textile, apparel and furniture-making industries disappear," McClatchy noted. "The Midwestern Rust Belt and areas of the Northeast also have been hard hit as economic restructuring and foreign competition have forced numerous plant closings. At the same time, low-skilled immigrants with impoverished family members are increasingly drawn to the South and Midwest to work in meatpacking, food processing and agricultural industries."[24]

In Illinois, the rate of extreme poverty is the highest in the hard-hit Midwest, with more than 700,000 people in such straits, according to the Heartland Alliance for Human Needs & Human Rights, an advocacy group in Chicago. A family of four living in extreme poverty in Bellevue, Ill., would have monthly expenses of $2,394 but monthly income of only $833, the group says.[25]

But some researchers see little or no evidence that severe poverty is on the rise. Robert Rector, a senior policy analyst at the conservative Heritage Foundation, said "he's seen no data that suggest increasing deprivation among the very poor," according to the McClatchy report.

Rector "questioned the growth of severe poverty, saying that census data become less accurate farther down the income ladder. He said many poor people, particularly single mothers with boyfriends, underreport their income by not including cash gifts and loans."[26]

Such skeptical views extend beyond the severely poor. "While real material hardship certainly does occur, it is limited in scope and severity," Rector told a congressional panel this year. "Most of America's 'poor' live in material conditions that would be judged as comfortable or well-off just a few generations ago. Today, the expenditures per person of the lowest-income one-fifth . . . of households equal those of the median American household in the early 1970s, after adjusting for inflation."[27]

In fact, many more consumer items are within reach of a wider segment of the population — even the poor — than they were 30 or 40 years ago, thanks in part to globalization and the spread of discount retailers. But the cost of necessities such as health care and shelter have exploded, taking a much higher proportion of income than they once did.

Indeed, while the poor may have more material goods than in the past, many analysts say poverty is much more complicated than comparisons with earlier eras might suggest.

"On the one hand, the poor have vastly more consumer goods than a generation ago — TVs, cars, washing machines, dishwashers in many cases," says Hacker of Yale University. "But at the same time, if you think about where they are relative to middle-class Americans, to say nothing of those at the top, they're much further behind."

A major portion of the spending done by poor people is for basics, especially housing, transportation, child care and health care, and the poor have had a tough time keeping up with those costs, Hacker says. What's more, "the consumption of the poor is supported by higher levels of debt that can leave them extremely vulnerable."

And those most vulnerable are people who live in severe poverty. From 2000 to 2004, its prevalence rose sharply. The risk of extreme poverty is significantly higher for children than adults, and it is higher for African-Americans and Hispanics than for whites or Asian-Americans, according to the study in the *American Journal of Preventive Medicine.*

"Millions of Americans, overrepresented by children and minorities, have entered conditions of extreme poverty," the study said. "After 2000, Americans subsisting under these conditions grew as a class more than any other segment of the population."[28]

Reducing severe poverty is a daunting challenge that has spurred an outpouring of policy proposals from all sides of the political spectrum.

In Savannah, Dodd's project — called Step Up, Savannah's Poverty Reduction Initiative — represents one of the nation's most ambitious local anti-poverty efforts. Formed in 2004, it is a collaboration of more than 80 organizations representing business, local government, nonprofit organizations, neighborhood groups and others. It receives donations from several major foundations as well as other sources, including businesses.

Step Up's methods include asking employers and business executives to role play for a few hours what impoverished residents experience every day. "These things are quite eye-opening for a lot of people," Dodd says. The "poverty simulation" exercise reveals "how frustrating the system is to navigate if you're making minimum wage, if you don't have the skills, and how hard it is to keep a job with what you're getting paid. There's transportation obstacles, crime," and other impediments.[29]

The exercise "provides a common frame of reference for the community and demystifies myths" about poverty, adds Dodd, who points out that welfare reform has led to a 70 percent reduction in government subsidies for the city's poor in the past seven years.[30]

Step Up's goals include expanding poor people's access to good jobs and quality health care, training them for career-level positions and expanding access to the EITC.

The effort grew from a realization that "we hadn't had a decline in poverty in 30 years," Dodd says. "People

Step Up Savannah, one of the nation's most ambitious local anti-poverty efforts, is a collaboration of organizations from business, government, education and the nonprofit sector that helps residents of high-poverty neighborhoods become self-sufficient.

Courtesy Step Up Savannah

realized we'd thrown millions of dollars at this but hadn't had the impact we needed to have."

For all the project's earnestness, though, it remains unclear whether Step Up will succeed. "What I always tell people," says Dodd, "is we don't have it all figured out yet."

Has welfare reform reduced entrenched poverty?

In August 1996, President Bill Clinton's signature ended a six-decade practice of guaranteeing cash assistance to the poor. A new system required most people who get aid to work within two years of receiving it. The revised law also limited most aid to a total of five years. And it turned over to states and localities much of the control over how federal poverty money is dispensed.[31]

More then a decade later, experts are still debating whether the poor are better off.

Ron Haskins, a former Ways and Means Committee staff member who played a key role in the welfare overhaul, has written that "above all, welfare reform showed that work — even low-wage work — provides a more durable foundation for social policy than handouts."[32]

"Before welfare reform," Haskins, now a senior fellow at the Brookings Institution, said last year, "the main goal of state welfare programs was simply to give out money. But now the message families receive when they apply for welfare is that they need a job, that the 'welfare' program is there to help them find one and that they can receive cash benefits for a maximum of five years. As a result, welfare rolls plunged by over 60 percent, as many as 2 million mothers entered the labor force, earnings for females heading families increased while their income from welfare payments fell, and child poverty declined every year between 1993 and 2000. By the late 1990s, both black child poverty and poverty among children in female-headed families had reached their lowest levels ever."

Even after four years of increased child poverty following the 2001 recession, Haskins said, the rate of child poverty was still 20 percent lower than in 1993.

Haskins went on to say that "the success of welfare reform was created both by welfare reforms itself and by the work-support programs that provided tax credits, health insurance, nutrition supplements and child care to low-income working families."[33]

Yet, despite what many see as its positive effects, welfare reform remains a mixed bag. It is not clear, for example, to what degree welfare reform itself, along with its time limits on benefits, caused poverty rates to fall and work rates to rise.

"Welfare reform, and in particular the onset of time limits, arrived in the midst of an extremely tight labor market and a flourishing economy," says Katherine Newman, a professor of sociology and public affairs at Princeton University.

"So how much the shift toward work was attributable to the pull of a growing economy and [demand for] labor is very hard to sort out," she continues. "My sense is that welfare reform had something to do with it, but it's hardly the whole story. A lot had to do with favorable market conditions."

The Center on Budget and Policy Priorities, a Washington think tank, last year noted, among other negative trends, that while child poverty declined in the 1990s, as Haskins pointed out, it nonetheless rose sharply after 2000, as did the number of children living in severe poverty.[34] (*See sidebar, see p. 168.*)

Many anti-poverty advocates say even though welfare reform put more people to work, further steps are needed to ensure that families can climb out of poverty and stay there, and that poor children are protected.

Timothy M. Smeeding, director of the Center for Policy Research at Syracuse University, says welfare reform "turned the welfare poor into the working poor.

You've got more self-respect, you're earning it, but the effect on kids is mixed." He calls for a system that will "make work pay," where "you go out and you work, you show the effort, you put in 1,000 hours, and we'll find a way to make sure you've got $15,000 or $20,000 and you're not poor."

In Wisconsin — where some of the earliest efforts at welfare reform took place — the rate of growth in the number of people living in poverty was higher in 2003-2004 than in any other state.[35] Richard Schlimm, executive director of the Wisconsin Community Action Program Association, a statewide association of community-action and anti-poverty groups, says welfare reform simply "has not worked," in reducing poverty in his state.

"Certainly it was the right thing to do, to get people working," Schlimm says. "But I've always believed poor people want to work, and they prefer work over welfare....We successfully achieved the elimination of welfare, but I maintain that we had the wrong goal. The goal was to reduce poverty, and if we kept that in our sights we would have focused a whole lot [more] funding on that than we did."

Would more government spending on poverty help?

While welfare reform encouraged work and reduced government caseloads, many experts say the fight against poverty has only begun.

Some argue that reducing poverty depends in large measure on the poor exercising greater personal responsibility. "While it is often argued that the U.S. devotes far fewer resources to social welfare spending than other rich nations, the facts show otherwise," Rector of the Heritage Foundation said. "The good news is that remaining poverty can readily be reduced further, particularly among children. There are two main reasons that American children are poor: Their parents don't work much, and fathers are absent from the home."[36]

Others say more government spending on anti-poverty programs is the key. Schlimm, at the Wisconsin Community Action Program Association, says that to reduce poverty, the nation needs political leadership coupled with "a massive investment" in affordable housing, accessible health care, education and job creation for the poor. "Let's face it, we have committed massive investments in Iraq," he says, "and [with] half of that — even a fourth of that — focused on poverty in the United States, we could make remarkable strides."

Smeeding, the Syracuse University policy researcher, says U.S. poverty could be cut by a third to a half with an outlay of $45 billion to $60 billion a year, focused on three things: child care for working mothers, guaranteed child support for mothers who have established paternity with fathers who can't or won't pay because of disability or prison, and an expansion of the EITC.

Lawrence Mead, a professor of politics at New York University, advocates a stick-and-carrot approach with low-income men. "In 2005, there were more than 7 million poor men ages 16 to 50 in the United States, and only half of them worked at all," Mead wrote. "Among black men in poverty, nearly two-thirds were idle, and their employment has fallen steadily in recent decades."

Mead proposes using the child-support and criminal-justice systems to promote work among poor males. "Right now, these institutions depress male work levels by locking men up and by garnishing their wages if they do work," he wrote. "But they could be used to promote work. For example, men in arrears on their child support could be assigned to government-run work programs, as could parolees with employment problems. These men — about 1.5 million each year — would have to show up and work regularly — on penalty of going to jail. Both groups might also receive wage subsidies. The combination might instill more regular work habits."

Mandatory work for 1.5 million men would run $2 billion to $5 billion annually, according to Mead. "In return, governments could collect more in child support and spend less on incarceration."[37]

"Everyone recognizes that men are the frontier," Mead says. The ultimate goal, he says, should be to both reward and enforce work in ways the current system doesn't do now.

While spending on new programs is one approach to fighting poverty, some argue the solution isn't more outlays for anti-poverty programs but rather a mix of free-market capitalism and charity.

"Despite nearly $9 trillion in total welfare spending since Lyndon B. Johnson declared [the] War on Poverty in 1964, the poverty rate is perilously close to where it was when we began, more than 40 years ago," wrote Michael D. Tanner, director of health and welfare studies for the conservative Cato Institute think tank.

"Clearly we are doing something wrong. Throwing money at the problem has neither reduced poverty nor made the poor self-sufficient. . . . [I]f we have learned anything by now, it is that there are limits to what government programs — even reformed ones — can do to address the root causes of poverty.

"Observers have known for a long time that the surest ways to stay out of poverty are to finish school; not get pregnant outside marriage; and get a job, any job, and stick with it. That means that if we wish to fight poverty, we must end those government policies — high taxes and regulatory excess — that inhibit growth and job creation. We must protect capital investment and give people the opportunity to start new businesses. We must reform our failed government school system to encourage competition and choice. We must encourage the poor to save and invest.

"More importantly, the real work of fighting poverty must come not from the government, but from the engines of civil society. . . . [P]rivate charities are far more effective than government welfare programs."[38]

BACKGROUND

Warring on Poverty

Concerns about work, hardship and who deserves help go back to the roots of the Republic. The Virginia Assembly of 1619 decreed that a person found guilty of idleness would be forced to work under a master "til he shewe apparant signes of amendment."[39]

In the 19th century, poorhouses sprang up to accommodate a growing tide of desperate people flooding the cities from the countryside. Poverty flourished along with widespread indifference to the plight of the needy. After the Civil War the journalist and political economist Henry George called the United States a place where "amid the greatest accumulations of wealth, men die of starvation, and puny infants suckle dry breasts."[40]

Later came the first rudimentary efforts to measure poverty. In 1904 the social worker Robert Hunter set what might have been the first national poverty line — $460 per year for a five-member family in the Northern industrial states and $300 for a family in the South.[41]

In the post-World War I boom years, some Americans enjoyed unprecedented comfort and wealth, but poverty

CHRONOLOGY

1950s-1960s *Many Americans enjoy a post-war economic boom, but poverty persists. Poverty rate is 22.4 percent in 1959.*

1962 Michael Harrington's book *The Other America* helps spur President Lyndon B. Johnson's War on Poverty. . . . Welfare program is renamed Aid to Families with Dependent Children (AFDC).

1964 Congress establishes permanent food stamp program. . . . Federal government develops income thresholds to define poverty in American society.

1965 Congress enacts Medicaid to provide health care to low-income people.

1967 Congress establishes the Work Incentive Program, requiring states to establish job-training programs for adults receiving welfare.

1969 President Richard M. Nixon calls hunger in America an "embarrassing and intolerable" national shame.

1970s *The energy crisis, recessions and industrial restructuring put new strains on the poor.*

1975 Congress approves Earned Income Tax Credit (EITC), partly to offset the burden of Social Security taxes on low-income families and to provide an incentive to work.

1980s *Poverty programs of the 1960s and '70s come under scrutiny from the Reagan administration.*

1981 Congress cuts cash benefits for the working poor and lets states require welfare recipients to work.

1988 President Ronald Reagan signs Family Support Act, requiring states to implement education, job training and placement programs for welfare recipients.

1990s *Clinton administration pushes Congress to pass massive welfare reforms.*

1992 Democratic presidential candidate Bill Clinton pledges to "end welfare as we know it."

1993 Clinton expands EITC.

1996 Congress ends 60-year welfare entitlement program, passing a reform law that imposes work requirements and puts time limits on cash benefits.

1997 Federal minimum wage rises to $5.15 an hour.

1997 State Children's Health Insurance Program (SCHIP) is created.

1999 The government of British Prime Minister Tony Blair introduces a plan to end child poverty in Britain by 2020, spurring calls for a similar effort in the United States.

2000s *Hurricane Katrina devastates Gulf Coast, putting spotlight on poverty.*

2000 Federal poverty rate falls to 11.3 percent, lowest since 1974.

2004 Federal appeals court upholds the "living wage" law in Berkeley, Calif., rejecting the first major challenge to civic ordinances requiring contractors to pay above-poverty wages. . . . Poverty rate climbs to 12.7 percent

Aug. 29, 2005 Hurricane Katrina hits New Orleans.

2006 Congress reauthorizes Temporary Assistance for Needy Families (TANF) as part of Deficit Reduction Act.

2007 McClatchy Newspapers analysis finds that percentage of poor Americans living in severe poverty reached a 32-year high in 2005. . . . Congress spars with the Bush administration over expansion of SCHIP. . . . House Ways and Means Committee hearings focus on poverty and inequality. . . . Democratic presidential candidate John Edwards takes a three-day, 1,800-mile "Road to One America" poverty tour. . . . Federal minimum wage rises for the first time in a decade to $5.85 an hour; it goes to $6.55 in summer 2008 and $7.25 in summer 2009. . . . Poverty rate falls to 12.3 percent.

wracked much of the nation. Between 1918 and 1929, some 10 million families were poor. By 1933, in the depths of the Great Depression, a fourth of the labor force was without jobs, and an estimated 15 million families — half the American population — lived in poverty.[42]

World War II jump-started the U.S. economy, and in the 1950s and early '60s many Americans enjoyed middle-class prosperity. But not all saw their living standards rise. Poverty persisted and grew, much of it concentrated in the rural South, Appalachia and the gritty urban cores of the industrial North. Many Americans blamed the poor for their plight, dismissing racism, educational inequality and other entrenched societal ills as major factors in perpetuating poverty.

In 1962 Michael Harrington wrote in his ground-breaking book *The Other America: Poverty in the United States:*

"There are sociological and political reasons why poverty is not seen; and there are misconceptions and prejudices that literally blind the eyes. . . . Here is the most familiar version of social blindness: 'The poor are that way because they are afraid of work. And anyway they all have big cars. If they were like me (or my father or my grandfather), they could pay their own way. But they prefer to live on the dole and cheat the taxpayers.'

"This theory," Harrington went on, "usually thought of as a virtuous and moral statement, is one of the means of making it impossible for the poor ever to pay their way. . . . [T]he real explanation of why the poor are where they are is that they made the mistake of being born to the wrong parents, in the wrong section of the country, in the wrong industry or in the wrong racial or ethnic group. Once that mistake has been made, they could have been paragons of will and morality, but most of them would never even have had a chance to get out of the other America."[43]

By 1962, more than a fifth of Americans were living in poverty. Harrington's book helped spur Washington to act.[44]

A few months before his assassination, President John F. Kennedy directed his Council of Economic Advisers to study domestic poverty and recommend ways to fight it.[45]

Kennedy's successor, President Lyndon B. Johnson, followed through, declaring in his first State of the Union address, on Jan. 8, 1964, "unconditional war on poverty in America." Later that year Congress established the Office of Economic Opportunity, which attacked poverty through a phalanx of new programs, from Head Start — a school-readiness effort — to Job Corps, a training program for teens and young adults.[46] Johnson's fight against poverty also included a wide range of "Great Society" programs, from the 1964 Food Stamp Act to Medicare and Medicaid.

The War on Poverty persisted under the Nixon administration, which broadened the Food Stamp program and saw the passage of the Supplemental Security Income program for disabled people, among others. Even so, President Richard M. Nixon sought to dismantle the Office of Economic Opportunity, disbursing many of its programs among various federal agencies. The office was finally closed by President Gerald R. Ford in 1975.

Under Attack

By the 1980s and the start of the Reagan administration, poverty programs were under full-scale attack. The poverty rate, which dipped to just over 11 percent in the early 1970s, hit 15.2 percent in 1983. Conservatives, impatient with the Johnson-era philosophy of federally funded social aid for the poor, charged that the government's expensive programs were making poverty and dependence worse rather than better.

"[S]ome years ago, the federal government declared War on Poverty, and poverty won," Reagan famously said in his 1988 State of the Union address. "Today the federal government has 59 major welfare programs and spends more than $100 billion a year on them. What has all this money done? Well, too often it has only made poverty harder to escape. Federal welfare programs have created a massive social problem. With the best of intentions, government created a poverty trap that wreaks havoc on the very support system the poor need most to lift themselves out of poverty: the family."

The Reagan administration argued "that the social policies enacted in the 1960s and '70s had undermined the functioning of the nation's basic institutions and, by encouraging permissiveness, non-work and welfare dependence, had led to marital breakup, non-marital childbearing and the erosion of individual initiative," according to the University of Michigan's Danziger and Robert H. Haveman, a professor of economics and public affairs at the University of Wisconsin.

Military Families Face Financial Strain

"This spring our caseload doubled."

Meredith Leyva's work with military families recently has led her to a troubling conclusion: Poverty is growing among the ranks of deployed service members, especially those who have been seriously injured in Iraq or Afghanistan.

"This spring our caseload of both military families and wounded warriors doubled," says Leyva, who is the founder of Operation Homefront, a Santa Ana, Calif., charity that helps military families through 31 chapters nationwide. And, adds Leyva, whose husband is a Navy physician, "We saw a significant change in the types of cases. We're now seeing many more complicated and high-dollar crises that are compounded by deployment after deployment."

Operation Homefront served approximately 1,700 families of wounded service members in 2006,

Meredith Leyva, founder of Operation Homefront.

Leyva says, and "over half and possibly more were living in poverty."

As for the 1.5-million-member military as a whole, however, little if any hard data exist on the extent of poverty in military families during the current conflict. Much of the government information on issues like food stamp use among military families predates the war.

Indeed, the financial health of military families can be a highly complicated and nuanced issue to analyze, even leaving aside the struggles of those dealing with catastrophic injury. "By any traditional measure of poverty..., military families are a lot better off than their civilian peers based on such things as age and education," says Joyce Raezer, chief operating officer of the National Military Family Association, a policy advocacy group in Alexandria, Va.

Still, she says some military families may be on the "financial edge," often because "they're young and financially inexperienced" and perhaps "prey for financial predators." Others may be strained by relocation demands that put them in temporary financial straits, she says.

"My sense is that you don't have folks living in poverty so that day in and day out things are inadequate," says Raezer. "But it can be episodic, where they're strapped for cash because of the military lifestyle, financial inexperience and predators."

Most military families are ineligible for food stamps because the military housing allowance puts them over the eligibility threshold, Raezer notes.

Even so, in fiscal 2006 food-stamp redemptions at military commissaries rose about $2.3 million over the previous year, to $26.2 million. While it was not clear what caused the increase, three military stores affected by Hurricane Katrina and other storms accounted for more than 80 percent of the increase.[1]

In May, U.S. Reps. James McGovern, D-Mass., and Jo Ann Emerson, R-Mo., introduced a bill that would expand

"The Reagan philosophy was that tax cuts and spending cuts would increase the rate of economic growth, and that the poor would ultimately benefit through the increased employment and earnings that would follow such growth," they wrote. "However, a deep recession in the early 1980s increased poverty, and the subsequent economic growth did not 'trickle down.' Although the economy expanded for many years in the 1980s, the wage rates of low- and medium-skilled male workers did not. On the other hand, the earnings of those in the upper part of the income distribution grew rapidly."[47]

Welfare Reform

The 1980s laid the groundwork for the radical shift in anti-poverty policy that was to come during the Clinton era. In 1993 Clinton pushed through a record expansion spending for federal nutrition programs, including a provision that would exclude combat-related military pay from income calculations for food-stamp eligibility.[2]

National Guard and active-duty families can feel financial strain differently. Lt. Col. Joseph Schweikert, state family program director for the Illinois National Guard, says "there are definitely families that go through financial hardships, sometimes due to deployments. But it varies from soldier to soldier, family to family. Some make more while deployed."

Nonetheless, at least 30 percent of Guard soldiers suffer a financial loss when deployed, he says.

Because the Guard offers a college-scholarship program, many young soldiers enlist, get a degree and then enter a well-paying career field. When they are mobilized, their pay may drop sharply. "It causes the family to go through a lot of hardships," Schweikert says, especially if the soldier doesn't have savings or a spouse's income to rely on.

Still, he suggests, many Guard members can be more stable financially than active-duty troops. Guard soldiers tend to be older and to have established civilian careers. Moreover, a working spouse will not have had to uproot periodically from a job, as often happens within the active-duty forces.

"In active duty, a lot of time you have to transfer from base to base, and it's hard to establish a long-term career," Schweikert says.

Nonetheless, military families in both the Guard and regular forces may find it hard to avoid financial ruin, especially in cases of serious injury suffered in war.

When a soldier is deployed, a spouse may have to pay others to do jobs the soldier performed at home, such as

Wounded soldiers and their families attend a get-together sponsored by the Texas chapter of Operation Homefront at Brooke Army Medical Center at Fort Sam Houston.

mowing the lawn and maintaining the car, Leyva says. And if a soldier is wounded, she says, "his pay immediately drops while the expenses skyrocket." Often, a spouse takes leave from a job or quits altogether to be at the wounded soldier's bedside or to help the soldier through rehabilitation, spending long days or weeks away from home.

"Service members were never paid well," Leyva says, "but these extraordinary crises certainly overwhelm."

Leyva fears that poverty among veterans will skyrocket in the wake of the current war, as it did after the Vietnam conflict. "I think we're going to see a whole new generation of disabled veterans that are sort of the mirror images of the Vietnam veterans," she says. "It's as much about mental as physical wounds," she says, and it could lead to a new "generation of poverty."

---

[1] Karen Jowers, "Storms May Have Spurred Jump in Food-Stamp Use," *Air Force Times*, July 5, 2007, www.navytimes.com.

[2] The Feeding America's Family Act, HR 2129.

of the Earned Income Tax Credit. Then, Clinton signed the Personal Responsibility and Work Opportunity Reconciliation Act of 1996 — otherwise known as the Welfare Reform Act.

The move to overhaul welfare outraged some. Georgetown University's Edelman resigned from the Clinton administration in protest. In a blistering critique, Edelman wrote that the measure would lead to "more malnutrition

and more crime, increased infant mortality and increased drug and alcohol abuse" and "increased family violence and abuse against children and women."[48]

But others have praised the reform measure. What the Clinton bill did, a *Boston Globe* columnist opined on the act's 10th anniversary, "was end the condescending attitude that the poor were incapable of improving their situation, and that 'compassion' consisted of supplying money

Did Recent Reforms Help Needy Families?

Bush administration tightened TANF work requirements.

Mention welfare reform to a political observer, and it is Bill Clinton who typically comes to mind. It was candidate Clinton who pledged to "end welfare as we know it" and President Clinton who signed the landmark welfare reform act into law in 1996.

But the Bush era also has engineered significant reforms in the welfare system, changes that could have far-reaching effects on the nation's poor.

The most important came with last year's congressional reauthorization of Temporary Assistance for Needy Families (TANF), the federal block-grant program that replaced the old welfare system.

The reauthorization strengthened work requirements and closed a loophole so that separate state-funded TANF programs have to be included in work-participation calculations.

"In effect, the Bush administration and Congress put teeth back into TANF work requirements but set difficult benchmarks for state programs that are working with adult populations experiencing many barriers to employment," Scott W. Allard, an assistant professor of political science and public policy at Brown University, noted recently.[1]

Others looking back on more than a decade of welfare reform worry the recent changes in the welfare rules could make poverty trends worse. Two analysts at the Center on Budget and Policy Priorities, Sharon Parrott, director of the center's Welfare Reform and Income Support Division, and senior researcher Arloc Sherman, argue that even though changes in TANF a decade ago "played a role in reducing poverty and raising employment rates during the 1990s, our safety net for the poorest families with children has weakened dramatically."[2]

Among the trends they pointed to: child poverty fell in the 1990s, but began rising after 2000, and the number of children in "deep" poverty rose; the number of jobless single mothers receiving no government cash assistance has risen significantly, and TANF now helps a far smaller share of families that qualify for the program than it used to help.

Last year's reauthorization could weaken the safety net even more, the two analysts suggested. Welfare reauthorization requires states to place a much bigger portion of their TANF caseloads in work activities and restricts the kind of activities that can count toward state work-participation requirements, Parrott and Sherman noted. "In many cases,

indefinitely to women who had children, but no husbands or jobs." The bill "replaced deadly condescension with respect."[49]

Still, while welfare caseloads plummeted, poverty persisted, even among those who joined the labor force.

"Basically, things are better than most people thought," Danziger says today. "On average, welfare recipients did much better moving from welfare to work, in part because the minimum wage was increased in 1997, the Earned Income Tax Credit expanded so much in the early '90s, states put so much into child-care subsidies, and the State Children's Health Insurance Program (SCHIP) came in. But the poverty rate among single mothers remains very high, and there's nothing new on the horizon."

Danziger noted in a 2006 paper that as many as 30 percent of single mothers who left welfare and took jobs are out of work in any given month.[50]

Advocates point out that it is possible to make real gains against poverty — and not just gains in cutting welfare caseloads. They point to big strides against child poverty in Britain, where in 1999 Prime Minister Tony Blair pledged to end child poverty by 2020.

'Elusive Dream'

But in cities and towns across America, President Johnson's 1964 pledge "not only to relieve the symptom of poverty but to cure it and, above all, to prevent it" remains an elusive dream.[51]

The loss of manufacturing jobs — and the stability and safety net they once provided — is a big reason the dream remains out of reach.

In Wisconsin, a state of 5.6 million people, the poverty rate shot from 8.2 percent to 11 percent over five years, says the Wisconsin Community Action Program

state programs designed to address two of the biggest problems that have emerged over TANF's first decade — that parents who leave welfare for work often earn low wages and have unstable employment, and that many families with the greatest barriers to employment are being left behind — will no longer count toward states' work requirements," they wrote.

"In fact, the cheapest and easiest way for a state to meet the new work rules would simply be to assist fewer poor families, especially the families with barriers to employment who need the most help."

On top of that, the amount of basic federal block-grant funds for states has not been adjusted since 1996 and has lost 22 percent of its value to inflation, Parrott and Sherman wrote.

Some observers are more sanguine about the course of welfare reform. Writing in a "point-counterpoint" format with Parrott and Sherman, Lawrence Mead, a professor of politics at New York University and an architect of welfare reform, describes it as an "incomplete triumph." He says reform achieved its two main goals: Work levels rose sharply among poor mothers, the main beneficiaries of welfare. And caseloads plummeted.

Still, Mead says that the reform effort has had limitations. For one thing, he says, it did not create a system that promotes work on an ongoing basis through a combination of government incentives and emphasis on personal responsibility. He notes that 40 percent of those who have left welfare have not gone to work, and many welfare recipients have moved in and out of jobs.

Nor did welfare reform ensure that people leaving welfare for jobs will have enough income to live on, Mead says. "The situation has improved, but not enough."

And welfare reform did not adequately address the employment challenges among poor men, many of whom are fathers in welfare families, Mead says.

Nonetheless, Mead is hopeful the limitations of welfare reform can be addressed at least partly through engagement by the poor in the political process. Because more of the poor are working or moving toward work, they are in a stronger position to demand changes, such as payment of living wages, than they were under the old entitlement system of welfare, Mead says.

First, though, the poor must assert themselves both on the job and in the political sphere, he says.

"Finally," he writes, "what reform enforced was not work, but citizenship."[3]

---

[1] Scott W. Allard, "The Changing Face of Welfare During the Bush Administration," *Publius*, June 22, 2007.

[2] Sharon Parrott and Arloc Sherman, "Point-Counterpoint," in Richard P. Nathan, editor, "Welfare Reform After Ten Years: Strengths and Weaknesses," *Journal of Policy Analysis and Management*, Vol. 26, No. 2, 2007.

[3] Lawrence Mead, "Point-Counterpoint," in *ibid*.

Association's Schlimm. "I'm 58 and have lived in Wisconsin all my life, and it's very unusual to see those kinds of numbers," he says. It is the "loss of good jobs, manufacturing jobs" that is to blame.

"A lot of Wisconsin's good jobs support the auto industry," he continues. "And we're a paper-making state. Many of the papermakers moved. . . . When I got out of college, you could go to a paper mill, and if it didn't work out, you could drive a couple of blocks down the street and find work with another company. In 1968 they paid $6 to $7 an hour. Now they pay $25. They're very coveted jobs. But there aren't as many of them. The economy hasn't been able to replace those very good jobs."

What matters most in the fight against poverty, many advocates contend, is leadership and political will.

The No. 1 problem is leadership, says David Bradley, executive director of the National Community Action Foundation. "We're not talking billions of dollars. We're talking receptivity to looking at ideas."

Bradley notes that the Johnson-era Office of Economic Opportunity was a laboratory for anti-poverty innovations. "For many years we've not had the federal government willing to fund and be experimental in partnering in new ideas on poverty. A lot of ideas start at the grass roots. I see incredible projects out there but no mechanism to duplicate them nationwide."

At the same time, Bradley laments that some in both political parties believe none of the ideas from the 1960s are worth keeping. "I find it frustrating that some candidates who are talking about poverty view anything that's gone on previously as not successful or not innovative or creative enough," he says. "If you're a program that started in 1964 or 1965, that doesn't mean by definition that you're still not innovative in your community."

Bradley is cautiously optimistic that a renewed commitment to fighting poverty is afoot in the nation. Political leaders in both parties are talking about the issue and the government's role in bringing about solutions, he points out.

But that will happen, Bradley says, only if solutions are not overpromised, the effort is bipartisan, innovation and creativity are part of the approach, sufficient government money is available and, "most important, if there is a general acceptance that the federal government wants to be a positive partner.

"It can be a partner that requires accountability," he says, "but a partner nevertheless."

CURRENT SITUATION

Presidential Race

It remains unclear how much traction the poverty theme will have in the 2008 presidential race. But as the campaign began moving into high gear this summer, poverty — and what to do about it — has been high on the list of priorities among several leading Democratic candidates, most notably Edwards and Obama.

Edwards has set the ambitious goal of cutting poverty by a third within a decade and ending it within 30 years. Echoing President Johnson's Great Society program, Edwards proposes a "Working Society" where "everyone who is able to work hard will be expected to work and, in turn, be rewarded for it."

To attack poverty, Edwards is pushing more than a dozen ideas, from raising the minimum wage, fighting predatory lending and reducing teen pregnancy to creating a million temporary "stepping stone" jobs for those having difficulty finding other work.

Obama has his own long list of proposals. He also backs a transitional jobs program and a minimum-wage increase, for example, along with such steps as improving transportation access for the working poor and helping ex-prisoners find jobs.

But deeper differences exist in the two candidates' approaches. "Edwards has focused on the malignant effects of the concentration of poverty in inner cities," *The Washington Post* noted. "He has argued for dispersing low-income families by replacing public housing with a greatly expanded rental voucher program to allow families to move where there are more jobs and better schools." Obama, on the other hand, has "presented a sharply different overall objective: fixing inner-city areas so they become places where families have a shot at prospering, without having to move."[52]

Part of what is noteworthy about the Edwards and Obama proposals is that they exist at all. Many Democratic candidates, including Sen. Clinton, have focused on the plight of the middle class rather than the poor. "Since the late 1980s," the columnist E. J. Dionne Jr. noted, "Democrats have been obsessed with the middle class for reasons of simple math: no middle-class votes, no electoral victories."[53]

With the exception of recent comments by former Republican Bloomberg of New York, GOP rhetoric on poverty has not been nearly as prevalent as the Democrats'. In January, President Bush acknowledged that "income inequality is real," suggesting his administration might be poised to do more on poverty and perhaps get ahead of Democrats on the issue.[54] But more recently the administration has resisted congressional efforts to expand the SCHIP program, which benefits poor children.

Meanwhile, Republican presidential hopeful Mitt Romney echoed the longstanding conservative criticism of Democrat-backed social policies, declaring that Democrats are "thinking about big government, big welfare, big taxes, Big Brother."[55]

Anti-Poverty Proposals

In recent months several think tanks and advocacy groups have turned out policy proposals for reducing poverty. In April the liberal Center for American Progress advanced a dozen key steps to cut poverty in half in the next decade, including raising the minimum wage to half the average hourly wage, expanding the EITC and Child Tax Credit, promoting unionization, guaranteeing child-care assistance to low-income families and creating 2 million new housing vouchers "designed to help people live in opportunity-rich areas."

The center's main recommendations would cost roughly $90 billion annually — "a significant cost," it conceded, "but one that is necessary and could be readily funded through a fairer tax system." Spending $90 billion a year "would represent about 0.8 percent of the nation's gross domestic product, which is a fraction of the money spent on tax changes that benefited primarily the wealthy in recent years."

Should immigration be reduced to protect the jobs of native-born poor?

YES — Steven A. Camarota
Director of Research,
Center for Immigration Studies

From testimony prepared for House Judiciary Committee, May 9, 2007

There is no evidence of a labor shortage, especially at the bottom end of the labor market where immigrants are most concentrated. . . . There is a good deal of research showing that immigration has contributed to the decline in employment and wages for less-educated natives. . . . All research indicates that less-educated immigrants consume much more in government services than they pay in taxes. Thus, not only does such immigration harm America's poor, it also burdens taxpayers. . . .

While the number of immigrants is very large . . . the impact on the overall economy or on the share of the population that is of working age is actually very small. And these effects are even smaller when one focuses only on illegal aliens, who comprise one-fourth to one-third of all immigrants. While the impact on the economy . . . may be tiny, the effect on some Americans, particular workers at the bottom of the labor market may be quite large. These workers are especially vulnerable to immigrant competition because wages for these jobs are already low, and immigrants are heavily concentrated in less-skilled and lower-paying jobs. . . .

It probably makes more sense for policymakers to focus on the winners and losers from immigration. The big losers are natives working in low-skilled, low-wage jobs. Of course, technological change and increased trade also have reduced the labor market opportunities for low-wage workers in the United States. But immigration is different because it is a discretionary policy that can be altered. On the other hand, immigrants are the big winners, as are owners of capital and skilled workers, but their gains are tiny relative to their income.

In the end, arguments for or against immigration are as much political and moral as they are economic. The latest research indicates that we can reduce immigration secure in the knowledge that it will not harm the economy. Doing so makes sense if we are very concerned about low-wage and less-skilled workers in the United States. On the other hand, if one places a high priority on helping unskilled workers in other countries, then allowing in a large number of such workers should continue.

Of course, only an infinitesimal proportion of the world's poor could ever come to this country even under the most open immigration policy one might imagine. Those who support the current high level of unskilled legal and illegal immigration should at least do so with an understanding that those American workers harmed by the policies they favor are already the poorest and most vulnerable.

NO — Gerald D. Jaynes
Professor of Economics and
African-American Studies, Yale University

From testimony before House Subcommittee on Immigration, Citizenship, Refugees, Border Security, and International Law, May 3, 2007

We can acknowledge that immigration probably hurts the employment and wages of some less-educated citizens and still conclude immigration is a net benefit for the United States. The most methodologically sound estimates of the net effects of immigration on the nation conclude that the United States, as a whole, benefits from contemporary immigration. Properly measured, this conclusion means that during a period of time reasonably long enough to allow immigrants to adjust to their new situations, they produce more national income than they consume in government services.

Confusion about this issue is caused by some analysts' failure to make appropriate distinctions between immigration's impact on specific local governments and groups and its impact on the whole nation. Although benefits of immigration — such as lower prices for consumer and producer goods and services, greater profits and tax revenues — accrue to the nation as a whole, nearly all of the costs for public services consumed by immigrants are borne by localities and specific demographic groups. . . . Even so, inappropriate methods of analysis have led some analysts to overstate the costs of immigration even at the local level. . . .

On average, Americans receive positive economic benefits from immigration, but, at least in the short run, residents of particular localities and members of certain groups may lose. . . .

Democratic concepts of justice suggest the losses of a few should not override the gains of the many. Democratic concepts of justice also demand that society's least-advantaged members should not be paying for the immigration benefits enjoyed by the entire nation. A democratic society benefiting from immigration and debating how to reshape its immigration policies should also be discussing social policies to compensate less-skilled workers through combinations of better training, relocation and educational opportunities. . . .

[T]he evidence supports the conclusion that from an economic standpoint immigration's broader benefits to the nation outweigh its costs. An assessment of the effects of immigration on the employment prospects of less-educated native-born workers is that the effect is negative but modest, and probably is significant in some specific industries and geographic locations. . . . However, it is just as likely that the relative importance of less-educated young native [workers'] job losses due to the competition of immigrants is swamped by a constellation of other factors diminishing their economic status.

The Urban Institute estimated that four of the center's recommendations — on the minimum wage, EITC, child tax credit and child care — would cut poverty by about a fourth. Moreover, it said, both child poverty and extreme poverty would fall.[56]

A Brookings Institution proposal to "reinvigorate the fight for greater opportunity" includes seven recommendations for the next U.S. president, from strengthening work requirements in government-assistance programs, promoting marriage and funding teen pregnancy-prevention efforts to subsidizing child care for low-wage workers, increasing the minimum wage and expanding the EITC.

"We need a new generation of anti-poverty policies that focus on requiring and rewarding work, reversing the breakdown of the family and improving educational outcomes," the proposal states. The $38.6 billion per year cost should not be incurred, the authors say, unless it "can be fully covered by eliminating spending or tax preferences in other areas."[57]

Many advocates emphasize the need to help poor people build their assets, such as savings accounts and home equity, as a way of propelling them out of poverty. Also key, they say, is the need to spend more on early-childhood programs to help keep youngsters from falling into poverty in the first place.

"Universal high-quality early childhood education is the single most powerful investment we could make in insuring poverty doesn't strike the next generation," says Newman of Princeton University.

Tax Policy

Proposals to adjust federal tax policy to help lift the poor into the economic mainstream are among those getting the most attention. Much of the discussion has focused on expansion of the child and earned income tax credits.

A letter sent to members of Congress last spring by hundreds of advocacy groups urged expansion of the child credit, which can reduce the tax liability of families with children. "The current income threshold — in 2007, it is $11,750 — excludes 10 million children whose families are too poor to claim the credit," the letter stated. "The threshold keeps rising with inflation, increasing the tax burden on the poor and dropping many families from the benefit altogether."

The letter added that according to the Tax Policy Center, operated by the Urban Institute and Brookings Institution,

"half of all African-American children, 46 percent of Hispanic children and 18 percent of white children received either no Child Tax Credit or a reduced amount in 2005 because their families' earnings were too low."[58]

Along with the child credit, the EITC is widely cited as ripe for expansion.

Created in 1975 to protect low-wage workers from rising payroll taxes, the credit has been expanded several times, under both Republican and Democratic administrations. More than 20 million families benefit from more than $40 billion in credits today, according to Brookings' Berube. Most of those eligible for the credit have children under age 18 living at home and earn less than $35,000, according to Berube. In 2004 the average claimant received a credit of about $1,800.[59]

While claims of abuse have been leveled at the tax credit, it has generally been popular across the political spectrum because it encourages work, helps the needy and does not levy a cost on wealthier taxpayers.[60]

But anti-poverty advocates say the tax credit could be even more effective by making it easier for families with two earners to get the credit and extending it to single workers in their late teens and early 20s.[61]

"Childless adults are the only group of working tax filers who begin to owe federal income taxes before their incomes reach the poverty line," says the letter to members of Congress. Workers in that category got an average credit of only $230 last year, the letter said. "Increasing the amount of the credit for low-income workers not living with children would increase work incentives and economic security for millions of Americans working in low-wage jobs."

Making poor people aware of the tax credit is also an obstacle that must be overcome, advocates say. Many people who are eligible for the credit don't claim it, sometimes because of language or educational barriers.

Dodd, at Step Up in Savannah, says the Internal Revenue Service said $10 million to $12 million in credits go unclaimed in his city alone.

States and Localities

As federal policymakers wrestle with the poverty issue, states and localities are making inroads of their own. Mayor Bloomberg has been promoting a plan to pay poor families in New York up to $5,000 a year to meet such goals as attending parent-teacher meetings, getting medical checkups and holding full-time jobs. Patterned after a Mexican initiative, the plan aims to help poor families make better long-range decisions and break cycles of poverty and dependence that can last generations.[62]

Other efforts are afoot in the states. A proposed bill in the California Assembly, for example, would establish an advisory Childhood Poverty Council to develop a plan to reduce child poverty in the state by half by 2017 and eliminate it by 2027.[63]

Not all such steps pan out, though. In 2004, Connecticut passed legislation committing the state to a 50 percent reduction in child poverty by 2014, but child poverty has risen since then, an official of the Connecticut Association for Community Action complained this summer, blaming the failure to enact a state-funded EITC.[64]

As states seek ways to reduce the number of poor within their borders, they also are trying to adjust to the stiffer work requirements that Congress enacted last year when it reauthorized welfare reform.[65]

The new rules are forcing some states to adapt in creative ways. In California, for example, where less than a fourth of welfare recipients work enough hours to meet federal requirements, officials are moving some teenage parents, older parents and disabled people into separate programs paid entirely by state funds so they aren't counted in federal work-participation calculations.

Arkansas, on the other hand, has been sending monthly checks to the working poor. "Arkansas eventually aims to artificially swell its welfare population from 8,000 families to as many as 11,000 and raise the work-participation rate by at least 11 percent," according to a press report. "Officials hope the extra cash will also keep the workers employed."[66]

The tougher work rules have upset poverty advocates, who argue they damage efforts to help those most vulnerable or lacking in skills to prepare for the job market. "Some of the changes made it almost impossible in some ways for people to use the system to get out of poverty," said Rep. McDermott, the Washington Democrat.[67]

But others defend the approach. "The bottom line is that the only real way to get out of poverty is to find a job," said Rep. Wally Herger, a California Republican who chaired the House subcommittee that worked on last year's reauthorization. "There's always the line, 'Well, some people can't do it.' What that's really doing is selling those people short."[68]

OUTLOOK
Ominous Signs

The outlook for real progress against domestic poverty is mixed, especially in the near term.

On one hand, concerns about poverty, income inequality and declining mobility are playing a bigger role on the national scene than they have in years. The kind of political momentum that spurred the War on Poverty in the 1960s may be emerging again — albeit in a more muted fashion and with a different set of policy proposals.

But big obstacles remain, especially funding. Congress would face difficult fiscal choices if it sought to enact any major anti-poverty program, many analysts point out. Even the Democratic majority, which has long pushed for more spending for social programs, would face major barriers.

"The Democrats have committed to pay-as-you-go budgeting, so I don't think we'll have a major push on anti-poverty [programs] or on programs designed to help the poor and middle class" over the next four to eight years, says Yale's Hacker. "That's part of the reason for the public's frustration — we're hamstrung by the budgetary situation."

At the same time, a number of ominous developments have been occurring that suggest the poor will have an even rougher time financially than they have in recent years. The explosion in mortgage foreclosures, rising prices for basics like gasoline and milk and the ever-present threat of recession and layoffs all conspire most heavily against those with the fewest resources. Recently, job growth and expansion in the service sector have both been weaker than expected, indicating tougher times ahead for those on the economic margins.

Coupled with the uncertain economic outlook is the unresolved issue of immigration. Some analysts are less concerned about illegal immigrants taking low-paying jobs from native-born Americans as they are about the chance that immigrant groups will become mired in permanent poverty because of out-of-wedlock births and other social problems.

"In the long term," says Mead of New York University, "overcoming poverty probably does depend on restricting immigration" to 1970 levels. Curbing immigration, he says, not only would make more entry-level jobs available to native-born men — the group that Mead sees as a priority for anti-poverty action — but also help keep a new underclass from developing even as the nation struggles to reduce poverty in the established population.

As scholars and activists look ahead, some express optimism, as Lyndon Johnson once did, that poverty not only can be substantially reduced but actually eliminated. Others note that Johnson's vow to eliminate poverty raised expectations that were never satisfied.

"I think the poor are always going to be with us," says Bradley of the National Community Action Foundation. "Can we substantially reduce poverty? Yes. But the [idea] that somehow certain programs are going to eradicate poverty in America is just unrealistic."

NOTES

1. Testimony before House Ways and Means Subcommittee on Income Security and Family Support, "Hearing on Economic Opportunity and Poverty in America," Feb. 13, 2007.

2. Figures reflect U.S. Census Bureau data for 2006. For background, see Kathy Koch, "Child Poverty," *CQ Researcher*, April 7, 2000, pp. 281-304.

3. Timothy M. Smeeding, testimony before House Ways and Means Subcommittee on Income Security and Family Support, "Hearing on Economic Opportunity and Poverty in America," Feb. 13, 2007. The study is based on Smeeding's calculations from the Luxembourg Income Study.

4. Quoted in Bob Herbert, "The Millions Left Out," *The New York Times*, May 12, 2007, p. A25.

5. Tony Pugh, "U.S. Economy Leaving Record Numbers in Severe Poverty," McClatchy Newspapers, Feb. 22, 2007, updated May 25, 2007.

6. Aviva Aron-Dine, "New Data Show Income Concentration Jumped Again in 2005," Center on Budget and Policy Priorities, March 29, 2007, www.cbpp.org/3-29-07inc.htm.

7. David Cay Johnston, "Income Gap Is Widening, Data Shows," *The New York Times*, March 29, 2007, p. C1.

8. "Panel Study of Income Dynamics; Cross-National Equivalent File," Cornell University. Cited in John Edwards, Marion Crain and Arne L. Kalleberg, eds., *Ending Poverty in America: How to Restore the American Dream* (2007), The New Press, published in conjunction with the Center on Poverty, Work and Opportunity, University of North Carolina at Chapel Hill. Data are from Jacob S. Hacker, "The Risky Outlook for Middle-Class America," Chapter 5, p. 72.

9. Mark R. Rank, "Toward a New Understanding of American Poverty," *Journal of Law & Policy*, Vol. 20:17, p. 33, http://law.wustl.edu/Journal/20/p17Rankbookpage.pdf.

10. Steven Greenhouse, "A Unified Voice Argues the Case for U.S. Manufacturing," *The New York Times*, April 26, 2007, p. C2.

11. Katrina vanden Heuvel, "Twelve Steps to Cutting Poverty in Half," Blog: Editor's Cut, *The Nation*, April 30, 2007, www.thenation.com/blogs/edcut?pid=190867.

12. Patrick Healy, "Clinton Vows Middle Class Will Not Be 'Invisible' to Her," *The New York Times*, March 11, 2007, www.nyt.com.

13. Quoted in Alec MacGillis, "Obama Says He, Too, Is a Poverty Fighter," *The Washington Post*, July 19, 2007, p. 4A.

14. Jackie Calmes, "Edwards's Theme: U.S. Poverty," *The Wall Street Journal Online*, Dec. 28, 2006.

15. Edward Luce, "Bloomberg urges US to extend anti-poverty scheme," *FT.com* (*Financial Times*), Aug. 29, 2007.

16. "McDermott Announces Hearing on Proposals for Reducing Poverty," press release, House Ways and Means Subcommittee on Income Security and Family Support, April 26, 2007.

17. Mike Dorning, "Will Poverty Make Political Comeback?" *Chicago Tribune*, June 3, 2007, p. 4.

18. Gallup Poll, June 11-14, 2007.

19. Jon Cohen, "Despite Focus on Poverty, Edwards Trails Among the Poor," *The Washington Post*, July 11, 2007, p. 7A.

20. Testimony before House Committee on Ways and Means, "Hearing on the Economic and Societal Costs of Poverty," Jan. 24, 2007.

21. Steven H. Woolf, Robert E. Johnson and H. Jack Geiger, "The Rising Prevalence of Severe Poverty in

America: A Growing Threat to Public Health," *American Journal of Preventive Medicine*, Vol. 31, Issue 4, October 2006, p. 332.

22. Quoted in "Statement of Child Welfare League of America," House Ways and Means Subcommittee on Income Security and Family Support, "Hearing on Economic Opportunity and Poverty in America," Feb. 13, 2007. According to the statement, Conley's comment came in an ABC television profile of poverty in Camden, N.J., broadcast in January 2007.

23. Testimony before House Ways and Means Subcommittee on Income Security and Family Support, Feb. 13, 2007. Berube said concentrated poverty is defined by Paul Jargowsky of the University of Texas-Dallas as neighborhoods where at least 40 percent of individuals live below the poverty line.

24. Pugh, *op. cit.*

25. Nell McNamara and Doug Schenkelberg, *Extreme Poverty & Human Rights: A Primer* (2007), Mid-America Institute on Poverty of Heartland Alliance for Human Needs & Human Rights. For the Bellevue data, the report cites Pennsylvania State University, "Poverty in America (n.d.) Living Wage Calculator," retrieved Nov. 15, 2006, from www .livingwage.geog.psu.edu/.

26. Pugh, *op. cit.*

27. Testimony before House Ways and Means Subcommittee on Income Security and Family Support, Feb. 13, 2007.

28. Woolf, *et al.*, *op. cit.*

29. Peter Katel, "Minimum Wage," *CQ Researcher*, Dec. 16, 2005, pp. 1053-1076.

30. Sarah Glazer, "Welfare Reform," *CQ Researcher*, Aug. 3, 2001, pp. 601-632.

31. Dan Froomkin, "Welfare's Changing Face," www .Washingtonpost.com/wp-srv/politics/special/ welfare/welfare.htm, updated July 23, 1998.

32. Ron Haskins, "Welfare Check," *The Wall Street Journal*, July 27, 2006, accessed at www.brookings.edu.

33. "Interview: Welfare Reform, 10 Years Later," *The Examiner*, Aug. 24, 2006, accessed at www .brookings.edu.

34. Sharon Parrott and Arloc Sherman, "TANF at 10: Program Results are More Mixed Than Often Understood," Center on Budget and Policy Priorities, Aug. 17, 2006.

35. Wisconsin Council on Children & Families, "Wisconsin Ranks First in Growth in Poverty: Census Bureau Reports," press release, Aug. 30, 2005. See also testimony of Richard Schlimm, House Ways and Means Committee, "Hearing on the Economic and Societal Costs of Poverty," Jan. 24, 2007.

36. Testimony before House Subcommittee on Income Security and Family Support, Feb. 13, 2007.

37. Lawrence Mead, "And Now, 'Welfare Reform' for Men," *The Washington Post*, March 20, 2007, p. 19A.

38. Michael D. Tanner, "More Welfare, More Poverty," *The Monitor* (McAllen, Texas), Sept. 8, 2006.

39. Proceedings of the Virginia Assembly, 1619.

40. Henry George, "Progress and Poverty," first printed in 1879. Quoted in H. B. Shaffer, "Persistence of Poverty," *Editorial Research Reports*, Feb. 5, 1964, available at *CQ Researcher Plus Archive*, www.cqpress .com.

41. Gordon M. Fisher, "From Hunter to Orshansky: An Overview of (Unofficial) Poverty Lines in the United States from 1904 to 1965-Summary, March 1994, retrieved at http://aspe.hhs.gov/poverty/papers/ htrssmiv.htm.

42. *CQ Researcher, op. cit.*

43. Michael Harrington, *The Other America: Poverty in the United States* (1962), pp. 14-15.

44. U.S. Census data show the poverty rate for individuals was 22.2 percent in 1960; 21.9 percent in 1961; 21 percent in 1962; 19.5 percent in 1963; and 19 percent in 1964. For families the rate ranged from 20.7 percent to 17.4 percent in that period.

45. See H. B. Shaffer, "Status of War on Poverty," in *Editorial Research Reports*, Jan. 25, 1967, available at *CQ Researcher Plus Archive*, www.cqpress.com.

46. Marcia Clemmitt, "Evaluating Head Start," *CQ Researcher*, Aug. 26, 2005, pp. 685-708.

47. Sheldon H. Danziger and Robert H. Haveman, eds., *Understanding Poverty* (2001), Russell Sage Foundation and Harvard University Press, pp. 4 and 5.

48. Peter Edelman, "The Worst Thing Bill Clinton Has Done," *The Atlantic Monthly*, March 1997.

49. Jeff Jacoby, "Wefare Reform Success," *The Boston Globe*, Sept. 13, 2006, p. 9A.

50. Sheldon H. Danziger, "Fighting Poverty Revisited: What did researchers know 40 years ago? What do we know today?," *Focus*, University of Wisconsin-Madison, Institute for Research on Poverty, Spring-Summer 2007, p. 3.

51. Lyndon B. Johnson, "Annual Message to Congress on the State of the Union," Jan. 8, 1964.

52. MacGillis, *op. cit.*

53. E.J. Dionne Jr., "Making the Poor Visible," *The Washington Post*, July 20, 2007, p. A19.

54. Mary H. Cooper, "Income Inequality," *CQ Researcher*, April 17, 1998, pp. 337-360.

55. www.mittromney.com.

56. Mark Greenberg, Indivar Dutta-Gupta and Elisa Minoff, "From Poverty to Prosperity: A National Strategy to Cut Poverty in Half," Center for American Progress, April 2007, www.americanprogress.org/issues/2007/04/poverty_report.html.

57. Ron Haskins and Isabel V. Sawhill, "Attacking Poverty and Inequality," Brookings Institution, Opportunity 08, in partnership with ABC News, February 2007, www.opportunity08.org/Issues/OurSociety/31/r1/Default.aspx.

58. Coalition on Human Needs, "Nearly 900 Organizations Sign Letter to Congress in Support of Expanding Tax Credits for the Poor," May 25, 2007, www.chn.org. The letter, dated May 24, 2007, was accessed at www.chn.org/pdf/2007/ctceitcletter.pdf.

59. Alan Berube, "Using the Earned Income Tax Credit to Stimulate Local Economies," Brookings Institution, www.brookings.org.

60. Adriel Bettelheim, "The Social Side of Tax Breaks," *CQ Weekly*, Feb. 5, 2007.

61. *Ibid.*

62. Diane Cardwell, "City to Reward Poor for Doing Right Thing," *The New York Times*, March 30, 2007, p. 1B.

63. The bill is AB 1118.

64. David MacDonald, communications director, Connecticut Association for Community Action, letter to the editor of the *Hartford Courant*, June 27, 2007, p. 8A.

65. Clea Benson, "States Scramble to Adapt To New Welfare Rules," *CQ Weekly*, June 25, 2007, p. 1907.

66. *Ibid.*

67. *Ibid.*

68. *Ibid.*

BIBLIOGRAPHY

Books

Danziger, Sheldon H., and Robert H. Haveman, eds., *Understanding Poverty,* **Russell Sage Foundation and Harvard University Press, 2001.**
Writings on domestic poverty range from the evolution of anti-poverty programs to health policy for the poor. Danziger is a professor of social work and public policy at the University of Michigan, Haveman, a professor of economics and public affairs at the University of Wisconsin, Madison.

DeParle, Jason, *American Dream: Three Women, Ten Kids, and a Nation's Drive to End Welfare,* **Viking Adult, 2004.**
A reporter looks at the effort to overhaul the American welfare system through the lives of three former welfare mothers.

Edwards, John, Marion Crain and Arne L. Kalleberg, eds., *Ending Poverty in America,* **New Press, 2007.**
Co-edited and with a conclusion by Democratic presidential candidate Edwards, this collection of articles reflects a progressive economic agenda.

Haskins, Ron, *Work Over Welfare: The Inside Story of the 1996 Welfare Reform Law,* **Brookings Institution Press, 2006.**
A former Republican committee staffer and a chief architect of welfare reform, Haskins tells the story of the political debates leading up to the historic welfare overhaul.

Articles

Bai, Matt, "The Poverty Platform," *New York Times Magazine,* **June 10, 2007.**
Taking a close look at presidential candidate John Edwards' focus on the poor, Bai says "the main economic debate in Democratic Washington" focuses on "the tools

of economic policy — taxes, trade, welfare — and how to use them."

Dorning, Mike, "Will Poverty Make Political Comeback?" *Chicago Tribune*, June 3, 2007.
Since the 1960s, Dorning notes, "leading presidential candidates generally have not focused on the plight of the poor as a central issue."

Reports and Studies

Children's Defense Fund, **"The State of America's Children 2005."**
Marian Wright Edelman, founder and president of the Children's Defense Fund, writes, "Far less wealthy industrialized countries have committed to end child poverty, while the United States is sliding backwards."

Congressional Budget Office, **"Changes in the Economic Resources of Low-Income Households with Children,"** May 2007.
This study charts income changes among the poor from the early 1990s.

Greenberg, Mark, Indivar Dutta-Gupta and Elisa Minoff, "From Poverty to Prosperity: A National Strategy to Cut Poverty in Half," *Center for American Progress*, April 2007.
The think tank's Task Force on Poverty says the United States should set a goal of halving poverty over the next decade.

Harrison, David, and Bob Watrus, "On Getting Out–and Staying Out–of Poverty: The Complex Causes of and Responses to Poverty in the Northwest," *Northwest Area Foundation*, 2004.
An estimated 2 million people live in poverty in the Northwest, more than 900,000 of them in severe poverty.

McNamara, Nell, and Doug Schenkelberg, "Extreme Poverty & Human Rights: A Primer," *Heartland Alliance for Human Needs & Human Rights*, 2007.
A guidebook explains how human rights advocacy can combat both global and domestic poverty.

Meyer, Bruce D., and James X. Sullivan, "Three Decades of Consumption and Income Poverty," *National Poverty Center Working Paper Series*, September 2006.
The study examines poverty measurement in the United States from 1972 through 2004 and how poverty rates have changed over the years.

Rector, Robert, "How Poor Are America's Poor? Examining the 'Plague' of Poverty in America," *Heritage Foundation*, Aug. 27, 2007.
A senior research fellow at the conservative think tank writes that " 'the plague' of American poverty might not be as 'terrible' or 'incredible' as candidate [John] Edwards contends."

Toldson, Ivory A., and Elsie L. Scott, "Poverty, Race and Policy," *Congressional Black Caucus Foundation*, 2006.
The four-part report explores affordable-housing policy, wealth-accumulation needs and strategies for reducing poverty and unemployment.

Woolf, Steven H., Robert E. Johnson and H. Jack Geiger, "The Rising Prevalence of Severe Poverty in America: A Growing Threat to Public Health," *American Journal of Preventive Medicine*, October 2006.
Woolf, a professor of family medicine, epidemiology and community health at Virginia Commonwealth University and lead author of this study, says the growth in severe poverty and other trends "have disturbing implications for society and public health."

For More Information

Center for American Progress, 1333 H St., N.W., 10th Floor, Washington, DC 20005; (202) 682-1611; www .americanprogress.org. A liberal think tank that issued a report and recommendations on poverty this year.

Coalition on Human Needs, 1120 Connecticut Ave., N.W., Suite 910, Washington, DC 20036; (202) 223-2532; www.chn.org. An alliance of organizations that promote policies to help low-income people and others in need.

Economic Policy Institute, 1333 H St., N.W., Suite 300, East Tower, Washington, DC 20005-4707; (202) 775-8810; www.epi.org. A think tank that studies policies related to the economy, work and the interests of low- and middle-income people.

Heritage Foundation, 214 Massachusetts Ave., N.E., Washington, DC 20002-4999; (202) 546-4400; www .heritage.org. A conservative think tank that studies poverty and other public-policy issues.

Institute for Research on Poverty, University of Wisconsin-Madison, 1180 Observatory Dr., 3412 Social Science Building, Madison, WI 53706-1393; (608) 262-6358; www.irp.wisc.edu. Studies the causes and consequences of poverty.

Mid-America Institute on Poverty, 4411 North Ravenswood Ave., Chicago, IL 60640; (773) 336-6084; www.heartlandalliance.org. A research arm of Heartland Alliance, which provides services for low-income individuals.

National Community Action Foundation, 810 First St., N.E., Suite 530, Washington, DC 20002; (202) 842-2092; www.ncaf.org. Advocates for the nation's community-action agencies.

Step Up, Savannah's Poverty Reduction Initiative, 101 East Bay St., Savannah, GA 31401; (912) 644-6420; www.stepupsavannah .org. A coalition of more than 80 local business, government and nonprofit organizations seeking to reduce poverty.

U.S. Census Bureau, 4600 Silver Hill Road, Suitland, MD 20746; www.census.gov. Maintains extensive recent and historical data on poverty and demographics.

University of North Carolina Center on Poverty, Work and Opportunity, UNC School of Law, Van Heck-Wettach Hall, 100 Ridge Road, CB#3380, Chapel Hill, N.C. 27599-3380; (919) 962-5106; www.law.unc.edu/centers/ poverty/default.aspx. A national forum for scholars, policy-makers and others interested in poverty, established by presidential candidate John Edwards.

Urban Institute, 2100 M St., N.W., Washington, DC 20037; (202) 833-7200; www.urban.org. Studies welfare and low-income families among a range of issues.

8

Hunger in America

How Bad Is the Problem?

Kathy Koch

Eight-year-old David Hatfield offers a mealtime prayer at a Kids Café in Cincinnati, housed in a local church. The nationwide program to feed children in poor neighborhoods is sponsored by ConAgra Foods Inc. and America's Second Harvest.

From *CQ Researcher*,
December 22, 2000.

A t a church in the Mid-west recently, a group of men gathered to pack holiday food baskets for the hungry. "These were the kind of big-hearted guys who would do anything for anybody," a church volunteer recalls.

Despite their magnanimity, however, several of the volunteers had uncharitable thoughts about the needy, saying they had caused their own problems with their unwise spending habits. "They actually said that the reason people are hungry or can't afford food in America is because they shop in convenience stores," the worker says. "It drove me nuts. That myth has been disproved."

Several private and government studies have indeed debunked the myth that the disadvantaged aren't careful shoppers, but the misperception lingers, says Sue Hofer, a spokeswoman for America's Second Harvest, the nation's largest private, domestic, hunger-relief organization.

Overcoming skepticism about the causes of hunger in America is one of the biggest problems facing those who strive to alleviate it. "It's a real problem for emergency food banks, especially at this time of year," Hofer says, when pantries depend on year-end drives for up to a third of their annual food supply.

Food banks aren't alone in fighting skepticism about hunger. Support for the federal food stamp program — the nation's flagship nutrition-assistance system — waxes and wanes because of the same doubts. Advocates for the hungry say Americans are often ambivalent about offering help — torn between their sense of duty and their innate suspicion that anyone needing a handout amid America's abundance must be either lazy or a cheat.

Measuring Hunger in the United States

An average of 9.7 percent of U.S. households (about 10 million households) did not always have access to enough food to meet basic needs in the period 1996-98. Eleven states in the West and South had rates of "food insecurity" significantly above the national average.

Prevalence of Food Insecurity
(Average Percentage of Households Per State, 1996-98)

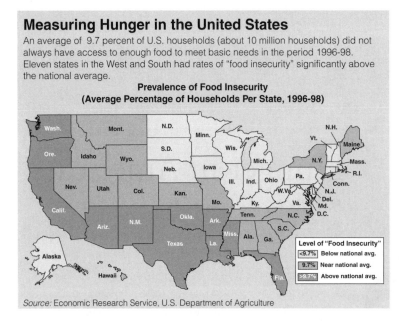

Source: Economic Research Service, U.S. Department of Agriculture

"Such ambivalence suggests a certain underlying doubt that significant numbers of people are truly hungry," writes Peter K. Eisinger, a professor of urban affairs at Wayne State University in Detroit and author of *Toward an End to Hunger in America.*[1]

But recently released annual reports from Catholic Charities USA and the U.S. Conference of Mayors say the problem is real. Among the findings:

- Requests for emergency food aid in selected cities regularly surveyed by the mayors increased an average of 17 percent from 1998 to 1999, the second-highest increase since 1992.[2]
- Families with children comprised 62 percent of those requesting emergency food in 1999, up 16 percent — the highest increase since 1991, according to the mayors.[3]
- Nearly a third, 32 percent, of the adults requesting emergency food were employed.[4]
- Requests for emergency food aid from elderly citizens increased 9 percent, the mayors found.[5]
- In 100 percent of the cities surveyed by the mayors, emergency food assistance was relied on both for emergencies and as a steady source of food over long periods of time.
- Almost 6 million persons received emergency food services in 1999 from Catholic Charities, up 32 percent from 1998 to 1999.[6]

Several other studies in recent years have confirmed that children and the working poor make up a growing portion of the hungry in America. For instance, the Chicago-based America's Second Harvest, which provides food to more than 25 million clients each year through its network of more than 200 food banks and food-recovery organizations, found in a 1998 survey that nearly 38 percent of its clients were 17 years old or younger. Plus, at least one adult was working in nearly 40 percent of the households served by the network.

"We've seen a real shift in who we serve," says Doug O'Brien, director of public policy and research at Second Harvest. "A decade ago, it was almost always homeless, single men and chronic substance abusers. Now we have children and working families at soup kitchens."

In addition, the most comprehensive study ever done on childhood hunger in the United States, by the Food Research and Action Center (FRAC), found that 29 percent of children under 12 in the early 1990s lived in families coping with hunger or the risk of hunger during some part of at least one month of the year.[7]

Finally, the U.S. Agriculture Department found that in 1999 some 31 million people — including 12 million children — lived in households that were "food insecure," those with a limited ability to acquire enough food to meet their basic needs in socially acceptable ways. That amounted to 10.1 percent of all U.S. households and an increase of 5 million people over 1997. The study also found that more than 7.5 million people lived in homes where someone in the household went without food involuntarily, the government's official definition of hunger.

Although hunger rates in America have been slowly falling over the long term, they are higher than in other industrialized countries. And anti-hunger advocates argue that hunger and food insecurity are unacceptable because they cause serious adverse health, educational and developmental consequences. "The pace of improvement in hunger is just too slow compared to the roaring economy," said Lynn Parker, FRAC's director of child nutrition.[8]

"When people who are working full time have to go to a church pantry to put food on their tables, something is terribly wrong," O'Brien says.

He and others who fight hunger say the biggest causes of hunger in America today are not the spending habits of low-income Americans but low-paying jobs, unemployment, high housing and utility costs, poverty, substance abuse, cutbacks in food stamp benefits and meager benefits in public-assistance programs compared to other industrial countries. Particularly troubling, they say, is a precipitous 27 percent drop in participation in the federal food stamp program over the three years immediately following the 1996 overhaul of the welfare program.[9]

As America's first line of defense against hunger, the food stamp program is an important support for families making the transition from welfare to self-sufficiency. It provides benefits worth an average of $2.34 a day per person, redeemable only for food. Yet since 1996, participation has fallen three times as fast as the poverty rate, suggesting that many poor families left the program even though they were still eligible for food stamps.

Agriculture Secretary Dan Glickman is concerned that with 31 million "food insecure" Americans, the number of food stamp participants has dropped to 17 million. Although the improved economy is partly responsible for the decline, some was also caused by Congress' decision in 1996 to suddenly withhold food stamps from non-citizen immigrants. In addition, overzealous state and local governments have cut benefits more than the law permits, advocates for the hungry say. And states and local officials have erected new bureaucratic hurdles for applicants, they point out, while some states simply aren't telling people leaving welfare that they are still eligible for food stamps.

"Unfortunately, many families that have left the [welfare] rolls are unaware that they may continue to be eligible for food stamps," Glickman said in a July 12 letter asking governors to help ensure that all families needing assistance have access to the program.

Children are suffering disproportionately from the drop in food stamp participation, according to the General Accounting Office (GAO), which said that in 1997 children accounted for 48 percent of the decrease in participation. "Children's participation in the food stamp program has dropped more sharply than the number of children living in poverty, indicating a growing gap between need and assistance," the GAO said.[10]

Letter carriers open a giant mailbox to help kick off the annual Stamp Out Hunger food drive to restock food banks across the country. Campbell Soup Co. donated 1 million pounds of canned goods.

Newsmakers/William Thomas Cain

"We're not making any progress in fighting hunger because cuts in the food stamp program are offsetting the positive effects of the economic boom," complains FRAC President James Weill.

Other causes of hunger among low-income working families are the "stratospheric cost of housing," the cost of quality child care and the absence of reliable transportation to work, 68 members of Congress said in a "Dear Colleague" letter in October. They called the persistence of hunger and food insecurity in America "particularly troubling in this time of great prosperity."

The same month, Congress passed a measure relaxing food stamp eligibility rules. Signed into law on Oct. 28, it is expected to provide $1.6 billion more in food stamp benefits over five years, increase benefits for needy families and allow new families to participate in the program.

The new law allows applicants to own a reliable car and still be eligible for food stamps. Low-income families need a car to get to work, but many families who have one are disqualified from food stamp participation because of artificially low limits on the value of a reliable car, proponents of the legislation argued.

"The act...[also] will allow more low-income families with high housing costs to apply for food stamps," said President Clinton, as he signed the bill. "The...changes mean that families do not have to choose among buying food, paying their housing costs or having a more reliable car."

Why People Need Food Assistance

The two most frequently cited reasons people go to church pantries are that they are not earning enough or are recently unemployed. Among those at soup kitchens, long-term unemployement is by far the most often cited reason.

What Clients Say	Where They Go for Food	
	Church Pantry	Food Kitchen
Recent unemployment	53.7%	35.7%
Long-term unemployment	35.2	51.9
Working/need more money	57.3	40.5
High fixed expenses	22.4	19.3
Other help inadequate	35.6	35.4
Bureaucratic hassles	15.5	12.7
High cost of child care	3.3	3.2
No child care/can't work	2.6	2.0
Divorce/separation/ death of spouse	14.0	7.3
Illness/medical problem	23.2	25.9
Disability/handicap	18.1	23.2
Emergency/crisis	35.5	28.3

Source: America's Second Harvest, Nov. 8, 2000 (www.secondharvest.org)

Clinton further relaxed federal food stamp rules on Nov. 18, allowing states to make the program more user-friendly for working families. The regulations allow states to provide three months of guaranteed benefits to people leaving welfare for work and eliminate the time-consuming requirement that recipients reapply for benefits every three months and verify their income monthly.

But advocates for hunger relief call for more action, including reauthorization of the food stamp program in the next Congress. As social-policy experts and lawmakers debate the issue, here are some of the questions being asked:

Is there a serious hunger problem in America today?

Robert Rector, a senior research fellow at the conservative Heritage Foundation, disputes hunger activists' claim that nearly a third of American children are hungry or "at risk" of hunger. "Far from being a widespread crisis, hunger is a problem very limited in scope and duration," Rector says, citing government statistics.

A 1995 Department of Health and Human Services (HHS) report shows that the vast majority of American families — 96 percent — have "enough food to eat," he says. According to the survey, he says, only one-half of 1 percent said they "often" don't have enough to eat, and about 3 percent "sometimes" don't have enough food, the survey showed.[11]

"American children, both rich and poor, are remarkably well fed and well nourished," Rector says. "The average amount of protein, vitamins and minerals consumed by poor children is virtually identical with that of middle-class children."

Douglas Besharov, a welfare expert at the conservative American Enterprise Institute (AEI), concurs, adding, "If there is a problem, it's much smaller than it's ever been in our history. Obesity is a bigger problem among the poor in America today than hunger."

Indeed, Rector says that nearly half of those claiming they don't have enough to eat are actually overweight. "Obesity is most common among the tiny group claiming they 'often' lack food," he says. Moreover, he contends, poor Americans suffer from health problems caused primarily from overconsumption of food, not food scarcity. The average poor child's daily food intake greatly exceeds recommended norms and includes more than twice the recommended daily allowance of protein, he points out.

Compared with 50 years ago, today's children are neither stunted nor too skinny, he says. The average, low-income 18-year-old boy today is an inch taller and 10 pounds heavier than the typical middle-class 18-year-old in the late 1950s, he adds.

But Second Harvest's O'Brien claims Rector uses "salad-bar science" to make his points. "He takes a little from here, and a little from there, mixes it together and comes up with a bad conclusion."

O'Brien says Rector not only "co-mingles the data" from various studies but also relies on decade-old data that many leading researchers say were not designed to measure hunger. "In other words, his conclusions are just plain wrong," O'Brien says.

The 1988-89 data used in the HHS survey cited by Rector has since been supplanted by information collected between 1995 and 1998 in the Census Bureau's annual Current Population Survey (CPS), says O'Brien. The most recent version of that survey, published in 1998, found that 11.2 million people — not counting the homeless — experienced hunger due to inadequate resources. It also found that nearly 12 percent of U.S. households, or 35 million people, were "food insecure."[12]

O'Brien points out that numerous studies by non-governmental organizations and academics have also confirmed statistically significant rates of food insecurity and hunger. Among others, he cites a recent National Survey of America's Families by the Urban Institute, which found that half of all families who earn up to twice the poverty threshold were worried about obtaining food.

J. Larry Brown, executive director of the Center on Hunger and Poverty at Brandeis University in Waltham, Mass., says the Census Bureau's survey, the Food Security Supplement, uses a "widely accepted, highly reliable" method for measuring the severity of food insecurity and hunger in U.S. households. He points out that Tufts University School of Nutrition researchers John T. Cook and Katie S. Martin also dispute the claim that because the average nutrient intakes of poor and non-poor children are about the same over time, there is no connection between poverty and poor nutrition. They argue that overall nutrient adequacy depends upon the actual distribution and frequency of nutrient intake over time — not the average intake.

In a proportional analysis of the same data used by Rector, Cook and Martin concluded that, "millions of poor American children have significantly inadequate dietary intakes."[13]

For instance, they say the diets of poor children from ages 1 to 5 are seriously deficient in 10 out of 16 major nutrients compared with non-poor children. Poor children are also two-and-a-half times as likely as wealthier children to have substandard caloric intakes and six times

as likely to have substandard intakes of magnesium and vitamin A. In addition, half of the nation's poor children are deficient in zinc, 40 percent in iron and more than a third in vitamin E.[14]

In addition, they conclude, protein intake is not a sound indicator of overall nutrition. "Reliance on protein as an indicator of the adequacy of nutrient intake is inconsistent with current nutrition science, which emphasizes the importance of a much wider range of nutrients in human health," they wrote.[15]

Brown adds that although obesity is a serious national health problem for Americans at all income levels, recent studies show that obesity among the poor can result from periodic episodes of insufficient food intake and can mask serious nutrient deficiencies. (*See sidebar, p. 192.*)

"The weight of the evidence clearly shows that we have a hunger problem in this country," Brown says. "Working people who are otherwise playing by the rules can't afford shelter, clothes and food for their families."

Besharov says increasingly long lines at emergency food banks are not an accurate measure of hunger. Rather, he says, "The lines at the soup kitchens are driven by the availability of free food. If you give food away, people will come and get it."

But anti-hunger advocates bristle at the suggestion that people stand in food lines to get bargains. "That's absurd," Brown says. "Does the ordinary middle-class American drag his kids down to stand in line at a food bank when he hears free cheese is being given away? Of course not. It's degrading to stand in a food line. People who say that are contaminating the public discourse with seat-of-the-pants opinions."

Should food stamps be easier to obtain?

Only 40 percent of those served by Second Harvest's food banks receive food stamps, even though most emergency-food recipients are income-eligible. And since welfare reform was adopted in 1996, more people who are otherwise eligible for food stamps have been walking away from applying for them. Instead, they have been depending more on soup kitchens and food banks.

One reason for the switch, anti-hunger advocates say, is the nature of the food stamp bureaucracy. Designed initially to serve the unemployed, the program has never been user-friendly for working people, and has become even less so in recent years.

Second Harvest reviewed food stamp application procedures and found that they were so cumbersome and complex that they discourage thousands of eligible participants from even applying. Among other things, the group found that the applications are too long — up to 36 pages.[16]

They are also difficult to read and complete, with language and verification procedures so complex they "put the Internal Revenue Service to shame," the report says. Some applications also stigmatize and intimidate the applicant. For instance, the California application warns that anyone who does not "follow food stamp rules" may be fined up to $250,000 and/or sent to jail/prison for 20 years.[17]

The applications also ask intrusive and unnecessary questions about income that in some cases are forbidden by federal law, O'Brien says. Sixteen states are either fingerprinting applicants or are considering it. Others contact an applicant's employer and/or landlord; require personal references, credit checks and home visits. He says the average application takes five hours to fill out and at least two visits — which can last a half-day each — to the local food stamp agency. Often applicants must return in person every three months to reverify that their salary hasn't changed.

"What employer will put up with that number of absences from an employee?" O'Brien asks. "And is it worth it to miss work, possibly losing wages or putting your job in jeopardy, just for $18 a week per person in benefits?"

States also use tactics with low-income people that they would never try to use with middle-class Americans, O'Brien says. "Would the government ask a middle-class American to be fingerprinted and certify answers to 30 pages of intrusive questions in order to obtain a gun permit?" he asks. "Yet these people are being asked to endure such indignities — not in order to carry a deadly weapon, but to get food for their children."

In short, the report says, the process creates "a chilling atmosphere for families seeking food security."[18]

State officials say the lengthy applications, background checks and fingerprinting are needed to prevent fraud. "The federal government puts the onus on the states if they pay too much or too little," O'Brien says. "That's what leads the states to go through this ridiculous process."

The good news, he says, is that since the report came out about a dozen states have begun trying to streamline their application procedures. And, if adopted by the states, the measures recently announced by Clinton will go a long way toward reducing other barriers, advocates for the hungry say.

But food stamp critics say that rather than being easier to get, they should be harder to obtain. Rector favors work requirements imposed on all recipients. "The basic principle of welfare reform is that it's not good to reward idleness," he says. "The food stamp program is run just the opposite."

O'Brien points out that since the 1980s, applicants who are able have been required to work — or at least register for work — to receive food stamps. And the 1996 welfare reforms required able-bodied applicants ages 18 to 50 without dependent children to work. It also limited their eligibility for food stamps to three months in any 36-month period. Only the elderly, the disabled, pregnant women and parents caring for a dependent child are exempted, O'Brien points out. "So, I would say Mr. Rector's concern has been met," he says.

But Rector stresses that he would like to see "real, effective work requirements" imposed, not "nominal requirements that mean nothing." He says the pre-1996 welfare program had "all kinds of nominal behavior requirements" that were meaningless in practice. "We must decide if we want food stamps to continue operating in the old Great Society model."

Rector points out that able-bodied persons without children — the only ones currently required to work — are effectively exempt from the work requirement during the first three or six months they are on the rolls. He also questions how many hours recipients are actually working. "A lot of able-bodied people getting food stamps are not even working 20 hours a week," he says.

Yet anti-hunger advocates say it's not necessary to require food stamp recipients to work because many are already working, and some even have two jobs. For instance, at least 6,300 enlisted members of the U.S. armed forces need food stamps to get by, they point out.

But Rector claims anti-hunger advocates like to focus on food-aid recipients who are working because they arouse the most sympathy with the public. He questions Second Harvest's estimate that 38 percent of its food-bank clients are working. "How do they know for a fact that their clients are working?" Rector asks. "Do they demand to see their salary stubs? No."

He points out, for instance, that according to Department of Agriculture figures only 26 percent of food stamp households have any earned income.[19]

Lisa Oliphant, entitlements policy analyst with the libertarian Cato Institute, would also like to see food stamps harder to obtain. "Right now, they are quite easy to obtain," she says. "In fact, in some communities, relying on food stamps has become a way of life."

She wants the program to be scrapped entirely because it encourages dependence. "I would rather not have a food stamp program at all," she says. "We shouldn't make poverty more comfortable."

Instead of simplifying food stamp application procedures, the government should make it easier for private-sector alternatives — like food banks — to flourish, she says.

She disagrees with those who argue that no working family should have to stand in a line for handouts. "Standing in line at a food bank is less dignified than getting food stamps," she concedes. "That's why it induces less dependence than food stamps do." The discomfort recipients feel standing in food lines is healthy, she says, because it may encourage them to find better ways to meet their needs themselves.

Oliphant doesn't believe that working parents really need to go to food banks. Even if they have a minimum-wage job, she says, they should be able to make ends meet by accessing the "vast safety net of supplemental, non-cash benefits" available to working families, such as food stamps, child care and housing subsidies, Medicaid and the Earned Income Tax Credit. "The benefits are definitely generous enough," she says.

However, O'Brien points out that most of those programs are grossly underutilized, partly because they have never been fully funded. Moreover, there is no peer-reviewed evidence showing that food stamps create dependence, he says. The 8 million people who have dropped out of the food stamp program since 1996 indicate just the opposite, he says.

That drop greatly exceeds both the number of people leaving poverty and those the government calls food insecure. "If the program were creating dependence, one would presume that the poor — seemingly dependent — would stay in the program," he says.

Should food stamps be available to all legal immigrants?

When Congress passed the welfare-reform law in 1996, it barred all legal immigrants, including those already in the United States at the time, from receiving food stamps or Social Security benefits unless they were U.S. citizens. New immigrants were prohibited from receiving food stamps or other welfare benefits until they became citizens, a process that can take up to seven years.

Even as he signed the bill into law on Aug. 22, President Clinton decried the non-citizen provisions and promised to reverse them in future legislation. Since then, Congress has restored food stamp eligibility for roughly 225,000 legal immigrants who were living in the United States when the law was enacted and were either elderly, disabled, under age 18 or active or former members of the U.S. military.

But nearly a million legal immigrants are still barred from receiving food stamps, even though many are working and paying taxes. The Clinton administration has supported measures to restore their eligibility, but Congress has refused to pass them.

Despite strong bipartisan support, a few powerful Republican congressional opponents have successfully blocked the measures. The lawmakers, all House committee or subcommittee chairmen representing Southern states, argue that allowing legal immigrants to receive food stamps is tantamount to "expanding welfare."

The group includes Virginians Thomas J. Bliley Jr. and Robert W. Goodlatte and three members representing border states with significant Hispanic immigration problems: Texans Bill Archer and Lamar Smith and E. Clay Shaw Jr. of Florida.

"We should promote the assimilation of newcomers as productive members of society and not wards of the welfare state," they argued in an Oct. 6 letter to House Speaker J. Dennis Hastert of Illinois. "We think critically important to ensure that non-citizens come to America for opportunity and not for welfare."

An accompanying position statement said, "The United States welcomes hard-working immigrants, but we cannot afford to be a welfare magnet or a retirement home for the entire world."

They pointed out that when immigrants apply for resident visas, both they and their sponsors swear that

Major Domestic Food Aid Programs

- **Food Stamp Program** — Provides participants with electronic debit cards containing an average value of $72.70 a month per person. The maximum allowed for a family of three is $341 and $434 for a family of four. To qualify, a four-person household's gross annual income must be less than $22,176. According to the Agriculture Department, 80 percent of food stamp benefits go to households with children and senior citizens. The average length of participation is less than two years, and half of all new recipients stay in the program less than six months. The federal government pays 100 percent of the cost of food stamps, but only half of the administrative costs; the states administer the program and pay the other half. In fiscal 1997, the total federal share of food stamp costs was $21.4 billion.

- **National School Lunch Program** — Created by Congress in 1946 after many World War II draftees were rejected for military service because they were malnourished. It reimburses schools for providing needy children with lunches containing at least a third or more of the Recommended Dietary Allowance (RDA) of key nutrients. Today more than 15 million low-income children receive free or reduced-price lunches each school day. To qualify for free meals, the child's household income can't be more than 130 percent of the federal poverty level, or the household must be receiving food stamps or welfare. In 1997, the program cost the federal government $5.5 billion.

- **School Breakfast Program** — Created in 1966, it reimburses public and private schools and residential child-care institutions for serving breakfast to low-income students. Studies show that poor children who participate in a breakfast program achieve higher standardized test scores than poor children who do not. For free meals, a child's household income must be less than 130 percent of poverty; for reduced-price meals, it must be below 185 percent of the poverty line. In 1998 more than 7 million children in 68,426 schools received free or reduced-price breakfasts. In 1997 the federal share of the program was $1.2 billion.

- **Summer Food Service Program for Children** — Created in 1968, the program pays eligible sponsoring organizations to serve meals when school is not in

they will not apply for welfare benefits or food stamps. Their sponsors also swear that they have the wherewithal, if necessary, to support the immigrants. "If we don't have provisions like this, a person could come in and not be able to support himself and then go on to sponsor others who can't support themselves," says John Lampman, a press spokesman for Smith.

Oliphant also argues that reinstating benefits for legal immigrants is tantamount to expanding welfare. "We need to shrink our welfare state," she says, "not expand it."

"Government welfare assistance should not be a right," she adds. "After all, people are not forced to go hungry if they can't get food stamps. There are private charities in almost every neighborhood." She suggests that instead of making food stamps available for non-citizens, the government should direct them to private food banks.

But FRAC's Weill says barring legal immigrants from food is a "self-defeating, stupid policy." The 1996 law caused hardship for many immigrant families, he says,

citing a 1998 study showing that legal immigrants who lost food stamp benefits suffered far greater rates of hunger and food insecurity than the general population.

In addition, many of those families have children who were born here and are U.S. citizens and thus eligible for food stamps. But Agriculture Department statistics show that many immigrant families with U.S.-born children aren't getting food stamps for their eligible children. Between summer 1994 and summer 1997, food stamp participation among children born in the U.S. to legal immigrant parents fell more than twice as fast as participation among children with native-born parents, the Agriculture Department says.

In addition, when the federal government cut off legal immigrants, it shifted the responsibility and cost for those needing food to the state governments, complains Sheri Steisel, senior director of the human-services committee of the National Conference of State Legislatures (NCSL).

"It amounted to an unfunded mandate for state tax-payers and state governments," she says. "The federal

session to low-income children, usually in conjunction with educational, developmental and recreational activities at schools, residential camps or youth sports programs. In addition, anyone attending a school program for people with disabilities, regardless of age, may participate. In 1998, more than 2.2 million children received meals under the program; about 15 percent of those received free or reduced-price school lunches during the school year. In 1998, the program cost the federal government $261 million.

■ **Special Supplemental Nutrition Program For Women, Infants And Children (WIC)** — Established in 1972, the program provides prescribed foods, nutrition education and access to health care to low-income pregnant women, new mothers, infants and children under age 5. By increasing the number of women receiving prenatal care, the program reduces the incidence of low birth weight and fetal mortality, reduces anemia and enhances the nutritional quality of participants' diets. Every dollar spent on WIC saves between $1.77 and $3.13 in Medicaid costs for newborns and their mothers, according to the Agriculture Department. Participants' household incomes must be under 185 percent of poverty and they must be certified by a

health professional to be either homeless or migrants or to have inadequate diets, abnormal weight gains during pregnancy, histories of high-risk pregnancies or the children are stunted, underweight or anemic. In fiscal 1997, WIC provided food and services for more than 7.4 million women, infants, and children and cost $3.8 billion.

■ **Child and Adult Care Food Program (CACFP)** — Established in 1968 to provide federal funds for meals and snacks for low-income recipients in public and nonprofit child-care centers and after-school programs and in adult day-care centers that serve chronically impaired adults or people over age 60. In 1997, more than 2.4 million preschool children and more than 52,000 elderly persons received meals and snacks under the program, and 1.5 billion meals and snacks were served in after-school programs. In 1997, the CACFP cost $1.6 billion.

■ **The Emergency Food Assistance Program** — Authorized in 1981 to distribute surplus commodities to states for low-income households and emergency food providers. An estimated 3.8 million households were served by TEFAP in 1997. Each state determines its own criteria for household eligibility. In 1997, federal funding for TEFAP was $179 million.

government allowed these people to come here through its own immigration laws and then left the states to pay for their social services." Noting that many state constitutions prohibit states from treating citizens any differently from non-citizens, she said, "States had to create their own food stamp programs to handle this need."

She particularly angers when lawmakers and others call food stamps a welfare program. "This is a hunger-relief program. It is very different from the welfare program," she insists. "These people work and pay taxes and contribute to the system. They should be allowed to access these programs."

Anti-hunger advocates say reinstating the benefits for legal immigrants is not only morally right but also economically wise. It would pay off in improved health, productivity and learning capacity of immigrant children — many of whom are citizens.

Weill says many things can happen to an immigrant waiting to become a citizen. "Some folks may lose their

jobs or their sponsors or may suddenly find themselves otherwise down on their luck," he says.

Punishing them for that, Brown says, is counterproductive in the long run. "What message are we sending to the children of a working, legal immigrant if he is forced to go to a food bank to feed his family? Why should that child want to grow up and play by the rules?"

BACKGROUND

Early Food Aid

Food-assistance programs have been administered by the Agriculture Department since 1935, when they were initiated largely to get rid of surplus agricultural commodities and to help support farm income, according to Eisinger.[20]

In fact, the food stamp program, which has become the nation's primary safety net for millions of low-income families, was launched in 1939, at the end of the

AP/Iowa City Gazette

High school students in Iowa City sort food they collected in November for the city's Crisis Center Food Bank. Six eastern Iowa high schools collected 19 tons of food for the center.

Great Depression, as a limited, four-year program to eliminate farm surplus. At its peak, it served only 4 million people.

The program was terminated after the onset of World War II, when feeding millions of troops made the problem of surplus-crop disposal disappear, along with most unemployment and poverty. Nonetheless, several members of Congress continued to push for a food stamp program throughout the 1950s. A 1959 farm bill amendment finally authorized the Agriculture Department to establish one.

However, the department never exercised that authority until 1961, shortly after President John F. Kennedy took office. As a member of the Senate, Kennedy had introduced some of the unsuccessful food stamp bills during the 1950s, and a food stamp proposal was included in the 1960 Democratic presidential campaign platform.

In one of his first official acts, Kennedy ordered the Agriculture secretary to immediately "expand and improve the program of food distribution throughout the United States." He also ordered establishment of a pilot food stamp program in West Virginia, Pennsylvania, eastern Kentucky, northern Minnesota, southern Illinois and Detroit.[21]

After Kennedy was assassinated, President Lyndon B. Johnson argued for a food stamp program as part of his War on Poverty. "We want no American in this country to go hungry," Johnson said. "We have the knowledge,

the compassion and the resources to banish hunger and to do away with malnutrition."[22] In 1964, a bipartisan coalition of urban Northerners and rural Southerners in Congress was able to establish a permanent food stamp program.

Hunger in America was further thrust into the limelight in 1967, following a visit to the Mississippi Delta by a Senate subcommittee on poverty led by Democratic Sens. Joseph Clark of Pennsylvania and Robert F. Kennedy of New York, the slain president's brother. During subcommittee hearings after the trip, a doctor testified that the malnutrition he observed in the Delta was as bad or worse than what he had seen in Africa and Aden.[23]

In 1968, a self-appointed Citizens' Board of Inquiry into Hunger and Malnutrition in the United States released a report, "Hunger, U.S.A.," identifying 280 "hunger counties" where both childhood mortality rates and the percentage of the population below the poverty line were double the national average.[24]

About the same time, a CBS television documentary, "Hunger in America," looked at serious malnutrition problems in the South and Southwest. In Alabama's cotton country, a reporter said, "Slow starvation has become part of the Southern way of life."[25]

Both houses of Congress immediately held hearings, and the Senate Select Committee on Nutrition and Human Needs was established.

Moral Issue

For both Republican and Democratic presidents, the persistence of hunger in a country of overwhelming agricultural abundance had become a moral issue. In 1969, just before convening the first White House conference on food and hunger, President Richard M. Nixon told Congress that hunger in America was an "embarrassing and intolerable" national shame.[26] Likewise, a task force convened in the 1980s during the Ronald Reagan administration concluded, "Hunger is simply not acceptable in our society."[27]

However, Americans were still often ambivalent about the causes of hunger, Eisinger points out. As a result, Congress has often liberalized the program at the same time that it has imposed new restrictions.

For instance, when the current program structure was established during President Jimmy Carter's administration in 1977, Congress eliminated the requirement that

C H R O N O L O G Y

1960s *Permanent food stamp program is established. Congressional committees and television documentaries expose hunger in Deep South and Appalachia.*

1961 President John F. Kennedy orders Agriculture secretary to expand food-distribution programs and establish pilot food stamp program in six regions.

1964 Congress establishes permanent food stamp program after President Lyndon B. Johnson declares "unconditional war on poverty."

1966 Congress creates school breakfast program.

April 1967 Senate subcommittee on poverty visits Mississippi Delta.

1968 Citizens' board identifies 280 "hunger counties." Television documentary exposes malnutrition in South and Southwest. Congress establishes Summer Food Service Program for Children and the Child and Adult Care Food Program.

1969 President Richard M. Nixon calls hunger in America an "embarrassing and intolerable" national shame at first White House conference on hunger.

1970s *Congress expands some federal welfare programs.*

1972 Special Supplemental Nutrition Program For Women, Infants And Children (WIC) is established.

1974 Earned-income tax credit (EITC) enacted to provide tax refunds for the working poor.

1975 School breakfast program permanently authorized.

1977 Current food stamp program structure is established, but Congress tightens eligibility.

1980-81 *Manufacturing decline eliminates thousands of jobs. Congress broadens food stamp eligibility requirements three times.*

1981 Temporary Emergency Food Assistance Program is established to distribute surplus commodities to the needy.

1990s-2000s *Food stamp participation reaches record levels in the early 1990s, but Congress cuts food stamp benefits as part of welfare reform.*

August 1993 Childhood Hunger Relief Act improves access and benefits for families on food stamps. Congress and newly elected President Bill Clinton promise to fully fund WIC and expand school breakfast and summer food programs by 1996.

1994 New Republican majority in Congress debates ways to cut social programs and reform welfare.

1995 Slightly more than 10 percent of the U.S. population is receiving food stamps, costing $24.6 billion a year. Clinton proposes raising minimum wage to $5.15 an hour.

1996 Congress raises minimum wage to $4.75 per hour and reforms welfare, making deep cuts in the food stamp program and the school breakfast and summer food programs.

1997-1998 Congress restores food stamp eligibility to young, elderly and disabled immigrants and restarts some school, summer and adult-care food programs.

Sept. 1, 1997 Minimum wage increased to $5.15. Federal share of food stamps drops to $21.4 billion.

1998 Poverty and unemployment decline amid economic boom, but food stamp participation declines faster than poverty. Private charities report surge in requests for emergency food.

October 2000 Congress relaxes food stamp eligibility but refuses to restore food stamps for non-citizens.

December 2000 U.S. Conference of Mayors and Catholic Charities USA report continuing increase in requests for food aid.

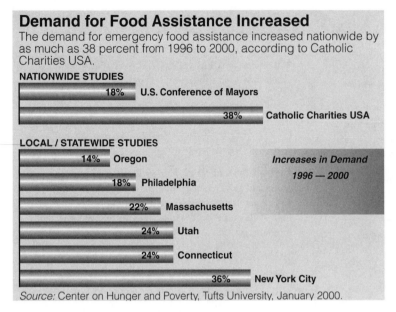

Demand for Food Assistance Increased

The demand for emergency food assistance increased nationwide by as much as 38 percent from 1996 to 2000, according to Catholic Charities USA.

NATIONWIDE STUDIES

- 18% U.S. Conference of Mayors
- 38% Catholic Charities USA

LOCAL / STATEWIDE STUDIES

- 14% Oregon
- 18% Philadelphia
- 22% Massachusetts
- 24% Utah
- 24% Connecticut
- 36% New York City

Increases in Demand 1996 — 2000

Source: Center on Hunger and Poverty, Tufts University, January 2000.

and Congress promised to fully fund WIC by 1996, and Congress promised to expand the school breakfast and summer food programs.

In a dramatic reversal, the 1996 welfare-reform legislation made deep cuts in the food stamp program, eliminated proposed expansion funds and cut funds for the Child and Adult Care Food Program, which provides meals and snacks for low-income recipients child and adult day care.

After intensive lobbying by hunger advocates, Congress in 1997 and '98 improved the school breakfast, summer food and child and adult-care food programs and restored food stamp eligibility to young, elderly or disabled immigrants who were in the country as of Aug. 22, 1996.

Nevertheless, state and local governments and private charities continued to complain they were increasingly unable to shoulder the burden caused by federal and state cutbacks in social services. When states make severe cuts in human services programs, soup kitchens and emergency food banks find donations unpredictable despite growing demand for aid.

Meanwhile, the gap between the richest Americans and everyone else became wider than it had been since the end of World II, and the disparity grew significantly between 1992 and 1994. According to a Census Bureau report, the average income of households in the top 20 percent has increased by more than 40 percent since 1968, while the average income of households in the bottom 20 percent grew by only 8 percent.

As reasons for the low income growth among the poor, the Census Bureau report cites the shift away from high-wage manufacturing jobs; a decline in the number of unionized workers as companies increasingly use temporary employees; an increased reliance on high-tech jobs requiring higher skills and education; intensified global competition; and the decline in the real value of the minimum wage.

The Economic Policy Institute's 1998 "State of Working America" report cites the same factors as

recipients make minimum cash payment for food stamps. But in the same law they removed more than a half-million people from the food stamp rolls by scrapping the automatic eligibility of anyone receiving welfare and disability benefits.

After that, Congress would alternate between reducing benefits and liberalizing them. In the early Reagan administration, benefits were reduced and strikers and college students were disqualified from receiving them. Then, after a sharp economic downturn in the early 1980s, Congress broadened eligibility requirements in 1985, '87 and '88. In 1993, after the recession of the late '80s and early '90s during the presidency of George Bush, eligibility was again relaxed.

The combination of broader eligibility and successive recessions drove food stamp participation to record levels by the early 1990s. By 1995, the year before welfare was reformed, 26.6 million Americans — slightly more than 10 percent of the population — were receiving food stamps, at an annual cost of $24.6 billion.

Hunger in the '90s

In the early 1990s, advocates for the hungry were hopeful about renewed interest among policy-makers in improving food-assistance programs. In 1993, the Mickey Leland Childhood Hunger Relief Act improved access and benefits for food stamp families. President Clinton

putting pressure on struggling families. It also found that while real wages grew significantly at all levels during the last two years, the increases have not been enough to counteract the two-decade-long pattern of stagnant and declining wages. Between 1989 and 1997, hourly wages for the bottom 60 percent of all workers stagnated or fell, after adjusting for inflation.

"Considering these circumstances, maintaining and strengthening the social safety net is essential," says FRAC.[28]

CURRENT SITUATION

Pressure on Congress

President Clinton's new, relaxed federal food stamp regulations are major improvements, say those who work on hunger relief, but now the states must translate the new rules into actual policy changes at local welfare offices. In addition, the Agriculture Department must re-examine its rules that sanction states that overpay or underpay food stamp benefits, says O'Brien of Second Harvest, because such rules prompted many states to impose the onerous bureaucratic requirements in the first place.

Steisel of the National Conference of State Legislatures thinks states will immediately start amending their rules to reflect the new federal changes. "There's a lot of state concern about removing barriers to food stamp eligibility," she says, "especially if it helps the working poor stay off welfare."

> 'We need to put hunger back on the national agenda. If we can't work to wipe out hunger in times of national plenty, when will we?'
>
> — *Sen. Byron L. Dorgan, D-N.D.*

For instance, she says, many states have created various incentives for people to donate their used cars to former welfare recipients who need them to get to work. "But the federal rules were so inflexible and out-of-date that people were bumped off the food stamp program just because they accepted a donation of a reliable used car," she says.

While waiting for states to change their rules, advocates for the hungry are starting to drum up congressional support for expanding the federal food stamp program when it comes up for reauthorization in the next Congress.

To dramatize the continuing problem of hunger amid prosperity, Democratic lawmakers held an unusual field hearing on Dec. 1, just a few blocks from the marbled halls of the Capitol — in a chilly food-storage room in the D.C. Central Kitchen, a privately run soup kitchen.

Surrounded by boxes of soup cans stacked to the ceiling, Rep. Tony P. Hall, D-Ohio, spoke of a recent trip to Appalachia where he saw 450 families waiting in line for food. "It was unbelievable," he said, adding that many senior citizens have to choose between buying medicine and eating.[29]

Hall, who once went on a hunger strike for 22 days to protest the way the federal government treats the hungry, was joined by Democratic Sen. Byron L. Dorgan of North Dakota, who helped organize the meeting, and Rep. Eva Clayton, D-N.C. "We need to put hunger back on the national agenda," Dorgan said. "If we can't work to wipe out hunger in times of national plenty, when will we?"[30]

The Farm Belt senator added, "Hunger is still with us, despite America's current robust prosperity, and ironically, it occurs at a time when America's family farmers are told the food they produce in such abundance has no value."[31]

Dorgan and Hall called for a renewed focus on hunger during the incoming 107th Congress, when the food stamp program comes up for reauthorization and both parties will be battling over how to spend surpluses anticipated to reach $4.6 trillion over the next decade.

Relief groups and social-service organizations have suggested, among other things, improving supervision and care for people leaving welfare for work, expanding pilot school breakfast programs nationwide, increasing business involvement in feeding the hungry, funding school-based community nutrition centers and modifying farming laws so that surplus crops are not wasted.

Eisinger of Wayne State University suggests more outreach, such as assigning food stamp caseworkers to large emergency food pantries and soup kitchens. "It wouldn't even require extra employees," he says, "because you could have existing county food stamp administrators do outreach one or two days a week."

O'Brien would also like to see all federal nutrition-assistance programs expanded and funded at higher levels. In particular, he calls for expansion of food stamp

Poverty Gets the Blame...

Hunger in America does not look the same as it does in the Third World.

"Hunger in this society has a different face than hunger does in Somalia," says Peter K. Eisinger, a professor of urban affairs at Wayne State University in Detroit and author of *Toward an End to Hunger in America*. "We don't have gaunt and listless children with distended bellies with flies swarming around them."

In fact, hungry Americans are often overweight. "The poor are most likely to be overweight," says Robert Rector, a senior research fellow at the conservative Heritage Foundation. "In fact, nearly half of the people who claim on government surveys that they 'lack enough food' are overweight."

Obesity occurs disproportionately among the poor, he says, pointing out that nearly half of poor adult women are overweight, compared with a third of non-poor women, and obesity is most common among poor children. "A recent medical study of low-income black and Hispanic students in Central Harlem found that 25 percent were 'obese,' and more than half were 'super-obese,'" he says.

Many blame the poor's overreliance on fatty foods, which are cheaper than low-fat foods. But Rector blames simple overeating. "Government data show that the amount of vitamins, minerals and protein per calorie of food eaten is the same for poor and middle-class Americans," he says. "And the diets of poor people, on average, are no higher in fat than the diets of the middle class."

The exception, he concedes, are some inner-city poor, who eat too much fast food, he says. "A diet laden

Poor people are often overweight because they eat at fast-food restaurants, which offer a cheap source of calories, nutritionists say. President Clinton snacks at a McDonald's in Little Rock, Ark.

AP Photo/Greg Gibson

with 'Big Macs' and 'Super-Size Fries' isn't healthy, but it's also not proof of a lack of money to buy healthy food," he says.

But Eileen Kennedy, acting undersecretary of Agriculture for research, education and economics, says, "Rector is just wrong. It's naïve to think that just because you are obese you don't have a problem of food insecurity and hunger. Obesity is the result of an overall poor lifestyle, which is heavily driven by poverty."

She agrees that a disproportionate share of the overweight population lives in low-income neighborhoods. The reasons are complex, and partly explained by an emerging body of research called the fetal-origin-of-disease theory, she says. That theory explains the biological mechanisms for how hunger and obesity can occur simultaneously.

The research, which she says is "getting stronger by the day," shows a strong link between low birth weight and chronic disease. "In other words, if a child is nutritionally deprived during its fetal development, it can be pre-programmed to have a greater risk for chronic diseases like hyper-tension and obesity later in life," she says. Current scientific thinking views obesity as a disease, she points out.

In addition, healthy eating is not "income neutral" as Rector implies, Kennedy says. The poor try to maximize their energy — or caloric — intake with the least amount of money, she says. "And the cheapest source of calories is fat."

eligibility to include any household making 150-180 percent of the poverty level. The current cutoff is 130 percent over the level.

But the Heritage Foundation's Rector opposes expanding the food stamp program unless its benefits are linked to work requirements. "Just giving out more of the old-fashioned dole doesn't work," he says. "We already did that for 30 years."

The food stamp program, like all means-tested programs, he says, is inherently flawed, because it penalizes low-income

...for Obesity Among the Poor

Getting maximum calories from lean meat and fresh fruit and vegetables is more expensive, she says. For instance, a kid can get a large hamburger, containing 1,000 calories, for 99 cents at a fast-food restaurant. One would have to buy about 15 apples, at a much higher price, to get the same number of calories, she says.

Getting enough exercise to prevent weight gain is a luxury that eats up both time and money, she says. The average low-income single mom — who may be working two or three jobs, or working and trying to go back to school while raising children — doesn't have time or money to work out in a gym like the typical upper-income suburban housewife, she says.

The United States is not the only country experiencing an epidemic of obesity among the poor, Kennedy says. Some of the poorest countries in the world — India, China, other parts of Asia and sub-Saharan Africa are experiencing similar epidemics, she says. Obesity increases when people migrate from jobs on the farm to sedentary desk jobs in urban areas, she points out.

The increase of women in the world's work force also contributes to obesity problems, she says. Cooking from scratch using less-fattening raw ingredients requires the luxury of time that many workers, particularly working mothers, don't have, she says.

That's a major reason, along with a lack of exercise, why obesity is on the increase among all American children — and not just poor children, says Raj Anand, executive director of the Agriculture Department's Center for Nutrition Policy and Promotion.

"American kids are taking in more calories — by eating a lot more junk food, soda pop and fast food — and exercising less," he says. "It's not rocket science. When your energy intake, in the form of calories, exceeds your output, or exercise, you get fat."

A double cheeseburger at a fast-food restaurant supplies more than 1,500 calories, plus a large amount of fat.

AP Photo/Greg Gibson

Kids today eat more calories than they did in the 1950s, but only one state in the nation — Illinois — still requires physical education for all grade levels, he points out.

Anand blames too much TV and computer time, coupled with constant snacking and an overreliance on high-fat, convenience and fast-food meals. In addition, portion sizes in American restaurants have increased. "Everything is super-sized and half-liters now," which is particularly fattening when it is high-sugar soft drinks, he says.

"A child can consume a couple hundred calories in a soft drink, but the body still feels hungry," he says, "because the human mind does not perceive a soft drink as food. So kids will still eat the requisite number of calories to satisfy their hunger, plus the extra calories in the soft drink."

Another reason more poor people are overweight, he says, is a lack of education. "Studies show there is a direct relationship between healthy eating and the amount of education a person has," he says. "People who have gone to college eat better than those who have only gone to high school."

Yet there is no major government program to promote healthy eating among children, he complains. For instance, his center gets $2.5 million a year to research and develop healthy dietary guidelines. "But we don't get a single penny to aggressively promote those guidelines through a general education campaign, except to post it on the Agriculture Department's Web site," he says.[1]

"Meanwhile, kids are constantly bombarded with millions of dollars' worth of advertising for fast foods and sugary cereals," he says.

[1] The Agriculture Department's Web site is: www.usda.gov.

women who get married to a working spouse. "The lower the earnings or income of the applicant, the higher their benefits are," he says. "So it discriminates against marriage."

A better way to target the working poor, he says, is to make the earned income tax credit (EITC) — the annual tax refund paid to low-income taxpayers with children — payable on an ongoing quarterly "forward" basis, so workers could receive the refunds throughout the work year. "There are various discussions going on about making EITC a quarterly concurrent payment," he says.

Is there a real hunger problem in America?

YES   DOUG O'BRIEN
Director of Public Policy and Research, America's Second Harvest

Written for *The CQ Researcher,* December 2000

Despite strong economic growth and sharply declining welfare and food stamp caseloads over the past five years, an estimated 10.1 percent of all U.S. households, including 31 million people, were food insecure in 1999. That means that at some time during the previous 12 months they were uncertain of having, or unable to acquire, sufficient food to meet their basic needs due to inadequate financial resources. Approximately 3 million households with more than 9 million people were food insecure with hunger, meaning that individuals in the household went involuntarily without food due to a lack of financial resources.

The prevalence estimates are based on data collected from 1995 through 1999 in the Food Security Supplements to the Census Bureau's annual "Current Population Survey" (CPS). Utilizing a widely accepted standard definition of food insecurity and hunger, the supplement represents a highly reliable statistical measurement method producing a detailed scale for measuring the level of severity of food insecurity and hunger in U.S. households.

Augmenting the federal government's estimates of food insecurity and hunger are numerous studies by non-governmental organizations and academics that have confirmed statistically significant rates of food insecurity and hunger. One such example is the Urban Institute's National Survey of America's Families, a nationally representative survey, which found that half of all families at 200 percent of poverty and below had concerns with food shortages or difficulty obtaining food.

Although obesity is a serious national health problem for many Americans regardless of income, obesity among the poor may also indicate an adaptive response to periodic episodes of insufficient food intake. Recent research indicates that the incidence of obesity may mask serious nutrient deficiencies among poor children. Compared to non-poor children ages 1 to 5, the diets of poor children were seriously compromised in 10 of 16 critical nutrients essential for normal development; and the proportion of poor children with substandard intakes of food energy is more than two-and-a-half times as great as for non-poor children.

The greater body of scientific evidence strongly indicates that hunger and food insecurity remain serious, although solvable, problems for millions of poor and vulnerable Americans.

NO   ROBERT RECTOR
Senior Research Fellow, The Heritage Foundation

Written for *The CQ Researcher,* December 2000

According to the government's own data, there isn't a hunger problem. U.S. Department of Health and Human Services surveys show, for example, that 96 percent of American families report that they have "enough food to eat." About 3 percent say they "sometimes" don't have enough food. Only one-half of 1 percent say they "often" don't have enough food. Ironically, nearly half of the people who claim they don't have "enough food" are actually overweight. Obesity is most common among the tiny group claiming they "often" lack food.

Political activists claim that nearly one-third of American children are hungry or "at risk" of hunger. But, in reality, American children, both rich and poor, are remarkably well fed and well nourished. The average amount of protein, vitamins and minerals consumed by poor children is virtually identical with that of middle-class children. In most cases, average consumption greatly exceeds recommended norms. For example, poor children, on average, take in more than 200 percent of the recommended daily allowance of protein, a relatively expensive nutrient.

Health problems relating to the underconsumption of food are scarce among both poor and middle-class children. Thinness (low weight for height) and stunting (low height for age) are virtually non-existent within both groups. In fact, by the time poor boys reach age 18, they are, on average, one inch taller and 10 pounds heavier than the typical middle-class boy of the same age in the late 1950s.

Poor Americans do face health problems related to diet, but these arise primarily from the overconsumption of food, not food scarcity. In a nation burdened by a superabundance of calories, the poor are most likely to be overweight. Nearly half of poor adult women are overweight, compared with a third of non-poor women. Health experts in recent years have expressed concern about the rapid growth of obesity among American children. Unfortunately, obesity is most common among poor children.

Many believe that money shortages force the poor to eat unhealthy diets, low in nutriments and high in fat. Again, government data contradict that view. None of this means that there is no hunger in America. But far from being a widespread crisis, hunger is a problem very limited in scope and duration. More important, when significant hunger does occur, it is likely to be linked to behavioral problems within a family that are far more significant than simple food shortages.

Still others are discussing turning the food stamp program into a block-grant system, says Rector, in which the federal government sends the funds to the states, which would be free to distribute the money as they see fit.

But FRAC President Weill says he hopes the more bipartisan makeup of the new Congress will lead to a "strengthening" of the program, rather than a "drastic, negative process like block-granting it." He says block-granting any program eliminates protections that set federal minimum standards and eligibility requirements. It was tried in the early days of the program, he points out, and resulted in some states having dramatically higher and lower benefit levels.

"It would end the food stamp program as the key to our basic safety net," he says. "That was one of the implicit agreements in the '96 [welfare reform] law — that food stamps and Medicaid would not be block-granted."

Aid for Immigrants?

The next Congress will undoubtedly be asked to restore food stamps for legal immigrants, say advocates for the hungry.

"Obviously we think it's long overdue, given the broad support the measure has in both the House and Senate," Weill says.

The measure's prospects may be brighter in the new Congress. "Such a measure would be a good vehicle to demonstrate bipartisanship, especially if we can get the next president on board," says a House Agriculture Appropriations Subcommittee aide.

Plus, two of the five Republican committee chairmen who blocked the measure in the current Congress are retiring — Ways and Means Chairman Archer and Commerce Committee Chairman Bliley. New committee chairmen are not expected to be named until Jan. 4.

In addition, the measure is popular among Hispanic voters, an increasingly significant voting bloc that neither party wants to alienate.[32] "Given the growing power of that group of voters, nobody really wants to get out in front on withholding food stamps from legal immigrants," says another House staffer.

"The political dynamic now is very different from what it was in 1996," Steisel says.

Another measure that will no doubt be back on Congress' plate is a bill that has been proposed before but never enacted. It would allow small businesses to deduct the fair market value of in-kind gifts to the needy. For example, right now only large corporations can deduct donations to food banks.

"It's crazy," says Second Harvest's O'Brien. "If Pizza Hut Inc. donates tomato sauce to a local food bank, it gets to deduct the value of that donation from its taxes. But if a local Pizza Hut restaurant makes the same donation, it doesn't."

OUTLOOK
Search for Solutions

Anti-hunger advocates say that if Congress really wanted to, it could eliminate hunger in America within a short period of time for a relatively small amount of money. "It's a readily achievable goal, if we had the political will to do it," says FRAC's Weill.

"Of all the social problems in America, hunger is the easiest to fix," says O'Brien of Second Harvest. "The various federal nutrition programs are already in place and working fairly well. They just need to be fully funded to cover all those who are already eligible and expanded to cover working poor families."

He continues, "Are we doing our society any good by targeting only the very poorest of the poor? Shouldn't we target the working poor as well? That's what the big debate will be about in the future."

Weill says it would only take "a tiny fraction" of the anticipated surplus to end hunger in America.

But Rector says the way to solve the nation's hunger problem is to adopt policies that encourage full-time work and married parenthood. "I would also like to see the EITC increased for married couples with children," he says. "Then they can get free food at food banks to top off their incomes."

However, academics argue that over the long term, significant structural improvements targeted at the poor should be made in the underpinning of the nation's economy. A study released last January by the Center on Hunger and Poverty said neither the current food stamp

Kids' Cafés Fill Hungry Tummies

When the young-sters arrive at the after-school program at the Garfield Terrace public housing project in northwest Washington, D.C., they get a nutritious snack. And if their parents can't pick them up until after dinnertime, they get a hot meal.

The meals are provided free through a nationwide program called Kids' Cafes, sponsored by Omaha-based ConAgra Foods Inc. and America's Second Harvest, the nation's largest hunger-relief organization.

"Without this program, a lot of children wouldn't get an evening meal," says Sarah Letterner, Kids' Café coordinator in Washington.

Letterner says kids are especially needy in low-income places like Garfield Terrace, which is blue-collar and pre-dominantly African-American. Often the parents are work-ing, but their salaries don't stretch far enough to completely cover their expenses for housing, utilities, clothes and food.

"Some parents have two jobs, or they are trying to go back to school, or they have to take a couple of buses to get home from work, so they aren't home in time to fix the kids dinner," Letterner says. And some are substance abusers, she says. "Sometimes kids even come in looking for food on Saturdays."

For whatever reason, say anti-hunger advocates, many American children don't receive an evening meal on a regu-lar basis. And while many of the children receive school lunches and breakfasts, schools don't serve dinner, and most are closed in the summer — leaving a gnawing hole in the

To provide evening meals for needy children, ConAgra and America's Second Harvest have established 350 Kids Cafés at existing after-school programs around the country.

nation's child hunger problem, advocates for the hungry say.

To attack this unmet need, ConAgra and local food banks organized by Second Harvest have estab-lished 350 "Kids Cafés" at existing after-school programs in 29 states across the country.

Housed in Boys and Girls Clubs, churches, schools and community centers, the "cafes" dish up nutri-tious snacks or hot meals, or both, while the kids are doing their homework or taking part in other after-school activities. The Garfield facility is served by the Capital Area Food Bank.

Kids' Cafes are part of an $11 million, three-year pro-gram called Feeding Children Better, in which ConAgra provides refrigerated trucks and/or cash grants to local food banks to provide free food to after-school programs.

The program is the largest corporate initiative dedicated solely to childhood hunger in the United States. The first Kids' Café was opened in Savannah, Ga., in 1989 by the Second Harvest Food Bank of Coastal Georgia, after two young brothers were discovered late one night in the kitchen of their housing project's community center. The older boy had broken into the kitchen in search of food.

ConAgra and Second Harvest are also launching a pub-lic-service advertising campaign with the Ad Council, start-ing in January, to focus attention on childhood hunger. "Hunger is a critical issue in the United States, and steps such as these will ensure that no child grows up hungry," says Deborah Leff, president of Second Harvest.

program nor private emergency food providers can be expected to resolve the underlying causes of hunger and food insecurity in America.[33]

"Fundamentally, these problems are manifestations of poverty and household economic insecurity," said the

study. Because key elements of the New Deal have been dismantled and other elements are out of date, the nation lacks a "cohesive social welfare policy," it continued.[34] Over the long run, the report recommended that a new social-policy framework should include:

- A revamped insurance system, with better unemployment insurance and portable benefits.
- More comprehensive income and tax programs that help families supplement their earnings and stabilize their financial circumstances.
- Policies that promote the accumulation of household assets and ensure economic security among low-income families similar to the policies that built the middle class.

Without fundamental changes, says the center's Brown, "The real question we have to answer is, 'Do we want America to continue to be a soup-kitchen society?'"

NOTES

1. Peter K. Eisinger, *Toward an End to Hunger in America* (1998).
2. "A Status Report on Hunger and Homelessness in America's Cities 2000," U.S. Conference of Mayors, December 2000.
3. *Ibid.*
4. *Ibid.*
5. *Ibid.*
6. "1999 National Survey of Services to Families and Communities," Catholic Charities USA, December 2000.
7. Wehler, C.A., *et. al.*, "Community Childhood Hunger Identification Project: A Survey of Childhood Hunger in the U.S.," Food Research and Action Center, 1995.
8. From a FRAC press release, Sept. 8, 2000.
9. Kathy Koch, "Child Poverty," *The CQ Researcher*, April 7, 2000, pp. 281-304; Christopher Conte, "Welfare, Work and the States," *The CQ Researcher*, Dec. 6, 1996, pp. 1057-1080; Kenneth Jost, "States and Federalism," *The CQ Researcher*, Sept. 13, 1996, pp. 793-816.
10. "Food Stamp Program: Various Factors Have Led to Declining Participation," (Letter Report), General Accounting Office, July 2, 1999.
11. "Third Report on Nutrition Monitoring in the United States," Interagency Board National Health and Evaluation Survey, Vol. 5, 1995, p. VA95.
12. Steven Carlson, Margaret Andrews and Gary Bickel, "Measuring Food Insecurity and Hunger in the U.S.: Development of a National Benchmark and Prevalence Estimates," presented at the American Society for Nutritional Sciences' symposium "Advances in Measuring Food Insecurity in the U.S.," April 18-22, 1998, San Francisco.
13. "Differences In Nutrient Adequacy Among Poor and Non-Poor Children," Tufts University School of Nutrition Center on Hunger, Poverty & Nutrition Policy, March 1995.
14. *Ibid.*
15. *Ibid.*
16. Doug O'Brien *et. al.*, "The Red Tape Divide," America's Second Harvest, October 2000.
17. *Ibid.*
18. *Ibid.*, p. 28.
19. According to USDA's "Characteristics of Food Stamp Households for Fiscal Year 1998."
20. Eisinger, *op. cit.*, p. 42.
21. *Ibid.*, p. 38.
22. Quoted in Elizabeth Drew, "Going Hungry in America," *The Atlantic*, December 1968, p. 58.
23. *Congressional Record*, April 7, 1964, p. 7159.
24. Eisinger, *op. cit.*, p. 12.
25. *Ibid.*, p. 13.
26. Richard M. Nixon, "Message of the President to Congress," May 6, 1969, contained in White House Conference on Food Nutrition and Health, Final Report (1970).
27. Report of the President's Task Force on Food Assistance (January 1984), p. 2.
28. FRAC Web site: www.frac.org.
29. Quoted in Eunice Moscoso, "Lawmakers get up-close and personal with hunger," *The Atlanta Constitution*, Dec. 5, 2000.
30. *Ibid.*
31. Quoted in Spencer S. Hsu, "Advocates Call for Renewed Effort to Feed Hungry," *The Washington Post*, Dec. 5, 2000.
32. David Masci, "Hispanic-Americans' New Clout," *The CQ Researcher*, Sept. 18, 1998, pp. 809-832.

33. Sandra H. Venner, *et al.*, "Paradox of Our Times: Hunger in a Strong Economy," Center on Hunger and Poverty, Tufts University, January 2000.

34. *Ibid.*

BIBLIOGRAPHY

Books

Eisinger, Peter K., *Toward an End to Hunger in America*, **Brookings Institution Press, 1998.**
A Wayne State University professor of urban affairs discusses the history of the nation's food-assistance programs and the public's continuing, albeit ambivalent, efforts to eliminate hunger in America.

Poppendieck, Janet, *Sweet Charity: Emergency Food and the End of Entitlement*, **Viking, 1998.**
The director of the Center for the Study of Family Policy at Hunter College argues that America's drive to end hunger has taken a wrong turn by trying to shift away from entitlements toward a patchwork quilt of stopgap charitable efforts.

Reports and Studies

"A Status Report on Hunger and Homelessness in America's Cities 2000," U.S. Conference of Mayors, December 2000.
This annual survey by officials in selected cities estimates that during the past year requests for emergency food assistance increased by about 17 percent, the second highest rate of increase since 1992.

Andrews, Margaret, *et. al.*, "Household Food Security in the United States, 1999," U.S. Department of Agriculture, Food Assistance and Nutrition Research Report No. 8, fall 2000.
The most recent data on food security in America finds that 31 million Americans were "food insecure" last year.

Cook, John T., and Katie S. Martin, "Differences In Nutrient Adequacy Among Poor and Non-Poor Children," Tufts University School of Nutrition Center on Hunger, Poverty & Nutrition Policy, March 1995.
Tufts University researchers conclude that "millions of poor American children have significantly inadequate dietary intakes."

"Food Stamp Program: Various Factors Have Led to Declining Participation," (Letter Report), General Accounting Office, July 2,1999.
A GAO report found that in 1997 children accounted for 48 percent of the drop in participation in the food stamp program, more dramatic than the drop in the number of children living in poverty.

"Hunger 1997: The Faces and the Facts," Second Harvest National Food Bank Network, March 1998.
This survey by the nation's largest food bank network found that its providers serve more than 25.7 million people in a year.

"1999 National Survey of Services to Families and Communities," Catholic Charities USA, December 2000.
This annual survey of participating charities found that in 1999 the number of clients seeking emergency food services increased 32 percent over 1998.

Nord, Mark, *et. al.*, "Prevalence of Food Insecurity and Hunger, by State, 1996-1998," U.S. Department of Agriculture, Economic Research Service, 1998.
This state-by-state report shows that the greatest food insecurity in America occurs in 11 states located in an arc along the western and southern borders and in the District of Columbia.

O'Brien, Doug, *et. al.*, "The Red Tape Divide," America's Second Harvest, October 2000.
This state-by-state review of food stamp application procedures found them to be so cumbersome, complex and intrusive that they discourage thousands of eligible participants from even applying.

Rector, Robert, *et. al.*, "The Extent of Material Hardship and Poverty in the United States," The Heritage Foundation, Sept. 3, 1999.
Citing Department of Health and Human Services statistics, a senior research fellow at the conservative think tank disputes hunger activists' claim that there is a hunger crisis in America.

Wehler, C.A., *et. al.*, "Community Childhood Hunger Identification Project: A Survey of Childhood Hunger in the U.S.," Food Research and Action Center, 1995.

The most comprehensive study ever done on childhood hunger in the United States found that 29 percent of children under 12 lived in households coping with hunger or the risk of hunger.

Wilde, Parke, *et al.*, "The Decline in Food Stamp Program Participation in the 1990s," U.S. **Department of Agriculture, Food Assistance and Nutrition Research Report No. 7, June 2000.**

This report examines the recent unprecedented decline in participation in the food stamp program from 27.5 million participants in 1994 to 18.2 million participants in 1999.

For More Information

America's Second Harvest, 116 S. Michigan Ave., Suite 4, Chicago, Ill. 60603; (312) 263-2303; www.secondharvest .org. The nation's largest domestic hunger-relief organization distributes 1.4 billion pounds of food to 26 million people each year, including 8 million children, through its network of more than 200 food banks and food-rescue programs.

Catholic Charities USA, 1731 King St., Suite 200, Alexandria, Va. 22314; (703) 549-1390; www.catholiccharitiesusa .org. This coalition of private agencies and institutions provides social services — including adoption, education, counseling, food and housing — to persons of all backgrounds.

Food Research and Action Center, 1875 Connecticut Ave., N.W., Suite 540, Washington, D.C. 20009-5728; (202) 986-2200; www.frac.org. Founded in 1970 as a public interest law firm, FRAC is now a nonprofit, nonpartisan public interest advocacy, research and legal center that works

to end hunger and poverty in the U.S. It also serves as the hub of an anti-hunger network of thousands of individuals and agencies across the country.

The Heritage Foundation, 214 Massachusetts Ave., N.E., Washington, D.C. 20002-4999; (202) 546-4400; www.heritage. org. This public policy research organization conducts research and analysis and sponsors lectures, debates and public policy forums advocating individual freedom, limited government, the free market system and a strong national defense.

U.S. Conference of Mayors, 1620 Eye Street, N.W., Washington, D.C. 20006; (202) 293-7330; www.usmayors .org. This nonpartisan organization of mayors from cities with populations over 30,000 promotes city-federal cooperation and serves as a clearinghouse for information on urban and suburban problems. It favors reinstating food stamps for non-citizens.

9

Welfare Reform

Are Former Welfare Recipients Better Off Today?

Sarah Glazer

Marquita Chisholm, 27, left, was cut off from welfare last fall and began working for McDonald's in Cleveland. But when she had her third child, she quit her job. McDonald's wanted to hire her back, but she could not find child care. On her lap is daughter Rainah. They are being visited by social worker Diana Merriweather.

A fter more than five years on welfare, Connie Rounds — the divorced mother of two teenagers — went to work as an aide at a residential facility for the elderly in Oregon. It was 1998, and she was paid $6.30 an hour.[1]

When Rounds' boss required her to work overtime, her income went over the monthly eligibility limit for Medicaid and state health insurance, a major disaster for Rounds, who is in her 40s and suffers from chronic health problems.

Losing health insurance saddled Rounds with more than $3,000 in medical bills, which she must pay from a monthly income that has no room for luxuries. After her old car gave out, Rounds purchased a better used car, which put her over the eligibility limit for food stamps.* For several months, Rounds had to choose between buying the daily pain killers that enabled her to work or paying for basic expenses such as car insurance, the electric bill for her trailer and food.

Although her income has gone up $1.60 an hour since she started working, Rounds and her family are no better off financially than when she first left welfare because her increased wages make her ineligible for health insurance and food stamps.[2]

When Rounds first left welfare, she only worked half-time. One of her teenage daughters was doing poorly in school, smoking and staying out late. About a year ago, Rounds began working 32 hours a week to boost her income, but she worried about

From *CQ Researcher*, August 3, 2001.

*Last October Congress raised the cap on how much cars owned by food stamp recipients could be worth without disqualifying them from the program.

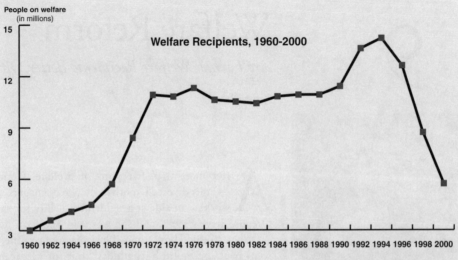

Welfare Rolls Have Been Declining

The nation's welfare rolls have dropped by more than half from their peak of 14.2 million recipients in 1994 — two years before the 1996 welfare reform bill passed. Conservatives tend to credit the law's toughened time limits and work requirements, which many states had already enacted on a trial basis. Liberals generally credit a strong economy that provided a wealth of low-wage jobs. Economists credit both factors.

People on welfare (in millions)

Welfare Recipients, 1960-2000

Source: Administration for Children and Families, Department of Health and Human Services

losing time she could spend with her daughter. The extra hours also kept Rounds continually exhausted and strapped for time to complete a recertification course she needed to qualify for a higher-paying job as a licensed practical nurse.

Looking back, Rounds feels lucky that welfare enabled her to stay home with her children when they were young. That's something her co-workers are not able to do under the tougher work requirements that came with the sweeping welfare reforms passed in 1996. Citing a co-worker whose milk dried up because she had to work when her nursing baby was 3 months old, Rounds says, "Working full-time is too hard when you are a single parent."[3]

When Congress passed the welfare reform bill, conservatives had high hopes for breaking what they saw as a culture of dependence on welfare while liberals predicted destitute children in the streets. Now, five years later, the liberals' dire predictions of vastly increased poverty have not come to pass. But experts disagree whether the dramatic behavioral changes touted by reform

advocates are the result of a newfound work ethic triggered by the law or were the result of the booming economy.

Moreover, the complex process of leaving welfare has raised new issues. As Rounds' story illustrates, the average $6.75 per hour wage earned by former welfare mothers is so low that many are no better off than when they were on welfare.[4] And if a welfare mother loses welfare-associated benefits, like health insurance and food stamps, she can end up even worse off. In addition, long working hours — coupled with obstacles to obtaining child-care subsidies promised when the law was passed — often result in children and teens being left unsupervised.

Studies have found that teens with parents in early welfare-to-work programs did worse in school and had more behavior problems than adolescents in other welfare households, perhaps because working parents have less time to monitor their teens' behavior and may saddle them with more responsibilities at home.[5] By contrast, studies of elementary children have found either positive or neutral effects on children's behavior and school performance, which some researchers attribute to the boost in pride a working mother passes on to her young children.[6]

The landmark 1996 law — officially the Personal Responsibility and Work Opportunity Reconciliation Act (PRWORA) — ended the open-ended entitlement to cash benefits, guaranteed to single mothers under the old welfare system. Now no one can receive a monthly welfare check for more than five years in a lifetime, except in hardship cases as defined by the states. However, states were allowed to impose even earlier deadlines, and some did so. The law also required welfare recipients to work, or be involved in activities leading to work, within two years after receiving welfare.

Federal welfare funding to the states, which had been based on the welfare population in each state, was converted to a single block grant of $16.5 billion annually over six years to be distributed to all the states. Because the block grant expires in October 2002, Congress is expected to revisit many of these issues when lawmakers reauthorize the program next year.

Nationally, welfare reform has had dramatic effects: Welfare rolls have declined by more than half since their peak in 1994; more poor, single mothers are working than ever before; single-parent families are seeing their earnings rise and child poverty is at its lowest level ever.

But plenty of problems remain, in addition to low wages and lost health benefits for some:

- About half the welfare recipients who left welfare in 1996 and 1997 had lower household incomes in the year they left — more than $50 a month lower — than their last months on the rolls, according to a study based on a national sample of more than 30,000 households.[7]
- Some welfare recipients have lower net earnings than they had on welfare because they do not keep their job for the entire year, or they lose food stamps and Medicaid, sometimes erroneously, when they leave the welfare rolls.
- Up to a third of those who left welfare for low-wage jobs were back on welfare within a year, largely because of the lack of steady work and the difficulty of keeping a job while maintaining a patchwork of child-care arrangements.[8]

Welfare to Work Partnership

Johnnie Cartledge, Cessna Aircraft Co. plant manager in Wichita, Kan., teaches blueprint reading to former welfare recipients and recovering substance abusers who are training to be aircraft mechanics. The Cessna program is part of the Welfare to Work Partnership, a nonprofit association of businesses that helps retrain former welfare recipients.

- About 40 percent of former recipients who have left the welfare rolls are not working, leaving welfare officials scratching their heads as to how they are surviving.

Nevertheless, champions of welfare reform say the law's success should be judged by the dramatic number of recipients who have gone to work, not by how many are still in poverty.

"Welfare reform is about altering the culture of poverty, not reducing poverty," argued journalist Mickey Kaus, a long-time critic of welfare, at a recent Brookings Institution forum.[9] Rather than achieve "equal income" for the poor, he writes, the aim is to provide "equal respect . . . the respect our society reserves for workers, even if they gain not a cent of income."[10]

"We're showing that — at least in a good economy — we can promote work," boasts Ron Haskins, a senior fellow at Brookings who helped write the 1996 law as former chief welfare adviser to Republicans on the House Ways and Means Committee. "We've had a huge impact," he says, noting that never-married mothers are now more likely to be working than receiving welfare — a reversal from pre-reform years.

Some reform advocates say that even if former welfare recipients are worse off in the short-term, the long-term

Out-of-Wedlock Births Stopped Rising

The steady rise in out-of-wedlock births flattened out in 1994, but experts are unsure what role the 1996 welfare reform bill or earlier state reforms played. Some experts suggest that increased use of the contraceptive Depo Provera and concern about AIDS and other sexually transmitted diseases played the key role.

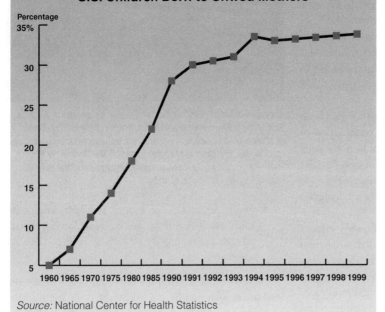

U.S. Children Born to Unwed Mothers

Source: National Center for Health Statistics

they passed. "It's hard to argue there's an increase in material hardship through this period," he concedes. "That's telling me that the gloom-and-doom set — of whom I number myself — overdid it a bit."

Nevertheless, say welfare reform critics, the largest economic expansion in decades has been far more influential in getting welfare recipients into the work force than any cultural conversion to the work ethic. Contrary to the popular stereotype, critics argue that many welfare moms had prior work experience, only used welfare between jobs and would have left the welfare rolls even without welfare reform.

"I don't think these welfare mothers were as out-to-lunch as conservatives think," Jencks says. He says the welfare rolls shrank so rapidly because state welfare offices discouraged new applicants from coming onto the rolls by requiring them to seek employment first.

Many experts worry about what will happen if there is a recession. Typically, a 1 percent rise in unemployment translates into a 5 percent rise in the welfare rolls for single mothers and a 10 to 15 percent rise for married couples, notes economist Rebecca Blank, dean of the Gerald R. Ford School of Public Policy at the University of Michigan. And, if families that lose their jobs come knocking at the welfare office doors, they may be turned away if they have reached their five-year time limit. Furthermore, many won't qualify for unemployment insurance because they only had part-time jobs or won't have worked long enough.

An economic downturn could be devastating to poor children, who compose about two-thirds of the welfare caseload, notes Ann Segal, former deputy assistant secretary for policy initiatives in the Health and Human Services Department under President Bill Clinton. "What happens when the time limits come and Mom can't find a job?" asks Segal, who now

dismantling of a system that encouraged an urban underclass of idle, unmarried mothers is worth it, citing the leveling off in the 1990s of births to unmarried mothers.

Skeptics doubt it was the welfare law that caused out-of-wedlock births to level off, noting that the percent of single-mother births leveled off in 1994 — more than two years before the law was enacted. But reformers point out that during the early '90s — when the unwed-births began declining — many states already were experimenting with time limits and work requirements for welfare recipients.

Even so, the huge increases in homelessness, foster care and hunger that liberals predicted would follow welfare reform have not materialized, admits Christopher Jencks, a sociologist at Harvard University's John F. Kennedy School of Government, who opposed the reforms when

studies children's issues for the David and Lucile Packard Foundation in Los Altos, Calif. "I can't believe the country would write off that number of children. It's a scary thought to me."

Conservatives say state and federal governments haven't "written off" anybody. Instead, they have more than doubled the amount spent on the poor over the $30 billion per year they spent on the old welfare program at its peak. Total aid to the working poor increased to about $65 billion by 1999, primarily through state and federal earned-income tax credits (EITC) — tax refunds only available to low-income working families. A mother with two children leaving welfare and earning $10,000 a year can supplement her income by $4,000 in cash from the tax credit and by more than $2,000 in food stamps, bringing her total income to $16,000 — lifting her above the official poverty line. But in most states that income is still marginal. A child-care crisis, broken-down car or ailing family member could cause a newly working parent to lose that first job. "They're one disaster away from destitution," Blank says.

When re-funding for welfare reform comes up for debate next year, Congress is expected to clash over how much federal money states should continue to receive for welfare. Democrats are expected to push for more exemptions from the time limits, while Republicans are likely to seek measures encouraging marriage and discouraging out-of-wedlock births — two goals of the 1996 law that the Bush administration strongly supports.

As lawmakers and policy experts debate the law, here are some of the issues they will tackle:

Did welfare reform move recipients off the welfare rolls and into employment?

After years of steady increases, the nation's welfare rolls have dropped by more than half from their peak of 5.1 million families in 1994. But the downward trend began more than two years before the 1996 federal welfare reform bill passed and several years before most states implemented those reforms. Does the welfare reform bill deserve the credit?

Conservatives tend to credit the law's toughened time limits and work requirements for transforming welfare recipients' attitudes toward work. Liberals generally give more weight to the strong economy, which provided a flood of low-wage jobs and the lowest unemployment

Doris Saunders, mother of five, tells a Welfare to Work Partnership conference in Washington, D.C., last May about her journey from being a welfare recipient to manager of special projects at the Sears store in New Castle, Del.

rate in 25 years. Economists credit a mixture of both factors.

The employment rate among never-married mothers, who typically have little education or work experience and spent the most time on welfare, shot up to 65 percent in 1999, compared with 49 percent in 1996.[11] New York University politics Professor Lawrence M. Mead III, who has long criticized welfare's failure to emphasize work, cites those statistics as evidence of the success of the welfare reform program, called Temporary Assistance for Needy Families (TANF). "It's the first large increase in work levels since the 1960s," he says. "A key part of that story is eliminating the welfare entitlement and requiring adults to function. There's no denying the success of TANF."

Ironically, most people left the rolls long before time limits actually begin to kick in this fall, which Mead attributes to the word getting out on the street that the deadlines were approaching.

"You make it no longer acceptable to be dependent, and a lot of people get the message," Mead says. "Now the caseworkers are saying, 'The clock is ticking. You should bank your hours because you're really going to need them.'" By "banking hours," recipients conserve their lifetime limit of five years of welfare eligibility for a future emergency, such as a health problem or getting laid off or fired.

But sociologist Jencks says conservatives are wrong to think the law somehow transformed welfare mothers

How Much Is Welfare Worth?

The monthly welfare benefit for a single parent with two children ranges from a low of $120 per month in Mississippi to a high of $923 in Alaska, according to Pamela Loprest, a welfare expert and senior research associate at the Urban Institute. Pennsylvania, which lies in the middle of the TANF (temporary assistance for needy families) benefits range, pays $403 per month. The monthly food stamp grant for a single mother with two children and no work income would add approximately $330. Only about a quarter of TANF recipients receive a government housing subsidy. Ron Haskins of the Brookings Institution estimates the annual value of Medicaid insurance at about $4,000. But liberal experts are reluctant to place a dollar value on Medicaid since it does not add dollars to a family's income that can be spent on something else like food. Also, its value is highly dependent on the health of an individual family.

1996, the nation experienced its lowest unemployment rate in 25 years: The annual rate fell from 6.9 percent in 1993 to 4 percent in 2000. And during this longest-running expansion in U.S. history, real hourly wages for the lowest-paid workers (adjusted for inflation) began to rise after falling for two consecutive decades.[14]

Mark Greenberg, a senior attorney at the liberal Center for Law and Social Policy who opposed welfare reform, worries about what will happen in a recession. "The way the welfare system has worked during a strong economy gives us very little information about what the picture will be in a deteriorating economy," he says.

Experts from both camps agree that a large chunk of the declining caseloads is attributable to recently passed laws that make work pay, such as expanding the EITC. The credit, available only to low-wage workers with children, can have as much value as a $2 per-hour raise. Some call the EITC the government's largest anti-poverty program.

Other policies that helped the working poor include health insurance for low-income children not receiving welfare, increased spending on child-care subsidies and increased earned-income "disregards," which permit welfare recipients to keep more of their earnings while remaining on welfare.[15]

In a recent summary of economic studies, Douglas J. Besharov, a resident scholar at the conservative American Enterprise Institute (AEI), concluded that aid to the working poor explained 30 percent to 45 percent of the caseload decline. He thinks welfare reform accounted for another 30 percent to 45 percent of the drop, and credits the healthy economy with 15 percent to 25 percent of it.[16]

Conservatives like Haskins say that if the booming economy were mainly or even solely responsible for the dropping welfare rolls, past economic booms should have produced similar reductions, but they didn't. Instead, caseloads rose even in the best labor markets. During economic expansion in the 1980s, when the American economy added 20 million jobs, welfare rolls

from idlers into workers for the first time. "Even without welfare reform, nearly half the single mothers on the rolls in 1994 would have left by 1999 simply because their children grew older, they found work or they got married," he says. However, he concedes that without welfare reform most of the mothers who left welfare would have been replaced by other mothers who had just had their first baby, split up with their husband or lost their job.[12]

Welfare reform made its biggest difference in state welfare offices, which tended to open fewer new cases. In some states, caseworkers handed newspaper "Help Wanted" sections to applicants, telling them to return after making 30 calls, Jencks says. A lot of mothers never came back, he thinks, and word of mouth probably discouraged other mothers from applying.

Moreover, work is not foreign to most welfare mothers, he contends. According to survey data, 60 percent of all welfare recipients had worked in the previous two years. "Making Ends Meet," a study of 214 welfare-reliant women in four cities, found that mothers had an average of five years of job experience. But the mothers who were on welfare had concluded that returning to the kinds of jobs they had in the past would not make them better off or that the job might vanish and leave them without income to support their small children. Many had plans to return to work when their children were older.[13]

Critics of welfare reform say the economy has been so strong in recent years that it's hard to know what the law's effect would have been in its absence. After

still grew by nearly half a million families, notes Haskins, of Brookings. [17] Similarly, caseloads continued to rise by 700,000 families between December 1991 and March 1994, the first couple of years of the most recent recovery, even as the economy added 6 million jobs.

Welfare rolls did not begin their sustained decline until 1994, when more than half the states implemented work-requirement programs that predated the 1996 reforms. In the 1990s, Haskins argues, it was the new welfare-assistance deadlines and tougher work requirements that pushed families into the job market.

A report just released by the conservative Manhattan Institute in New York City concludes that TANF accounts for more than half the decline in welfare participation and more than 60 percent of the rise in employment among single mothers. By contrast, the report by two Baruch College economists also finds that the booming economy of the 1990s explains less than 20 percent of either trend. [18]

Many economists argue that it was both the booming economy and the harder line coming from welfare offices. In 1999, the Council of Economic Advisers (CEA) estimated that welfare reform accounted for one-third of the caseload reduction from 1996 to 1998, and the robust economy for about 10 percent.

By contrast, from 1993 to 1996, when unemployment was dropping even more sharply, most of the decline was due to the strong labor market, the CEA concluded. Tough, new state work requirements during that period accounted for only about 10 percent of the drop, the CEA said. Increases in state and federal minimum wages also accounted for about 10 percent of the caseload decline, the CEA said. [19]

"The bottom line is we could not have had the dramatic decline in caseloads if we hadn't had the biggest social policy change in decades," says the University of Michigan's Blank, a former CEA member under President Clinton, who counts herself as one of the early liberal skeptics of welfare reform. She says the reforms were more successful than she expected because "states have been more serious than I expected in…changing their bureaucracies."

Are welfare recipients and their children better off after they leave the rolls?

Much of the upcoming reauthorization debate will no doubt center on whether those leaving welfare are better

Welfare to Work Partnership

Former welfare recipients tell their stories at a 1999 Faces of Welfare Reform panel in Chicago, Ill., during a seminar sponsored by the Welfare to Work Partnership. From the left are New York City Citigroup office manager Gail Hagan; Chicago Sears sales associate Kelly Shaheed; Cessna Aircraft assembly mechanic Chris Wilcox and CEO of Children of the Rainbow Day Care Center Gale Walker. Local NBC-TV anchorman Art Norman, right, hosted the discussion.

off than they were while receiving benefits. No one disputes that as the caseload declined, so did overall child poverty. By 1999, child poverty had fallen to its lowest rate since the government started measuring it in 1979 — to 19.6 percent of all children (14 million children), compared with the peak of 26.3 percent in 1993. [20] Black child poverty declined more in 1997 and 1999 than in any previous year, reaching its lowest level ever in 1999. [21]

But, these numbers don't tell the story of those at the bottom of the income scale. Welfare-reform critic Wendell E. Primus, director of income security at the Center on Budget and Policy Priorities, stresses that the decline in poverty has not been as steep as the drop in the welfare caseload. And deep poverty — defined as having an income below 50 percent of the poverty level — has been growing. [22]

Female-headed families appear to be leaving welfare because they can earn more money now than before, Primus points out. Earnings have risen for the bottom 40 percent of these families, and annual earnings for the bottom 20 percent increased nearly 82 percent from 1993 to 1999. Earnings for the next lowest 20 percent rose almost 100 percent. [23]

Wisconsin's 'Workfare' Experiment...

Policy-makers have long flocked to Wisconsin to figure out how the state managed to cut its welfare rolls more than any other urban state in the nation.[1] Wisconsin has reduced its monthly caseload by more than 93 percent since 1987, when it began its first experiments with a work-based system.[2]

"Welfare is gone in Wisconsin," says Demetra Smith Nightingale, director of the Welfare and Training Research program at the Urban Institute in Washington, D.C., who has surveyed research on the state's welfare experiment. About 85 percent of Wisconsin's welfare cases are now concentrated in Milwaukee, a heavily black and Hispanic city that is one of the most depressed in the nation.[3]

Wisconsin abolished the welfare entitlement check altogether in 1997 and replaced it with a new program called Wisconsin Works, or W-2. It requires virtually everyone to work and pays a cash subsidy only to those in government jobs or treatment programs. Almost everyone has to work — including the disabled, drug abusers and mothers with young children.[4]

Then-Gov. Tommy G. Thompson, who oversaw the creation of the program before being tapped by President Bush as secretary of Health and Human Services, calls his state's program "the standard for welfare reform in America." Conservatives have hailed the state's tough work policies and the influence of conservative theorist Charles Murray, who has argued that traditional welfare created a culture of non-work among the poor.[5]

But what often gets overlooked in the political compromise brokered between a Republican governor and Democratic legislators is financial help for low-income workers on a scale so generous that it has been compared with a European welfare state.[6]

Wisconsin subsidizes child care and health care for all working families with incomes up to 165 percent of poverty — not just former welfare recipients — adds a state tax credit on top of the federal earned-income tax credit and has massively increased health insurance for children.

Many were opposed to Wisconsin's groundbreaking welfare reform program. The state began experimenting with a work-based system in 1987, but it abolished the welfare entitlement check altogether in 1997 and replaced it with a new program called Wisconsin Works, or W-2. A Milwaukee group called Welfare Warriors shows its concern about the 1997 policy change.

"They're more progressive on the services side while tougher on the work side" than any other state, Nightingale says.

"W-2 redefined who the government helped," says Milwaukee Director of Administration David Riemer, one of the Democratic architects of the program. "The old AFDC [Aid to Families with Dependent Children] system was very narrow: It took the poorest of single parents and ignored all above the poverty line and ignored people with no kids. W-2 created a de facto entitlement to child care and health care for the entire working poor."

In his 1988 book *The Prisoners of Welfare: Liberating America's Poor from Unemployment and Low Wages*, Riemer argued for replacing government aid with government jobs as a progressive goal. Today, he contends that Wisconsin's program approaches the liberal ideal of providing a guaranteed minimum income for the working poor.

"The key to political success in Wisconsin was a concordat where the Democrats abandoned the idea of entitlement to welfare and the Republicans abandoned the idea of downsizing government," says Lawrence M. Mead, a professor of politics at New York University, who is writing a book on the Wisconsin experience. "They junked the old system and created a new one that is simultaneously very severe and very generous. It says, 'You've got to work, but if you work, we'll help you in all these ways.'"

However, only a small proportion of the working poor take advantage of all the generous supports, according to Lois Quinn, senior research scientist at the University of Wisconsin-Milwaukee Employment and Training Institute, which has been studying W-2. Child-care subsidies, for example, reach less than one-quarter of the eligible children in Milwaukee, according to the institute. "There's been a dramatic increase in child care, but it's not serving the majority of working poor families. And it's not going to, because it would break the bank," says Quinn, who doubts

...Miracle or Mirage?

the legislature would support the funding if all eligible families claimed it.

Although the legislature initially passed what looked like massive increases in spending for the poor, the welfare caseload plunged so dramatically that the program quickly became self-financing, Mead says.[7]

"Gov. Thompson went out in a burst of glory because he had these programs that looked like they served the entire working poor," Quinn says, "but the price tag, had it been utilized, would have been very expensive."

One reason more eligible parents don't take advantage of the child-care subsidies is that many of them — especially former welfare mothers — rely

Health and Human Services Dept.

As Wisconsin governor, Tommy G. Thompson, now secretary of Health and Human Services, pushed through landmark welfare reforms.

on informal babysitting arrangements with neighbors and relatives, which often don't qualify for subsidies.

Wisconsin's child-care subsidies go only to licensed or certified day care. Few qualified centers stay open on nights and weekends, when many former welfare mothers work in fast food, retail and nursing homes. They "need you on the weekend and maybe Tuesday night because Becky can't come in. Informal care is about the only thing that works for that," Quinn says. Only 24 licensed child-care providers with 458 slots were open after 7 p.m. in Milwaukee's central city, according to an institute study conducted from 1996 to 1999.[8]

Moreover, former welfare recipients have a hard time keeping steady work. The Urban Institute reported that while at least 75 percent of former recipients work some of each year after they leave the rolls, less than half are continuously employed.[9] And a study by the University of Wisconsin-Madison found that more than 60 percent of those who left welfare in 1995 and 1997 remained in poverty.[10]

In addition, as Wisconsin gets down to a welfare population that may be hard to employ, people are hitting the 24-month point without getting jobs. "What does it mean

for the safety net?" Nightingale asks.

Riemer contends that as a result of W-2, Milwaukee's low-income population is better off. Some data bear out his contention. In nine Milwaukee neighborhoods with the highest concentrations of former welfare families, incomes have risen since the advent of W-2, and the number of single parents filing income taxes continues to increase, according to Quinn.

But, Quinn notes, "The largest [income] increases came before welfare reform in Milwaukee County, likely due to the economy" in Wisconsin, which has been blessed with a low unemployment rate following W-2. Currently, Quinn reports, the number of working poor families is declining in Mil-waukee. But the number of near-poor (earning incomes at 100 to 125 percent of poverty) is growing. "The big challenge," she says, "will be moving beyond that."

---

[1] Lawrence M. Mead, "The Politics of Welfare Reform in Wisconsin," *Polity*, summer 2000.

[2] Tommy G. Thompson, "Welfare Reform's Next Step," *Brookings Review*, summer 2001, pp. 2-3.

[3] Amy L. Sherman, "The Lessons of W-2," *Public Interest*, summer 2000, p. 36.

[4] *Ibid.*

[5] Mead, *op. cit.*

[6] *Ibid.*

[7] Mead, *op. cit.*

[8] John Pawasarat and Lois M. Quinn, "Impact of Welfare Reform on Child Care Subsidies in Milwaukee County, 1996-1999," October 1999, University of Wisconsin-Milwaukee Employment and Training Institute; www.uwm.edu/Dept/ETI.

[9] Demetra Smith Nightingale and Kelly S. Mikelson, *An Overview of Research Related to Wisconsin Works (W-2)*, Urban Institute, March 2000; http://urban.org/welfare/wisc_works.html.

[10] Maria Cancian *et al.*, *Before and After TANF: The Economic Well-Being of Women Leaving Welfare*, May 2000, Institute for Research on Poverty, University of Wisconsin-Madison.

National Archives

President Franklin D. Roosevelt delivers one of his popular "Fireside Chats" in 1937. Two years earlier, Congress passed the Aid to Dependent Children program to help widows with children.

Despite the higher incomes, those leaving welfare more recently appear to be having a harder time making ends meet in some respects. According to a recent study by the Urban Institute, a liberal Washington-based think tank, about a third of those who left welfare in both 1997 and 1999 say they have had to skip or scrimp on meals in the past year. The study also found that the most recent welfare-leavers tend to have more health problems than those who left earlier.

Furthermore, rising housing costs appear to be causing trouble for the most recent welfare graduates. A significantly higher percentage of those who left welfare in 1999 have housing worries. Forty-six percent were unable to pay mortgage, rent or utility bills in the past year, compared with 39 percent of those who left welfare in 1997. The study suggested that this could reflect rising housing costs driven up by tight housing markets.[24]

In addition, many of those who left welfare earliest may have been less capable of working than more recent leavers. Many left welfare not to work, but because their benefits were terminated when they failed to meet welfare reform's work requirements or because health problems prevented them from working.[25]

Furthermore, critics of reform say that once work expenses like child care and transportation are factored in, many families are only marginally better off when they leave welfare, and some are actually worse off. For instance, the poorest two-fifths of families headed by single mothers increased their average earnings by about $2,783 per family between 1995 and 1999, but their disposable incomes increased only $643 after inflation and work expenses were factored in, according to Primus.

Moreover, those at the very bottom of the income ladder — 700,000 families — appear to be worse off, he says. The average disposable income of the poorest one-fifth of single mothers fell 3 percent in real terms from 1995 to 1999, he notes.

Primus also notes that while some working families leaving welfare are making higher incomes on paper, their net earnings are less. For instance, some do not continue to receive Medicaid and food stamps for which they are eligible, or their rising incomes make them ineligible for such supports. Or they fail to work a full year, either because their jobs are unstable or their lives are too chaotic.

The Urban Institute found after researching welfare families in 12 states that many families leaving welfare are eligible for food stamps but aren't receiving them. Families leaving welfare often lose both their Medicaid and food stamps, either because they don't know they are still eligible or because claiming them requires repeated in-person visits to a welfare office during work hours.[26]

A recent University of Wisconsin study found that less than a third of the mothers who left welfare for work in that state had higher incomes a year later, and more than 60 percent remained in poverty because the loss of food stamps and other benefits outweighed their increased earnings.[27] "The glass is half-full," says Maria Cancian, lead author of the study and a professor of public affairs and social work at the University of Wisconsin-Madison. "You've seen big increases in employment and earnings. But these women are not [earning] incomes to bring children out of poverty."

Even with higher wages, many of these women rarely reach above $10 an hour, Cancian says. Many have sporadic employment because either the job does not last a full year or personal crises force them to quit before the year is out. Other studies show that about 20 percent of mothers leaving welfare go through long periods without work, and many more are sporadically unemployed.[28]

Still another study found that about half of the women who left welfare remained below the poverty level 18-21 months later, primarily because only a minority got good-quality jobs with benefits, reliable hours and decent wages, says Sandra Morgen, director of the University of Oregon's Center for the Study of Women in Society, which conducted the study for Oregon state.[29] "What we've done in most states is force people into a problematic labor force," she says.

In addition, small raises frequently cause these mothers to become ineligible for food stamps and Medicaid. And because state-required copayments for child care are based on income, a small wage increase can jack up the copayment so high that mothers are forced to "pull the kid out of decent child care and stick him with grandma or the boyfriend," she adds.

The study also raised serious concerns about the poor quality of child care that former welfare mothers can afford and the precarious, patched-together arrangements many moms rely upon. If one thing goes wrong in that complicated structure, Morgen says, it can lead to job loss. "We have families who wake up at 5:30 a.m. to take a sleeping kid to Aunt Lola, who gets the kid to school; someone else picks the kid up and later takes the kid somewhere else," she says. "The kid may have three different child-care arrangements, and if any one of them gets screwed up, it can send the whole system out of whack." In addition, for many women, child care becomes unaffordable in the summer when children need all-day care.

"An awful lot of families want to work and think they're better off. But a significant percentage — who don't want to be working and think their kids need them — think they're worse off," Morgen says.

But welfare-reform advocates say that even if newly working mothers are poor, it is better than being on the dole because it boosts their self-esteem, creates a better role-model for their children and gives them a first step toward a better job.

Welfare critic Mead argues that, "over several years, if people keep working, they usually do escape poverty. But it's a long and painful climb."

The University of Michigan's Blank suggests that even if a former welfare mother loses her first job, she may persist in looking for a second job because she will have figured out how to cope with child care and transportation.

Robert Rector, a senior research fellow at the conservative Heritage Foundation, disputes the idea that a family's income determines a child's well being. "The worst thing about welfare is that it destroyed the marital and work ethic and damaged children's life prospects," Rector says. "A child in a working single-mother household will do better than where the mother is collecting a welfare check."

But the research on children of working mothers remains equivocal. About half the studies find significant improvements in children's behavior or academic achievement, while the other half find no effects.[30]

Another puzzle is the so-called "missing 40 percent." When Congress takes a close look at welfare funding next year, it will no doubt look at the large percentage of women who do not go to work after leaving welfare, according to a recent analysis by AEI scholar Besharov. Studies suggest that some have other forms of government aid or are getting help from family members, friends or boyfriends.

But Harvard's Jencks thinks the non-working welfare-leavers may be the one-third or more of welfare recipients who are unemployable because of poor job skills, mental health issues or drug problems. Democrats are expected to question whether this unemployable population will need more assistance to stay out of dire poverty after their five-year limits expire. If they are unable to exploit a social network, Jencks suggests, this population will be worse off after the time limits hit.

BACKGROUND

Widows' Relief

The original aim of cash welfare in the 1930s was to enable widows to stay home and raise their children. In 1935, Congress passed the Aid to Dependent Children bill. The goal, as stated in a report to President Franklin D. Roosevelt, was to "release from the wage-earning role the person whose natural function is to give her children the physical and affectionate guardianship necessary . . . but more affirmatively to rear [her children] into citizens capable of contributing to society."[31]

But in the 1970s, when the single-mother population rose dramatically and became dominated by divorced,

1930s *During President Franklin D. Roosevelt's administration, widows are classed with the disabled as unable to work.*

1935 Congress passes Aid to Dependent Children to help widows with children.

1936 Less than 1 percent of families with children are on welfare.

1960s *Welfare rolls surge, welfare-rights movement reduces welfare's stigma, divorce and illegitimate birth rates rise.*

1962 Welfare program is renamed Aid to Families with Dependent Children (AFDC).

1964 President Lyndon B. Johnson declares "war on poverty," establishing anti-poverty programs.

1970s *As the U.S. economy slows, Congress begins tightening eligibility for welfare and requiring more AFDC parents to take jobs or enroll in job training.*

1971 Congress requires all AFDC parents to register for work or job training unless they have children under age 6.

1974 The earned-income tax credit is enacted to provide tax refunds for the working poor.

1980s *The federal government starts granting waivers to states to experiment with welfare-to-work programs.*

July 31, 1981 Congress cuts cash benefits for the working poor and allows states to require welfare recipients to work.

Oct. 31, 1988 President Ronald Reagan signs the Family Support Act requiring states to implement education, job training and placement programs for welfare recipients.

1990s *Most states are allowed to experiment with work requirements and penalties. Congress passes major welfare-reform bill. Poverty and unemployment drop to historic lows.*

1992 Democratic presidential candidate Bill Clinton promises to "end welfare as we know it."

1993 Newly elected President Clinton raises the amount paid to poor working families under the earned-income tax credit.

1994 Welfare rolls reach peak of 5.1 million families. Republican majority takes over Congress and begins debating ways to reform welfare.

1996 President Clinton signs the landmark welfare-reform law on Aug. 26 removing the open-ended entitlement to welfare and converting the program to a block grant to states. Congress raises the minimum wage from $4.25 to $4.75 an hour.

Sept. 1, 1997 The minimum wage is increased again to $5.15 an hour. Falling welfare caseloads enable states to begin amassing a $5 billion surplus in unspent federal welfare funds.

1998 Child poverty drops to its lowest level since 1989.

1999 Employment of never-married single mothers rises to all-time high of 65 percent.

2000s *Amid historic lows in welfare cases and unemployment, Congress prepares to debate welfare-reform reauthorization.*

September 2000 Welfare caseload drops to 2.2 million families, a 50 percent decrease from its 1994 peak. Jobless rate drops to historic low of 4 percent.

October 2001 Five-year time limit on welfare benefits begins to kick in.

Oct. 1, 2002 Congress must reauthorize welfare-reform legislation.

separated and never-married women, Americans became increasingly hostile to aid for single mothers. In the 1930s, single mothers were grouped with the aged and disabled as citizens who should not be asked to work, and most married mothers did not work at the time. By the 1990s, work had become the norm for U.S. mothers.

Polls consistently show that two-thirds or more of Americans support policies to help "the poor" who cannot help themselves, especially children and the disabled. But the same number also say they do not support "welfare."[32] And polls show that Americans have traditionally opposed government aid for the able-bodied.[33] As the public increasingly perceived single mothers as fully capable of working, opposition seemed to mount in tandem with growing welfare rolls.

For nearly 60 years, it seemed that welfare rolls could only grow, regardless of the economy's health. Except for a few brief declines, the rolls grew from 147,000 families in 1936 to about 5 million in 1994 — from less than 1 percent of the families with children to about 15 percent.

After President Lyndon B. Johnson declared war on poverty in 1964, the rolls surged 230 percent from 1963 to 1973. The rise largely reflected two factors, according to the AEI's Besharov: administrative changes that made it easier for income-eligible families to get benefits, and the welfare-rights movement, which removed some of the stigma of being on welfare.[34] But this period also saw a rise in divorce and concern about the decline of traditional families.

After remaining roughly steady for the next 15 years, the welfare rolls shot up 34 percent between 1989 and 1994. Fears that welfare was discouraging work and encouraging illegitimate births resurfaced with new urgency during this period. Much of the caseload rise was due to the major economic downturn of the late 1980s and early '90s, according to Besharov. But there were other important influences: a spike in out-of-wedlock births, government efforts to get single mothers to sign up for Medicaid — and therefore also for welfare benefits — and an increase in child-only welfare cases, perhaps resulting from the crack epidemic that rendered addicted parents incapable of caring for their children.[35]

Since the 1970s, welfare policy has been "a tug-of-war between those trying to protect children and families from penury and those who believe that welfare dependency is even worse for families than poverty is," writes Gordon Berlin, senior vice president at the Manpower

AP Photo/Al Behrman

Welfare reform has been so successful at pushing adults into work in some states that their welfare rolls now consist mostly of children who are in the custody of someone other than their biological parents. Dea Shanute, 2, went to live with her disabled grandmother, Betty Burke, when her mother could no longer care for her. Burke receives $116 a month from the state to care for the child.

Demonstration Research Corporation, and author of numerous welfare studies.[36] But until the 1990s, he notes, neither side gained much of an edge in changing welfare.

Until the early 1970s, most changes in the program — renamed Aid to Families with Dependent Children (AFDC) in 1962 — tended to expand eligibility and liberalize benefits. Grants grew slightly during the 1970s and '80s, but not enough to keep up with inflation.

Beginning around 1972, as the economy slowed and poverty increased, public resentment grew against the tax burden needed to support large federal anti-poverty programs. Efforts to reform welfare over the next 20 years revolved around reducing benefits, tightening eligibility and requiring more AFDC parents to take jobs or enroll in job training.

Child Poverty and Welfare Caseloads Declined

Child poverty and welfare caseloads both declined after passage of the 1996 welfare-reform law. By 1999, child poverty was at its lowest rate since the government started measuring it in 1979 — 19.6 percent of all children (14 million children), compared with the peak of 26.3 percent in 1993. Black child poverty reached its lowest level ever in 1999. However, welfare-reform critics say that the decline in poverty has not been as steep as the drop in caseloads.

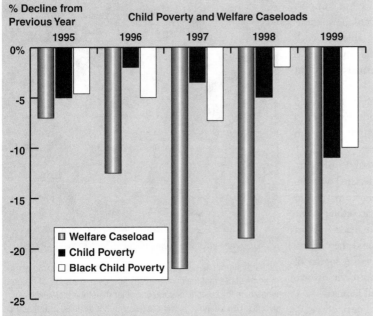

Child Poverty and Welfare Caseloads

% Decline from Previous Year

- Welfare Caseload
- Child Poverty
- Black Child Poverty

Sources: Congressional Research Service; Census Bureau; Wendell E. Primus, Center on Budget and Policy Priorities, "TANF Reauthorization," National Governors Association Briefing, June 6, 2001, Washington, D.C.

But none of the changes dramatically affected welfare caseloads. In a last-ditch effort Congress passed the Family Support Act of 1988, requiring states to place most mothers with children over age 3 in education, work or training.

The public's dissatisfaction with welfare stemmed partly from the growing size and costs of AFDC and partly from resentment that it was supporting a large proportion of unwed mothers, most of whom were assumed to be African-Americans. In fact, more whites than blacks received AFDC.[37] In addition, by the 1990s it had become more common for mothers to work than to stay home — a reversal from the societal position of mothers in 1935.

Welfare Reform

On the presidential campaign trail in 1992, Democratic candidate Clinton promised to "end welfare as we know it." After the election, his administration granted waivers from federal welfare regulations to many states, allowing them to experiment with toughening work requirements and imposing time limits on benefits. Both approaches became cornerstones of the Republican-backed 1996 welfare-reform law.

The changes ultimately adopted were based more on a Republican plan than on an administration bill. Both bills imposed time limits on benefits, but the Clinton proposal included an entitlement to a public job afterward, and that was not in the final bill. The Republican bill changed the program from one in which all recipients were entitled to a benefit under AFDC — and states received open-ended funds as their caseload grew — to a capped block grant, which gave states an incentive to cut caseloads because they would get to keep any unspent money.

It was largely this change — and the fear that states would not have either the money or the incentive to support welfare recipients adequately — that led to several high-profile resignations of welfare policy-makers from Clinton's Department of Health and Human Services (HHS), including Primus.

TANF was seen as a cut in federal funding because states would get funding based on their 1995 caseloads, recalls Greenberg, of the Center for Law and Social Policy. "Our question was: How will states manage with fixed funding and rising caseloads? But caseloads had begun falling in 1994, so TANF resulted in a significant increase in funding to the states," he says. "If you compare TANF to AFDC in 1997, the states had an additional $4.7 billion."

The result was more positive than Greenberg had expected, he says, because the states used the extra money to support families leaving the welfare rolls with additional child-care subsidies, child health insurance and other assistance, ameliorating the dire situation foreseen under low wages.

A recent study in Cleveland, Los Angeles, Miami-Dade and Philadelphia concluded that "the worst fears'" of welfare reform's critics — that states would slash benefits and services — "have not materialized." On the contrary, the study found, states are actually keeping some people longer on the rolls because they are permitting working people both to earn money and receive cash assistance. Under the old rules, a mother would be cut from the rolls once her caseworker discovered she had a job that earned significant income.[38]

The Working Poor

The massive increases in aid to the working poor initiated by Clinton and passed by the Republican Congress also helped prevent the grim forecast of the bill's opponents. Such subsidies now exceed the amount spent on the old AFDC program.

The most important support is the EITC, available only to working parents. Between 1993 and 1999, the income supplement for a single mother of two more than doubled from $1,700 to about $3,900 per year.[39]

Clinton also pushed through a two-stage increase in the minimum wage — from $4.25 to $4.75 an hour in 1996 to the current $5.15 an hour in 1997. In addition, real hourly wages for the lowest-paid workers began to rise after falling for two consecutive decades.[40] The prospects for welfare-leavers also brightened during this period as the annual unemployment rate fell from 6.9 percent in 1993 to 4 percent in 2000, its lowest rate ever.

Child care and Medicaid subsidies also expanded to record highs. Between 1996 and 1999, millions more children have become eligible for health insurance through the Medicaid program, and child-care subsidies have been expanded, essentially becoming an entitlement for families leaving welfare. Total annual federal and state child-care expenditures rose from $8 billion to more than $12 billion from 1993 to 1999, Besharov calculates, providing subsidies for more than 1 million additional children.[41]

However, advocates for the poor say child-care subsidies often buy poor quality care, and that only a fraction of the eligible low-income families take advantage of them.

CURRENT SITUATION

Reauthorizing TANF

Because the states' TANF block grant of $16.5 billion annually for six years expires in October 2002, the welfare-reform law must be reauthorized before then. Some hearings have been held, but serious legislative action is not expected until late this year or early next year.

The size of the block grant is the biggest issue to be resolved. Because the grant was established before caseloads plummeted, several states have had large unspent surpluses. In 1999, federal lawmakers were shocked to learn not only that there was an unprecedented $7.4 billion in federal welfare funds sitting unspent, left over from fiscal 1997 and 1998, but also that some states had used their surpluses for non-welfare uses like reducing middle-class taxes.[42]

Since then, much of the surplus has melted away, with only about 4 percent remaining unobligated, says Gretchen Odegard, legislative director for human services at the National Governors' Association (NGA). Moreover, many states are holding their surpluses in reserve in case of an economic downturn. Others are using them to provide child care and transportation for the newly working poor.

"Those structures are in place," Odegard says. "They're the reason the funding needs to continue. The governors will fight reductions in funding."

While Republican lawmakers are likely to argue that the unspent surpluses indicate that federal welfare assistance should be cut, Democrats will argue that states should keep the money as a contingency fund for leaner times or for child care and health insurance for the working poor.

Time limits are another major issue to be debated. Democrats and liberals are expected to propose more generous exemptions from TANF's five-year time limit for former recipients working part-time or completing their education and job training, as well as those considered the hardest-to-employ. Some studies suggest that many who are still on welfare are currently unemployable due to multiple problems, including drug or alcohol addiction, depression, disabled children and lack of work experience.[43]

'I'm Grateful I'm Not on Welfare Today' ...

When New York City's welfare office told Gregory Cannon he would have to clean city buildings to work off his $34 weekly welfare check, he bought crack cocaine with the bus fare they gave him. Today Cannon is drug free and working, thanks to Binding Together Inc. (BTI), a job-training program for former welfare recipients.

"I had plenty of jobs where I told off the boss and walked away," he says. "At Binding Together, I learned to get along with people. BTI gave me what [New York City's Work Experience Program] didn't — pride and dignity."

Binding Together mainly serves the hard-to-employ. About 75 percent of its trainees have prison records, and many were drug users. But in the past two years, clients have had multiple problems — including lower literacy levels, untreated mental health problems and less experience living a sober life, according to Program Director Angelia Holloway.

Because New York state limits how long an individual can receive welfare assistance — including time spent in

Two hundred former welfare recipients and other hard-to-employ people a year learn to operate sophisticated copiers at a training program run by Binding Together Inc. in New York City.

Binding Together Inc.

drug treatment — many people now arrive at the program with much shorter periods of sobriety under their belt — as little as three months compared with 18 months previously. Thus, they still have to learn basic skills like getting along with co-workers and arriving at work on time. The program is also finding higher rates of depression and learning disabilities. The average reading level has dropped — from eighth grade to about a fifth-grade level. And the program is getting an increasing number of women navigating their first job for whom child care is a major logistical issue.

Nationally, some welfare experts expect to see more such problems as the country's welfare caseload shrinks to a hard core of people who have little work experience and multiple health and substance-abuse problems.

As a result, BTI does a lot more counseling and hand-holding to get people ready for work, Holloway says. Constance Hayes, 40, who came to BTI directly from a drug-treatment program, says she was "still in a shell" when she first arrived. "Since I've been here," she says, "I'm able to open up and socialize better with people. BTI taught me I

States already are permitted to exempt up to 20 percent of their caseloads. So far, few states have defined who will be eligible for exemptions. According to ongoing research, a significant number of people who do not qualify for disability benefits, such as people undergoing treatment for cancer, cannot meet existing work requirements.[44]

Republicans are expected to argue that the 20 percent exemption should be sufficient to take care of problem cases.

Work Requirements

TANF required welfare recipients to work — or take up to 12 months of vocational education — within two

years of receiving benefits. States were required to have half of their recipients involved in such activities by 2002.

Because caseloads have fallen so dramatically — more than 50 percent in some states — states have been able to meet those targets without having to create the kinds of extensive work programs envisioned by the bill. Republicans, led by HHS Secretary Tommy G. Thompson, argue that states should not be released from the requirement to establish good work or work-plus-training programs.

Democrats will argue that the bill should have a broader definition of what qualifies as work, including

...Job-Training Graduate Says

can live in a productive way and can get money." She is counting on BTI to find her a copying job for about $8 an hour.

Several recent BTI graduates say they were motivated to find job training because they could barely make ends meet on welfare, and they knew their time limits on welfare assistance were approaching.

Desiree Dennis, 39, the mother of five, had been on public assistance for more than seven years when New York City assigned her a "workfare" job cleaning highways. She found the work "disgusting and degrading," and decided to find a job-training program. She recently started working as a copier operator at a print shop next door to Binding Together.

Yet at the $8 hourly wages typically paid to copy operators, some mothers aren't much better off than on welfare. Joann Gonzalez, 25, who was on public assistance for almost eight years, decided to get job training because she couldn't support her two children on the $390 per month she received from workfare for collecting trash in city offices. "I just decided to get up and start working because public assistance wasn't giving me enough money to live off," she says.

Vanessa Ratliff, a mother of three, now works at BTI after abusing drugs and receiving welfare for 20 years.

Binding Together Inc.

Gonzalez had not looked for work when her children were younger, she says, because she had no job experience and lacked a high school diploma. After training at BTI, she got work in January as a copy operator. She makes $220 a week, working from 2-10 p.m. That sum is quickly gobbled up by the $150 she pays to her babysitter and her $75 contribution to her subsidized rent. "I can't live off $220," she says. "Besides the rent and the light bill, you've got expenses for the kids: clothes, school pictures, notebooks." But her husband recently moved back in with her, which makes the job viable. He picks the kids up at 9 p.m. from the babysitter when he gets home from his job.

Graduates generally agree there should be time limits on welfare.

Vanessa Ratliff, 40, a mother of three, described herself as a "dedicated and sincere" cocaine user since high school. Today she works at BTI. "I'm grateful I'm not on welfare today," she says. "I was on it for a good 20 years, and it was OK with me. It shouldn't be that way, where I should be comfortable on it for 20 years."

---

a broader definition of what kind of education is allowed. Republicans are likely to argue that only work works, pointing to past failures of government-funded job-training programs.

Democrats also would like to see the law include an explicit new goal: reducing poverty. The law should not just aim to get a welfare recipient the first job available, but a well-paying job, they will contend.

Most states have allowed welfare recipients to keep most of their earnings from a job — up to a certain salary — without losing supplemental cash support.[45] Democrats will argue that recipients who are in the transition between welfare and work should not have to risk hitting their five-year time limit on assistance and becoming ineligible for benefits if they need them in the future.

There is also a growing momentum in both parties in Congress to let welfare mothers keep a larger share of child-support payments paid by absent fathers. Under current law, the state and federal governments retain all of a father's child-support payments while mothers are on welfare and about half the payments on overdue child support after mothers leave welfare. The provision has discouraged some unwed mothers from cooperating with state and federal agencies trying to find so-called "deadbeat dads," because often the father is paying some support to the mother unofficially.

Are Welfare Time Limits Unfair?

Two of the most controversial provisions of the 1996 welfare reform law were its five-year time limit on benefits and financial penalties for families not complying with the work requirements.

So far it is hard to gauge the effects of the time limits, since most families have left the rolls before their time limits kick in. Many families, however, will be affected starting this October and in subsequent years.

Although time limits are unlikely to be challenged, Democrats are expected to push for provisions to soften the limits' effects.

A recent University of Michigan study found high rates of depression and physical health problems among Michigan welfare recipients. Moreover, the women who reported the problems tended to work fewer months out of the year. High school dropouts and those with little work experience tended to have trouble keeping a job.[1]

Democrats will point to such studies to argue that a high proportion of welfare recipients may not be able to start working before the time limits hit and that exceptions should be made for hardship cases.

But Republicans can be expected to resist. Ron Haskins, former chief welfare adviser to Republicans on the House Ways and Means Committee when they were crafting the welfare reform bill and currently a senior fellow at the Brookings Institution, notes that current law permits states to exempt 20 percent of their caseload from the time limit. "There's no evidence that any state will press up against the time limit," he says. Moreover, he points out that a surprisingly high proportion of women with mental health and other problems manage to work at least part of the year, suggesting they may not have insuperable barriers to work.

The changes Democrats are expected to propose include:

- Stopping the clock on the five-year time limit for welfare recipients who are working but still receiving TANF (temporary assistance to needy families) benefits. Under some state policies, recipients continue to receive reduced welfare benefits while working to encourage their transition to working. Democrats will argue that such recipients should not be penalized by lifetime welfare limits while they are making the transition toward self-sufficiency and that states should have the option of subsidizing low wages.
- Changing the basis for the 20 percent hardship exemption. Under the law, states are currently permitted to exempt 20 percent of their welfare caseload from the time limits. Few states have actually defined who will

Both conservative and liberal advocacy groups argue that families should get more of these collections in order to benefit the children involved.

Non-custodial fathers of children on welfare often do not pay child-support regularly because they are unemployed or employed in low-wage jobs. Helping such fathers get good-paying jobs is high on the agenda of several progressive groups, who point out that most federal employment efforts have so far been aimed only at mothers.

Unwed Mothers

Promoting marriage and reducing out-of-wedlock pregnancies ranked among the 1996 law's key goals. The virtual disappearance of married families from many poor, urban neighborhoods worries the administration, according to HHS Secretary Thompson, who pushed through one of the earliest welfare-to-work experiments as governor of Wisconsin. (*See sidebar, p. 208.*) "The nation has clearly had major success in rolling back the culture of not working," he wrote in a recent article, "but the incidence of single-parent families, especially those formed by births outside of marriage, is still too high."[46]

Any proposals delving into the private arena of marriage, however, will be viewed as government intrusion and likely will face strong opposition from the National Organization for Women (NOW) and other progressive groups. It's not clear what proposals might be offered, other than exhorting the states to try harder to reduce unmarried births and possibly setting aside a fixed pot of money to encourage state experiments.

Although many states have used federal funds — provided under the 1996 law — to prevent teen pregnancy, congressional Republicans are disappointed at how little states have done to promote marriage. Lawmakers are

count under the 20 percent. Democrats will argue that the 20 percent should be based on the higher caseloads states had at the time of welfare reform's passage, not today's drastically reduced caseloads. Such a recalculation would permit a higher number of recipients to be exempted from the time limits.

- Loosening restrictions on training and education. Under current law, welfare recipients are permitted to enroll in vocational education for a maximum of one year under the federal work requirement. Democrats will argue that welfare recipients should be allowed to extend their education for longer than that and for a wider array of educational programs, such as college and English classes, before facing sanctions for not participating in work.

Advocates working with the poor at the community level say they're opposed to the entire concept of time limits. "Poverty doesn't have time limits, so helping people shouldn't have time limits," says Don Friedman, senior policy analyst with the Community Food Resource Center, a social service agency in New York City. "It's inhumane and outrageous to arbitrarily decide someone isn't entitled to assistance."

Friedman claims that, in practice, the time-limit exemptions aren't helping the people they should. For example, New York City requires even people with serious disabilities to come into its offices to be re-evaluated to see if they are exempt from the time limits. "I predict 10

percent of the caseload will be sanctioned for non-participation because they can't understand the rules or they can't make it in," he says.

For Nancy Nay, who suffers from sickle cell anemia and cancer, it is not clear that she can be defined as one of the 20 percent of hardship cases, because the number of slots keeps shrinking as the caseload declines, *The New York Times* recently reported.[2]

Federal law also allows states to exempt welfare mothers who are coping with domestic violence. But in New York, which opted for such a provision, more than half the women were never screened for domestic violence, and of those who said they were victims fewer than half were referred for help, according to Marcellene Hearn, an attorney at the NOW Legal Defense and Education Fund.

"Many states have adopted laws that are pretty good" for welfare recipients who are victims of domestic violence, Hearn says, but "caseworkers are just not following through."

---

[1] Mary Corcoran *et al.*, University of Michigan Program on Poverty and Social Welfare Policy, "Predictors of Work Among TANF Recipients: Do Health, Mental Health and Domestic Violence Problems Limit Employment?" Unpublished paper for Brookings Institution press briefing, May 21, 2001.

[2] Nina Bernstein, "As Welfare Deadline Looms, Answers Don't Seem So Easy," *The New York Times*, June 25, 2001, p. A1.

expected to discuss whether states should be offered federal money to encourage more marriage. Rector of the Heritage Foundation proposes paying a $1,000 annual bonus over five years to reward at-risk women who wait to have a child until they are 20 and married — as long as they remain married and off welfare for five years.

Most states have been leery of plunging into this controversial territory, although West Virginia adds a $100 marriage incentive to the monthly cash welfare benefit of any family that includes a legally married man and women living together.[47]

Timothy Case of the NOW Legal Defense and Education Fund condemns both West Virginia's approach and Rector's proposal as "rank discrimination against families where parents are unmarried. The government should not try to coerce people into marrying. Marrying or not marrying is a private decision."

Rector argues that welfare currently creates a "profound [financial] anti-marriage incentive," even though mothers are no longer required to be unmarried in order to qualify for benefits. As long as a man earning $7-$8 an hour doesn't marry the woman he loves who is on welfare, she keeps her benefits. Once they marry, his income gets counted, pushing the wife over the income eligibility line and forcing her to lose almost all benefits, Rector observes.

Eloise Anderson, former director of social services for California's welfare system, argues that the married family environment prepares a child for citizenship and adulthood "better than any other social arrangement." She is among those who have proposed that unmarried couples be urged to consider marriage in the hospital as soon as their child is born.[48]

Wade F. Horn, who as President Bush's new assistant secretary of HHS for children and families will administer

TANF Provisions for Reauthorization

Here are the major funding provisions of the current TANF (temporary aid to needy families) program, which Congress must reauthorize by Oct. 1, 2002.

Provision	Description	Funding	In Baseline?
Basic TANF block grant to states	To help needy children, reduce non-marital births and other purposes	$16.5 billion annually, FY1996-FY2002	Yes
Illegitimacy bonus for up to 5 states	To reward greatest reductions in out-of-wedlock birth rates	$100 million annually, FY1999-FY2002	Yes
Performance bonuses	To reward high performance by states	$1 billion for FY1999-FY2003	Yes
Population and poverty adjustor for 17 states	Grants for states with high population growth and low welfare spending	Up to a total of $80 million for FY1998-FY2001	No
Contingency fund	Matching grants for needy states	$2 billion for FY1997-FY2001	No
Native Americans	Grants for tribes	$7.6 million annually, FY1997-FY2002	Yes
Territories	Grants for TANF, foster care and other programs	About $116 million, FY1997-FY2002	Yes
Loan fund	Interest-bearing loans for state welfare programs	Total amount of loans may not exceed $1.7 billion	Yes
Medicaid for families leaving welfare	Federal payments for up to 12 months of Medicaid	About $0.5 billion per year	Yes
Additional Medicaid costs	Funds to compensate for computing Medicaid eligibility	$500 million total	No
Research by Census Bureau	To study impact of TANF on poor families	$10 million annually, FY1996-FY2002	No
Research by Dept. of HHS	Funds to study costs/benefits of TANF	$15 million annually, FY1997-FY2002	No

Source: Brookings Institution

Note: If a TANF provision is in the baseline, then Congress will not need to find a funding mechanism (either a tax increase or a program cut) to reauthorize the provision. If funding is not in the baseline, Congress must find a funding mechanism.

TANF at a Glance

The 1996 welfare-reform law replaced the old AFDC (Aid for Families with Dependent Children) program with the radically different TANF program (temporary aid to needy families). TANF's five key provisions are:

1) The individual entitlement to benefits provided by AFDC was repealed. The right to cash welfare was replaced by a system of mutual responsibilities in which cash benefits are conditioned on attempts to prepare for self-support.

2) The funding mechanism of open-ended federal payments for every person added to the welfare rolls by states was replaced by a block grant with a fixed amount of funding for each state for 6 years. States were given far more discretion than under AFDC law, to spend funds for purposes other than cash assistance, such as transportation, wages subsidies, pregnancy prevention and family formation.

3) States were required to place an escalating percentage of their caseload in work programs.

4) Financial sanctions were placed both on states and individuals who fail to meet the work standards. In the case of individuals, states must reduce the cash TANF benefit and sometimes the food stamp benefit of adults who fail to meet the work requirements designed by states. Similarly, the federal government will reduce the block grant of states that fail to meet the percentage work requirement. This requirement stipulates that states must have 50 percent of their caseload involved in work programs for a minimum of 30 hours per week by 2002.

5) States are generally not allowed to use federal dollars to pay the benefits of families who have been on welfare for more than 5 years.

TANF, actively supports government programs advocating marriage. He points out that most children born in single-parent families will experience poverty before they turn 11 and that fatherless children are more likely to fail at school, engage in early sexual activity and develop drug and alcohol problems.[49]

In hospital interviews conducted in a national survey, 80 percent of unwed couples reported being "romantically involved" at the "magic moment" of their child's birth.[50] Usually it is the father's poverty or unemployment that prevents them from marrying, says study co-author Sara S. McClanahan, a professor of sociology and public affairs at Princeton University's Woodrow Wilson School of Public and International Affairs. "I don't think signing them up for marriage will solve the problem. They're just going to split up," unless the husband's unemployment and the couple's lack of parenting and relationship skills are addressed, she says.

Other welfare experts worry that such policies could have dire consequences if the father is physically abusive. It's also not clear that marriage produces better futures for children or if the kinds of couples who decide to get married already have the kinds of relationship and parenting skills that are better for children.

AEI's Besharov suggests that increased use of the long-acting contraceptive Depo Provera and concern about

AIDS probably has had a larger influence on curbing out-of-wedlock births than any changes in welfare policy. It's too early to say, many agree, whether welfare reform can affect sexual behavior.

OUTLOOK

Decline Tapering Off?

Many welfare experts are concerned that as welfare rolls fall the population of recipients will be composed increasingly of those who are harder to employ. But statistics paint a mixed picture.

For example, it now appears that less than 10 percent of the welfare population has a drug abuse problem, far lower than the 25 percent assumed during the welfare-reform debate, notes Peter Reuter, a visiting scholar at the Urban Institute. And, he adds, it's not clear that addiction should keep welfare recipients from working. "Most people who have substance abuse problems who are not on welfare are employed," Reuter says. "They find jobs and on the whole keep them."

Moreover, Urban Institute studies have found that 1999 welfare recipients were no more disadvantaged than those on the rolls two years earlier.[51] One reason may be that those least able to work have been among the first

Child-Care Aid Goes Unused

Most former welfare recipients who are working do not receive the child-care subsidies they are eligible to receive. In many parts of the country, subsidies go to less than one-third of the former recipients, according to a study by the liberal Center for Law and Social Policy (CLASP).[1]

Study co-author Mark Greenberg, a senior CLASP attorney, says 40 percent are simply unaware that they could get child-care assistance. When families leave welfare, the state welfare office may not know that they have gone to work and may not get an opportunity to inform parents face-to-face that the aid is available. Meanwhile, parents receiving or just leaving welfare are actually more likely to receive child-care subsidies than other poor parents, probably because they have greater contact with government offices.

Many parents don't apply for the subsidy because states often don't pay for the kind of informal, unlicensed care that many welfare recipients must rely upon to cover their night and weekend work shifts, when few child-care centers are open. By contrast, families that are receiving the subsidies are more likely to use organized, center-based care than those using a neighbor or relative. Still other families may be overwhelmed by the administrative and paperwork hassles of applying for the aid.

The child-care subsidy, which varies from state to state, may not be enough to provide a mother with the child care of her choice. The federal government requires each state to pay a day-care subsidy high enough to meet the fees at 75 percent of that state's child-care providers, based on the most recent market survey. But only 23 percent of the states meet this requirement, Greenberg says.

According to the Department of Health and Human Services, only 12 percent of the 15 million eligible low-income children benefit from the major source of federal child-care funds — the $13.9 billion, six-year Child Care and Development Block Grant. Another study, of low-income workers in Santa Clara, Calif., showed that a third of the parents were unable to work because they could not afford child care, while another third reduced their work hours.[2]

The child-care block grant is underutilized because it does not provide enough federal funding to cover all the eligible families, so there are few state outreach or information programs aimed at getting more families signed up for benefits, Greenberg says. "Why have a big outreach campaign if you can't respond to the need?" he asks.

About 20 percent of federal welfare funds, called Temporary Aid to Needy Families (TANF), now goes to paying for child care, Greenberg says. Much of that comes from surpluses of federal welfare money realized by the states after their caseloads declined dramatically following reform efforts. But the number of children benefiting from the child-care subsidy hasn't increased as fast as the number of mothers leaving welfare to go to work.

If Republicans succeed in cutting TANF during the welfare-reform reauthorization next year, it could have a "huge impact on the child-care system," Greenberg says.

---

[1] Rachel Schumacher and Mark Greenberg, "Child Care After Leaving Welfare: Early Evidence from State Studies," October 1999; www.clasp.org.

[2] Linda Giannarelli and James Barsimantov, "Child Care Expenses of America's Families," December 2000, Urban Institute; www.urban.org. Spending was $3.45 billion in 2000. See U.S. Department of Health and Human Services, "Fact Sheet: Administration for Children and Families Child Care Development Fund," Jan. 23, 2001, www.acf.dhhs.gov, and HHS press release, "New Statistics Show Only Small Percentage of Eligible Families Receive Child Care Help," Dec. 6, 2000.

---

forced off the rolls by work requirements, while those with jobs sometimes are permitted to stay on the rolls under new state rules.

However, some employers and job-training companies say they're now seeing a less educated, more troubled population, with higher levels of depression among former welfare recipients undergoing job training or entering the work force.

"Businesses we work with say they are having a more difficult time finding work-ready applicants [among former welfare recipients] than two or three years ago," says Dorian Friedman, vice president for policy at the Welfare to Work Partnership in Washington, D.C. The partnership is comprised of employers committed to hiring ex-welfare recipients.

At CVS drugstores, which have hired some 12,000 former welfare recipients, newer applicants have lower literacy levels and are more likely to have prison records, notes Wendy Ardagna, who specialized in working with former welfare recipients at CVS and is now on loan to the Welfare to Work Partnership.

Nevertheless, companies will continue to be interested in hiring former welfare recipients because they foresee

Should the government encourage welfare recipients to marry?

YES

Wade F. Horn
Assistant Secretary for Children and Families,
Department of Health and Human Services

NO

Jacqueline K. Payne, policy attorney, and
Martha Davis, legal director
NOW Legal Defense and Education Fund

From the *Brookings Review*, summer 2001

Testimony Submitted to House Ways and
Means Human Resources Subcommittee hearing, June 28, 2001

Marriage is in trouble, especially in low-income communities. It is no accident that communities with lower marriage rates have higher rates of social pathology. Unfortunately, [federal and state governments] have been reluctant even to mention the word, let alone do something to encourage it. Public policy...needs to show that [society] values marriage by rewarding those who choose it....

Congress should make clear that the intent of the 1996 [welfare reform] law was to promote marriage, not cohabitation or visits by non-resident parents....

Second, states should be required to indicate how they will use Temporary Aid to Needy Families (TANF) funds to encourage marriage. Anyone who has ever spent any time in a state welfare office can attest to the...not-so-subtle message that marriage is neither expected nor valued.

Third, Congress should reduce the financial disincentives for marriage [by requiring states] to eliminate the anti-marriage rules...in the old [welfare] program. The law that established the TANF block grant to states allowed, but did not require, states to eliminate the old rules. Congress should also reduce or eliminate financial penalties for marriage in other programs, like the earned-income tax credit.

Fourth, Congress should implement marriage incentives, [such as] suspending collection of child-support arrearages if the biological parents get married...and requiring states to provide a cash bonus to single welfare mothers who marry the child's father.

Fifth, Congress should fund programs that enhance the marital and parenting skills of high-risk families. Many men and women lack [such skills] because they grew up in broken homes without positive role models [or]...had inadequate or abusive parents themselves. Congress should provide resources to religious and civic groups offering meaningful premarital education to low-income couples applying for or on public assistance.

Finally, [Congress should] earmark some TANF funds for a broad-based public awareness campaign to publicize the importance of marriage and the skills necessary to form and sustain healthy marriages.

When it comes to promoting healthy, mutually satisfying marriages, doing nothing hasn't worked. Perhaps doing something might.

Marriage is not the solution for everyone, nor is it the solution to poverty. Our country consists of diverse family structures: those in which parents are married, single, remarried, gay and lesbian, foster and adoptive. These families...deserve to be valued and respected as they are.

Marriage is a constitutionally protected choice. The Supreme Court has long recognized an individual's right to privacy regarding decisions to marry and reproduce as "one of the basic civil rights of man, fundamental to our very existence and survival." (*Skinner v. Oklahoma*) Significantly, this constitutional right equally protects the choice not to marry. This right of privacy protects an individual from substantial governmental intrusion into this private decision. Marriage promotion mandates in [proposed] bills essentially coerce economically vulnerable individuals to trade in their fundamental right to privacy regarding marital decisions in exchange for receiving job and life-skills training....

Supportive services should be made available to all families, regardless of their marital status or family composition, including services to help improve employment opportunities, budget finances, promote non-violent behavior, improve relationships and provide financial support to children. Where parents choose to engage in an intimate relationship, resources should be available to help ensure that it is a safe, loving and healthy one.

Promotion of marriage requirements endangers lives. Violence against women both makes women poor and keeps them poor. Over 50 percent of homeless women and children cite domestic violence as the reason they are homeless. Many depend on welfare to provide an escape from the abuse. [Studies] demonstrate that a significant proportion of the welfare caseload — consistently between 15 percent and 25 percent — consists of current victims of serious domestic violence.

For these women and their children, the cost of freedom and safety has been poverty. Marriage is not the solution to their economic insecurity. For them marriage could mean death; it will almost undoubtedly mean economic dependence on the abuser or economic instability due to the abuse.

Where the very lives of these women and children are at stake, we cannot afford to encourage the involvement of [abusive] fathers without taking every reasonable precaution, and without recognizing that in some cases father involvement is not appropriate.

a shortage of entry-level workers at least through 2020, according to Ardagna. Former long-time welfare recipients may have trouble getting promotions and more pay, she says, because of their low level of education — frequently no more than an eighth-grade reading level.

Political Consensus?

Both liberals and conservatives say they detect an increased willingness among legislators and voters to improve the lot of the working poor, who enjoy much greater support in national polls than non-working welfare recipients.[52]

"If you redefine single moms as working, the public's willingness to support them increases," says Harvard's Jencks, who argues for raising the minimum wage and increasing child-care subsidies.

By transforming so much of the welfare population into the working poor, conservatives may have handed liberals the kind of consensus they need to get more government help for workers.

As evidence, welfare critic Mead of New York University notes that some provisions in the tax-cut bill recently signed by President Bush were aimed at helping the working poor. The bill increased by $88 billion over 10 years the tax refunds that low-income families with children will receive.[53]

A similar consensus is gathering in the states, where governors will fight to keep the programs they established to subsidize health insurance and child care.

Many experts think the consensus will spill over to the reauthorization of the food stamp program, which also comes up for review next year. Advocates for the hungry would like to see it made easier for the working poor to receive food stamps, and for restrictions on working families to be relaxed.[54]

In a supreme political irony, Mead foresees enlarged support for improving job quality through an increased minimum wage and other pro-labor measures traditionally associated with the political left — as a result of welfare reform's conversion of welfare mothers to workers.

"Now we're going back to the 'me too' politics of the 1950s and '60s, where Republicans were competing with Democrats to do good things for ordinary people," Mead predicts. "We're going to see child care and all kinds of things coming from Washington to help out all those struggling workers."

"But," he points out, "if they had not become workers it would never have happened."

NOTES

1. Connie Rounds is a fictitious name used in the following report to protect the confidentiality of the person interviewed by the study authors. Center for the Study of Women in Society Welfare Research Team, University of Oregon, "Oregon Families Who Left Temporary Assistance to Needy Families (TANF) or Food Stamps: A Study of Economic and Family Well-Being from 1998 to 2000, January 2001," Vol. II, pp. 65-68.

2. *Ibid.*

3. *Ibid.*, p. 67. For background on the 1996 law, see Christopher Conte, "Welfare, Work and the States," *The CQ Researcher,* Dec. 6, 1996, pp. 1057-1080.

4. Ron Haskins et al., *Welfare Reform: An Overview of Effects to Date,* January 2001, Policy Brief No. 1, Brookings Institution.

5. Tamar Lewin, "Surprising Result in Welfare-to-Work Studies," *The New York Times,* July 31, 2001, p. A16.

6. Pamela Morris et al., "Welfare Reform's Effects on Children," *Poverty Research News,* Joint Center for Poverty Research, July-August 2001, pp. 5-9; www.jcpr.org.

7. Richard Bavier, "An Early Look at Welfare Reform in the Survey of Income and Program Participation," *Monthly Labor Review,* forthcoming.

8. House Ways and Means Committee, *2000 Greenbook.*

9. Kaus spoke at a Brookings Institution forum on May 17, 2001, in Washington, D.C.: "Beyond Welfare Reform — Next Steps for Combating Poverty in the U.S." Transcript at www.brook.edu/com/transcripts/20010517/htm

10. Mickey Kaus, "Further Steps toward the Work-Ethic State," *Brookings Review,* summer 2001, pp. 43-47.

11. Ron Haskins, "Giving is Not Enough," *Brookings Review,* summer 2001, pp. 13-15.

12. Christopher Jencks and Joseph Swingle, "Without a Net," *The Prospect Online,* Jan. 3, 2000; www.prospect.org.

13. Kathryn Edin and Laura Lein, *Making Ends Meet: How Single Mothers Survive Welfare and Low-Wage*

Work (1997), pp. 63-64. National Survey data cited in Edin is from the Panel Study of Income Dynamics.

14. Wendell Primus, "What Next for Welfare Reform? A Vision for Assisting Families," *Brookings Review,* summer 2001, pp. 17-19.

15. *Ibid.*

16. Douglas J. Besharov and Peter Germanis, "Welfare Reform-Four Years Later," *The Public Interest,* summer 2000, pp. 17-35.

17. Haskins, op. cit.

18. June E. O'Neill and M. Anne Hill, *Gaining Ground? Measuring the Impact of Welfare Reform on Welfare and Work,* July 2001, The Manhattan Institute; www.manhattan-institute.org

19. The White House, "The Effects of Welfare Policy and the Economic Expansion on Welfare Caseloads: An Update," Council of Economic Advisers, August 3, 1999; http://clinton4.nara.gov/WH/EOP/CEA/html/welfare/.

20. Wendell E. Primus, Center on Budget and Policy Priorities, "TANF Reauthorization," NGA Briefing, June 6, 2001, Washington, D.C. According to Primus, counting the additional income received by low-income families from tax and government benefits, the percentage of children in poverty is even lower — 12.9 percent in 1999, compared to 20 percent in 1993.

21. *Ibid.*

22. *Ibid.*

23. Haskings *et al., op. cit.,* p. 5.

24. Pamela Loprest, *How are Families that Left Welfare Doing? A Comparison of Early and Recent Welfare Leavers,* April 2001, pp. 5-6.

25. *Ibid.,* p. 6.

26. Ron Haskins, Isabel Sawhill and Kent Weaver, "Welfare Reform Reauthorization: An Overview of Problems and Issues," *Welfare Reform and Beyond Policy Brief No. 2,* January 2001, Brookings Institution.

27. Maria Cancian et al., "Before and After TANF: The Economic Well-Being of Women Leaving Welfare," Institute for Research on Poverty, *Special Report No. 17,* May 2000.

28. Haskins *et al., op. cit., Policy Brief No. 2,* p. 4.

29. Center for the Study of Women in Society, *op. cit.*

30. Haskins *et al., op. cit., Policy Brief No. 1,* pp. 6-7.

31. "Report of the Committee on Economic Security," January 1935, cited in John E. Hansan and Robert Morris, eds., *Welfare Reform,* 1996-2000 (1999), p. 6.

32. Gordon Berlin, "Tug-of-War," *Brookings Review,* summer 2001, p. 35.

33. *Ibid.,* pp. 9-10.

34. Besharov, *op. cit.,* p. 18.

35. *Ibid.,* pp. 18-19.

36. Berlin, *op. cit.*

37. In 1992, 38.9 percent of families receiving AFDC were white, 37 percent were black and 17.8 percent were Hispanic. See Hansan and Morris, *op. cit.,* p. 9.

38. Manpower Demonstration Research Corporation, "Big Cities and Welfare Reform: Early Implementation and Ethnographic Findings from the Project on Devolution and Urban Change," April 1999; www.mdrc.org.

39. Besharov, *op. cit.,* p. 24.

40. The hourly wage rate for the 20th percentile rose from $6.58 in 1993 to $7.13 in 2000 for female workers. See Primus, *op. cit.*

41. Besharov, *op. cit.*

42. For background, see Kathy Koch, "Child Poverty," *The CQ Researcher,* April 7, 2000, p. 295.

43. Haskins, *op. cit.,* p, 4.

44. Berlin, *op. cit.,* p. 38.

45. *Ibid.*

46. Tommy G. Thompson, "Welfare Reform's Next Step," *Brookings Review,* summer 2001, pp. 2-3.

47. See testimony of Theodora Ooms, senior policy analyst, Center for Law and Social Policy, before the House Committee on Ways and Means Subcommittee on Human Resources, May 22, 2001; www.clasp.org/marriagepolicy/toomstestimony.htm.

48. Anderson quote is from the May 17 Brookings forum; www.brook.edu/com/transcripts/20010517.htm.

49. Wade F. Horn and Isabel V. Sawhill, *Making Room for Daddy: Fathers, Marriage, and Welfare Reform,* Brookings Institution, written for the New World of Welfare Conference, February 2001, p. 2.

50. This analysis comes from a new study "Fragile Families and Child Well-Being," which will follow 3,600 children born to unmarried parents and 1,100 children born to married parents in 20 cities. Information about the study is at http://opr.princeton.edu/circw/ff.

51. See Sheila R. Zedlewski and Donald W. Alderson, "Before and After Reform: How Have Families on Welfare Changed?" The Urban Institute, April 2001.

52. "A National Survey of American Attitudes Towards Low-Wage Workers and Welfare Reform," April 27-30, 2000, by Lake Snell Perry and Associates; http://www.jff.org/pdfs%20and%20downloads/FinalSurvey Data.pdf.

53. See Robert Greenstein, *The Changes the New Tax Law Makes in Refundable Tax Credits for Low-Income Working Families,* Center on Budget and Policy Priorities, June 18, 2001; http://www.cbpp.org/6-14-01tax.htm.

54. See Kathy Koch, "Hunger in America," *The CQ Researcher,* Dec. 22, 2000, pp. 1048-1051.

BIBLIOGRAPHY

Books

Edin, Kathryn, and Laura Lein, *Making Ends Meet,* Russell Sage Foundation, 1997.

Hundreds of interviews convince the authors that poor single mothers are usually worse off once they leave welfare for low-wage jobs.

Articles

Besharov, Douglas J., and Peter Germanis, "Welfare Reform — Four Years Later," The Public Interest, summer 2000, pp. 17-35.

Besharov, a scholar at the American Enterprise Institute, and Germanis, assistant director of the University of Maryland's Welfare Reform Academy, largely credit falling welfare rolls to the good economy and government supports to the working poor.

Boo, Katherine, "After Welfare," The New Yorker, April 9, 2001, pp. 93-107.

The profile of this single mother who made it off welfare by working two full-time jobs has raised questions about whether children and teens are better off when their mothers are in the work force.

Haskins, Ron, "Giving is not Enough," Brookings Review, summer 2001, pp. 12-15.

Haskins, a principal aide to House Republicans in the crafting of the welfare reform bill, argues that the 1996 law produced the reductions in the caseload and record high employment levels among single mothers.

Primus, Wendell, "What Next for Welfare Reform?" Brookings Review, summer 2001, pp. 16-19.

Primus, who resigned in protest from the Clinton administration over the 1996 welfare reform law and is now at the liberal Center for Budget and Policy Priorities, argues that the reauthorization bill should shift its focus from reducing caseloads to reducing poverty.

Sawhill, Isabel, "From Welfare to Work," Brookings Review, summer 2001, pp. 4-8.

In this special issue devoted to welfare reform, the senior Brookings Institution fellow summarizes the broad range of views on welfare reform.

Sherman, Amy L., "The Lessons of W-2," The Public Interest, summer 2000, pp. 36-48.

This positive report assesses Wisconsin's work-based welfare experience, which reduced welfare caseloads by more than 80 percent.

Reports and Studies

Boushey, Heather, and Bethney Gundersen, "When Work Just Isn't Enough: Measuring Hardships Faced by Families after Moving from Welfare to Work," Economic Policy Institute, June 2001. http://epinet.org.

Families who have left welfare experience levels of hardship similar to other poor families.

Center for the Study of Women in Society, Welfare Research Team, University of Oregon, "Oregon Families Who Left Temporary Assistance to Needy Families (TANF) or Food Stamps: A Study of Economic and Family Well-Being from 1998 to 2000," January 2001.

About half the women had incomes below the poverty level a year and a half after leaving welfare. Volume 2 contains individual profiles of women interviewed.

Haskins, Ron, Isabel Sawhill and Kent Weaver, "Welfare Reform: An Overview of Effects to Date," Policy Brief No. 1, The Brookings Institution, January 2001.

A former architect of the welfare-reform bill and a liberal economist summarize the effects of the 1996 welfare reform law.

Haskins, Ron, Isabel Sawhill and Kent Weaver, "Welfare Reform Reauthorization: An Overview of Problems and Issues," Policy Brief No. 2, The Brookings Institution, January 2001.

A good summary of issues likely to be debated in Congress during the welfare-reform bill's reauthorization.

Horn, Wade F., and Isabel V. Sawhill, "Making Room for Daddy: Fathers, Marriage, and Welfare Reform," The Brookings Institution, February 2001.

Horn, President Bush's new assistant secretary for children and families, and Brookings scholar Sawhill argue that public policy must help "bring fathers back into the family picture."

Loprest, Pamela, "How are Families that Left Welfare Doing? A Comparison of Early and Recent Welfare Leavers," The Urban Institute, April 2001.

This report finds little evidence that recent welfare leavers are less capable of working than those who left several years earlier.

Rector, Robert, "Issues 2000, Welfare: Broadening the Reform," Heritage Foundation.

A scholar at the conservative foundation argues that the welfare system "bribed individuals" into having children out of wedlock.

For More Information

Brookings Institution, 1775 Massachusetts Ave., N.W., Washington, D.C. 20036; (202) 797-6105; www .brookings.edu/wrb. This think tank's Welfare and Beyond project sponsors forums and issues reports on controversial issues relating to welfare reform and the upcoming reauthorization bill.

Center on Budget and Policy Priorities, 820 First St., N.E., Suite 510, Washington, D.C. 20002; (202) 408-1080; www.cbpp.org. This nonpartisan research group analyzes government policies affecting low-income Americans and has been in the forefront in arguing that the poorest families are worse off after welfare reform.

Center for Community Change/National Campaign for Jobs and Income Support, 1000 Wisconsin Ave., N.W., Washington, D.C. 20007; www.communitychange.org. The center and the National Campaign represent grassroots welfare-rights advocates across the country and have released reports critical of state welfare-reform efforts.

Center on Law and Social Policy, 1616 P St., N.W., Washington, D.C. 20036; (202) 328-5140; www.clasp.org. CLASP is a research and advocacy organization for the poor that provides analyses of many welfare-related issues from a perspective that is critical of welfare reform.

Heritage Foundation, 214 Massachusetts Ave., N.E., Washington, D.C. 20002; (202) 546-4400; www.heritage .org. This conservative think tank has been a vocal critic of welfare and a supporter of policies to encourage marriage in welfare-prone communities.

House Human Resources Subcommittee, House Ways and Means Committee, U.S. House of Representatives; www.house.gov/ways_means/humres.htm#Human ResourcesHearings. This subcommittee has primary jurisdiction over welfare in the House. Its Web site includes links to hearing documents and witness testimony.

Joint Center for Poverty Research, Northwestern University/University of Chicago, 2046 Sheridan Rd., Evanston, Ill. 60208; (773) 271-0611; www.jcpr.org. The center summarizes its own and others' research on welfare reform in its newsletter.

Manpower Demonstration Research Corp. (MDRC), 16 E. 34th St., New York, N.Y. 10016; (212) 532-3200; www .mdrc.org. This nonprofit, nonpartisan research organization has a reputation for objective, influential studies of welfare and welfare reform.

Senate Finance Committee, U.S. Senate; www.senate. gov/~finance/. The committee with primary jurisdiction over welfare reform in the Senate is expected to hold hearings on welfare reform as the reauthorization deadline approaches.

Urban Institute, 2100 M St., N.W., Washington, D.C. 20037; (202) 833-7200; www.urban.org. This nonpartisan think tank has issued numerous influential reports regarding welfare reform.

U.S. Department of Health and Human Services, Administration for Children and Families (ACF), 901 D St., S.W., Washington, D.C. 20447; (202) 401-9215; www .acf.dhhs.gov. ACF is the federal agency with primary jurisdiction over temporary aid to needy families. Its welfare reform Web site includes links to HHS policy documents and data.

Social Security Reform

10

How Should America's Retirement System Be Saved?

Mary H. Cooper

President Bush tells the National Summit on Retirement Savings he favors allowing workers to invest part of their Social Security payroll taxes in stocks. Democratic presidential nominee John Kerry opposes so-called privatization plans.

From *CQ Researcher*, September. 24, 2004.

Demographers often describe the huge generation of baby boomers as a pig in a python, a population bulge so big it dwarfs both their parents' generation and their children's.

By most measures, the 77 million Americans born during the prosperous postwar period from 1946 to 1964 have dominated culture and politics. New schools rose to accommodate them; their protests ended the Vietnam War; and their tastes drove entertainment and consumer trends.

Now, as they near retirement, baby boomers may have yet another profound influence on American society: They could bankrupt the 70-year-old Social Security system.

"As the baby boomers start to retire, if the economy is slowing and the deficit is still bad, there's going to be some serious concern about whether or not they're even going to get all of their benefits," says Jeff Lemieux, executive director of the nonpartisan Centrist Policy Network, which analyzes Social Security reform proposals.

Only about 60 percent of the 47 million people who now receive Social Security benefits are retired, but the boomers' retirement will swell those ranks to the breaking point. Barring changes to current law, the Social Security trust fund will run out of money by 2053, according to the nonpartisan Congressional Budget Office (CBO).[1]

Demographers have warned for several decades that Social Security could not long survive the boomers' retirement without significant changes in the way the system collects and disburses revenue.[2] Spawned by the hardships of the Great Depression, Social Security was designed as a "pay-as-you-go" system, collecting

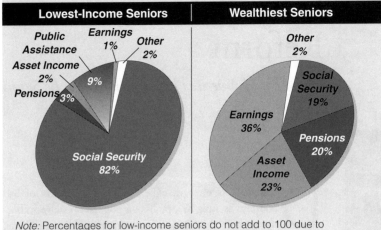

Low-Income Retirees Depend on Social Security

Low-income seniors received 82 percent of their retirement income from Social Security in 2001, while wealthy seniors depended on Social Security for only 19 percent of their income.

Sources of Income for Seniors, 2001

Lowest-Income Seniors

- Public Assistance
- Earnings 1%
- Other 2%
- Asset Income 2%
- Pensions 3%
- 9%
- Social Security 82%

Wealthiest Seniors

- Other 2%
- Social Security 19%
- Earnings 36%
- Pensions 20%
- Asset Income 23%

Note: Percentages for low-income seniors do not add to 100 due to rounding.

Source: "Income of the Aged Chartbook, 2001," Social Security Administration, 2003

payroll taxes from current workers and employers and using those funds to pay benefits to current retirees. Historically, the system stayed in the black because Social Security had a relatively large work force and small elderly population. In 1950, for example, 16 workers supported every retiree — more than enough to cover benefits. (*See graphs, p. 234.*)

Indeed, since 1983 payroll taxes have exceeded benefits paid, resulting in large surpluses in Social Security "trust funds" — the accounts used to pay benefits.[3] Money not needed to pay current benefits is invested in special-issue U.S. Treasury bonds. In early 2004, the Social Security system held $1.5 trillion in such bonds, which produced more than $80 billion a year in interest.

Over the years, the government has tapped into the trust funds to pay for unrelated programs, promising to pay the money back. But the boomers had fewer children than their parents, resulting in the "baby bust" of the 1970s and '80s. Thus, by 2040, when the last boomers will be well into retirement, only two workers will be supporting each Social Security recipient — too few to pay

scheduled benefits at current tax rates.

Compounding the system's financial problems, medical advances have raised life expectancy, so future retirees will live longer and collect Social Security benefits longer than their predecessors. In fact, the combined impact of a larger retiree population and increased longevity suggests that Social Security's financial problems may outlive the boomers.

"This is not just a temporary problem that will go away when we get over the baby-boom bulge," says Michael Tanner, director of health and welfare studies at the libertarian Cato Institute. Rather than a "pig in a python," the boomers are "more like a python swallowing a telephone pole. The situation will never improve because life expectancies will continue to increase, while birth rates will likely continue to decline."

Policymakers have been reluctant to take on the politically thankless task of reforming Social Security. Indeed, the program is so popular it's known as the electrified "third rail" of U.S. politics — touching it can be political suicide. But with the approach of 2008, when the first boomers become eligible for Social Security benefits, politicians are acknowledging the system must be changed if it is to survive.*

The question is how. Early in his administration, President Bush set up a commission that recommended ways to "privatize" part of Social Security by allowing workers to invest a small portion of their payroll contributions in stocks held in personal investment accounts. The theory was that stocks would return higher dividends than the government's conservative bond investments.

Support for personal investment accounts runs high among conservatives eager to reduce the size and role of government in general — a sentiment famously characterized

---

* Retiring workers may begin to receive reduced benefits at age 62. They receive full benefits by deferring retirement until their normal retirement age of 66.

by Grover Norquist, president of Americans for Tax Reform: "I don't want to abolish government; I simply want to reduce it to the size where I can drag it into the bathroom and drown it in the bathtub."[4]

Some proposals to privatize Social Security reflect the view that the private-enterprise system is a superior source of financial security for retirees than a government-funded entitlement program. Peter J. Ferrara, an associate law professor at the George Mason University School of Law, in Arlington, Va., and a former senior policy adviser on Social Security for Norquist's organization, has authored a plan that relies heavily on private investments. "Even though the stock market has a lot of ups and downs, over a lifetime of investment workers are certainly going to end up with a lot more through a system like this than they would under the pay-as-you-go Social Security system," Ferrara says.

Outlays to Surpass Revenues in 15 Years

Social Security benefit payments will exceed revenues coming into the system beginning in 2019, according to Congressional Budget Office predictions. The revenue shortfall will force the program to pay benefits by drawing down its trust funds, which are expected to run dry by 2053.

Social Security Outlays and Revenues, 2003 to 2100
(As a percentage of gross domestic product)

Source: Congressional Budget Office, "The Outlook for Social Security," June 2004

Critics, including many Democrats, say personal accounts amount to a backdoor assault on one of the country's most successful entitlement programs. "What the folks who want to drown government in the bathtub are really trying to do with privatization is bankrupt the federal government," says Joan Entmacher, vice president for economic security at the National Women's Law Center, a Washington advocacy group. "It's terrifying."

The "dirty little secret" about personal investment accounts, she continues, is that rather than improving Social Security's long-term financial shortfall, "they would make it worse." A full 85 percent of payroll taxes paid by all of today's workers "go to pay benefits for our fathers, our grandmothers and the kid down the street whose parents were killed. If — instead of going into the Social Security trust fund — that money goes into private accounts [unavailable to Social Security], how are we going to pay those benefits?"

The stock market's recent plunge and recent corporate and stock market scandals that resulted in thousands of

Americans losing their retirement nest-eggs raise more red flags for critics of privatization plans.[5] Further, corporate America is abandoning traditional, defined-benefit pension plans in favor of defined-contribution schemes like 401(k)s that shift pension investment risks to workers, making Social Security the only secure source of retirement income that retirees can count on, they say.[6]

"In today's 401(k) world, 40 percent of workers work for employers who don't even offer a 401(k) plan, and fewer than 50 percent of private-sector workers take advantage of those plans," says Christian Weller, senior economist at the Center for American Progress, a liberal think tank in Washington. "Even those who favor privatization are aware of Social Security's value as an insurance system."

To date, the contenders in this fall's presidential election have taken a cautious approach to Social Security reform. Even Bush, who earlier spearheaded the call for privatization, has downplayed the issue. Sen. John Kerry, D-Mass., the Democratic nominee, rejects Bush's privatization

Major Proposals to Reform Social Security

Proposals to reform Social Security are designed to eliminate the funding gap that the program likely would face over the next several decades as baby boomers start retiring in droves.

Plans to "privatize" Social Security would supplement the current system, which pays defined, or guaranteed, benefits, with a voluntary system enabling workers to shift part of their payroll-tax contribution into government-managed personal investment accounts.[1] Returns on those investments would replace part of the defined benefits provided to retirees who choose to participate. Most of the plans offer several investment options in index funds, like the existing federal Thrift Savings Plan (TSP) that covers government employees. The plans differ in the amount of transition costs they entail, which result from the diversion of payroll-tax revenue from the Social Security trust funds to personal accounts.* Most plans include benefit cuts with or without payroll-tax increases. Among the plans being debated are proposals from:

Rep. Paul Ryan, R-Wis., and Sen. John Sununu, R-N.H. — Based on a proposal by Peter J. Ferrara of George Mason University, the plan allows workers to divert an average of 6.4 percent of earnings into a personal investment account, more than any other major proposal. It would not cut Social Security benefits or raise payroll taxes. Workers who choose to stay with the current Social Security system would receive the benefits promised under current law; those who open investment accounts would be guaranteed to receive at least as much as they would receive in benefits under current law. The plan incurs much higher transition costs than other major proposals, according to Centrists.org, a nonpartisan group that analyzes public policy.[2]

Michael Tanner, Cato Institute — Workers could divert half of their payroll taxes — 6.2 percent — to private accounts. (The other half would pay disability and survivor benefits and part of the transition costs.) Workers who choose the private accounts would forgo the accrual of future traditional Social Security benefits. Workers who remain in the traditional Social Security system would receive benefits payable with the current level of revenue. The government would guarantee that workers' retirement incomes would be at least 120 percent of the poverty level. The plan requires Congress to figure out how to pay for remaining transition costs, suggesting cutting corporate subsidies and redirecting the savings to Social Security.[3]

President's Commission to Strengthen Social Security — The most closely watched of the commission's three proposals, Model 2, would allow workers to place up to 4 percent or $1,000 per year of payroll taxes into personal investment accounts, with the remainder going to the Social Security trust funds to pay current beneficiaries. Once retired, account holders would receive reduced benefits, based on the total amount diverted into their personal accounts. The plan would offer several investment options for Social Security retirement accounts, and those who fail to stipulate their investment allocations would have their holdings split among stocks and bonds. The plan would reduce retirees' initial benefits but continue to allow later benefits to rise with inflation.

Sen. Lindsey Graham, R-S.C. — Workers under age 55 either could "pay to stay" in the current system or join a hybrid system with personal accounts similar to the TSP. (Workers over 55 would remain in the current system.) Eligible workers could stay in the current system by paying an additional payroll tax of 2 percent. The hybrid system would pay lower benefits but increased minimum benefits for low-income workers. The government would match voluntary contributions up to $500 for workers making less

scheme for Social Security but has yet to offer a detailed plan to resolve the system's impending funding shortfall. And neither candidate is thought likely to offer a detailed solution to the shortfall before the election.

"The candidates have been quiet on Social Security all year, and that's largely because it's an election year," says Jeffrey R. Brown, a Social Security expert and professor of finance at the University of Illinois, Urbana-Champaign. "This, more than any other issue, is a topic that is difficult to express nuanced views about in a way that is easily digested by the electorate."

But even if both candidates continue to dodge the issue through the November elections, the next administration will face fundamental choices about the best way to ensure the system's long-term survival. Meanwhile, these are some of the questions policymakers are asking:

Does Social Security face an immediate funding crisis?

Government analysts predict that Social Security will begin taking in less revenue than it pays out in benefits in about 15 years. After that, the system will be able to

than $30,000 a year and guarantee a minimum benefit. Centrists.org calls the proposal moderately sized and somewhat more progressive — lower-income workers get relatively higher benefits, and higher-income workers get relatively lower benefits — than under current law, but with significant transition costs.

Reps. Jim Kolbe, R-Ariz., and Charles Stenholm, D-Texas — Beginning in 2006, workers under 55 could redirect 3 percent of their first $10,000 in earnings and 2 percent of their remaining taxable earnings to personal accounts. (For someone earning $30,000, the amount that could be invested would be about $733.) The government would match 50 percent of the contributions for workers earning less than $30,000 a year. Low-wage workers would receive a new minimum benefit. It would speed up the increase in Social Security's normal retirement age to 67 by 2011, with a small reduction in benefits for workers who retire early and a small increase in benefits for those who work beyond the normal retirement age. Centrists.org describes this personal-account plan as moderately sized, probably more progressive than current law and better than Graham's plan at limiting and paying for transition costs.

Laurence J. Kotlikoff, economist, Boston University, and Scott Burns, finance columnist — A new "personal security system" (PSS) would replace the retirement portion of Social Security (survivor and disability insurance would remain unchanged). The retirement portion of Social Security would cease to collect revenue, and a new federal retail sales tax would be used to pay off the transition costs. Current retirees would continue to receive their promised benefits, and current workers, once they retire, would receive all the benefits owed them as of the plan's imple-

mentation date. Workers continue to pay payroll taxes to cover Social Security's survivor and disability benefits; the portion of payroll taxes no longer collected for Social Security's retirement system would go instead to PSS accounts. The government guarantees the principal amount that workers contribute to their PSS accounts.[4]

Robert M. Ball, former Social Security commissioner — Retains the system's current structure with minor benefit cuts and tax increases and offers private investment accounts. Part of the Social Security trust funds, now held only in Treasury bonds, would be invested in a broad index of stocks, overseen by a Federal Reserve-type board. Workers could choose to invest up to an additional 2 percent of their earnings in supplemental retirement savings accounts administered by Social Security.

Peter Orszag and Peter Diamond, economists, Brookings Institution — Plan offers no personal accounts and relies on tax increases to solve Social Security's funding shortfall, with a gradual increase in the $87,900 cap on taxable income and a new tax of 3 percent on earnings above the cap. It cuts benefits for higher-income workers and raises benefits for low-income workers, widows and widowers and workers qualifying for disability benefits. With no personal accounts, there are no transition costs. Centrists.org says the plan's downside is its permanent increase in the payroll tax, and that overall the plan is probably more progressive than current law.

---

[1] Social Security payroll taxes currently total 12.4 percent of earnings up to $87,900, half of which are paid by employers and half by employees.

[2] Centrists.org. The Web site provides assessments of most major Social Security reform proposals.

[3] See Michael Tanner, "Cato's Plan for Reforming Social Security," *Cato Policy Report*, May/June 2004, p. 3.

[4] See Laurence J. Kotlikoff and Scott Burns, *The Coming Generational Storm* (2004), pp. 155-162.

---

* Transition costs are the payroll tax revenues diverted to private accounts and thus unavailable to pay benefits under the existing system.

---

continue paying scheduled benefits for another three decades by drawing down the surplus in the Social Security trust funds. Around the middle of the century, however, that cushion will run out.

"We have a huge fiscal gap, a huge generational imbalance, which has been built up over years through this pay-as-you-go program," says Laurence J. Kotlikoff, an economics professor at Boston University. "It's now time for us to recognize that fact and collectively deal with it." In his recently published *The Coming Generational Storm*, Kotlikoff says it's not the boomers, but their children

and grandchildren, who stand to suffer if Social Security reform is put off any longer.[7] "We do need social insurance; we just need to pay for it," he says. "And we can't let one generation's social insurance be paid for by bankrupting another generation."

Social Security's funding shortfall is even more worrisome, some analysts say, in the context of a rapidly worsening federal budget deficit and even graver financial shortfalls facing Medicare and Medicaid, the federal programs that provide health insurance program for seniors and the poor, respectively.[8]

Fewer Workers Support Each Beneficiary

The number of workers paying into Social Security per beneficiary has dropped from 16 in 1950 to 3.3 today. In 2033, only two workers will be supporting each beneficiary, severely straining Social Security's financial soundness.

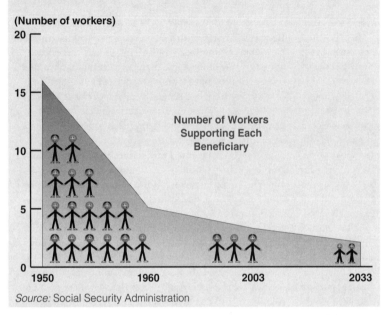

(Number of workers)

Number of Workers Supporting Each Beneficiary

1950   1960   2003   2033

Source: Social Security Administration

"People often say that no action is taken until a crisis is upon us," says Maya MacGuineas, executive director of the Committee for a Responsible Federal Budget, a bipartisan, nonprofit group in Washington. "Today that crisis is really upon us. We have structural budget deficits, a huge deficit in Social Security and even larger deficits in our health-care programs. Then we have tax cuts that they're talking about making permanent with no plan for how to pay for them. Hopefully, this will push Congress to come up with a real kind of budget agreement, which is what we need to get back on the path towards fiscal soundness."

But other experts say predictions of Social Security's impending demise are overblown. "It's very important to consider the financial problems that Social Security is supposed to encounter from a long-term perspective," says Weller of the Center for American Progress. He points out that in their most recent annual report on the program's financial sustainability, the Social Security trustees predicted that the costs associated with the baby boomers'

retirement would level off by about 2038. "Once the baby boomers have all died off, the program's cost stabilizes," he says. "Other than this demographic bulge, there's nothing really that makes the system unsustainable."

In fact, supporters of Social Security's current funding mechanism say calls for diverting payroll tax revenues to private investment accounts are little more than fear-mongering on the part of those, like Norquist, who want to reduce the size of the government. "This is precisely a backdoor way of achieving that goal," says Entmacher of the National Women's Law Center. "While we might want to make some adjustments to the payroll tax, Social Security really is in a strong financial position."

Entmacher cites annual reports by the Social Security trustees and the recent CBO report as evidence that the system's projected shortfalls hardly amount to a crisis. The trustees' most recent annual report, published in March, predicted that the system's trust funds won't run out until 2042, 13 years later than the 2029 date the trustees forecasted in 1997, thanks in part to rising real wages since 1997.[9] And the CBO was even more optimistic, predicting the program wouldn't run out of trust fund money until 2052. "The privatizers aren't able to sell fear because the CBO confirms that Social Security can pay 100 percent of benefits until 2052," Entmacher says. "That's 50 more years."

But long before the trust funds actually run out of money, the surplus will begin to shrink. It's uncertain exactly when the system will begin paying more in benefits than it collects in payroll taxes — the trustees predict that will occur in 2018; the CBO says it won't happen until 2019. Such differences among the official forecasts are unimportant, some experts say. "The evidence is overwhelming that we are going to begin to run large deficits in the Social Security system sometime in the next two decades," says Brown of the University of Illinois. "Whether it's in 2018 or 2019, once we pass over into that period, absent some sort of a change in the way the system is structured, those deficits are going to grow larger every year."

Indeed, while experts differ widely over the gravity of Social Security's funding shortfall and the best way to solve it, everyone agrees that some adjustments are needed to ensure the system's long-term survival. They also agree that the sooner lawmakers make those changes, the easier it will be to pay for them. "There's no miracle here," says Alicia Munnell, director of the Center for Retirement Research at Boston College. "We just have to bite the bullet and acknowledge that it's going to require money. Then we can talk about what's the best way to do it."

Inaction — the path taken thus far — is no longer a viable option, most experts agree. "We could do nothing for a couple of decades, but then we would have very few options on the table apart from big tax increases or big benefit cuts," Brown says. "To do nothing is completely irresponsible and unrealistic."

Would privatization be good for future retirees?

Most proposals to privatize Social Security are voluntary and would allow workers to invest part of the money they now contribute as payroll taxes in stocks, bonds or a mix of the two, in privately held, government-administered accounts. In return, they would receive smaller monthly benefits when they retire than they would under the current system. Current beneficiaries and workers nearing retirement would retain promised benefits under most proposals.

Beyond those general terms, however, privatization schemes vary widely. The most sweeping proposal — by George Mason's Ferrara — would require the federal government to guarantee that beneficiaries' personal accounts return no less than the benefits they would have received through Social Security under current law.

"Even if Social Security could pay all its promised benefits, the real rate of return for most workers would be no more than 1.5 percent," says Ferrara. "The long-term return on stocks after inflation is 7 to 7.5 percent. So even if stocks during certain periods go up or down, the large gulf between private capital returns and the pay-as-you-go return means that we can take the risk off the worker so that he's guaranteed current-law benefits in any event."

Those higher investment returns, supporters of this approach maintain, will translate into greater consumer

Former Enron employee Gwen Gray cries after telling union officials in Washington about her job layoff and her husband's death. The failure of many corporate pension funds has complicated the debate over Social Security reform.

spending, boosting the overall U.S. economy. But critics say Ferrara's plan could bankrupt the system because it relies too heavily on the consistently robust growth of the stock market, an assumption they say is invalidated by the recent volatility of stock prices. "Peter Ferrara's proposal is a prime example of the notion that somehow privatization will accelerate economic growth and that over the long run it will ultimately pay for itself," says Weller of the Center for American Progress. "That's just silly economics."

Under some privatization proposals, administrative costs — mainly fees charged by brokers to manage workers' personal accounts — could reduce participants' account balances at retirement by as much as 30 percent, according to CBO estimates.[10] Boston University's Kotlikoff would reduce that burden by offering a single, internationally diversified portfolio. "This plan offers private investment in a collective, global mutual fund of stocks and bonds," he says. "Instead of having everybody investing on their own and paying whatever fees their brokers want to charge, everybody in our plan would be invested in exactly the same portfolio, and the whole thing would be administered by the Social Security Administration."

But critics say privatization would divert revenue from the Social Security trust funds to private accounts, reducing the amount of money available to pay benefits to current beneficiaries. Over time, when workers holding personal investment accounts retire and use the returns on those investments as part of their retirement income, privatization could save the system money. But until then, the payroll taxes diverted to those accounts would be a drain on Social Security, commonly described as the "transition costs" of privatization.

"Giving workers accounts costs money in the short run, because at the same time you're funding those accounts you're also paying Social Security benefits," says Lemieux of the Centrist Policy Network. "It's only in the long run, when people holding personal accounts get smaller regular Social Security benefits, that the savings to the system begin to take effect."

Many experts assess the viability of privatization plans according to the magnitude of the transition costs they would incur. Ferrara's plan has attracted the broadest criticism from supporters of Social Security because it would allow workers to divert a larger portion of their payroll to private accounts. "Some of the more conservative Republicans are entertaining a pie-in-the-sky or free-lunch proposal," says Lemieux. "This plan is just nuts. The transition costs would be so enormous they would greatly upset capital markets and possibly the economy. Over the next 75 years, Ferrara's plan would cost more than current law, and it would raise Social Security spending much higher than it would get even after all the baby boomers retire."

Other critics say privatization is the wrong approach to solving Social Security's funding problem because it undermines the federally guaranteed program at a time when other sources of retiree income are becoming less certain. U.S. employers are abandoning traditional, defined-benefit pension plans, which promise a monthly payment for life, in favor of defined-contribution plans, which shift the investment risk to the employee and future retiree.[11] Moreover, because employees generally are not required to participate in the defined-contribution plans — known as 401(k) plans — it's usually the lower-paid or less-educated workers who fare the worst, because they either feel they can't afford to set aside money for retirement or are unaware of the need to do so.

"We need a part of our retirement income that's secure and that we can count on," says Entmacher of the National Women's Law Center. "So much risk is already being shifted to workers, while employers are bearing less and less of that risk in private pensions. For that reason, we need Social Security to really be secure."

But many analysts who dismiss sweeping reforms such as Ferrara's still favor partial privatization as the only way to ensure Social Security's long-range survival. In addition, some proposals — such as one introduced by Reps. Jim Kolbe, R-Ariz., and Charles W. Stenholm, D-Texas — seek to enhance the system's progressivity by tailoring it in favor of low-income workers.* "The good reform proposals don't cut benefits so much for people who earned small amounts during their working careers, and they specifically boost personal accounts for those people," Lemieux says. "So I feel pretty confident that they would be even more progressive than current law."

Are benefit cuts or payroll-tax increases better alternatives to privatization?

Reducing benefits or increasing payroll taxes are the only alternatives to partial privatization to resolve Social Security's funding shortfall.

Lawmakers cut benefits in 1983 by gradually raising the age at which retirees become eligible to receive full benefits. Under current law, only workers born before 1938 may begin receiving benefits at the traditional eligibility age of 65. Anticipating Americans' increasing longevity, Congress phased in a gradual increase in the eligibility age, which eventually will reach 67 for those born after 1959. Workers of all ages may continue to take early retirement at 62 with reduced benefits, based on the expectation that they will receive them for a longer time than if they began receiving them at their normal retirement age.

Federal Reserve Board Chairman Alan Greenspan has suggested that the retirement age continue to increase to reflect longer life expectancies. But many analysts say further benefit cuts would deal an unacceptable blow to the entitlement program's promise to keep retirees and the disabled out of poverty.

"Social Security is already a bare-bones system," says Weller, of the Center for American Progress, who calculates that each one-year increase in the normal retirement age amounts to an 8 percent benefit cut. "About a third of households enter retirement woefully inadequately prepared, often with just Social Security to live on, which was never the intention. Cutting back Social Security benefits from their already low level is a dangerous proposition."

---

* Progressivity means that poor workers get proportionally more benefits than wealthy ones.

Some reform proposals would cut benefits less directly by changing the way they are calculated. Currently, Social Security adjusts benefits based on two formulas: Initial benefits are adjusted to reflect average wage increases in the economy, based on a wage-indexation formula, and subsequent benefits are adjusted for inflation using the cost-of-living index. But some reform plans would eliminate wage indexation and adjust benefits according to consumer price increases alone. "That would shrink the replacement ratio [the portion of pre-retirement earnings beneficiaries receive each month] of Social Security over time, from about 40 percent [of workers' earnings] right now to 20 percent or less within the next two or three decades," says Weller. "That's basically death by a thousand cuts, because every year relative benefits would be cut a little bit more. That's just a recipe for disaster."

Some analysts say changing the ways benefits are indexed is not only necessary but also fair. "You can call it a benefit cut, or you can call it a reduction in the growth of benefits," says Brown of the University of Illinois. "If you have future benefits grow with inflation rather than with real wage growth, future generations will continue to pay the current 12.4 percent payroll tax, but their benefits will grow with inflation and nothing more. Over 60 years, that would rebalance the system and do it in a very gradual way. People who are near retirement wouldn't be greatly affected, while people in their 20s and 30s today would have plenty of time to adjust. That would be a lot more feasible politically than cutting everybody's benefits today."

Others say increasing the payroll tax would make Social Security solvent over time. Today workers and employers split the cost of Social Security, with each paying 6.2 percent of workers' earnings, up to a maximum of $87,900 a year. Earnings above that cap are not subject to the payroll tax. Some analysts say raising the wage cap would be the fairest solution to the system's funding problems.

"Why should a secretary pay the Social Security tax on 100 percent of her income while her boss, who is more likely to be male, only pays tax on a portion of his?" asks Entmacher of the National Women's Law Center.

Some proposals, including the Kolbe-Stenholm bill, would increase tax payments by raising the earnings cap. "Most of the reform community is actually in favor of that to some extent," says Lemieux, including some privatizers who see an increase in the wage cap as a necessary means to cover the transition costs resulting from any shift to private accounts. "These transition costs amount to over a trillion dollars over the next 10 years, and we'd have to pay for that somehow."

Munnell, of the Center for Retirement Research, points out that benefits are already going to diminish, even without any additional changes to the system, thanks to the rising retirement age, an increase in Medicare premiums and the taxation of Social Security benefits.[12] Medicare Part B premiums, which are automatically deducted from Social Security benefits, are expected to rise from 6 percent of benefits for someone retiring today to 9 percent for those retiring in 2030. Because Social Security benefits are taxed at a fixed rate, and future benefits will rise with inflation, the number of beneficiaries whose benefits will be taxed will grow over time.

"It's quite reasonable to fix the current system and keep its existing structure, but you need more money or benefit cuts to do that," Munnell says. "My preference is more money, because I'm not sure we want wage-replacement rates to go down further than they're already scheduled to go."

She supports an increase in the taxable-wage base, which former Social Security Commissioner Robert M. Ball and a few other reformers have proposed. "This can easily be done without going to personal accounts."

BACKGROUND

Roots in Industrialization

Social Security began during the Depression, but the concept of a publicly funded safety net to protect citizens from poverty is rooted in longstanding theory and practice. In his pamphlet, "Agrarian Justice," written shortly after the Revolutionary War, American patriot Thomas Paine described a social program to ensure the economic well being of the young and the elderly. Paine proposed creating a fund, financed through an inheritance tax, to provide a single payment of 15 pounds sterling to citizens reaching age 21, to help them get started in life, and annual benefits of 10 pounds sterling to everyone 50 and older to prevent poverty in old age.

CHRONOLOGY

1930s *Social Security is created to combat widespread poverty during the Great Depression.*

Aug. 14, 1935 President Franklin D. Roosevelt signs the Social Security Act, the nation's first major anti-poverty insurance program providing benefits to older Americans.

1939 Ida May Fuller of Ludlow, Vt., becomes the first retiree to receive a monthly Social Security check. Social Security is expanded to provide benefits to workers' survivors and the disabled.

1940s-1960s *A postwar population boom sets the stage for Social Security's future funding shortfall.*

1946 The first year of the baby boom starts a demographic bulge that will last for the next 18 years.

1950 Cost-of-living adjustments are applied to Social Security to protect benefits from inflation. . . . There are 16 workers for every retiree in the United States, more than enough to cover Social Security benefits.

1954 Congress expands Social Security to include benefits for disabled older workers and disabled adult dependents.

1960 Disability insurance is extended to cover disabled workers of all ages and their dependents.

1961 All workers are permitted to receive reduced, early-retirement benefits at age 62.

July 30, 1965 Medicare, the most far-reaching change to the Social Security system, becomes law, providing health insurance to Americans ages 65 and older.

1970s-1980s *Concern mounts over Social Security's solvency, as demographers warn of the coming baby-boom bulge.*

1972 Social Security's new Supplemental Security Income (SSI) program provides additional benefits to poor seniors

and begins covering the blind and the disabled — groups previously served by the states and localities.

1977 As Social Security benefit expenditures rapidly mount due to expanded coverage, Congress raises payroll taxes and increases the wage base — the maximum earnings subject to Social Security taxes — to restore the trust funds' financial soundness.

1983 Congress authorizes taxation of Social Security benefits, brings federal employees into the system and calls for an increase in the normal retirement age from 65 to 67, beginning in the 21st century.

2000s *Privatization proposals gather momentum.*

2001 President Bush's Commission to Strengthen Social Security recommends ways to reform the program that would introduce personal investment accounts.

2008 The first baby boomers reach age 62, making them eligible to receive reduced, early-retirement Social Security benefits.

2009 The normal retirement age — the age at which retirees may receive full Social Security benefits — rises to 66.

2012 The first baby boomers turn 66, enabling them to receive full Social Security benefits.

2019 Social Security begins paying more in benefits than it receives in payroll tax revenues, forcing it to draw down its trust funds in order to pay benefits, according to Congressional Budget Office (CBO) predictions.

2027 The normal retirement age rises to 67.

2040 With most boomers well into retirement, there are just two workers for each Social Security recipient, too few to pay scheduled benefits at current tax rates.

2052 The Social Security trust funds will run out of money, the CBO predicts.

Benefits Crucial to Older Women

Almost two-thirds of U.S. retirees now rely on Social Security for most of their income, largely due to the decline of traditional pensions in recent decades.

Social Security is especially vital for elderly women, but it does less to meet women's retirement needs than it does for men. Because of their longevity and work patterns, "women rely much more heavily on Social Security than men do for their economic security in old age," says Joan Entmacher, vice president for economic security at the National Women's Law Center.

The average American woman who reaches age 65 will live for another 20 years, four years longer than her male counterpart. But after her spouse dies, a widow receives only half her husbands' benefits, leaving her with reduced income to cover the higher medical costs that typically come with old age. Single women often fare even worse, having only their own benefits to live on in retirement.

Women also have fewer alternative sources of income during retirement than men, so they're more dependent on Social Security. They tend to accumulate less in savings and pension credits than men during their working years, mainly because they are more likely to work part time or take time off to raise children.[1]

Indeed, women typically work for 32 years, compared with 44 years for men. Part-time employment generally pays less than full-time work, and rarely provides pension coverage. Full-time female workers still make 75 cents for every dollar earned by men, a wage gap that makes it harder for women to save money for retirement. Because traditional pension benefits usually are calculated on the basis of years worked and earnings, even women with full pension coverage tend to receive lower benefits during retirement than their male counterparts.

Advocates of Social Security privatization say allowing women to save part of their payroll taxes in managed retirement investment accounts would help them prepare for a more comfortable old age.

But many women's-rights activists say privatization would further erode women's retirement security. For one thing, the current system favors lower-income recipients, a group that includes a disproportionate share of women. "Social Security has a progressive benefit formula, so that lower earners get a higher percentage of their pre-retirement earnings as benefits," says Alicia Munnell, director of the Center for Retirement Research at Boston College. "So to the extent that we move away from that benefit formula and into individual accounts, women would be hurt."

Another advantage of Social Security as it's currently designed is the automatic cost-of-living increase, which protects benefits from inflation. Virtually no private investment scheme or annuity offers such protection. "Because women live much longer than men, Social Security's inflation-indexed annuities are particularly valuable for women," Munnell says. "Again, to the extent that you move away from that, women will be hurt."

[1] See Alicia H. Munnell, "Why Are So Many Older Women Poor? Just the Facts on Retirement Issues," Center for Retirement Research at Boston College, April 2004.

Paine's idea never made its way into public policy. Before the Industrial Revolution drew workers off the farms and into urban factories, in fact, people who could no longer work as a result of injury or old age relied on family for support and care. But the move to cities eroded that safety net, as extended families broke up into smaller, "nuclear" households composed of only parents and their children. Charities and a patchwork of state welfare programs were a poor substitute for family-based support.[13]

Only one segment of American society — war veterans — enjoyed government-provided income protection. The first solders' pension program started in 1776, before the signing of the Declaration of Independence.

The Civil War Pension program, created in 1862, initially provided benefits to combat-disabled Union veterans and to widows and orphans of Union soldiers killed in action. Confederate veterans and their dependents received no benefits. The program was expanded in 1906 to include all surviving Union veterans and their widows. The last Civil War Pension recipient, a woman who married an elderly veteran while in her teens, died earlier this year.[14]

Working Americans became eligible for old-age benefits with the advent of company pensions, first introduced in 1882 by the Alfred Dolge Co., a piano and organ manufacturer. But private pensions were slow to gain

Average Low-Wage Worker Receives $701 Monthly

A typical low-wage worker who retired at age 65 in 2003 received $701 a month from Social Security, compared to $1,721 received by the average high-wage earner. Workers can maximize their monthly income by working until age 70 before claiming benefits.

Typical Social Security Benefits, 2003

Earnings	Age 62	Age 65	Age 70
Low	$572	$701	$833
Average	943	1,158	1,387
High	1,236	1,513	1,786
Maximum	1,404	1,721	2,045

Source: "Fast Facts & Figures About Social Security, 2003," Social Security Administration

acceptance. In 1900, only five companies in the United States offered pensions to workers.

Meanwhile, the steady move to cities, the breakdown of the extended family, increasing reliance on wage income for survival, together with an increase in life expectancy, were undermining the living standards of older Americans. By 1920, more people were living in cities than on farms. The vast majority of aging workers were simply fired when they were no longer able to perform up to standard. With no one to care for them and no income, millions of former workers faced the prospect of dying in poverty. Because of improvements in sanitation and health care, life expectancy increased by 10 years between 1900 and 1930, the fastest increase in recorded history. By 1935, the number of elderly Americans had reached nearly 8 million at a time when the traditional sources of care for this population were fast disappearing.

The plight of America's growing elderly population deteriorated even more rapidly after Oct. 24, 1929, when the stock market crashed, setting off the Great Depression. More than a quarter of working Americans lost their jobs, about 10,000 banks failed, and the gross national product — the value of economic output — plummeted from $150 billion before the crash to just $55 billion in 1932.

With few federal resources available to fight poverty, President Herbert Hoover (1929-33) called on Americans to volunteer their services and charitable contributions to

alleviate the plight of the unemployed and the elderly. But with so much of the population facing financial hardship, Hoover's call went largely unanswered, leaving it up to the states to support the poor and elderly. By the 1930s, most states had established limited workers' compensation programs and state old-age "pensions" for older Americans who met financial-need standards. But these programs were of little value; none offered more than $1 a day to qualified beneficiaries.

As Congress began considering proposals for a new nationwide old-age safety net, conservative lawmakers favored adopting the state model, arguing that its need-based structure would limit the scope of the program and make it easy to end it once the economy recovered. But as the Depression persisted, calls for a different approach to social welfare — one that would reflect the permanent societal changes wrought by industrialization — began to take hold.

Social Security Act

President Franklin D. Roosevelt (1933-45) took office promising to shift the model for federal economic security policy from the state-based welfare assistance programs to new federal programs similar to "social insurance" plans then prevalent in Europe. First adopted in 1889 in Chancellor Otto von Bismarck's Germany, social insurance plans worked like commercial insurance plans, collecting premiums, or taxes, from a large pool of individuals (in this case working-age citizens) to pay benefits to those who meet eligibility conditions, such as disability and old age.

On June 8, 1934, Roosevelt announced his support for a similar approach in the United States. "Security was attained in the earlier days through the interdependence of members of families upon each other and of the families within a small community upon each other," he said in an address to Congress. "The complexities of great communities and of organized industry make less real these simple means of security. Therefore, we are compelled to employ the active interest of the nation as a whole through government in order to encourage a greater security for each individual who composes it."

Roosevelt sought to placate critics of such an expanded role for the federal government by adding: "This seeking for a greater measure of welfare and happiness does not indicate a change in values. It is rather a return to values lost in the course of our economic development and expansion."

On Aug. 14, 1935, Roosevelt signed into law the Social Security Act, which codified various recommendations of the presidential Committee on Economic Security. The new law created a social insurance program to pay retired workers age 65 or older a steady income for the rest of their lives.

"We can never insure 100 percent of the population against 100 percent of the hazards and vicissitudes of life," Roosevelt said. "But we have tried to frame a law which will give some measure of protection to the average citizen and to his family against the loss of a job and against poverty-ridden old age."

Though the law fell short of some supporters' goals, it provided the basic structure for today's Social Security program. Initially it paid benefits only to covered workers when they retired at 65. And, unlike the state old-age pension plans, it was funded through a contributory system, in which future beneficiaries contribute to their own retirement through payroll deductions made during their working lives. The law established a Social Security Board, made up of three presidential appointees, to administer the new program, but the Social Security Administration (SSA) replaced it in 1946, later incorporated into the Department of Health and Human Services.

America's Changing Population

Most Americans were under age 50 at the end of the 19th century. But by 2080, because of the coming retirement of the baby boomers, longer life expectancies and the popularity of smaller families, there will be relatively fewer young people and more Americans over 50 — creating a demographic bulge resembling a "python swallowing a telephone pole," according to some demographers.

Makeup of U.S. Population, by Age and Gender

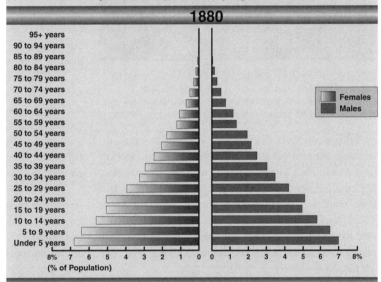

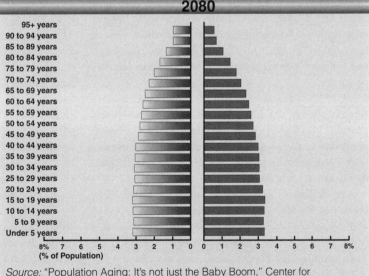

Source: "Population Aging: It's not just the Baby Boom," Center for Retirement Research

President Franklin D. Roosevelt signs the Social Security Act on Aug. 14, 1935. "We have tried to . . . give some measure of protection to the average citizen and to his family against the loss of a job and against poverty-ridden old age," he said.

Within two years all employers were registered, workers were assigned Social Security numbers and field offices were built. On Jan. 1, 1937, workers began acquiring credits toward their old-age benefits, and they and their employers began paying payroll taxes, known as FICA taxes (after the Federal Insurance Contributions Act, which authorized their collection). FICA taxes were placed in dedicated Social Security trust funds, to be used for paying benefits.

For the first three years Social Security paid each beneficiary a small, single, lump-sum payment because early recipients had not paid enough into the system to be vested for monthly benefits. By 1940, the trust funds had collected enough revenues to begin paying monthly payments.

In 1939 Congress expanded Social Security to cover workers' spouses, children under 18 and aged parents and provided survivors' benefits in the event of a worker's premature death. Lawmakers thus transformed the program from a retirement system for workers into a broader family income-security system.

The first retiree to receive a monthly Social Security check was Ida May Fuller of Ludlow, Vt., who retired in 1939 at age 65. Because of Social Security's pay-as-you-go financing arrangement, the retired legal secretary got a great return on her contribution. After contributing just $24.75 into the system over three years, she collected $22,888.92 in Social Security benefits before she died in 1975 at 100.

Later Amendments

By 1950, inflation had eaten away at the value of Social Security benefits, so Congress incorporated cost-of-living allowances (COLAs) that provided retroactive adjustments for beneficiaries in 1950 and 1952. A 1972 amendment made the COLA provision permanent.

Then, in 1954 Congress expanded the program to include disability insurance, initially limited to disabled older workers and disabled adult dependents. In September 1960, President Dwight D. Eisenhower (1953-61) signed into law an amendment extending coverage to all disabled workers and their dependents.

In 1956, Congress reduced from 65 to 62 the age at which women could choose to begin receiving their old-age benefits. Women who took the earlier benefits would receive smaller monthly checks, based on the actuarial notion that they would receive benefits for a longer period of time than if they waited until age 65. The same early-retirement option was extended to men in 1961.

In the 1960s, building on Roosevelt's vision of a strong governmental role in protecting Americans from poverty, President Lyndon B. Johnson launched a series of federal programs — known as the Great Society — including measures that strengthened the safety net provided by Social Security.

Johnson's primary proposal was Medicare — the federal program that provides health insurance to nearly all Americans age 65 and older. Signed into law on July 30, 1965, Medicare would become the most far-reaching change to the Social Security system. Within the next three years, nearly 20 million Americans enrolled in Medicare.

By the end of the 1960s there were calls to bring the old state and local welfare programs into the federal Social Security system to reduce waste and redundancy. In 1969, President Richard M. Nixon (1969-74) called on Congress to "bring reason, order and purpose into a tangle of overlapping programs."

The 1972 Social Security Amendments brought three "adult categories" — needy aged, blind and disabled — previously served by the states and localities with partial federal funding — under a single new Social Security program called Supplemental Security Income (SSI). More than 3 million people were shifted from the state welfare rolls to SSI.

The 1972 amendments also increased Social Security benefits for elderly widows and widowers, extended Medicare to individuals receiving disability benefits and those with chronic renal disease and increased Social Security benefits for workers who delay retirement past age 65.

Concerns about Social Security's soundness began to surface in the late 1970s. An economy beset by "stagflation" — inflation and minimal economic growth — and the demographic time bomb posed by the baby boom fueled predictions that the trust funds would soon be exhausted. To address the coming shortfall, Congress passed the 1977 Social Security Amendments, which increased the payroll tax, increased the maximum earnings subject to Social Security taxes and adjusted the way COLAs and the wage base are calculated. These changes restored the trust funds' long-term financial soundness for the next 50 years.

But within only a few years Social Security faced a serious short-term funding crisis due to the rapid growth in benefit expenditures. The crisis prompted President Ronald Reagan (1981-89) to appoint a panel headed by Greenspan (who began his tenure as Federal Reserve chairman in 1987) to recommend changes to the system. The 1983 amendments, based on those recommendations, authorized taxation of Social Security benefits, brought federal employees into the system and called for the gradual increase in the normal retirement age from 65 to 66 in 2009 and 67 in 2027.

Reagan oversaw the beginnings of a shift in philosophy toward the social safety net that had protected Americans from poverty since the Great Depression. He repeatedly called for tightening eligibility standards for welfare programs, decrying "welfare queens" he said were working the system to gain a free ride at the expense of honest, hardworking Americans. In 1995 Republicans took control of Congress, and began passing laws reflecting this philosophical shift.

The 1996 Contract with America Advancement Act, signed by Democratic President Bill Clinton on March 29, for the first time disqualified applicants for disability benefits under Social Security or SSI if drug or alcohol addiction contributed to their disabilities. The Personal Responsibility and Work Opportunity Act, signed five months later, ended the unlimited welfare entitlements provided under the Aid to Families with Dependent

Privatization supporters say stocks typically return higher dividends than the government's conservative bond investments. But critics say the stock market's recent plunge and numerous corporate and stock market scandals make personal investment accounts too risky for average workers.

Children program that had been established by the 1935 Social Security Act.

The 1996 law limited the amount of time beneficiaries could receive welfare benefits and required recipients to work; it also ended SSI eligibility for most legal non-citizen aliens and tightened up eligibility standards for disabled children. After public outcry, Congress later relaxed some of the new restrictions on non-citizens and children.

Clinton signed two other bills aimed at encouraging Social Security beneficiaries to work. The 1999 Ticket to Work and Work Incentives Improvement Act established a new program providing vocational rehabilitation and employment services to help disability beneficiaries find productive work. The 2000 Senior Citizens' Freedom to Work Act allowed workers to receive benefits even if they continued to work past the normal retirement age.

CURRENT SITUATION

Privatization

When he made his acceptance speech at the Republican National Convention on Sept. 2, President Bush said, "We'll always keep the promise of Social Security for our older workers. With the huge baby-boom generation approaching retirement, many of our children and grandchildren understandably worry whether Social Security will be there when they need it. We must strengthen Social Security by allowing younger workers to save some

AT ISSUE

Is privatization the best way to save Social Security?

YES
Peter J. Ferrara
*Senior fellow, Institute
for Policy Innovation*

From testimony before the Senate Special
Committee on Aging, June 15, 2004.

I'm here to discuss . . . providing a progressive option for
personal retirement accounts as a choice as compared to
Social Security. The option . . . is designed to be progressive,
which means lower-income workers can contribute a higher
percentage of their taxes to the account than higher-income
workers.

The option provides [for] . . . an average of 6.4 percent of
the 12.4 percent [payroll-tax contribution] to go into personal
accounts, a much larger account than has been proposed
before. . . . The proposal makes no change in disability and
survivors' benefits, and there is no change in Social Security
benefits otherwise for anybody at any point — now or in the
future. Because the advantages of a large personal account are
so great, no other changes are necessary. . . . It preserves
within the personal account the progressivity of Social Security
so workers across the board would gain roughly the same
percentage. . . .

There are five ways this proposal enhances progressivity for
low- and moderate-income workers. First of all, it sharply
increases future retirement benefits. . . . Large accounts do that
much more than any other alternative because they're able to
take more advantage of the better return in the private sector, so
they provide very sharp increases. . . . [Workers who] invest over
a lifetime, half-and-half in stocks and bonds at standard, market-
investment returns, I calculate would gain a benefit increase of
two-thirds compared to currently promised Social Security
benefits. . . .

For most workers today, the real rate of return promised by
Social Security — let alone what it could pay — is 1 to 1.5 percent. The long-term, real rate of return on corporate bonds is 3 to
3.5 percent. On stocks, I think the record will bear out 7 to 7.5
percent, so [there will be] much higher returns. And you see
what we've done here is a vast improvement both on the basis of
adequacy and of equity, because the returns are much higher, the
future benefits are higher.

Also, under the reform plan low- and moderate-income
workers would gain much greater accumulations of personal
wealth than under Social Security. The chief actuary of Social
Security has already officially scored this plan. He estimates
that by 15 years after the reform plan is adopted working
people would have gained $7 trillion in today's dollars in their
own personal accounts. [T]his is the greatest advantage and
breakthrough for working people that we could possibly adopt
today.

NO
Christian Weller
*Senior economist, Center
for American Progress*

From testimony before the Senate
Special Committee on Aging, June 15, 2004

Privatization as an alternative to fixing Social Security within the
parameters of the system is too risky and too costly, especially
for low-income families.

Usually 80 percent of pre-retirement income is considered
adequate for a decent standard of living. A substantial minority of
households, typically one-third, falls short of this standard. The
shortfalls are especially large for minorities, single women, workers with less education and low-wage workers. To make ends meet
in retirement, these households will have to curtail their consumption, often severely, and rely on public assistance in retirement.

Retirement income adequacy also has worsened for the typical household over the past few years. Underlying this trend are
three factors. First, pension coverage has remained low and
declined in recent years. Second, retirement wealth has become
increasingly unequally distributed. And, third, with the proliferation of defined-contribution plans, such as 401(k) plans, risks
have shifted onto workers.

Against this backdrop, Social Security gains in relative importance. Its coverage is almost universal, [and] its benefits favor
lifetime earners and [have] guaranteed, lifetime, inflation-
adjusted benefits. Part of Social Security's importance results . .
. from its other benefits, in particular disability and survivorship
benefits. These benefits are often also at stake when Social
Security benefits are reduced to pay for privatization. But we've
got to keep in mind that Social Security benefits are bare bones.
The average replacement ratio [the percentage of one's pre-
retirement earnings provided by Social Security] in the United
States is about half of that in Germany or Italy, and the average
monthly benefit [for Social Security] was about $850 in 2002.

Social Security benefits were 80 percent of retirement income
for households in the bottom 40 percent of the income distribution in 2000, meaning that the private sector is still not doing its
job to help low-income workers. Yet Social Security trustees predict a financial shortfall in the long run. It is anticipated that by
2042 Social Security will have exhausted its trust funds and that
tax revenue will cover only two-thirds of promised benefits. An
immediate and permanent increase of the payroll tax by 1.9 percent would allow Social Security to cover all of that shortfall. . . .

With privatization, insurance is replaced with savings
accounts. That is, the risks are privatized. These risks include the
risk of misjudging the market and investing in losing assets.
Another risk is the possibility of financial markets staying low for
long periods of time. Moreover, workers face the risk that they
will exhaust their savings during their retirement.

of their taxes in a personal account, a nest egg you can call your own and government can never take away."

President Bush's support for shifting part of the Social Security tax revenues into personal accounts marks another philosophical departure from the social-insurance concept championed by Roosevelt. Like many of his supporters, Bush has often called for reducing the size of the federal government. As the main entitlement programs in the federal budget, Social Security and Medicare are prime targets for this effort.

Bush announced during his January 2001 inaugural address that he intended to reform Social Security and Medicare. That May he appointed the President's Commission to Strengthen Social Security and directed it to recommend ways to reform the program that would ensure three major goals: preserve the benefits of current retirees and those nearing retirement; return Social Security to sound financial footing; and enable younger workers to invest part of their payroll taxes in individual savings accounts outside of the Social Security system.

Supporters of the current system immediately denounced the commission as a rubber stamp for privatization. "The president, his staff and his allies are already committed to privatization," declared the liberal Campaign for America's Future after the commission was created. "Calling their process of arranging the details a 'commission' is an attempt to mislead the public about its process and purpose. In reality, it will amount to no more than a collection of individuals who support privatization."[15]

Treasury Secretary Paul H. O'Neill responded by defining Social Security as "a revolutionary idea for its time" that was fast running out of money. "This is all about happy times and doing the right thing while our generation is able to act," he said.[16]

The commission's final report, issued in December 2001, recommended several measures to meet Bush's goals. It offered three different models to ensure that Social Security would remain afloat over the long term. Model 2 of the report, widely viewed as the likely basis for the Bush administration's reform proposal, if it wins a second term, would eliminate wage indexation and rely entirely on consumer prices to adjust future benefits. Apart from changing the benefits formula, Model 2 would retain the current system for all who prefer it while allowing workers who wish to set up a private investment account with part of their payroll-tax contribution to do so.

Several reform plans have been introduced in recent months — including the Kolbe-Stenholm bill and one authored by Sen. Lindsey Graham, R-S.C. — both of which would provide for moderately sized, progressive personal accounts. In July, Rep. Paul Ryan, R-Wis., introduced a bill that incorporates Ferrara's more-radical privatization plan. "We're going to try to translate that into a very broad co-sponsorship on the Hill," George Mason University's Ferrara says, "ultimately with the goal of presenting it to the administration and making the case to them that this is, in fact, what they should adopt."

But with much of Congress facing re-election and concerns about the wars against Iraq and terrorism, proposals to overhaul Social Security have yet to receive extensive congressional consideration. Other than being introduced, says Lemieux of the Centrist Policy Network, "there hasn't been a lot of legislative activity on Social Security."

Eroding Pensions

Recent trends in private pension coverage add additional uncertainties to the debate over Social Security reform. Many traditional pension funds have been failing, threatening a major source of retirement income for American workers. Most recently, in a move that may be emulated by other troubled companies, United Airlines is considering scrapping its defined-benefit pension plan, which covers 120,000 workers, as part of a bankruptcy proceeding. The federal Pension Benefit Guaranty Corp. (PBGC), which protects pension benefits from corporate bankruptcies, would assume the airline's $8.3 billion pension obligations, but the move likely would mean reduced benefits for United workers. If other companies follow United's lead, the PBGC could be unable to cover benefits, requiring a taxpayer bailout reminiscent of the savings and loan crisis of the 1980s.[17]

That prospect — or the possibility that many retirees may stop receiving their pension checks altogether — gained further credence with a new study that concludes the agency will go broke by 2023 if pension funds continue to fail at the pace of recent years.[18]

Meanwhile, a study by Munnell, of the Center for Retirement Research, documents the inability of 401(k)s and other defined-contribution plans to fill the gap created as private companies scale back or abandon their traditional pension programs. Despite the popularity of 401(k)s, she found that less than half of American workers are covered by an employer-provided pension plan, a figure that hasn't changed since 1979. And only one in four workers whose employers do offer 401(k)s chooses to participate in the plan, and fewer than one in 10 contribute the maximum allowable portion of their income. In addition, many employers offering 401(k)s have responded to hard economic times by cutting their matching contributions to the plans.[19]

These findings constitute a strong case against relying on private markets to solve Social Security's funding problems, Munnell says.

"We were stunned to find out what a poor mechanism 401(k) plans are, as currently structured, to provide retirement income," she says. Like 401(k)s, private investment accounts within Social Security require workers to be involved in the management of their retirement incomes, she notes. "These financial decisions are hard for people to make. They're not trained to do it, they don't have the time to do it, and to shift an even greater burden to the individual doesn't make any sense."

Ferrara says his plan addresses those concerns. "We designed the investment structure of the fund to make it easy for unsophisticated investors," he says. "There would be a list of private, managed investment funds approved and regulated by the government expressly for this purpose, and the investor only needs to pick one of those funds. Then the managers of those funds make all the sophisticated investment decisions for the investor."

Budget Concerns

When President Bush announced the formation of his Commission to Strengthen Social Security in May 2001, he said federal budget surpluses were enough to cover any costs incurred by the transition to a partially privatized system. "Our government will run large budget surpluses over the next 10 years," Bush said. "These surpluses provide an opportunity to move to a stronger Social Security system."[20]

That was before the terrorist attacks of Sept. 11, 2001. Since then, administration-supported tax cuts coupled with spending for counterterrorism initiatives and the war against Iraq have obliterated the budget surplus. This year, the deficit is expected to reach a record high of $445 billion, up from $375 billion in fiscal 2003.

Bush's initiative to add a drug benefit to Medicare, signed into law Dec. 8, 2003, will place an additional drain on the federal budget. The Medicare Prescription Drug, Improvement and Modernization Act, which would expand the federal health insurance program for some 41 million elderly and disabled Americans by offering partial coverage of prescription drug costs, is now expected to cost $534 billion over the next 10 years, $134 billion more than the administration had originally claimed.[21]

"Congress is still in shock and denial about the deteriorating budget," says Lemieux of the Centrist Policy Network. "They're still doing things the way they did a couple of years ago, when they thought they had a budget surplus and could pass tax cuts without paying for them and keep spending growing fast."

In light of the budget deficit, some analysts say moderate privatization plans offer a promising solution to Social Security's funding shortfall. "We have Medicare and Medicaid growing much faster than the gross domestic product, and we're looking at a very uncertain future in terms of how much money we're going to be spending on homeland security, defense and other programs," says University of Illinois Social Security expert Brown. He supports the commission's Model 2 plan for partial privatization of Social Security. "We have to put some serious constraints on how quickly Social Security can grow."

An essential and fair cost-saving element of the plan, Brown says, is its elimination of wage indexation in calculating initial benefits. "I don't see why the program has to grow faster than inflation," he says. "Why should my children get Social Security benefits that, after adjusting for inflation, are 30 percent higher than mine, even if we're [making the same amount of money today?]"

But other experts say the case for privatization evaporated with the federal budget surplus. "When some of the privatization proposals were developed we had a surplus, and they said we could take some of the surplus and use it to create private accounts," says Entmacher, of the National Women's Law Center. "Well, hello, not only is there no surplus anymore, but we're running gigantic deficits as far as the eye can see, and privatization actually makes it worse."

OUTLOOK
Campaign Debate

As the November presidential election nears, both major candidates are declaring their support for Social Security but skirting the details of plans to ensure the program survives the baby boomers' retirement.

Bush continues to push for partial privatization through private investment accounts, and he has not ruled out raising the retirement age. "It's very important in the Social Security system to say to boomers like me, nothing's going to change," Bush said at a campaign rally in Wheeling, W.Va. "We're in good shape. But if you're a younger worker, you better listen very carefully to the presidential debates on Social Security. The fiscal solvency of Social Security is in doubt for the young workers coming up. Therefore, I think young workers ought to be able to own a personal retirement account, a personal savings account, in order for Social Security to work."

Candidate Kerry opposes privatization, raising the retirement age or cutting payments. "As president, I will not privatize Social Security," Kerry said in accepting his party's nomination in July. "I will not cut benefits. And together, we will make sure that senior citizens never have to cut their pills in half because they can't afford lifesaving medicine."

The Democratic Party platform pledges to support "reform" but to fight privatization of either Social Security or Medicare. But it has provided no details about how to strengthen either program beyond fiscal discipline for Social Security and expanded prescription-drug coverage for Medicare.[22]

"I don't see anything that either the Republicans or the Democrats are advocating right now that would really responsibly deal with the long-term problems either with Social Security or Medicare," says Kotlikoff of Boston University. "The privatization proposal that the president is likely to propose if he's re-elected could well make things worse because it could cut taxes by more than it cuts benefits."

Meanwhile, Federal Reserve Chairman Greenspan is trying to heat up the debate by warning policymakers that reforms are urgently needed. "We owe it to our retirees to promise only the benefits that can be delivered," he said, suggesting that even the boomers — not just their children — may be in for an ugly surprise if changes are postponed much longer. "If we have promised more than our economy has the ability to deliver . . . as I fear we may have, we must recalibrate our public programs so that pending retirees have time to adjust through other channels. . . . If we delay, the adjustments could be abrupt and painful."[23]

Most analysts hope that the candidates will heed that warning and inform voters of their plans to resolve Social Security's fiscal problems as the campaign progresses. "Even if they don't provide highly detailed proposals, both candidates need to flesh out how they would reform the program," says MacGuineas of the Committee for a Responsible Budget. "If someone wants to lead this country, we need to know how they would fix the federal government's largest program. That's something the voters should have insight on."

NOTES

1. Congressional Budget Office, "The Outlook for Social Security," June 2004.

2. For background, see Adriel Bettelheim, "Saving Social Security," *The CQ Researcher*, Oct. 2, 1998, pp. 857-880.

3. See David Cay Johnston, "The Social Security Promise Not Yet Kept," *The New York Times*, Feb. 29, 2004.

4. From an interview with Mara Liasson, "Morning Edition," National Public Radio, May 25, 2001.

5. For background, see Kenneth Jost, "Corporate Crime," *The CQ Researcher*, Oct. 11, 2002, pp. 817-840, and David Masci, "Stock Market Troubles," *The CQ Researcher*, Jan. 16, 2004, pp. 25-48.

6. For background, see Mary H. Cooper, "Retirement Security," *The CQ Researcher*, May 31, 2002, pp. 481-504.

7. Laurence J. Kotlikoff and Scott Burns, *The Coming Generational Storm* (2004).

8. For background, see Adriel Bettelheim, "Medicare Reform," *The CQ Researcher*, Aug. 22, 2003, pp. 673-696; and Rebecca Adams, "Medicaid Reform," *The CQ Researcher*, July 16, 2004, pp. 589-612.

9. For more information on these estimates, see Thomas J. Healey, "Social Security's Surprising Turn," *The Washington Post*, June 25, 2004.

10. Congressional Budget Office, "Administrative Costs of Private Accounts in Social Security," March 2004.

11. See Cooper, *op. cit.*

12. See Alicia H. Munnell, "Just the Facts: The Declining Role of Social Security," Center for Retirement Research, February 2003.

13. Unless otherwise noted, information in this section is drawn from Social Security Online, "Brief History," March 2003.

14. Melissa Nelson, "Woman Recognized as Confederate Widow," The Associated Press, June 15, 2004.

15. Campaign for America's Future, press advisory, May 2, 2001.

16. Quoted in Glenn Kessler, "O'Neill Faults 'No Assets' Social Security," *The Washington Post*, June 19, 2001, p. E1.

17. See Mary Williams Walsh, "Bailout Feared if Airlines Shed Their Pensions," *The New York Times*, Aug. 1, 2004, p. A1.

18. Douglas J. Elliott, "PBGC: When Will the Cash Run Out?" Center on Federal Financial Institutions, Sept. 13, 2004.

19. Alicia H. Munnell and Anika Sundén, *Coming Up Short: The Challenge of 401(k) Plans* (2004).

20. From remarks in the Rose Garden, May 2, 2001.

21. See Walter Shapiro, "Politicians Fool Only Themselves with Medicare Bribe," *USA Today*, Aug. 13, 2004. For background, see Bettelheim, "Medicare Reform," *op. cit.*

22. See Dan Balz, "Democratic Platform Assails Administration," *The Washington Post*, July 4, 2004, p. A4.

23. Quoted in Martin Crutsinger, "Social Security Crisis Warned," The Associated Press, Aug. 28, 2004.

BIBLIOGRAPHY

Books

Katz, Michael B., *In the Shadow of the Poorhouse: A Social History of Welfare in America, Basic Books,* **1996.**
A professor of history from the University of Pennsylvania traces the development of social policy in the United States, including Social Security.

Kotlikoff, Laurence J., and Scott Burns, *The Coming Generational Storm: What You Need to Know about America's Economic Future, MIT Press,* **2004.**

A Boston University economist (Kotlikoff) and a finance columnist (Burns) suggest how Social Security and Medicare can survive the onslaught of 77 million retiring baby boomers and how individuals can protect their private savings.

Articles

Kirchoff, Sue, "Greenspan Urges Cuts to Benefits for Retirees," *USA Today,* **Aug. 30, 2004.**
Federal Reserve Chairman Alan Greenspan renews his controversial call to reduce Social Security benefits, even for baby boomers nearing retirement, to save the system from collapse.

Krugman, Paul, "Maestro of Chutzpah," *The New York Times,* **March 2, 2004.**
The liberal columnist argues that in the face of deepening federal budget deficits, Federal Reserve Chairman Greenspan should drop his call to cut Social Security benefits and instead push for a repeal or roll-back of the Bush-supported tax cuts that he says primarily benefit wealthy Americans.

McNeil, Donald G., Jr., "Demographic 'Bomb' May Only Go 'Pop!'" *The New York Times,* **Aug. 29, 2004, "Week in Review," p. 1.**
Falling birth rates are lessening the threat of global overpopulation and fueling concern over the negative impact of aging populations, especially in industrialized countries.

Porter, Eduardo, "Coming Soon: The Vanishing Work Force," *The New York Times,* **Aug. 29, 2004, Section 3, p. 1.**
The coming retirement of millions of baby boomers will create shortages of skilled workers in many fields and may force many boomers to postpone retirement.

Tanner, Michael, "Cato's Plan for Reforming Social Security," *Cato Policy Report,* **May/June 2004, p. 3.**
The libertarian think tank's solution for Social Security's shortfall is a combination of personal investment accounts and reduced benefits.

Reports and Studies

Congressional Budget Office, **"The Outlook for Social Security,"** **June 2004.**
The CBO predicts Social Security's financial shortfall is not as imminent as earlier estimates indicated: Payments will start exceeding revenues in 2019, but the trust funds will not run out of money to pay benefits until 2052.

—, "Social Security: A Primer," September 2001.
This exhaustive analysis provides historical background, a description of Social Security's organization and programs and options for its future.

Favreault, Melissa M., and Frank J. Sammartino, "The Impact of Social Security Reform on Low-Income and Older Women," *Urban Institute,* **July 2002.**
Social Security benefits affect women of different ages, marital status and income levels in different ways. The authors point out the impact of several reform options on older women.

Ferrara, Peter, "A Progressive Proposal for Social Security Private Accounts," *IPI Reports, Institute for Policy Innovation,* **June 13, 2003.**
The most far-reaching and controversial of the major privatization plans would allow workers to divert a large portion of their payroll-tax contributions to private accounts.

Munnell, Alicia H., "Population and Aging: It's Not Just the Baby Boom," *Issue Brief, Center for Retirement Research,* **April 2004.**

The director of the Boston College-based center warns that the baby boomers' retirements will radically change U.S. society. Low birth rates since the mid-1960s and steady increases in longevity ensure that the United States will remain an aging society for the foreseeable future.

President's Commission to Strengthen Social Security, **"Strengthening Social Security and Creating Personal Wealth for All Americans," December 2001.**
The panel appointed by President Bush to devise ways to incorporate personal investment accounts into Social Security offers three main alternatives, one of which is expected to provide the model for a legislative proposal in 2005 if Bush wins re-election.

Social Security Administration, **"The Future of Social Security," January 2004.**
The report outlines current funding problems facing the program and proposals to allow workers to use part of their payroll-tax contributions to fund personal investment accounts.

For More Information

Cato Institute, 1000 Massachusetts Ave., N.W., Washington, DC 20001; (202) 842-0200; www.cato.org. This libertarian think tank supports the introduction of private investment accounts to Social Security.

Center for American Progress, 805 15th St., N.W., Washington, DC 20005; (202) 682-1611; www.americanprogress.org. A liberal think tank that supports the current structure of Social Security and opposes efforts to privatize them.

Center for Retirement Research, Boston College, Fulton Hall 550, 140 Commonwealth Ave., Chestnut Hill, MA 02467; (617) 552-1762; www.bc.edu/centers.crr. Directed by Alicia Munnell, a former research director at the Federal Reserve Bank of Boston, the center studies issues related to Social Security and other sources of retirement income.

Centrist Policy Network Inc., 236 Massachusetts Ave., N.E., Suite 205, Washington, DC 20002; (202) 546-4090; www.centrists.org. A nonpartisan group that analyzes most of the major proposals to reform Social Security.

Committee for a Responsible Federal Budget, 163 Connecticut Ave., N.W., 7th floor, Washington, DC 20009; (202) 986-6599; www.crfb.org. This nonprofit group analyzes all aspects of the federal budget and supports policies, including Social Security reform proposals, that strive to avoid deficit spending.

Institute for Policy Innovation, 1660 S. Stemmons Freeway, Suite 475, Lewisville, TX 75067; (972) 874-5139; www.ipi.org. A conservative group that supports Social Security privatization and other initiatives to reduce the size of the federal government.

National Women's Law Center, 11 Dupont Circle, N.W., Suite 80, Washington, DC 20036; (202) 588-5180; www.nwlc.org. A nonprofit group that analyzes the impact of public policy, including Social Security, on women and criticizes privatization efforts that would erode benefits to elderly women.

Social Security Administration, 6401 Security Blvd., Baltimore, MD 21235; (410) 965-3120; www.ssa.gov. The federal agency that administers Social Security and Medicare.

Child Welfare Reform

Will Recent Changes Make At-Risk Children Safer?

Tom Price

Sally Ann Schofield was sentenced in Augusta, Maine, to 20 years in prison for killing her 5-year-old foster child in 2002. Logan Marr suffocated after being bound to a highchair with 42 feet of duct tape. More than 900,000 children were abused or neglected in the United States in 2003 and 1,390 died. Today about a half-million children live in foster homes under the jurisdiction of state child welfare agencies.

From *CQ Researcher*, April 22, 2005.

D aisy Perales, a 5-year-old San Antonio girl, died on Dec. 1, 2004, a week after she was found unconscious and bleeding, with head trauma, bruises, a fractured rib and a lacerated spleen. She weighed just 20 pounds.

Texas Child Protective Services had investigated her family seven times. Daisy was one of more than 500 Texas children to die of abuse or neglect from 2002 to mid-2004. The agency had looked into at least 137 of the cases.[1]

At the beginning of 2003, in Newark, N.J., police entered a locked basement to find Raheem Williams, 7, and Tyrone Hill, 4. Both were starving and covered with burns and excrement. The next day, police found the body of Raheem's twin, who had been dead for more than 30 days. The state Department of Youth and Family Services had received repeated warnings that the children were being abused.[2]

"Our system is broken, and we need to make monumental changes," New Jersey Human Services Commissioner James Davy declared a year later, after more scandals surfaced.[3]

A decade earlier, police in Chicago had discovered 19 children, ages 1 to 14, living in a filthy two-bedroom apartment with a half-dozen adults. Police described a horrific scene of dirty diapers, spoiled food, roaches and dog and rat droppings. One child had cigarette burns, cuts and bruises. The Illinois Department of Children and Family Services had been in contact with six of the children.[4] Following the discovery, the department placed the children with various caregivers, later admitting it had lost track of them. The department eventually confessed it had a backlog of

U.S. Probe Faults State Programs

No state child welfare programs fully comply with federal child safety standards, according to a three-year investigation by the Bush administration. Sixteen states did not meet any of the seven federal standards (below) used to assess children's programs, and no state met more than two of the standards.

States That Did Not Meet Any Federal Standards
(dark gray)

Federal Child Safety Standards for State Agencies

1) Children are first and foremost protected from abuse and neglect.

2) Children are safely maintained in their homes whenever possible and appropriate.

3) Children have permanency and stability in their living situations.

4) The continuity of family relationships and connections is preserved for children.

5) Families have enhanced capacity to provide for their children's needs.

6) Children receive appropriate services to meet their educational needs.

7) Children receive adequate services to meet their physical and mental health needs.

Source: U.S. Department of Health and Human Services

4,320 uninvestigated complaints of abused or neglected children.

But then consider these hopeful signs of reform:

- Legislation being considered in Texas this year would increase spending on child welfare programs, improve training for caseworkers and encourage the administration to reduce caseloads. Republican Gov. Rick Perry calls reform an "emergency issue."[5]
- New Jersey is planning to hire hundreds of new child welfare workers, speed investigations and reduce

caseloads to no more than 25 children or 15 families per worker — down from the current maximum of more than 40 children and 20 families. Children who have lived in institutions for 18 months or more will be moved into "familylike" settings. An independent committee of child welfare experts, appointed in a lawsuit settlement, has approved the plan.[6]

- And Illinois has been transformed into "sort of the gold standard" for child welfare, in the words of Sue Badeau, deputy director of the Pew Commission on Children in Foster Care, a bipartisan group of political leaders and child welfare experts that promotes child welfare reform. After the state's child welfare scandal in the mid-1990s, new leadership and a new philosophy have turned the Illinois system around, says Mark Testa, co-director of the University of Illinois' Children and Family Research Center and former research director of the state children's services department.

The department reduced caseloads and focused on keeping families together or quickly placing children in alternative permanent-living situations. It obtained federal waivers from regulations preventing subsidies for placements with relatives, such as grandparents or aunts and uncles. As a result, Illinois has reduced the number of children in foster care from 52,000 in 1997 to fewer than 17,000 today, according to Testa.

So it goes in the American child welfare system: Scandal triggers public outrage which spurs reform, leaving children's advocates and child welfare workers constantly ricocheting between hope and despair. Meanwhile, more than 900,000 American children age 17 and younger were abused or neglected in 2003.[7]

"Reading the newspapers of late has been more like reading a horror novel, with case after case of abuse and neglect," said Texas state Sen. Jane Nelson, reflecting the nationwide despair generated by the unending reports of children who were mistreated while supposedly being protected by state agencies charged with doing so.[8] But, as the Republican author of reform legislation, Nelson also represents the potential for improvement that gives advocates hope.

Not a single state received a passing grade last year when the U.S. Health and Human Services Department (HHS) completed its review of state and local child welfare systems, and 16 states did not meet *any* of the seven federal child-care standards used to evaluate the programs. But the first eight states given follow-up reviews met all their initial targets for improvement,

Nearly 1 Million Children Are Maltreated

More than 900,000 children in the United States were victims of abuse or neglect in 2003, about a 5 percent increase over the 1990 total. Most of the cases involved neglect, but 19 percent involved physical abuse and 10 percent sexual abuse.

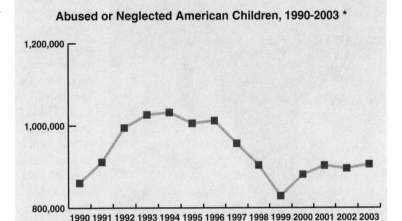

Abused or Neglected American Children, 1990-2003 *

*2003 is the most recent year for which data are available

Source: Child Trends Data Bank, based on Department of Health and Human Services Reports, 1990-2003

says Wade F. Horn, the department's assistant secretary for children and families.*[9]

State and local officials throughout the country agree on the need for substantial improvements in their child welfare systems, and even critics acknowledge that significant improvements are under way. Private organizations are adding to the ferment, from public-interest law firms demanding reforms in court to foundations that are supporting innovation. The Bush administration has offered up its plan for restructuring federal funding of child welfare, and both Republicans and Democrats in Congress agree not only on the need for reform but also on how that reform should be carried out.

"The consensus is: Where we can, we should protect the family," says Fred H. Wulczyn, an assistant professor at the Columbia University School of Social Work and a research fellow at the University of Chicago's Chapin Hall Center for Children. "Where we need to place kids in

---

* The states are: Arizona, Delaware, Indiana, Kansas, Massachusetts, Minnesota, Oregon and Vermont.

Foster child Daphane Irvin, a senior at Chicago's South Shore High School, hopes to become an actress. Only 2 percent (1,900) of all foster care adoptions in 2002 were older teens, ages 16 to 18. Another 19,500 teens "aged out" of foster care without being adopted and must face the transition to adulthood alone.

Getty Images/Melanie Stetson Freeman

foster care, we should proceed to permanent placement — such as with adoptive parents — as soon as possible."

Child welfare workers, government officials and children's advocates agree that it's best for children to live with their parents in healthy families, and that agencies should help families stay together. When children must be removed from their parents because of abuse or neglect, it's best to quickly return the children home safely or to place them permanently with adoptive parents or relatives.

Failure to do so can have disastrous consequences, as Maryland residents learned in early April.

Maryland houses 2,700 children in 330 privately operated group homes that are not adequately supervised by state agencies, according to an investigation by *The Baltimore Sun*.[10] In some of those homes, children have been denied needed medical treatment, served inadequate food, assaulted by employees and even supplied by employees with illegal drugs. At least 15 group home residents have died since 1998.

Children often are placed in group homes — which cost the state far more than foster family homes — when there is no other place for them. "There were some providers who were good, but there were others who we would have chosen not to be bothered with, but we had no choice," said Gloria Slade, former child placement supervisor for the Baltimore Social Services Department.

Maryland Human Resources Secretary Christopher J. McCabe said the state will recruit more foster parents to reduce the need for group homes. But Charlie Cooper, who manages the Maryland Citizens' Review Board for Children, said the state must offer a wider range of children's services.[11]

"You have a lot of things going on at the same time" to improve services to children, says Susan Notkin, director of the Center for Community Partnerships in Child Welfare, a nonprofit organization that funds and consults with agencies implementing innovative programs. "A lot of innovation is being tested. There's a lot of interest in looking at the financing."

Madelyn Freundlich, policy director for Children's Rights, a New York-based advocacy organization, agrees. "There is a lot of energy in the field right now," she says. "There has been a joining together of public agencies and the private sector to really look at foster care, and there is a growing awareness among the general public about foster care and the support needed to provide the right services for kids and families."

But the challenge is complex. And the road from good intentions to effective accomplishments is neither short nor straight. There are stark disagreements about how much spending should be increased (or whether it should be increased at all), how much federal control should be exercised over federally funded state and local programs, and which reform proposals are most likely to be effective.

Widespread agreement on the need for reform represents just "superficial consensus," says Douglas J.

Besharov, director of the American Enterprise Institute's (AEI) Social and Individual Responsibility Project and a former director of the U.S. Center on Child Abuse and Neglect.

"The Democrats who say they want to give states more flexibility want to make it open-ended [entitlement] spending," Besharov, a University of Maryland public affairs professor, says. "This is just an excuse to put in more money, while Republicans say they're looking for ways to cap expenditures. It's just like we're all in favor of long life and fighting cancer, but getting from here to there requires a lot more agreement than what I see."

As the nation struggles to help children from troubled families, here are some of the questions child welfare experts are trying to answer:

Do state and local governments do enough to keep families together?

Most headline-grabbing child welfare horror stories spring from parents mistreating children whom the system has failed to protect. But many child welfare experts believe the more common problem stems from agencies removing children from parents too frequently. It's not that the children didn't need protection but that agencies failed to provide early services that could have kept the kids safe and at home.

In fact, concern about taking children from their parents is so prevalent that a common measure of agency success is reducing the number of youngsters removed from their homes. Several private organizations are promoting reforms designed to improve services to troubled families before the children have to be removed. But there's still a long way to go.

Illinois' newfound reputation for quality stems in part from cutting its foster care population by two-thirds since the mid-1990s and removing fewer than half as many children from their parents each year, Testa says. Improvement in New York City's system is marked by a foster care caseload that dropped from just under 50,000 in the mid-1990s to just below 20,000 today, according to Columbia University's Wulczyn.

Nationwide, the foster care caseload also is declining, but it did not peak as early and is not falling as rapidly as in Illinois and New York. In 1999, nearly 570,000 American children lived in foster homes — an historic high. That number dropped to just above 520,000 in

2003, the most recent figure available. But the dip wasn't because fewer children were removed from their homes; it was because states did a better job of returning foster children to their parents or placing them in other permanent homes.[12]

Because child welfare systems differ from state to state, Wulczyn says, "it's hard to come up with one overarching statement about where the system is, except to say that it's not as good as it should be, but it's better than it was."

Illinois succeeds, Testa says, because it is "doing a better job making family assessments, working with families who can take care of their kids in the home and not putting those children unnecessarily into foster care." Child welfare experts would like to see that approach expanded throughout the country.

"Most places do not have the services and support that families need, so they would never get put into the child welfare system in the first place," says Judy Meltzer, deputy director of the Center for the Study of Social Policy, who serves on panels monitoring court-ordered reforms in New Jersey and Washington, D.C. "The infrastructure does a really bad job of being able to reach out and work with families before they get to the point where crises occur and kids have to be removed from their homes."

Meltzer and others say that even the best child welfare agencies can't provide those services by themselves. "If we think child welfare agencies alone will do it, we will always be stuck," says Wanda Mial, senior associate for child welfare at the Annie E. Casey Foundation, a leading operator and funder of programs for disadvantaged children.

"Government can't do it alone," either, says Notkin, whose Center for Community Partnerships promotes cooperation among many public and private organizations.

Parental substance abuse causes or exacerbates 70 percent of child neglect or abuse incidents, says Kathryn Brohl, author of the 2004 book *The New Miracle Workers: Overcoming Contemporary Challenges in Child Welfare Work*.[13] Abuse also stems from poverty, poor housing, ill health, lack of child care, parental incompetence, domestic violence, arrest and imprisonment, Brohl adds. Some children enter the child welfare system because they run afoul of authorities by committing a crime or frequently skipping school, says Mial, a former child welfare worker in Philadelphia.

Judges' Hearings Help Kids Feel Loved

"So, I [see] you want to be a cosmetologist," Judge Patricia Martin Bishop said to the teenager sitting before her. "What's that?" the girl asked.

"Someone who fixes your hair, does your nails — things like that," Bishop replied.

"I can't even do my own hair," the girl exclaimed. "I want to be a lawyer."

Bishop, the presiding judge in the Child Protection Division of Cook County Circuit Court in Chicago, looked at the girl's caseworker, who explained why she had changed the girl's answer on a questionnaire about her future. "I changed it to cosmetologist because she's reading at such a low level she'll never be a lawyer."

But Bishop quickly set the caseworker straight: "I'm not convinced she can't become a lawyer until we help her get through high school and give her the support she needs to get into college and get her through college and get her through law school. Until we've made some concerted effort to help her achieve her dreams, I'm not prepared to channel her to our dreams for her."

That moment, Bishop says, demonstrated exactly why she created "benchmark hearings" for teenagers.

Since 1997, Illinois has reduced its foster care rolls from 52,000 to fewer than 17,000, thus reducing demands on the court. Bishop was able to relieve Judge Patricia Brown Holmes of her regular caseload, and now they both conduct special hearings for unadopted teens about to leave foster care for independence.

The benchmark hearings are held when the child is 14, 16 and 17$\frac{1}{2}$. The children, as well as their caseworkers, teachers, doctors, coaches and other adults with whom they have important relationships, attend the meetings, which can last up to two hours. "I require the psychiatrist to face me and tell my why this kid's on meds," the judge explains. "I make the basketball coach come in and tell me how basketball helps or hurts this kid."

Every Illinois foster child attends a juvenile court hearing every six months, but they can be brief, Bishop says. The benchmark meetings tend to be longer because the judges want to get a clear picture of the child's capabilities and needs.

"The idea is to look at kids more holistically," Bishop explains, "to coordinate with the agencies, to help [the teens] for the present and for their dreams for the future. If there are unresolved issues after a benchmark hearing,

---

To avoid removing children from their parents in these circumstances, Brohl and other experts say, child welfare workers must be able to call on other agencies to address such problems as soon as they are discovered — or even before.

According to social psychologist Kristin Anderson Moore, who heads the Child Trends research organization, the most effective ways to deter child abuse and neglect include "helping people establish healthy marriages before they have children, helping teenagers delay child-bearing and helping parents delay having second births."

Some "very rigorous studies" have shown that starting home-visitation programs shortly after birth can reduce abuse and neglect by 50 percent, says Shay Bilchik, president of the Child Welfare League of America. A visiting nurse trains new parents, monitors the well being of the child and arranges for additional services needed by the family. "If you track those babies

15 years down the road," Bilchik says, "home visitation has been shown to reduce those babies' entering into the criminal world."

Rep. Wally Herger, R-Calif., chairman of the House Ways and Means subcommittee that oversees child welfare, noted that the federal government spends 10 times as much on state and local foster care and adoption services as it does on programs designed to hold families together.

"As a result," he said, "rather than focusing on the prevention of abuse and neglect, today's funding structure encourages the removal of children and breakup of families. That is unacceptable."[14]

There are deep disagreements about how that problem should be fixed, however.

"I don't have any doubt Wally cares about kids," says Rep. Jim McDermott of Washington, the ranking Democrat on Herger's subcommittee. "It's a question of how you do it."

I keep it on my benchmark calendar and have follow-up hearings."

The needs for follow-up can vary widely. "A girl came to one of my benchmarks wearing sandals and a short skirt in dead of winter," the judge says. "She had moved from one group home to another, and her allowance hadn't kept up with her so she couldn't buy the things she needed. I kept the case on my benchmark hearing calendar until we were able to resolve the allowance problem."

At another hearing, Bishop discovered that a boy had maintained a relationship with his mother, whose parental rights had been terminated years before — a not uncommon occurrence. "His mother had continued drugging," Bishop says. "My position was, if he's maintained this relationship it's incumbent upon us to make it work as best we can. We put the mother back into [drug-treatment] services. She got clean. We sent this kid back home before he turned 18."

Presiding Judge Patricia Martin Bishop of Chicago created "benchmark" hearings to protect teens' rights — and their dreams.

Cook County Courthouse

Adolescents need relationships that will help them make the transition to adulthood when they leave foster care, Bishop explains. Sometimes the relationship can be as unlikely as with a drug-addicted mother who had lost her parental rights. Sometimes it can continue to be the child welfare system.

Bishop is authorized to keep a foster child within the jurisdiction of the Department of Children and Family Services until age 21. And, using private donations, the department can even provide higher-education assistance until age 23.

Bishop doesn't have empirical data to establish the value of benchmark hearings, but she has heard encouraging anecdotes. "Lawyers who didn't want to do this now are requesting that I extend this down to age 12," she says. "Kids come and say, 'I want Judge Holmes to have my case, or Judge Bishop to have my case.'

"The state is such a poor parent. We [judges] can look a child in the eye and talk about what he or she hopes to do in the future. They feel as if they're heard. They feel as if they've gotten attention. They feel loved."

Does the federal government give state and local child welfare agencies enough financial support and flexibility?

As they lobbied on Capitol Hill last month, volunteers from the Child Welfare League of America boldly proclaimed their top legislative priority on oversized campaign buttons pinned to their lapels: "No caps on kids!"

The slogan is shorthand for their opposition to President Bush's proposal to convert the main source of federal child welfare funding — the foster care entitlement — into a flexible, capped block grant, or a single grant that the states can spend in various innovative ways with less federal control.

Under current law, states are entitled to federal reimbursement for every foster child whose parents would have qualified for welfare under the old Aid to Families with Dependent Children program in 1996. Overall, the federal government pays about half the nation's $22 billion child welfare bill, according to an Urban Institute study, while the rest comes from state and local governments.[15]

The welfare league argues that not only should the existing entitlement regime be preserved but also that the federal government should increase spending on various child welfare programs.

However, HHS Assistant Secretary Horn says groups like the Child Welfare League "live in a dream world where money grows on trees," adding that he himself prefers to live "in the world of the achievable."

Both sides agree that child welfare agencies should be able to spend more federal money on helping families stay together and on alternatives to traditional foster care, which receives the bulk of federal aid today. The administration contends this can be accomplished by letting states spend their existing federal foster care allotment for other activities, such as helping troubled families or supporting guardians. But many child welfare

Number of Foster Kids Has Declined

The number of foster children began declining after peaking in 1999, due largely to a rise in adoptions. Even so, more than a half-million American children were in foster care in 2003, a 31 percent increase over 1990.

Number of Foster Children Ages 17 and Under, 1990-2003*

Number of Foster Children

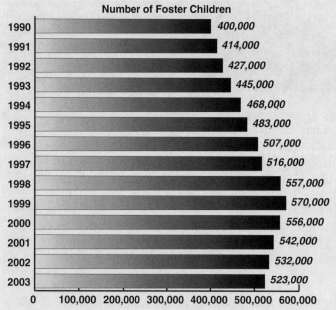

Year	Number
1990	400,000
1991	414,000
1992	427,000
1993	445,000
1994	468,000
1995	483,000
1996	507,000
1997	516,000
1998	557,000
1999	570,000
2000	556,000
2001	542,000
2002	532,000
2003	523,000

0   100,000   200,000   300,000   400,000   500,000   600,000

* 2003 is the most recent year for which data are available

Source: Child Trends Data Bank, based on Department of Health and Human Services Reports, 1990-2003

advocates argue that the agencies need more money and warn that eliminating the entitlement could leave them with less in the long run.

The administration proposes giving states the option of accepting a block grant that could be spent on foster care and other services. Unlike the entitlement, the grant would not rise and fall with changes in the foster care caseload. For the first five years, each state would receive the same amount it would have received under the entitlement program based on the caseload change during the previous five years. That means states that had declining caseloads would receive less federal money. After five years, Congress would decide how to continue to fund the program.

Some states have implemented well-regarded innovations by obtaining waivers from federal regulations, leading administration officials to contend that allowing flexibility works. Pointing to the drop in welfare rolls that followed similar welfare reforms in the mid-1990s, the administration also argues that flexibility allows the states to be more effective while cutting costs.[16]

"We think if states are better able to focus money on prevention — which is cheaper than intervention — there would be less need for expensive out-of-home-care, in the same way that when states focused on work instead of simply cash, welfare caseloads declined," Horn says.

States would be hard pressed to shift money from foster care to other services, however, because child welfare systems already are underfunded, contends Liz Meitner, vice president for government affairs at the Child Welfare League. "We think a better strategy is to increase investments for prevention that will ultimately reduce the number of kids in foster care," Meitner says.

The Pew Commission on Children in Foster Care proposed maintaining the entitlement and beefing up federal aid while increasing flexibility.[17]

The commission calculated it would cost $1.6 billion annually just to extend federal aid to all foster children. Acknowledging the pressure to contain federal spending, the commission proposed extending aid to all but cutting the amount given for each child, so total federal aid would not rise. The commission suggested hiking other, more flexible, federal grants by $200 million the first year and by 2 percent above inflation in later years.

"Every child who experiences abuse or neglect deserves the protection of both the federal and state governments," said commission Chairman Bill Frenzel, former Republican representative from Minnesota, making a key argument against ending the entitlement.[18]

"Child welfare has traditionally been the safety net for vulnerable children and families," Freundlich of Children's Rights says. "It does not have waiting lists. It's had to be there for the children."

Block grant opponents point to the crack cocaine epidemic that devastated many families and caused child welfare caseloads to soar in the 1980s and '90s. Without the entitlement, states would have had to spend much more of their own money or agencies could not have cared for all the children coming through their doors. Many warn methamphetamine abuse could become the next crack. They also note that, over time, block grant programs haven't kept pace with inflation, and funding for some has declined.

The Social Services Block Grant, for example, dropped from $3 billion in 1981 to $1.7 billion in 2003, according to the Child Welfare League. Had it tracked inflation, she says, it now would total more than $6 billion.

But Assistant HHS Secretary Horn replies that if states reduce foster rolls they would receive more money through a block grant program than through an entitlement program. That's because the entitlement, which is based on the number of children served, would drop if the rolls dropped, while the block grant would not. If caseloads rise significantly, he adds, the administration plan includes an emergency fund that states could tap.

The federal government can't afford to give states both flexibility and an entitlement, the American Enterprise Institute's Besharov argues. "The only way to give states flexibility in a federal grant program is to cap it. Otherwise, they will steal you blind."

Besharov suggests extending the waiver option, which gives the states supervised flexibility, and "tying it to rigorous evaluations" to document what works best.

Testa, of the Children and Family Research Center, also supports more waivers, although he doesn't share Besharov's fear of entitlements. "We have to invest a lot more in demonstrations that will prove what works," he says. "We should be giving states permission to innovate but requiring them to demonstrate that what they're doing is working."

Because states have to match the federal funds under current law, he adds, they will not be motivated to spend more than they need.

Does the child welfare system prepare foster adolescents for adulthood?

Mary Lee's foster care judicial reviews always seemed the same. She'd wait for hours in the courthouse, then have what felt like a one-minute session during which the judge would "pat me on the back and say everything's great."

Then, when she was 16, a judge actually asked: "Mary, what do you want for your life?" And she told him.

"I said I want a family," she recalls. "I want to be adopted. I want to know that when I go to college I'm going to have a family to come home to, that I'm going to have a dad to walk me down the aisle and grandparents for my children. And if I stay in foster care, when I leave I'm not going to have anything. I'm going to be totally on my own."

A week before her 18th birthday, after five years in foster care, Mary was adopted by Scott Lee, her caseworker, and his wife in Montgomery County, Tenn. Now 23, Mary has graduated from Vanderbilt University and plans to attend law school. She traces her good life and bright future to that moment the judge asked her about her dreams.

"Adoption is not about your childhood," she explains. "It's about the rest of your life. You always need a mom and a dad. You always need your grandparents. You always need the family support."

Mary's happy-ending story is, unfortunately, rare. According to the latest available statistics, 92,000 teens ages 16 to 18 lived in foster homes in 2002 — 17 percent of the total foster population. Just 1,300 of them were adopted that year — 2 percent of all foster care adoptions. That same year, 19,500 teens "aged out" of foster care, usually by turning 18, and many of them faced the transition to adulthood the way Mary Lee feared she would face it — alone.[19]

Four years after leaving foster care, nearly half of these older teens had not graduated from high school, a quarter had been homeless, 40 percent had become parents and fewer than a fifth were self-supporting, according to the Jim Casey Youth Opportunities Initiative, which works with those young people.[20]

"Effective middle-class families parent their kids into their 20s, and these kids are cut off at 18," Moore of Child Trends notes. "From age 18 to 24 is a time kids need contact and care and monitoring from adults."

CHRONOLOGY

1800-1900 *Charitable organizations open "orphan asylums." Courts allow child protection societies to remove children from homes. Later, child-protection organizations pay families to take in homeless children.*

1853 Children's Aid Society of New York is founded and begins sending homeless children to Western families on "orphan" or "baby" trains in 1854.

1872 New York Foundling Asylum begins putting unwanted infants and toddlers on westbound "baby trains."

1900-1930s *First juvenile courts created. Child welfare agencies increase supervision of foster homes.*

1912 U.S. Children's Bureau established.

1935 Social Security Act provides federal funds for rural children's services, social-worker training.

1960-1970s *Federal role expands, focus intensifies on preserving families and alternatives to adoption.*

1961 Federal aid extended to poor foster children; more children's services are offered in urban and rural areas.

1962-69 Child-care professionals are required to report suspected abuse.

1974 Child Abuse Prevention and Treatment Act provides federal funds for protecting endangered children.

1976-79 Child welfare agencies try to reduce need for foster care. California, New York and Illinois subsidize adoptions.

1977 Foster care caseloads total about 550,000.

1980s-2000 *Single-parent households, unmarried births, child abuse and neglect reports all soar. Demands for reform increase. Lawsuits force improvements in state and local child welfare systems.*

1980 Congress creates federal adoption-assistance program. Social Security Act becomes main source of federal child welfare support.

1986 Foster caseload drops below 300,000; crack cocaine epidemic soon causes foster care rolls to soar.

1993 Federal government grants waivers for states to test innovative child welfare services.

1993-94 Discovery of 19 children living in squalor, death of another, spur shakeup of Illinois child welfare system.

1995 Foster caseloads hit nearly 500,000.

1997 Adoption and Safe Families Act increases federal support for adoption, family preservation.

1999 Foster caseloads peak at 570,000. Federal government increases aid for youths aging out of foster care.

2000s *Courts get federal money to reduce abuse and neglect backlogs, improve information technology.*

2001 Federal government offers new education assistance for aging-out youths.

2002 Authorities report 900,000 confirmed cases of child abuse or neglect nationwide, including 1,390 deaths.

2003 Foster rolls decline to 525,000. General Accounting Office says high caseloads and low salaries inhibit recruitment and retention of effective child welfare workers.

2004 Concern arises that a methamphetamine epidemic could raise foster care rolls. Pew Commission on Children in Foster Care argues that states need more child welfare money and flexibility. About 20 states receive waivers to offer support services not normally funded by federal programs.

2005 President Bush asks that federal foster care funding be converted to block grants. Illinois, now representing child welfare's "gold standard," cuts foster care population by two-thirds since mid-1990s and reduces average caseload from more than 50 to fewer than 20.

After Chris Brooks left foster care in Nevada at age 19, he slept in a car and on friends' couches. At age 18, Terry Harrak figured out how to sleep and scrounge food amid the bustle of a busy hospital in Northern Virginia.

But both Chris' and Terry's stories have happy endings, thanks to serendipitous relationships with caring adults. A professor studying homeless youth "took me under his wing" and "became kind of like an uncle," Chris says. Now 23, he attends college in Las Vegas and mentors homeless youth. While living in a shelter, Terry met a Child Welfare League staff member who was looking for homeless young people to testify before Congress. Now 25, she attends college and works as the league's youth leadership coordinator, staffing an advisory council on which Chris and Mary serve.

Chris and Terry both say they were ill-prepared for independent living. And both cite the need for ongoing relationships and training in such basic skills as balancing a checkbook, filling out a tax form and applying for college aid.

"Historically, in child welfare we never thought about the permanent lifetime relationships that these kids need," says Gary Stangler, head of the Casey program for older teens and former director of the Missouri Social Services Department. "If we got them to age 18 alive, we did our job.

"Adoption, especially the older you get, is difficult and uncommon. So the solution was training for independent living, which is the opposite of permanent lifetime relationships."

Stangler has observed "an awakening to the fact that we were doing a very poor job for kids once they left the foster care system without the support we take for granted for our own kids." Slowly, he says, things are getting better.

Legislation passed in 1999 provides federal aid for housing and education for former foster youths, but many young people do not know how to apply for it. States are allowed to keep them on Medicaid beyond age 18, but most don't. Private organizations and some states are helping older teens build the adult relationships they need. And a few courts are institutionalizing the kind of court procedure that turned Mary Lee's life around.

In Chicago, the Cook County Circuit Court's Child Protection Division conducts "benchmark hearings" when foster children turn 14 and 16 and six months before they age out. (*See story, p. 256.*) The hearings can last up to two hours. Participants include the most important individuals in the children's lives, such as caseworkers, teachers, doctors and adults with whom the children have or might build long-lasting relationships.

"All of us were grappling with how could we, the court, get a handle on this road to being independent," says Patricia Martin Bishop, the division's presiding judge, who established the hearings. "The thought was, if we had more time to concentrate on each of these kids, we'd get a better handle on what needs they have that aren't met."

Among the questions Bishop requires the children to answer during the hearings: "What do you want to do when you get out of school? What do you intend to do with your life?"

BACKGROUND

Orphan Trains

In the beginning, America's child welfare system provided a kind of residential vocational education: Families took in needy children, then fed, clothed and trained them in a trade. Such apprenticeships were common, even for youngsters who were not parentless or poor. But it was considered an especially attractive way to place orphans and other children whose parents couldn't care for them. The child got a home and learned a trade; the host family benefited from the child's work.[21]

In the early 19th century, religious and charitable organizations began opening orphan asylums, which became the most common means of caring for children without parents between 1830 and 1860.

Also in mid-century, Charles Lorring Brace organized the Children's Aid Society of New York, which created the "orphan train" or "baby train" movement. Urban centers like New York attracted hordes of immigrants who took difficult, dangerous and sometimes deadly jobs. Diseases like typhoid, diphtheria and cholera also hit the poor especially hard. Deceased adults left orphans or

How Illinois Reformed a Broken System

Clearer information is needed

Three times, the Illinois Children and Family Services Department took Joseph Wallace away from his mentally ill mother, and three times the youngster was returned to her. There was no fourth time, because on April 19, 1993, she tied an extension cord around the 3-year-old's neck and hanged him from a transom in their Chicago apartment.[1]

Early the next year, Chicago police discovered 19 children living in a squalid, two-bedroom apartment with a half-dozen adults. Again, the department knew about six of the children but had left them with their mothers.[2]

Although the tragedies were only tiny tips of an enormous iceberg of bureaucratic failure, they shined a media spotlight on the Illinois child welfare system and outraged the public. In the end, they spurred dramatic reforms in the system, making it a font of successful innovation.

"They've addressed preventing kids from coming into foster care in the first place, as well as strengthening reunification for children who return home safely and strengthening alternative forms of permanency through subsidized guardianship and adoption," says Sue Badeau, deputy director of the Pew Commission on Foster Care, who says the system is now the "gold standard" of child care.

The Illinois system was "sort of average" in the 1980s, became "a mess" by the mid-'90s and now is one of the best, says Jill Duerr Berrick, associate dean of the School of Social Welfare at the University of California, Berkeley. "We've seen tremendous innovation coming out of Illinois."

Illinois probably ran America's worst child welfare system in the mid-1990s, says Mark Testa, co-director of the University of Illinois' Children and Family Research Center. It had the nation's highest prevalence of children in foster care — 17.1 per 1,000 — where they remained in care longer than children in other states. The total foster care rolls soared from 20,000 in the late-'80s to 52,000 in 1997. But when horror stories repeatedly hit the media, public outrage triggered changes.

Feeling intense pressure from the public, the state legislature and a lawsuit by the American Civil Liberties Union, Republican Gov. Jim Edgar appointed a new department director, Jess McDonald. He launched a comprehensive overhaul of the system and hired Testa as in-house research director.

"Lawsuits are critical to reform," says Marcia Robinson Lowry, executive director of Children's Rights, a New York organization that sues local and state governments to get them to improve child welfare systems. "There is sustained pressure for reform because of a court order."

McDonald and Testa discovered a system engaged in self-destruction. It was taking custody of thousands of children who didn't need to be removed from their homes, which limited caseworkers' ability to take care of children who really were in danger.

"The state was stepping in and taking these kids into protective custody because they were living with someone other than their parents — grandmother, aunt, uncle —

single parents who couldn't support their children. And as immigrants or the offspring of immigrants, many of the children had no extended families they could turn to for support.

Besides worrying about the children's well being, Brace warned they might grow up to be violent criminals, referring to them as the "dangerous classes." He convinced businessmen to support shipping the children west, where they presumably would live healthy and wholesome lives on farms.

The first orphan train carried children to Dowagiac, Mich., in 1854. Over the next 80 years, some 150,000 to 200,000 children were shipped to states in the West.

In 1872, the New York Foundling Asylum, which took in unwanted babies, began putting infants and toddlers on the trains, a practice that lasted into the 20th century. As in colonial days, the farmers benefited from the labor of the children they took in.

In the 1870s growing public concern about child abuse and neglect spurred the founding of societies for the prevention of cruelty to children, and courts began to empower them to remove children from neglectful homes.

What we now know as foster care took root in the last two decades of the 19th century, when some child protection organizations began to pay families to take in homeless children so the children would not have to work.

even though they were living safely," Testa explains. "Children were building up in long-term foster care because there were no pathways for moving kids into more permanent homes, and folks weren't asking the relatives if they were willing to adopt. There was this myopia of only recognizing nuclear families, and if you're not in a nuclear family you're taken into the child welfare system."

The new managers forced the department to stop taking children who were living safely with relatives and start offering those families services available to nuclear families. "That reduced the number of kids coming into foster care right off the bat," Testa says. "But large numbers were still remaining in long-term foster care, so moving kids out needed attention."

The Illinois child welfare system delivers most foster care services through private contractors rather than local government agencies. "The financial incentives were all geared toward keeping kids in foster care," Testa explains, because they were paid only for foster children. "There was no reward for moving kids into permanent homes."

The state began paying incentives for adoption and reunification with parents, and the foster rolls dropped again.

The state also sought a waiver from federal rules in order to use some of its federal foster care funds to subsidize guardianships. Guardianship does not require termination of parental rights as adoption does, but it creates a permanent relationship between the child and the guardian and removes state supervision. Many relatives willing to care for children do not want to adopt, Testa says, because that would require termination of the biological parents' rights.

Since obtaining the waiver in 1997, Illinois has moved more than 8,000 children from foster care to guardianship, Testa says, reducing state costs and freeing caseworkers to concentrate on families that really are in trouble. During the decade of reform, the average worker's caseload has dropped from more than 50 cases to fewer than 20, Testa says.

"Illinois takes far fewer kids into foster care than many other states," he explains, "because we're doing a better job making family assessments and working with families who can take care of their kids with some help."

Now the department's biggest challenge is helping older adolescents who remain in foster care and are less likely to be adopted. "The solution is to attach every child as early as possible to a permanent family, a mentor, someone who's going to care about them," Testa says.

One hurdle to adoption is that older adolescents lose foster services that help in the transition to adulthood. The department has obtained a new federal waiver to extend those services after adoption or while the child is in guardianship. The department also is working with universities to support former foster children while they're in school. And it's developed a program to recruit families to host college students during vacations and to maintain connections with them during the school year.

"The Illinois system has not achieved perfection," Berrick says, "but it's certainly made a remarkable turnaround."

---

[1] Phillip J. O'Connor and Zay N. Smith, "Woman Charged In Son's Hanging," *Chicago Sun-Times*, April 20, 1993, p. 3.

[2] Phillip J. O'Connor and Ray Long, "Police Rescue 19 Kids In Filthy Apartment," *Chicago Sun-Times*, Feb. 2, 1994, p. 1; Colin McMahon and Susan Kuczka, "19 Kids Found In Filth," *Chicago Tribune*, Feb. 2, 1994, p. 1.

As the century neared its end, states began to organize charity boards that tended to favor home placements over institutional care.

The modern child welfare system began taking shape in the early 20th century. In 1912, the federal government created the U.S. Children's Bureau, now part of the Health and Human Services Department, to conduct research and distribute information to state children's agencies. States began to create separate juvenile court systems, which ordered more children into government care. In the 1920s, child welfare agencies began to exercise greater supervision of foster homes. And the New Deal brought federal money into the picture.

The Social Security Act of 1935 made the Children's Bureau responsible for administering the new Aid to Dependent Children program, later known as Aid to Families with Dependent Children, or AFDC. Congress intended the program to preserve poor families that otherwise might not be able to afford to keep their children at home. Aimed primarily at widowed mothers, it supported state aid programs for children living with a parent or other relative. States also received federal assistance to establish or strengthen children's services in rural areas and to train child welfare workers.

The federal government didn't extend aid to foster children and to urban services until 1961. To receive that

Linda and Mike Hurley and adopted daughter Courtney pose for their first family photo after signing adoption documents in Tampa on June 4, 2004. Child welfare agencies around the nation are seeking adoptive parents or guardians to help older foster children make the transition to adulthood.

aid, the foster child had to come from a family with income low enough to qualify for AFDC. Assistance also was offered for a broader range of child services, including family preservation.

Child Abuse and Crack

Also during the early 1960s, Denver physician Henry Kempe called public attention to the "battered child syndrome," revealing that many hospitalized youngsters whose injuries had been attributed to accidents actually had been abused by a parent or other caregiver. Before the decade ended, all 50 states passed laws requiring doctors, teachers and other child-care professionals to report suspected abuse. Congress followed suit in 1974 with the Child Abuse Prevention and Treatment Act (CAPTA), which provided federal funds for child protection services, including procedures for reporting and investigating abuse and protecting endangered children.

During the late-'70s, child welfare agencies began focusing on moving children from foster care into permanent homes and on helping families avoid the need for out-of-home placements in the first place. Advocates of the shift in focus said it was better for children and would cost less than foster care.

Congress established a national adoption-information exchange program in 1978. California, New York and Illinois became the first states to subsidize adoptions in order to counteract the financial penalty suffered by foster parents who lose their foster payments when they finally adopt their foster children.

In 1980, Congress created a federal adoption-assistance program and merged it with the old AFDC foster care funds. Known as Title IV-E of the Social Security Act, it is now the main source of federal support for child welfare. The law required states to make "reasonable efforts" to keep children with their parents or return them as soon as possible. When families couldn't be reunited, the law declared placement with relatives or adoption to be superior to long-term foster care.

These efforts collided with the crack cocaine epidemic and other social pathologies from the mid-1980s through early-'90s.

From 1980 to 1994, single-parent households increased from 22 percent to 31 percent of all families. Births to unmarried teens soared from 27.6 per 1,000 females in 1980 to 44.6 in 1992. In 1993, 2.9 million child abuse and neglect reports were filed, up from 1.7 million in 1984.[22]

Foster caseloads — which dropped from a little more than 500,000 in 1977 to fewer than 300,000 in 1986 — soared back to nearly 500,000 by 1995.[23]

Federal and state governments, with support and prodding from private organizations, continued to press for family preservation and adoption as better alternatives to foster care.

In 1993, Congress authorized $1 billion over five years to help states strengthen troubled families. More federal money was distributed to help courts improve their handling of foster care and adoption cases. Congress gave the Health and Human Services secretary authority to grant waivers so states could use federal child welfare grants to finance innovative programs.

President Clinton declared adoption to be a national priority in 1996, saying "no child should be uncertain about what 'family' or 'parent' or 'home' means." The 1997 Adoption and Safe Families Act provided more incentives for adoption and family preservation. The Foster Care Independence Act of 1999 increased federal funding for counseling and other services for youths making the transition from foster care to adulthood. The money could be used for housing and other living expenses, and states could extend Medicaid coverage beyond the youths' 18th birthday.

In 2000 Congress authorized federal aid to help courts reduce backlogs of abuse and neglect cases and improve information technology systems. New federal educational assistance for so-called aging-out youths — those leaving the system — was authorized in 2001.

CURRENT SITUATION

Rigid Rules and Budgets

When Katie Sutton's grandchildren wanted to sleep over at a friend's house, Philadelphia child welfare caseworkers had to investigate the friend's family first. If she wanted to take a child to the doctor, she had to get a caseworker's instructions. When she wanted to take them across the nearby border into New Jersey, she had to get a caseworker's permission.

To Sutton, who had custody of five grandchildren as a foster parent, this was more than a nuisance.

Investigating a friend's family felt like "a way of invading their privacy and just automatically assuming that they have a bad background," she explained. For the grandchildren, the frequent involvement of caseworkers sent the message that "we're foster care kids, we don't belong anywhere, we have a label and we're different from everyone else."[24]

The children don't feel different anymore, because Sutton has become their permanent legal guardian, and they have left government supervision behind them. She hadn't wanted to adopt because she didn't want to terminate her son's parental rights. He's not a bad father, she said, just immature and emotionally and financially unable to care for his offspring. She couldn't afford to keep them outside the foster care system until Pennsylvania offered to subsidize her guardianship.

Her story encapsulates the state of the U.S. child welfare system today. Rigid rules and tight budgets make it difficult for agencies to tailor services to the specific needs of individual children and families.

Caseloads Are Double Recommended Levels

The average American child welfare caseworker oversees two-dozen or more children — twice as many as child advocate and accreditation organizations recommend. Some caseworkers manage as many as 110 cases.

Number of cases per child welfare worker

Category	Number of cases
CWLA* standard	12-15
COA** standard	1-18
Average caseload per worker	24-31

* Child Welfare League of America

** Council on Accreditation for Children and Family Services

Source: "HHS Could Play a Greater Role in Helping Child Welfare Agencies Recruit and Retain Staff," U.S. General Accounting Office, March 2003

But federal, state and local governments — often in cooperation with private organizations — are moving toward more flexible policies that emphasize holding families together and placing children in alternative permanent homes when that's not possible.

It's common for relatives not to want to adopt, even when they're willing to make permanent homes for grandchildren, nieces or nephews, Testa at the University of Illinois says. "They don't want to get embroiled in an adversarial battle with a daughter or sister," he explains. "Many of them feel it's odd that they'd have to adopt someone to whom they were already related."

Stephen McCall of Brooklyn, N.Y., has been a foster parent for five years for, from left, Marshawn, Maleek, Brandon and Marcus. New York's child welfare agency is encouraging more potential foster parents to take adolescent and special-needs children.

In Sutton's case, Pennsylvania uses state funds to help her give the grandchildren a stable home. Sixteen other states do the same, while nine redirect surpluses from their share of the federal welfare program. Another nine have negotiated waivers with the HHS to spend some of their federal foster-care funds on subsidies for guardians.[25]

Waivers have become an important vehicle for reform of the child welfare system, just as they were for welfare reform in the mid-1990s. About 20 states have used them in varied ways, including for guardian assistance, drug-abuse treatment for parents, training of staff in private and public child services agencies, adoption promotion and other services to children and families not covered by federal foster care assistance.[26]

Whole Child Approach

Some state and local agencies have teamed up with private organizations and volunteers to improve the way they do business.

Some 70,000 volunteer court-appointed special advocates — or CASAs — represent the interests of children under court supervision throughout the country, for instance. Started in Seattle in 1976, the CASA movement has grown to 930 local programs that are united in the National Court Appointed Special Advocate Association. [27] The volunteer builds a relationship with a child and tells the court whether the child is receiving the care and services the judge has ordered.

Child welfare workers often don't have enough time to keep close watch on the children in their charge, says Kenneth J. Sherk, who helps lead an organization that supports CASAs and children in the Phoenix-area child welfare system. "They're overworked and underpaid and all bogged down in red tape, and often as not things just don't get done for these kids," Sherk explains. "The CASAs tell the court and the Foster Care Review Board here when a child needs counseling, dental work, new clothes, school books — the basic needs."

In 2002 child welfare agencies in St. Louis, Louisville, Cedar Rapids, Iowa, and Jacksonville, Fla., agreed to work with the Center for Community Partnerships in Child Welfare. The center funds and advises efforts to bring a broad array of public and private organizations and individuals together to help troubled families. It's now working in 80 communities, Director Notkin says.

"The problems of families at risk of child abuse and neglect are complex," Notkin explains. "Therefore, it's necessary to develop a neighborhood network of services and support that involves public agencies, private agencies, nonprofits, the business community, the faith community, neighbors and relatives."

The center also stresses creation of a unique plan for each family, Notkin says. "If substance abuse is a problem, make sure someone from substance-abuse treatment is at the table," she explains. "If job training is needed, the job-training folks need to be there."

A key component is the participation of neighborhood volunteers who may tutor the parents in the skills of parenting, help to care for the children and help integrate the family into the community. "Our fundamental principle is that in order to have safe children we need strong families, and strong families need healthy communities that they're connected to," Notkin says.

Comprehensive approaches must be advocated, says Rosemary Chalk, director of the National Academy of Sciences Board on Children, Youth and Families, because "there's no sense of overall accountability for the whole child within the child welfare system."

"We know these kids are in bad shape and in many cases may have serious health problems or serious educational deficits," she explains. "But no one is stepping up and saying we're prepared to deal with the whole child."

Such services work, child welfare experts say, but the demand exceeds the supply. In a study of mothers who

Should states be allowed to convert federal foster care funds into capped block grants?

YES

Wade F. Horn, Ph.D.
*Assistant Secretary for Children and Families,
U.S. Department of Health and
Human Services*

Written for *The CQ Researcher*, April 2005

States should be allowed to convert the Title IV-E foster care entitlement program into a flexible, alternative-financing structure. President Bush's proposed Child Welfare Program Option would allow them to do that. But the president's proposal is not a block grant. Its very name, Child Welfare Program Option, says it all: It is an option. If a state does not believe it is in its best interest to participate in this alternative, it may continue to participate in the current title IV-E entitlement program.

The states for many years have criticized the Title IV-E program as too restrictive. For instance, it only provides funds for the maintenance of foster children who have been removed from a home that would have been eligible for assistance under the old welfare program and for child welfare training. Under current law, Title IV-E funds cannot be used for services that might prevent a child from being placed in foster care in the first place, that might facilitate a child's returning home or that might help move the child to another permanent placement.

Under the proposed Program Option, states could choose to administer their program more flexibly, with a fixed allocation of funds over a five-year period. States would be able to use funds for foster care payments, prevention activities, permanency efforts, case management, administrative activities and training of child welfare staff. They would be able to develop innovative systems for preventing child abuse and neglect, keeping families and children safely together and quickly moving children toward adoption and permanency. They also would be freed from burdensome income-eligibility provisions that continue to be linked to the old welfare program.

Although states would have greater flexibility in how they use funds, they would still be held accountable for positive results. They would continue to be required to participate in Child and Family Services Reviews and to maintain the child safety protections, such as conducting criminal-background checks and licensing foster care providers, obtaining judicial oversight for removal and permanency decisions, developing case plans for all foster children and prohibiting race-based discrimination in placements. States also would be required to maintain their existing level of investment in the program.

Thus, the proposal allows — but does not force — states to enhance their child welfare services while relieving them of unnecessary administrative burdens. This option for flexible funding represents good public policy.

NO

Shay Bilchik
*President and CEO,
Child Welfare League of America*

Written for *The CQ Researcher*, April 2005

It is too common an occurrence to read a newspaper or listen to the news and learn about yet another seriously abused or neglected child or a child welfare system struggling to protect the children in its care. Recently, every state, the District of Columbia and Puerto Rico had the performance of their child welfare system measured as a part of a federal review. States fell short in a variety of areas, including having excessive caseloads, inadequate supervision, inadequate training and lack of treatment services.

Each of these shortcomings relates to a failure to provide resources that would support high-quality performance — resources that should be provided through investments made by the federal, state and local governments responsible for protecting abused and neglected children.

Yearly, states confirm nearly 900,000 reports of abuse and neglect. There are more than 550,000 children in the nation's foster care system. Too many of these children stay in foster care far longer than necessary because of the lack of appropriate support services. In fact, nearly 40 percent of abused and neglected children don't receive treatment to address the emotional trauma they have experienced. In addition, much of this abuse could have been avoided through prevention services.

There is indeed a need for greater flexibility in the use of federal funds to help address these service gaps. Proposals that condition flexibility on capping federal funding, however, are shortsighted and reflect a lack of responsiveness to the results of the federal review. While it may seem difficult to argue against an option being presented to the states that trades funding level for flexibility, it actually is quite easy when it is being presented as the federal government's solution to the problems facing our nation's child welfare system. Such a proposal is tantamount to a freeze on the federal commitment to protecting children and contradicts the vital role that the federal government plays in keeping children safe.

Flexibility is needed, but new federal investments are also needed so that fewer children are hurt and more parents can safely care for their children. The federal review clearly tells us that this is the case. It seems a fair demand, therefore, that our federal leaders bring forward a reform proposal that presents serious solutions to the trauma and horror that confront our abused and neglected children — and no less.

AP Photo/Elise Amendola

A mourner leaves the funeral service of Dontel Jeffers, 4, in Boston's Dorchester section on March 16, 2005, wearing a photo of the abused child on his shirt. Dontel died in a foster home where he had been placed by the Department of Social Services. The boy's relatives claim his foster mother beat him.

received drug abuse treatment, for example, slightly more than half had custody of their children before entering treatment while three-quarters had custody six months after completing treatment, the Child Welfare League reported. Three-quarters of parents with children in the child welfare system need treatment, the league said, but only a little more than 30 percent receive it.[28]

In 2003 authorities received about 2 million child abuse or neglect reports involving more than 3 million children. Agencies found that more than 900,000 of the children had been neglected or abused and that 1,390 had died. Most of the confirmed cases involved neglect, but 19 percent involved physical abuse and 10 percent sexual abuse.[29]

Although most agencies prefer to keep children with their parents, about 525,000 lived in foster homes in 2003, a number that has steadily declined since peaking at 570,000 in 1999. The Congressional Budget Office estimates that the number of federally supported foster care children will drop from 229,000 this year to 225,000 next year and 162,000 by 2015. Because federal aid goes only to children from families with very low income, only about half of the foster caseload receives a federal subsidy.[30]

Many child welfare workers complain that this caseload exceeds the capabilities of the work force, and the Government Accountability Office (GAO) has endorsed that view. "A stable and highly skilled child welfare work force is necessary to effectively provide child welfare services," Congress' nonpartisan investigating arm said in a 2003 report.[31] However, workers' salaries tend to be too low to attract and maintain a well-qualified staff, and caseloads tend to be higher than those recommended by widely recognized standards, the agency found. (*See graph, p. 265.*)

"Large caseloads and worker turnover delay the timeliness of investigations and limit the frequency of worker visits with children," the GAO said.[32] In reviewing the performance of state child welfare agencies, HHS attributed many deficiencies to high caseloads and inadequate training.[33]

The Child Welfare League suggests a caseload of 12 to 15 children per worker, and the Council on Accreditation for Children and Family Services recommends no more than 18, GAO said. [34] Actual caseloads last year ranged from nine to 80, with medians ranging from 18 to 38 depending on the type of cases a worker was handling, according to a survey by the American Public Human Services Association.[35]

Beginning caseworkers earned a median salary of about $28,500 in 2002, and the most experienced workers about $47,000, the Child Welfare League reported.[36] Child welfare administrators complain about losing workers to jobs in schools, where the workers can continue to work with children while earning more in a safer environment.[37] Child welfare staff turnover ranges from 30 to 40 percent annually.

To induce workers to stay in their jobs, Rep. Stephanie Tubbs, D-Ohio, has introduced legislation to forgive their college loans. Ohio Republican Rep. Mike DeWine introduced a similar bill in the previous Congress but had not done so again this year.

OUTLOOK

Hope and Fear

Children's advocates view the future of child welfare with optimism and concern. Their hope springs from the reform movements spurring changes in many state and local programs, the trends in child welfare policies that seem to be moving in effective directions and the agreement among liberals and conservatives that more attention must be focused on early services to troubled families and speedy placement of foster children into permanent homes.

They worry that the federal financial squeeze might strangle child welfare funding and that a threatened increase in methamphetamine addiction could imitate the devastating crack cocaine epidemic of the 1980s and '90s and cause caseloads to soar once more.

"You have a lot of things going on, a lot of innovation being tested, a lot of interest in looking at the financing," says Notkin, of the Center for Community Partnerships in Child Welfare. "You also have, in the last few years, some really horrific stories coming to the attention of the public that dramatize the crisis in child welfare.

"The question is whether there will be enough political will to honestly confront the problems of the child welfare system, which are reflective of and connected to other problems in our society."

The Child Welfare League's Bilchik foresees "a three- to five-year window where we're going to see tremendous change in practice and a continuing push for reduction of federal support. Either states are going to ratchet up their support in tough economic times or we're going to see a reduction in the level and quality of care.

"I think we're going to go through another cycle where they push for less investment, which will result in more harm for children and that will lead to recognition that more resources are needed," he says. "At the same time, good practices will be adopted as we get better at keeping kids closer to home, reducing the number of times they move and placing them more often with kin."

Columbia University's Wulczyn predicts foster care rolls will shrink because "we're doing a better job of providing appropriate services," but he adds a caveat: "as long as we don't experience an unexpected social upheaval that mimics the crack cocaine epidemic."

The Casey Foundation's Stangler expects agencies to do "a much better job of promoting permanency arrangements for older youth. And I expect states to get better at connecting the dots between emancipating youth, education and the work force."

He looks to expansion of current programs through which families volunteer to provide home-like relationships to former foster children, offering them a place to come home to during college vacations, for instance, and adults to whom they can turn for parent-like guidance year-round.

An important challenge, says Meltzer, of the Center for the Study of Social Policy, is getting other parts of society to solve problems that shouldn't have been left to child welfare agencies to fix. "Ultimately, the child welfare systems have become services of last resort for a lot of problems related to poverty, mental health and substance abuse," she explains. "Figuring out how you build up resources so fewer kids and families need child welfare intervention is where you want to go."

HHS Assistant Secretary Horn is confident that the government and child welfare community know more today than 15 years ago about how to prevent child abuse and neglect. "I'm very encouraged by the renewed focus on helping families form and sustain healthy marriages," he adds, "because two parents in a healthy marriage don't come home one day and decide to abuse and neglect their children. Parents in unhealthy, dysfunctional and violent households do."

Rep. McDermott concedes the possibility of "some improvements here or there. But, if you're digging the kind of debt hole we've created, the first ones who are sacrificed into the hole are the kids."

"Republicans and Democrats do care a lot about kids," says Mial of the Casey Foundation. "What it comes down to is how well connected are they to what's happening."

Research and education are needed, for child welfare workers as well as for politicians, she adds.

And despite Horn's optimism about knowledge gained in the last 15 years, she says, "We know how to send kids to adoption. We don't necessarily know how to keep kids in a family or how to reunite them with their family."

NOTES

1. Lomi Kriel, "Bill to Overhaul Kid Agency Is Filed," *San Antonio Express-News*, Feb. 4, 2005, p. A8. And

Robert T. Garrett, "New bill on child abuse proposed; Police would become involved in most reports of juvenile injuries," *The Dallas Morning News*, Dec. 2, 2004, p. A4.

2. Suzanne Smalley and Brian Braiker, "Suffer the Children," *Newsweek*, Jan. 20, 2003, p. 32.

3. Leslie Kaufman, "State Agency For Children Fails Its Tests, U.S. Says," *The New York Times*, May 22, 2004, p B5.

4. Phillip J. O'Connor and Ray Long, "Police Rescue 19 Kids In Filthy Apartment," *Chicago Sun-Times*, Feb. 2, 1994, p. 1; Colin McMahon and Susan Kuczka, "19 Kids Found In Filth," *Chicago Tribune*, Feb. 2, 1994, p. 1.

5. Michelle M. Martinez, "Senators Giving CPS Reform Bill a Thumbs up," *Austin American-Statesman*, March 3, 2005, p. B1; "Senators Approve Protective Services Bill," *Austin American-Statesman*, March 4, 2005, p. B6.

6. Richard Lezin Jones, "Child Welfare Plan Approved," *The New York Times*, June 13, 2004, Section 14NJ, p. 6; Jones, "Monitor Approves Child Welfare Plan," *The New York Times*, June 10, 2004, p. B4; Jones, "New Jersey Plans to Lighten Load for Child Welfare Workers," *The New York Times*, June 9, 2004, p. B5; Jones, "Plan for New Jersey Foster Care Removes Many From Institutions," *The New York Times*, Feb. 16, 2004, p. B1.

7. "The Number and Rate of Foster Children Ages 17 and Under, 1990-2003," Child Trends Data Bank, available at www.childtrendsdatabank.org.

8. Robert T. Garrett, "Changes Urged for Care Agencies," *The Dallas Morning News*, Dec. 8, 2004, p. 4A.

9. "Trends in Foster Care and Adoption," U.S. Department of Health and Human Services, Administration for Children and Families, August 2004, available at www.acf.dhhs.gov/programs/cb/dis/afcars/publications/afcars.htm.

10. Jonathan D. Rockoff and John B. O'Donnell, "State's Lax Oversight Puts Fragile Children at Risk," *The Baltimore Sun*, April 10, 2005, p. 1A. Additional stories in the series, "A Failure To Protect Maryland's Troubled Group Homes," published April 11-13.

11. Rockoff and O'Donnell, "Leaders Vow To Fix Group Homes," April 14, 2005, p. 1A.

12. Child Welfare League of America press release, 2004.

13. House Ways and Means Committee, Human Resources Subcommittee, "Hearing to Examine Child Welfare Reform Proposals," July 13, 2004, transcript and documents available at http://waysandmeans.house.gov/hearings.asp?formmode=detail&hearing=161&comm=2.

14. Roseana Bess and Cynthia Andrews Scarcella, "Child Welfare Spending During a Time of Fiscal Stress," Urban Institute, Dec. 31, 2004, available at www.urban.org/url.cfm?ID=411124.

15. "Budget in Brief, Fiscal Year 2006," U.S. Department of Health and Human Services, pp. 6 and 98, available at http://hhs.gov/budget/06budget/FY2006BudgetinBrief.pdf.

16. For background, see Sarah Glazer, "Welfare Reform," *The CQ Researcher*, Aug. 3, 2001, pp. 601-632.

17. "Fostering the future: Safety, Permanence and Well-Being for Children in Foster Care," Pew Commission on Children in Foster Care, May 18, 2004, available at http://pewfostercare.org/research/docs/Final Report.pdf.

18. House Ways and Means subcommittee hearing, *op. cit.*

19. "The AFCARS Report" (Adoption and Foster Care Analysis and Reporting System), U.S. Department of Health and Human Services, August 2004, available at www.acf.dhhs.gov/programs/cb/publications/afcars/report9.pdf.

20. www.jimcaseyyouth.org/about.htm.

21. Except where noted, information for this section is drawn from these sources: Rachel S. Cox, "Foster Care Reform," *The CQ Researcher*, Jan. 9, 1998. Kasia O'Neill Murray and Sarah Gesirich, "A Brief Legislative History of the Child Welfare System," Pew Commission on Children in Foster Care, available at http://pewfostercare.org/research/docs/Legislative .pdf; Mary-Liz Shaw, "Artist Recalls the Rough Rumbling of the Orphan Trains," *Milwaukee Journal Sentinel*, Feb. 2, p. E1; Mary Ellen Johnson, "Orphan Train Movement: A history of the Orphan Trains Era in American History," Orphan Train Heritage Society

of America, available at www.orphantrainriders.com/otm11.html.

22. "National Study of Protective, Preventive and Reunification Services Delivered to Children and Their Families," U.S. Department of Health and Human Services, 1994, available at www.acf.hhs.gov/programs/cb/publications/97natstudy/introduc.htm#CW.

23. Margaret LaRaviere, "A Brief History of Federal Child Welfare Legislation and Policy (1935-2000)," the Center for Community Partnerships in Child Welfare, Nov. 18, 2002, available at www.cssp.org/uploadFiles/paper1.doc.

24. Press conference, Washington, D.C., Oct. 13, 2004, transcript, pp. 7-9, available at www.fosteringresults.org/results/press/pewpress_10-13-04_fednewsbureau.pdf.

25. *Ibid.*, p.12, for updated waiver figure. Also: Mark Testa, Nancy Sidote Salyers and Mike Shaver, "Family Ties: Supporting Permanence for Children in Safe and Stable Foster Care With Relatives and Other Caregivers," Children and Family Research Center, School of Social Work, University of Illinois at Urbana-Champaign, Oct. 2004, p. 5, available at www.fosteringresults.org/results/reports/pewreports_10-13-04_alreadyhome.pdf.

26. "Summary of Title IV-E Child Welfare Waiver Demonstration Projects," U.S. Health and Human Services Department, May 2004, available at www.acf.hhs.gov/programs/cb/initiatives/cwwaiver/summary.htm.

27. "History of CASA." Available at www. casanet.org/download/ncasa_publications/history-casa.pdf.

28. "The Nation's Children 2005," the Child Welfare League of America, pp. 2-3.

29. *Ibid.*, p. 1. Also: "Child Maltreatment 2002," Health and Human Services Department, available at www.acf.hhs.gov/programs/cb/publications/cm02/summary.htm.

30. Child Trends Data Bank, *op. cit.* Also: "CBO Baseline for Foster Care and Adoption Assistance," Congressional Budget Office, March 2005, available at www.cbo.gov/factsheets/2005/FosterCare.PDF.

31. "HHS Could Play a Greater Role in Helping Child Welfare Agencies Recruit and Retain Staff," General

Accounting Office, (now called the Government Accountability Office) March 2003, available at www.gao.gov/new.items/d03357.pdf.

32. *Ibid*, pp. 3-4.

33. *Ibid*, p. 21.

34. *Ibid*, p. 14.

35. "Report From the 2004 Child Welfare Workforce Survey: State Agency Findings," American Public Human Services Association, February 2005, p. 22, available at www.aphsa.org/ Home/Doc/Workforce%20Report%202005.pdf.

36. Child Welfare League of America National Data Analysis System, available at www.ndas.cwla.org/data_stats/access/predefined/Report.asp?ReportID=86.

37. General Accounting Office, *op. cit.*, pp. 3, 11.

BIBLIOGRAPHY

Books

Brohl, Kathryn, *The New Miracle Workers: Overcoming Contemporary Challenges in Child Welfare Work,* *CLWA Press,* **2004.**
A veteran child welfare worker and family therapist explains new challenges facing workers and administrators, including meeting legislature-imposed timelines for case management, working collaboratively with clients, understanding diverse cultures and nontraditional families, keeping up with research, improving pay and training and overcoming worker burnout.

Geen, Rob, editor, *Kinship Care: Making the Most of a Valuable Resource, Urban Institute Press,* **2003.**
A collection of essays edited by an Urban Institute researcher examines how child welfare agencies are using relatives as foster parents, how this differs from traditional foster care, and how the caregivers describe their experiences.

Shirk, Martha, and Gary Stangler, *On Their Own: What Happens to Kids When They Age Out of the Foster Care System, Westview Press,* **2004.**
A journalist (Shirk) and the former director of the Missouri Social Services Department (Stangler) who now runs a program for older foster children offer alternately inspiring and heartrending stories of 10 young

people who must leave foster care and learn to live on their own without the family and community relationships that most young people lean on as they make the transition from teen to adult.

Articles

Campbell, Joel, "Encourage Access to Juvenile Courts: The Time Is Right for Lifting Juvenile Court and Child Welfare System Secrecy," *The Quill*, Aug. 1, 2004, p. 36.

A leader of the Society of Professional Journalists' Freedom of Information Committee argues that one way to improve the child welfare system is to let the news media into juvenile courts.

Colloff, Pamela, "Life and Meth," *Texas Monthly*, June 2004, p. 120.

Methamphetamine is destroying families in East Texas — an epidemic child welfare authorities worry could spike foster care rolls nationwide.

Humes, Edward, "The Unwanted," *Los Angeles Magazine*, Jan. 1, 2003, p. 64.

The reporter exposes a dysfunctional Los Angeles children's home.

Rockoff, Jonathan D., and John B. O'Donnell, "A Failure to Protect Maryland's Troubled Group Homes," *The Baltimore Sun*, April 10-13, 2005.

In a four-part exposé, the authors reveal child abuse, neglect and even death within Maryland's state-supervised group homes for children.

Reports and Studies

"Fostering the Future: Safety, Permanence and Well-Being for Children in Foster Care," the *Pew Commission on Children in Foster Care*, May 18, 2004, available at http://pewfostercare.org/research/docs/FinalReport.pdf.

This influential report by a blue-ribbon panel headed by two former U.S. representatives — Republican Bill Frenzel of Minnesota and Democrat William H. Gray III of Pennsylvania — explores the need to improve the child welfare system. The commission argues for more flexibility and more federal funds while acknowledging need to moderate federal spending.

"HHS Could Play a Greater Role in Helping Child Welfare Agencies Recruit and Retain Staff," *General Accounting Office* (now the Government Accountability Office), March 2003, available at www.gao.gov/new.items/d03357.pdf.

A report by Congress' nonpartisan investigating arm presents evidence that child welfare agencies' effectiveness suffers because caseworkers are underpaid and given too many cases to manage.

Testa, Mark F., "Encouraging Child Welfare Innovation through IV-E Waivers," *Children and Family Research Center, School of Social Work, University of Illinois at Urbana-Champaign*, January 2005; http://cfrcwww.social.uiuc.edu/briefpdfs/cfrc.

An academic study by the former research director of the Illinois Department of Children and Family Services examines how states have used waivers of federal regulations to spend federal funds on innovative programs and suggests how to use waivers more effectively. Testa is co-director of the University of Illinois' Children and Family Research Center.

Vandivere, Sharon, Rosemary Chalk and Kristin Anderson Moore, "Children in Foster Homes: How Are They Faring?" *Child Trends Research Brief*, December 2003; www.childtrends.org/files/FosterHomesRB.pdf.

An analysis of surveys of children and families concludes that foster children are less healthy than other children, have more developmental and behavioral problems and often have problems in school.

For More Information

Annie E. Casey Foundation, 701 St. Paul St., Baltimore, MD 21202; (410) 547-6600; www.aecf.org. Advocates, conducts research and supports programs to benefit disadvantaged children and families; known for its Kids Count Data Book, an annual compilation of state-by-state statistics.

Child Trends, 4301 Connecticut Ave., N.W., Suite 100, Washington, DC 20008; (202) 572-6000; www.childtrends. org. Conducts research about children and publishes reports and statistics on its Child Trends Data Bank.

Child Welfare League of America, 440 First St., N.W., Washington, DC 20001; (202) 638-2952; www.cwla.org. America's oldest and largest child welfare organization advocates, suggests standards and educates welfare workers.

Children and Family Research Center, University of Illinois, 1203 W. Oregon St., Urbana, IL 61801; (217) 333-5837; http://cfrcwww.social.uiuc.edu. Leading university-based institution for studying children, families and child welfare services.

Children's Bureau, 370 L'Enfant Promenade, S.W., Washington, DC 20447; (202) 205-8618; www.acf.hhs .gov/programs/cb. Agency of the U.S. Health and Human Services Department that supports states' delivery of child welfare services, publishes reports and data on its Web site, maintains hotlines for reporting child and domestic abuse and runaway, missing or exploited children (1-800-4ACHILD).

National Court Appointed Special Advocate (CASA) Association, 100 W. Harrison, North Tower, Suite 500, Seattle WA 98119; (800) 628-3233; www.nationalcasa.org. Provides leadership, consultation and resources for more than 900 CASA programs across the country whose nearly 70,000 volunteers serve as advocates for 280,000 abused or neglected children.

Pew Commission on Foster Care, 2233 Wisconsin Ave., N.W., Washington, DC 20007; (202) 687-0948; www .pewfostercare.org. Blue-ribbon, bipartisan panel that proposed more federal funding and more flexibility for states to spend it.

12

Universal Coverage

Will All Americans Finally Get Health Insurance?

Marcia Clemmitt

Many working Americans, like Daniel and Mindy Shea, of Cincinnati, are un- or under-insured. Young workers are hit especially hard: In 2004, a third of Americans ages 19-24 were uninsured. Only 61 percent of Americans under age 65 obtain health insurance through their employers. As health costs rise and incomes sag, more and more companies are dropping coverage, especially restaurants and small businesses.

From *CQ Researcher*,
March 30, 2007.

When Emily, a 24-year-old graduate student, discovered a lump on her thigh, her doctor told her to get an MRI to find out whether it was cancerous. But Emily's student-insurance policy didn't cover the $2,000 procedure, so she skipped it.[1]

Several weeks later, during outpatient surgery to remove the lump, Emily's surgeon found a rare, invasive cancer underneath the benign lump — with only a 20 to 40 percent survival rate. The skipped MRI could have detected the cancer much sooner, improving her chances for recovery.

Emily pieced together payment for her treatment from her school insurance, two state public-aid programs and a monthly payment plan that ate up more than 40 percent of her take-home income. But a year later she learned that annual health premiums for all students at her school would rise by 19 percent because a few, like her, had racked up high expenses. The price hike led many more students to skip purchasing the coverage altogether.

Advocates say such stories are a good reason why Congress should enact a universal health-insurance program. While Congress has been expanding public health insurance programs covering the very poor — especially children and their mothers — students and lower-income workers increasingly are losing coverage or are finding, like Emily, that they can't afford adequate coverage.

Today, 45 million Americans — about 15.3 percent of the population — lack health insurance, usually due to job loss, student status, early retirement or because they have entry-level jobs

Cost of Premiums Rising Rapidly

The average annual cost of family health coverage has risen more than 50 percent since 2001, to $11,500, and is expected to exceed $18,000 in the next five years. Most of the cost is borne by the employer.

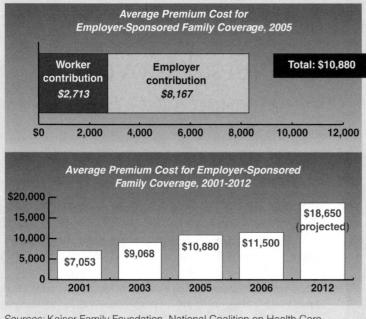

Average Premium Cost for Employer-Sponsored Family Coverage, 2005

| Worker contribution $2,713 | Employer contribution $8,167 | Total: $10,880 |

Average Premium Cost for Employer-Sponsored Family Coverage, 2001-2012

| 2001 | 2003 | 2005 | 2006 | 2012 |
| $7,053 | $9,068 | $10,880 | $11,500 | $18,650 (projected) |

Sources: Kaiser Family Foundation, National Coalition on Health Care

"Health insurance expenses are the fastest-growing cost component for employers," according to the National Coalition on Health Care. "Unless something changes dramatically, health insurance costs will overtake profits by 2008."[6]

"If there's one thing that can bankrupt America, it's health care," warns U.S. Comptroller General David Walker, chief of the Government Accountability Office, Congress' non-partisan auditing arm. And in response to those who say the United States can "grow" its way out of uninsurance by creating more and better jobs with coverage benefits, he states flatly: "Anybody that tells you we are going to grow our way out of this . . . probably isn't very proficient at math."[7]

While the public often pictures the uninsured as being unemployed, the fact is that most un- and under-insured Americans have jobs. Only 61 percent of Americans under age 65 obtain health insurance through their employers — down from 69 percent in 2000. And as health costs rise and incomes sag, more and more companies are dropping coverage, especially very small businesses. Because insurers raise premium prices for high-cost groups — as happened with Emily's grad-school coverage — small companies whose employees get seriously ill or injured or pregnant often find themselves priced out of coverage altogether.

Now some states are trying to create new sources of affordable coverage. Massachusetts is launching a universal-coverage plan in 2007 that has bipartisan support, and Republican California Gov. Arnold Schwarzenegger hopes to enact a similar measure. At the federal level, no new initiatives are expected this year — except for a probable expansion of children's coverage — but many expect universal coverage to be a major theme in the 2008 presidential election.

America's creeping lack of health coverage constitutes a crisis for the uninsured, even as the skyrocketing cost of

or work in a service industry or a small business. Only about 40 percent of businesses employing low-wage or part-time workers offer health benefits, and at $11,480 a year, the average family's health-insurance premium now costs more than a minimum-wage worker makes in a year. Young workers are hit especially hard: In 2004, more than a third of Americans between the ages of 19 and 24 were uninsured.[2] And in the construction and service industries, only 80 percent of the managers have health coverage.[3]

And the situation is only expected to get worse. U.S. health spending is expected to double by 2015 — to more than $12,300 per person.[4] As health-care costs skyrocket, so does the cost of health insurance, whether purchased by individuals or by employers. Between 2000 and 2006, health premiums for employer-sponsored insurance jumped 87 percent, far outpacing inflation's 18 percent overall increase.[5]

health care makes it inevitable that even more people will be uninsured in the future. If health premiums continue rising at their current rate, about 56 million Americans are predicted to be uninsured by 2013 — 11 million more than today, according to a University of California at San Diego study.[8] The increase will cause 4,500 additional unnecessary deaths per year and $16 billion to $32 billion in lost economic productivity and other "human capital," the study says.[9]

The leading public myth about the uninsured is that "people without health insurance get the medical care they need," said Arthur Kellerman, chairman of Emory University's Department of Emergency Medicine and co-chairman of an Institute of Medicine (IOM) panel that has called for universal coverage by 2010.[10]

In fact, the uninsured seldom receive appropriate care at the appropriate time, said Kellerman. "The uninsured are less likely to see a doctor or be able to identify a regular source of medical care and are less likely to receive preventive services," he said.[11] And uninsured children admitted to a hospital due to an injury are twice as likely to die and 46 percent less likely to receive rehabilitation after hospitalization, according to a recent study by the consumer advocacy group Families USA.[12]

The growing number of uninsured Americans also pushes up the cost of publicly subsidized health insurance like Medicare, the panel said. Working-age uninsured patients with uncontrolled diabetes or high blood pressure eventually enter the health system sicker than they would have been had they been insured.[13] And about 20 percent of those with schizophrenia and bipolar disorder are uninsured and end up in jail or prison when their untreated conditions trigger illegal behavior, said the panel.[14]

Adding to the problem, manufacturing and unionized jobs were the mainstay of job-based coverage, but their numbers have been dropping for 20 years. "I suspect you're going to see wholesale withdrawal of employer-sponsored health care" for anyone earning less than twice federal poverty-level wages, said National Governors Association Executive Director Ray Scheppach.[15]

"Economic security, jobs, health care and retirement security — those are all now one and the same issue," says Henry Simmons, president of the National Coalition on Health Care, which includes employers, unions and academic and other groups advocating universal coverage.

Pension investment funds have recently realized that skyrocketing health-care costs could bankrupt Americans' future if they are not checked, says Simmons. Since Medicare covers only some of the health services needed by retirees, virtually all elderly people who can afford it also purchase private supplemental insurance to fill the gaps. But pension-fund investors are finding no investments that grow fast enough to allow retirees' savings income to keep up with the anticipated soaring cost of future Medicare and supplemental-coverage premiums.

While no one expects significant action from Congress until after the 2008 presidential election, federal

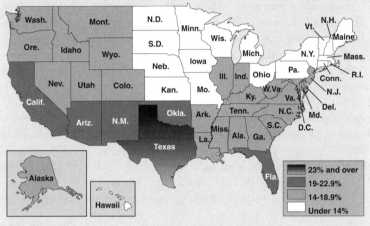

Americans Without Health Insurance

In 25 states, between 14 percent and 19 percent of the adults ages 18-64 did not have health insurance in 2005. States with high levels of uninsured residents typically have minimal state and employer insurance coverage.

Percentage of People Ages 18-64 Without Insurance, 2005

- 23% and over
- 19-22.9%
- 14-18.9%
- Under 14%

Source: Kaiser Family Foundation, statehealthfacts.org, 2005

policymakers increasingly acknowledge a need for action. Consensus appears to be growing for some type of hybrid universal coverage that combines public and private insurance.

"In the past the debate got bogged down because different groups wanted their first-priority proposal only," says Ron Pollack, founding executive director of Families USA. "One group would say, 'Coverage must be financed through public programs,' while another would say, 'There should be no government action in the marketplace,' And since everyone's second-favorite program was the status quo, nothing happened."

But that decades-old logjam may be breaking up, as advocates on all sides of the issue creep closer to one another in their proposals. "The very grand visions on both sides" — a single-payer government system or relying on individuals saving money for their own care via Health Savings Accounts (HSAs) — "are both completely impossible in our political system," says Yale University Professor of Political Science Jacob Hacker.

Even President George W. Bush, a longtime proponent of individually purchased HSAs, softened that stance in his most recent proposal. Bush's fiscal 2008 budget plan would offer similar tax breaks to those buying all kinds of health insurance, not just HSAs, either as individuals or through employers.

Paul Ginsburg, president of the nonpartisan research group Center for Studying Health System Change, says critics rightly point out that Bush's tax break doesn't target lower-income people who are most in danger of losing coverage. Nevertheless, "eventually, the Democrats may see that the president has given them something — a revenue source" to help pay for expanding coverage, he says.

So far, every Democrat who has announced he or she will run for president has declared a commitment to universal coverage, tying the issue to the country's overall economic health, but only former Sen. John Edwards, D-N.C., has announced a specific coverage plan. "The U.S. auto industry is struggling, in part because of the rising cost of health care that this administration has done nothing to address," newly announced Democratic candidate Sen. Barack Obama, D-Ill., said last November. "I have long proposed that the government make a deal with the Big Three automakers that will pay for a portion of their retiree health costs if they agree to invest those savings in fuel-efficient technologies." Health-care costs account for approximately $1,000 of the cost of each car produced by the America's largest automakers — more than they spend on steel.[16]

Among Republican presidential candidates, former Massachusetts Gov. Mitt Romney last year backed legislation intended to achieve universal coverage in his state, and former House Speaker Newt Gingrich, who has not yet thrown his hat into the presidential ring, also has called for systemic reforms in the health-care system.

While a consensus may be developing on the need for some kind of universal coverage, many contentious debates remain. For example, both the right and the left have criticized the California and Massachusetts plans for requiring individuals to buy health insurance, just as drivers are required to carry automobile insurance.

Nevertheless, many believe the country is on the verge of a focused, national debate on universal coverage. "In 2008, universal coverage will be up there with Iraq as top election issues," says Pollack.

As policymakers gear up for that debate, here are some of the questions being asked:

Can America afford universal health coverage?

Critics of universal-insurance proposals have long argued that while expanding coverage is desirable, covering everyone would simply cost too much.[17] Universal-coverage advocates, however, argue that current administrative expenses are high partly because the United States has a piecemeal system with many uninsured.

"It is impossible to get everybody covered," former Senate Majority Leader Bill Frist, R-Tenn., a transplant surgeon, said in 2004.[18] State efforts have shown that universal coverage is not financially feasible, he said.

For example, his home state of Tennessee managed to cover about 93 percent of residents — a national high — by having Medicaid cover both the uninsured and the uninsurable. But "in attempting to do this the state is going bankrupt," he said, "and there is a major effort to backtrack."[19]

Universal-coverage plans generally are "unrealistic," said former Health and Human Services Secretary Tommy G. Thompson. I just don't think it's in the cards. . . . "I don't think that administratively or legislatively it's feasible."[20]

While few politicians today will say America cannot afford universal coverage, both sides agree that the costs will be high. A study by the liberal Urban Institute says that in 2004 universal coverage would have added about $48 billion to the $125 billion the nation spent on health care for uninsured people — most of which was paid out of pocket by the uninsured or was delivered without compensation by doctors and hospitals.[21] A proposed universal-coverage plan for Maryland would raise that state's health spending by some $2.5 billion per year, while a Minnesota proposal to cover the state's 383,000 uninsured is projected to cost an estimated $663-$852 million in new annual funding.[22]

Most proposals for universal coverage call for increased government spending. And finding those dollars will be tough, given that the federal budget and many state budgets are facing substantial deficits.[23]

"The public sector has fewer resources" now compared to when the issue was debated previously, says Ginsburg, of the Center for Studying Health System Change. A lack of willingness or ability to commit new revenue has doomed at least one state plan, he adds. When Maine launched a universal-coverage initiative in 2003, the state "put almost no money in and got almost nothing out," he says.

The Democratic presidential hopefuls who have called for universal coverage "will be desperate for revenues when they put out their plans," says Robert Blendon, professor of health policy and management at the Harvard School of Public Health. "Money is going to be hard to come by. We've got defense costs that are very, very high."

A 2006 Massachusetts law requiring every resident to purchase subsidized coverage — unless that coverage is "unaffordable" — is already running into an affordability crisis, said Jonathan Gruber, a professor of economics at the Massachusetts Institute of Technology.[24] The state has said it would subsidize only those who earn up to three times the federal poverty level (about $30,000 for an individual and $60,000 for a family of four), said Gruber. But "at three times poverty, health insurance is still expensive. . . . It's not feasible to have someone spend 20, 30 or 40 percent of income on health insurance."[25]

While some say universal coverage is too expensive for America, many economists point out that industrialized nations with universal coverage spend less per capita on health care than the United States. In 2004, for instance, the United States spent $6,102 per capita on health care

while Australia spent $3,120; Denmark, $2,881; Germany, $3,043; Luxembourg, $5,089; Sweden, $2,825 and Switzerland, $4,077.[26]

Not only are Americans paying more for health care than those in any other industrialized country, but they are getting lower-quality care — by some measurements — than consumers in countries with universal coverage. While new drugs and technology have improved longevity and quality of life for many Americans, the United States is ranked 37th by the World Health Organization in overall quality of care, based on adult and infant mortality rates. The United States also ranks 24th among industrialized nations in life expectancy.[27]

Those stark realities, coupled with the fact that U.S. health-care costs are spiraling out of control, lead a growing number of analysts to argue that the United States can't afford not to have universal coverage.

"I've always believed universal coverage would carry significant costs and would bring daunting . . . economic challenges," said Harold Pollack, associate professor at the University of Chicago School of Social Service Administration.[28] But recently, he says, he has decided "there is no alternative" to pushing forward with universal insurance. "The current system is no longer able to accomplish important things we expect from our health care."[29]

Former Gov. John Kitzhaber, D-Ore. — an emergency-room physician who now heads the Oregon-based Archimedes Project, a health-reform initiative — agrees. Economic growth depends on good health for all, he said. Good health "is the first rung on the ladder of opportunity . . . the cornerstone of a democratic society, allowing people to . . . be productive and to take advantage of the opportunities of upward mobility."[30]

Others argue that having more than 15 percent of the population uninsured means that all Americans pay more for health care. "The uninsured are one of the inefficiencies" driving health costs into the unaffordable range, says Robert Greenstein, executive director of the liberal Center on Budget and Policy Priorities.

"Reining in health-care cost growth" — which soared by 7 percent last year alone — is a prerequisite for universal coverage, says Robert Laszewski, an independent health-care consultant and a former health-insurance executive. Health-insurance premiums grow even faster than costs, and neither government subsidies nor the

Universal Coverage Faces Financial Obstacles

Reducing health-care costs is the big challenge

Now that Americans appear to be reaching some consensus on the need for universal health coverage, major hidden obstacles — all involving money — must be overcome. Among those thorny financial issues are questions over who is going to pay for the coverage, how can affordable access be ensured for all and how can overall health-care costs be reduced.

Perhaps the most controversial issue is who will pay for the coverage. In 2005, employers paid 75 percent of workers' health-premium costs — about $500 billion compared to the approximately $170 billion that workers paid.[1] That's "most of the money outside the government that's spent on health care," says Stanley Dorn, a senior research associate at the liberal Urban Institute. To work, any universal-coverage plan will have to either continue to use those employer contributions or come up with a suitable replacement for them.

That's why many universal-coverage proposals ask employers for financial contributions. But making those contributions both fair and adequate is difficult, mainly because businesses vary so widely in what they pay today: Many contribute nothing, but others pay hundreds of millions of dollars each year.

Dorn says policymakers may want to consider asking all employers to pay a set amount into a general pool but vary the amount by companies' line of business and their geographical location. That way, companies that compete with one another would share the same burden.

Lawmakers also must figure out how to ensure affordable access to all. Many Republican proposals for expanding coverage rely on tax subsidies to help more people buy individual health policies. Because such coverage wouldn't be tied to a job, it would be "portable," so employees who switch or lose jobs would not be without insurance.

But buying individual health insurance can be far more expensive than purchasing through an employer because insurers don't "pool" risks the way they do for workers under employer-based policies. So individual purchasers pay based on their family's health status and age, which makes it the most expensive way to buy health insurance. Moreover, insurers won't even sell coverage to some people because the companies themselves consider it unaffordable.

"The words 'kinda crummy' come to mind when I think of the individual market," said former Maryland Insurance Commissioner Steve Larsen, now a private attorney. For example, a case of mononucleosis and a chronic condition like hay fever is enough for some insurers to deem a potential buyer unaffordable. "And if you have any type of serious mental illness, forget it," he said.[2] A study by the Georgetown University Institute for Health Care Research and Policy found that a 62-year-old overweight moderate smoker with controlled high blood pressure was deemed an unaffordable risk 55 percent of the times he sought individual health coverage.[3]

incomes of lower-wage working people can keep up with the current growth rate for long, he says.

If coverage expansion were accompanied by efforts to rein in spending and improve care, "there's absolutely no doubt that you can have universal coverage without substantially raised costs," says Simmons, president of the National Coalition on Health Care. "Every other country does it" already, he says.

Universal coverage is needed to "get a [health-care] market that works," he adds. "You can't fix the issue of cost" — which affects everyone, insured and uninsured — "without universal coverage," he says. Absent a universal-coverage requirement, "what markets do is avoid risk," such as when insurance companies develop marketing and risk-assessment procedures to avoid selling policies to

sick people. "It's an open-and-shut case that universal coverage is cheaper and better" than the status quo.

Getting everyone covered and specifying uniform benefit packages would create a huge, immediate, one-time financial saving, Simmons says. "Automatically, you're talking about hundreds of billions of dollars" in savings that "every other nation has already captured," partly accounting for lower costs abroad.

Should Americans depend on states to expand coverage?

In recent years, states have been far more active than the federal government in expanding health coverage. Massachusetts and Vermont passed universal-coverage laws in 2006, and Illinois created a program to cover all

Buying an individual policy is more affordable for the young and healthy, says health-care consultant Robert Laszewski. His 20-something son found an individual health policy for $150 a month several years ago, but "if he was 58 years old, his premium would have been $1,500," he says. "If you're going to do universal health care, you can't age-rate premiums or bar people based on pre-existing conditions."

No matter how widely risk is shared, however, behind the high cost of insurance lurks the ever-rising cost of health care. "The 10,000-pound elephant in the room is cost," says Laszewski.

Health-care costs have been growing faster than the entire economy or any other sector in it for the past 45 years, says Gail Wilensky, a senior fellow at the nonprofit health-education foundation Project HOPE and former head of Medicaid and Medicare. "They can't go on doing it for the next 30 years" without crippling other parts of the economy, she says.

U.S. health-care costs are the world's highest because of insurers' high administrative and marketing costs and because American doctors and medical suppliers enjoy higher profits and salaries than their counterparts in other industrialized countries.[4]

In today's fragmented insurance system, insurers' efforts to attract the healthiest, cheapest customers add extra overall costs, point out Paul Menzel, a philosophy professor at Pacific Lutheran University in Tacoma, Wash., and Donald W. Light, professor of comparative health care at the University of Pennsylvania.[5] For example, they wrote, a Seattle survey found that 2,277 people were covered by 755 different policies linked to 189 different health-care plans.

"The $420 billion (31 percent!) paid [annually] for managing, marketing and profiting from the current fragmented system could be drastically cut" if insurers had to take all comers rather than carefully jiggering their policies, premiums and marketing strategies to attract only the healthiest, least expensive buyers, they said.

A key is to cut spending on care by "learning more about what works for whom," says Wilensky. But getting that information requires investment, she says.

In addition to cutting excess services, says Laszewski, making coverage affordable will ultimately mean sacrificing some of the health-care industry's high profits and salaries. International comparisons show that other countries spend less on health care while delivering the same amount or even more services to patients.

Americans don't understand that controlling cost is crucial to sustaining the health system, let alone expanding coverage, says Laszewski. "I'll bet you if you told consumers that if they lost their jobs, replacing their insurance would cost $15,000 or $16,000 a year, they'd understand that," he says.

---

[1] Aaron Catlin, Cathy Cowan, Stephen Heffler and Benjamin Washington, "National Health Spending in 2005: The Slowdown Continues," *Health Affairs*, January/February 2007, p. 148.

[2] Quoted in "Reinsurance for Individual Market Pricks Up Many Ears," *Medicine & Health*, "Perspectives," Oct. 28, 2002.

[3] "Hay Fever? Bum Knee? Buying Individual Coverage May Be Dicey," *Medicine & Health*, June 25, 2001.

[4] For background, see Marcia Clemmitt, "Rising Health Costs," *CQ Researcher*, April 7, 2006, pp. 289-312.

[5] Paul Menzel and Donald W. Light, "A Conservative Case for Universal Access to Health Care," *The Hastings Center Report*, July 1, 2006, p. 36.

---

children. Other proposals are being discussed in state legislatures this spring.[31]

States' uninsured populations vary widely around the country, so they are the natural venue for expanding coverage, say some analysts. "All states face different challenges in reducing the number of uninsured residents," so "imposing a one-size-fits-all program" at the federal level "will not work," said Arthur Garson, dean of the University of Virginia School of Medicine.[32]

With no national consensus emerging on how to cover the uninsured, encouraging state action is the only way forward, said Stuart M. Butler, vice president for domestic and economic policy at the conservative Heritage Foundation. "Successful welfare reform started in the states," and coverage could be expanded by removing federal roadblocks and offering federal incentives to states "to try proposals currently bottled up in Congress."[33]

In California over the past year, the Republican governor, Democratic legislators and top executives from the state's largest private insurer all proposed universal-coverage plans, though none has yet been enacted. The California-based Kaiser Foundation Health Plan offered a plan that would provide "near-universal coverage" within two years to California's 5 million uninsured — who represent a whopping 10 percent of all uninsured Americans. "Despite the greater dimensions of the problem in California, we believe that a state-based solution is possible," wrote Kaiser executives.[34]

Private Insurance Coverage Dropped

The percentage of people with private health insurance dropped by 8 percentage points from 1987 to 2005 (right). At the same time, the percentage of people insured by either government or private insurance dropped 3 percentage points (left). As people lost private coverage, government picked up the slack to keep as many people insured as possible.

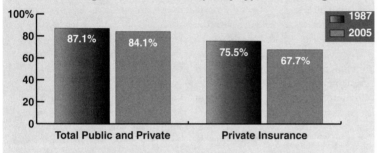

Percentage of Uninsured People by Type of Coverage

Source: U.S. Census Bureau, "Historical Health Insurance Tables"

While federal laws restrict states' ability to expand Medicaid and set rules for employer-sponsored coverage, that hasn't stopped some states from expanding coverage, says Stanley Dorn, a senior research associate at the liberal Urban Institute. In the early 1990s, for example, Minnesota and Washington state both "implemented coverage systems that succeeded brilliantly," he says.

Regardless of whether they succeed completely, state initiatives provide models and impetus for future national efforts, say many analysts. "The state action provides great momentum," says Dorn.

"States are hugely important," says Hacker at Yale University. "When two Republican governors" — Romney and Schwarzenegger — "break with the national party to propose universal coverage, that's a huge boost," he says.

Ginsburg, of the Center for Studying Health System Change, says the 2006 Massachusetts law has been a catalyst — "the answer to political gridlock." It is supported by both Republicans, who've traditionally been skeptical of universal coverage, and liberal Democrats who favor a single-payer system, he says.

The flurry of major state proposals shows the nation is ready for change, he says, even though "the federal government has been dysfunctional on domestic issues

for many years." He predicts "a few more states" will expand coverage soon, but many states are limited in what they can accomplish.

All states can't emulate the Massachusetts model, said James J. Mongan, chief executive of the New England-based hospital and physician network Partners HealthCare, because Massachusetts is very different from most other states.[35]

"We started with half the problem solved," said Mongan, a former congressional health aide who also worked in the Carter administration. Only about 10 percent of Massachusetts residents were uninsured, compared to uninsurance rates in other states of 25 percent and higher. And the state was already spending more than $500 million annually to compensate hospitals for treating the uninsured.[36]

"Federal action ultimately [will] be essential," said Shoshanna Sofaer, professor of health policy at Baruch College in New York City and a member of the IOM insurance panel. States don't have the steady financing or the legal flexibility to expand coverage to all of their residents. One roadblock, she said, is the federal Employee Retirement Income Security Act (ERISA), which limits states' power to control insurance.[37]

"The best thing states can do is set up role models," says Brandeis University Professor of Health Policy Stuart Altman. "You can't design true national health insurance state by state, because you'd get past a few states, then stop."

While states' efforts are important, says the National Coalition on Health Care's Simmons, "we don't think that any single state, no matter how large," can accomplish universal coverage of its residents "without major federal policy changes." Many governors agree and acted on their own only because they're frustrated with a lack of federal action, he says.

Furthermore, even if all states achieved universal coverage, the result would be a cost-increasing nightmare — the last thing the health system needs, says Simmons. "If you think we have administrative complexity now, imagine 50 individual state programs."

Should individuals be required to buy health insurance?

At the turn of the new century, few people were advocating that all Americans be required to buy health insurance, but in recent years such voices have grown louder. With interest growing in a system that subsidizes the cost of private coverage, advocates say unless everyone participates no functioning insurance market can develop. Insurance is designed to even out annual health costs for everyone by having everyone pay similar amounts into an overall pool each year, whether they are healthy in that particular year or facing an unexpected sickness or injury.

But opponents on the left say mandating insurance is unfair to lower-income families who can't afford even heavily subsidized private insurance. And conservative critics say a requirement to purchase is undue government intrusion into private life.

"You can talk until you're blue in the face about risk pools and actuarial tables and all the green-eyeshade reasons that the health insurers need everyone to participate in order to write affordable policies. I understand all that, and I basically don't care," wrote lawyer and policy blogger David Kravitz about Massachusetts' new buying requirement. "It is fundamentally wrong to force people to buy an expensive product in the private market, simply as a condition of existing in this state," he wrote on the Blue Mass Group policy blog.[38]

Monitoring who is obeying the requirement and determining subsidy sizes creates "one more aspect of citizens' lives" that government would monitor, complains Michael D. Tanner, director of health and welfare studies at the libertarian Cato Institute. A mandate would also be extremely difficult to enforce, he says.

"An individual mandate crosses an important line: accepting the principle that it is the government's responsibility to ensure that every American has health insurance," said Tanner. "In doing so, it opens the door to widespread regulation of the health-care industry and political interference in personal health-care decisions. The result will be a slow but steady spiral downward toward a government-run national health-care system."[39]

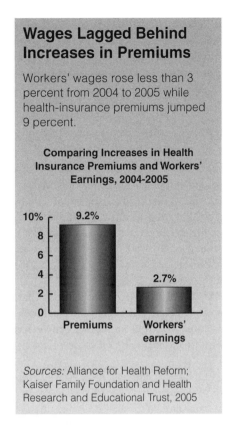

Wages Lagged Behind Increases in Premiums

Workers' wages rose less than 3 percent from 2004 to 2005 while health-insurance premiums jumped 9 percent.

Comparing Increases in Health Insurance Premiums and Workers' Earnings, 2004-2005

Sources: Alliance for Health Reform; Kaiser Family Foundation and Health Research and Educational Trust, 2005

Advocates of a mandate argue that if government can require automobile insurance to ensure that costs are paid when drivers cause accidents, then health insurance shouldn't be any different, notes Tanner. But economists say there are some key differences between the two kinds of coverage. For example, few people will drive more recklessly just because they have auto insurance. But the prevalence of generous health insurance has been shown to encourage patients to seek — and doctors to prescribe — more and sometimes unnecessary or unduly expensive treatments.[40]

Nevertheless, policymakers from both parties increasingly consider mandating health insurance "an essential accommodation to limited public resources," explains Ginsburg of the Center for Studying Health System Change. In 2004, for instance, then-Senate Majority Leader Frist said "higher-income Americans have a societal and a personal responsibility to cover in some way themselves and their children."[41] If those who can afford coverage don't enroll, the government should enroll them automatically in a high-deductible insurance plan that covers catastrophic expenses and obtain the payment for the premiums at tax time, Frist said. And the mandate should apply to the "very, very rich" initially, then expand over time, he said.[42]

Requiring everyone to buy coverage ensures that those with lower medical needs will pay premiums alongside those with expensive illnesses, analysts point out. "If the government says an insurance company must take whoever comes their way, they couldn't predict risk and might go broke" if only sicker people enrolled, says Marian R. Mulkey, senior program officer at the California Healthcare Foundation, which funds health-care research. A mandate like the one Schwarzenegger proposes "relieves this concern of insurers, who are businesses and must be on solid financial footing to offer benefits."

The Medicare drug benefit works similarly, says health-care consultant Laszewski. Medicare doesn't require seniors to enroll but strongly encourages it by imposing a financial penalty on those who wait to sign up, he says.

The drug benefit "created a huge pool of people from age 65 to 95," he explains. "And you allowed people in at the same rates no matter what their age or pre-existing condition, so long as they signed up as soon as they became eligible."

The proof of that approach is in the pudding, he says. Private insurers have "flooded the market with plans," and people are not faced with steeply escalating premiums as they age or their health worsens, he says.

BACKGROUND

America vs. Europe

From the beginning, America differed sharply from other industrialized nations in its approach to health insurance. While Europe turned to social insurance, in which all residents pay into a common fund that provides population-wide benefits, American physicians resisted, fearing such an approach would encourage government influence over the practice of medicine.[43]

The development of the American workplace-based insurance system echoed "themes that distinguish the more general history of the United States," wrote Rosemary

A. Stevens, University of Pennsylvania professor emeritus of the history of science. Social insurance was trumped by "the commitment to private solutions to public needs" and "the belief in local initiatives wherever possible."[44]

As the 19th century ended, Europeans leaned more toward "social democracy" — the belief the free market cannot supply certain human necessities, such as a minimum income to purchase food, clothing, housing and access to health services. Governments were seen as necessary to guarantee those needs, explains Thomas Bodenheimer, adjunct professor of community medicine at the University of California, San Francisco.[45]

In the late 1800s a conservative German government enacted the first social-insurance programs in hopes of heading off a wholesale movement toward more radical socialism with government ownership of industries. Supported by mandatory contributions from all citizens, the first programs paid out when people lost their livelihood through unemployment, disability or retirement. In 1883, Germany added health care to its social-insurance offerings, though with a twist. Unlike other programs, health insurance was run by privately operated "sickness funds." Social insurance, including for health care, soon became the European norm.

In the United States, lawmakers debated social insurance for decades and ultimately used it for a few programs. But health insurance remained a voluntary purchase, managed by private companies.

American liberals argued that social insurance for health would unite the entire population into a single risk pool and serve everyone's long-term interest, according to Bodenheimer. Though younger people would pay for older people, and healthy people for sick people, this would even out in the end, progressives argued, since the young will one day be old and the healthy injured or sick.[46]

But conservatives answered that it's unfair to force young people to subsidize health care for older, sicker neighbors and that people will spend more prudently on medical care if they buy their own.

Sickness Insurance

The private market for what we call health insurance today — policies that pay medical bills — grew slowly, mainly because health costs were low, even in the early 20th century. Before 1920, there were virtually no

CHRONOLOGY

1880s-1920s *Most European countries adopt compulsory health insurance.*

1895 German physicist William Roentgen discovers the X-ray, ushering in the age of modern medicine and rising health-care costs.

1920 Public commissions in California, New Jersey, Ohio and New York recommend universal state health coverage.

1926 The private Committee on the Cost of Medical Care (CCMC) endorses developing private health insurance; American Medical Association (AMA) opposes the idea.

1929 The first hospital prepayment insurance plan is launched for school teachers in Dallas, Texas.

1930s-1940s *Private hospital prepayment insurance spreads around the country, as hospitals worry they'll go under when poor patients don't pay. Congress and legislatures in at least eight states debate but don't enact compulsory health insurance.*

1935 Attempts to include health coverage in the new Social Security Act are unsuccessful.

1943 The first measure calling for compulsory national health insurance is introduced in Congress. . . . National War Labor Board declares employer contributions to insurance income-tax free, enabling companies to offer health insurance to attract workers.

1950s-1960s *Health spending and consumption rise rapidly, and workplace-based health insurance spreads. Medicare and Medicaid are enacted for the poor and elderly.*

1970s-1980s *Worries grow about health care becoming unaffordable. Presidents Nixon and Carter propose universal health coverage and health-care price controls. Cost controls reduce federal spending on Medicare, but doctors and hospitals shift their costs to employers.*

1990s *Federal government expands Medicaid and enacts a new children's health program, but employers begin dropping health benefits. Washington lawmakers shy away from large-scale coverage expansion after President Clinton's ambitious attempt to enact universal coverage fails.*

Sept. 22, 1993 Clinton unveils sweeping plan to reform U.S. health-care system.

Sept. 26, 1994 After a year of fierce debate, Senate leaders declare Clinton's bill dead.

1996 Congress enacts Health Insurance Portability and Accountability Act to make employer-provided coverage transferable between jobs and more accessible to the self-employed.

1997 Congress enacts State Children's Health Insurance Program (SCHIP) to help states cover children from low-income families.

2000s *As health costs and the ranks of the uninsured rise, Congress mulls new tax deductions and credits to help consumers buy coverage; interest grows in compulsory insurance.*

2002 Congress enacts Health Care Tax Credit, available to those who lose their jobs due to foreign competition.

2006 Massachusetts enacts universal-coverage plan requiring all residents to buy health insurance. . . . Vermont enacts voluntary coverage plan with subsidized insurance and medical cost trimming. . . . Maryland plan to force large employers to supply coverage or pay into a state insurance pool is struck down in federal court.

2007 President Bush proposes replacing the tax break received by those with employer-based coverage with a tax deduction available to everyone. . . . Gov. Arnold Schwarzenegger, R-Calif., proposes universal, state-subsidized health insurance. . . . Advocates press Congress to expand SCHIP to more children and parents.

Looking Into the Future of Health Coverage

New proposals offer new approaches

With the number of uninsured Americans creeping inexorably upward, universal coverage is likely to become a hot political issue in the 2008 presidential campaign. While former Sen. John Edwards, D-N.C., is the only candidate to have offered a specific plan so far, the state and federal plans being considered contain some new wrinkles that might help policymakers reach a compromise on how to expand coverage.

Massachusetts — A 2006 state law requires all residents to buy insurance, beginning this year, or pay a penalty. Massachusetts will subsidize premiums for those earning under 300 percent of poverty level (about $60,000 for a family of four) and waive the coverage requirement if no "affordable" policies are available.

Coverage will be sold through a state-operated market, the Massachusetts Health Insurance Connector, and the state is negotiating with insurers to get affordable premiums for comprehensive policies, something that's proven to be more of an uphill struggle than lawmakers imagined.

"Massachusetts decided consciously not to grapple with rising health-care costs and decided to do it later," says Paul Ginsburg, president of the Center for Studying Health System Change, a nonpartisan research group. "Now they're having a problem with the bids coming in higher than expected."

That decision may have doomed the plan, says Robert Laszewski, a consultant and former insurance executive. Annual health-insurance premiums for the average Massachusetts family had already reached $15,000 a few years ago — higher than the current national family average of $12,000 — in part because of the state's high-cost

academic medical centers and plethora of physicians, he points out. "Yet the Massachusetts legislature came up with $200 a month" — $2,400 a year — "as a reasonable premium for their plan," he laments. "The chances that the law will ever be implemented are slim."

California — In January, Gov. Arnold Schwarzenegger unveiled a universal-coverage plan that also would require all residents to buy a minimal level of coverage. Public programs would be expanded to cover the lowest-income Californians, and subsidies would help others buy private insurance.

Insurers would offer policies to all comers, at state-approved rates. Employers with 10 or more workers would pay at least 4 percent of payroll for health insurance or pay that amount into a state pool. To trim costs, insurers would be required to spend at least 85 percent of every premium dollar on patient care.

To entice more hospitals and doctors to participate in California's subsidized Medi-Cal program, the state would increase payments to participating providers. This would also eliminate what Schwarzenegger calls the "hidden tax" — low public-program payments and uncompensated care for uninsured people that providers now pass along as higher prices to paying patients. The Medi-Cal pay boost would be funded by a tax on non-participant doctors and hospitals.

Some employers are skeptical of the plan, which must be approved by the California legislature. The plan would help companies that already provide health benefits because it would force their competitors to ante up for health care also, said Scott Hauge, president of the advocacy group Small Business California. But that could be perceived as

antibiotics and few effective drugs, and X-rays had been discovered only in 1895. Most of the financial burden from illness was due to lost wages, so insurers sold income-protection "sickness" or "accident" insurance.

The first such policy was sold in 1850 by the Massachusetts-based Franklin Health Assurance Company. For a 15-cent premium, the policy paid $200 if its holder was injured in a railway or steamboat accident.[47]

Some employers offered sickness insurance as a worker benefit. In 1910, the catalog store Montgomery

Ward and Co. established a group insurance plan to pay half of an ill or injured employee's salary.[48] In 1918, the Dallas, Texas, school system established sickness insurance to protect teachers against impoverishment during the great influenza epidemic.[49]

The mining, railway, and lumber industries led the way in establishing insurance plans more similar to modern HMOs (health maintenance organizations), paying medical costs. Their workers faced serious health risks and labored in remote locations where traditional care wasn't

unfair by some companies with young workers, whose "invincibility-of-youth syndrome" means they'd prefer cash to health benefits they believe they don't need, he said.[1]

Insurers are expected to balk at being forced to spend 85 percent of premiums on patient care, says Laszewski. "Wellpoint, California's biggest [for-profit] insurer, puts 80 cents on the dollar toward care, holding on to a full 20 cents for profits and administration," he says. Nevertheless, "everybody knows that it can be done for less. In Medicare, 95 cents on every dollar goes to patient care."

President George W. Bush — The president wants to replace the current unlimited government subsidy for employer-sponsored health coverage with a flat standard deduction available to everyone who buys at least catastrophic health coverage on their own or through an employer. Federal funds would be available for states to improve their markets for individual health policies, where people would shop for non-workplace coverage.

Economists praise Bush for proposing to replace the government's current subsidy for health insurance — the exclusion from taxable wages of employer-sponsored coverage — with more widely available assistance. But some critics on both the left and right agree the proposal doesn't target the people most in need of subsidies and doesn't help create enough affordable coverage for them to buy.

"Replacing the current tax treatment with a new standard deduction is a big step in the right direction," said Heritage Foundation Vice President Stuart M. Butler and Senior Policy Analyst Nina Owcharenko.

Former Sen. John Edwards, D-N.C., is the first presidential candidate to propose a detailed universal health-care plan.

Nevertheless, "an even better step would be to replace it with a tax credit," which would help lower-income families who are least likely to have insurance, they said. Unlike tax credits, which benefit everyone equally, Bush's proposed deduction has a much higher dollar value for higher-income people.[2]

The Edwards plan — The presidential candidate also proposes an individual mandate, but the requirement would only kick in once new, affordable coverage options are available and employers are either contributing to a general pool or helping their own workers buy coverage through new, regional nonprofit purchasing pools known as "health markets." The federal government would help states or groups of states set up such health markets, which would offer a choice of competing health policies. Unlike most current proposals, the health markets would offer all buyers — in addition to private coverage — a public-insurance plan modeled on Medicare.

"Let's have real competition between public and private systems," says Yale University Professor of Political Science Jacob Hacker, who consulted with Edwards on the proposal. "If you put a level playing field between the public and private sectors" — as in the health markets — the public programs "might turn out to be cheaper. If that happens over time, people would vote with their feet," he says.

[1] Renuka Rayasam, "Schwarzenegger Health Plan Raises Doubts." *U.S. News & World Report*, Jan. 10, 2007, www.usnews.com/usnews/biztech/smallbizscene/070110/schwarzenegger_health_plan_rai.htm.

[2] Stuart M. Butler and Nina Owcharenko, "Making Health Care Affordable: Bush's Bold Health Tax Reform Plan," *WebMemo No. 1316*, Heritage Foundation, Jan. 22, 2007.

available. So companies established clinics that prepaid doctors fixed monthly fees to provide care.

Nevertheless, between 1910 and 1920, near the end of the so-called Progressive Era in American politics, "government-sponsored health insurance seemed a practical possibility in the United States," according to the University of Pennsylvania's Stevens. In 1920, expert panels in four large states — California, New Jersey, Ohio and New York — recommended universal state-sponsored health insurance.[50]

However, doctors, hospitals and insurance companies feared if universal coverage was adopted they would lose control and cash. The chairman of Ohio's commission complained about "the confusion into which the public mind had been thrown by the misleading, malicious and false statements emanating from an interested and active commercial insurance opposition."[51]

Soon, popular support for government-sponsored insurance dropped to a low level again, as financial worry receded in the 1920s economic boom. In the overall

Stakeholder Groups May Balk at Changes

They fear paying more, losing coverage

As costs and the ranks of the uninsured soar, there's plenty not to like about the current health-care system. Nevertheless, many longtime stakeholders fear change. As has often happened in the past, insurance companies, health providers, employers and those with expansive work-based health coverage all may balk at the changes universal coverage may bring.

"You often see interest groups wearing a cloak of ideology," saying they oppose a reform plan on economic or philosophical grounds when they're really protecting their money, says Stanley Dorn, a senior research associate at the liberal Urban Institute.

For example, he says, during the bitter debate over President Bill Clinton's universal-coverage plan in the early 1990s, "you had companies that didn't provide insurance to their workers and knew they could lose money" if the proposal succeeded. "But they didn't talk about that. They talked about how evil it would be for the government to take over the health system."

Various employer groups are likely to weigh in on both sides of the debate. Those who offer health coverage as a benefit today are more likely to embrace the change, although they may still be hesitant to endorse all universal-coverage proposals, says Paul Ginsburg, president of the Center for Studying Health System Change, a nonpartisan research group. "They'd like to get out of the business of coverage long term, but the issue has always been whether they'd end up paying more in taxes" for a new universal coverage system than they spend now to provide benefits, he says.

Large, unionized employers like U.S. automakers initially supported the Clinton plan in 1993, said Walter Mahan, former vice president for public policy of DaimlerChrysler Corp.[1] Employers who didn't offer health benefits strongly opposed the Clinton plan, which, like many universal-coverage plans today, asked all businesses to chip in, including those that didn't offer health benefits before.

Caught somewhat off guard by ferocious opposition from businesses that didn't offer coverage — like restaurants and soda manufacturers — architects of the Clinton plan reduced the payments required from companies that had not previously offered coverage and hiked the amount asked from employers who offered coverage. Complaining of unfairness, unionized employers then pulled their support, said Mahan. The bad news for the new crop of reformers:

prosperity of that decade, the medical system flourished, and hospitals built new wings in the mood of general optimism.

By 1929, however, more than a third of hospital beds were empty, and many hospitals struggled to pay off the loans that had funded expansion. Baylor University Hospital in Dallas, for example, had $1.5 million in overdue loan payments for construction and was behind in other bills. "Baylor was just 30 days ahead of the sheriff," said one observer.[52] Baylor's crisis led to health insurance as we know it today.

In search of cash, Baylor made common cause with local employers. In late 1929, the Dallas school system set up a hospital-service prepayment plan that operated alongside its sick-benefit fund. For a monthly premium of 50 cents, teachers would get free hospitalization for 21 days and a one-third discount on additional days. Benefits became effective on Dec. 20, 1929, less than two months after the stock market crash.[53]

A few days later, elementary-school teacher Alma Dickson slipped on an icy sidewalk and broke her ankle.[54] Hospitalized with a cast, Dickson became the first patient in the first prepaid hospitalization plan, the forerunner of today's Blue Cross system.[55]

By 1935, 19 such plans had been created in 13 states, as hospitals struggled to stay afloat during the Great Depression.[56]

But many influential physicians argued that "prepayment" threatened professional independence. Recommendations that the nation adopt insurance to protect people against the rising cost of care amounted to "socialism and communism — inciting to revolution," wrote Morris Fishbein, editor of the *Journal of the American Medical Association.*[57]

Workplace Plans

During the 1930s, as businesses folded and millions sank into poverty, the United States made its largest-ever foray in social insurance.

More and more companies have been dropping coverage since then, so the constituency of businesses not offering coverage "is stronger now," he said.[2]

Insurers may have the biggest stake in the current system. Most analysts say proposals that would abolish private insurance in favor of a government-run universal plan modeled on Medicare are politically impossible today. However, most reform plans would force insurers to cover potentially sicker beneficiaries than most do today and would tighten rules for selling and marketing insurance policies.

Many insurers mistrust changes because the current employer-based system works well for them by weeding out the sickest populations, said former Rep. William Thomas, R-Calif., who chaired the House Ways and Means Committee. Employed people "have to get up every morning, go to work and carry out difficult and complex tasks." They're essentially prescreened to be, on average, healthier than the general population and thus easier to cover and still earn profits, he said.[3]

Insurers also distrust government-run "insurance exchanges" in many universal-coverage plans that would establish standard benefit packages, ensure affordability and replace insurers' marketing with government-scrutinized plan descriptions. Insurers have "traditionally hated" government limits on their marketing, says Dorn.

Finally, virtually all economists say any health system reform must include cost cutting, including reining in salaries and profits of doctors, hospitals and drug manufacturers. Some proposals ask providers to put money in up front to support coverage proposals. Providers always push back against such steps.

For example, when Democratic Maine Gov. John Baldacci unveiled a universal-coverage program in 2003, he included a tax on insurance premiums along with both voluntary and mandatory price caps on many health services, without which the governor said the program could not survive. Maine's hospitals said they couldn't survive having prices capped.

"That cannot happen . . . without irreparably harming Maine's hospitals," said Warren Kessler, a consultant and former head of the Maine General Medical Center in Augusta.[4]

Finally, those who currently have good coverage are sensitive to any proposal that might make their own insurance worse or cost more. Interest groups like insurers and doctors who oppose any new plan "just have to play on the public's fear of losing what they now have," says Dorn.

---

[1] "Universal Coverage: It Can't Happen Here . . . Or Can It?" *Medicine & Health Perspectives*, March 31, 2003.

[2] Quoted in *ibid.*

[3] Quoted in "Thomas Takes Aim Again at Tax-Favored Employer Coverage," *Medicine & Health*, Feb. 16, 2004.

[4] Quoted in "Baldacci Says Everyone Must Give a Little to Fund Care," *Medicine & Health*, May 12, 2003.

Developed by Democratic President Franklin D. Roosevelt and enacted in 1935, Social Security is a mandatory, universal system that provides income support for retirees, severely disabled people, widows and under-age bereaved children. During the debate over passage, activists argued for including health insurance, but the administration declined, in part because it feared the contentious health issue might doom the whole plan.[58]

Later, members of Congress made unsuccessful attempts to extend social-insurance to health in 1943, 1945, 1947, 1949 and 1957. Nevertheless, by 1966, 81 percent of Americans had hospitalization insurance — mostly offered through their workplaces and often as a result of labor union demands — compared to only 9 percent in 1940.[59]

Unlike today, from 1940 to 1966 large unionized companies dominated the economy. Offered as a worker benefit, employer-sponsored health plans successfully pooled the risk and contributions of many employees in order to keep individuals' costs low and uniform, even in years when they had accidents or illness. And, since the sickest people are unlikely to be employed, relying on workplace-based plans allowed private insurers to more easily predict and control costs.

As the primary source of Americans' health insurance, the still union-dominated U.S. auto industry has evolved over the years into "a social-insurance system that sells cars to finance itself," said Princeton University economics Professor Uwe Reinhardt.[60]

But even in the early days, employer-provided insurance had limits. Many retired people, very low-income families and the disabled never had workplace-based insurance and were too poor to buy individual policies, for which they would be charged premiums based on health status.

After several years of debate, Congress in 1965 enacted a new compulsory, universal insurance plan — the Medicare program — to provide health coverage for elderly and some disabled people and Medicaid to provide health care for the poorest mothers with children, elderly and the disabled.

Coverage Declines

With Medicare and Medicaid in place, most Americans had access to health care.

Nevertheless, health spending was rising sharply, and Presidents Richard M. Nixon and Jimmy Carter both proposed reforms to keep care affordable, including universal coverage. Neither plan gained traction, however.

Gradually, the higher costs and the changed nature of American business began to erode the work-based insurance system.

"Forty years ago, the largest private employer was AT&T, a regulated monopoly with guaranteed profits," wrote Stanford University Professor Emeritus Victor Fuchs and Ezekiel Emanuel, chairman of clinical bioethics at the National Institutes of Health. "If health-insurance premiums rose, they could easily be passed on to telephone subscribers."[61]

That changed, however, as union membership began declining in the 1980s, and manufacturing jobs began migrating overseas and U.S. companies had to compete with foreign competitors that don't offer health benefits. More and more Americans ended up working in the largely non-unionized service industry, which offered few benefits.

"Today, the largest private employer is Wal-Mart, which despite its size faces intense competition daily from a host of other retail outlets," Fuchs and Emanuel wrote. "When they offer health insurance, it must come out of their workers' wages; for minimum-wage employees, this is not possible."[62]

Over the past two decades, employer-sponsored coverage has gradually waned, along with the number of insured Americans. Government programs have grown and picked up some of the slack, however.

In 1987, fully 87.1 percent of Americans were insured, with 75.7 percent insured through private, mostly employer-sponsored, coverage. By 1999, the percentage of insured Americans had dropped to 85.5.percent, 71.8 percent through private coverage. In 2005, the overall percentage had dropped to 84.1 percent — 67.7 percent with private insurance.[63] (*See graph, p. 282.*)

In the face of declining coverage, proposals to expand coverage have been advanced repeatedly by the White House, members of Congress, state and local governments and others. Only some small-scale efforts have gone anywhere, however.

In 1994, Tennessee used federal Medicaid dollars and state funding to create TennCare. State officials hoped money-saving HMOs could provide coverage to many lower-income people and sicker Tennesseans, who were ineligible for Medicaid and couldn't afford insurance on their own.

For a few years, the program saved money and enrolled 500,000 residents who would otherwise have been uninsured. But the federal government had agreed to contribute funding for only 1.5 million people, and when enrollment exceeded that cap, TennCare refused to accept new applicants and struggled financially. For the past several years, TennCare has fought to survive, plagued by charges of poor care at its HMOs and disputes with the federal government over funds.

Clinton Plan

The highest-profile recent effort to enact a universal health care plan was President Bill Clinton's ambitious proposal to restructure the nation's health care system, unveiled on Sept. 22, 1993. His Health Security Act was proposed at a time when the uninsured ranks had swelled to 40 million, and polls showed that up to two-thirds of Americans favored tax-financed national health insurance.[64] Yet, within a year Senate Democrats had pronounced the plan dead, the victim of bruising attacks by business, insurers and medical providers.[65]

Five days after his inauguration, Clinton announced that first lady Hillary Rodham Clinton would chair a health-care task force made up of Cabinet members and White House staffers. It held hearings for a year and produced a plan to attain universal coverage mainly through expanded private coverage. It aimed to offer people a choice of affordable coverage while maintaining the existing private insurance industry and holding down health-cost growth.

To do that, the Clinton panel proposed creating regional government-managed insurance markets to negotiate health-care and premium prices and insurance-benefit packages and to oversee insurance marketing. It also called for annual caps on health-coverage cost increases, and a requirement that all employers contribute to the cost of coverage.

But opposition soon grew from businesses that believed they had more to lose than to gain from change. Employers who didn't offer coverage balked at proposed fees to help finance the plan. Insurers objected to regulations aimed at keeping them from skimming off healthy customers. After 10 months of strenuous campaigns by opponents, public approval had dropped to a lukewarm 40 percent.[66] (*See sidebar, p. 288.*)

Former first lady Clinton — now the Democratic senator from New York who is running for president — has assured voters she still believes in universal health coverage, but she has not yet announced a specific plan. "I think she's learned her lesson" and likely will propose something "not quite as big and ambitious" this time, says Brandeis' Altman.

For the next decade the dramatic failure of the Clinton plan frightened lawmakers away from the issue, while conservative lawmakers said the booming 1990s economy would enable the United States to "grow its way" out of uninsurance by creating more and better jobs with coverage benefits.

But that did not turn out to be the case. From 1997 to 2001, the economy boomed and jobs were created, but rates of employer-sponsored health insurance did not rise. The late '90s experience "tells us that relying on economic growth alone to reduce the number of uninsured won't work," said Ginsburg at the Center for Studying Health System Change.[67]

Since Clinton's efforts, Congress enacted two coverage expansions. The State Children's Health Insurance Program (SCHIP) was enacted in 1997. The Clinton administration and a bipartisan group of lawmakers led by Sens. Edward M. Kennedy, D-Mass., and Orrin G. Hatch, R-Utah, gave states federal matching funds to expand coverage for children in low-income families. Today, SCHIP operates in all states, making nearly all otherwise uninsured children with family incomes up to twice the poverty level eligible for public coverage.

With Republicans dominating the White House and Congress, most recent debate over coverage has focused on tax incentives to help Americans buy insurance. Criticized by lawmakers of both parties for offering too-small tax breaks in its early proposals, the Bush administration has gradually expanded its plan each year but has seen none enacted.

The only federal health-coverage expansion enacted in this decade was a tax credit to assist workers unemployed due to competition from international trade, enacted in 2002 after a long contentious delay. But the credit has reached only 10 to 20 percent of those eligible for it, says the Urban Institute's Dorn, which he calls a "tragic" outcome for states like North Carolina, where it was intended to help people facing "the largest layoff in the state's history — the closing of the textile mills."

The program failed to catch on because its premiums are too high, he says. "It's not realistic to ask people to pay 35 percent of premiums when they're not working" when working people pay only 15 to 25 percent of theirs, he says. In addition, the tax credit in most states could only be used for individual policies, whose premiums generally are based on age and health status. "Even with a 65 percent subsidy, people were facing an unaffordable $1,000 a month premium."

Over the past decade, some congressional Republicans also have proposed allowing business and professional groups to offer association health plans (AHPs), which would enable small businesses and the self-employed to band together to buy health insurance free from the state regulations that apply to individual and small-group insurance plans, which AHP advocates say unduly drive up coverage costs for small business.

In the 1970s Congress waived state insurance regulation for large employers to encourage them to provide coverage for workers. But today both Democratic and some Republican lawmakers staunchly oppose allowing AHPs the same freedom. AHP opponents argue that it is too easy for such loosely formed groups to skim off workers most likely to be healthy and low-cost, which would raise premium costs even higher for those left behind.

Meanwhile, outside of legislative chambers advocates increasingly have been calling for universal coverage. In 2004, a three-year-long Institute of Medicine study declared that eroding coverage poses such a threat that the federal government must launch a "firm and explicit" plan to achieve universal coverage by 2010.[68]

Many analysts agree that universal coverage has been stalled not because of a lack of knowledge of how to accomplish it but because lawmakers lack the will to demand sacrifices. (*See sidebar, p. 280.*)

There are "at least four ways" to get universal coverage, says Simmons of the National Coalition on Health Care. "This problem is solvable. It does not require atomic science."

CURRENT SITUATION

Interest Grows

A few states are moving forward with universal-coverage plans, but little action is expected on Capitol Hill this year. Meanwhile, all Democratic contenders for the 2008 presidential nomination have advocated universal coverage, although only former Sen. Edwards has offered a specific plan so far. (*See sidebar, p. 286.*)

While few expect federal action until after the next president takes office in 2009, many Washington hands think the tide finally may be turning.

"One big difference between now and several years ago is that there is a loss of faith in employer-provided coverage as capable of covering everyone, including from unions and key business groups" who have been its strongest supporters, says Yale's Hacker.

Coalitions of interest groups have come together in 2007 to announce support for universal coverage. In January, the Health Coverage Coalition for the Uninsured (HCCU) advocated a phased-in approach to universal coverage, beginning with an expansion of SCHIP and creation of tax credits for families with incomes up to about $60,000, and then creating similar programs for childless adults.[69]

The coalition includes groups that have traditionally sparred over health care, including Families USA, the retiree organization AARP, the American Medical Association, the American Hospital Association and the health-insurance lobby America's Health Insurance Plans. "Organizations that have never spoken to one another in a friendly manner are now talking about this, and that has transformed the debate," says Pollack of Families USA.

Others aren't convinced. The HCCU's "rhetoric was wonderful," says Altman of Brandeis. "But the result shows how little they actually agree on."

But Pollack says the coalition's proposal is a "sequential" plan that will follow expansion of the children's program — expected to be enacted this year — with a move to universal coverage after that.

In February the Service Employees International Union joined with Wal-Mart, an employer whose limited health benefits have been sharply criticized by the union, to form the Better Health Care Together group, calling for "quality, affordable" universal health care by 2012. The group plans a national summit this spring to rally support but has not announced a proposal, saying only that it supports joint public and private-sector efforts.[70]

But Dana Rezaie, a Wal-Mart shelf stocker in Fridley, Minn., says, "anybody can say they support something. They need to show they really do." After six years at the store, the widowed mother of three says she can't afford Wal-Mart's health plan.[71]

Congress is reviewing President Bush's fiscal 2008 budget, which proposes a new version of his tax-based coverage-expansion proposals. Bush would ditch the current tax break Americans receive for employer-sponsored coverage and replace it with a more general tax break that would apply both to employer coverage and to insurance purchased individually.

The plan gets points from Greenstein at the Center on Budget and Policy Priorities for tackling the unfairness of the current tax treatment of insurance, which penalizes those who purchase insurance on their own. But the plan "has an Achilles' heel," Greenstein says, since it doesn't encourage pooling sicker and healthier people to spread costs and skews its tax benefits toward higher-income people.

Nevertheless, Pollack does not expect "a serious productive debate on universal coverage" in 2007, with a presidential campaign heating up. However, he does expect Congress to reauthorize — and possibly expand — the 10-year-old SCHIP program "before the end of the calendar year."

The Bush budget recommends funding SCHIP leanly, by not offering federal assistance, for example, to the 14 states anticipating shortfalls in their 2007 SCHIP budgets. But both political parties strongly support SCHIP and are likely to ride to the rescue. Sen. Gordon Smith, R-Ore., has called for doubling the federal cigarette tax to pay for the aid.[72]

State Steps

As health insurance gains momentum as a public issue, many states are flirting with expanding coverage, and three are struggling to get universal coverage off the ground.

Massachusetts was first out of the gate, enacting a plan in 2006 that will require residents to buy health insurance, often with government assistance. A state-operated clearinghouse — the Health Insurance Connector — will help consumers comparison-shop for affordable coverage. So

Should Congress enact President Bush's tax proposal for expanding health coverage?

YES

Stuart M. Butler, Vice President
Nina Owcharenko, Senior Policy Analyst
The Heritage Foundation

From the foundation's Web site, January 2007

President Bush's proposal to reform the tax treatment of health care takes a bold step toward fixing America's health system by widening the availability of affordable and "portable" health plans and by defusing some of the pressure that currently leads to higher health costs.

Although some Americans would have more of their compensation subject to taxes, this proposal is no more a tax increase than limiting or ending tax deductions to move toward a flatter tax system. It would remove distortions and inequities and make tax relief for health insurance more widely available.

While the proposal can be improved in ways that would further reduce uninsurance, it is a big step toward sound tax and health policy. It would treat all Americans equally by ending the tax discrimination against families who buy their own health insurance, either because they do not have insurance offered by employers or because they prefer other coverage.

Ending that discrimination would have the added advantage of stimulating wider choice and greater competition in health coverage, which will help moderate the growth in costs. It would also make it easier for families to keep their chosen plan from job to job, reducing the loss of coverage that often accompanies job changes.

The president's proposal could be improved. While replacing the tax treatment with a new standard deduction is a big step in the right direction, an even better step would be to replace it with a tax credit more like the current child tax credit — at least for those buying health coverage outside their place of work. A tax credit would especially help lower-income families. With a deduction, many families would still be unable to afford basic coverage, but a credit set at a flat dollar amount or a high percentage of premium costs would make coverage more affordable.

A tax credit could be grafted onto the president's current proposal and would strengthen it considerably.

By taking this step, Congress can help make the tax treatment of health care more equitable and efficient, help more Americans choose the coverage they want and retain it from job to job and begin to reduce the tax-break-induced pressure that is a factor in rising health costs.

NO

Karen Davis
President, The Commonwealth Fund

From the fund's Web site, January 2007

While it is encouraging that President Bush made health care a theme of the State of the Union address, his proposal to offer tax deductions to those who buy health insurance would do little to cover the nation's 45 million uninsured.

Under the president's proposal, Americans with employer-provided health insurance would have the employer contribution counted as taxable income. But anyone with health coverage — whether provided by an employer or purchased individually — would have the first $7,500 of income excluded from income and payroll taxes or, in the case of families, the first $15,000 of income.

Those purchasing coverage in the individual market would get a new tax break, as would those whose employer contribution currently is less than the new standard deduction for health insurance.

The proposal would increase taxes on workers whose employers contribute more to health insurance than the premium "cap" allows, such as those that serve a large number of older workers. The administration estimates this change would translate into a tax increase for about 20 percent of employees. However, this could rise to more than half of employees by 2013, if increases in health-insurance premiums continue to outpace general inflation. In addition, the president proposes diverting federal funds from public hospitals to state programs for the uninsured.

Although the plan would offer subsidies to people looking to buy insurance on the private market, it would fail to assist most of the uninsured. Insurance premiums would still be unaffordable for Americans with modest or low incomes. And the tax increase for employees would likely lead to the erosion of employer-sponsored health insurance over time.

The proposal wouldn't do anything to make individual coverage available or affordable for those with modest incomes or health problems. The Commonwealth Fund found that one-fifth of people who had sought coverage in the individual health-insurance market in the last three years were denied coverage because of health problems or were charged a higher premium. The proposal, unlike plans in California and Massachusetts, does not require insurers to cover everyone.

Nor would the proposal likely help the currently uninsured. More than 55 percent of the uninsured have such low incomes that they pay no taxes, while another 40 percent are in the 10-to-15-percent tax bracket and would not benefit substantially from the tax deductions.

far, however, the state is struggling to define benefit packages that insurers can sell at "affordable" prices.

Meanwhile, the California legislature is considering Gov. Schwarzenegger's proposal to require individuals to buy coverage. The plan would be funded with contributions from multiple sources, including government, individuals, employers, insurers and health-care providers.

Vermont's new Catamount Health program will focus first on promoting information technology and other reforms to shave administrative costs and an evidence-based standard of care "community by community," says Emory University's Thorpe, who consulted on the program. Then the state will turn to expanding coverage.

In Texas, where more than 25 percent of the population is uninsured, Republican Gov. Rick Perry is looking for revenue sources to subsidize more coverage. In February he proposed selling off the state lottery and putting part of the proceeds in an endowment fund to expand insurance coverage.[73]

Last year, Rhode Island began requiring insurers to develop "wellness benefit" policies to help individuals and small businesses afford at least basic coverage.[74]

OUTLOOK

Health Politics

Consensus has been building around proposals that link public subsidies to private coverage. But it remains an open question whether Congress will finally enact a universal-coverage plan, which undoubtedly would shift some resources and benefits away from currently insured people and health providers.

Some interest groups that helped bring down the Clinton plan have softened their stance, says Ginsburg at the Center for Studying Health System Change. In Massachusetts, he points out, insurers have accepted the new state-run insurance marketplace, even though in the past they would have preferred to send out their own people to market policies and avoid head-to-head consumer comparisons of plans. But insurers realize that their long-time bread and butter — employer-sponsored coverage — "has topped out," Ginsburg says, so they anticipate no growth unless they embrace government-sponsored expansions.

"There's [been] a dramatic change in national political attitudes," says Simmons of the National Coalition on Health Care. One "truly remarkable thing is that every Democratic and some Republican candidates now say we have to achieve universal coverage."

But others say the country may still not be ready to make the concessions needed.

"It's not clear to me that life has changed very much," says Altman of Brandeis. Forces that have resisted change in the past "are stronger today," and "you have very weak leadership" from the White House and Congress.

Endorsement by Democratic presidential hopefuls doesn't necessarily mean much, says Harvard's Blendon. "Democratic primary voters disproportionately care about this," he says. But different priorities will prevail in the general election. "The biggest thing on everyone's mind is casualties in Iraq."

Furthermore, Americans generally "do not want an alternative health system," he continues. "They want to fix the one they have."

Unfortunately for politicians, the simplest, catchiest sound bite on health reform involves covering the uninsured, but that doesn't "play politically," says Blendon. While people do want everyone to have access to health care, "what they want most is cheaper premiums for themselves."

NOTES

1. Jay Himmelstein, "Bleeding-Edge Benefits," *Health Affairs*, November/December 2006, p. 1656.

2. Jeffrey A. Rhoades, "The Uninsured in America, 2004: Estimates for the U.S. Civilian Non-institutionalized Population Under Age 65," *Medical Expenditure Panel Survey Statistical Brief #83*, June 2005, Agency for Healthcare Research and Quality.

3. Diane Rowland, executive vice president, Henry J. Kaiser Foundation, "Health Care: Squeezing the Middle Class With More Costs and Less Coverage," testimony before House Ways and Means Committee, Jan. 31, 2007; for background, see Keith Epstein, "Covering the Uninsured," *CQ Researcher*, June 14, 2002, pp. 521-544.

4. Christine Borger, *et al.*, "Health Spending Projections Through 2015: Changes on the Horizon," *Health Affairs* Web site, Feb. 22, 2006.

5. Rowland testimony, *op. cit.*

6. "Facts on Health Care Costs," National Coalition on Health Care, www.nchc.org.

7. Quoted in Steven Taub and David Cook, "Health Care Can Bankrupt America," CFO.com, March 6, 2007, For background, see Michael E. Chernew, Richard A. Hirth and David M. Cutler, "Increased Spending on Health Care: How Much Can the United States Afford?" *Health Affairs*, July/August 2003.

8. Todd Gilmer and Richard Kronick, "It's the Premiums, Stupid: Projections of the Uninsured Through 2013," *Health Affairs*, April 5, 2005, www.health affairs.org.

9. *Ibid.*

10. "Coverage Matters: Insurance and Health Care," statement of Arthur L. Kellerman, co-chairman, Consequences of Uninsurance Committee, Institute of Medicine, www7.nationalacademies.org/ocga/ testimony/Uninsured_and_Affordable_Health_ Care_Coverage.asp.

11. Quoted in "IOM Uninsured Report Cites Rising Costs, Attacks Myths." *Medicine & Health*, Oct. 15, 2001.

12. "The Great Divide: When Kids Get Sick, Insurance Matters," Families USA, March 1, 2007, www .familiesusa.org/assets/pdfs/the-great-divide.pdf.

13. "Expanding Coverage Is Worth It for All, IOM Panel Insists," *Medicine & Health*, June 30, 2003.

14. *Ibid.* For background, see Marcia Clemmitt, "Prison Health Care," *CQ Researcher*, Jan. 5, 2007, pp. 1-24.

15. Quoted in "States Scramble for Ways to Cover Working Uninsured," *Medicine & Health*, "Perspectives," Feb. 8, 2005.

16. Barack Obama, "Obama Statement on President's Meeting with Big Three Automakers," press release, Nov. 14, 2006, http://obama.senate.gov.

17. For background, see Marcia Clemmitt, "Rising Health Costs," *CQ Researcher*, April 7, 2006, pp. 289-312.

18. Quoted in "Frist: 100 Percent Coverage Impossible, 93 Percent Not Working So Well Either," *Medicine & Health*, Feb. 9, 2004.

19. Quoted in *ibid.*

20. Quoted in "Who Should Pay for Health Care?" PBS Newshour Extra online, Jan. 19, 2004, www.pbs.org/ newshour/extra/features/jan-june04/uninsured_1-19 .html.

21. Jack Hadley and John Holahan, "The Cost of Care for the Uninsured: What Do We Spend, Who Pays, and What Would Full Coverage Add to Medical Spending?" The Kaiser Commission on Medicaid and the Uninsured, May 10, 2004, p. 5.

22. "Maryland Universal Coverage Plan Estimated to Cost $2.5 Billion," *Healthcare News*, News-Medical. Net, Feb. 21, 2007, www.news-medical.net; also see "How Much Would It Cost to Cover the Uninsured In Minnesota? Preliminary Estimates," Minnesota Department of Health, Health Economics program, July 2006.

23. For background, see Marcia Clemmitt, "Budget Deficit," *CQ Researcher*, Dec. 9, 2005, p. 1029-1052,

24. "Universal Coverage Rx: Tax-Code Changes, Money, Insurance Pools and a Mandates," interview with Jonathan Gruber, "On My Mind: Conversations with Economists," University of Michigan Economic Research Initiative on the Uninsured, www.umich.edu.

25. *Ibid.*

26. "Health Expenditure," Organization for Economic Cooperation and Development, www.oecd.org/doc ument/16/0,2340,en_2649_37407_2085200_1_1_ 1_37407,00.html; also see Rhoades, *op. cit.*

27. See Clemmitt, "Rising Health Costs," *op. cit.*

28. "Pushed to the Edge: The Added Burdens Vulnerable Populations Face When Uninsured," interview with Harold Pollack, "On My Mind: Conversations With Economists," University of Michigan Economic Research Initiative on the Uninsured, www.umich.edu.

29. *Ibid.*

30. John Kitzhaber, "Why Start With the Health Care Crisis?" The Archimedes Movement, www.JoinAM .org.

31. "Access to Healthcare and the Uninsured," National Conference of States Legislatures, www.ncsl.org/ programs/health/h-prmary.htm.

32. Arthur Garson, "Help States Cover the Uninsured," *Roanoke Times*, May 26, 2006.

33. Stuart M. Butler, "The Voinovich-Bingaman Bill: Letting the States Take the Lead in Extending Health Insurance," *Web Memo No. 1128*, The Heritage Foundation, June 15, 2006.

34. George C. Halvorson, Francis J. Crosson and Steve Zatkin, "A Proposal to Cover the Uninsured in California," *Health Affairs*, Dec. 12, 2006, www .healthaffairs.org.

35. Quoted in Christopher Rowland, "Mass. Health Plan Seems Unlikely to Be U.S. Model," *The Boston Globe*, April 14, 2006.

36. *Ibid.*

37. Quoted in "IOM Panel Demands Universal Coverage by 2010," *Medicine & Health*, "Perspectives," Jan. 19, 2004.

38. David Kravitz, "The Individual Mandate Still Sucks," Blue Mass Group, Jan. 30, 2007, www .bluemassgroup.com.

39. Michael D. Tanner, "Individual Mandates for Health Insurance: Slippery Slope to National Health Care," *Policy Analysis No. 565*, Cato Institute, April 5, 2006, www.cato.org.

40. "Problems of Risk and Uncertainty," The Economics of Health Care, Office of Health Economics, p. 26, www.oheschools.org/ohech3pg3.html.

41. Quoted in "Frist: Limit Tax Exclusion for Employer-Based Coverage," *Medicine & Health*, July 19, 2004.

42. *Ibid.*

43. For background, see Anne-Emmanuel Birn, Theodore M. Brown, Elizabeth Fee and Walter J. Lear, "Struggles for National Health Reform in the United States," *American Journal of Public Health*, January 2003, p. 86; Laura A. Scofea, "The Development and Growth of Employer-Provided Health Insurance," *Monthly Labor Review*, March 1994, p. 3; Thomas Bodenheimer, "The Political Divide in Health Care: A Liberal Perspective," *Health Affairs*, November/December 2005, p. 1426.

44. Rosemary Stevens, foreword to Robert Cunningham III and Robert M. Cunningham, Jr., *The Blues: A History of the Blue Cross and Blue Shield System* (1997), p. vii.

45. Bodenheimer, *op. cit.*, p. 1426.

46. *Ibid.*, p. 1432.

47. Scofea, *op. cit.*, p. 3.

48. *Ibid.*

49. Cunningham and Cunningham, *op. cit.*, p. 5.

50. Stevens, *op. cit.*, p. vii.

51. Quoted in Scofea, *op. cit.*

52. Quoted in Cunningham and Cunningham, *op. cit.*, p. 4.

53. *Ibid.*, p. 6.

54. "Dallas School Teachers, 1928," Rootsweb.com; http://freepages.history.rootsweb.com/~jwheat/ teachersdal28.html.

55. Cunningham and Cunningham, *op. cit.*, p. 6. For background, see also "Sickness insurance and group hospitalization," *Editorial Research Reports*, July 9, 1934, from *CQ Researcher Plus Archive*, http:// library.cqpress.com.

56. Scofea, *op. cit.*

57. Quoted in Cunningham and Cunningham, *op. cit.*, p. 18.

58. For background, see "Federal Assistance to the Aged," Nov. 12, 1934, in *Editorial Research Reports*, available from *CQ Researcher Plus Archive*, http:// library.cqpress.com.

59. Cunningham and Cunningham, *op. cit.*

60. Quoted in Danny Hakim, 'Health Costs Soaring, Automakers Are to Begin Labor Talks," *The New York Times*, July 14, 2003, p. C1.

61. Victor R. Fuchs and Ezekiel J. Emanuel, "Health Care Reform: Why? What? When?" *Health Affairs*, November/December 2005, p. 1400.

62. *Ibid.* For background, see Brian Hansen, "Big-Box Stores," *CQ Researcher*, Sept. 10, 2004, pp. 733-756.

63. "Historical Health Insurance Tables," U.S. Census Bureau, www.census.gov.

64. Bridget Harrison, "A Historical Survey of National Health Movements and Public Opinion in the United States," *Journal of the American Medical Association*, March 5, 2003, p. 1163.

65. For background, see "Health-Care Debate Takes Off," *1993 CQ Almanac*, pp. 335-347, and "Clinton's Health Care Plan Laid to Rest," *1994 CQ Almanac*, pp. 319-353.

66. Harrison, *op. cit.*

67. "Rising Tide of Late '90s Lifted Few Uninsured Boats," *Medicine & Health*, Aug. 6, 2002.

68. "IOM Panel Demands Universal Coverage by 2010," *op. cit.*

69. "Unprecedented Alliance of Health Care Leaders Announces Historic Agreement," Health Coverage Coalition for the Uninsured, press release, Jan. 18, 2007, www.coalitionfortheuninsured.org.

70. Dan Caterinicchia, "Rivals Want Health Care for All," *Columbus Dispatch* [Ohio], Feb. 8, 2007.

71. Quoted in *ibid.*

72. Alex Wayne, "War Supplemental To Include Money for Children's Health Insurance Program" *Congressional Quarterly Healthbeat*, Feb. 27, 2007.

73. Quoted in The Associated Press, "Texas Governor Has Funding Idea: Sell the Lottery," *The Washington Post*, Feb. 7, 2007, p. A7.

74. "Rhode Island: Making Affordable, Quality-Focused Health Coverage Available to Small Businesses," *States in Action: A Bimonthly Look at Innovations in Health Policy*, The Commonwealth Fund, January/February 2007.

BIBLIOGRAPHY

Books

Derickson, Alan, *Health Security for All: Dreams of Universal Health Care in America,* **Johns Hopkins University Press, 2005.**
A professor of history at Pennsylvania State University examines the ideas and advocates behind the numerous 20th-century proposals for universal health care in the United States.

Funigello, Philip J., *Chronic Politics: Health Care Security from FDR to George W. Bush,* **University Press of Kansas, 2005.**
A professor emeritus of history at the College of William and Mary describes the politics behind a half-century of failed attempts at major health reform.

Gordon, Colin, *Dead on Arrival: The Politics of Health Care in Twentieth-Century America,* **Princeton University Press, 2003.**
A professor of history at the University of Iowa explains how numerous private interests — from physicians desiring autonomy to employers seeking to cement employer-employee relationships — have helped halt development of universal health coverage in America.

Mayes, Rick, *Universal Coverage: The Elusive Quest for National Health Insurance,* **University of Michigan Press, 2005.**
An assistant professor of public policy at Virginia's University of Richmond explains how politics and earlier policy choices regarding the U.S. health system shape the range of possibilities available for future reforms.

Richmond, Julius B., and Rashi Fein, *The Health Care Mess: How We Got Into It and What It Will Take to Get Out,* **Harvard University Press, 2005.**
Two Harvard Medical School professors recount the history of American medicine and trends in financing health care and conclude that the United States could afford universal health coverage.

Swartz, Katherine, *Reinsuring Health: Why More Middle-Class People Are Uninsured and What Government Can Do,* **Russell Sage Foundation, 2006.**
A professor of health policy and economics at the Harvard School of Public Health argues that more people could buy insurance and coverage would be cheaper if the federal government offered insurance companies financial protection for the highest-cost illnesses.

Articles

Appleby, Julie, "Health Coverage Reform Follows State-by-State Path," *USA Today,* **April 5, 2006.**
States take different approaches to expanding health coverage as worry over lack of insurance grows.

Gladwell, Malcolm, "The Moral Hazard Myth," *The New Yorker,* **Aug. 29, 2005.**
Some fear that large-scale expansion of health coverage would encourage patients to rack up higher amounts of useless health-care spending.

Holt, Matthew, "Policy: Why Is Fixing American Health Care So Difficult?" *The Health Care Blog,* **Oct. 16, 2006; www.thehealthcareblog.com/the_health_care_blog/2006/10/abc_news_why_is.html#comment-2418315.**

An independent health-care consultant — along with blog comments by analysts, businesspeople and members of the public — describes and discusses the interest-group politics that shape the universal-coverage debate.

Holt, Matthew, "Risky Business: Bush's Health Care Plan," *Spot-On Blog,* **Jan. 25, 2007; www.spot-on.com/ archives/holt/2007/01/bush_tax_deductions_and_the_ lo.html.**

An independent health-care consultant explains the concept of risk-pooling for insurance and the current tax break already enjoyed by workers with employer-sponsored coverage.

Reports and Studies

"Covering America: Real Remedies for the Uninsured," Vols. 1 and 2, *Economic and Social Research Institute,* **June 2001 and November 2002.**

Economists assembled by a non-partisan think tank analyze multiple proposals for achieving universal coverage.

"Insuring America's Health: Principles and Recommendations," *Institute of Medicine Committee on the Consequences of Uninsurance, National Academies Press,* **2004.**

In its sixth and final report, an expert panel urges federal lawmakers to create a plan for insuring the entire population by 2010.

Burton, Alice, Isabel Friedenzoh and Enrique Martinez-Vidal, "State Strategies to Expand Health Insurance Coverage: Trends and Lessons for Policymakers," *The Commonwealth Fund,* **January 2007.**

Analysts summarize recent state initiatives to extend health coverage to more adults and children.

Haase, Leif Wellington, *A New Deal for Health: How to Cover Everyone and Get Medical Costs Under Control, The Century Foundation,* **April 2005.**

A health analyst for the nonprofit group outlines cost, quality and coverage issues that the group says make it necessary for the United States to switch to universal coverage.

For More Information

Alliance for Health Reform, 1444 I St., N.W., Suite 910, Washington, DC 20005; (202) 789-2300; www .allhealth.org. Nonpartisan, nonprofit group that disseminates information about policy options for expanding coverage.

Economic Research Institute on the Uninsured, www. umich.edu/~eriu. Researchers at the University of Michigan who conduct economic analyses of the hows and whys of uninsurance and coverage-expansion proposals.

Families USA, 1201 New York Ave., N.W., Suite 1100, Washington, DC 20005; (202) 628-3030; www.familie-susa.org/contact-us.html. A nonprofit group that advocates for large-scale expansion of affordable health coverage.

The Health Care Blog, www.thehealthcareblog.com. Blog published by health-care consultant Matthew Holt; analyzes coverage proposals and other insurance issues.

Heritage Foundation, 214 Massachusetts Ave., N.E., Washington, DC 20002-4999; (202) 546-4400; www .heritage.org. Conservative think tank that supports state-organized purchasing groups for health care.

Kaiser Family Foundation, 1330 G St., N.W., Washington, DC 20005; (202) 347-5270; www.kff.org. Nonprofit private foundation that collects data and conducts research on the uninsured.

National Coalition on Health Care, 1200 G St., N.W., Suite 750, Washington, DC 20005; (202) 638-7151; www .nchc.org. Nonprofit, nonpartisan group that supports universal coverage; made up of labor, business and consumer groups, insurers and health providers' associations.

Physicians for a National Health Program, 29 E. Madison, Suite 602, Chicago, IL 60602; (312) 782-6006; www.pnhp.org. Nonprofit group that advocates for single-payer national health insurance.

13

Wounded Veterans

Is America Shortchanging Vets on Health Care?

Peter Katel

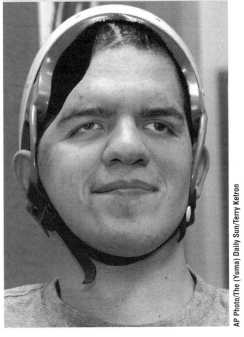

U.S. Army Sgt. Frank Sandoval, 27, died in June after struggling for nearly two years to recover from a massive head injury. Traumatic brain injury (TBI) has been called the signature wound of the Iraq War because of the numerous roadside bombs and rocket-propelled grenades used against U.S. troops. Critics have blasted the Veterans Affairs Department for being unprepared to deal with the large number of TBI patients and their families.

AP Photo/The (Yuma) Daily Sun/Terry Ketron

From *CQ Researcher*,
August 31, 2007.

S gt. Garrett Anderson of the Illinois National Guard lost his right arm in Iraq. But after coming home, he faced another battle — with the Department of Veterans Affairs (VA).

Anderson also suffers from traumatic brain injury and is riddled with shrapnel, but the VA rated him 90 percent disabled, although VA guidelines call for a 100 percent disability rating. Incredibly, his evaluation report said, "Shrapnel injury not related to combat."

Anderson laughed at first. Then he got angry. "After everything I went through, this is the last thing I wanted to happen," he says. The 90 percent rating meant disability payments of $1,600 a month instead of $2,600 (plus relief from paying property taxes).

Clearly, Anderson hadn't joined the Guard with a body full of shrapnel. But the VA said shrapnel wasn't mentioned in his battle-care records.

Well, no wonder, says L. Tammy Duckworth, director of Illinois' Department of Veterans Affairs, "They were too busy saving his life!"

Anderson finally got his 100 percent rating after he, his wife and top Illinois politicians spent nearly a year appealing the VA. (*See sidebar, p. 314.*)

Anderson is one of many veterans forced to run a benefits obstacle course through the VA bureaucracy. But in early 2007, a devastating exposé in *The Washington Post* revealed new problems being faced by wounded veterans of the fighting in Iraq and Afghanistan.[1] At Walter Reed Army Medical Center, just a few miles from the Capitol, recovering outpatient vets were coping with moldy, vermin-infested outpatient housing and overworked, sometimes incompetent, staff.[2]

Record Number of Troops Wounded in Iraq

An unprecedented number of American soldiers have been injured in the fighting in Iraq and Afghanistan compared with the number killed — by far the highest killed-to-wounded ratio in U.S. military history. More than 50,500 soldiers suffered non-mortal wounds and more than 3,000 were killed — a ratio of 16 wounded for every fatality. The high number of wounded reflects the effectiveness of military medicine as well as the widespread use of IEDs (improvised explosive devices) and similar anti-personnel weapons.

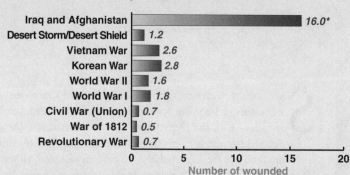

Number of Wounded Soldiers per Fatality in Major American Wars

War	Number of wounded
Iraq and Afghanistan	16.0*
Desert Storm/Desert Shield	1.2
Vietnam War	2.6
Korean War	2.8
World War II	1.6
World War I	1.8
Civil War (Union)	0.7
War of 1812	0.5
Revolutionary War	0.7

* Using the Pentagon's narrower definition of wounded personnel, the ratio is 8 wounded per fatality.

Source: Linda Bilmes, "Soldiers Returning from Iraq and Afghanistan: The Long-term Costs of Providing Veterans Medical Care and Disability Benefits," John F. Kennedy School of Government, Harvard University, January 2007

In the glare of TV news cameras, the Pentagon rushed repair crews to the center, and new Defense Secretary Robert Gates cleaned house, too, firing the secretary of the Army, Walter Reed's commander and the Army's surgeon general. In July, President George W. Bush accepted the resignation of the Veterans Affairs secretary.[3]

But Walter Reed was just the beginning. ABC News reported soon afterward that the Pentagon and VA weren't coping with a surge in traumatic brain injury (TBI), the signature wound of the Iraq and Afghanistan wars because of the large number of IEDs (improvised explosive devices) and rocket-propelled grenades aimed at U.S. troops.[4]

"In prior conflicts, TBI was present in at least 14-20 percent of surviving combat casualties," according to the Pentagon's Defense and Veterans Brain Injury Center. "Preliminary information from the current conflict in the

Middle East suggests that this number is now much higher."[5]

In 2006, the VA's own Inspector General's Office had blasted the agency's long-term management of TBI patients and their families.[6] "We've got a lot of work to do" on TBI, new Army Secretary Preston "Pete" Geren told a Senate confirmation hearing in June 2007.[7]

"The system is breaking at the seams and cries out for real, radical change," says House Veterans Affairs Chairman Bob Filner, D-Calif. "We have increasing needs for Vietnam veterans, but we are still treating World War II vets, plus we have an incredible onslaught from Iraq and Afghanistan with injuries never foreseen."[8]

Congressional Republicans charge critics with trying to transform problems into catastrophe. "It's part of political gamesmanship by Democrats to say that the administration has failed veterans," Sen. Larry E. Craig, R-Idaho, said shortly before his resignation from the Senate Veterans' Affairs Committee, where he was the ranking Republican. "They want to cause a confidence crisis in the country for their personal, political gain."*

As of Aug. 7, the government said 13,163 service members had been wounded in Iraq and Afghanistan badly enough not to be returned to duty within 72 hours; another 15,588 were wounded and returned to duty.[9]

Some experts say, however, that the toll is far greater. Linda Bilmes, a professor of budgeting and public finance at Harvard's Kennedy School of Government, cites Pentagon reports showing about 63,000 casualties, once non-combat injuries and wounds that didn't require medical air transport are included. The Defense Department, saying it didn't want to mislead the public

---

* On Aug. 29, Craig resigned all his committee leadership posts following news he had pleaded guilty to a disorderly conduct charge stemming from his arrest during a sex sting in a men's room at the Minneapolis-St. Paul International Airport.

about the war's toll, changed its main casualty Web site in January 2007 to show only combat injuries.[10]

In March President Bush named a blue-ribbon commission* to study the care system for wounded military personnel, chaired by former Sen. Bob Dole, R-Kan., a wounded World War II veteran, and Donna Shalala, president of the University of Miami and a former secretary of Health and Human Services.[11] Among its six major recommendations:

- Simplify the disability-ratings system;
- Assign a care coordinator to each seriously wounded service member;
- Improve care for post-traumatic stress disorder (PTSD) and TBI; and
- Increase support for relatives to care for wounded service members, including expansion of the Family Medical Leave Act.[12]

More Than 3,000 Soldiers Seriously Wounded

Of the 1.5 million service members who have served in either Iraq or Afghanistan, more than 3,000 have been seriously injured, including more than 2,700 with traumatic brain injury (TBI).

Number of service members deployed	1,500,000
Air evacuated for illness or injuries	37,851
Wounded in action	28,000
Treated and returned to duty within 72 hours	23,270
Seriously injured	3,082*
Traumatic brain injuries	2,726
Amputations	644
Serious burns	598
Polytrauma	391
Spinal cord injuries	94
Blindness	48

* Recipients of Traumatic Servicemembers' Group Life Insurance

Note: A wounded service member can appear in more than one category.

Source: President's Commission on Care for America's Returning Wounded Warriors, "Serve, Support, Simplify," July 2007

Bush ordered the Defense and Veterans Affairs secretaries to carry out the recommendations "so that we can say with certainty that any soldier who has been hurt will get the best possible care and treatment that this government can offer."[13]

But Rep. Filner rebukes the commission for not going further. "Now is the time to shake up the system," he says, arguing for automatic VA coverage for all veterans. Presently, they get two years of automatic health coverage after discharge; afterwards, vets must prove their medical conditions resulted from their service.

In principle, all of the nation's 24.5 million veterans are eligible for lifetime VA medical treatment. In reality, the agency has to ration care based on its annual appropriations and only provides care to about 5 million vets. Veterans'

organizations have long demanded "mandatory" funding of the agency so that all veterans could get care.[14]

But commission co-chair Shalala says panel members focused on immediately achievable results. "We wanted to make recommendations that would actually affect the people who were injured in those wars," she says. "We were focused on what the system could absorb."

Trends both on the battlefield and at home underlie the clash over veterans' care. Medical advances have cut the fatality rate among wounded soldiers to 9 percent, compared to almost double that during Vietnam and 23 percent in World War II.[15]

Moreover, many veterans are coming home with multiple amputations and severe brain injuries. "We have survivors now who come to us with medical conditions, rehab needs, multiple impairments that we've not seen before," Lucille "Lu" Beck, chief consultant to the VA for rehabilitative services, told *USA Today.*[16]

The psychological toll is also heavy. More than one-third of Army and Marine troops have consulted

---

* The nine-member commission included two wounded Iraq vets: Marc Giammateo, now a Harvard Business School student; and Jose Ramos, a student at George Mason University in Fairfax, Va.; and Tammy Edwards of Cibolo, Texas, the wife of an Army sergeant severely burned in a car bombing.

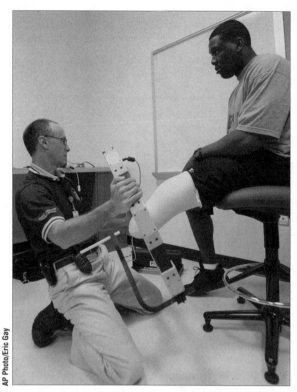

AP Photo/Eric Gay

Sgt. Tawan Williamson gets fitted for a prosthetic leg at Brooke Army Medical Center in San Antonio in March. Williamson was wounded by a bomb that blew up his Humvee in June 2006. This fall he expects to become an Army job counselor and affirmative action officer. In a new policy, the military is putting many more amputees back on active duty.

mental-health professionals on return from Iraq, according to a recent study, and 19 percent "screened positive for a mental health concern."[17]

Indeed, a Pentagon task force acknowledged in June that as many as one-half of active duty and Reserve fighters deployed to combat zones reported various mental health symptoms, including possible PTSD. "But most report they have not yet sought help for these problems," the task force said.[18]

A major reason for the non-reporting may lie in the negative responses soldiers receive from their superiors. Army Spec. Alex Lotero of Fort Carson, Colo., said in May he was cursed at and accused of insubordination when doctors' appointments for treatment of nightmares forced him to miss training.

"They belittled my condition," he said.[19]

"I'm one of the few — of the people I served with — who's gone and got help for it," says Army National Guard Sgt. Patrick Campbell, legislative director of Iraq and Afghanistan Veterans of America, and a former medic in Baghdad. If everyone who needed help all of a sudden asked for help, the system would break under the pressure."

Another sign of post-combat problems is suicide. Neither the VA nor the Pentagon tracks suicide among veterans, though news accounts report several. However, the Defense Department does keep figures on active-duty suicides. A Pentagon report in August disclosed 99 suicides among active-duty Army troops, mostly in Iraq, in 2006, up from 88 in 2005.[20]

The VA supports pending legislation that would focus new attention on preventing suicide among vets suffering post-traumatic stress (*see p. 313*). And Defense and VA officials say they're adding resources to meet the demand for PTSD treatment.

But veterans filing claims for disability payments from the VA — based on PTSD and all other injuries — face waiting periods that average 127 days; and those who appeal the initial rulings spend an average of nearly two years — 657 days — waiting for a decision. "That is absolutely unacceptable," says Paul Sullivan, a former VA staffer who is director of Veterans for Common Sense, an advocacy organization that filed a class-action lawsuit in July in federal district court in California challenging treatment of veterans.[21]

Former Spec. Luis Calderon, 22, of Puerto Rico, became a quadriplegic after a wall fell on him in Baghdad; he had to wait months for his VA benefits and now feels abandoned by the military.[22] National Guard Staff Sgt. Jim Sparks, 43, a police detective in Fairfax, Va., says he had to wait a year for hearing aids after he was injured in an IED attack in Ramadi on Jan. 17, 2006.

"The VA said I didn't need hearing aids. I called back," says Sparks, whose age and experience as a policeman may have equipped him to deal with red tape.

"Care for the wounded is strapped right now," he says. "I've heard lots of talk [of improvement] but not seen a lot of action. I'm not so worried about me, but the 18- and 19-year-old guys I serve with — having them lose a leg or arm or eye and having to deal with insufficient care."

As debate about veterans' care continues, here are some of the questions being asked:

Does the Dole-Shalala commission have the best plan for improving veterans' care?

"The United States has a very spotty record in terms of looking after veterans," says sociologist David Segal, who heads the University of Maryland's Center for Research on Military Organization. "Vietnam veterans did not do well. Veterans are doing badly again because the government, not having anticipated the size of duration of the current engagement, grossly underestimated the number of veterans it was going to have to deal with, and did not understand what we are going to face in terms of experiences — psychiatric and physical."

But Rep. Steve Buyer, R-Ind., the top Republican on the House Veterans' Affairs Committee, notes that today there is no hostility toward Iraq veterans.

"That's a change," he says, attributing the shift in part to bad consciences of Vietnam War protesters — "who in later years feel pretty guilty about their behavior in their youth. I compliment them."

But skeptics say that good feelings alone won't provide the care veterans need.

After the Dole-Shalala commission issued its report on July 25, White House Press Secretary Tony Snow said flatly that President Bush is "not going to be making recommendations; he's not going to be issuing calls for actions," But the following day, Bush said he stood behind the report's recommendations.[23]

The commission reported problems in:

- Coordinating care and patient information by the Defense and Veterans Affairs departments, whose procedures now often leave veterans in limbo between the two agencies.
- Reconciling the differing Defense and Veterans Affairs standards for evaluating veterans' disabilities.
- Treating post-traumatic stress disorder (PTSD) and traumatic brain injury (TBI), due to a lack of staff specialists.
- Supporting family members of wounded soldiers, even as relatives are uprooting themselves for months at a time to help loved ones recover.
- Transferring patient information from the military to the VA.

The report also urged that Walter Reed Medical Center — scheduled for closing in 2012 — be maintained in top shape, with first-rate staff, until then.

Above all, the commission advocated focusing the military- and veterans-care system squarely on the patient: "The tendency to make systems too complex and rule-bound must be countered . . . [Patients'] needs and aspirations should inform the medical care and disability systems."

The commission's conclusions reflected testimony and reports by numerous veterans-advocacy organizations and news media. "It represents very much a consensus view," says Thomas Donnelly, an expert on military affairs at the conservative American Enterprise Institute. "I can't imagine that it's going to cause a whole lot of controversy."

Yet some influential experts argue that the commission didn't seize the moment. "What they are doing is letting the two biggest bureaucracies in the federal government, Defense and Veterans Affairs, continue with some improvements — but not enough to meet what is an emergency situation," says House Veterans Affairs Chairman Filner.

The commission's recommendations aren't bad, Filner says, just too cautious. "I wish they would have issued a clarion call that this is a disaster — a Katrina-like disaster."

Republican Rep. Buyer scoffs at the notion of a system in crisis. "The use of that language indicates someone who is ignorant of the present health system," he says. "Someone saying that is not credible. That's someone who would be from the outside and does not know, or from inside who hasn't invested time" in understanding the system.

Buyer says the Dole-Shalala commission did zero in on some of the top problems in veterans' care — above all the call for a patient-centered philosophy. The Defense and Veterans Affairs departments tend to use budgetary justifications for limiting veterans' options he says. "We take that wounded warrior, and in sub-acute care, we send them back to their homes — and home may be two or three or four hours from a military medical facility. And when they're so distant, we ought to be able to contract for that care," Buyer says. "Sometimes the green-eyeshade guys start making decisions based on dollars, not on patients."

Still, Buyer says, the notion of a system in disaster obscures progress that is being made. "The cooperation

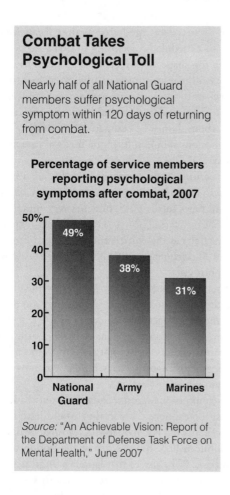

Combat Takes Psychological Toll

Nearly half of all National Guard members suffer psychological symptom within 120 days of returning from combat.

Percentage of service members reporting psychological symptoms after combat, 2007

National Guard: 49%
Army: 38%
Marines: 31%

Source: "An Achievable Vision: Report of the Department of Defense Task Force on Mental Health," June 2007

Senate Veterans Affairs Committee Chairman Daniel K. Akaka, D-Hawaii, however, argues the Dole-Shalala panel "was given far too little time, but they made the best of it." The recommendation for cutting through the red tape that clogs ex-soldiers' transitions from the military to the Veterans Affairs Department is on target, and so are the commission's other proposals, he says.

Are veterans being shortchanged by DoD and VA to save money?

Dozens of hours of House and Senate committee hearings held this year on treatment of wounded soldiers and veterans featured exchanges on an explosive topic — whether care was being withheld in order to save money.

James Terry Scott, a retired Army lieutenant general, told a joint hearing of the Senate Veterans Affairs and Armed Services committees on April 12 that Department of Defense (DoD) standards for evaluating the extent of a service member's disabilities apparently vary according to what the Pentagon can afford. "It is apparent that DoD has a strong incentive to rate [disability] less than 30 percent so that only severance pay is awarded," said Scott, who heads the Veterans Disability Benefits Commission, which Congress created in 2004 to recommend changes in the compensation system for wounded veterans.[24]

Army Secretary Geren responded that no such incentive existed. "Any government program, the more people who avail themselves of the benefits . . . it's going to cause that program to cost more," he said. "But I don't think there's any evidence to show that the people who make the decision on those evaluation boards are influenced by that at all."[25]

But Deputy Defense Secretary Gordon England added that he wasn't certain about financial constraints. "So, yes, it's probably appropriate to step back and make absolutely certain that that is the case, that we are not unduly constraining the system because of funding."[26]

Medical treatment for serious wounds gets virtually unanimous praise.

But a string of official studies have concluded that the Defense and Veterans Affairs departments haven't been able to meet the demand for mental health services for Iraq and Afghanistan veterans.

The Government Accountability Office (GAO) in 2006 concluded that only 22 percent of the troops who

between DoD and VA improves every day," he says. "Has it achieved satisfaction? I don't know if we can get there. That's Valhalla. But there's not a society that invests more in caring for wounded warriors. That doesn't mean there aren't hiccups along the way."

But Stephen L. Robinson, a former Army Airborne Ranger and Ranger instructor who is one of the nation's most active veterans' advocates, argues that veterans are facing more than hiccups. The commission "missed an opportunity to put out a charge to the nation and create a bipartisan movement that everyone can get behind," he says. "It was an opportunity to bring the nation together for a common cause." Robinson now serves on the staff of ONE Freedom, a Boulder, Colo.-based nonprofit that has developed stress-reduction programs for returning veterans.

served in Afghanistan or Iraq and seemed at risk for PTSD were referred for more detailed evaluations: "DoD cannot provide reasonable assurance that . . . service members who need referrals receive them."[27]

Similarly for the VA, the GAO in 2005 questioned "VA's capacity to meet veterans' needs for PTSD services."[28]

Moreover, hundreds of service members have been discharged for "personality disorder" after seeking PTSD treatment. Army veteran Jonathan Town told the House Veterans Affairs Committee in July that after suffering PTSD symptoms following a rocket attack in 2004, he was discharged with a "personality disorder," which left him ineligible for benefits, including treatment, although the doctor who made the diagnosis told him he would be covered. "I never realized everything that was said to me during that day were all lies," Town said.[29]

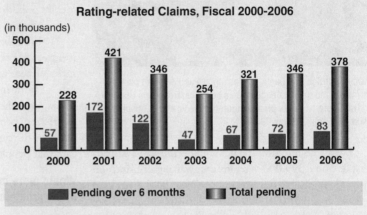

Backlog of Disability Ratings Claims Grew

The number of pending rating-related claims handled by the Department of Veterans Affairs has increased by 66 percent since 2000, to 378,000 claims in 2006. Claims pending for over six months rose 45 percent, from 57,000 in 2000 to 83,000 last year. Resolution of claims appeals "remains a lengthy process," according to the Government Accountability Office, taking an average of 657 days in fiscal 2006.

Rating-related Claims, Fiscal 2000-2006
(in thousands)

Pending over 6 months   **Total pending**

Source: "Veterans' Disability Benefits: Long-Standing Claims Processing Challenges Persist," Government Accountability Office, March 7, 2007

Pentagon officials at the hearing didn't challenge Town's account. Bruce Crow, the psychology consultant to Army Surgeon General Gale Pollock, is reviewing the records of the 295 service members discharged for personality disorder last year after serving in a combat zone. "To the uniformed, civilian and contract health-care professionals that care for these soldiers," he said, "the thought of even one soldier being inappropriately discharged for personality disorder is disturbing."[30]

Meanwhile, a pending amendment to the National Defense Authorization Act sponsored by Sen. Patty Murray, D-Wash., and five colleagues would block personality-disorder discharges until an independent discharge review board is established. "We need to ensure these discharges are medically accurate and that service members are not being denied the treatment or benefits they deserve," Murray said.[31]

The Dole-Shalala commission also explored concerns about payments of promised bonuses. "We learned that service members' remaining enlistment bonuses were not

being paid when they were injured and medically retired or separated from active duty," the commission said. After the commission stepped in, withheld bonuses were paid retroactive to 2001.[32]

With the PTSD issue getting growing attention, Antoinette Zeiss, the VA's deputy chief consultant for mental health, told the House Oversight and Government Reform Committee in May that the department had "improved capacity and access, supporting hiring, so far, of over 1,000 new mental health professionals, with more in the pipeline."[33]

The following month, however, the DoD's Task Force on Mental Health reported that some veterans who needed attention may have been left waiting indefinitely. The panel cited the frequency with which PTSD symptoms appear after expiration of the two-year period in which vets are automatically eligible for treatment. Consequently, "Someone may enter the system without special eligibility, be assigned low priority and not be able to access mental health care while waiting for the outcome" of the evaluation process.[34]

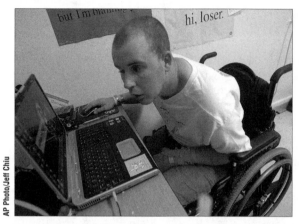

Army Staff Sgt. Eric Cagle, 27, lost an eye and suffered partial paralysis and brain damage when a bomb destroyed his Humvee in Iraq. Here he works on a computer at the veterans' hospital in Palo Alto, Calif., in July 2006.

There's no question the demand on the VA is considerable. Some 399,000 veterans are awaiting decisions on how their disabilities are rated. Overall, the backlog stands at about 629,000 cases, if simple requests are included, such as changes in benefits because a child has been born.

Former Army First Lt. Brady van Engelen, who served a tour in Iraq in 2003-2004 in the 1st Armored Division, says he received no follow-up medical attention after he was treated at Walter Reed for a bullet wound from a sniper that tore through the side of his head under the lip of his helmet. "They just didn't account for the number of walking wounded that would walk out of this war," he says. "Maybe they just didn't think about it."

Testifying before the House committee last March, he called veterans care a "broken system."[35]

While the system's defenders acknowledge rules and procedures can complicate veterans' lives, they reject talk of a financial emergency. "When I hear these complaints about a shortage of funds for VA, I just shake my head in astonishment," said Sen. Craig in an e-mail. "We are on our way to spending at least $86 billion next year — increasing spending on veterans by more than 77 percent since 2001."

Yet, Craig adds, "What do we hear from our friends on the other side of the aisle: 'VA funding is woefully inadequate.' It's an easy sell that just doesn't jibe with reality." So far, he says, citing the Dole-Shalala report, there

are about 6,000 seriously wounded U.S. Iraq-Afghanistan veterans. A cohort of that size "should not be overwhelming the VA system," Craig says. "And they aren't."

Indeed, Michael Kussman, acting VA undersecretary for health, testified in March there will be an estimated 263,000 Iraq and Afghanistan veteran patients next fiscal year (including the 6,000 seriously wounded) out of a total population of 5.8 million veterans receiving VA treatment. "So it's a relatively small number . . . We are ideally poised to be able to take care of the patients as they transition out" of the full-time military.[36]

"I think we're doing a good job with the physical injuries that we can see," Veterans advocate Robinson says. "Where we're falling down is the unseen wounds of war — both in traumatic brain injury as a result of the blasts, and the psychological toll of the war. It's very clear; every commission, every report has said that we do not have the capacity to deliver the kind of mental health care that people are demanding."

Would more money solve most of the problems with veterans' care?

Those who say there's a crisis in veterans' care as well as those who argue there is certainly a problem — just not a crisis — agree more money is needed.

But agreement ends at how the money should be allocated — and whether it would solve *most* of the problems.

"Most" is the key word. Uwe E. Reinhardt, a professor of political economy at Princeton University and a leading expert on health-care finance, told the Senate Veterans Affairs Committee in July that economic inequities in the larger society show up in the veterans-care debate as well. Referring to his son, a Marine captain who was wounded in Afghanistan, Reinhardt said: "When we went to [the military hospital in] Landstuhl [Germany] to visit our son, I asked myself, 'How easy is it actually for people from the lower economic strata to fly to Landstuhl?' My wife and I just jumped on the plane and flew there and stayed in a hotel . . . Those visits are crucial to the healing. So it is a real problem." No one on the committee responded.[37]

Conservative military-affairs analyst Donnelly, for his part, has no doubt that funding is the issue. "There are bureaucratic snafus, no doubt," he says. "But in general terms, this is a case of, 'You get what you pay for.' "

A supporter of the war in Iraq, Donnelly blames some of the veterans' problems on the initial planners and strategists of the war. "It's pretty clear that, for whatever reason, nobody really anticipated that there would be so many casualties. Nobody intended or thought or imagined that serious fighting was going to go on as long as it has. There was a sense of denial."

As a result, says Segal at the University of Maryland's Center for Research on Military Organization, "There has to be a change in our thinking about what is going in Afghanistan and Iraq. There has been an unwillingness to admit the number of psychological casualties coming out of this war."

The unique conditions that troops are encountering in both countries are behind the upsurge in PTSD claims, Segal argues. "In past conflicts, there were tremendous differences in exposure to psychological trauma between combat troops and support troops. Now, it doesn't matter. Now people in logistics and other support functions are seeing more combat than in past wars. Basically, once you put boots on the ground in Iraq, you're in a combat zone."

Nonetheless, money still seems to be the solution, according to Senate Veterans Affairs Committee Chairman Akaka. "There are larger concerns about how DoD and VA cooperate," he acknowledges. "But funding is at the heart of many of the known shortcomings. In recent years, the administration has not requested sufficient funding for VA health care.

"Veterans are coming home with PTSD and other invisible wounds like TBI, and the VA should have been prepared for them, but they are not."

A World War II veteran, Akaka advocates so-called "mandatory" funding for VA health care, or funding independent of annual appropriations from Congress. Other Democrats active in veterans' affairs urge the same approach.

"They don't have money to take care of every veteran," says Duckworth, who lost both legs when the Black Hawk helicopter she was piloting in Iraq as a major in the Illinois National Guard was shot down. "If funding were mandatory, every veteran who has a service-connected disability would have the care that this country promised them. That is what the American people think they're getting."

Rep. Buyer, the senior Republican on House Veterans Affairs, calls the mandatory approach irresponsible. "If

you put me on a mandatory-funding glide path, what incentives do I have for improvement? Why do I have to create efficiencies? I think it would be very bad judgment and bad policy to take advantage of the American people's compassion toward our wounded warriors."

But Chairman Filner argues that mandatory funding would bring a welcome simplicity to the regulation-filled world of veterans' care. "I would like to break through the system and say, 'Give me your discharge papers and you're in,'" Filner says. "We'd be saving so much on bureaucracy. All the issues that Vietnam veterans and World War II veterans have — a guy claims his Parkinson's disease is a result of Agent Orange. Just accept the claim. They fought for us, they're ill, let's treat them."

Sen. Craig dismisses such talk as facile, given the enormous demands on the budget created by other "mandatory" funding arrangements. "We already have three very large programs that are considered to be funded by 'mandatory spending' — namely Social Security, Medicare and Medicaid," he says by e-mail. "And notable economic experts . . . have been warning us that unless we make changes to those systems soon [they] will crowd out every other federal program — including defense and homeland security."

BACKGROUND

The 'Great War'

Many of the 4 million American veterans of the American Expeditionary Force who came home from the World War I battlefields of France, Belgium and Germany — and the 3 million more who never saw action — re-entered civilian life with high expectations.[38]

It was a bittersweet homecoming for many. Not only were jobs scarce, but corruption in the Veterans Bureau diverted most of the money that Congress allocated for wounded and disabled ex-soldiers. For example, Congress authorized $33 million for veterans' hospitals, but only 200 new beds were produced.

Shortchanging the wounded was especially grievous due to the devastating after-effects of a frightening new weapon — poison gas. About 27 percent of all fatal and non-fatal casualties were caused by gas, a modern military historian calculates.[39]

CHRONOLOGY

1918-1950 *Treatment of veterans evolves from limited benefits and care after World War I to society-changing benefits after the second global conflict.*

1921 President Warren G. Harding forms the Veterans Bureau, which soon becomes notorious for limited accomplishments and widespread corruption.

1924 Congress enacts bonus to compensate veterans for the higher pay that civilian defense factory workers received.

1932 Army veterans demanding an early payout of the bonus to help them weather the Depression march on Washington and set up "Hooverville" encampment.... Repression of the "bonus army" on orders from Republican President Herbert Hoover helps Democrat Franklin D. Roosevelt win the presidency.

1945 Roosevelt and Congress, determined to avoid a repeat of the "bonus march" debacle, create the GI Bill.... Millions of veterans take advantage of its benefits to attend college and buy homes, vastly expanding the nation's middle class.

1950s-1980s *The atmosphere toward veterans chills slightly after the Korean War and more so after the Vietnam War, leaving a lasting bitterness among the vets.*

1953 Veterans returning from the three-year Korean conflict get a new, less generous GI Bill but are not welcomed as warmly as World War II vets.

1960s-1984 Returning Vietnam vets encounter attitudes ranging from indifference to hostility.... Thousands begin developing symptoms linked to exposure to the defoliant Agent Orange.

1967 Vietnam Veterans Against the War (VVAW) is founded.

1970 Following an article in *The New Yorker,* Senate Subcommittee on the Environment holds hearings on Agent Orange.... Soon after, Defense Department bans use of dioxin, the chemical used in the defoliant.

April 1971 Veterans at VVAW demonstration in Washington — including future Sen. John Kerry, D-Mass. — protest the war by tossing their medals onto the Capitol steps.

Nov. 13, 1982 Vietnam Veterans Memorial — "The Wall" — opens on the National Mall bearing the names of 58,249 dead or missing servicemen and women.

1984 Veterans claiming serious illness from dioxin sue the government.

1990s-Present

1992 Veterans of the 1990-91 Persian Gulf War begin reporting ailments collectively dubbed "Gulf War syndrome" and attributed to possible chemical exposure.

1997 Medical researchers report in the *Journal of the American Medical Association* "Gulf War syndrome" results from exposure to combinations of pesticide and nerve gas.

2003 Improvised explosive devices (IEDs) begin wreaking havoc on American troops — including multiple loss of limbs.

Dec. 22, 2005 Army Reserve Spc. Joshua Omvig, 22, of Grundy Center, Iowa, commits suicide after an 11-month tour in Iraq; his parents say he was suffering from post-traumatic stress disorder (PTSD).

2006 Government Accountability Office says military efforts to treat PTSD symptoms fall short.... Joshua Omvig Veterans Suicide Prevention Act introduced in House in July, charges VA with setting up a program to screen and monitor for suicide risk.

2007 *Washington Post* series reports shocking conditions for outpatients at Walter Reed Army Medical Center.... Army secretary and two top medical officers are forced out.... Presidential panel recommends simplification of disability-rating process and other changes in veterans'-care system.... Congress takes up raft of legislation on veterans' benefits.... Bush administration and Congress move toward possible showdown over veterans'-care spending.

Veterans also noticed that the $60 they got when mustering out added up to little compared with bonuses of up to $14 a day that wartime defense-factory workers had received. In 1924, Congress created a bonus-pay system to compensate vets for the higher civilian incentives they'd missed out on. The bonus was calculated at $1.25 for each day served overseas, and $1 a day for those who stayed stateside.

But there was a catch. The money would be paid out in bonds that would mature in 1945. And after the stock market crash of 1929 launched the Great Depression, vets desperately needed their bonus money immediately.

In 1932, groups of struggling ex-soldiers, along with their wives and children, began gathering in Washington. Eventually numbering as many as 40,000 men, women and children, the Bonus Expeditionary Force (BEF) camped across the Anacostia River from the Capitol. They called their shantytown "Hooverville," in a sarcastic salute to President Herbert Hoover, who rejected their bonus demands.

In July, troops led by Gen. Douglas MacArthur destroyed the encampment and routed the protesters. The ugly spectacle of mounted American troops charging into unarmed veterans and their families helped Democrat Franklin D. Roosevelt defeat Hoover in the 1932 presidential election.

GI Bill Benefits

World War II marked the beginning of a change in views about war and its effects on fighters. Early in the war, in 1942, anti-aircraft artillery crews were told, for example, "if a soldier was a man he would not permit his self-respect to admit an anxiety neurosis or to show fear," a military historian has written. Yet, as the fighting ground on in Europe and the Pacific, commanders and physicians came to accept that combat could cause psychiatric casualties.[40]

By the time the war ended, there was greater acceptance of the strains that fighting could place on the spirit, not to mention the political lessons learned from the "bonus marchers" debacle. Even before the final victory, the Roosevelt administration and Congress had created one of the most far-reaching pieces of social legislation ever enacted: the GI Bill of Rights.

The 1944 law provided funding for veterans to attend college or trade school and buy homes with no down payments and low-interest loans. The postwar economic boom and the simultaneous expansion of the college-educated middle class grew directly out of the "GI Bill," as it was widely known. By 1947, just two years after the war's end, 1 million vets had purchased homes, giving rise to the suburbs. By 1949, average annual income reached double the 1939 level.

The GI Bill even addressed the likelihood that many veterans would need to readjust gradually to civilian life, providing $20 a week for unemployment compensation for up to 52 weeks — a provision promptly dubbed the "52/20 club."

"If it wasn't for the GI Bill I wouldn't be here," says Sen. Akaka, who graduated from the University of Hawaii in 1952 after serving in the Army from 1945-1947. He adds that his fellow Hawaiian senator, Daniel K. Inouye, who lost an arm during combat in Italy, also went on to college and law school on the GI Bill. "We need to add that back as a program," Akaka says.

But even the nation's warm embrace of World War II vets couldn't banish the strains that fighting had placed on them. In the 1990s, a team of researchers predicted in the *American Journal of Psychiatry* that 15 years after combat, "a subject would experience physical decline or death." In some veterans, they hypothesized, physical symptoms may have resulted from inability to talk about what they went through.[41]

Korea to Vietnam

None of the wars that followed saw veterans greeted as warmly as those coming back from World War II.

The first to note the chill were veterans of the much less popular Korean War, a brutal, 1950-1953 conflict in which the United States beat back an invasion of South Korea by communist North Korea, aided by China.

Although Korea veterans did receive benefits, they were less generous than those provided by the original GI Bill. Korea vets also had to cope with a perceived blot on their collective reputation. Some of the 4,000 Americans held captive in grim prison camps succumbed to North Korean torture and allowed themselves to be put on display in propaganda films or broadcasts.

Seeing civilians neither sympathetic nor well-informed about the war, Korean War vets tried their best to fade into society. But during and after America's next big conflict — in Vietnam — veterans stayed vocal and visible enough to keep their generation of ex-soldiers on the sociopolitical radar screen for decades.

Recruiters Turn to Fail-Safe Approach

Big cash bonuses help reach quotas.

Times are tough for military recruiters. A steady stream of stories of veterans coming home with limbs missing, brains injured or nerves shattered — and government bungling in vets' care — have left the Defense Department reaching for a traditional tool of companies with hard-to-fill jobs: cold, hard cash.

In July, after missing its combined May and June recruitment goal of 13,900 by 10 percent — 1,400 enlistees — the Army started offering "quick ship" bonuses of $20,000 each to recruits who agree to report for combat training by the end of September, which is also the end of the federal fiscal year.[1]

The incentive worked. Recruiters signed up 9,972 young men and women in July, exceeding their 9,750-recruit goal for the month and reversing a worrisome trend in which the Army failed to meet its targets for the previous two months.

The extent to which veterans' problems are playing a role in discouraging enlistment and re-enlistment, however, hasn't been established.

"I don't think it's possible to make a really clear connection," says Thomas Donnelly, a military-affairs specialist at the conservative American Enterprise Institute. But the realities of the war itself are clearly weighing more heavily on America's youth, says Donnelly, citing talks about the war with his 19- and 21-year-old sons, both in college — "the

kind a lot of families are having with their kids," says Donnelly, who did not serve in the military.

Some veterans' activists go further, arguing that the public focus on mishandled treatment of veterans inevitably is making itself felt in the military's manpower problems.

"There have been plenty of stories about veterans," says Stephen L. Robinson, a former Army Airborne Ranger and Ranger instructor. "The best way to make sure that we always have an all-volunteer Army is to keep our promises that we will use them judiciously and appropriately, give them the things they need to succeed — and take care of them should they become injured in war. It's the best recruiting tool there is. When we fail, we see results in recruiting and retention."

As Maj. Gen. Thomas P. Bostick, who heads the Army Recruiting Command at Fort Knox, Ky., told the House Armed Services Committee in August: "We are recruiting during a period of protracted combat. Today's recruiting environment is incredibly challenging."[2]

Still, the Army is doing better in keeping those already in uniform — meeting 101 percent of the retention goal for the active-duty force, 119 percent for the Army Reserve, and 107 percent for the Army National Guard.

"I still think there are lots of young guys who are passionate about serving," says Army National Guard Staff Sgt. Jim Sparks, who is training for his third combat deployment.

Like the rest of American society in the 1960s and '70s, veterans split into pro- and anti-war camps. Vietnam Veterans Against the War (VVAW), founded in 1967, soon formed part of a movement whose biggest constituency was college students who had avoided the draft. For all of its visibility, though, VVAW clearly occupied a minority position among the 3.4 million Americans who served in Southeast Asia during the war.[42]

Most Vietnam veterans didn't get tickertape parades welcoming them home. But the amount of hostility they encountered is still hotly debated. As recently as this year, the dispute has come to center on what is seen as the signature insult of the times: spitting.

Richard H. Taylor, a Vietnam vet, writes in a new book of a vet who reported trying to enroll in a California

college. "A young woman and two young men approached him. . . . She screamed at him, calling him a baby-killer; one of the guys with her spit on him."[43]

Although such accounts are plentiful, Jack Shafer, a media columnist for *Slate*, an online magazine, provoked a series of angry replies when he described the frequent accounts of returning veterans being spat upon as an "urban myth."

"I've yet to locate a news account that documents a specific spit altercation or a police or court paper trail that would back the accusations," Shafer wrote.[44]

The division between pro-war and anti-war Vietnam vets faded somewhat as veterans ran into issues that affected them both.

One was the level of care provided by the VA. "Veterans considered VA hospitals the last resort for medical care,"

"You see them wearing baggy pants and listening to gangsta rap — but their [dedicated] service gives you faith in youth, it really gives you back that feel-good sensation about the younger crowd, the new generation."

And Sparks himself, an ex-Marine, volunteered for service even though it costs him the overtime pay that makes up an appreciable part of his family's income. He is a detective in Fairfax County, Va. "I really consider it an honor to wear the uniform; I really enjoy serving."

Enthusiasm aside, money is playing a role for at least some service members opting to stay in uniform. "I only re-enlisted this time for college," Marine Cpl. Cara Tighe told *Army Times*, referring to the $10,000 bonus she got for re-upping. She has no plans to do so again.[3]

Defense experts note the cost of such sweeteners is skyrocketing. "Spending on enlistment and recruitment bonuses tripled from $328 million before the war in Iraq to over $1 billion in 2006," Lawrence J. Korb, military strategy director at the Center for American Progress, a liberal think tank, told the House Armed Services Committee in July. Korb is a Vietnam-era Navy veteran and former Defense official in the Reagan administration.[4]

Nor is the retention picture uniformly bright. Retention among West Point graduates has reached its lowest point in

Gunnery Sgt. Brian Bensen, a Marine recruiter in Belle Vernon, Pa., has a quota of two recruits per month.

Getty Images/*Christian Science Monitor*/Mary Knox Merrill

30 years, Korb said. And he cited indications that the strain of repeated combat deployments is provoking an increase in post-traumatic stress disorder symptoms among service members deployed repeatedly to Iraq and Afghanistan.

Veterans' issues aside, the realities of the war itself are looming large for potential recruits and their families, says Donnelly. "Everybody knows that if you join the military now you're going to war,"he says. "It's a more sobering proposition. You're not joining so much for career development."

[1] See Josh White, "Many Take Army's 'Quick Ship' Bonus," *The Washington Post*, Aug. 27, 2007, p. A1; Thom Shanker, "Army, Shedding a Slump, Met July Recruiting Goal," *The New York Times*, Aug. 11, 2007, p. A8.

[2] See "Army Recruiting and Retention," House Armed Services Committee, Committee testimony, Aug. 1, 2007.

[3] Quoted in Rick Maze and William H. McMichael, "Here today . . . gone tomorrow?; Turning tide of war may drain bonus pool," *Army Times*, July 30, 2007, p. A14. Also, "Retention Remains High Military-Wide, Including in Combat Zone," *CQ Federal Department and Agency Documents*, July 11, 2007.

[4] See "Troop Deployment Policy," House Armed Services Committee, Committee testimony (written), July 27, 2007.

Taylor writes. "Medical care in combat was crude, but fast, effective and always there. But at VA hospitals they could die in a waiting room, and no one would notice."[45]

The second unifying issue was the chemical defoliant dioxin — Agent Orange — which had been sprayed from U.S. aircraft to destroy jungle canopy that gave cover to the enemy. In 1970, Thomas Whiteside reported in *The New Yorker* that scientific evidence linked Agent Orange to cancer.[46]

The article led to hearings by the Senate Subcommittee on the Environment, after which the Pentagon quit using Agent Orange.[47] But the ban didn't help those already exposed. Starting in the late 1970s, a wave of diseases including leukemia began striking Vietnam veterans. Some medical experts traced the origins to dioxin. Veterans filed

the first class-action lawsuit arising from dioxin exposure in 1984. Veterans have largely prevailed in court, but the Veterans Affairs Department has been fighting to limit benefits.

As recently as July, the 9th U.S. Circuit Court of Appeals in San Francisco threw out the government's appeal of a decision ordering retroactive disability payments to veterans suffering from leukemia linked to dioxin exposure.

"What is difficult for us to comprehend is why the Department of Veterans Affairs, having entered into a settlement agreement and agreed to a consent order some 16 years ago, continues to resist its implementation so vigorously, as well as to resist equally vigorously the payment of desperately needed benefits to Vietnam War veterans who fought for their country and suffered grievous

The scandal over conditions at Walter Reed Army Medical Center led Defense Secretary Robert M. Gates to fire Maj. Gen. George Weightman, commander of the center, right, and Army Surgeon General Lt. General Kevin C. Kiley. Above, they testify before a House Government Reform and Oversight subcommittee on March 5, 2007.

injury as a result of our government's own conduct," Judge Stephen Reinhardt wrote in the decision.[48]

Along with Agent Orange, homelessness also is often associated with Vietnam veterans. The nation's homeless population seemed to grow during the 1970s and '80s, and many homeless men were believed to be vets suffering from the effects of combat. Recent studies suggest the link between Vietnam and homelessness is weaker than popularly believed. "Vietnam era veterans, who are often thought to be the most overrepresented group of homeless veterans, were barely more likely to be homeless than non-veterans (1.01 times)," the Congressional Research Service reported in May, citing a 1994 study using 1980s data.[49]

Gulf War and Beyond

The 1990-1991 Persian Gulf War, pitting a U.S.-assembled coalition against the forces of Iraqi leader Saddam Hussein, was the shortest of all major post-Vietnam conflicts, with the ground war lasting just 100 hours.

A relatively small number of troops — 382 — died in the war zone. But soon after returning stateside about 100,000 of the 694,000 troops who served in the Gulf began reporting symptoms such as joint pain, chronic fatigue, aches and fevers.[50]

As with Agent Orange, Veterans department officials resisted compensating veterans suffering from what came to be collectively defined as Gulf War Syndrome.

Veterans and some scientists speculated the cause was exposure to destroyed Iraqi supplies of sarin nerve gas, to insect repellents or to the nerve-gas antidote pyridostigmine bromide — separately or together.

In 2004, a government-sponsored committee gave credence to the chemical-exposure hypothesis and to the theory that the ailments reflected neurological damage. A "probable link" exists between the exposure and the damage to vets' brains, the panel said.[51]

But two years later, a committee appointed by the non-governmental Institute of Medicine reached a different conclusion. "We can't identify a Gulf War syndrome," said Lynn R. Goldman, a physician and epidemiologist who headed the committee. The committee did find that Gulf War vets suffered PTSD and depression two to three times more frequently than ex-soldiers from other conflicts. The panel noted researchers were hampered by a lack of hard data on Gulf War troops' chemical exposure.[52]

Less than a month after the 9/11 terrorist attacks, the United States launched Operation Enduring Freedom to chase the Taliban regime from Afghanistan. On March 19, 2003, the Bush administration launched Operation Iraqi Freedom to oust Saddam.

By August 2003, American commanders in Iraq realized that the deadliest weapon they faced was the improvised explosive device (IED) — "the insurgents' weapon of choice," the *Los Angeles Times* reported. Generally made with artillery shells, IEDs were hidden under or alongside roads and highways. Set off by remote control, the biggest IEDs could even immobilize tanks, to say nothing of the destruction they could wreak on the ubiquitous unarmored Humvees.[53]

As the war ground on, National Guard and Reserve troops were thrown into battle. Along with active-duty troops, they found themselves deployed to Iraq and Afghanistan two and even three times.

For Army troops, war-zone deployments lasted 12 months (the Marine Corps mostly keeps to its standard seven-month combat tours). In April, Defense Secretary Gates ordered that Army tours be lengthened to 15 months, and some commanders warned troops to expect 18-month deployments.[54]

As reports mounted of the growing number of veterans with severe physical and psychological injuries, and of strains on families' lives, the series of articles on failures in veterans' services *The Washington Post* began on Feb. 18, 2007, prompted a round of hearings, formation of a blue-ribbon commission and more widespread journalistic probing. Among other disclosures, journalists highlighted complaints by Guardsmen and Reservists that they were forced to wait months for medical care and benefits.[55]

CURRENT SITUATION

Congress Reacts

Lawmakers are responding to a cascade of studies, news reports and committee testimony with bills that would change virtually every aspect of the veterans-care system. House Veterans Affairs Chairman Filner says he's considering side-by-side bills separately embodying the recommendations of the Dole-Shalala commission and the sweeping changes he advocates, including guaranteed health care for all veterans.

Congress' single biggest move is a spending bill — still awaiting final action — on veterans and military construction. The House passed its version of the legislation on June 15, the day after the Senate Appropriations Committee approved a similar measure. Details differ from bill to bill, but both call for spending about $4 billion more than the Bush administration requested for VA benefits and medical care. A full Senate vote — followed by reconciliation of differences with the House legislation — was pending as Congress prepared to go back into session after Labor Day. Bush has threatened to veto other spending bills to make room for the higher spending levels the veterans' legislation calls for — unless lawmakers themselves do the cutting.[56]

Meanwhile, the Senate already has passed legislation initially sparked by *The Post's* Walter Reed exposé. Shortly before taking its summer recess, the Senate passed the "Wounded Warrior Act," which would set up a hotline for reporting deficient conditions, improve training of caregivers and step up congressional oversight.

The Senate bill contains some departures from the version that originated in the House, including the addition of a military pay raise. A conference to resolve differences in the two versions has yet to be scheduled.[57]

Other legislation growing directly out of the present wars would step up efforts at suicide prevention. The Joshua Omvig Veterans Suicide Prevention Act, named after a 22-year-old Iowa veteran who killed himself in 2005 on return from Iraq, would require screening of all patients at VA centers for suicide potential, and the monitoring of those at risk. The bill has passed the House, where its sponsor was Rep. Leonard Boswell, D-Iowa; it is pending in the Senate, where Tom Harkin, also an Iowa Democrat, is the sponsor.[58]

"The VA endorses the bill," Ira Katz, the agency's mental health director, testified. "We are already implementing almost all of that bill with existing legislative authority. We're committed to doing everything possible to prevent veteran suicide."[59]

Meanwhile, proposed legislation would protect veterans who interrupted their educations to serve in the armed forces from being penalized by schools and school lenders. The bills were introduced in late June in the Senate by Sherrod Brown, D-Ohio, and in the House by Susan Davis, D-Calif. Campbell, of the Iraq and Afghanistan Veterans of America, drafted the bill based on his own experience. Returning to law school, he found that he'd used up his repayment grace period while serving in Iraq. The bill would extend the repayment period to 13 months. And schools would be required to refund unused tuition and to guarantee re-entry to returning veterans.[60]

Other bills pending in the Senate include a proposal by Senate Veterans Affairs Chairman Akaka to increase services to veterans with TBI. The bill would authorize $48 million for VA programs to improve the quality of life for veterans who are too impaired to manage daily life on their own.

"There must be new approaches to best meet the health-care needs of these veterans," Akaka said.[61]

The legislation also includes a measure calling for restoration of VA health care to so-called "Priority 8" veterans, those whose relatively high incomes and lack of service-connected disabilities led the VA to cut them off from care in 2003.[62]

The health care-restoration provision sparked a partisan fight in the Senate Veterans' Affairs Committee, as the panel prepared final versions of legislation. "I was elected to change the priorities of this country," Sen. Bernard Sanders, I-Vt., said in support of the measure, adding that he opposed the Bush administration tax cuts that benefited

A Wounded Vet Comes Home

"I expected better treatment."

Coming home from Iraq has been difficult for Sgt. Garrett Anderson, a 30-year-old National Guardsman from Champaign, Ill. The wounds bothered him, of course, but it was the red tape that really hurt.

A sniper for the Army's 130th Infantry, Anderson was wounded in Abu Ghraib province in October 2005 after an IED exploded next to his armored Humvee. He lost part of his right arm in the explosion, which also shattered his jaw and eye socket and left him with traumatic brain injury (TBI) and shrapnel throughout his body.

He arrived at Washington's Walter Reed Army Medical Center three days later and remained there for seven months. He has nothing but praise for the nurses and doctors in his amputee ward. His encounter with the VA would be another matter.

After Anderson retired from the Army in June 2006, he immediately filed a disability claim with the VA. That was when the battle on the home front began.

"The VA officers who were assigned to help me were completely helpless," Anderson recalls. "They did nothing for me. The paperwork they filled out for me wasn't thorough enough." As a result, six months would pass until his first VA medical appointment.

More bad news followed. Last March, the VA declined to give Anderson a 100 percent disability rating, although he appeared eligible under VA regulations. "Shrapnel injury not related to combat," the VA letter said. His claim on his brain injury was denied as well. He later learned the shrapnel injuries were disallowed because they were not officially documented in his care report.

Instead, he was given a 90 percent disability rating, which entitled him to $1,600 from the government every month, significantly less than the $2,600 for a 100 percent rating.

Anderson was appalled. "Oh, I laughed to the point of anger when I saw that letter," he recalls. "After everything I had to go through, this was the last thing I wanted to happen. I expected better treatment."

The 10 percent difference would burden his wife, Samantha, and baby daughter as well. Anderson, who is now working with Sen. Richard J. Durbin, D-Ill., on improving veterans' health care, hopes to attend college by using the educational benefits given to veterans. His wife,

the wealthy. "Tax breaks to Paris Hilton's parents" is one of those priorities in need of change, Sanders said.[63]

Idaho Republican Craig says the legislation would flood the VA system with 17 million new patients — the now-excluded Priority 8 vets — endangering care for veterans in greater need. "This is the wrong focus at the wrong time," he said. His attempt to eliminate the provision failed.[64]

Calling All Civilians

As the Bush administration and Congress respond to calls to improve the veterans-care system, a growing number of veterans' advocates are urging citizens to mobilize to help veterans rejoin the civilian world.

House Veterans' Affairs Chairman Filner argues that the Bush administration is resisting making sweeping changes. "They're trying to low-key it," he says. "The president has sort of walled off the war from our national consciousness. We don't see the injuries, the caskets."

Idaho Republican Craig contends veterans are getting the help they need. "Citizens' groups have cropped up around the country to help veterans, and their efforts have been highlighted by the Department of Defense." He cites a Pentagon Web site, "America Supports You," that provides links to organizations aimed at boosting the morale of troops overseas and their families. The site also includes links to organizations that help veterans meet potential employers and that build or remodel homes for disabled veterans.[65]

But Sparks, the Army sergeant training for his third deployment to a war zone since the 9/11 terrorist attacks, says he sees little sign that the public at large is engaged in the struggle that the troops on the ground are waging. "People are getting a little weary of the war," he says. "The general populace isn't affected by it. We forget 9/11 and all the U.N. resolutions that were in place on Saddam."

Some veterans' advocates also argue that efforts such as the Pentagon's Web-based outreach program haven't

however, was not entitled to spousal educational benefits, which are only available to spouses of vets with a 100 percent disability rating.

After some lobbying from Sen. Durbin and Rep. Timothy V. Johnson, R-Ill., plus extensive media coverage and research on the disability process by his wife, the VA in June reclassified Anderson as 100 percent disabled — a year after his initial claim.

Back home in Champaign, Ill., Sgt. Garrett Anderson and his wife and child visit with Sen. Ricahrd J. Durbin, who helped with his benefits appeal.

"Sgt. Garrett Anderson's 100 percent rating is well deserved and long overdue," says Durbin. "It is unacceptable that an American soldier who fought [and] came home wounded had to spend the next year of his life fighting for proper care and compensation."

The Andersons are relieved, but not everything has been resolved. Mrs. Anderson, who is attending law school, has submitted a request for spousal educational reimbursement going back to June 2006 — when disability was claimed — but she has yet to receive any compensation.

"An injury [forces] the uninjured spouse to seek employment that can financially support the family," she says in an e-mail. . . . "This cannot be done without some sort of post high school education, and unless the veteran has received a 100 percent rating from the VA, the family will suffer great difficulty in trying to recover financially after an injury."

Thanks to the new disability rating, she is eligible to receive an additional $800 per month in educational assistance.

Anderson joined the Army for its sense of brotherhood and camaraderie. And, bureaucratic obstacles with the VA notwithstanding, he has no regrets.

"No question. I still feel my duty to my country was worth it," he says. "I would definitely do it all over again.

"My problem is simply with the bureaucratic system."

— *Darrell Dela Rosa*

penetrated the national consciousness. "Unless you know a soldier who's been injured, you do not understand the depth of their need," says Robinson of ONE Freedom. Like many others in the veterans' community, he observes that the 1.5 million military personnel who have served or are serving in Iraq and Afghanistan don't even amount to 1 percent of a nation of 300 million people. "Most of America assumes they go to war, they come home, go to the VA to get what they need and we've done what we're supposed to do."

But, he argues, only the civilian world can provide the depth of support that returning veterans need. "I don't think that any program that DoD or VA has can be as complete as a community that wraps its arms around you. We need to engage the nation in the communities where the soldiers live to help them return from war and help them reintegrate into society in a meaningful way."

In Los Angeles, the director of a residential program for homeless veterans — many of them Vietnam veterans

with drug problems, PTSD and other psychological war wounds — speaks in almost identical terms. "I just don't think the VA is capable of the kind of extreme reform that is needed to address this population," says Toni Reinis, executive director of New Directions, which operates on government contracts, private grants and its own enterprises — including a diner that residents operate.[66]

"We need to make sure that, when they are released from the military, they're not just dumped — as our Vietnam vets were — on the streets of America," Reinis says. "We need to make sure that there's a strong connection with families, and that families know what to expect — what the symptoms are of depression and PTSD."

Whether civilians reach out now, or leave veterans' care to the government, the non-military majority will be involved in veterans' matters in any case. Testifying about psychological effects of the present wars on those fighting them, Thomas Insel, director of the National Institute of

AT ISSUE

Do today's veterans face a health-care crisis?

YES

Rep. Bob Filner, D-Calif.
Chairman, House Committee on
Veterans' Affairs

Written for *CQ Researcher*, August 2007

The nation's veterans' health-care system is strained to the breaking point. America has a moral and legal obligation to provide care for our nation's veterans. Veterans have kept their promise to serve our nation, and we must keep our promises to our veterans.

As chairman of the House Veterans' Affairs Committee, I have met with individual veterans, heard the testimony of veterans' service organizations and held town hall meetings across the country, and I am told that veterans are falling through the cracks and that more funding is needed to provide care to our veterans.

This administration does not understand that treating our veterans is part of the cost of war. The reality is that this administration did not ask for enough funding to begin addressing the problems faced by veterans. Any planned military surge must be accompanied by a funding surge for health care for veterans.

Our troops come back with post-traumatic stress disorder and can get no services. They come back with dental problems and have to wait a year for an appointment. The average wait for veterans to receive their earned benefits is 177 days.

Today, many of our service members return from Afghanistan and Iraq without legs and arms. They return with many and varied physical and mental health-care needs. Today, many of our veterans live longer and need long-term care — and we should be prepared to provide for them. Today, we have people that have died while waiting for their veterans' benefit claim to be adjudicated. People have lost their homes because they could not afford them. The backlog of claims is a disgrace.

The VA is meant to be an advocate for veterans but is too often seen as an adversary of veterans.

In June, the House of Representatives passed a bill that provides for the largest increase in funding for veterans' health care in the 77-year history of the VA. This bill provides the resources and support to the VA so that veterans can receive the treatment they have been promised. This bill provides the necessary resources to improve health care and expand mental health services. This bill invests in the hiring and training of new claims processors to reduce the VA benefits backlog. This bill will mean increased funding to address the repair and maintenance needs of VA facilities.

The work of this Congress can only begin to address the crisis faced by our veterans. It is our moral obligation to do more — and we must keep our promises to the men and women who have defended our country.

NO

Rep. Steve Buyer, R-Ind.
Ranking Member, House Committee on
Veterans' Affairs

Written for *CQ Researcher*, August 2007

The Department of Veterans Affairs provides health care to 5.5 million patients. As of July 2007, Iraq and Afghanistan veterans made up about 5 percent of the total, 96 percent of whom were seen by the VA on an outpatient basis.

Since eligibility reform in 1996, Congress and two administrations have worked effectively to provide quality care for veterans who need it most. Eligibility reform was designed to strike a balance, maintaining a patient base large and varied enough to keep clinicians in practice, without straining the system and compromising quality with excessive enrollments by those who need VA care least.

The nation can be proud of an aging VA workforce, whose men and women have dedicated their lives to care for all veterans. The health-care system they helped build provides excellent care to a well-defined population, but it is not designed to handle a huge influx of non-service-connected patients. That is why former VA Secretary Anthony Principi, to prevent this type of potential crisis in a time of war, suspended enrollment of new "Priority 8" veterans.

We must preserve quality care for VA's core constituency — veterans with service-connected disabilities and illnesses, those with catastrophic disabilities such as blindness and paralysis and the poor. While veterans of Iraq and Afghanistan seeking VA care represent a small percentage of the department's patient base, they do present new challenges — not problems. Responding to the increase of traumatic brain injury (TBI), Congress created four VA polytrauma rehabilitation centers in 2004. These centers have so far treated just over 400 TBI patients. Mental health will continue to receive increased funding to improve access and care. Each war brings its unique challenges, but our obligation to the veterans who have served us in every generation does not vary.

Fulfilling that obligation requires us to remain cognizant of the pressures on the system and sensitive to the influence of patient flow on quality. We will be vigilant in improving transitions, electronic medical records, sub-acute care, administrative support, disability evaluations and medical modernization and research.

The VA has earned its reputation for providing excellent care to our nation's veterans who need it most. If anything will put VA health care into crisis, it would be enrolling millions of non-service-connected patients — who already have access to other health-care options — into a system that is not prepared to receive them.

Mental Health, told the House Oversight and Government Reform Committee in May, "This is not simply a problem for the VA or for DoD. . . . Much of the burden of illness will spill over to the public sector to mental health care in the civilian sector."[67]

OUTLOOK

More Money?

Some observers say that widespread support — at least on the political level — for improved veterans' care bodes well for the future.

"There's no constituency for treating these wounded warriors badly," says Shalala, co-chair of the president's commission on veterans' care. "With all the fussing that's going on, the bureaucracy doesn't want that, Congress doesn't want it, the American people don't want it. Everybody wants to make certain we've done our best. I'm quite optimistic."

Former First Lt. van Engelen, who was treated for a sniper wound at Walter Reed, agrees. "It doesn't matter which organization I speak to, no matter how far left or how far right, regardless of their views of the war, none of them are going to turn down services for a veteran, especially a wounded veteran."

However, double-amputee Tammy Duckworth, at the Illinois' veterans' affairs department, sounds a downbeat note. "I think we're going to forget about the vets," she says. Only two possibilities exist to counter that trend, she says.

One would be veterans putting more pressure on the system to pay attention to their needs. As a state veterans' official, she feels pressure to get things done quickly. "I feel that I have two or three years, if that, to set up programs to make sure that we take care of veterans into the future," she says. "If that doesn't happen now, I can't see that anyone will be going back in 10 years to take action."

Sullivan of Veterans for Common Sense, which filed a class-action suit in California on behalf of veterans, agrees that now is the time to expand or initiate programs. "We have to increase capacity so that veterans see the doctor right away and get their disability payments right away. If we don't fix that now, there will be a social catastrophe — alcohol abuse, drug abuse, DUIs, homelessness."

Army Capt. Ian Perry tries out a one-handed keyboard at a career fair at Walter Reed Army Medical Center in June 2007. Perry was injured in April in a rocket attack while patrolling in Mahmoudiyah, Iraq.

Worries over the future hinge in large part on whether more money will be available. The Kennedy School's Bilmes, who is forecasting the possible financial consequences of the fighting in Iraq and Afghanistan, calculates a low-end cost of $350 billion in lifetime medical and disability expenses for all wounded veterans. The underlying assumption is that no more troops are deployed and that the pattern of claims matches that of Gulf War veterans. At the high end, if 200,000 to 500,000 more troops are sent into the field, the lifetime costs could rise to $663 billion.[68]

Democratic supporters of mandatory funding cite Bilmes' study to make their case. At a Senate Veterans' Affairs hearing in July, however, Republican Sen. Craig warned that mandatory funding inevitably would raise taxes. "But there have been incredible improvements over the past 10 years in VA's health-care delivery system," Craig explained in an e-mail. "To suggest that the system is broken and therefore we need to change the funding model is simply, in my opinion, an exaggeration of the reality at hand."

Princeton health-care economist Reinhardt agreed that taxes will go up whether or not mandatory funding is enacted. In any event, he told the committee, prospects for the new generation of veterans appear dim, if recent history is any guide. His physician daughter, he noted, treats homeless men, many of them Vietnam veterans.

And Reinhardt recounted what he told his son when he was considering enlisting in the Marine Corps: "My experience has been that soldiers are usually not well-treated by their society."[69]

NOTES

1. For the number of military personnel deployed in Iraq and Afghanistan, see "Serve, Support, Simplify: Report of the President's Commission on Care for America's Returning Wounded Warriors," July 2007, p. 2, www.pccww.gov/docs/Kit/Main_Book_CC%5BJULY 26%5D.pdf.

2. See Dana Priest and Anne Hull, "Soldiers Face Neglect, Frustration at Army's Top Medical Facility," *The Washington Post*, Feb. 18, 2007, p. A1.

3. See Thom Shanker and David Stout, "Chief Army Medical Officer Ousted in Walter Reed Furor," *The New York Times*, March 13, 2007, p. A13. For Nicholson resignation, see Christopher Lee, "VA Secretary is Ending a Trying Tenure," *The Washington Post*, July 17, 2007, p. A3.

4. See Nancy Chandross, "Bob Woodruff: Turning Personal Injury Into Public Inquiry," ABC News, Feb. 26, 2007 (site provides links to Web video of Woodruff's reports), http://abcnews.go.com/WNT/Story?id=2904214&page=1.

5. See "Blast Injury" in "Defense and Veterans Brain Injury Center," undated, www.dvbic.org.

6. See "Health Status of and Services for Operation Enduring Freedom/Operation Iraqi Freedom Veterans after Traumatic Brain Injury Rehabilitation," Department of Veterans Affairs, Office of the Inspector General, July 12, 2006, www.va.gov/oig/54/reports/VAOIG-05-01818-165.pdf.

7. See "Senate Armed Services Committee Holds Hearing on the Nomination of Preston Geren to be Secretary of the Army," *Congressional Transcripts*, June 19, 2007.

8. Other commissions that reported on veterans care-related matters include the Department of Defense Task Force on Mental Health; the Institute of Medicine; the President's Task Force on Returning Global War on Terror Heroes; the Independent Review Group (examining Walter Reed Army Medical Center and National Naval Medical Center). All are listed in "Serve, Support, Simplify," *op. cit.*, p. 29.

9. See the Pentagon Web site, www.defenselink.mil/news/casualty.pdf.

10. See Denise Grady, "U.S. Reconfigures the Way Casualty Totals Are Given," *The New York Times*, Feb. 2, 2007, p. A17. Also see "Operation Iraqi Freedom U.S. Casualty Status, Operation Enduring Freedom Casualty Status," (updated weekly), www.defenselink.mil/news/casualty.pdf; "Global War on Terrorism — Operation Iraqi Freedom, By Casualty Category Within Service," (updated weekly), http://siadapp.dmdc.osd.mil/personnel/CASUALTY/OIF-Total.pdf; "Global War on Terrorism — Operation Enduring Freedom," siadapp.dmdc.osd.mil/personnel/CASUALTY/WOTSUM.pdf.

11. See "Serve, Support, Simplify," *op. cit.*, pp. 5-11.

12. See "Commissioners," in President's Commission on Care for America's Returning Wounded Warriors," 2007, www.pccww.gov/Commissioners.html.

13. Quoted in James Gerstenzang, "Panel urges better care for war vets," *Los Angeles Times*, July 26, p. A10.

14. See Sidath Viranga Panangala, "Veterans' Health Care Issues in the 109th Congress," Congressional Research Service, updated Oct. 26, 2006, pp. 25-27, www.fas.org/sgp/crs/misc/RL32 961.pdf.

15. See Brian J. Eastridge M.D., *et al.*, "Trauma System Development in a Theater of War: Experiences From Operation Iraqi Freedom and Operation Enduring Freedom," *The Journal of Trauma*, December 2006, www.usaisr.amedd.army.mil/gwot/Combat%20Trauma%20System.pdf.

16. Quoted in Gregg Zoroya, "Families bear catastrophic war wounds," *USA Today*, Sept. 25, 2006, p. A8.

17. See Charles W. Hoge M.D., *et al.*, "Mental Health Problems, Use of Mental Health Services, and Attrition From Military Service After Returning From Deployment to Iraq or Afghanistan," *Journal of the American Medical Association*, March 1, 2006, p. 1023.

18. See "An Achievable Vision: Report of the Department of Defense Task Force on Mental Health," June 2007, p. 5, www.ha.osd.mil/dhb/mhtf/MHTF-Report-Final.pdf.

19. Quoted in Dan Frosch, "Fighting the Terror of Battles That Rage in Soldiers' Heads," *The New York Times*, May 13, 2007, p. A18.

20. See "High Rate of Suicide Seen in Soldiers," *Los Angeles Times* (The Associated Press), Aug. 11, 2007, p. A13. "Global War on Terrorism — Operation Iraqi Freedom . . ." and ". . . Operation Enduring Freedom," *op. cit.* See also, Jennifer C. Kerr, "The battle within: Iraq vet suicides," *Marine Corps Times* (The Associated Press), May 28, 2007.

21. For statistics on claims handling, see Daniel Bertoni, "Veterans Disability Benefits: Long-Standing Claims Processing Challenges Persist," Government Accountability Office, testimony before Senate Veterans' Affairs Committee, March 7, 2007, www.gao.gov/new.items/d07512t.pdf. The complaint, *Veterans for Common Sense, et al., v. R. James Nicholson,* et al., C 07 3758, is available at www.mofo.com/docs/pdf/PTSD070723.pdf.

22. Holland Carter, "Words Unspoken Are Rendered on War's Faces," *The New York Times*, Aug. 22, 2007, p. B1.

23. Quoted in Steve Vogel, "Overhaul Urged in Care for Soldiers," *The Washington Post*, July 26, 2007, p. A1.

24. See "Senate Armed Services and Veterans' Affairs Committees Hold Joint Hearing on Disabled Veterans," *Congressional Transcripts*, April 12, 2007.

25. *Ibid.*

26. *Ibid.*

27. See "Post-Traumatic Stress Disorder: DoD Needs to Identify the Factors Its Providers Use to Make Mental Health Evaluation Referrals for Servicemembers," Government Accountability Office, May 2006, p. 21.

28. See "VA Health Care: VA Should Expedite the Implementation of Recommendations Needed to Improve Post-Traumatic Stress Disorder Services," Government Accountability Office, February 2005, p. 5.

29. See "Post-Traumatic Stress Disorder," House Veterans' Affairs Committee, written committee testimony, July 25, 2007.

30. *Ibid.*

31. "Sens. Murray, Obama, Bond, Boxer, McCaskill Introduce Amendment to Temporarily Decrease Military Personality Disorder Discharges," *US Fed News*, July 12, 2007.

32. See "Final Report Draft — The President's Commission on Care for America's Returning Wounded Warriors," July 24, 2007, p. 24, www.usatoday.com/news/pdf/07%2025%202007%20wounded%20warriors.pdf.

33. See "House Oversight and Government Reform Committee Holds Hearing on U.S. Military Mental Health," *Congressional Transcripts*, May 24, 2007.

34. "An Achievable Vision," *op. cit.*, p. 30.

35. "Veterans Affairs Claims Process," House Veterans' Affairs Committee, written committee testimony, March 13, 2007.

36. See House Veterans' Affairs Committee, "Subcommittee on Oversight and Investigations Holds Hearing on Impact of Poor Conditions on Soldiers Leaving Service," *Congressional Transcripts*, March 8, 2007.

37. See "Senate Veterans' Affairs Committee Holds Hearing on Veterans' Affairs Health Care Funding," *Congressional Transcripts*, July 25, 2007.

38. Unless otherwise noted, this section is drawn from Richard H. Taylor, "Homeward Bound: American Veterans Return From War," 2007. See also William Triplett, "Treatment of Veterans," *CQ Researcher*, Nov. 19, 2004, pp. 973-996.

39. See Maj. Charles E. Heller, "Chemical Warfare in World War I: The American Experience, 1917 — 1918," Combat Studies Institute, U.S. Army Command and General Staff College, Fort Leavenworth, Kansas, September 1984, www-cgsc.army.mil/carl/resources/csi/Heller/HELLER.asp#5.%20The%20Quick%20and%20the%20Dead:%20The%20AEF%20on%20the%20Chemical%20Battlefield.

40. Roger J. Spiller, "Shellshock," *American Heritage*, May-June 1990, www.americanheritage.com/articles/magazine/ah/1990/4/1990_4_74.shtml.

41. See Glen H. Elder Jr., Ph.D, *et al.*, "Linking Combat and Physical Health: The Legacy of World War II in Men's Lives," *American Journal of Psychiatry*, March 1997, p. 330, http://ajp.psychiatryonline.org/cgi/reprint/154/3/330.

42. For statistics on military service during the Vietnam era, see "Fact Sheet: America's Wars," Department of Veterans Affairs, November 2006, www1.va.gov/opa/fact/amwars.asp.

43. See Taylor, *op. cit.*, p. 134.

44. See Jack Shafer, "Spitfire," *Slate*, Feb. 5, 2007, www.slate.com/id/2159099/.

45. See Taylor, *op. cit.*, p. 135.

46. See Thomas Whiteside, "Defoliation," *The New Yorker*, Feb. 7, 1970, www.vietnam.ttu.edu/star/images/225/2250209003.pdf.

47. See Douglas Martin, "Thomas Whiteside, 79, Dies," *The New York Times*, Oct. 12, 1997, p. A44.

48. Quoted in Henry Weinstein, "VA rebuked for balking on Agent Orange care," *Los Angeles Times*, July 20, 2007, p. B1. For full text of the decision, see *Nehmer, et al., v. Department of Veterans Affairs*, United States Court of Appeal for the 9th Circuit, July 19, 2007, www.ca9.uscourts.gov/ca9/newopinions.nsf/28D4FD1ECE6EEC3B8825731D0057D6DD/$file/0615179.pdf?openelement.

49. See Libby Perl, "Veterans and Homelessness," Congressional Research Service, May 31, 2007, p. 7, www.fas.org/sgp/crs/misc/RL34024.pdf.

50. See "Fact Sheet: America's Wars," *op. cit.*

51. Quoted in Scott Shane, "Chemicals Sickened Gulf War Veterans, Latest Study Finds," *The New York Times*, Oct. 15, 2004, p. A1.

52. Quoted in David Brown, "Panel Discounts Existence of Unique Gulf War Syndrome," *The Washington Post*, Sept. 13, 2006, p. A10.

53. See Edwin Chen, Chris Kraul and Patrick J. McDonnell, "Bush Pledges 'No Retreat' From Iraq," *Los Angeles Times*, Aug. 27, 2003, p. A1; Tom Squiteri, "Army Late with Orders for Armored Humvees," *USA Today*, March 28, 2005, p. A1.

54. See Ann Scott Tyson and Josh White, "Strained Army Extends Tours to 15 Months," *The Washington Post*, April 12, 2007, p. A1; Kimberly Johnson, "Conway: Corps sticking to 7-month tours," *Marine Corps Times*, July 12, 2007.

55. See Rone Tempest, "Injured Vet Faces Battle of Red Tape," *Los Angeles Times*, March 21, 2007, p. A1.

56. See John M. Donnelly and Josh Rogin, "Appropriators Call Bush's Bluff on VA," *CQ Weekly*, June 18, 2007, p. 1860; Josh Rogin, "Spending Measures Reflect Growing Need for Veterans' Health Care," *CQ Today*, June 15, 2007.

57. See John M. Donnelly and Kathleen Hunter, "Senate Passes Military Health Care Overhaul, Pay Raise," *CQ Today*, July 25, 2007.

58. See Patrick Yoest, "House Expected to Pass Trio of Bills Aimed at Improving Veterans' Benefits," *CQ Today*, March 20, 2007; "Bill at a Glance," March 21, 2007.

59. See House Veterans' Affairs Committee, March 8, 2007, *op. cit.*

60. See Rep. Susan Davis, *Congressional Record*, p. E1548, June 29, 2007.

61. Quoted in *Congressional Record*, Senate, April 26, 2007, p. S5211.

62. See Sara Lubbes, "Senate Committee Approves Five Veterans Measures," CQ Committee Coverage, June 27, 2007; Edward Walsh, "VA Cuts Some Veterans' Access to Health Care," *The Washington Post*, Jan. 17, 2003, p. A21.

63. Quoted in Lubbes, *op. cit.*

64. *Ibid.*

65. See "America Supports You," www.americasupportsyou.mil/americasupportsyou/.

66. See the organization's Web site at www. newdirections.org.

67. See "House Oversight and Government Reform Committee Holds Hearing on U.S. Military Mental Health," *Congressional Transcripts*, May 24, 2007.

68. See Linda Bilmes, "Soldiers Returning from Iraq and Afghanistan: The Long-term Costs of Providing Veterans Medical Care and Disability Benefits," Harvard University, John F. Kennedy School of Government, Faculty Research Working Papers Series, January 2007, pp. 16-17, http://ksgnotes1.harvard.edu/Research/wpaper.nsf/rwp/RWP07-001/$File/rwp_07_001_bilmes.pdf.

69. See Senate Veterans' Affairs Committee, July 25, 2007, *op. cit.*

BIBLIOGRAPHY

Books

Rieckhoff, Paul, *Chasing Ghosts — Failures and Faces in Iraq: A Soldier's Perspective, NAL Caliber,* 2006.
The founder of Iraq and Afghanistan Veterans of America chronicles his wartime experiences as a National Guard infantry lieutenant and his transformation into an anti-war activist.

Taylor, Richard H., with Sandra Wright Taylor, *Homeward Bound: American Veterans from War, Praeger Security International,* 2007.
A veteran of the Vietnam War traces the experiences of vets returning home from war, including those suffering from post-traumatic stress disorder (PTSD) after fighting in Iraq and Afghanistan.

Wood, Trish, *What Was Asked of Us: An Oral History of the Iraq War by the Soldiers Who Fought It, Little, Brown and Co.,* 2006.
An investigative reporter recounts veterans' combat experiences and examines life after war — including the account of helicopter pilot Tammy Duckworth, who was shot down and lost both legs.

Articles

The Associated Press, "Home from Iraq a Shattered Man," *Los Angeles Times,* July 1, 2007, p. A18.
A VA physician examines the injuries of Iraq veteran Joseph Briseno Jr., whom some consider the most severely injured American soldier in the war.

Glasser, Ronald, "A Shock Wave of Brain Injuries," *The Washington Post,* April 8, 2007, p. B1.
A physician who treated medically evacuated troops in Vietnam reports on the extent and effects of traumatic brain injury in the war in Iraq.

Kraul, Chris, "Veteran Medics Help Reduce Iraq Fatalities," *Los Angeles Times,* Feb. 12, 2006, p. A15.
An on-scene report from a combat hospital in Baghdad describes how surgeons are helping to vastly improve the odds of survival for severely wounded soldiers.

Perry, Tony, "War Injuries Strain Hospitals," *Los Angeles Times,* March 19, 2007, p. B3.
Military and VA hospitals in the San Diego area near major Navy and Marine bases are trying to cope with a growing number of patients.

Priest, Dana, and Anne Hull, "Soldiers Face Neglect, Frustration at Army's Top Medical Facility," *The Washington Post,* Feb. 18, 2007, p. A1.
Two reporters spent several months visiting recovering soldiers in a dilapidated outpatient residence at Walter Reed Army Medical Center to produce this dramatic series.

Priest, Dana, and Anne Hull, "The War Inside," *The Washington Post,* June 17, 2007, p. A1.
Priest and Hull examine the hardships of veterans trying to deal with post-traumatic stress disorder (PTSD) — often with little help from the VA.

Tempest, Rone, "Troops Get Help Battling Stress," *Los Angeles Times,* April 22, 2007, p. B1.
A pilot program embeds psychologists and social workers with Iraq National Guard veterans in an effort to detect and deal with PTSD.

Zucchino, David, "Injured in Iraq, a Soldier Reclaims His Independence," *Los Angeles Times,* July 4, 2006, p. A1.
A lengthy profile of a veteran who lost three limbs in Iraq provides a window into the life-long cost of war.

Reports and Studies

"An Achievable Vision: Report of the Department of Defense Task Force on Mental Health," June 2007, www.openminds.com/indres/070907mhtfreport.pdf.
A Pentagon panel takes a self-critical look at the availability of services for treating the psychological wounds of war.

"Serve, Support, Simplify," *Report of the President's Commission on Care for America's Returning Wounded Warriors,* July 2007, www.pccww.gov/docs/Kit/Main_Book_CC%5BJULY26%5D.pdf.
The Dole-Shalala commission proposes six recommendations designed to produce immediate improvements in the veterans' care system.

"Veterans' Disability Benefits: Claims Processing Challenges Persist," *Government Accountability Office,* March 2007, www.gao.gov/new.items/d07512t.pdf.

Daniel Bertoni, the Government Accountability Office's acting director for education, workforce and income security, tells lawmakers that the VA system has failed to meet its own goals for faster responses to veterans' applications in disability ratings-related matters.

Panangala, Sidath Viranga, "Veterans' Health Care Issues in the 109th Congress," *Congressional Research Service*, **Updated Oct. 26, 2006, www.fas.org/sgp/crs/misc/RL32961.pdf.**

A detailed explanation of the disability-ratings system and the ongoing debate over mandatory funding keep this report relevant even past the close of the 109th Congress.

For More Information

America Supports You, www.americasupportsyou.mil/americasupportsyou/index. A Defense Department-created program aimed at citizens and organizations who want to mount projects supporting troops and veterans.

Defense & Veterans Brain Injury Center, Building 1, Room B209, Walter Reed Army Medical Center, 6900 Georgia Ave., N.W., Washington, DC 20307; (202) 782-6345; www.dvbic.org. A Defense Department program for active-duty personnel and veterans that provides medical care, sponsors research and publishes information.

Iraq War Veterans Organization — Long War Veterans Organization, P.O. Box 571, Yucaipa, CA 92399; www.iraqwarveterans.org. Service organization for veterans of the present wars as well as those now serving.

National Veterans Legal Services Program, P.O. Box 65762, Washington, DC 20035; (202) 265-8305; www.nvlsp.org. Nonprofit organization that sues the government to obtain benefits for veterans and trains non-lawyer advocates to represent veterans before government agencies.

ONE Freedom, P.O. Box 7418, Boulder, CO 80306; (888) 334-8387; www.onefreedom.org. Nonprofit developer of programs aimed at helping veterans and their families manage post-combat stress.

Veterans for America, 1025 Vermont Ave., N.W., 7th Floor, Washington, DC 20005; (202) 483-9222; www.veteransforamerica.org. Advocacy organization whose purposes go beyond traditional veterans' issues, to include campaigning for humanitarian relief in war-ravaged countries.

Veterans for Common Sense, 1101 Pennsylvania Ave., S.E., Suite 203, Washington, DC 20003; www.veteransforcommonsense.org. Critically evaluates government programs.

Veterans of Foreign Wars, 406 West 34th St., Kansas City, MO 64111; (816) 756-3390; www.vfw.org. A longtime leader in veterans' affairs.

Veterans' Disability Benefits Commission, 1101 Pennsylvania Ave., N.W., 5th Floor, Washington, DC 20004; (202) 756-7729; www.vetscommission.org. Created by law to study the entire veterans' benefits system.

14

Ending Homelessness

Is the Problem Solvable?

William Triplett

A discarded couch offers a soft landing to a homeless man on Sunset Boulevard in Hollywood, Calif. The U.S. Conference of Mayors estimates 840,000 people are homeless in America each day, with up to 3 million homeless over the course of a year.

From *CQ Researcher*,
June 18, 2004.

City Commissioner Tomas Regalado advocates arresting anyone caught feeding the homeless in downtown Miami.[1]

In suburban Seattle, a homeless shelter has not brought the feared rise in crime, nor widespread opposition to its location.[2]

Outside Tucson, an elderly man and his 48-year-old son live in a filthy desert camp on the father's Social Security check and the son's panhandling, but neither has much interest in living in a shelter.[3]

In cities across the country, America's 2 to 3 million homeless people are increasingly visible — with all the complicated and sometimes contradictory realities associated with homelessness. In recent years, a shortage of affordable housing accompanied by a sluggish economy has put more Americans on the street, say advocates for the homeless. Meanwhile, requests for emergency shelter are up, but resources haven't kept pace, they say.

However, thanks to new research suggesting that homelessness could be solved if society addresses the many interrelated factors that cause it, advocates for the homeless are more optimistic now than perhaps ever before about the possibility of finally eliminating the perennial problem. But no consensus yet exists on a comprehensive approach to address all the causes.

Reflecting the new optimism, the Fannie Mae Foundation recently pledged $35 million in financing and challenge grants toward construction of new, subsidized housing. "In the late 1970s, we as a country were creating about 400,000 units of subsidized housing a year," says Paul Weech, director of market research and

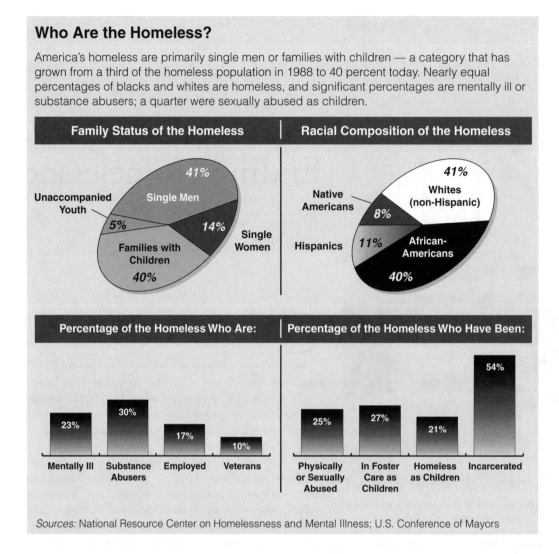

Who Are the Homeless?

America's homeless are primarily single men or families with children — a category that has grown from a third of the homeless population in 1988 to 40 percent today. Nearly equal percentages of blacks and whites are homeless, and significant percentages are mentally ill or substance abusers; a quarter were sexually abused as children.

Family Status of the Homeless

- Single Men 41%
- Single Women 14%
- Families with Children 40%
- Unaccompanied Youth 5%

Racial Composition of the Homeless

- Whites (non-Hispanic) 41%
- African-Americans 40%
- Hispanics 11%
- Native Americans 8%

Percentage of the Homeless Who Are:

- Mentally Ill 23%
- Substance Abusers 30%
- Employed 17%
- Veterans 10%

Percentage of the Homeless Who Have Been:

- Physically or Sexually Abused 25%
- In Foster Care as Children 27%
- Homeless as Children 21%
- Incarcerated 54%

Sources: National Resource Center on Homelessness and Mental Illness; U.S. Conference of Mayors

policy development at Fannie Mae (formerly the Federal National Mortgage Association). "For the last several years, it hasn't been above 60,000-70,000." Meanwhile, median housing prices rose 639 percent, contributing to a serious shortage of affordable housing nationwide.[4]

But according to Robert Rector, a senior research fellow at the conservative Heritage Foundation, homelessness is not just a housing problem. It is an "incidental symptom of other, more fundamental problems," like substance abuse or mental illness, he says. Homelessness exists "precisely because we have not succeeded in dealing with those other problems."

Fiscal conservatives maintain that with the federal government spending $3.2 billion a year on homelessness programs, anyone sleeping without a roof over his head should be held accountable for his behavior. But, they insist, anyone receiving a shelter berth should first earn it, even if that only means agreeing to take his antipsychotic medication.

But advocates for the homeless say that approach only works in some cases. "One size does not fit all," says Nan Roman, president of the National Alliance to End Homelessness, a nonprofit organization dedicated to mobilizing the nonprofit, public and private sectors to end homelessness within 10 years by addressing its root causes.

If one size does not fit all, it may be because the nation's homeless population is so diverse: 40 percent are families with children, 30 percent are substance abusers, 23 percent are severely mentally ill, 17 percent are employed and 10 percent are veterans.[5]

Despite the size and diversity of the problem, the federal government has never devoted enough resources to eliminate homelessness, and $3.2 billion really isn't enough, some advocates say.

Policy analysts and observers have only begun to understand the full complexity of homelessness in the last few years, many experts say. "People think that because they see people living on the streets, they understand homelessness," Roman says. "But so much of it is away from the public eye." To understand homelessness, she maintains, one needs to understand all the causes and effects of poverty.

Critics say the homeless — and their shelters — can drive down the value of real estate. And some homeless people refuse to go into shelters, often because of overcrowding or crime. But advocates question whether cities should be allowed to jail those who refuse to go to shelters, as some have chosen to do.

Experts also disagree about the size of the problem. The U.S. Conference of Mayors says 840,000 people are homeless on any given night, and that over the course of a year some 3 million people are homeless at one time or another.[6] Philip Mangano, executive director of the U.S. Interagency Council on Homelessness, estimates that 650,000 are homeless on any given night and 2 million to 2.5 million are without shelter at some point each year. Others say the U.S. Census Bureau's estimate of 470,000 people homeless on any given night is more realistic.[7]

Advocates say the numbers are increasing due to the recession, Congress' refusal to raise the minimum wage, rising unemployment and stricter welfare-eligibility requirements. They cite a recent Conference of Mayors survey showing that requests for shelter assistance in 2003 increased by 13 percent over the previous year.[8]

"Yes, [shelter requests] are up, but to some degree that reflects people moving from the streets to the shelters, and shelter availability fluctuates," notes Michael Tanner, director of health and welfare studies at the libertarian

President Bush greets volunteers during the December 2001 holidays at Martha's Table, a nonprofit in Washington, D.C., that feeds the homeless.

AFP Photo/Stephen Jaffe

Cato Institute, who maintains that the nation's homeless population has not changed appreciably in the last 20 years.

Even the definition of homelessness remains disputed. Some observers say it means residing in a shelter (or outdoors) for more than six months; others say anyone without a home is homeless.

Most agree, however, that the homeless population consists of two types: the episodic, or transitionally homeless, who are experiencing a bad run of luck but will soon be back on their feet, and the chronically homeless — usually substance abusers, the handicapped or the mentally ill.

While the chronically homeless account for only 10 to 20 percent of the homeless, they pose the biggest challenges, most advocates for the homeless agree. They also agree that unless governments at all levels adopt new, coordinated strategies, homelessness will never be eliminated.

In 2002 the Bush administration declared a commitment to ending chronic homelessness in 10 years, and is pressing Congress to pass the Samaritan Initiative, a bill aimed at providing $70 million for housing and attendant care specifically for the chronically homeless. But critics say because the proposal only addresses the 10-20 percent who are chronically homeless, it does not go far enough or is rooted in failed approaches.

"We agree with ending chronic homelessness," Roman says. "But that doesn't mean we shouldn't address needs of other homeless people."

Mangano, the administration's point man on homelessness, maintains that ending homelessness will be a slow, incremental process, given its relatively low priority among lawmakers preoccupied with the war on terrorism and the occupation of Iraq. Addressing chronic homelessness is a sound first step, he says, because this subgroup consumes more than half the resources devoted to reducing homelessness.

Similarly, most agree that government — in particular, the federal government — should play the lead role in combating homelessness. But precisely what the government should do, and how much it should spend doing it, is still sharply contested. "In every respect, the private sector would probably do a better job than government," says Douglas Besharov, an expert on welfare at the American Enterprise Institute (AEI), a conservative think tank.

Meanwhile, public perceptions of homelessness have changed since the early 1980s, when the issue dominated media reports. General sympathy waned after years of federal programs and hundreds of local initiatives seemed to fail. In the mid-1990s, Congress limited welfare benefits, forcing some recipients off the program, and — according to homeless advocates, into the streets.[9] By decade's end, with the economy booming and unemployment low, many people assumed that if you were homeless, it was "your own damn fault."[10]

Cities began to rely more on law enforcement to deal with homelessness, such as anti-panhandling ordinances. Orlando, for instance, declared lying down on the sidewalk illegal.[11] In Manhattan, Mayor Rudolph W. Giuliani in 1999 ordered the arrest of any homeless person refusing to go into a city shelter.[12]

Some cities still criminalize homelessness, but because of the new research and the enthusiasm it has generated, alternatives are also developing.

As city officials and homeless advocates seek a solution to homelessness, here are some of the key questions under debate:

Is homelessness solvable?

"Absolutely," says Laurene Heybach, director of the Law Project at the Chicago Coalition for the Homeless. The key, she says, is to be clear about the ultimate goal. "Is it to solve every personal problem that every person who needs housing has? Not in my view, though I laud any program that assists people in overcoming their personal problems."

Heybach says history supports her viewpoint. "There was a time in our nation when many people with personal problems were housed." The rise of neoconservatism and its preference for private market forces over governmental programs has worsened the plight of the homeless, she argues. "There's been a tremendous loss of resources in [federally] funded programs since Ronald Reagan became president. We're in a neocon world now, which seeks to undo a number of programs that have worked very well over the years, though they've never been as big as they need to be."

For example, public housing projects have been extremely successful, she says, particularly for homeless children as well as the elderly and disabled. "Does that mean every public housing project is a success? Of course not. But neither is private housing. The private market can't solve the problem because it would be too expensive. In fact, the world is sliding backward because of a willingness to let market forces address homelessness."

But the AEI's Besharov thinks the homeless, like the poor, will always be with us. "It's a mistake to think we'll eradicate homelessness because there are always people who can't make it on their own" because of mental illness and alcoholism, he says.

"A certain level of homelessness is intractable," concurs Tanner of the Cato Institute. Since the first days of the Republic, he notes, "people lived on streets or in flophouses. Of course, you got a big explosion in the homeless population with deinstitutionalization [the widespread releasing of patients from state mental hospitals that began during the Kennedy administration] because those people used to be taken off the streets. You probably can help a few families of working poor who are temporarily having problems." But at least 400,000 people would still be homeless, he estimates.

The real obstacle to ending homelessness, he says, is often the homeless themselves. People experiencing temporary problems typically don't leave a shelter until they have a new permanent place to live. But substance abusers often will stay in a shelter for a few days, then leave to get drugs. "You can't tie people down and force them to stay," he says. "In winter, they'll stay longer because of the weather, but in summer, for some of these folks, life on the streets wasn't the worst thing in the world."

But homeless advocate Roman says the problem could be ended. "It's not that everyone's going to be living in a white house with a picket fence, but we don't have to have people living on the street or in shelters or transitional housing," she says. "And I don't think there are people who can't be helped. If people are rejecting what we're offering them" — such as refusing to enter shelters — "maybe we're not offering the right thing."

Homeless shelters, almost by definition, are only temporary accommodations, and many observers acknowledge a dire, nationwide shortage of affordable housing. According to Harvard University's Joint Center for Housing Studies, the total shortfall in low-cost rental housing was 4.7 million in 2002.[13]

Moreover, while the U.S. poverty rate declined slightly during the economic boom of the 1990s, it began to rise again in 2001, when the economy started to slow down rapidly. By 2003, almost 33 million Americans — 11.7 percent of the population — were living below the poverty line, according to census data.[14]

Thus, as the amount of affordable housing was decreasing, the number of poor people was increasing. With less money, poor families forced to choose between paying rent and buying groceries often opted for the food, ending up on the streets.

Until recently, one of the most effective antidotes to homelessness was single-room occupancy (SRO) housing, which offered simple but extended accommodations. "Even if you looked at Chicago 20 years ago," Heybach says, "we had lots of drunks on skid row, but they had a place to go at night because we had lots of SRO housing. But in the past 15 years, like in L.A. and San Francisco, SRO has disappeared."

Urban renewal and gentrification — replacing derelict buildings with expensive new offices or apartments — have eliminated much SRO housing and other traditional shelter space. And as advocacy groups have tried to establish new shelters in neighborhoods, residents often have raised the now-ubiquitous cry: "Not in My Back Yard!" (NIMBY).

"We had a struggle about two years ago," Heybach says. "A church proposed to convert a building into

housing for recovering substance-abusing women who were homeless. There was lots of community opposition, and at the zoning hearing, people in this wealthy community were testifying that here would be people who we knew had used drugs. The very people articulating this were completely oblivious to the fact that on any given Friday night in this same community, many people with good jobs use drugs in their private residences."

"People are all for low-income housing as long as it is not in their suburb," Tanner observes.

Are we doing the right things to combat homelessness?

A few years ago, Amy Sherman, a senior fellow at the Hudson Institute and an urban policy adviser at Trinity Presbyterian Church in Charlottesville, Va., stopped her car to help a woman holding a sign that read, "Homeless. Please Help." Sherman offered to take her to a clean, safe Salvation Army shelter, but the woman said she and her husband were fine sleeping under some nearby trees.

Sherman took the woman shopping, buying her food, clothing and some bug spray. Later, she visited the couple at their makeshift campsite, giving the husband job leads. Then one day they were gone.[15]

Some advocates would say that by offering tangible help, Sherman did exactly the right thing. But as she later wrote, "I'm convinced that handouts are basically wrongheaded." She shares author James L. Payne's view that handouts "demean recipients by implying [they] can't meet their own needs. [Handouts] can enable dysfunctional behavior and can be disincentives to work."[16]

By contrast, as Payne writes, " 'expectant giving' — a contribution that demands a constructive response from the supplicant — affirms people's God-given dignity and capacities. It's a 'hand-up,' not a handout."[17]

But the American social welfare system generally offers handouts, Sherman points out. The main reason for this, she says, is that "hand-up giving requires far more time, thought and personal investment than sympathetic [handout] giving. It's much easier to toss the homeless a few dollars than to build a relationship with them [that] can address the root causes of their condition."[18]

Critics of many programs targeting the homeless agree, saying the predominant strategy has only enabled the homeless by merely "warehousing" them and

Crackdown in San Francisco

It used to pay to be homeless in San Francisco. For years, the city gave homeless people up to $410 a month. This past spring, about 2,500 of the city's estimated 9,500 homeless were receiving checks.[1]

"I was in Nebraska," a new arrival said in 2002, "and I met some guys on freight trains. They said, 'Hey, let's go to San Francisco. They give you a check.' I said, 'Why do they give you a check?' They said, 'Because you're homeless.' I said, 'I don't believe this.' "[2]

But it was true. A local television station even secretly videotaped some homeless people cashing their checks and then buying drugs or alcohol.[3]

Last month city officials began reducing the monthly homeless allowances to as little as $59 and instead will offer housing coupled with mental health and substance-abuse services. The new Care Not Cash program is similar to the Bush administration's proposed permanent supportive housing (PSH) program, a centerpiece of the administration's plan to ending chronic homelessness in 10 years.

Care Not Cash had a difficult birth. When an outline of the program was put on a ballot by then Supervisor Gavin Newsom two years ago as Proposition N, nearly 60 percent of residents voted for it. But the San Francisco Coalition on Homelessness, among others, denounced the measure as "another example of an aspiring politician using the homeless to advance his career." Another city official pointed out that the housing and services being promised by Care Not Cash did not yet exist.[4]

Proponents countered that the housing and services would be funded by the estimated $13.2 million in savings expected from reducing the monthly cash payments. However, the following year a homeless woman and an advocate for the poor challenged the validity of the Proposition N vote in court. A San Francisco judge ruled in their favor, saying that "only the city's elected Board of Supervisors, not voters, had the authority to reduce payments to the homeless."[5]

The program's proponents appealed, and in April an appeals court reversed the lower court's ruling. The vote was indeed valid, because it represented the will of the people, the court said.

Last month, San Francisco finally launched Care Not Cash by opening up two old residential hotels that the city had refurbished. Together, they have 154 rooms, one of which went to Cesar Ragsac, 53, who said he had been homeless since losing his electronics job nine years ago.

ignoring their personal problems. That's exactly what the nation's 50 federal programs, administered by eight different agencies, have done for the past 17 years, Housing Secretary Mel Martinez told the national convention of the National Alliance to End Homelessness shortly after he took office in 2001.

"Since 1987, the federal government has funneled more than $13 billion into easing the plight of the homeless . . . [b]ut we have not made much progress," he said. "It is time for the federal government to . . . invest in more permanent solutions [such as] moving the chronically homeless into permanent housing and permanent care." Martinez promised the administration would seek to remove Reagan-era "statutory barriers" that prevent the use of federal homeless dollars to develop housing.

But conservatives Rector and Besharov contend that homelessness is not, fundamentally, a housing problem. "Build a shelter, and it shall be filled, unless it is a rat hole," Besharov says. "If you build anything halfway decent and make it available for free, people are going to take it. It's just human nature. There'll always be shelters because they're too attractive, and they'll never kick people out."

"What we need in the shelters is a series of demands and requirements that begin to address the core reason why the individual is in the shelter," Rector says, such as requiring addicts to undergo a drug-withdrawal program and the mentally ill to take anti-psychotic medication as prescribed. "Unfortunately a lot of homeless shelters seem to just operate as dumping grounds," with no requirements.

Maria Foscarinis, executive director of the National Law Center on Homelessness and Poverty (NLCHP), argues that many existing programs have been successful. "They have just not been at a large enough scale to solve the whole problem. Individual problems get solved, but not the whole problem." For example, she says, "We know that providing rent subsidies to people who just

"This is one of the best things that ever happened to me," he said. "My own home. My own."[6]

The city hopes to have 900 more rooms available by the end of the year, but that means nearly 1,500 people now receiving checks will still be homeless — and receiving only $59 a month. City officials claim that even more housing and services will be created as the savings begin to accrue from the reduced monthly payments. By next year, city funding for new residences will total $10 million, they say.

Critics say that may be too little, too late. Some 8,500 San Franciscans would still be competing for approximately 2,250 emergency shelter beds and 1,200 transitional housing slots, according to the National Law Center for Homelessness and Poverty.[7]

On the day the city opened the first of the two hotels to accept residents, about 100 activists and homeless people demonstrated against Care Not Cash. A homeless woman dressed as a monkey said, "Homeless people are being used

Supporters of San Francisco's Care Not Cash program demonstrate during an address in May 2003 by then-mayoral candidate Gavin Newsom, who proposed the initiative.

like lab animals in experiments. Care Not Cash is the experiment. We are here because this is our Last Supper before being crucified by Care Not Cash."[8]

---

[1] Estimate of 9,500 from "Homelessness in the United States and the Human Right to Housing," National Law Center on Poverty and Homelessness, Jan. 14, 2004, p. 24. Some conservatives, however, estimate the city's homeless population is much closer to 6,000.

[2] Hank Plante, "5 Investigates: Can 'Care Not Cash' Help SF Homeless?", cbs5.com, Oct. 29, 2002; http://cbs5.com/news/local/2002/10/29/5_Investigates:_Can_'Care_Not_Cash'_Help_SF_Homeless%3F.html.

[3] Ibid.

[4] "San Francisco revamps homeless policy," CNN.com, Dec. 12, 2002; www.cnn.com/2002/US/West/12/12/homeless.evicted.ap.

[5] "Appeals Court Validates San Francisco's Homeless Initiative," The Associated Press, April 30, 2004.

[6] Kevin Fagan, "A home after years adrift — S.F. reduces payments to homeless people on welfare in exchange for providing housing," The San Francisco Chronicle, May 4, 2004, p. A1.

[7] National Law Center, op. cit.

[8] Fagan, op. cit.

---

need help with housing costs can end homelessness — studies document this."

"Many of the shelter-plus-care programs have been very successful," adds Heybach. Indeed, permanent supportive housing (PSH) programs that also offer complementary supportive services, such as mental health care and detox programs designed to address the causes of homelessness, are becoming increasingly popular. In fact, 60,000 such units have been opened nationwide in recent years.[19]

PSH figures prominently in the Bush administration's strategy to end chronic homelessness in 10 years. "When you put housing together with services for vulnerable populations, then there's a high retention rate of tenancy," says the Interagency Council's Mangano, noting that a 10-year-old PSH program in New York has shown that "over 90 percent of people deemed intractably homeless retain tenancy with supportive housing."

Rep. Rick Renzi, R-Ariz., responded to the administration with the Samaritan Initiative Act of 2004, which he introduced in the House on March 30. The bill calls for the Departments of Health and Human Services, Housing and Urban Development and Veterans Affairs to create housing that provides health care, mental health and substance-abuse treatment and other services for the chronically homeless.

Reactions to the bill have been mixed. Many advocates and political insiders support the bill in spirit, but some have interpreted the White House's request for $70 million in funding as a cynical contradiction of that spirit. "Everybody knows $70 million won't buy you much," says Rep. Barney Frank, D-Mass. "If the Bush administration got its way on homelessness, the situation would be worse, not better."

Mangano hopes the $70 million is only the beginning of a regular stream of funding that will grow bigger as PSH begins to show positive effects. "We know more

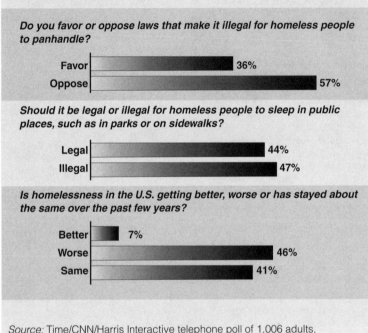

Majority Opposes Criminalizing Panhandling

A majority of Americans oppose criminalizing panhandling by the homeless, and nearly half think homelessness is getting worse, according to a recent poll.

Do you favor or oppose laws that make it illegal for homeless people to panhandle?

Favor — 36%
Oppose — 57%

Should it be legal or illegal for homeless people to sleep in public places, such as in parks or on sidewalks?

Legal — 44%
Illegal — 47%

Is homelessness in the U.S. getting better, worse or has stayed about the same over the past few years?

Better — 7%
Worse — 46%
Same — 41%

Source: Time/CNN/Harris Interactive telephone poll of 1,006 adults, Nov. 13-14, 2002. "Not sures" are not included.

Heybach says the administration's focus on the chronically homeless leaves her unconvinced of its sincerity. "A cynic would say that represents an effort to get the most visible off the streets. We think there has to be a plan to house everyone."

Should government play a stronger leadership role in fighting homelessness?

Ending homelessness requires a partnership involving a wide range of government and private groups, but with government — in particular, the federal government — acting as the leading player, says Rep. Julia Carson, D-Ind.

"When you have people homeless in a community, it affects the whole community," she says. "It becomes like a disease — it starts out and then spreads. In suburban Indianapolis around shopping centers I see people pushing carts hoping to get cast-offs. The city has a blueprint to end homelessness, but it relies on federal support."

The support comes from the McKinney Act, which President Reagan signed into law in 1987. Among other provisions, it created the Interagency Council on Homelessness to coordinate the activities of 15 federal agencies (now 20) and designated $1 billion in federal funding the first two years for emergency food, shelter, care, education and job training for the homeless.

But Carson wants to broaden the federal government's role beyond the McKinney Act or the proposed Samaritan Initiative. In July 2003 she introduced the Bringing America Home Act, which would amend the McKinney Act to include donation of surplus federal property to assist the homeless and attempts to establish affordable housing as a basic human right. (*See "At Issue," p. 339*) Lacking the administration's backing, however, the bill isn't moving through Congress as quickly as the Samaritan Initiative.

now about what works," he says, adding that political will to end homelessness is building, but only incrementally.

The focus on chronic homelessness is the first step in adopting a new, management-oriented strategy toward the problem. "We're not trying to service homeless people in place for years, as we have before," Mangano says. "We don't want to just fund more homeless programs because all you get are more homeless programs, and there are over 40,000 programs targeted to homeless people already."

As chronic homelessness shrinks, there will be more money to begin addressing the remaining homeless population, Mangano says. He notes that the chronically homeless account for no more than 10-20 percent of the total homeless population but absorb half the governmental resources devoted to the problem.

The NLCHP's Foscarinis also believes a full public-private partnership is necessary. "But the overwhelming responsibility is at the government level to make sure there's enough housing and other resources available to meet the basic needs of the poorest members of society," she says. But the policies needed to make those resources available aren't there yet, she says.

Indeed, says Heybach of the Chicago Coalition for the Homeless, the federal government should be doing the most to fight homelessness. "The federal government has put a lot of state and local entities into a fiscal crisis by grossly reducing taxes and raising the deficit and expenditures," she says. States simply can't afford to do enough. However, she cautions the federal government against any unilateral action. "Whatever they do must be in participation with those in the private sector and in advocacy groups who know about solutions."[20]

Mangano agrees the federal government could make a difference. But he also notes, "We've learned that no one level of government can get this job done alone."

The Interagency Council's leadership could best be used to build partnerships around the country, he says. An advocate on homelessness for more than two decades, Mangano is encouraging the nation's mayors to adopt 10-year plans to end chronic homelessness in conjunction with the administration's plan. To date, 117 mayors have adopted such plans, he says.

The Heritage Foundation's Rector stresses the government can do more, particularly in providing coordinated leadership involving shelters. "The general rule is that bad charity drives out good," he says. "If you have a few shelters in a community, and one of them tries to have rigorous behavioral requirements and the other shelters don't, guess who gets all the clients? It's very difficult for a private charity to run a constructive shelter program, one that's demanding, if down the street there's a bigger governmental facility that says, 'Hey, come on in and pass out!' "

Rector doesn't oppose the use of federal money as long as it's not wastefully spent. But historically, he says, federal spending on homelessness has achieved "nothing" at great expense.

Tanner of the Cato Institute says government at all levels needs to better recognize and address the ways in which government has contributed to homelessness through its zoning laws. "Are we zoning low-income housing out of existence?" he asks. He argues that local governments tend to bow to NIMBY pressure, which has helped restrict the amount of available affordable housing.

Advocates for the homeless also note that federal tax cuts have indirectly contributed to that loss of affordable housing by putting additional pressure on cash-strapped local governments, which often then turn to rezoning to enable gentrification of low-income areas, which increases local tax revenues.

"But I also think private charities and the private sector have enormous responsibility here, too," Tanner adds. "There are also issues of personal responsibility, and not just the individual's. It used to be that if your brother-in-law lost his job you put him on your couch. Now we send him to the shelter. We need to get back to taking care of each other."

For Besharov, government needs to play the leadership role because the private sector probably won't. "There are all sorts of reasons and challenges that make it difficult for the private sector to do it," including not having enough private money, he says. "But if there were enough of that, the private sector would do a better job than the government because in the end, judgments have to be made. Not about how much money to give, but about looking a homeless person in the eye and saying either, 'Get a job,' or, 'You need some counseling.' The private sector makes those judgments a lot better than the government."

Government certainly has a financial interest in ending homelessness. A recent study that followed 15 homeless people in San Diego for 18 months revealed that they were anything but inexpensive. Factoring in the number of ambulance rides and emergency-room services they needed, plus occasional law enforcement action, the cost to the city was $200,000 for each of the 15 people, according to Mangano.

"But at the end of 18 months, after $3 million was spent, these 15 people were in exactly the same situation they were at the beginning," Mangano says.

BACKGROUND

Perennial Problem

Homelessness has been a marginal feature of the American scene since the early days of the Republic. Over the

CHRONOLOGY

1930s *Stock market crash of 1929 wreaks economic havoc across the country.*

1933-1935 Federal Emergency Relief Administration (FERA) supplies shelter and other aid to the homeless.

1935 FERA is replaced by programs targeting individual needs. Works Progress Administration (WPA) creates jobs but requires applicants to meet strict residency tests.

1940s *World War II creates jobs nationwide, lessening the need for social programs.*

1949 Housing Act calls for "a decent home for every American."

1960s *Homelessness rises after years of seeming remission.*

1963 Community Health Centers Act deinstitutionalizes an estimated 430,000 mentally ill people.

1970s *Courts rule on homelessness for the first time.*

1972 Supreme Court decriminalizes vagrancy and declares laws making residency a condition for receiving public assistance unconstitutional.

Dec. 7, 1979 New York Supreme Court Justice Andrew R. Tyler declares in *Callahan v. Carey* that the state and the city must provide "clean bedding, wholesome food and adequate supervision and security" for the homeless.

1980s *Supplies of affordable housing begin to shrink as the nation awakens to the problems of homelessness.*

September 1982 Community for Creative Non-Violence estimates that 2.2 million Americans lack shelter.

October 1982 U.S. Conference of Mayors reports that cities are meeting only 43 percent of the demand for emergency services.

July 22, 1987 President Ronald Reagan signs into law the Stewart B. McKinney Homeless Assistance Act, which provides emergency shelters, job training and other programs.

1990s *Homelessness is increasingly perceived as a complex condition resistant to easy remedies.*

May 1992 Census Bureau says 459,000 persons are homeless; homeless advocates call the count far too low.

May 17, 1994 Interagency Council on the Homeless recommends "continuum of care" approach offering individuals and families a variety of services.

Dec. 6, 1995 President Clinton vetoes a balanced-budget bill that would have eliminated the preference for homeless-assistance groups in the disposal of surplus federal property.

Dec. 19, 1995 Conference of Mayors estimates that 24 percent of families' requests for emergency shelter were unmet in 1994.

1999 Fannie Mae Foundation finds that public housing has only "slight to modest" negative impact on property values.

2000s *New research leads to more effective strategies and approaches to fighting homelessness as private sector and government coordinate joint efforts.*

2002 Bush administration announces plan to end chronic homelessness in 10 years.

December 2003 Conference of Mayors' annual report on homelessness and poverty reveals that requests for emergency-shelter assistance increased an average of 13 percent in 25 cities.

January 2004 Bush administration's fiscal 2005 budget requests an increase of $113 million for affordable housing for low- and moderate-income individuals, and $70 million to fund the Samaritan Initiative; critics say the requests amount to a cutback and are too low to make a difference.

years, though, perceptions of the jobless and homeless poor have changed.

In the past, according to a 1993 study, "the public was willing to admit that social isolation, alcoholism, drug abuse and mental illness were closely associated with homelessness, and from time to time reformers have designed programs intended to address these problems, some punitive, some generous." Today, in contrast, "fearful of blaming the victim, most people prefer to deny these conditions and view homelessness as a single problem: being without a home."[21]

Borrowing from the British experience, Americans of a century ago drew a sharp distinction between the "deserving" and "undeserving" poor. The little available assistance for the poor went to those whose impoverished condition was deemed beyond their control, such as incurably ill and physically handicapped persons, widows and orphans and men who suddenly lost their jobs. Paupers, generally able-bodied men who refused to work, received only contempt.

Meanwhile, social and economic upheavals left deep scars. Many wounded Civil War veterans, unable to regain their bearings, joined the ranks of the itinerant poor, along with widows and orphans of men killed in the conflict.

The depressions that periodically shook post-Civil War economies plunged thousands of families into sudden indigence. Temple University historian Kenneth L. Kusmer noted that the "increasing number of homeless men during the very period when the United States was emerging as an industrial nation was no coincidence. The new vagrancy was an indigenous aspect of a country in rapid transition from an agricultural and small-town society to one centered in great cities."[22]

Before the 1930s, private charities and local governments furnished the bulk of services for poor, jobless and homeless people. But during the administration of Herbert Hoover, the Great Depression that followed the 1929 stock market crash overwhelmed the resources of traditional caregivers. As unemployment rose into double digits, breadlines and soup-kitchen queues grew steadily longer, while shantytowns derisively called "Hoovervilles" sprang up in large cities — including New York's Central Park.

Soon after Franklin D. Roosevelt took office as president in 1933, he initiated his New Deal program, in which the federal government began to assume a major role in combating poverty and homelessness. For instance,

the Federal Emergency Relief Administration supplied shelter, food, medical care, clothing, jobs and cash to the homeless. And the Works Progress Administration also created jobs available to the homeless.

Most of the emergency-relief programs established in the early years of the New Deal were discontinued when World War II started. With war-production plants operating at peak capacity, unemployment vanished. Joblessness remained at low levels after peace returned, especially during the 1950s. By that time, homelessness seemed confined to the alcoholic and mentally disturbed single men who frequented impoverished neighborhoods like Lower Manhattan's Bowery.

Before long, though, homelessness resurfaced as a national concern. Social historians date the turnabout from February 1963, when President John F. Kennedy urged the creation of a nationwide network of community mental health centers to replace the state mental hospitals housing more than 500,000 mentally ill and mentally retarded people, where numerous abuses had come to light.[23]

Congress acceded to Kennedy's request, but from the outset many patients did not receive the aftercare they needed. States shuttered the state mental hospitals but did not provide enough support for the community mental health centers to replace inpatient treatment. Thousands of former patients ended up on the streets or in jails or prisons.[24]

In the mid-1960s, President Lyndon B. Johnson launched his Great Society program, a large part of which included his famous "War on Poverty." While Johnson's anti-poverty programs did not include any specific initiatives targeted at homelessness, many of its provisions benefited homeless people.

In the 1970s the courts confronted homelessness for the first time. In January 1972, the U.S. Supreme Court unanimously upheld lower court rulings barring one-year welfare residency laws in New York and Connecticut. The following month, the high court struck down as unconstitutionally vague a Jacksonville ordinance against loafing, "nightwalking" or avoiding work. The decision voided vagrancy laws in many other cities and states.

Callahan v. Carey, the nation's first right-to-shelter lawsuit, was filed in New York State Supreme Court in 1979 by homeless advocate Robert M. Hayes. In a ruling handed down on Dec. 7, Justice Andrew R. Tyler ordered

At the end of the Great Depression in 1939, a homeless family walks along a highway near Brawley, Calif., on the way to San Diego, where the father hoped to get relief benefits. They were coming from Phoenix, Ariz., where they had picked cotton.

New York City and New York state to create 750 new beds for the "helpless and homeless men of the Bowery."

In the early 1970s, veterans returning from the Vietnam War — particularly those suffering from post-traumatic stress disorder or who had become addicted to heroin in Vietnam — added to the homeless population. "Between the wounds of war and not being able to find a place to deal with it, many veterans turned to substance abuse, which then turned into homelessness," says Sharon Hodge, associate director of Vietnam Veterans of America. Approximately 10 percent of the current homeless population are veterans, almost half of whom are believed to be Vietnam vets.[25]

In 1980, President Jimmy Carter signed the Mental Health Systems Act, which would have helped the mental-health treatment problems of the homeless. But the law was repealed the following year under the new Reagan administration. The Omnibus Budget Reconciliation Act of 1981 essentially restructured the nation's mental health system by shifting direct federal funding to a more flexible program of community block grants that states could apply to mental health treatment if they so chose. Under the new system, funding for community mental health in 1982 dropped 30 percent.[26]

In the early 1980s, panhandlers and shabbily dressed people sleeping on outdoor steam grates began to attract the anxious notice of city residents and the news media. At first, the development was blamed on the 1981-82 recession and the federal budget cuts. It was assumed that once the economy improved, the number of homeless people would decline.

When that failed to happen, social commentators had to look for more deep-seated causes. The introduction of highly addictive crack cocaine in the mid-1980s obviously was a major factor. But changes in the work force and in housing availability may have been even more disruptive.

Disappearing Housing

The unskilled day-labor jobs transients had long relied on were rapidly disappearing, as was much of the nation's stock of low-rent housing. Many apartments in public housing complexes were being boarded up because of vandalism or lack of maintenance. And in some cities, entire high-rise public housing projects were being demolished as uninhabitable. The combination of fewer bottom-tier jobs and fewer affordable-housing units evidently tipped thousands of poor people out of their homes and into the streets. By this time, the crack epidemic had also begun turning many vulnerable inner-city residents into addicts who either lost their homes or were kicked out by their families. Many housing projects degenerated into crack havens or were so plagued by drug-related crime that many residents moved away.

Loss of privately owned, low-income shelter compounded the problem. Rooming houses, once a common residential option in big cities, became an endangered housing species. Many of the structures, especially those in gentrified neighborhoods, were returned to single-family use and sold at handsome profits.

The supply of single-room occupancy (SRO) hotels has fallen sharply for the same reason. Since the 1970s, numerous SRO buildings have been transformed into upscale rental apartments or condominiums or torn down as unsalvageable.

Christopher Jencks, a sociology professor at Northwestern University, has argued that construction of "cubicle hotels" modeled on the flophouses of yore could do much to alleviate homelessness. Cubicle housing would "provoke opposition in some neighborhoods," but it would also cost far less to build and maintain than regular SRO rooms, he says.[27]

But no one knows how much cubicle housing would be needed because of widely divergent estimates of homelessness. The debate dates at least from 1980, when Mitch Snyder, a homeless activist with the Community for Creative Non-Violence (CCNV) in Washington, D.C., began to draw frequent media coverage. In a 1982 report, "Homelessness in America: A Forced March to Nowhere," Snyder and a colleague, Mary Ellen Hombs, estimated that 2.2 million people lacked shelter nationwide and predicted that the number would reach 3 million or more in 1983.

"Lacking better figures, others repeated this guess, usually without attribution," Jencks noted. "In due course, it became so familiar that many people treated it as a well-established fact."[28]

Congress Responds

Snyder played a pivotal role in pressuring Congress to approve the sweeping 1987 Stewart B. McKinney Homeless Assistance Act. McKinney, a Connecticut Republican who suffered from AIDS, had fought for the homeless and the poor. He died weeks before the law passed, not long after he had joined a handful of other members of Congress to sleep on heating grates in downtown Washington to publicize the plight of the homeless.[29]

The measure was introduced on Jan. 8, 1987, ending a seven-week protest at the U.S. Capitol by homeless advocates. CCNV members had camped out near the Capitol's east entrance since Thanksgiving Day 1986 next to a homemade statue honoring the homeless. Snyder had defied police and court orders to remove the figure.

Congress' action was also triggered in part by two reports released the previous December showing that the nation's homeless population grew by 25 percent in 1986, and that families with children were the fastest-growing segment of that population. Advocates for the homeless blamed cuts of more than 70 percent in federal subsidized housing programs since Reagan became president. The administration, however, blamed continuing deinstitutionalization of mental patients, job losses and the disappearance of low-income housing due to local redevelopment projects.[30]

The law authorized $443 million in homeless aid for fiscal 1987 and an additional $616 million for fiscal 1988. The Interagency Council on the Homeless established by the act was directed to coordinate federal programs for the homeless and report to Congress and the president on the homeless problem. It also established nearly 20 programs to aid the homeless, including emergency food and shelter, medical and mental-health care, permanent housing, education and job training. The law also directed the secretary of the Department of Housing and Urban Development (HUD) to make underused federal buildings available for the homeless.

On Nov. 29, 1993, a homeless woman, Yetta M. Adams, 43, was found dead on a bench outside the offices of HUD Secretary Henry G. Cisneros. The low temperature that morning had been 34, two degrees above the threshold that sends city workers around in vans picking up the homeless and taking them to shelters.[31]

Cisneros promptly advanced several hundred thousand dollars to Washington to upgrade its homeless-outreach efforts. He also promised $25 million more to other cities. At the end of the month, the Clinton administration announced grants of $411 million to fund 187 homeless-assistance programs in 44 states. California ($75 million) and New York ($75 million) were the principal beneficiaries.

Then, in May 1994, the administration issued a blueprint for trimming the U.S. homeless population by one-third. The report, called "Priority: Home! The Federal Plan to End Homelessness," proposed $900 million in new HUD spending for homeless aid, bringing the total to a record $2.15 billion in fiscal 1995. Donald Whitehead, executive director of the National Coalition for the Homeless (NCH), says that while HUD Secretary Andrew Cuomo was "very responsive to the need for homelessness initiatives," and many new programs were begun, "many other initiatives were never implemented [and] HUD ended up with no real substantial increase in new funding."

Meanwhile, Democrats tried unsuccessfully during the Clinton administration to raise the nation's $5.15 minimum wage by $1 an hour. Some low-wage workers often must decide between paying rent and buying groceries, Sen. Edward M. Kennedy, D-Mass., said during the Senate's 2000 debate on raising the wage. At $5.15 per hour, an employee would have to work 80 hours a week to afford the fair-market rent established by the federal government for assisted housing.[32]

Republicans have said they would favor raising the minimum wage if it is phased in slowly and is accompanied

Doe Fund

A formerly homeless man works cleaning streets in New York City after training by the Doe Fund's Ready, Willing and Able Program.

by tax breaks for small business, but the measure has been stalled in Congress for nearly four years.

Cities Respond

City governments, however, were adopting harsher policies. New York's Giuliani announced in May 2000 that homeless persons would have to participate in job training, drug treatment and other self-help programs in order to qualify for shelter and other services. And the city began denying shelter to families who turned down more than three apartments offered by the city.

But the Giuliani approach soon appeared benign compared with those adopted by some other cities. A survey of 49 cities released in 1994 found that 42 "pursued efforts to criminalize activities associated with homelessness," mostly through anti-panhandling ordinances, restrictions on occupying public spaces and police sweeps.[33]

The National Law Center on Homelessness and Poverty conceded that some concerns about the use of public space were legitimate. "Ultimately, no city resident — homeless or housed — wants people living and begging in the streets. But criminalizing these activities is not the solution. Instead of attacking homeless people, cities should attack homelessness."[34]

By the late 1990s and the start of the new millennium, consensus began to grow around causes of homelessness and workable solutions. For instance, homeless advocates once believed that substance abuse was a result of

homelessness, but researchers eventually found instead that it was a principal cause of homelessness. Similarly, the notion that housing alone was the biggest problem gave way to the realization that — for the chronically homeless, in particular — supportive services had to accompany a roof and a bed.

The Bush administration also signaled a new attitude toward chronic homelessness when it claimed that the problem could indeed be eliminated. Throughout most of the 1990s, many politicians, researchers, analysts and even much of the general public had begun to view homelessness as intractable, causing many people to suffer so-called compassion fatigue.

But, as new research developed, the realization emerged that previous strategies were wrong or misdirected or, in the opinion of some, simply underfunded.

CURRENT SITUATION

Pending Bills

Rep. Renzi's pending Samaritan Initiative Act, cosponsored by 14 Republicans and two Democrats, is expected to clear Congress this year, given its strong White House support.

The $70 million requested by the White House for the program would be dispersed through three agencies: $50 million from HUD, $10 million from the Department of Health and Human Services and $10 million from the Department of Veterans Affairs.

Permanent supportive housing — the centerpiece of the initiative — was once derided as too costly by many members of Congress. But recent research has helped to change minds on both sides of the aisle.[35]

For example, a study of homeless facilities in New York showed that each chronically homeless person with severe mental illness cost the city on average almost $41,000 a year in shelter, corrections and health services. But residents in permanent supportive housing needed costly acute-care far less frequently, nearly offsetting the extra cost of PSH.[36]

By contrast, Rep. Carson's proposed Bringing America Home Act, cosponsored by 42 Democrats and an Independent, is far more ambitious than the Samaritan Initiative. It would establish a National Housing Trust Fund to underwrite construction and maintenance of

1.5 million affordable homes over the next 10 years. The bill would also provide job training and public transportation for the working homeless or those seeking work; child-care vouchers for working homeless parents; and emergency funding for families facing eviction. It also includes provisions on health, income and civil rights.

"We as a Congress need to look at everything that promotes homelessness and see what we can do to counteract it, if at all possible," Carson says. At the moment, the bill "is just hanging around," she says. "But we're getting more members interested in it once they understand the need for it, and that's a slow process."

> **"For the third year in a row, the budget fails to demonstrate how the administration plans to implement its own goals of ending homelessness by 2012."**
>
> **— National Alliance to End Homelessness**

Cutting Vouchers

Advocates for the homeless are disappointed in the Bush administration's fiscal 2005 budget for federal programs at agencies that deal with the homeless.

"For the third year in a row, the budget fails to demonstrate, with either resources or a strategy, how the administration plans to implement its own goal of ending chronic homelessness by 2012," the National Alliance to End Homelessness said after the budget was released on Feb. 2. The group said the $70 million requested for the Samaritan Initiative was "wholly inadequate to the goal."

The administration's proposal would provide up to $2 billion less than is needed to maintain subsidized-rent vouchers — called Section 8 vouchers — at current levels, causing 250,000 households to lose federal housing aid, the group said.

But HUD spokesman Brian Sullivan says the administration is trying to hold the line on Section 8 spending, while providing a "record level" — about $1.3 billion — for homelessness.

That's not enough, maintains Foscarinis, of the National Law Center on Homelessness and Poverty. She cites last year's Conference of Mayors survey showing that more than 80 percent of cities surveyed had been forced to turn away homeless families in 2003, and expected unmet needs to increase in 2004.[37]

And holding the line on rent subsidies amounts to a cutback, say advocates for the homeless, because the ranks of the homeless are growing. "Losing that funding is going to do a lot of harm," says Roman of the National Alliance to End Homelessness. "The administration has committed to ending chronic homelessness in 10 years. It's going to be difficult to see how that's accomplished with their plans for Section 8."

But the Heritage Foundation's Rector strongly disagrees. "Section 8 is a bad program," he says. "In many respects it serves an able-bodied population similar to the [Temporary Assistance to Needy Families] program, but in TANF there are requirements to become self-sufficient. No requirements like that are in Section 8. This is essentially an old-style, War-on-Poverty, one-way handout program that facilitates dependence and certainly needs to be radically reformed."

Mangano of the Interagency Council agrees. "When I was an advocate in Massachusetts, for years I advocated for an increase in Section 8 funding. Very rarely did that happen. So one of the first things I did when I got to Washington was to look at Section 8, and I found that every year between $700 million and $1.2 billion of Section 8 resources were returned."

The money couldn't be used for a variety of reasons, Mangano says. For example, Section 8 vouchers cannot be applied to rents above a certain amount, and in some areas the rental markets had risen too high. Mangano immediately went to the White House Office of Management and Budget (OMB) to ask for some of the returned Section 8 funding to be made available for the Interagency Council on the Homeless for redistribution to other programs for the homeless.

"They told me that the reversion of Section 8 resources was so chronic that they already reprogrammed that money. Every year, they made the money available, but knowing about a billion was coming back, they allotted it elsewhere. So in that moment, it dawned on me, that in all those years I was begging for more Section 8 money, the policymakers' view of Section 8 was that it was a very dysfunctional program. And I then understood that something needed to be done to repair it."

In reducing the Section 8 subsidy, the Bush administration has only "made a corrective," Mangano says. "The

How You Can Help

America may have a shortage of shelter for the homeless, but it doesn't lack for programs to help. An estimated 40,000 public and private programs are dedicated to fighting homelessness.

For would-be volunteers, the key to success is to think specifically, according to the National Coalition for the Homeless (NCH). For instance, many shelters require filing, clerical or typing help. Many also need basic labor — sorting clothing, washing dishes, chopping vegetables. Volunteers should also consider whether they prefer working with individuals or groups, with men or women, with adults or children.

Start by contacting your local public housing authority or visit the NCH Web site (www.nationalhomeless.org/state/), which lists nearly 400 different advocacy groups across the country, to find out which goods or services are most needed in your area.

Ideally, you should say not only how you could best help but also when and for how long. Shelters and service providers are almost perpetually understaffed and underfunded, and providing as much information up front about what you can do saves them valuable time.

Here are some specific suggestions for volunteering from the NCH and National Alliance to End Homelessness:

- Volunteer for an evening or overnight shift at a shelter.
- Help build or renovate a house or shelter for the homeless.
- Assist with catering, plumbing, accounting, management, carpentry, public relations, fundraising, legal work, health care, dentistry, writing, child care, counseling, tutoring or mentoring.

- Offer to organize an event at a shelter, such as a board game or chess night, an open-mike poetry reading, a guest storytelling or musical performance or even a holiday party.
- Train homeless people for jobs.
- Register homeless people to vote.
- Donate food and used clothing.

Also consider becoming a part-time advocate by attending neighborhood and public meetings to speak in favor of low-income housing and shelters as well as homelessness-prevention programs. The implications of these measures are often complicated and not well understood by the general public; someone who knows their advantages and disadvantages can have a definite positive impact on any relevant vote or decision.

Call or write local officials and leaders to involve them on the issue. Are the area media covering homelessness sufficiently? If not, let them know. If yes, also let them know — the press often will continue reporting on stories they know are getting favorable attention.

Several advocacy groups also urge volunteers to contact their congressional representatives. For example, the National Student Campaign Against Hunger and Homelessness is currently asking visitors to its Web site to e-mail Washington with requests to support full federal funding for Section 8 housing.

For more specific advice on how to help, visit either www.nationalhomeless.org/help.html or www.naeh.org/do/index.htm.

---

hope is that the dire predictions of the sky falling will not be true. What will be true is what HUD and OMB are saying: That reform will allow the program to serve more people."

John Kerry, the presumptive Democratic nominee for president, has criticized the Bush administration for "working to dismantle many federal programs that help Americans find affordable housing." Citing statistics from the National Housing Conference, a nonprofit organization devoted to maintaining affordable housing, Kerry notes that more than 14 million working families were spending more than half of their income for housing in 2001. He further claims the administration's 2004 budget

has worsened the problem by eliminating housing-assistance programs that help low-income families as well as the elderly and disabled.[38]

Local Alternatives

Some cities have begun developing alternative means of addressing homelessness. "Criminalizing [homelessness] continues and in some cases has gotten worse, but some cities are looking for a more constructive approach," The NLCHP's Foscarinis says. For instance, experts say Columbus, Ohio, has taken a model approach to homelessness, combining input from local officials and business leaders with up-to-date research and meticulous planning.

Is affordable housing a human right?

YES
Maria Foscarinis
Executive Director, National Law Center on Homelessness and Poverty

Written for *The CQ Researcher*, June 2004

Over 50 years ago, the United States took the lead in drafting the Universal Declaration of Human Rights (UDHR). Adopted by the international community in 1948, it states:

"Everyone has the right to a standard of living adequate for the health and well being of himself and his family, including…housing."

The right to housing is recognized in numerous subsequent treaties, including three that have been signed and ratified by the United States. As defined in human rights law, affordability is included as a component of the right.

Under the right to housing, each nation must maximize available resources to implement the right "progressively but fully." Implementing the right in the United States would not require government to provide free housing for everyone, but would require implementing a housing policy that ensures adequate housing for all — through subsidies, private-sector incentives, tax credits or a combination of means.

It would also require the United States to make implementation a priority and allocate resources accordingly. In effect, it would require our government to live up to the goal stated by Congress in the 1949 Housing Act: "The implementation as soon as feasible of a decent home and suitable living environment for every American family."

Yet today, due to inadequate funding, only about 25 percent of those low-income people eligible for federal housing assistance receive it. In contrast, the homeowners' tax deduction is available to all who qualify. Recognizing housing as a human right would mean extending housing benefits — of various kinds — to all, eliminating this inequity.

The universality of human rights can help counter the assumption that government involvement in housing benefits only the poor and broaden support for housing programs.

Economic and social rights are entwined with civil and political rights — and responsibilities. Nelson Mandela recently noted "the critical importance of social and economic rights in building true democracies," and observed, "this is nowhere more evident than in the right to housing. . . . Everyone needs a place which is a home."

Implementing the commitment to housing in the UDHR would make a positive difference in the lives of millions of Americans — and help re-establish the United States as a world leader in human rights.

NO
Michael Tanner
Director, Health and Welfare Studies Cato Institute

Written for *The CQ Researcher*, June 2004

Affordable housing for every American is a desirable goal for public policy. But not every good policy can be translated into questions of human rights.

When properly defined, rights do not conflict. That is because rights are essentially negative in character. My exercise of my rights in no ways infringes on your exercise of your rights. Your only obligation is negative, to refrain from interfering with my exercise of rights. Thus, my right to speak freely requires no action on your part, takes nothing away from you. My right exists independent of you. Your only obligation is not to stop me from speaking.

But the same is not true of a right to affordable housing. It would impose a positive obligation. In order for me to exercise my right, something must be taken away from you. That may be your property, directly through taxes, or indirectly through limits on what you can charge for rent. But in theory, my claim on you could go still further. Suppose there simply was not enough housing being built. If housing is a right, I would have the authority to conscript you to become a carpenter.

This can be expanded even further. Rights are universal, not subject to national borders. Therefore, if housing is a right, people's property and liberty would be subject to appropriation not just to solve homelessness in this country, but until every person worldwide had housing.

And, of course, one shudders at the definitional question. What qualifies as housing sufficient to satisfy the right? A mud hut, a single room, a ranch-style bungalow?

Beyond the philosophical, there are practical questions involved. Simply declaring something a "right" does nothing to actually solve the problems leading to homelessness. Homelessness is not simply a question of lack of money or lack of inexpensive housing. The majority of homeless suffer from mental illness and/or drug and alcohol problems. If given a house or apartment today, many would be homeless again tomorrow.

The problems underlying homelessness are complex and the solutions subject to considerable debate. That is a debate worth having, but it is a debate that is not advanced by defining housing as a human right.

Bowery Mission

Homeless men receive computer training and employment counseling at New York City's Bowery Mission, in addition to meals, shelter and showers.

Advocates also hail "inclusionary zoning" initiatives adopted by some cities, which require high-rise developers to also erect low-cost housing elsewhere. "It's a great way to bring in the private sector to create more affordable housing without spending government dollars," Foscarinis says.

Other cities are focusing on preventive measures, such as targeting help to those already in the welfare system who are at risk of becoming homeless. In the absence of an increase in the minimum wage, Whitehead of the NCH says, several states, counties and cities around the country have passed living-wage ordinances as a way to prevent homelessness.[39]

While the federal government still holds the line on increasing the national minimum wage, he nonetheless believes that "as more of these ordinances are passed locally, we'll probably see an increase in the minimum wage. Not in the near future, but maybe the medium future."

Fannie Mae's Weech is optimistic. "There's a lot happening — a sense that this is the right thing to do — and that creates the sense of synergy and political will" to end homelessness, he says. "It will be very hard and resources required will be significant, but at the same time it feels like a very different environment from the one in which people said, 'This is an intractable problem!' "

OUTLOOK
Good News, Bad News

Optimism is indeed in the air, but so is pessimism.

"There's lots of opportunity," says Roman of the National Alliance to End Homelessness. For instance, if the Samaritan Initiative proves successful it could mean substantial federal funding for permanent supportive housing. And the Fannie Mae Foundation's recent pledge of $35 million for PSH programs could spur similar initiatives by other foundations.

"On the other hand, we kind of take three steps forward and two back, like with Section 8, so it's hard to know whether we'll end up ahead or behind," Roman says. "If we focus on end-game strategies, on prevention, on getting people out of the [temporary shelter] system faster, we're going to be better off than we would have been if we didn't do it. But if we can't make some key steps forward, like straightening out the Section 8 thing, then we're not going to end homelessness."

Foscarinis of the National Law Center on Homelessness and Poverty also sees a "good-news, bad-news" future. Federal appropriations for homelessness are low, she concedes, but the issue is getting increasing attention. "State and local governments are at least saying they want to end it, and even at the federal level there's a stated commitment to ending at least part of homelessness."

Rep. Carson, however, says, "I really don't see anything changing much. We're arguing the budget now, and it's a no-caring budget. As long as we keep misspending money, then we're not making an investment in human capital, as we should be."

The Cato Institute's Tanner also doubts the situation will change appreciably, but for different reasons. The recently improving economy will help families who had lost jobs "but [not] the chronic folks," he says.

But before the government starts "another round of spending on this," he insists, "there needs to be a rethinking of what it is we're trying to do. Do we want people off the streets temporarily so they don't freeze to death? Good idea. Or do we want to bring these people into the mainstream of society? If so, good luck. You're not going to see any large-scale changes over the next year or five years."

Politics and other vested interests are the two largest obstacles to improving the situation, says the Heritage Foundation's Rector. He chuckles on hearing that the Bush administration has proposed $70 million to address chronic homelessness, saying, "That's essentially the way these issues always get stuck. Welfare reform is a good paradigm for this. For almost 15 years, the liberals in Congress would say, 'Well, maybe having women on welfare work is a good idea, but you're going to have to fork up a lot of money for that.' And Republicans would say, 'We're not going to fork up any additional money for anything.'

"The reality is welfare reform was essentially self-funding," he continues. "The program was pretty expensive before reform, but when you put requirements on people, the numbers on the rolls dropped, and you were able to divert all those funds into things like day care. So, essentially it was a funding diversion. It would probably be similar with homelessness.

"The problem is that on a rhetorical level, everyone accepts the idea that we should no longer be giving . . . one-way handouts," he continues. "But as soon as you talk about [imposing] work or behavioral requirements, you immediately run into the same vested interests that opposed welfare reform."

Some advocates for the homeless and analysts — mostly liberals — still debate the success of welfare reform.[40] But even independent observers admit that, despite the promise of some new approaches and programs to end homelessness, success is hardly guaranteed.

Those approaches and programs "are extremely ambitious, requiring major changes to a variety of famously intractable social welfare and other public systems, not to mention significant allocation or reallocation of resources," writes Dennis P. Culhane, a welfare policy expert at the University of Pennsylvania.

"And the pitfalls are many — political and economic constraints can limit implementation, unintended consequences can undermine achievement of goals and external forces can overwhelm the best of intentions."[41]

But Housing Secretary Martinez is undaunted. "It will take optimism — and a healthy dose of strength, patience and persistence — to wrestle homelessness from our cities," Martinez says. "But these are qualities Americans have in abundance."

NOTES

1. "Feeding Homeless on the Street Opposed," *The Miami Herald*, May 24, 2004, p. B3.

2. Keith Ervin and Justin Mayo, "Tent City Doesn't Seem to Affect Crime Rates," *The Seattle Times*, May 21, 2004, p. B1.

3. Sheryl Kornman, "Homing in on Homeless," *Tucson Citizen*, April 29, 2004, p. 1A.

4. National Association of Realtors.

5. Conference of Mayors, *op. cit.*

6. U.S. Conference of Mayors, Sodexho, "Homelessness and Hunger Survey," December 2003.

7. Nina Bernstein, "Deep Poverty and Illness Found Among Homeless," *The New York Times*, Dec. 8, 1999, p. A16.

8. Conference of Mayors, *op. cit.*

9. For background, see "Welfare Reform," *The CQ Researcher*, Aug. 3, 2001, pp. 601-632.

10. Jennifer A. Hurley, ed., *The Homeless: Opposing Viewpoints* (2002), p. 13.

11. Mary E. Williams, ed., *Poverty and the Homeless* (2004), p. 14.

12. Hurley, *op. cit.*, p. 13.

13. "The State of the Nation's Housing 2003," Joint Center for Housing Studies, Harvard University, 2003, cited in *Homelessness in the United States and the Human Right to Housing*, National Law Center on Homelessness and Poverty, January 2004, p. i.

14. Williams, *op. cit.*, p. 17.

15. Amy L. Sherman, "Expectant Giving," *Christian Century*, vol. 116, Feb. 24, 1999, p. 206, reprinted in Williams, *op. cit.*, p. 166.

16. *Ibid.*

17. Quoted in *ibid*, p. 167.

18. *Ibid.*

19. Joel Stein, "The Real Face of Homelessness," *Time*, Jan. 20, 2003, p. 52.

20. For background see William Triplett, "State Budget Crisis," *The CQ Researcher*, Oct. 3, 2003, pp. 821-844.

21. Alice S. Baum and Donald W. Burnes, *A Nation in Denial: The Truth about Homelessness* (1993), p. 91.

22. Quoted by Rick Beard in *On Being Homeless: Historical Perspectives* (1987), p. 23.

23. For background, see Jane Tanner, "Mental Illness Medication Debate," *The CQ Researcher*, Feb. 6, 2004, pp. 101-124.

24. See Bob Prentice, "Homelessness and Public Policy," in *Nursing and Health Care for the Homeless*, Juanita K. Hunter, ed. (1993), p. 21.

25. See "Background and Statistics" page on Web site of National Coalition of Homeless Veterans; www .nchv.org/background.cfm.

26. Tanner, *op. cit.*

27. Christopher Jencks, "Housing the Homeless," *The New York Review of Books*, May 12, 1994, p. 43.

28. Christopher Jencks, "The Homeless," *The New York Review of Books*, April 21, 1994, p. 20.

29. For background, see *Congressional Quarterly Almanac* (1987), p. 53.

30. *Ibid.*, pp. 508-509.

31. Henry G. Cisneros, "The Lonely Death on my Doorstep," *The Washington Post*, Dec. 5, 1993, p. C1.

32. For background, see Kathy Koch, "Child Poverty," *The CQ Researcher*, April 7, 2000, pp. 281-304.

33. National Law Center on Homelessness and Poverty, *No Homeless People Allowed*, December 1994, p. i.

34. *Ibid.*, p. ii, vi.

35. The Democratic cosponsors are Michael E. Capuano, Mass., and Jim Matheson, Utah.

36. Dennis P. Culhane, "New Strategies and Collaborations Target Homelessness," *Housing Facts & Findings*, Fannie Mae Foundation, 2002; www.fanniemaefoundation .org/programs/hff/v4i5-strategies.shtml.

37. "2004 Appropriations Fail to Keep Pace with Homelessness," press release, National Law Center on Homelessness and Poverty, Jan. 23, 2004.

38. Statement is found at http://kerry.senate.gov/band-width/issues/housing.html.

39. For background, see Jane Tanner, "Living-Wage Movement," *The CQ Researcher*, Sept. 27, 2002, pp. 769-792.

40. For background, see Sarah Glazer, "Welfare Reform," *The CQ Researcher*, Aug. 3, 2001, pp. 601-632.

41. Culhane, *op. cit.*

BIBLIOGRAPHY

Books

Anderson, Leon, and David A. Snow, *Down on Their Luck: A Study of Homeless Street People*, University of California Press, 1993.
Two sociology professors contend "any serious attempt to alleviate the problem of homelessness in the United States must move beyond a perspective based on individual pathology." Anderson is at Ohio State, Snow at the University of California, Irvine.

Burnes, Donald W., and Alice S. Baum, *A Nation in Denial: The Truth About Homelessness*, Westview Press, 1993.
Two homeless advocates dismiss claims that homelessness results from "lack of affordable housing, poverty, declining social benefits, and the nature of America's political and economic systems."

Hopper, Kim, *Reckoning with Homelessness*, Cornell University Press, 2003.
A research scientist at Columbia University analyzes the social and legal factors that cause or contribute to homelessness and the accomplishments and challenges of advocacy.

Hurley, Jennifer A., ed., *The Homeless: Opposing Viewpoints*, Greenhaven Press, 2002.
Essays, speeches, articles and book excerpts explore the big questions: Is homelessness a serious problem? What are its causes? How should society deal with it?

Williams, Mary E., ed., *Poverty and the Homeless*, Greenhaven Press, 2004.
A collection of articles explores whether unconditional charity is a positive or negative influence on reducing homelessness, and other questions.

Articles

Adams, Stacy Hawkins, "A New Light on the Homeless/ Study Attempts to Capture Information that could find ways to Prevent the Problem," *Richmond Times Dispatch*, April 9, 2004.
A focused research effort reveals that the demographics of the homeless in Richmond are not what officials have long believed them to be.

Bornemann, Thomas H., "Mental Health System Needs a Life," *The Washington Post*, May 29, 2004.
The director of the mental health program at the Carter Center argues that fragmentation of the mental health care system causes homelessness and other problems.

Hamill, Pete, "How to Save the Homeless — and Ourselves," *New York*, Sept. 20, 1993.
Hamill describes why many New Yorkers no longer sympathize with the homeless.

Jencks, Christopher, "The Homeless" and "Housing the Homeless," *The New York Review of Books*, April 21, 1994, and May 12, 1994.
A Northwestern University sociology professor examines the varying estimates of the U.S. homeless population.

Tunkieicz, Jennie, "Consolidation of emergency shelter services studied; Groups also want to address root causes of homelessness," *The Milwaukee Journal*, April 25, 2004.
Officials in Racine County, Wis., are joining together to evaluate and coordinate new integrated efforts to end homelessness in 10 years, beginning with a change in the way city shelters operate.

Von Bergen, Jane M., "The Job/Dancing with the Monster that Makes People Homeless; Navigating banking, bureaucracies to help the desperate," *The Philadelphia Inquirer*, May 31, 2004.
A city housing official disparages welfare policies that effectively "put people in situations where they [have] to turn to crime."

Reports and Studies

"Annual Report 2002," *National Alliance to End Homelessness*, July 2002.
A leading advocacy group says its blueprint for ending homelessness in 10 years is gaining increasing acceptance.

"Homelessness in the United States and the Human Right to Housing," *National Law Center on Homelessness and Poverty*, Jan. 14, 2004.
The advocacy group says "homelessness and the shortage of affordable housing that is its leading cause are growing crises in the United States."

"Hunger and Homelessness Survey 2003," *U.S. Conference of Mayors, Sodexho*, December 2003.
A survey of 25 cities concludes that homelessness rose last year.

Lee, Chang-Moo, Dennis P. Culhane and Susan M. Wachter, "The Differential Impacts of Federally Assisted Housing Programs on Nearby Property Values: A Philadelphia Case Study," *Housing Policy Debate*, Vol. 10, issue 1, Fannie Mae Foundation, 1999.
A study shows public housing has only a slight to moderate negative effect on surrounding real estate prices.

For More Information

American Bar Association Commission on Homelessness and Poverty, 740 15th St., N.W., Washington, DC 20005; (202) 662-1694; www.abanet.org/homeless/. Fosters pro bono legal programs for the homeless and educates the public about the legal problems of the very poor.

Beyond Shelter, 3255 Wilshire Blvd., Suite 815, Los Angeles, CA 90010; (213) 252-0772; www.beyondshelter.org. Combats chronic poverty, welfare dependency and homelessness among families with children.

Corporation for Supportive Housing, 50 Broadway, 17th Fl., New York, NY 10004; (212) 986-2966; www.csh.org. Supports the expansion of permanent housing opportunities linked to comprehensive services for people with chronic health challenges.

National Alliance to End Homelessness, 1518 K St., N.W., Washington, DC 20005; (202) 638-1526; www.naeh.org. Seeks to form a public-private partnership to reduce homelessness.

National Coalition for Homeless Veterans, 333-1/2 Pennsylvania Ave., S.E., Washington, DC 20003; (202) 546-1969; www.nchv.org. Works with government and community groups to build the capacity of service providers.

National Coalition for the Homeless, 1012 14th St., N.W., Suite 600, Washington, DC 20005; (202) 737-6444; www.nationalhomeless.org. Seeks to end homelessness through public education, grass-roots organizing and technical assistance.

National Law Center on Homelessness and Poverty, 918 F St., N.W., Suite 412, Washington, DC 20004-1406; (202) 638-2535; www.nlchp.org. Monitors legislation affecting the homeless.

U.S. Conference of Mayors Task Force on Hunger and Homelessness, 1620 Eye St., N.W., 4th floor, Washington, DC 20006; (202) 293-7330; http://usmayors.org. Studies trends in hunger, homelessness and community programs that address homelessness and hunger in U.S. cities.

U.S. Department of Housing and Urban Development, Special Needs Assistance Programs, HUD Building, Room 7262, Washington, DC 20410; (202) 708-4300; www.hud.gov/homeless/index.cfm. Promotes cooperation among federal agencies on homelessness issues.

15

Caring for the Elderly

Who Will Pay for Care of Aging Baby Boomers?

Marcia Clemmitt

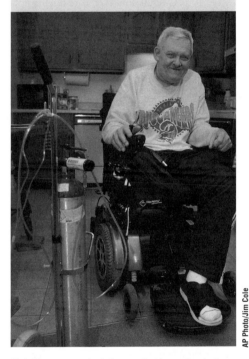

AP Photo/Jim Cole

Dick Peterson needs daily care, but he prefers to live at home in Concord, N.H., rather than in a nursing home. While more elderly Americans are being cared for outside of nursing homes, they may not be getting better care. Assisted-living facilities do not follow the federal standards set for nursing homes, and home-based care is difficult to monitor.

From *CQ Researcher*,
October 13, 2006.

W hen 87-year-old Germaine Morsilli entered Hillside Health Center nursing home in Providence, R.I., in 2000, she could still take care of many of her own needs. But dementia caused the retired factory worker to forget to eat so often that she was in danger of malnutrition.

Morsilli took a turn for the worse in 2002, when she fell and fractured her left hip while dancing to Christmas music. Bedridden for several months, Morsilli developed serious bedsores. Nearly a year later, health department inspectors found her lying on urine-soaked sheets, and at high risk of infection.

The inspectors gave Hillside time to correct the many problems they found. But in February 2004 Morsilli's worsening bedsores prompted health officials to declare her in "immediate jeopardy" and transfer her to another home. But they still did not close Hillside, despite repeated observations of similar poor care for other residents.

Morsilli's daughter later said she wished she had moved her mother sooner but, like the state, she'd hoped Hillside would do better. Besides, she said, "you don't know how much worse the next nursing home might be."[1]

Morsilli died soon after she was moved, and in May 2004 Hillside's owners closed the facility, leaving $82,250 in state fines unpaid.

Stories of horrific conditions in nursing homes have made headlines for decades, and probably contributed to a growing trend in long-term care (LTC) for the elderly. Over the past 20 years, elder care has been gradually shifting from nursing homes to home-based

Elderly Population to Double by 2050

The number of Americans 65 or older will more than double between 2000 and 2050, and the number 85 or older will grow fivefold.

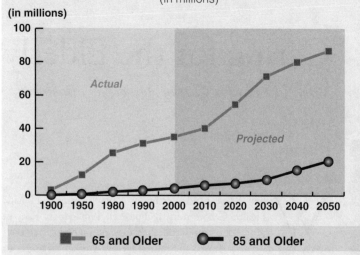

Number of Persons 65 and Older and 85 and Older
(in millions)

Source: Congressional Budget Office, "Financing Long-term Care for the Elderly," 2004

With the federal government paying more attention to specific care-quality issues — such as the number of residents who spend most of their time in bed — nursing-home care has improved recently by some measures, says Harrington. The percentage of residents spending most of their time in bed dropped by more than a third between 1999 and 2005, and the percentage of residents kept in physical restraints also dropped by more than a third, partly because some states have outlawed the practice.[4]

Overall, however, care quality still is not only deficient but getting worse. In 2005, for example, nearly 35 percent of nursing homes violated food-sanitation standards, and quality-of-care violations rose from 21 percent to 29.5 percent of all nursing homes.[5]

And while more seniors are being cared for outside of nursing homes, there's little reason to believe they are getting better-quality care. Assisted-living facilities do not have to comply with the same quality standards that Congress set for nursing homes in 1987, and it's very difficult to monitor quality in home-based care.

For example, in a Tucson, Ariz., assisted-living center an elderly woman died in December 2005 after she was given her husband's medication instead of her own for 38 days.[6]

"To me, assisted living's problems are the same as in nursing homes," says Toby Edelman, a senior policy attorney at the Center for Medicare Advocacy. Consumers do not know that there are no federal quality standards for assisted-living facilities, she says, and state regulators "are all over the place" — some relatively vigilant, some not.

The root of the quality problems, many agree, is a long-running — and worsening — shortage of trained staff. LTC "is a quintessential person-on-person service, and I think in the long run the staffing issue is going to swamp everything else," says Joshua M. Wiener, program director for aging, disability and LTC at the North

care and assisted-living centers, which offer less direct patient care than nursing homes.

"Nursing-home use rates for people 85 years and older are half of what they were 25 years ago," says Lisa Alecxih, vice president of the Falls Church, Va.-based Lewin Group consultancy. Altogether, about 6 million elderly Americans use some form of LTC, including around half of those age 85 or older.[2]

Perhaps because the more able-bodied seniors are being cared for at home and in assisted-living centers, a larger proportion of nursing-home residents today are the most vulnerable elders — those with dementia or other debilitating conditions. From 1999 to 2005, the percentage of nursing-home residents with dementia, including Alzheimer's disease, grew from 41.4 percent to 45.4 percent, according to Charlene Harrington, a professor of sociology and nursing at the University of California in San Francisco.[3] Those with other psychiatric diagnoses rose from 13.8 percent to 19.7 percent of residents.

Carolina-based nonprofit research organization RTI International.

But today's LTC manpower problems are nothing compared to the "huge shortages of manpower" expected when the over-85 population swells from 4.2 million in 2000 to a projected 21 million by 2050, says James Tallon, president of the United Hospital Fund (UHF) of New York and chairman of the Kaiser Commission on Medicaid and the Uninsured.[7]

To train and retain more and better staff, "there will need to be a shifting of resources into the sector," says Christine Bishop, a professor at Brandeis University's Heller School of Social Policy and Management.

Meanwhile, "you've got the perfect political crime going on," says Leonard Fishman, president of Boston's Hebrew SeniorLife eldercare system. "Elected officials get up on their soapboxes and complain about LTC quality. But when their own reports tell them you need more staffing — which means more money — they won't do it."

Americans spent $135 billion for LTC in 2003 — of which Medicaid paid $47.3 billion, individuals paid $44 billion, Medicare paid for $33.6 billion and private insurance paid $5.6 billion.[8] (*See graph, p. 349.*)

Aside from finding the money for higher-quality care, paying for any care at all will be an enormous challenge as the elderly make up an increasingly larger share of the population. A nursing home costs $72,000 a year, on average, but can run much higher in some metropolitan areas. Home health care can run as high as $25,000 a year for four hours of care a day, while assisted living — which often provides no special services — averages $20,000 to $30,000 a year, according to Molly O'Malley, senior policy analyst for the nonprofit Kaiser Family Foundation (KFF).

And although LTC can cost as much as hospital and physician care, in the U.S. system the two are treated differently. Medical care is paid through insurance,

10 Million Americans Need Long-Term Care

Nearly 10 million Americans — 62 percent of whom were 65 or older — needed long-term-care services in 2000; the other 38 percent were disabled. More than 80 percent lived in their homes and communities, rather than in nursing homes.

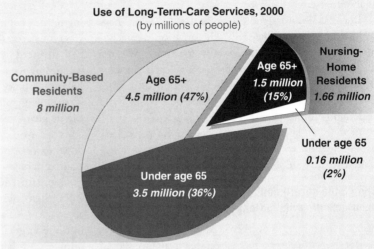

Use of Long-Term-Care Services, 2000
(by millions of people)

Community-Based Residents
8 million

Age 65+
4.5 million (47%)

Under age 65
3.5 million (36%)

Age 65+
1.5 million (15%)

Nursing-Home Residents
1.66 million

Under age 65
0.16 million (2%)

Source: The Henry J. Kaiser Family Foundation, Kaiser Commission on Medicaid Facts, July 2006

which spreads the largely unpredictable risk of illness over a large group and protects those unlucky enough to become ill from shouldering all the costs. But only a handful of Americans carry private LTC insurance, and Medicaid — the federal program that pays for nursing-home care — is a welfare program that requires people to impoverish themselves before they can get public help.

Some analysts say the government should establish a mandatory public LTC insurance program — modeled on Social Security — to spread the risk across the population. "If elderly people smoke and go to the hospital, we pay" through Medicare, says Richard Kaplan, a professor of tax law at the University of Illinois College of Law. "But if somebody doesn't smoke but gets the 'wrong' disease, such as Alzheimer's, they bear the burden themselves. We're discriminating in favor of the diseases people might have prevented themselves."

Others say a tax-supported program is not feasible in today's budgetary and political climates. "If we continue to take it back to that discussion, it'll be wheel-spinning," says Mark Meiners, director of George Mason University's Center for Health Policy, Research and Ethics. It's more realistic to help people share the risk by strongly encouraging them to purchase private LTC insurance, he says.

Whether we opt for one of those plans or a hybrid, serious debate over our LTC future should begin today, analysts agree.

But LTC is easy to ignore, says Kaplan. "We don't have a Hurricane Katrina," he says. "The situation is cataclysmic, but it's cataclysmic one family at a time." When a loved one develops Alzheimer's disease, "each family is devastated emotionally and financially," but "until there is a critical mass of interest there won't be a policy," and each family "thinks that they're the only ones."

As families, lawmakers and advocates for the elderly debate how to pay for and ensure the quality of long-term care, here are some of the questions being asked:

Should the government establish a mandatory insurance program for long-term care?

Just as homeowners know they need to insure their homes against fire, virtually everyone agrees that insurance should protect Americans against at least some long-term-care costs. It is much more likely, however, that people will need long-term care than that their homes will catch fire.

While LTC insurance is generally considered expensive, economists point out that it is not expensive if you are one of the unlucky ones who end up needing it for an extended period of time. For instance, the average person turning 65 in 2005 will spend $47,000 for long-term care over their lifetime. But that average masks a huge, unpredictable difference among people. Only 58 percent will spend anything on LTC, while another 19 percent will spend less than $10,000. However, an unlucky 5 percent will spend $250,000 or more. (*See graph, p. 358.*)

"This is not something that people can save for," says Brandeis' Bishop, arguing that either public or private LTC insurance is crucial.

Yet private LTC insurance can be expensive, costing on average $1,600 a year for an individual policy or $600 for an employer-based policy.[9] The high cost prompts some LTC advocates to argue that the federal government should require and subsidize an LTC insurance program. Others say similar federal initiatives — such as Medicare — have been poorly managed and wasteful and that private LTC insurance alone can do the job.

Private LTC insurance "is affordable for only 10 percent to 20 percent" of the elderly, making "federal involvement . . . essential" to "assure access to long-term care without making families face impoverishment," said a long-term-care study panel of the National Academy of Social Insurance.[10]

A federal program could operate in two ways, according to the panel. Like Social Security, it could guarantee "everyone access to a basic, limited, long-term-care benefit" financed by a special tax and supplemented by private insurance for higher-income people and additional public assistance for lower-income people. Or the federal government could expand current Medicaid LTC coverage by guaranteeing government assistance to pay LTC costs to anyone, once they had spent their own resources down to a nationally established minimum. People who wanted to protect more of their assets could buy private LTC insurance as a supplement.[11]

"Other countries have demonstrated that either approach — or a hybrid of the two — can target benefits to those in greatest need, retain personal responsibility through cost sharing and control costs," said the panel.[12]

"The debate about the aged is a social-insurance debate," not a matter for private markets to handle, says Tallon, of the Kaiser Commission on Medicaid and the Uninsured. "No market will be as successful as mandatory resource pooling."

"Most people don't think about LTC until it affects them. Then they ask, 'Where is the government?' " says Kaplan, at the University of Illinois. Still, the idea of a dedicated payroll tax to fund LTC coverage remains generally unpopular, he says, adding that he doubts whether even Medicare, with its payroll-tax financing, would be enacted in today's anti-tax atmosphere.

Nevertheless, says Kaplan, because needing LTC is a risk, not a certainty, and is expensive, "it is a classic instance of what should be covered by social insurance," like Medicare or Social Security.

Kaplan argues that the private LTC insurance industry's track record so far doesn't offer much hope that it will be a viable financing vehicle in the future. Many smaller companies in the field have gone out of the business, for example. "That leaves a question in people's minds about whether the insurance companies will even be around" when care is needed, decades down the line, says Kaplan. Even mammoth TIAA-CREF — which manages financial planning for the education and non-profit communities — entered and then left the private LTC insurance business, he points out.

"And other companies have raised rates even on existing policies," making the private LTC insurance market unstable and scaring away people who might otherwise buy coverage, Kaplan says.

Opponents of government action say existing government insurance initiatives, such as Medicare, are themselves on the brink of failure and that no more such programs should be attempted. To see the futility of expanding the government's presence into LTC, "you have to look 20 years ahead, when Medicare and Social Security will be in the last stages of collapse, and Medicaid will be history," says Stephen A. Moses, president of the Seattle-based Center for Long-Term Care Reform, who advocates more private financing of LTC.

The bottom line, says RTI's Wiener, is that "Congress and the president are not open to anything that would expand the government role."

Meanwhile, private LTC insurance sales are flat. About 95 percent of people between the ages of 45 and 64 with annual incomes over $20,000 are uninsured for LTC — unchanged since 2003, according to the Long Term Care Group, an El Segundo, Calif., company that provides administrative services to the LTC insurance industry. Among people age 65 and over, about 85 percent lack coverage, an increase from the 82 percent who lacked coverage in 2003.[13]

"Sales have not gone up," and insurers are reaching "only about 5 to 10 percent of the potential market," says Jodi Anatole, vice president for LTC for the MetLife insurance company.

Thus, "if you're not going to expand Medicare [to insure LTC], then you need to do something to make private insurance more palatable," says Kaplan. "LTC insurance is all over the map on benefits," he explains, making it hard for potential buyers even to figure out what a plan offers. If the government stepped in to

Government Pays for Most Long-Term Care

Sixty percent of all long-term-care expenditures for the elderly — $80.9 billion — were paid for by Medicaid and Medicare in 2004. Out-of-pocket expenditures by the elderly — mainly for institutional care — amounted to about $44 billion.

Who Pays for Long-Term Care for the Elderly
(in $ billions, 2004)

Payment Source	Institutional Care	Home Care	Total
Medicaid	$36.5	$10.8	$47.3
Medicare	15.9	17.7	33.6
Private Insurance	2.4	3.3	5.6
Out of Pocket	35.7	8.3	44.0
Other	2.0	2.5	4.4
Total	**$92.4**	**$42.5**	**$134.9**

Note: Numbers do not add exactly due to rounding.

Source: Congressional Budget Office, "Financing Long-term Care for the Elderly," 2004

require that policies be sold in standardized packages, "insurers could compete on price," potentially enticing more consumers to buy, he says.

Many analysts say neither an all-public nor an all-private LTC financing system will work and that hybrid solutions are needed. "A social-insurance program wouldn't solve the whole problem," says William J. Scanlon, a research professor at Georgetown University's Institute for Health Care Research and Policy. That's because no government-sponsored program could guarantee more than a very basic level of care universally, and many people expect far more, Scanlon says.

He suggests developing a plan similar to retirement financing, where Social Security provides basic support, and employer-sponsored retirement plans and personal savings add extra layers of funds.

Alternatively, the government might "say to everybody, 'You should have a year's worth of [private] LTC coverage,'" says George Mason University's Meiners. People could get public subsidies if they needed more, he says.

Are government and private industry doing enough to promote high-quality LTC?

Since Congress mandated improvements in nursing-home quality in 1987, federal, state and industry initiatives have aimed to make LTC safer. But while most experts agree that some of the most egregious problems — such as fatal fires — are less frequent today, critics say serious problems still exist. Moreover, the critics say the problems could worsen as nursing homes are replaced by largely unregulated home- and community-based care and assisted-living facilities.

Before Congress passed the Omnibus Budget Reconciliation Act of 1987 (OBRA), conditions in nursing homes "were pretty darned bad," says Edward Miller, an assistant professor of public policy at Brown University. "No matter how bad they are now, they were a heck of a lot worse."

New regulations "have improved quality in measurable ways," such as reducing the number of patients placed in restraints, Bishop and three Brandeis colleagues wrote in a 2005 report to the National Commission for Quality Long-Term Care. Furthermore, they wrote, national standards have become "ever more demanding," covering issues ranging from basic safety concerns to pain treatment.[14]

In addition, the Bill Clinton and George W. Bush administrations have pushed to post information about the quality of care at various nursing homes on the government's Nursing Home Compare Web site, says Wiener.*

Perhaps as a result of all these efforts, the most recent data show that the average number of nursing-home deficiencies cited by state inspectors dropped in 2005, says the University of California's Harrington. After increasing from 5.7 deficiencies per nursing home to 9.2 between 1999 and 2004, deficiencies dropped to 7.1 per nursing home in 2005.[15]

But Harrington fears that the statistics indicate only that state inspectors are "issuing fewer citations" rather than that homes are better. "It is unlikely that quality has improved," she says.

Other critics agree. "Even where we see progress, we worry that some of it may be artificial," says Georgetown's Scanlon. "Our ability to detect problems" is not uniform across the country.

In fact, state inspectors say they are not well trained and have told Congress they are pressured to understate problems because the LTC industry has political clout with state lawmakers, says Janet C. Wells, director of

public policy at the National Citizens' Coalition for Nursing Home Reform. "Study after study shows that surveyors are undercoding" — or understating the severity of deficiencies, she says.

"There is no ambiguity in problems that we do find," Scanlon says. For example, 10 to 15 percent of all nursing homes — between 1,500 and 2,000 homes nationwide, serving perhaps 200,000 residents — are cited persistently for deficiencies. That fact alone means that, "putting all gray areas aside, we've got a problem." Likewise, the Brandeis analysts cited "the continued presence of quality deficiencies" and the slow pace of adoption of "state-of-the-art care processes."[16]

Meanwhile, the jury is still out on initiatives like Nursing Home Compare. Adequate information on how to buy quality doesn't yet exist, says Wells. For example, the government is only in the earliest stages of collecting staffing information about individual homes.

"A family should know staffing data when they consider a home," Wells says. "Currently, we don't have it."

The biggest barrier to delivering high-quality LTC is retaining good workers, which is nearly impossible today, say many analysts. To keep trained staff, they need higher pay and health insurance, says RTI International's Wiener. Furthermore, "there's no career path" for direct-care workers like nursing assistants. "People don't have control over their work. The conventional wisdom is that wages get people in the door, but to keep them you need to redesign the job."

Turnover ranges from 50 percent to more than 100 percent annually in LTC jobs, says Miller. "We are woefully understaffed in gerontology at all levels," including registered nurses and even nursing-home administrators, he says. Among administrators, for example, very few are certified, and without qualified leadership quality initiatives are harder to sustain, he adds.

Retirement of older workers and potential limits on immigration could worsen the problem. "We have been heavily dependent on an immigrant work force," says Fishman, of Boston's Hebrew SeniorLife System. And, "when you look at the number of people retiring in this field, I think that's going to be a train wreck," he says.

"We need to quasi-professionalize these front-line workers" in line with quality-improvement models that have worked in other service industries like banking, says Bishop.

---

* The site is www.Medicare.gov/NHCompare.

Caring for Elderly Is a Global Challenge

Most industrialized countries have a significantly larger proportion of elderly citizens than the United States. As a result, they have enacted insurance systems to cover all long-term-care (LTC) costs and focused on making housing senior-friendly.

For example, in 2003 people 65 and older were about 12 percent of the U.S. population but nearly 19 percent of the population in Japan and Italy. In most European countries 15 percent or more were 65-plus.[1]

"Germany, Japan, the Netherlands, Luxembourg — all have social insurance for LTC," says Joshua M. Wiener, program director for aging, disability and LTC at RTI International, a North Carolina-based nonprofit research organization. "If you look across the world, wherever they have programs and services for LTC, it's overwhelmingly a government responsibility."

When Japan launched its universal government-funded LTC program in 2000, many doubted the government's ability to fund it. But, "many Japanese have now accepted the important role" of the program in easing burdens on elders and their families, said Tatsuo Honda, director of the department of planning at Japan's National Institute of Population and Social Security Research.[2]

While national insurance programs in many countries help spread financial risk, they now must grapple with the need to control costs, even as elderly populations keep growing.

Some advocates of private LTC insurance doubt public programs can ever hold down spending. "Has anyone run the numbers for the difference between promises made through Japan's social-insurance programs . . . and the country's ability to keep those promises?" asks Stephen A. Moses, president of the Seattle-based Center for Long-Term Care Reform, which advocates private LTC.[3]

"In the absence of a private market for services in which supply and demand set prices and determine priorities, governments are hopelessly at a loss to decide the best services to offer and the proper prices to charge for them," Moses says.

Cost-control initiatives are only in their infancy, and many focus on keeping elderly people healthier longer and providing more options for them to remain at home.

For example, Germany recently cut elders' use of more expensive medical institutions like nursing homes by paying for home-based care, including paying family members and friends for their assistance.[4] The Netherlands is stressing home-based care and is mulling incentives to encourage

patients and health providers to opt for more cost-efficient care when possible.[5]

New Zealand and Japan are among the nations beefing up preventive-health services, such as exercise and nutrition programs for elders who still need only minor assistance.[6] Japan's program also provides recipients with a once-in-a-lifetime subsidy to modify their existing homes so they can remain there longer, even with disabilities, said Honda.[7]

Housing that helps seniors feel independent and integrates their lives with overall community life is important to keeping seniors healthier longer, according to some analysts. "If you go to northern Europe" — mainly Scandinavia — "and talk about elder care, you hear about it as a housing issue," says Leonard M. Fishman, president of the Hebrew SeniorLife elder-care system in Boston. Higher-quality, more efficient elder care can be attained if elders can live on their own in housing clustered near senior services that provide both care and opportunities to stay active in community life, he says.

In Finland, senior buildings in urban areas are called "service homes," says Fishman. "The first floor has a dining room, lecture halls, rooms for doctors to come in and conduct exams. Then, on the floors above are housing units" designed to help preserve elders' independence, with rooms where "it's easy to roll your wheelchair into the showers," for example.

Perhaps most important, most senior housing in northern Europe has "dining facilities that are open to the public," where neighbors frequently join residents for dinner, Fishman says. Linking elder housing to the community at large helps ensure that the elder facility maintains high quality and that residents don't lapse into learned helplessness that worsens their health, Fishman says. "Every decent institution has its windows and doors open."

---

[1] "Older Americans 2004: Key Indicators of Well-Being," Federal Interagency Forum on Aging-Related Statistics, www.agingstats.gov.

[2] Quoted in "Interview With Mr. Tatsuo Honda," *Long-Term Care Trends*, AARP, Aug. 25, 2006, www.aarp.org.

[3] Stephen A. Moses, "Kaigo-Jigoku (LTC Hell) and What Japan's Doing About It: Valuable Lessons for the U.S. and Vice Versa," www.centerltc.com.

[4] *Proceedings*, AARP International Forum on Long-Term Care, AARP Global Aging Program, 2003, p. 4, www.aarp.org/international.

[5] *Ibid.*, p. 5.

[6] *Ibid.*, p. 9.

[7] "Interview with Mr. Tatsuo Honda," *op. cit.*

Medicaid Spending Tripled on Long-Term Care

Medicaid spending on long-term care was $95 billion in 2005, nearly triple the 1991 amount. The portion spent on home- and community-based care has risen steadily during the period, to 37 percent of total expenditures.

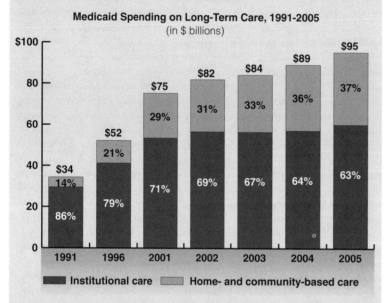

Medicaid Spending on Long-Term Care, 1991-2005
(in $ billions)

Legend: ■ Institutional care   ■ Home- and community-based care

Source: The Henry J. Kaiser Family Foundation, "Kaiser Commission on Medicaid Facts," July 2006

monitoring," which could leave problems undiscovered, says Georgetown University's Scanlon.

Dementia is an unsolved quality problem in all venues, says Stephen McConnell, vice president for advocacy and public policy at the Alzheimer's Association. Health care "costs Medicare three times as much for a person with dementia," presumably a strong incentive to manage it well, says McConnell.

But many elderly patients aren't being screened for dementia in Medicare's new chronic-care initiatives, which are intended to keep seniors healthier longer, he says. In addition, doctors aren't paid for long-enough office visits to communicate adequately with both dementia patients and their family caregivers, he says. These failures to take dementia into account gravely diminish care quality.

"If you manage diabetes, for example, and don't recognize dementia, your diabetes management will fail," McConnell says.

Unionization also could help, she says. "Unionization gives workers more of a voice," she says, often resulting in better treatment for the industry, such as higher government reimbursement.

Many people view home care or assisted-living facilities as offering superior quality, but watchdogs caution that care quality outside of nursing homes may be even worse. Unlike a decade ago, many people with serious disabilities, including dementia, now reside in assisted-living centers, says Edelman, at the Center for Medicare Advocacy. But those facilities haven't increased their staffs to meet the higher needs of this population since they aren't required to meet the same federal standards as nursing homes, she says.

"In a nursing home, at least there's an R.N. on the day staff," she points out.

Home-based services are delivered all over the community on hard-to-predict schedules, "so we do less

Are the government and private industry doing enough to promote home- and community-based care?

State and federal officials are trying to provide more elder-care services in homes and neighborhoods, where it is significantly cheaper than in nursing homes. Home care costs up to $25,000 a year for four hours of care per day, compared to $72,000 a year for the average nursing home.

But critics worry that states' home-and-community-based-services initiatives (HCBS) focus too much on cutting costs and do not offer counseling and consumer information to help family caregivers.

Over the past decade, Medicaid LTC expenditures have shifted away from nursing homes and toward HCBS. According to the Kaiser Commission on Medicaid and the Uninsured, in 1994 about 61 percent of Medicaid LTC spending went to nursing homes while 19 percent went to HCBS home-health agencies and personal-care assistants. By 2004, nursing homes' share of LTC expenditures had shrunk to 51 percent, while 36 percent went to HCBS.[17]

"Other options are there, they're viable, and people are using them," says the Lewin Group's Alecxih.

Much of the shift involves care of younger physically or mentally disabled people, says RTI International's Wiener. Currently, about two-thirds of Medicaid LTC spending goes to institutions and about one-third to home-based services — but only 20 percent of that third goes toward caring for the elderly.

"There has been a revolution in favor of HCBS" for those with intellectual disabilities, Wiener says. In some areas, such as Washington state, home care "is the dominant form of care" — even for the elderly.

Last year nearly three-quarters of the states added new HCBS services or expanded eligibility for their HCBS programs, according to the Kaiser Family Foundation's O'Malley.

But their efforts fall short in some key areas, say some advocates. Besides a shortage of workers" for HCBS, "turnover rates are high, and there are job vacancies. . . . Some areas like Wisconsin and the District of Columbia would like to expand HCBS but can't find enough workers," says Wiener.

It would help enormously if states provided databases or statewide information centers to help elderly residents and their families find people who provide home-care or community services, such as adult day care, transportation or respite care, says Susan C. Reinhard, director of the Center for State Health Policy at Rutgers University.

"Information is a big deal" when it comes to sustaining the elderly in their own homes rather than moving them to institutions, says Penny Feldman, vice president for research and evaluation at the Visiting Nurse Service of New York. "We pay a lot of lip service to it but don't do much."

People can better "age in place" if they have power and a voice in changes, according to advocates. "We are so used to taking a very paternalistic approach to these services," says Fredda W. Vladeck, director of the United Hospital Funds' Aging in Place Initiative. For instance, younger seniors could help drive older seniors to shopping and doctors' appointments, and seniors could form "social-action groups" to petition city governments to change a bus route, Vladeck says. "The more you empower seniors to take some ownership of this, the

A staff expert in exercise physiology gives residents a workout at the Jack Satter House, an apartment facility for seniors in Revere, Mass., operated by Hebrew SeniorLife, which specializes in improving the quality of life for elderly people in the Greater Boston area.

better," but that goal may take more than a generation to realize, she says.

Family caregivers also need to be brought into the discussion, say advocates. "In the material out there on HCBS, there is very little reference to families or friends," says Carol Levine, director of the United Hospital Fund's Families and Health Care Project. Yet, "who do they think is going to do the caring?" asks Levine, a caregiver for her husband, who was severely injured in a 1990 car accident.

Hired "aides can't be there 24 hours a day," she continues, citing a recent study showing that family members contribute 80 percent of the labor involved in home care for stroke victims, even those with paid helpers.

Nevertheless, Levine says, families "are almost always left out of policy discussions," have little access to respite services for needed breaks and are seldom given any training. That's in major contrast to the United Kingdom, for example, where family caregivers are entitled by law to take time off from work and to receive an official assessment of their assets and needs as caregivers, Levine says.

Social-service workers with the ill and elderly "have figured this out," she says. "But the medical side is still resistant" to actively engaging families in discussions about care.

"There is the idea that everybody in nursing homes can just end up in HCBS, but that's wrong," says McConnell, of the Alzheimer's Association. "We're a bit of a lone voice in the disability community, but we believe very strongly that when dementia reaches a certain point" — such as "when a wife's health fails from the strain of caring for her husband" — institutional care is necessary.

By pushing too hard for home care, "in some cases we're just shifting the cost to families," McConnell says. "And families already do a lot."

BACKGROUND

Family Matters

Elder care is a relatively new problem in history, largely because as late as 1900 few people lived to retirement age, and average life expectancy was 47.[18] But with people over age 85 today making up the fastest-growing population in industrialized countries, worries about how to provide seniors with health care and other assistance are becoming increasingly acute.[19]

One of the most hotly debated issues in the United States is how to balance individual responsibility with society's responsibility to care for those who've worked a lifetime but now face limited incomes and frailty. In addition, ensuring quality of care for elders is a perennial concern.

In the Middle Ages church law held children responsible for caring for their parents, based on the Bible's commandments to honor one's parents. The church also forbade others in the community from turning away poor, elderly parents seeking help.[20]

But when Protestant reformers like John Calvin and Martin Luther split the Catholic Church, they diluted the influence of church law. In 1601, England's so-called Elizabethan Poor Law first outlined society's legal obligations to manage poverty: Poor, elderly parents were expected to live with their children, and the community would assist the parents only after their children had used up their financial means.[21]

The American Colonies adopted the Poor Law. But other aspects of 18th- and 19th-century life also contributed to sustaining the principle that families should care for their own, according to Alvin Schorr, a liberal social reformer and long-time federal bureaucrat who also served as dean of the New York University School of Social Work.[22]

For example, farms and businesses generally were family-owned enterprises, and parents usually continued to control those properties until they died, wrote Schorr. So children were bound to their parents "in an economic unit by more than filial feeling or social pressure." Parental ownership gave adult children a strong monetary incentive to shoulder as much parental care as they could, according to Schorr.[23]

After the Colonies became the United States, Northeastern states — with a strong English Puritan tradition — required children to take responsibility for elderly parents, according to Schorr. But states to the south and west did not. As the economy shifted away from family-controlled enterprises, it grew less clear that adult children would shoulder the care for their elderly parents, Schorr wrote.

Economic changes aside, as the elderly population grew during the 20th century its burgeoning numbers helped turn elder care into a major issue. In 1900, only about 100,000 Americans were over 85. By 2000, that population had grown to 4.2 million; by 2050 it is expected to jump fivefold — to about 21 million.[24]

Among those turning 65 this year, nearly 70 percent will need some form of LTC, according to health policy professors Peter Kemper, of Pennsylvania State University, Harriet L. Komisar of Georgetown University and the Lewin Group's Alecxih. Twenty percent will need at least five years of LTC, while 31 percent won't need any, according to the analysis.[25]

But since no one can confidently predict his own need for LTC and because it is so expensive, most economists believe insurance — not savings — should pay for it.

Think of it like fire insurance, says Kemper. "There is a risk of your house burning down, but it's a relatively low probability. If it does burn down, though, you need a heck of a lot of money to pay for it," he says. "You can't expect everybody to have enough money in the bank. That's unreasonable. What insurance does is say that, on average, the cost of financing fires across a whole group is a pretty small amount [per person], so let everybody in the group pay that," and everyone will be shielded from substantial loss.

Unlike fire risk, LTC risk "is largely uninsured," says Kemper. Instead, the burden is borne in large part by individual "families providing care for elderly relatives," he says — a private responsibility that "is distributed very unequally."

CHRONOLOGY

1950s-1960s *Lawmakers seek to ensure nursing-home residents' safety after fires at several nursing homes kill patients, and the federal government begins paying for nursing-home care.*

1954 First national inventory of nursing homes finds many safety and quality-of-care problems.

1960 Senate report says 44 percent of nursing homes do not meet basic safety standards.

1965 Congress enacts Medicare — which covers only short, post-hospitalization nursing-home care — and Medicaid, through which states may cover long-term nursing-home care for the poor.

1970s-1980s *Demand for long-term care (LTC) grows as elderly population swells. Some older nursing homes close as government tightens safety rules.*

1970 The number of Americans age 85 or over — those most likely to need LTC — reaches 1 million.

1971 Federal officials establish national standards for nursing-home safety. President Richard M. Nixon beefs up safety enforcement, convenes the first White House Conference on Aging.

1975 Twelve consumer groups form National Citizen's Coalition for Nursing Home Reform to promote safe, high-quality care.

1981 Congress gives states the option of covering more home- and community-based LTC services under Medicaid.

1987 Congress establishes training and national minimum-staffing standards for nursing homes in the Omnibus Budget Reconciliation Act of 1987.

1990s *Interest grows in Medicaid-paid home- and community-based care; federal government begins developing quality measures for LTC. Four states establish experimental LTC Partnerships, promising LTC insurance purchasers that*

after their private benefits are exhausted they may access Medicaid LTC without divesting themselves of assets.

1993 Fearing that LTC Partnerships benefit only high-income people, Congress limits them to four states.

1994 Medicaid spends $8.4 billion on home-delivered services.

1996 Congress allows taxpayers to deduct private LTC insurance premiums from their taxes and makes it a crime to give away assets in order to quality for Medicaid LTC.

1999 A new series of government reports finds continuing quality problems in nursing homes, including tying up and drugging residents to control them.

2000s *Quality concerns continue as the elderly population grows faster than younger age groups; LTC staffing shortages loom.*

2000 Congress creates a small program of state grants to offer paid respite services and other help to family caregivers. Over-85 population rises to 4.2 million.

2002 Private LTC insurance is made available to federal employees. The federal government launches its Nursing Home Compare Web site, reporting individual homes' scores on quality measures.

2003 Medicaid pays $86.3 billion for LTC — 47.4 percent of the total amount Americans spent for long-term care.

2004 Medicaid spends $31.6 billion on home-delivered care, 36 percent of its LTC budget. Private LTC insurance pays about 4 percent of total LTC costs.

2006 The Deficit Reduction Act tightens financial-eligibility requirements for Medicaid LTC, makes it easier for states to offer Medicaid-paid home-based care and lifts the ban on states establishing LTC Partnerships. . . . Nursing-home care costs, on average, about $70,000 a year. . . . Thirty-eight states expand Medicaid coverage of home-delivered LTC services.

2050 The number of Americans age 65 or older will top 86 million — more than double the number in 2000.

They Work Hard for a Living

After caring for his dying mother, Thomas E. Gass, a former Catholic seminarian and halfway-house director, decided to translate his family experience into a new job as a nursing-home aide.[1]

A worker shortage plagues long-term care (LTC), and it is expected to worsen over the next few decades. Hard work, low pay and bad working conditions would make it hard to retain enough qualified workers even if the elderly population wasn't about to explode, analysts say.

The need for paid caregivers will increase by 39 percent between 2000 and 2010, but the population of 18-to-55-year-old women, who make up most of the LTC work force, will increase by only 1.25 percent over the period, according to the Bureau of Labor Statistics. Most workers in nursing homes and home-health agencies earn little more than the minimum wage, and few receive any benefits like health insurance.[2]

The work can be frustrating, dirty and sad, according to Gass' 2005 book about his experiences, *Nobody's Home: Candid Reflections of a Nursing Home Aide*.

Along with one other aide, Gass had three hours each morning to ready the 26 residents on his hall for breakfast. "On average, we are allowed 15 minutes to get each resident out of bed, toileted, dressed, coifed and wheeled or walked to breakfast. Every morning is a head-on collision against time," he wrote. "As a relatively well-paid aide, my cut is $6.90 an hour."[3]

One resident, Skooter, "is a graduate of Cambridge in his late eighties," wrote Gass. "He usually plays with his morning bowel movement, lightly smearing it on the bed sheets, the bed rails and himself. Sometimes he rubs it in his eyes. Nonetheless, he carries the bearing of a gentleman, always courteous and willing to help as best he can."[4]

Despite low pay and non-existent benefits, a good "direct care" worker needs to be patient, strong and perceptive to an unusual degree. "She's kind, she's empathetic, she's safe, and those are the attributes we look for," said Christie Overmyer, a supervisor at the Presbyterian SeniorCare facility in Oakmont, Pa., describing nurse's aide Barbara Bedillion.[5]

"I've always been a little sentimental about seeing my residents as individuals, always trying to do for them what I would want them to do for me, if our places were reversed," said Bedillion. But at 58, Bedillion, who's been on the job for 15 years, is one of the lucky ones. Presbyterian SeniorCare is among the elder-care facilities trying to reverse the industry trend of high staff turnover by improving the lives of its workers. Starting pay at the facility is $10.25 an hour, and workers who remain on the job for several years become eligible for health insurance and paid vacation.[6]

Experts know how to improve working conditions and retain LTC workers. Just treating them with the respect their front-line status deserves keeps many on the job, and research has "underscored the importance of including nursing assistants in care planning," according to Robyn I. Stone, executive director of the American Association of Homes and Services for the Aging's Institute for the Future of Aging Services, and Joshua M. Wiener, of RTI International, a North Carolina research organization. For example, they said, one study found that nursing homes in which supervisors accepted nursing assistants' advice or discussed care plans with the

Who Pays?

In Japan, Canada and most of Europe, governments have mandated nation- or province-wide LTC insurance programs financed in part with public funds. In the demographically younger United States, however, the question of whether LTC costs should be borne individually or across society has not even been openly debated, so the U.S. LTC system has developed by default.

Home-based care has been the "backbone of long-term care in this country," and family and friends provide about 80 percent of that care for free, says Kaplan of the University of Illinois. But providing that $306 billion worth of home-based care has become increasingly difficult as women join the work force, and adult children move away from their parents, he says.[26]

Americans spent $182 billion for LTC in 2003, of which Medicaid paid 47.4 percent, individuals paid 20.6 percent, Medicare paid for 17.8 percent and private insurance paid for 8.7 percent.[27]

However, 40 percent to 43 percent of all U.S. Medicaid expenditures went to non-elderly disabled

aides had turnover rates one-third lower than those without such practices.[7]

Better pay and benefits also help. For example, turnover rates in California declined after the Service Employees International Union organized 46,000 home-care workers in that state to bargain collectively for better wages and benefits. Full-time wages rose from around $6.15 an hour to between $8.45 and $10.50 an hour, according to a paper in the liberal journal *NewPolitics* by Brandynn Holgate and Jennifer Shea, doctoral candidates at the University of Massachusetts in Boston. Workers also got access to health insurance, transportation reimbursement and training.[8] Not surprisingly, turnover declined. For example, in San Francisco County, where wages doubled from $5 to $10 an hour between 1997 and 2002, the percentage of workers who stayed on their jobs for over a year increased from 39 percent to 74 percent.[9]

Change doesn't come easy, however, and efforts to give care workers more responsibility and respect sometimes run afoul of managers, such as registered nurses, who cling to the status quo.

For instance, the Green House Project — an experimental nursing home that originated in Tupelo, Miss. — rejected the traditional nurses'-aide model in favor of "universal workers," who receive more training, carry out a wider range

Former seminarian Thomas Gass, pictured with his pet falcon, writes about his work as a $6.90-an-hour nursing-home aide.

of tasks and have much more decision-making autonomy than traditional workers. The new role pleased the staff but ran into initial resistance among nurses, dietitians and other clinicians accustomed to being boss, according to Green House founders.[10]

However, based on promising results from Mississippi, the Green House model is spreading to other states.[11]

---

[1] Thomas Edward Gass, *Nobody's Home: Candid Reflections of a Nursing Home Aide* (2005), p. 1.

[2] *Occupational Outlook Handbook*, 2006-2007, Bureau of Labor Statistics.

[3] *Ibid.*, p. 13.

[4] *Ibid.*

[5] Quoted in Gary Rotstein, "Nursing Home Aide Has Empathy," *Pittsburgh Post-Gazette*, May 17, 2006.

[6] *Ibid.*

[7] Robyn I. Stone and Joshua M. Wiener, "Who Will Care for Us? Addressing the Long-Term Care Workforce Crisis." Urban Institute, posted to the Web Oct. 26, 2001, www.urban.org.

[8] Brandynn Holgate and Jennifer Shea, "SEIU Confronts the Home Care Crisis in California," *NewPolitics*, Summer 2005, www.wpunj.edu/newpol/issue41/.

[9] *Ibid.*

[10] Judith Rabig, William Thomas, Rosalie A. Kane, Lois J. Cutler and Steve McAlilly, "Radical Redesign of Nursing Homes: Applying the Green House Concept in Tupelo, Mississippi," *Practice Concepts*, The Gerontological Society of America, 2006, p. 533.

[11] *Ibid.*, p. 539.

---

people while elder care accounted for only 27 percent to 30 percent, according to an analysis by Bruce C. Vladeck, a former federal Medicare and Medicaid chief who is professor of health policy at New York City's Mount Sinai Medical Center. (He is married to the United Hospital Fund's Vladeck.)[28]

But Medicaid is a welfare program, not an insurance program. To qualify for LTC under Medicaid, an elderly person must either be too poor to afford LTC on their own or must "spend down" their income and assets to qualify.

"We've got a system where people routinely impoverish themselves" to pay for elder care, and "nobody likes that," says RTI International's Wiener, who favors a hybrid LTC system with government participation.

Medicaid's rules allow adult children to routinely commit what Moses, of the Center for Long-Term Care Reform, calls "financial abuse" on their elderly parents. The children hire lawyers to deplete the parents' estates of enough assets to make them eligible for Medicaid while preserving the children's inheritance in financial trusts, he explains. Moses advocates the voluntary purchase of

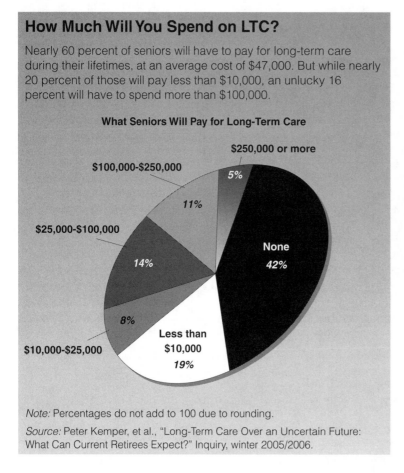

How Much Will You Spend on LTC?

Nearly 60 percent of seniors will have to pay for long-term care during their lifetimes, at an average cost of $47,000. But while nearly 20 percent of those will pay less than $10,000, an unlucky 16 percent will have to spend more than $100,000.

What Seniors Will Pay for Long-Term Care

$250,000 or more

$100,000-$250,000

5%

11%

$25,000-$100,000

None
42%

14%

8%

$10,000-$25,000

Less than
$10,000
19%

Note: Percentages do not add to 100 due to rounding.

Source: Peter Kemper, et al., "Long-Term Care Over an Uncertain Future: What Can Current Retirees Expect?" Inquiry, winter 2005/2006.

private insurance, with the government's role confined to helping the very poor pay for LTC.

So far, Washington has taken no significant action on LTC financing. Federal taxpayers are permitted to deduct premiums for private LTC insurance. But under current rules, a person with an adjusted gross income of $40,000 must have $3,000 in deductible medical expenses before he can claim any deduction for LTC premiums or any other medical expenses, according to Karen M. Ignagni, president of the industry association America's Health Insurance Plans. With such a high threshold, it's not surprising that "fewer than 5 percent of all tax returns" take these deductions, she said.[29]

Aging in Place

Throughout American history, lawmakers and advocates for the elderly have paid more attention to the quality of elder care than to financing it. As far back as Colonial times, local governments and charities ran poorhouses for those who couldn't care for themselves, often the elderly and the disabled.

Some 18th-century towns also offered "outdoor relief," a kind of community-based care as an alternative to literally going into the poorhouse. Home-based care also has a long history. As far back as 1909, the Metropolitan Life Insurance Co. offered coverage for nursing services delivered in patients' homes.

But many small, local LTC institutions couldn't cope with the scale of poverty that arrived in the 20th century, particularly during the Great Depression of the 1930s. State and federal governments assumed responsibility for elder-care financing, and eventually lawmakers tried to ensure that LTC institutions met basic quality and safety standards.

In the 1940s and '50s, for example, a number of fatal nursing-home fires led to an intensive national effort to develop state licensing standards for nursing homes.[30] After a 1960 Senate report found that 44 percent of nursing homes failed to meet minimum safety standards, Congress passed the Kerr-Mills Act, which gave states more federal matching funds to care for the poor and elderly and the "medically needy," whose severe health conditions drive them into poverty.[31]

In the early 1970s, shocking accounts of nursing-home abuses were brought to Congress' attention by a group of young female volunteers organized by consumer advocate Ralph Nader. The young women took jobs in or visited nursing homes in Washington, D.C., Connecticut, Maryland, New Jersey, New York and Virginia. "What we found in our study," the project's director told the Senate Special Committee on Aging, "was horrifying, disillusioning, heartbreaking and totally inexcusable."[32]

In 1971, six years after the Medicare and Medicaid programs were established, the federal government published national fire and safety standards that all nursing homes paid by Medicare and Medicaid were required to meet. The standards were four years in the making, and between 1969 and 1971 about 1,500 older nursing homes closed in expectation that they would not be able to meet the coming standards.

Since then, while worries about LTC quality have never disappeared, concern has gradually shifted from fire- and safety-code violations to quality of care. For example, a "litany of nursing-home abuses" laid out at a 1974 Senate hearing included improper use of physical restraints on patients and poor management of medications.[33]

In 1987, the Omnibus Budget Reconciliation Act mandated new minimum national standards for staffing nursing homes and training their staff. The bill also called for standardized assessments of the health and needs of nursing-home residents and stated that facilities should help residents attain "the highest practicable physical, mental and psychosocial well-being."[34]

Nevertheless, reports of quality problems in nursing homes persist. For example, a series of government reports between 1999 and 2003 provided "additional startling documentation of ongoing quality failures and continued public dissatisfaction," says a report to the National Commission for Quality Long-Term Care.[35]

At least partly in reaction to such longstanding complaints, the past 25 years have seen a gradual shift away from nursing home care into assisted living and home-based care. Among those age 85 and older, there are about the same number living in nursing homes today as 20 years ago, even though the over-85 population has doubled, says the Lewin Group's Alecxih.

Residents in assisted-living facilities today tend to have about the same level of disability as nursing-home residents had in past decades. "We have a million beds in assisted living today compared to a million-and-a-half in nursing homes, and many in the nursing homes are short-term patients, just off a hospital stay, not long-term residents," says Georgetown's Scanlon.

Various types of home-based care also are growing. For example, about 920,000 Medicaid beneficiaries receive care through state home-and-community-based services (HCBS) programs, 722,000 obtain care from home-health agencies and 683,000 receive personal, non-health assistance paid for by Medicaid. But, of course, many of these beneficiaries are non-elderly.[36]

Falling nursing-home occupancy rates could conceivably create what RTI International's Wiener calls a "market moment." Nursing homes "are more hungry for residents and could conceivably make quality improvements to attract them," he says.

Or low occupancy could have the opposite effect, creating some horrendous — and formerly unheard of — quality breaches, says Wells, at the National Citizens' Coalition for Nursing Home Reform. "While occupancy drops, facilities stay open, and that's where you may get the most horrible cases of abuse," she says. "To fill beds, they bring in people who are unsuitable residents, people with violent criminal histories, mental illness, sexual predators."

In Illinois, for example, more than 1,000 parolees, including sex offenders, were found to be among the state's 100,000 nursing-home residents this year, after a new law required criminal background checks of all residents. The law was prompted by an incident in which a convicted rapist groped a 77-year-old fellow resident in a Homewood, Ill., home.[37]

On the brighter side, LTC activists in recent years have developed several new types of elder facilities that may improve care. One such undertaking, called Green House homes, has shown promise in Mississippi. Self-contained houses accommodate about 10 residents cared for by nursing aides with advanced training and a visiting medical-support team.[38] Each house provides shared living space near residents' individual quarters, which has "worked well," according to a group of analysts that included the creators of the Green House concept, gerontologists Judith Rabig and William Thomas.

"Many elders stopped using wheelchairs because they were able to navigate the short distances in the house," and staff absenteeism and turnover is lower than in other nursing facilities, wrote Rabig and Thomas.[39] Additional Green House projects are planned in at least 10 states.[40]

CURRENT SITUATION

Deficit Reduction Act

Experts in LTC financing hope more Americans will buy private LTC insurance now that Congress has made it tougher to get Medicaid to pick up the tab for long-term care.

Turning Home Equity into Long-Term Care

The need for long-term care (LTC) most often hits late in life, when savings run low and many people live on fixed incomes. Most older people own their own homes, however, and some policymakers favor encouraging them to use their home equity to help pay for in-home care.

Eighty percent of those over age 65 own their homes, and nearly three-quarters have paid off their mortgages. Moreover, home equity is the major asset for most seniors: The median net worth of those age 75 and older is around $100,000, but only $19,000 of that is in non-housing assets like investments.[1]

Seniors' limited incomes and high home equity — and their preference for at-home LTC — lead some advocates to urge them to use so-called reverse mortgages — also called home-equity conversion mortgages — to pay for at-home care.

A senior over age 62 can qualify for a reverse mortgage by owning a home that is fully or nearly paid off.

Here's how it works: A bank lends money to the homeowner, either as fixed monthly cash payments or as a line of credit the homeowner can draw on. As long as homeowners remain in their house, they don't have to make any payments on the loan. After the homeowner either dies or sells the house, the bank recoups the payments made to the homeowner, plus the interest and finance charges due on the loan from the proceeds of the house sale.

Fifty-nine percent of older households — 14.2 million households — have sufficient housing assets to qualify for reverse mortgages, but about 3.8 million of those households have non-housing assets of $275,000 or more, which would make them unlikely to need a reverse mortgage, according to Georgetown University's Long-Term Care Financing Project.[2]

Tapping into home equity can give seniors "the purchasing power they need" to buy either LTC insurance or home-based "services they need to stay in their homes and out of nursing facilities," said Thomas Scully, former chief of the Medicare and Medicaid programs.[3]

A 2005 study funded by the federal Centers for Medicare and Medicaid Services "shows that reverse mortgages have significant potential to help many seniors," said James Firman, president and CEO of the National Council on Aging (NCOA), which published the study.[4]

But the mortgages can't help everyone, and they aren't the most efficient or effective financial tools, say many analysts. For example, the NCOA study cites "the need for strong consumer safeguards and lower transaction costs" to attract more users, said Firman.[5]

Reverse-mortgages "are very high-fee transactions," says Stephen I. Golant, a University of Florida professor of geography who studies elder housing issues. "A home may be worth $100,000, but you may get only $50,000 out of that, after fees and interest. That's a high price to pay for the privilege of remaining in your home."

Last February President Bush signed into law the Deficit Reduction Act (DRA), which included the most significant provisions ever aimed at boosting home-delivered care and the private LTC insurance market. Skeptics say, however, that while the law is designed to help trim government LTC spending, no one knows yet to what extent it will ultimately reshape the LTC landscape.

Passed in response to governors' warnings that rising Medicaid costs threaten to swamp their budgets, the law is expected to cut federal Medicaid spending by $43.2 billion between 2006 and 2014. At least $6.4 billion of that will come from tightening eligibility rules for LTC.[41]

"The DRA was the culmination of a decade of major work for me," says Moses, of the Center for Long-Term Care Reform. He has been one of the strongest voices urging lawmakers to make it harder for people to qualify for Medicaid-funded LTC because it would spur development of a strong, private LTC insurance market. "It's a virtual miracle that we got as much as we did" in the DRA, "though it doesn't go far enough," he says.

The law is designed to discourage people from counting on Medicaid to pay their LTC costs. Among other changes, the DRA bars anyone with more than $500,000 in home equity from qualifying for Medicaid nursing-home benefits. In the past, people were permitted to retain unlimited equity in their primary residence but had to exhaust other assets before qualifying for Medicaid LTC.

The law also imposes a much stiffer penalty on people who get rid of money or other assets, presumably in an effort to "spend down" to qualify for Medicaid LTC.

Since many seniors' homes have relatively low value, they still couldn't borrow enough money through a reverse mortgage to cover major episodes of LTC, according to independent health-policy consultant Mark Merlis, who wrote the Georgetown study. Forty-four percent of potential reverse-mortgage users could pay for 25 months of home care, the median length of time people use home-based LTC. But only 2 percent of likely reverse-mortgage purchasers would get enough from their loans to cover 51 months or more of home-based LTC, the amount used by 25 percent of people who use home care, Merlis wrote.[6]

And for many people, reverse mortgages may not be the best way to turn home equity into cash, say other analysts.

A better option for many seniors might be selling their houses and reinvesting the proceeds in a low-fee, income-producing fund that could help pay the rent in less expensive housing. "A significant share of older people . . . should not be encouraged to stay put," Golant says, because their old homes are too expensive, too big and too difficult to keep up. "It would probably be much better to have at least some older people in group housing or concentrated housing" near necessary services, such as grocery stores. That also would hold caregivers' travel costs down because they could visit several households at once, he adds.

There's one catch, however: Affordable housing is scarce, and senior-friendly housing is hard to find. "When it comes to adapting current housing, such as by adding grab bars [in bathrooms], we hear about it ad nauseam, but outside of the work of a few foundations, most of these simple things aren't being done," says Penny H. Feldman, vice president for research and evaluation at the Visiting Nurse Service of New York. Neither has affordable assisted living been made available in line with the demand, says Golant.

Affordable senior housing "is not that expensive," says Leonard Fishman, president of Hebrew SeniorLife, an elder-care system in Boston. "There's no big constituency demanding it, but it would be hard to find a more cost-effective change you can make."

But before the nation considers investing in affordable housing for seniors, says Golant, it needs to have a sensitive public-policy debate about two questions: "What's the best way for older people to translate their housing wealth into providing for their LTC? And should adult children expect to have their parents' houses passed on as part of their inheritance?"

[1] "Demographic Profile: Americans 65+," Mature Market Institute, MetLife, 2004.

[2] Mark Merlis, "Home-Equity Conversion Mortgages and Long-Term Care," Georgetown University Long-Term Care Financing Project, March 2005, www.ltc.georgetown.edu.

[3] Quoted in "Program Promotes Reverse Mortgages to Pay LTC," *Nursing Homes*, March 2004.

[4] "NCOA Study Shows Reverse Mortgages Can Help Seniors Pay for Long-Term Care at Home," press release, National Council on Aging, Jan. 26, 2005.

[5] *Ibid.*

[6] Merlis, *op. cit.*, p. 12.

States will now scrutinize the past five years — rather than three years — of seniors' financial transactions prior to Medicaid application for evidence of a spend-down, such as gifts to children or charities or sale of a car or summer cottage at below-market price to a relative. The new restrictions mean that applicants — even those who did not intentionally draw down their assets — will become ineligible for LTC payments for months or even years at the very time that they need to be admitted to a nursing home, say critics of the new rules.

People who help out in family emergencies and then suddenly find themselves needing assistance themselves, for example, are heavily penalized under the new law, said New York elder-care attorney Bernard A. Krooks.[42] For example, he said, a grandmother who pays $30,000 in vital bills over several years for a grown daughter with chronic-fatigue syndrome who's supporting two young children herself suffers a heart attack and a debilitating stroke. Two years later, after she's depleted all her financial assets and must turn to Medicaid, she finds that she is ineligible for many months because of the aid she gave her family within the last five years, Krooks said.

The law "suggests that the elderly can predict their medical and financial circumstances five years into the future," he said, and "will punish unwitting elders who have helped their families . . . and then experience medical events such as a stroke, hip fracture or Alzheimer's disease."[43]

The tougher eligibility rules are based on the argument that the Medicaid LTC benefit discourages people from buying private LTC insurance, even when they can afford it.

Residents at a Chicago nursing home have the luxury of ordering their meals from a menu. While care at nursing homes has improved by some measures, more than a third violated food-sanitation standards in 2005, and quality-of-care violations rose from 21 percent to 29.5 percent of all nursing homes.

Jeffrey Brown, an assistant professor of finance at the University of Illinois at Urbana-Champaign, calls Medicaid "an implicit tax on LTC insurance" because buyers of LTC insurance end up being ineligible for government Medicaid benefits that uninsured people at the same wealth level can obtain. "Most insurance doesn't take something away from you when you buy it," he says.

"We have a lot of people on Medicaid for LTC who would have, could have and should have been able to pay, had they taken the steps to do so," says Moses.

He acknowledges that there is "little empirical research" showing how many people illegitimately spend down money to qualify for Medicaid LTC. The phenomenon is "driven by adult children" of cognitively impaired parents who "hate to see their inheritance consumed" paying for private LTC, so they transfer and conceal their parents' assets so Medicaid will pay instead, Moses says.

Others disagree. The DRA provisions that tighten eligibility "won't make much difference" because "half a dozen studies show there is not much of this going on," says RTI International's Wiener.

A September 2005 report by the Government Accountability Office (GAO) found insufficient data to determine how much asset transfer occurs. In 2002, however, 22 percent of elderly households — about 6 million — reported that they'd transferred cash in the past two years, the GAO found.[44]

Most of the asset transfers occurred in higher-income households. While only about 10 percent of the lowest-income third of households were found to have transferred cash — in an average amount of $4,000 — more than 30 percent of the richest third had transferred cash — averaging more than $12,000 per household. And households with disabled elders, with the highest risk of needing LTC, "were less likely to transfer cash" than households with non-disabled elders, said the GAO.[45]

LTC Carrots

In response to longstanding pleas from state governments and disability advocates, the DRA allowed states to expand Medicaid coverage of home- and community-based elder care and simplified those procedures. It also stepped up a long-stalled initiative using positive reinforcement to entice people to buy private LTC insurance.

Most analysts agree that bolstering Medicaid programs offering home-and-community-based services (HCBS) will be good for many elderly and disabled people, but few studies give hard data.

But home-based care is generally more expensive than assisted living, and HCBS programs will only be as large as states can afford, some warn. The initiative "isn't going to go very far, because there isn't enough money," predicts Moses.

According to the disability community, many nursing-home residents could be moved back into their homes if more home-delivered services were available. But skeptics, like the United Hospital Fund's Tallon, say that might not be true for the elderly, given the current level of frailty among most nursing-home residents. "I'm not a great believer that most people in nursing homes don't belong there," he says.

The DRA also lifted a longstanding moratorium on long-term care partnerships — state programs that allow people to receive Medicaid LTC benefits without impoverishing themselves if they purchase private LTC insurance. Established in the late 1980s as a private research initiative, the partnerships were limited by Congress in 1993 to four states — California, Connecticut, Indiana and New York — because lawmakers feared that only wealthy people would benefit from the program because they are the only ones who can afford the high cost of LTC insurance.

Should the federal government establish a mandatory long-term-care insurance program?

YES

The Long-Term Care Study Panel, National Academy of Social Insurance

Judy Feder (L)
Co-Chair; Dean, Georgetown Public Policy Institute

Sheila P. Burke (R)
Co-Chair; Chief Operating Officer, Smithsonian Institution

From "Developing a Better Long-Term Care Policy," November 2005

Transforming long-term care ultimately requires fundamental reform of its financing and a substantial commitment of federal resources. Because the need for long-term care is a risk, not a certainty, it should be handled like other unpredictable and potentially catastrophic events — that is, through insurance.

Private long-term-care insurance, while growing, is affordable for only 10 to 20 percent of the elderly. To assure access without making families face impoverishment, federal involvement is therefore essential.

Creating an effective system requires a substantial new commitment of public resources, and — if benefits are to be adequate in all states — they must be federal resources. Expanded federal financing for long-term care could take a variety of forms and need not eliminate personal responsibility.

One approach, modeled on Social Security, would provide everyone access to a basic, limited, long-term-care benefit. Social insurance for long-term care could provide the same kind of basic protection. Individuals with sufficient income and assets could purchase private insurance to supplement the public program, while a safety-net program could help low-income people unable to afford private supplemental insurance.

Another approach would establish a national floor of income and asset protection that would reform or replace Medicaid. Such a program would assure everyone access to affordable, quality, long-term care without having to give up their life savings, as Medicaid requires today.

Other countries have demonstrated that either approach — or a hybrid of the two — can target benefits to those in greatest need, retain personal responsibility through cost-sharing and control costs. Analysis by the Organization for Economic Cooperation and Development in 19 countries finds a growing number [of nations] with universal public plans for financing long-term care.

Public protection does not imply the absence of private obligations, nor does it imply unlimited service or exploding costs. It aims to strike a fairer balance between public and private financing — relating personal contributions to ability to pay and targeting benefits to those in greatest need.

NO

Stephen A. Moses
President, Center for Long-Term Care Reform

From speech to insurers, posted at www.center ltc.com/speakers/what_i_believe_about_ltc.htm, Feb. 28, 2006

The personal tragedy of long-term care for individuals and families can be substantially relieved if people are able to pay privately for high-quality personal and respite care. The social tragedy of long-term care for America's aging population can be entirely averted by changing public policy so that fewer people end up dependent on underfinanced public welfare programs.

Friends and families provide most long-term care at no charge, but under enormous financial and emotional stress. The vast majority of all formal, compensated long-term-care services are paid for by Medicaid (welfare) or Medicare (social insurance). I believe that Medicaid routinely pays less than the cost of providing long-term care and that Medicare is slowly ratcheting down its reimbursement, while both programs impose heavier and heavier regulation on providers.

We're in [this mess] because 40 years ago the government started paying for nursing-home care without limiting its free and subsidized services to people in financial need. By making nursing-home care free, for all intents and purposes, the government impeded the development of a private market place for home- and community-based services. By subsidizing long-term care for middle- and upper-class Americans, the government impeded the development of a private insurance market to help pay for the kinds of services people prefer.

By becoming a single buyer of long-term care, the government artificially increased the demand for and the price of care beyond its ability to pay adequately. The resulting cost containment caused quality of care to decline and led directly to the overregulation that tied nursing homes and home-health agencies in bureaucratic knots.

If too much government financing has caused excessive dependency on inadequately financed institutional care, then the answer must lie in targeting scarce government resources to a smaller number of people truly in need.

When government programs have fewer people to serve, they will be better able to provide adequate reimbursement of higher quality. If they cannot ignore the risk and cost of long-term care, most people will save, invest and insure and thus be able to purchase red-carpet access to care in the private marketplace. When the government stops giving away what the long-term-care insurance industry and reverse-mortgage lenders are trying to sell, more people will buy those products.

Under the DRA, states now may offer Medicaid LTC coverage to consumers who exhaust their private LTC benefits. Such policyholders may retain assets worth the dollar value of their LTC policy. "The program has the merit of getting LTC insurance onto everybody's radar screen," says George Mason's Meiners, a key architect of the original partnership program. About 20 states reportedly are interested in establishing similar programs, but, "We aren't at a stage where you just turn a switch."

Moreover, the data on whether the partnerships work are "inconclusive," according to the National Conference of State Legislatures. So far, only 251 participants in the four states have exhausted their private coverage, and only 119 have accessed Medicaid — numbers too small to draw conclusions. Officers of Connecticut's program estimate it has saved the state $2.8 million.[46]

But MetLife's Anatole says the LTC insurance industry, which "pushed very hard" for the partnerships, is excited about the LTC insurance-education funding in the DRA law. Partnerships "may not be the be-all and end-all," but statistics show that insurers with a strong focus on LTC coverage have had stronger sales in the four partnership states, she says.

OUTLOOK

Higher and Higher

With the elderly population swelling, the cost of providing LTC in coming decades undoubtedly will rise dramatically. But it is difficult to predict how existing LTC delivery and financing systems may change to accommodate the deluge.

In the short run, Congress is expected to do little to address LTC financing and quality issues, although a few small but meaningful measures could be enacted in the next year or so.

A bill offering respite services for family caregivers of the elderly and ill of all ages has "lots of bipartisan support," says the Alzheimer's Association's McConnell. Expanding respite opportunities for families "plays right into the home-based-care trend, and it's not that expensive," he says.

The United Hospital Fund's Vladeck also predicts that some cities will experiment with NORCs — "naturally occurring retirement communities" — where seniors get help retooling their communities to facilitate "aging in place."[47] Advocates expect a nationwide NORC demonstration to be part of an eventual reauthorization of the Older Americans Act, which governs most of the country's programs for the elderly outside of Medicare, Medicaid and Social Security. It has been awaiting reauthorization for several years.

Eventually, however, sheer demographics will rivet Americans' attention to LTC. "The numbers . . . coming through the pipeline are pretty forbidding," says Georgetown University's Scanlon. And, as for LTC, "40 percent of the elderly think Medicare covers it, so there's a shock factor" when people discover that it doesn't.

Americans are "in denial of disability," says Kaplan of the University of Illinois, who favors an expansion of Medicare to include LTC. "But I don't have any fantasies about that happening any time soon. I don't know that Medicare itself would be enacted today."

Between 2000 and 2040, the share of the population age 65 and over will rise from 12.6 percent to 20.5 percent, according to the nonpartisan Congressional Budget Office. And since 55 percent of those age 85 and older have chronic physical impairment that makes it difficult to perform fundamental tasks required to live independently, like cooking or bathing, LTC spending is expected to reach $484 billion annually by 2040 — or about 2 percent of the nation's gross domestic product.[48]

Nevertheless, says UHF's Tallon, "When we're talking about health and health care, it's very hard to predict the future."

In the short term, he says, it's more important to recognize that "there is unmet need now" for LTC services. Thus, he suggests that policymakers put aside for now the debate on future LTC costs and ask instead, "Can you provide good LTC services today? If you can, that's the best step for the future."

NOTES

1. Quoted in Jennifer Levitz, "Resident #1," *Providence Journal*, Aug. 22, 2004.

2. Ellen O'Brien, "Long-Term Care: Understanding Medicaid's Role for the Elderly and Disabled," Kaiser Commission on Medicaid and the Uninsured, November 2005, p. 1.

3. Charlene Harrington, "Nursing Facilities, Staffing, Residents, and Facility Deficiencies, 1998 Through 2004," www.pascenter.org/documents/.

4. *Ibid.*

5. *Ibid.*

6. Jane Erikson, "Several Elder-Care Facilities Fined for Violations," *Arizona Daily Star*, Sept. 3, 2006.

7. "Older Americans 2004: Key Indicators of Well-Being," Federal Interagency Forum on Aging-Related Statistics, www.agingstats.gov.

8. Financing Long-Term Care for the Elderly, Congressional Budget Office, April 2004.

9. Marc A. Cohen, "Long-Term Care Insurance: Market Trends," address delivered to a Munich America Reassurance Co. conference, April 20, 2006.

10. "Developing a Better Long-Term Care Policy: A Vision and Strategy for America's Future," National Academy of Social Insurance, November 2005, p. iv.

11. *Ibid.* For background, see Mary H. Cooper, "Social Security Reform," *CQ Researcher*, Sept. 24, 2004, pp. 781-804; and Adriel Bettelheim, "Medicare Reform," *CQ Researcher*, Aug. 22, 2003, pp. 673-696.

12. *Ibid.*

13. "The Index of the Long Term Care Uninsured," Long Term Care Group, Inc., www.ltcg.com/INDEX%20of%20Long%20Term%20Care.pdf.

14. John Capitman, Walter Leutz, Christine Bishop and Rosemary Casler, "Long-Term Care Quality: Historical Overview and Current Initiatives," National Quality Forum, 2005, www.qualitylong-termcarecommission.org/reports/pdfs.

15. Harrington, *op. cit.*

16. Capitman, *et al.*, *op. cit.*, p. 1.

17. O'Brien, *op. cit.*

18. *Ibid.*

19. For background, see Capitman, *et al.*, *op. cit.*; and Karen Buhler-Wilkerson, *No Place Like Home: A History of Nursing and Home Care in the United States* (2003).

20. Alvin Schorr, "Thy Father and Thy Mother: A Second Look at Filial Responsibility and Family Policy," Government Printing Office, 1980, p. 7.

21. *Ibid.*

22. *Ibid*, p. 8.

23. *Ibid.*

24. "Older Americans 2004: Key Indicators of Well-Being," Federal Interagency Forum on Aging-Related Statistics, www.agingstats.gov.

25. Peter Kemper, Harriet L. Komisar and Lisa Alecxih, "Long-Term Care Over an Uncertain Future: What Can Current Retirees Expect?" *Inquiry*, winter 2005-2006, p. 335.

26. Carol Levine, director, Families and Health Care Project, United Hospital Fund, New York.

27. O'Brien, *op. cit.*, p. 4.

28. Bruce C. Vladeck, "Where the Action Really Is: Medicaid and the Disabled," *Health Affairs*, January/February 2003, p. 92.

29. Karen M. Ignagni, testimony before House Energy and Commerce Subcommittee on Health, April 27, 2005.

30. For background, see R. McNickle, "Older People," *Editorial Research Reports 1949* (Vol. II), available at CQ Researcher Plus Archive, at CQ Electronic Library, http://library.cqpress.com.

31. Capitman, *et al.*, *op. cit.*, p. 11. Also see H. B. Shaffer, "Nursing Homes and Medical Care," *Editorial Research Reports 1963* (Vol. II), available at CQ Researcher Plus Archive, CQ Electronic Library, http://library.cqpress.com.

32. For background, see H. B. Shaffer, "Plight of the Aged," *Editorial Research Reports 1971* (Vol. II), available at CQ Researcher Plus Archive, CQ Electronic Library, http://library.cqpress.com.

33. Capitman, *op. cit.*, p. 13.

34. *Ibid.*; see also R. K. Landers, "The Elderly in an Aging America," *Editorial Research Reports 1988* (Vol. II), available in *CQ Researcher Plus Archives*, CQ Electronic Library, http://library.cqpress.com.

35. *Ibid.*, Capitman.

36. O'Brien, *op. cit.*, p. 14.

37. Lori Rackl and Chris Fusco, "Background Checks Find 1,000 Felons in Nursing Homes," *Chicago Sun-Times*, July 21, 2006, p. 6.

38. Judith Rabig, William Thomas, Rosalie A. Kane, Lois J. Cutler and Steve McAlilly, "Radical Redesign of Nursing Homes: Applying the Green House Concept in Tupelo, Mississippi," *Practice Concepts*, The Gerontological Society of America, 2006, p. 533.

39. *Ibid.*, p. 538.

40. *Ibid.*, p. 539. The states are New York, Ohio, Arizona, Georgia, Nebraska, North Carolina, Florida, Michigan, Kansas and Hawaii.

41. "Deficit Reduction Act of 2005: Implications for Medicaid," Kaiser Commission on Medicaid and the Uninsured, February 2006.

42. Bernard A. Krooks, testimony delivered to the House Energy and Commerce Health Subcommittee, April 27, 2005.

43. *Ibid.*

44. "Transfers of Assets by Elderly Individuals to Obtain Long-Term Care Coverage," Government Accountability Office, September 2005.

45. *Ibid.*

46. Matthew Gever, "Long-Term Care Partnerships Could Bloom Again Under the DRA," National Conference of State Legislatures, www.mcsl.org.

47. For background, see H. B. Shaffer, "Housing for the Elderly," *Editorial Research Reports 1959* (Vol. I), available at CQ Researcher Plus Archive, CQ Electronic Library, http://library.cqpress.com.

48. Congressional Budget Office, *op. cit.*

BIBLIOGRAPHY

Books

Buhler-Wilkinson, Karen, *No Place Like Home: A History of Nursing and Home Care in the United States,* *The Johns Hopkins University Press,* **2003.**
A professor of community health at the University of Pennsylvania traces the history of home-delivered health care in the United States, comparing its relatively limited use to the much wider spread of residential health-care institutions.

Levine, Carol, and Thomas H. Murray, eds., *The Cultures of Caregiving: Conflict and Common Ground Among Families, Health Professionals, and Policy Makers, The Johns Hopkins University Press,* **2004.**
Murray, a bioethicist, and Levine, an advocate for family caregivers, assemble data, personal stories and essays that demonstrate the varying perspectives of family caregivers, medical personnel and health-care administrators.

Gass, Thomas Edward, *Nobody's Home: Candid Reflections of a Nursing Home Aide, ILR Press,* **2005.**
Gass describes the daily routines of his work and reflects on how quality of life could be improved for nursing-home residents.

Mezey, Mathy Doval, Barbara J. Berkman, Christopher M. Callahan and Ethel L. Mitty, eds., *The Encyclopedia of Elder Care, Prometheus Books,* **2004.**
Professors of medicine and nursing at various universities provide advice on health care for seniors and articles about the financing and delivery of long-term care for elderly people.

Articles

"Nursing Home Guide," *Consumer Reports,* **www .consumerreports.org/cro/health-fitness/nursing-home-guide/0608_nursing-home-guide.htm, September 2006.**
The nonprofit consumer-research group provides state-by-state listings of nursing homes that are likely to provide the best and the worst care; discusses how to choose high-quality long-term care; and analyzes how the federal government's Web site on nursing-home quality falls short.

Peck, Richard L., "Turning LTC Upside Down," *Nursing Homes,* **www.nursinghomesmagazine.com/ Past_Issues.htm?ID=4180, June 2005.**
In an interview, Leonard Fishman, former president of the American Association of Homes and Services for the Aging, describes current efforts to create a new continuum of senior-housing options to avoid institutionalization and improve elders' quality of life.

Reports and Studies

"Financing Long-Term Care for the Elderly," *Congressional Budget Office,* **April 2004.**
Congress' nonpartisan budget-analysis office analyzes trends in population aging, disability and long-term-care service delivery and discusses what they mean for future long-term-care costs in the United States.

Burke, Sheila P., Judith Feder and Paul N. Van de Water, eds., "Developing a Better Long-Term Care Policy: A Vision and Strategy for America's Future," *National Academy of Social Insurance,* **November 2005.**
Experts on public social-insurance programs discuss why the United States needs social insurance to finance future long-term-care needs.

Capitman, John, Walter Leutz, Christine Bishop and Rosemary Casler, "Long-Term Care Quality: Historical Overview and Current Initiatives," *National Quality Forum,* **2005.**
Professors of public policy at Brandeis University examine how standards for long-term-care quality have changed over the years and what steps federal and state governments have taken to measure and improve quality.

Johnson, Richard W., and Joshua M. Wiener, "A Profile of Frail Older Americans and Their Caregivers," *The Retirement Project, Urban Institute,* **February 2006.**
Analysts from a liberal-leaning think tank describe the demographic, financial and health-related characteristics of Americans who need long-term care and the friends and family who provide unpaid care for them.

O'Brien, Ellen, "Long-Term Care: Understanding Medicaid's Role for the Elderly and Disabled," *Kaiser Commission on Medicaid and the Uninsured,* **November 2005.**
A nonprofit research organization that studies health policy for low-income people describes Medicaid's role in paying for and delivering long-term care, including how state long-term-care programs vary.

Wunderlich, Gooloo S., and Peter O. Kohler, eds., "Improving the Quality of Long-Term Care," *National Academies Press,* **2001.**
An expert panel from the Institute of Medicine examines quality-of-care problems in nursing homes, home-health agencies and other long-term-care providers and proposes methods for beefing up staffing and setting and enforcing quality standards.

For More Information

AARP, 601 E St., N.W., Washington, DC 20049; (888) 687-2277; www.aarp.org. Formerly known as the American Association for Retired Persons, the organization conducts policy research and offers consumer information on long-term care.

Alzheimer's Association, 225 N. Michigan Ave., 17th Fl, Chicago, IL 60601-7633; (800) 272-3900; www.alz.org. Supports research on dementia and provides information about how long-term-care policies affect dementia sufferers and their families.

American Association of Homes and Services for the Aging, 2519 Connecticut Ave., N.W., Washington, DC 20008; (202) 783-2242; www.aahsa.org. Provides aging services to the elderly and conducts research on long-term care.

Center for Long-Term Care Reform, 2212 Queen Ave. North, #110, Seattle, WA 98109; (206) 283-7026; www.centerltc.com. Supports private long-term-care insurance and other private financing options for long-term care.

Family Caregivers Alliance, 180 Montgomery St., Suite 1100, San Francisco, CA 94104; (415) 434-3388; www.caregiver.org. Promotes development of programs at the local, state and national levels to support informal caregivers.

Kaiser Family Foundation, 1330 G St., N.W., Washington, DC 20005; (202) 347-5270; www.kff.org. Conducts and disseminates research on national health-care issues, including Medicaid and long-term care.

Medicaid Commission, Hubert H. Humphrey Building, 200 Independence Ave., S.W., Suite 450G, Washington, DC 20201; http://aspe.hhs.gov. Congress asked this expert panel to recommend policies by December 2006 that ensure long-term financial stability in Medicaid.

National Association for Home Care and Hospice, 228 Seventh St., S.E., Washington, DC 20003; (202) 547-7424; www.nahc.org. Provides information and advocacy on how long-term-care policies affect providers of home-delivered care.

National Citizens' Coalition for Nursing Home Reform, 1828 L St., N.W., Suite 801, Washington, DC 20036; (202) 332-2276; www.nccnhr.org. Advocates for better-quality nursing-home care and provides information about choosing nursing homes.

National Senior Citizens' Law Center, 1101 14th St., N.W., Suite 400, Washington, DC 20005; (202) 289-6976; www.nsclc.org. Advocates and litigates on behalf of low-income seniors and people with disabilities and provides consumer and policy information on long-term-care options.

United Hospital Fund, Empire State Building, 23rd Floor, 350 Fifth Ave., New York, NY 10118; (212) 494-0700; www.uhfnyc.org. Provides research and grant funding on health-care issues, including family caregiving and aging-in-place initiatives.

16

Aging Baby Boomers

Will the 'Youth Generation' Redefine Old Age?

Alan Greenblatt

Former mortgage broker Jamie Sims checks crawfish traps at her family's fish farm in Harrisburg, Ark., Sims, 44, is among the baby boomers who have left the "rat race" for less stressful jobs. Beginning in 2008, the oldest boomers will turn 62 — old enough to collect Social Security. In 2030, when the number of Americans over 65 hits 72 million, some experts predict dangerous strains on entitlement programs and the federal budget.

From *CQ Researcher*,
October 19, 2007.

Five years ago, Honda introduced a boxy SUV — the Element — with an ad campaign billing it as a combined "base camp" and "dorm room on wheels" and featuring images of 20-somethings cruising down to the beach.

But Honda's appeal to the youth market missed its target, triggering the interest of baby boomers instead. During its first year on the market, the average age of Element buyers was 42.[1]

Several other cars initially targeted at younger consumers have been "hijacked" by baby boomers — the generation of 78 million Americans born between 1946 and 1964 — including the Toyota Matrix, the Pontiac Vibe and the Dodge Neon.[2]

It's not surprising that the notably nostalgic boomer generation seeks out youthful, environmentally friendly products. Throughout their middle-age years, they have remained loyal to the music and culture of their youth as well as youthful in their habits, priorities and pursuits. "In their eagerness to live up to their label as the youth generation, boomers — with the help of marketers, to be sure — have created a youth-oriented consumer mindset that is proving difficult to shift," writes Diane Crispell, a consumer-behavior consultant associated with Cornell University.[3]

Since baby boomers apparently "never devised an exit strategy from their youth," as one wag put it, marketers and others wonder what they are going to be like as old people. Beginning in January 2008, the oldest boomers will turn 62 — old enough to start collecting Social Security. The nation's first baby boomer, in fact, just applied for Social Security benefits on Oct. 15, to great media fanfare. Kathleen Casey-Kirschling, 62, a retired schoolteacher in Cherry Hill, N.J., was born a second after the stroke of midnight

369

Number of Seniors Is Rising Rapidly

One in five Americans will be over age 65 by 2050. Such a profound demographic change raises fundamental questions about the federal government's ability to pay for all the aging boomers who will be depending on Social Security, Medicare and other entitlements.

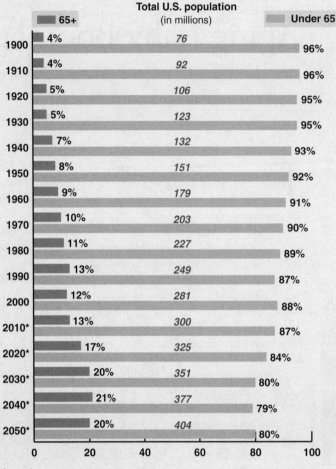

Percentage of People Age 65 and Older, 1900-2050

Total U.S. population (in millions)

Year	65+	Total (millions)	Under 65
1900	4%	76	96%
1910	4%	92	96%
1920	5%	106	95%
1930	5%	123	95%
1940	7%	132	93%
1950	8%	151	92%
1960	9%	179	91%
1970	10%	203	90%
1980	11%	227	89%
1990	13%	249	87%
2000	12%	281	88%
2010*	13%	300	87%
2020*	17%	325	84%
2030*	20%	351	80%
2040*	21%	377	79%
2050*	20%	404	80%

* projected

Percentages may not total 100 due to rounding.

Source: Robert B. Friedland and Laura Summer, "Demography Is Not Destiny, Revisited," Center on an Aging Society, Georgetown University, March 2005

on entitlement programs and the federal budget to a decline in the stock and housing markets as boomers start liquidating their assets.

But boomers are growing old at an opportune time. The nature of aging is changing. Many boomers feel younger than their parents did at the same age, and that's not just in their imaginations — or their consumer patterns. Life expectancy has gone up significantly during boomers' lifetimes, as has "health expectancy." Fewer seniors suffer from chronic disabilities than was the case 25 years ago, so millions of today's senior citizens — and the boomers who will follow — can lead active and productive lives until a later age.

Frieda Birnbaum, the 60-year-old New Jersey psychologist who gave birth to twins in May, is just an extreme example of how life milestones are shifting to later ages. The percentage of Americans working in their late 60s has shot up by more than half since 1985. And the percentage of those over 55 who say they are exercising 100 or more days per year has jumped 33 percent.[4]

"Compared to older people in the past, boomers will actually have a greater opportunity and ability to live a youthful old age," write J. Walker Smith and Anne Clurman, senior executives at the Yankelovich consumer research firm, which coined the term "baby boomer."[5]

"Four decades of Yankelovich research," they write in their new book, *Generation Ageless*, "has found one thing about boomers over and over again — an unwavering determination to not get old."[6]

Surveys conducted by AARP, the main advocacy organization for older Americans, show that up to 80 percent of boomers intend to work past 65. Many have expressed

on Jan. 1, 1946. By 2030, according to the Census Bureau, the number of Americans over 65 is expected to double — to 72 million. That demographic leap has led to a variety of dire predictions, from unbearable strains

the desire to pursue entirely new second careers, such as social work or teaching.

"Most previous generations thought about whether they're wealthy and able to leave trust funds," says Andrew Achenbaum, a historian of aging at the University of Houston. "Boomers think, 'I have to feel that I'm accomplishing something; I really am concerned about legacy.' Legacy has always been a minor motif, but it's going to be major with the boomers."

Less altruistic boomers will work simply to pay the bills. Taken together, boomers are affluent, but there are vast asset disparities within this huge cohort. Contrary to concerns about hostility between boomers and younger generations as Social Security and Medicare expenditures shoot up, New York University political scientist Paul C. Light noted, "It is far more likely that the baby boomers will divide against themselves in an intra-generational war between the haves and have-nots."[7]

Still, it remains an open question as to how much longer boomers will actually work — and whether those who want to work will be able to find work that's more "meaningful" or lucrative than, say, being a greeter at Wal-Mart.

Numerous nonprofits and job placement services have sprung up to help seniors interested in gainful employment, but some observers doubt boomers will be able to work much more than previous generations did during their retirement years. At the same time, some sectors — such as nursing and government — realize that boomers comprise a disproportionate share of their workforces so they are offering accommodations to keep seniors on longer. By 2010, an estimated 26 million workers will be 55 or over — a 46 percent increase since 2000.[8]

But surveys indicate that not all employers are eager to provide the flexibility senior workers say they want as they begin to dial back the number of hours they're willing to work. A few million boomers have already chosen to leave

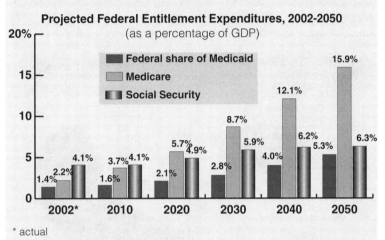

Entitlement Spending Will Skyrocket

The cost of the three key federal entitlement programs for older Americans is expected to increase dramatically in coming decades, reaching 28 percent of gross domestic product (GDP) by 2050. Comptroller General David M. Walker says the expected "tsunami of spending" threatens the nation's economic stability.

Projected Federal Entitlement Expenditures, 2002-2050
(as a percentage of GDP)

Legend:
- Federal share of Medicaid
- Medicare
- Social Security

Year	Federal share of Medicaid	Medicare	Social Security
2002*	1.4%	2.2%	4.1%
2010	1.6%	3.7%	4.1%
2020	2.1%	5.7%	4.9%
2030	2.8%	8.7%	5.9%
2040	4.0%	12.1%	6.2%
2050	5.3%	15.9%	6.3%

* actual

Source: Robert B. Friedland and Laura Summer, "Demography Is Not Destiny, Revisited," Center on an Aging Society, Georgetown University, March 2005

the workplace, and about 40 percent of retirees left their jobs involuntarily — due to layoffs or health issues.

However, when it comes to actually retiring, "There's a difference between saying it and doing it, and a difference between saying it and being able to do it," says Eric Kingson, a professor of social work at Syracuse University.

Still, it's clear boomers intend to age differently from their parents. They won't all be exercise demons or work full time. But because there are so many boomers, trends that take root among even a small percentage of them can have an outsized influence on society. "When we thought hula hoops were in, hula hoops were in," says Jerry Abramson, a boomer himself who sees the continuing influence of his generation at work in his capacity as mayor of Louisville, Ky. "When we thought bell bottoms were to be worn, they were worn." Today, he notes, "Boomers are changing housing patterns, recreation facilities and community-center programming."

"They've changed everything all along, haven't they," says Sara E. Rix, interim director of economic studies at AARP's Public Policy Institute. "I think they are going to

Seniors' Assets Total More Than $5 Trillion

Americans over age 65 hold one-fifth of the stocks and bonds owned by Americans — more than $5.25 trillion (left). According to a Government Accountability Office (GAO) study of current retirees, overall spending down of assets is slowing, and many retirees are actually continuing to purchase stocks. If baby boomers behave like current retirees, the GAO says, "a rapid and mass sell-off of financial assets seems unlikely." One-third of all baby boomers have no financial assets (right).

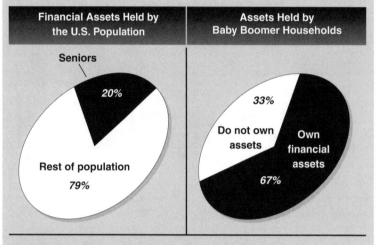

Financial Assets Held by the U.S. Population

Seniors
20%

Rest of population
79%

Assets Held by Baby Boomer Households

33%
Do not own assets

Own financial assets
67%

Percentages may not total 100 due to rounding.

Source: "Baby Boom Generation: Retirement of Baby Boomers Is Unlikely to Precipitate Dramatic Decline in Market Returns, but Broader Risks Threaten Retirement Security," Government Accountability Office, July 2006

see themselves as young for a much longer period of time and act accordingly."

Or as Birnbaum put it after her twins were born: "I don't feel like I'm 60. I don't know what 60 is meant to be."[9]

As boomers prepare to change the nature of senior citizenship — and as the nation prepares for them — here are the questions being debated:

Can boomers afford to retire?

Baby boomers owe their lives to affluence. The economic boom that followed World War II — when America dominated the global economy and wages skyrocketed — convinced millions of parents they could afford to raise multiple children.

As the resulting boomers grew up, the future continued to look promising. They were much more likely to attend and complete college than their parents, and few clouds darkened their economic horizon until the oil shocks and high inflation of the 1970s. As a result, boomers have been "one of the most prosperous generations in U.S. history," concludes a Congressional Budget Office study.[10]

But projections are mixed on whether boomers can afford to retire comfortably. Wealth in households headed by Americans 55 or over has doubled since 1989, reaching nearly $250,000 in 2004. During the same period, however, accumulated assets among those in their late 30s had dropped by more than 25 percent, to less than $50,000.[11]

Some boomers, however, are clearly struggling. "The top one-third of the boomers will have lots of choices, and the bottom one-third will be working until they drop just to keep food on the table," said Paul Hodge, chairman of the Global Generations Policy Institute at Harvard University.[12]

Waiting lists for affordable and subsidized senior housing have grown, while bankruptcy filings are rising faster for those 55 and older than for any other age group, due primarily to mortgage debt and health costs.[13]

And while boomers may be wealthy as a collective group, there is clearly a divide among them in terms of savings and wealth. The wealthiest 10 percent of boomers hold more than two-thirds of their generation's accumulated financial assets, says the Government Accountability Office (GAO).[14] And a substantial difference in wealth accumulation exists between older boomers (born between 1946 and 1954) and younger boomers (those born between 1955 and 1964), according to the Bureau of Labor Statistics.[15]

"Boomers have a hugely disproportionate amount of assets compared to the other generations," says Frederick R. Lynch, a sociologist at Claremont McKenna College in California and author of a forthcoming book about boomers. But about half of the boomers are vulnerable, in terms of retirement savings and retiree health benefits, he points out. "There's a whole working class — Joe Six-Pack America — even among the boomers."

Boomers should be better off in retirement than their parents because they have enjoyed higher per capita incomes and accumulated wealth at about the same rate as their parents. But some studies indicate that boomers have saved slightly less and spent a bit more than their forebears. One insurance ad noted, "The generation that 'wouldn't trust anyone over 30' never planned on a 30-year retirement."[16]

"Charge cards like VISA and MasterCard came into the market just when the boomers came out of college and started making money, so they've been in debt ever since," says Charles F. Longino Jr., director of the Reynolda Gerontology Program at Wake Forest University.

Boomers also tend to have more of their assets tied up in financial instruments such as stocks, which leaves them more vulnerable to economic cycles than previous generations. If there's a badly timed recession or stock market decline, Lynch says, "It's going to be really tough. They're betting on the market."

Some of the younger boomers may be vulnerable to the widespread switch in private pension plans from "defined-benefit" programs, which offered fixed, guaranteed payments throughout retirement, to "defined-contribution" plans (such as 401(k)s), which are stock-market-based accounts that can decline precipitously in value.[17]

"The risks of aging have shifted more to the individual," says Michael A. Smyer, codirector of the Center on Aging and Work at Boston College. "With the shift from defined-benefit to defined-contribution plans, the risk of planning for your future is more on your shoulders."

Rix, of AARP, says older Americans are also nervous about cuts in retiree health benefits, which may be why more seniors are working at least until 65, when they become eligible for Medicare. "Surveys overwhelmingly reveal that older workers expect to work in retirement, both for financial as well as non-financial reasons," she says. "But when pressed for the main reason, the financial reason rises to the top."

The proportion of Americans still working in their late 60s has been rising. In California, a study found that the proportion of people 55 to 69 who were working rose by about 10 percent between 1995 and 2006.[18]

The fact that boomers are expected to live longer than prior generations also prompts many to consider delaying retirement. Boomers "aren't saving and are really strapped," says Susan Krauss Whitbourne, a psychologist at the University of Massachusetts, Amherst who has studied boomers. "Now they're living longer, and the chickens have to come home to roost at some point."

But Yankelovich's Smith doubts claims that boomers haven't saved enough. "Compared to prior generations, boomers are in better shape financially," he says. "And, since they're not going to retire [at the traditional retirement age], those that predict doom and gloom are wrong."

Will boomers bankrupt America?

Like earlier generations, boomer seniors will depend heavily on government programs such as Social Security and Medicare, which have brought poverty rates among the over-65 population down from more than one-third in 1960 to just over 10 percent.[19] But with the number of seniors rising rapidly, can the federal government afford to pay for all the aging boomers who will be signing up?

Over the past two years, Comptroller General David M. Walker — the nation's top accountant — has been conducting his own "fiscal wake-up tour," crisscrossing the nation with a doomsday message for policy makers and the public about the government's long-term financial liabilities. "The most serious threat to the United States is not someone hiding in a cave in Afghanistan or Pakistan, but our own fiscal irresponsibility," he told CBS' "60 Minutes" in July.

His biggest worry: the federal entitlement programs designed to benefit seniors. "The first baby boomer will reach 62 and be eligible for early retirement or Social Security on Jan. 1, 2008," he said. The boomers will be eligible for Medicare three years later, and when they start retiring en masse it will create a potential "tsunami of spending that could swamp our ship of state."[20]

For years, economists have warned that the enormous boomer bulge in the senior population could impose enormous burdens on both the economy and government finances. Social Security and Medicare expenditures could rise from their current 8.5 percent of national economic output to 15 percent, according to the Congressional Budget Office (CBO). The federal debt

Many baby boomers are doing the things they couldn't afford in their youth, or during their working years. For Dean and Beverly Avery, of San Leandro, Calif., owning a 1966 Ford Mustang fulfilled a longtime dream.

could nearly double, rising from its current 37 percent of the economy to about 100 percent — a level previously reached only during World War II.[21]

But longstanding fears about the impact of this demographic upheaval on the stock market may not materialize, according to some experts. A GAO report concluded that retiring boomers will not suddenly sell off enormous amounts of stock market assets all at once. Because the boomer generation spans such a broad range of time — 1946 to 1964 — they will not all be retiring and liquidating at the same time. While the oldest boomers are on the cusp of Social Security eligibility, the youngest boomers will not reach 60 for another 15 years yet.[22]

"There will be no market meltdown — people don't all sell at once," says Barbara D. Bovbjerg, director of Education, Workforce and Income Security Issues at the GAO.

For similar reasons, some economists doubt that aging boomers will cause chaos in the housing market, since they won't be selling their homes all at once.

Similarly, there are fewer worries that millions of boomers reaching retirement age will cripple the nation's workforce, since many will continue working for some time, and replacements can be found for them in most fields. Fear of a coming labor shortage due to boomer retirements is "way overstated," says Peter Capelli, director of the human resources program at the University of Pennsylvania's Wharton School and author of an influential paper on the topic. "The biggest high-school class ever to graduate in the U.S. is the class that graduated this year, 2007."

But what about the impact of the boomer tsunami on entitlement programs for seniors? Like Comptroller General Walker, many observers worry that the number of seniors will increase exponentially as the number of workers paying taxes to support the entitlement programs dwindles. The ratio of seniors to working-age population (ages 25 to 64) will rise by 30 percent over each of the next two decades, says Dowell Myers, a demographer at the University of Southern California.

"I think it's going to be pretty bad," says Laurence J. Kotlikoff, an MIT economist and coauthor of *The Coming Generational Storm*, a 2004 book about the threat retired boomers represent to the entitlement programs. "The county is basically insolvent. We can't afford the policies we've got in place, let alone the projected growth."

Peter Diamond, a colleague of Kotlikoff at MIT who has written extensively about Social Security, is more sanguine. The baby boomers are already factored into Social Security projections, he notes. And, although the program's trust fund is expected to run out of money by 2040, Diamond and many other economists believe modest tweaking can keep the program in the black much longer.

But he does share widespread concerns that Medicare costs are rising at unsustainable rates, especially since the addition of a prescription-drug benefit that went into effect in 2006. Medicare and Medicaid, says GAO's Bovbjerg, are "the primary threat to the fiscal stability of the federal government."

Even those most pessimistic about Medicare costs believe the issue will have to be confronted, but in the broader context of the U.S. health system as a whole, not as a problem triggered just by boomer retirements.

Lynch, at Claremont McKenna College, agrees Medicare will be tougher to fix than Social Security but says both are more fixable than the "doomsday" economists believe. "The solution is that boomers will work longer and won't retire as early as prior generations," Lynch says. "The proportion of people retiring early is starting to decline."

Laura L. Carstensen, director of Stanford University's Center on Longevity, agrees that boomers will break the nation's bank — but only if the programs don't change and if boomers act like previous generations in terms of their retirement patterns — and she doubts either premise will come to pass.

"Boomers could [bankrupt the country] if . . . Social Security and Medicare don't change and people continue to retire at 65," Carstensen says. "But relatively modest changes could turn that around."

Will boomers change the nature of aging?

An old joke says old age is always 15 years away. Boomers seem to have taken that to heart. According to a 1996 survey, boomers believed old age began at age 79 — and at that time life expectancy was just over 76 years. As Smith and Clurman point out in *Generation Ageless*, boomers literally thought they'd die before they got old.[23]

"Boomers are not going to give up their aspirations for youthfulness," Smith says. "It is the defining characteristic of the boomer sensibility."

When approaching his own 60th birthday last year, President Bush, said he "used to think 60 was really old. Now I think it's young, don't you? It's not that old, it really isn't."[24]

Is Bush right? The fact that the boomers are "coming of old age" at a time when life expectancy is lengthening may pose some demographic and economic challenges. But many sociologists and gerontologists believe the generation that refuses to grow up can change — in healthy ways — how Americans think about aging.

"There's no question that we're going to change the meaning of late life," says Achenbaum, the University of Houston historian. "Chronological age, per se, is going to be a miserable predictor of what contingencies and opportunities might arise."

Today, the average man reaching 65 can expect to live for 17 more years, while women will live for 20.[25] People are not only living longer but in many cases are staying healthy longer. The rate of chronic disabilities is down to just 19 percent among those over 65, compared with 26 percent in 1982.[26]

U.S. Is 'Younger' Than Other Countries

The proportion of today's U.S. population 65 and older is smaller than in other industrialized nations and is projected to be even smaller in 2050. The elderly will be 21 percent of the U.S. population in 2050 compared with 30 percent or more in Japan, Italy and Germany. Population aging is a worldwide phenomenon, mostly due to declining fertility rates and increasing life expectancies.

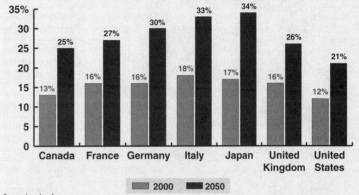

Percentage of Population Age 65 and Older, 2000 and 2050*
(in selected industrialized nations)

	2000	2050
Canada	13%	25%
France	16%	27%
Germany	16%	30%
Italy	18%	33%
Japan	17%	34%
United Kingdom	16%	26%
United States	12%	21%

* projected

Source: Robert B. Friedland and Laura Summer, "Demography Is Not Destiny, Revisited," Center on an Aging Society, Georgetown University, March 2005

"We get so many [article] pitches about people over 60 riding their bikes across the country, or running in 100-mile marathons, we have to tell them, 'Great, but this is not really news any more,' " said Margaret Guroff, health editor of *AARP* magazine.[27]

Not everyone is a marathoner, of course. But boomers, who created the jogging fad in the 1970s and turned aerobics into a multibillion-dollar industry in the 1980s, are now returning to fitness centers in record numbers.

They are also beginning to impose their preferences on a variety of services for seniors, demanding, for instance, that meals be less about gravy and more about fresh, healthy foods — organic, if possible, thank you very much.

Stanford psychologist Carstensen says boomers will update old-age behaviors and consumer demands — demanding, for instance, Starbucks coffee in nursing homes and cell phones designed so that "aging eyes can make out the numbers."

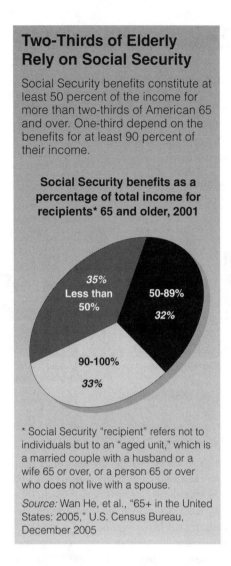

Two-Thirds of Elderly Rely on Social Security

Social Security benefits constitute at least 50 percent of the income for more than two-thirds of American 65 and over. One-third depend on the benefits for at least 90 percent of their income.

Social Security benefits as a percentage of total income for recipients* 65 and older, 2001

35% Less than 50%

50-89% 32%

90-100% 33%

* Social Security "recipient" refers not to individuals but to an "aged unit," which is a married couple with a husband or a wife 65 or over, or a person 65 or over who does not live with a spouse.

Source: Wan He, et al., "65+ in the United States: 2005," U.S. Census Bureau, December 2005

"We are offering more and more activities to keep the mind alert," said Becky Batta, director of a senior center in Annapolis, Md. "The baby boomers are coming and they demand it. They are completely different from other generations of seniors."[28]

But some research indicates boomers are less physically active than their parents and grandparents were at the same age, more likely to be sitting at a desk at work or in a car than actually working out. They also are more likely to suffer chronic problems such as high cholesterol and diabetes. Half of those 55 to 64 have high blood pressure, while 40 percent are obese, according to the Centers for Disease Control and Prevention.

"People are not as healthy as they approach retirement as they were in older generations," said Mark D. Hayward, a University of Texas sociologist. "It's very disturbing."[29]

"They talk to their fellow boomers and realize, I'm not the only one getting bad mammograms or having brittle bones," says Lynch, the Claremont McKenna sociologist. "They will realize there are some obstacles you can't overcome. Boomers are going to discover that if their biology says no, it's going to be no."

Nevertheless, Lynch and others believe boomers have redefined every stage of life they've entered, so being elderly should be no exception. And even if many inevitably fall prey to disease or age-related afflictions, millions will be healthier and more productive than society expects.

"Sheer numbers alone are going to cause a shift in attitudes and perception," says Rix of AARP. "When you see more older people who are active, vibrant and staying on the job, that will change perceptions about being older."

"Boomers are going to redefine what it means to be old and what it means to retire," says *Generation Ageless* coauthor Smith.

But that doesn't mean boomers can stay young forever. They may listen to cooler music than their parents did, but their ears are still getting older. About one in six boomers already suffers from hearing loss. In fact, the AARP reports, 10 million people between 45 and 64 suffer from hearing loss, compared to 9 million people over 65.[30] All those years of 115-decibel rock concerts and wearing a Walkman have taken their toll, experts say.

And while it's possible to retard the effects of aging through diet and exercise — which is why life expectancy keeps rising — it's not possible to turn back the clock. But that doesn't mean that being 60 will be the same experience that it was, say, in the 1960s.

"We hear 60 is the new 40," says Marc Freedman, CEO of Civic Ventures, a group that seeks to link seniors with job opportunities. "I'm convinced that 60 is the new 60 — that we're actually inventing a new stage of life now between the end of midlife careers and true old age and retirement."

BACKGROUND

'Fertility Splurge'

Following a long period of decline in birth rates — dating back to the Industrial Revolution — demographers in the 1930s predicted that the U.S. population would stagnate and was unlikely to rise above 150 million by century's end. But birth rates shot up immediately after World War II, quickly rising to more than 4 million births per year.

All told, about 76 million children were born in the United States between 1946 and 1964. (Several million have died, but immigrants have more than made up for those numbers.)

"Simply put, the baby boom was a 'disturbance' which emanated from a decade-and-a-half-long fertility splurge on the part of American couples," concluded the Population Research Bureau in 1980.[31]

Childbearing long delayed — first by the Depression and then by war — was put off no longer. Women married younger and had their first babies at an earlier age than at any time in modern history.[32] The fertility rate, which averaged 2.1 children per woman during the 1930s, peaked at 3.7 in the late 1950s. [33] The number of babies being born certainly surprised the General Electric Co. in January 1953. It promised five shares of stock to any employee who had a baby on Oct. 15, the company's 75th anniversary. GE expected maybe eight employees would qualify. Instead they had to hand over stock to 189 workers.[34]

But the baby boom of 1946 to 1964 was not simply triggered by the return of young soldiers from war. In fact, the boom accelerated through the 1950s. As the economy flourished and families moved to expansive new homes in suburbs, children became not just affordable but expected. As sociologist William Simon put it, those who didn't want children "were an embarrassed and embattled minority. It was almost evidence of a physical or mental deficiency."[35]

The time was ripe, economically, for many more people to have children than had done so during the Great Depression of the 1930s. The gross domestic product (GDP) expanded rapidly, growing from $227 billion in 1940 to $488 billion in 1960. Median family income and real wages climbed steadily due to tight labor markets, while inflation remained low. The Servicemembers'

Readjustment Act of 1944, commonly known as the GI Bill of Rights, helped more of the middle class buy their first homes and get college educations, significantly increasing their lifetime earnings.[36]

"Never had so many people, anywhere, been so well off," observed *U.S. News & World Report* in 1957.[37]

The increases in personal income and home ownership led to comfortable childhoods for millions of boomers in a largely peaceful and prosperous time, notable for its advances in medicine, such as the Salk polio vaccine of 1955.[38]

"Many American children, regardless of their family background, grew up during the baby boom with an expectation of nearly limitless growth and opportunity," wrote two University of Michigan social scientists in a recent essay.[39]

Those expectations were fueled by rising rates of education. Between 1955 and 1975, enrollment in elementary and high schools increased 41 percent. Not only were more students attending school but they were also spending more time in school than their parents or grandparents — 40 more days per school year, on average. Less than 20 percent of the school-age population had graduated from high school during the 1920s; by the 1970s more than 75 percent did.[40]

Near-universal high school — and the G.I. Bill's liberal higher-education benefits — led to a boom in college enrollments. From 1965 to 1980, college enrollment more than doubled, from 5.9 million to 12 million, making boomers the first generation in which vast numbers took college nearly for granted.[41]

Boomer Culture

Away from the schoolbooks, boomers were important and influential consumers. "They were the first generation of children to be isolated by Madison Avenue as an identifiable target," noted journalist Landon Y. Jones in his 1980 history of the boomers, *Great Expectations.* "From the cradle, the baby boomers had been surrounded by products created especially for them, from Silly Putty to Slinkys to skateboards. New products, new toys, new commercials, new fads [were] integral to the baby boomer experience."[42]

Boomers identified strongly with their favorite toys and trends. They grew up with TV — which evolved

CHRONOLOGY

1940s-1950s *High postwar birth rates fuel suburban growth.*

1946 First baby boomers are born.

1954 Bill Haley's "Rock Around the Clock" inaugurates the rock 'n' roll era that became symbolic of the baby boom generation.

1959 More than 50 million Americans are under age 14, representing 30 percent of the population.

1960s-1970s *Boomers continue to affect trends, increasing rates of college education and drug use.*

1960 A record 66.5 million Americans are employed. . . . Real wages are up almost 30 percent from 1940 levels. . . . Nine of 10 U.S. households have TVs. . . . Sun City opens in Arizona, pioneering the idea of a retirement community.

1963 In a defining moment for the generation, President John F. Kennedy is assassinated in Dallas.

1964 The Beatles appear on "The Ed Sullivan Show," attracting a record 70 million viewers. . . . Free Speech Movement at University of California, Berkeley launches era of student protests.

1965 Forty-one percent of all Americans are under age 20.

1968 Martin Luther King Jr. and Robert F. Kennedy are assassinated. . . . Antiwar protests spread worldwide.

1970 College enrollment reaches nearly 8 million, vs. 3.6 million in 1960. . . . First Earth Day ushers in modern environmental activism.

1973 Arab oil embargo triggers inflation.

1976 Writer Tom Wolfe names the "Me Decade."

1980s-1990s *Boomers set aside youthful rebelliousness to take a leading role in wealth creation and politics.*

1980 College enrollment reaches 12 million students.

1983 Congress raises age for full Social Security payments from 65 to 67.

1984 *Newsweek* declares it the "year of the yuppie," arguing that young, urban professionals are reshaping the economic and social landscapes.

1986 The Age Discrimination Employment Act is amended to eliminate mandatory retirement ages.

1990 One in two Americans lives in suburbs — double the 1950 ratio.

1992 Bill Clinton becomes first boomer president.

2000s *Oldest boomers enter their 60s, raising concerns about funds for their retirements.*

2000 For every American 65 or over there are 3.4 workers paying into Social Security — a ratio that will shrink to 2.0 by 2030.

2003 Congress passes prescription-drug benefit for seniors.

2005 President George W. Bush calls for privatizing Social Security, gets little support.

2006 President Bush, part of the baby boom generation's leading edge, turns 60. . . . Pension Protection Act allows workers to dip into their pensions while working past 62.

2007 Federal Reserve Chairman Ben S. Bernanke says Social Security and Medicare will swallow 15 percent of annual economic output by 2030. . . . Federal Aviation Administration proposes increasing retirement age for pilots from 60 to 65. . . . Survey finds older Americans enjoy active sex lives. . . .The nation's first baby boomer, Kathleen Casey-Kirschling, 62, a retired schoolteacher in Cherry Hill, N.J., applies for Social Security benefits.

Jan. 1, 2008 Oldest boomers turn 62, become eligible for Social Security.

2010 Number of workers 55 and over to hit 26 million — a 46 percent increase since 2000; number to reach 33 million by 2025.

from being a novelty at the start of the baby boom to a near-universal household appliance by its end. And the first rock records had a secret, defiant meaning for kids whose parents were listening to softer sounds. The success of Bill Haley's 1954 "Rock Around the Clock" was "the first inkling teenagers had that they might be a force to be reckoned with in numbers alone," wrote music critic Lillian Dixon.[43]

But not everything was sunshine and light. Part of the push toward education was fueled by competition in science and engineering with the Soviet Union, which challenged U.S. scientific superiority when it launched the world's first satellite, *Sputnik I*, into space on Oct. 4, 1957. And in a world in which youngsters practiced "duck and cover" drills at school and the government encouraged citizens to build bomb shelters in their back yards, the Cold War was ever-present in the boomer subconscious.

"The baby boomers never forgot the lesson that their world could someday end in a flash of light and heat while they were crouched helplessly in gyms and basements among heating ducts and spare blackboards," Jones writes.[44]

For many, the lesson of formative events such as the Cuban missile crisis of 1962 and the assassination of President John F. Kennedy the following year, was *carpe diem* — live for today. Perhaps partly as a result, the boomers developed an ethos that stressed the pursuit of personal fulfillment rather than focusing on mundane concerns, such as making a living.

Many rejected the "plastic" values of their parents. During the Free Speech Movement that began in 1964 at the University of California, Berkeley, protester Jack Weinberg told a reporter, "We have a saying in the movement, never trust anyone over 30," encapsulating an attitude that rejected the values of the past.[45]

The Free Speech Movement inaugurated an era of student protests, largely focusing on the war in Vietnam. Of the 27 million men who came of draft age from 1964 to 1973, only 11 million served in the military.[46] But protests seemed near-universal during the 1960s, especially in 1968 — the year anti-war demonstrators engaged in bloody clashes with police outside the Democratic National Convention in Chicago.

"After 1968, the antiwar demonstration was the standard adolescent rite of passage," recalled author Annie Gottlieb.[47]

The era's frequent protests — which included demands for equal rights for women and minorities — along with events such as the massive Woodstock rock concert in 1969 — gave visible representation to the enormous size of the baby boom generation. "If the baby boomers could not be heard as individuals, they were delivering a testimony of bodies that was deafening," Jones writes.[48]

From Me to Yuppies

While boomers may have been born due to social pressures and norms, as they grew up they continued to reject traditional social roles. Boomer women were more likely to work outside the home, and the percentage of women in the workforce skyrocketed. As adults, boomers were less likely than their parents to belong to a church, club or traditional nuclear family.

In previous generations, according to University of Massachusetts professor of psychology Whitbourne, the years from ages 30 to 65 were typically quiescent — a time to prepare for retirement and to anticipate and enjoy grandchildren. But as boomers entered adulthood in the 1970s, they remained disproportionately focused on themselves — a phenomenon dubbed by author Tom Wolfe the "me decade" in a celebrated 1976 *New York* article.

"The old alchemical dream was changing base metals into gold. The new alchemical dream is: changing one's personality — remaking, remodeling, elevating and polishing one's very self," Wolfe wrote.[49]

Not everyone fit that description, but many middle-aged boomers remained active, youth-oriented and in search of new challenges (and cosmetic surgery). The bestselling self-help book of the 1970s was *Looking Out for #1.*

"Boomers are America's self-absorbed generation," according to Leslie M. Harris, managing partner of Mature Marketing and Research in Teaneck, N.J. "For them, it wasn't enough to grow up, get married, become parents, be responsible and get off the stage as their parents did."[50] Instead, they wanted to stay in shape, protest a war, run a marathon or join a cult.

In 1985, *Time* magazine wished the boomers a happy early 40th by writing that "trendiness became a generational hallmark: From pot to yoga to jogging, they embraced the In thing of the moment and then quickly changed it for another."[51]

There's No Place Like Home

Cities are providing enhanced services to help seniors stay put.

Beacon Hill in Boston is home to the Massachusetts state capitol and once was home to the 19th-century novelists Henry James and Louisa May Alcott. Over the last few years, however, the swanky area has become known for something new — a concierge service that helps older residents continue to live independently in their own homes.

For up to $780 a year, Beacon Hill Village connects subscribers to carefully screened vendors who can provide them with nursing care, carpentry — or help chasing down a stray cat. The program has become a model for more than 100 such cooperative community efforts across the country.

Help with small tasks — getting to a grocery store or finding a tradesman who would otherwise be unwilling to come out for a small job — can help seniors stay in their own homes much longer. "A few neighborhood-based, relatively inexpensive strategies can have an enormous effect," said Philip McCallion, director of the Center for Excellence in Aging Services at the State University of New York in Albany. "If people don't feel so overwhelmed, they don't feel pushed into precipitous decisions that can't always be reversed."[1]

Beacon Hill residents are among the nation's most affluent — Sen. John F. Kerry, D-Mass., secured a $6 million mortgage on his townhouse there to keep his 2004 presidential campaign afloat. Most of the other areas where residents are setting up copycat programs are also well-to-do. But social-service agencies are launching similar ventures in lower-income areas as well.

With so many aging baby boomers, the nation is experiencing a new phenomenon: what sociologists call NORCs, or naturally occurring retirement communities. Although many seniors do retire to Sun Belt states — including Florida, Arizona and, increasingly, Nevada — they represent a tiny fraction of the senior population as a whole. As the number of senior citizens continues to rise, therefore, many more communities across the nation are having to adjust to offering the types of services older residents require.

"This whole idea of aging in place is important," says William H. Frey, a demographer at the Brookings Institution. "The fact is, most seniors don't move very far. If they do move, it's likely to be locally."[2]

Fewer than 2 percent of those 55 to 64 move across state lines in any given year — a number that grows smaller for those older than 65.[3] The senior population has doubled in recent years in Nevada, as it's become a magnet for seniors who want to follow the sun. But even in New York, which

This much-celebrated move toward self-centeredness may have been encouraged by the decade's economic downturns — among the first to confront the boomers. The 1973 embargo by oil-producing nations led to a period of high unemployment and rising inflation — and boomers faced stiff job competition due to their numbers. Indeed, the rising number of college graduates both lifted expectations and led to disappointment for those who found that a degree was no longer the automatic ticket to prosperity it had once been.

In 1975, some 2 million additional jobs were needed to keep up with population growth. Instead, the nation shed 1 million jobs in a recession, leading to an 8.5 percent unemployment rate.[52] In his history of the boomers, Steve Gillon writes, "A generation raised on the expectations of the good life would confront the cold, hard reality that their quality of life could actually decline."[53]

Things were never quite as rosy for the younger boomers who came of age in a less prosperous time. But by the time the older boomers began reaching their peak earning years in the 1980s — the era when they were dubbed "yuppies," for young, urban professionals — they had triggered a housing boom and were collecting half of all U.S. personal income.[54]

Boomer Critiques

Perhaps thanks to the advent of the birth control pill in 1960 and the fact that more women had careers of their own, boomers were slower to become parents than their parents had been. Between 1965 and 1976 — the era of

has the slowest projected growth among states in the 55-to-64 set, their numbers will still increase by 33 percent from 2000 to 2010.

Frey's research indicates that areas with strong job markets in recent decades now have plenty of people aging into the 55-to-64-year-old group. "In Georgia, for instance, the senior population will increase by more than 40 percent from 2010 to 2020 due to the aging of existing residents, vs. less than 3 percent due to migration," he writes.[4]

Many communities recognize they will have to gear up to offer enhanced services to an aging population. Staying at home is not only what seniors want but also something that can save governments money. The fastest-growing expense within Medicaid is nursing home care.

"The real future in the mayor business is changing demographics," says Louisville Mayor Jerry Abramson. "Aging boomers are changing housing patterns, public transportation and recreational facilities and community-center programming."

State and local governments have initiated many scattered programs to accommodate the rising population of seniors, from enlarged road signs on highways to "senior housing" zoning designations that allow small rental units. Many communities are expanding transportation programs to offer rides to those needing medical care — although few are as ambitious as the Northeastern Colorado Association of Local Governments, which provides heavily subsidized transportation to the sole dialysis center within a 9,500-square-mile region.

A 2005 survey by the National League of Cities found that more municipal officials were concerned about the increase in seniors (72 percent) than about other demographic issues such as growth and immigration.[5] In most communities, though, increased awareness of the need to step up services for seniors has not yet translated into much action. To some extent, that's because Congress approved aging-in-place pilot programs in its 2006 reauthorization of the Older Americans Act, but did not fund them.

Kate Sarosy, the mayor of Casper, Wyo., has been conducting a survey of local agencies to find out what they're doing for seniors and what they need to do to prepare for the coming wave.

"What we're finding is that they're all in a panic," Sarosy says. "They haven't begun to plan for baby boomers. They're having a hard enough time keeping up with their current seniors."

---

[1] Jane Gross, "A Grass-Roots Effort to Grow Old at Home," *The New York Times*, Aug. 14, 2007, p. A1.

[2] For more information, see Marcia Clemmitt, "Caring for the Elderly," *CQ Researcher*, Oct. 13, 2006, pp. 841-864.

[3] Jane Adler, "There's No Place Like Home for Aging Boomers," *Chicago Tribune*, Dec. 24, 2006, p. 4.

[4] William H. Frey, "Mapping the Growth of Older America: Seniors and Boomers in the Early 21st Century," The Brookings Institution, May 2007, p. 1.

[5] Haya El Nasser, "Cities Gird for Getting Grayer," *USA Today*, May 14, 2007, p. 1A.

---

the so-called baby bust — fertility dropped below replacement levels among whites.[55]

After just two decades, Americans were back to marrying later and producing fewer children. In 1990, only 32 percent of women 20-24 were married, compared to 70 percent in 1960.

But the baby bust was followed by the uptick known as the "echo boom," when many boomers became parents themselves, racking up 64 million live births between 1977 and 1993.[56]

The boomer's sense of individualism was not purely selfish. Last year, Leonard Steinhorn, a communications professor at American University, argued that the boomers made enormous strides in areas such as gender equality and environmental protection. "Boomers will never go

down in history as a generation that fought a great war to protect liberty," he wrote, "but boomers should go down in history as a generation that fought a great cultural war to expand and advance liberty."[57]

Steinhorn was writing in response to the 1989 book *Destructive Generation*, the 2000 *Esquire* article "The Worst Generation" and other critiques of boomers that blamed their personal habits and quest for self-fulfillment for every social ill from climbing divorce rates to teen drug use.

The debate about boomers' sex-drugs-and-rock-'n'-roll values became a recurring motif in politics — especially after Bill Clinton, who would become the first boomer president, emerged on the national stage in 1992. Political scientists have noted that the boomers failed to coalesce behind a single political party, with many growing more

Many Older Americans Continue Working

Traditional definition of 'retirement' is outmoded.

When Don Davidson was in his 50s, he decided it was time for a change. The longtime publishing executive's plan: turn his hobby — carpentry — into a business. Davidson pulled it off and now employs his two sons full time installing cabinets and refinishing furniture.[1]

Davidson is part of a growing trend of older workers who reach the traditional retirement age and decide to strike out in a new direction, rather than just withdraw from the workforce. "We now know that baby boomers are going to work longer than their parents did, whether they want to or not," writes Marc Freedman, founder of Civic Ventures, which promotes employment among older Americans. "Four out of five boomers consistently tell researchers that they expect to work well into what used to be known as the retirement years."[2]

The percentage of people in their late 60s who are working has increased from 18 percent in 1985 to nearly 30 percent in 2006, according to the Employee Benefit Research Institute, and it's a trend that's likely to continue. "The old, traditional definition of retirement doesn't work any more," says Sandra Timmermann, director of the MetLife Mature Market Institute, in Westport, Conn. "It's really no longer a fixed date."

A bipartisan group of senators has introduced legislation to provide a tax credit for employers who allow workers 62 and above to work flexible hours while retaining full pension and health-care benefits. The bill has not yet seen action, however.

"We're watching a very, very pleasant change occur, where industries that have traditionally relied on bright-eyed and bushy-tailed young people are now relying on older workers to do these jobs," said Bob Skladany, vice president of RetirementJobs.com., an online service that matches companies most-suited to older workers with seniors seeking a job or project that matches their lifestyle. "I think we're seeing the first wave of a fairly substantial shift."[3]

People are working past 65 for a number of reasons. Some simply need the money, recognizing that longer life expectancy leaves them with greater financial needs, as well as time on their hands. Meanwhile, some of the financial disincentives under Social Security and private pension laws that once penalized elderly people for working have been dropped. And many potential retirees relish the chance to do something different and, perhaps, more meaningful.

"Baby boomers grew up in the JFK era," says Frank Benest, city manager of Palo Alto, Calif., referring to John F. Kennedy, who served as president from 1961 to 1963 and challenged young Americans to give back to their country by volunteering. "They value the idea of contributing to their community. All of a sudden, they have the opportunity to do that."

Some economists are predicting that not only will boomers want to continue working but employers will need them. Within the next seven years, the number of workers age 55 and older will increase at four times the rate

fiscally conservative during the 1980s but remaining socially liberal, with views on race, AIDS, drugs and women's rights distinctly different from their parents' generation.

Yet, there were divisions — particularly over women's role in society. While most boomers celebrated the fact that a majority of women were working by the 1980s, in her address against the "counterculture" at the 1992 Republican National Convention Marilyn Quayle, wife of Vice President Dan Quayle, dismissed women who "wish to be liberated from their essential natures as women." Quayle noted that "Dan and I are members of the baby

boom generation, too," but "not everyone demonstrated, dropped out, took drugs, joined in the social revolution or dodged the draft."[58]

Former Kansas Sen. Bob Dole, the Republican presidential nominee in 1996, returned to the generational theme during his acceptance speech at the GOP convention, charging that the Clinton administration was made up of a soft "corps of the elite who never grew up, never did anything real, never suffered and never learned." That night, *Newsweek* reported, Clinton was celebrating his 50th birthday at a "plush summer home" in Jackson Hole, Wyo., singing Beatles songs.[59]

of the overall labor force. The Conference Board, a business research group, estimates that by 2010, 64 million workers — 40 percent of the nation's public and private workforce — will have reached retirement age.[4]

"Employers are going to need to find ways to engage older workers longer and more fully than has been the case in the past," says Michael A. Smyer, codirector of Boston College's Center on Aging and Work.

But others are more skeptical. A study released in May by a rival center at Boston College found that employers are "lukewarm" about retaining older workers.[5] Relatively few employers are interested in providing the flexible hours older workers desire — or paying for their health coverage, which can be more expensive than covering the young.

Some economists say the labor shortage predicted by demographers — created by the smaller generation that followed the boomers — should be manageable, especially given the global labor pool. Many retirees will be replaced in the workforce by immigrants — an advantage the U.S. has over other aging industrialized nations with less-open borders — while other jobs will be shipped abroad. And not all the boomers are going to hit retirement age at the same time.

In addition, a 2006 study by the consulting firm McKinsey & Co. found that 40 percent of current retirees left their jobs earlier than they had planned, either because of layoffs, downsizing or health reasons.[6] Given that several other studies have found that people often end up retiring earlier than they expected, from the employer point of view the need to keep aging boomers on the payroll is proving less pressing than some had expected.

Companies that have looked at the aging workforce have come to the conclusion that it isn't as big a

problem as they thought," says Mary Young, a senior researcher at the Conference Board. "It's much more manageable."

Young concedes the aging baby boomers will exacerbate existing shortages in professions such as nursing and teaching and create new ones in fields such as engineering and the utilities industry. Governments also employ a disproportionate share of older workers.

But what about the rest of the labor market? Aging workers are attractive to industries with high turnover, such as retail. Both CVS and Borders have programs that allow people to follow the seasons, working summers in the North and winters in the South. Not all employers are likely to be that flexible, however.

"Endless surveys have found contradictory conclusions," says Ron Manheimer, executive director of the Center for Creative Retirement at the University of North Carolina, Asheville. "Human-resources directors say seniors are loyal and reliable and have better customer-service attitudes — but they're not planning to hire them."

[1] Emily Brandon, "You Can Use This Time of Your Life for a Whole New Beginning," *U.S. News & World Report*, June 12, 2006, p. 55.

[2] Marc Freedman, *Encore: Finding Work That Matters in the Second Half of Life* (2007), p. 9.

[3] Jonathan Peterson, "Older Workers Becoming Valued Prize for Firms," *Chicago Tribune*, Sept. 10, 2007, p. 1.

[4] Christopher Conte, "Expert Exodus," *Governing*, February 2006, p. 22.

[5] Andrew D. Eschtruth, *et al.*, "Employers Lukewarm About Retaining Older Workers," Boston College Center for Retirement Research, May 2007.

[6] Sandra Block, "Off to Work They Go, Even After Retirement Age," *USA Today*, Aug. 31, 2007, p. 1B.

At his own nominating convention in 2000, George W. Bush echoed the points made by Quayle and Dole, seeking to castigate Democrats for the purported failings of the baby boom generation. "Our current president embodied the potential of a generation," Bush said. "So many talents, so much charm, such great skill. But in the end, to what end? So much promise, to no great purpose."[60]

But President Bush, of course, is a boomer — only five weeks older than Bill Clinton. "This year, the first of about 78 million baby boomers turn 60, including two of my dad's favorite people, me and President Clinton," Bush said during his 2006 State of the Union address. "This milestone

is more than a personal crisis. It is a national challenge. The retirement of the baby boom generation will put unprecedented strains on the federal government."[61]

Combined spending for Social Security, Medicare and Medicaid will consume 60 percent of the federal budget by 2030, Bush said, presenting future Congresses with "impossible choices — staggering tax increases, immense deficits or deep cuts in every category of spending."

Bush had spent a good chunk of 2005 touting his plan to revamp Social Security, meant to be the signature domestic achievement of his second term. But the plan — which would have allowed workers born after

1950 to put part of their payroll taxes into private investment accounts in exchange for cuts to traditional benefits — went nowhere. A Washington Post/ABC News Poll found that 58 percent of those surveyed said the more they heard about Bush's plan the less they liked it.[62]

CURRENT SITUATION

Entitlement Bills

Perhaps not coincidentally, the nation's budget-busting entitlement programs for seniors have barely been mentioned during the current run-up to the 2008 presidential campaign. Candidates are generally mum about how to deal with the fact that Social Security is expected to run through its surplus accounts by 2040 and Medicare and Medicaid — the federal government's two main federal health-care programs — pose an even more dire fiscal threat.[63]

President Bush has proposed a "means test" for the prescription-drug benefit under Medicare that he created in 2003. His idea is to charge higher premiums and deductibles for upper-income seniors. But the proposal died as part of his budget earlier this year, and the Senate voted down a similar idea in March.[64]

A pair of proposals are pending in Congress to create a commission to craft an entitlement-reform package that Congress and the next president would have to act upon. Bush had created a commission to address Social Security, but the current proposals would go further, tackling other entitlements as well. If approved, a new commission would be jointly appointed by the president and Congress and would likely craft a proposal that Congress would have to accept or reject, without amendment.

Some expect a solution for Medicare and Medicaid will be found within a broader discussion of reforming the U.S. health system. The three leading Democratic presidential candidates — Sens. Hillary Rodham Clinton and Barack Obama and former Sen. John Edwards — have all unveiled proposals for universal or near-universal health-coverage laws.

Clinton launched a plan in September that involved fewer government mandates than the universal-coverage package she designed as first lady in 1993. "I learned that people who are satisfied with their current coverage want assurances that they can keep it," she said. "Part of our

health-care system is the best in the world, and we should build on it; part of the system is broken, and we should fix it."[65]

Clinton's new plan, in fact, resembles a law passed in Massachusetts in 2006 that requires nearly all residents to buy private health insurance if they don't qualify for government-run coverage such as Medicaid. That bill was signed into law by Mitt Romney — then Massachusetts governor and now a leading GOP presidential candidate. The bill, along with other health-care expansion laws in Vermont and Maine, triggered a wave of activity among nearly two-dozen states that considered (but did not pass) universal health legislation this year.[66]

But Romney has not talked about his state's law much on the campaign trail this year, saying that he would prefer to leave it to states to create insurance mandates without prodding from Washington. Romney and the other Republican candidates have talked about problems with the U.S. health-care system but in general favor reforms within the insurance markets, states or the use of tax credits to resolve them, rather than any sort of new federal program.

Clearly, the fact that millions of boomers will soon reach retirement age has many economists worried about entitlement expenses and recommending cutting back coverage — or at least raising the age of eligibility. Federal Reserve Chairman Ben S. Bernanke told the Senate Budget Committee in January that by 2030 Social Security and Medicare will cost the equivalent of 15 percent of U.S. annual economic output — up from 8.5 percent today.

"The longer we wait [to make changes], the more severe, the more draconian, the more difficult the adjustment is going to be," Bernanke said. "I think the right time to start is about 10 years ago."[67]

Many of these financing problems, particularly in Social Security, are rooted in the fact that the ratio of workers to retirees is shrinking. There were 16.5 workers paying into the system for every Social Security beneficiary in 1950, but now there are only 3.3 workers for every retiree — a number that continues to decline.

One solution, AARP and other advocates for the elderly say, would be for boomers to work longer than their parents did. While the percentage of people in their late 60s still working has risen, they remain a minority. People working just a few years longer — and collecting fewer years worth of Social Security checks — could erase its

Do aging boomers pose a threat to fiscal solvency?

YES   David M. Walker
Comptroller General,
Government Accountability Office

From a speech delivered in Washington, D.C., Nov. 7, 2006

The United States government is on an imprudent and unsustainable fiscal path. We do not face an immediate crisis, but we face large and growing structural imbalances that are growing every second of every minute of every day due to continuing deficits, known demographic trends — the demographic tidal wave, the demographic tsunami which is represented by the retirement of the baby boom generation — and rising health-care costs.

Let me give you some numbers. In 1965, 43 percent of the federal government's budget was for defense. Fast-forward 40 years to 2005: It was down to 20 percent. Where did the money go? Social Security, Medicare and Medicaid. In 1965, we spent zero money on Medicare and Medicaid because they didn't exist. In 2005, 19 percent of the federal budget was for Medicare and Medicaid, and growing rapidly. In 1965, [Congress] got to decide how two-thirds of the money was going to be spent. In 2005, it was down to 39 percent; stated differently, 61 percent of the budget is on autopilot, and that number is going up every year.

You project it out for 75 years, which is what the Social Security and Medicare trustees are required to do every year. If you take the difference between what we promised and what's funded for Social Security and Medicare alone, you'll find that the total liabilities and unfunded commitments of the United States in the last five years have gone up from a little over $20 trillion — and you got to add 12 zeroes to the right of that 20 to get a feel for that number — to over $46 trillion in five years. It's going up every second of every minute of every day.

How much is $46 trillion? It's over 90 percent of the entire net worth of every American in the United States. It's $156,000 for every man, woman and child in the United States. People talk about eliminating the death tax. How about eliminating the birth burden, that $156,000? No wonder newborn babies cry. Somebody's giving them the bill.

Let's tell it like it is. This is mortgaging the future of our kids and grandkids, big time. And for the first time in the history of the United States, the baby boom generation, of which I am a member, may be the first generation in the history of this country to leave this country in a situation where their kids and grandkids will not have a higher quality of life. That is not acceptable, and we need to start doing something about it.

NO   Robert B. Friedland and Laura Summer
Center on an Aging Society,
Georgetown University

From *Demography Is Not Destiny, Revisited* (2005)

That our society is aging is well known. Media stories and political rhetoric abound concerning the impending demographic challenges as the population age 65 and older is anticipated to more than double by the year 2030. Much of the hand wringing concerns an expectation of dire fiscal consequences for publicly financed programs, such as Medicare and Social Security, of which older people tend to be the principal beneficiaries.

What is not said is that planning for the future on the basis of demographic projections alone is a fool's game. Population projections can be wrong, but even if they turn out to be correct, other factors, particularly those related to the economy and public policies, can have a decidedly greater impact on the future than simply the growing number of older people.

At any point in the past century, one could have easily anticipated a dramatic increase in the size and proportion of the population age 65 and older. Since 1900, the number of Americans age 65 and older has doubled three times. Since 1960, the population age 65 and older has doubled while the overall population has only grown 57 percent. However, since 1960 the nation's income (as measured by real gross domestic product) has nearly quadrupled.

Economic growth has made the nation more prosperous and has enabled many to enjoy a higher standard of living than would have been possible a generation earlier. . . .

There are legitimate reasons to be concerned about growth in federal entitlement spending, but there is more reason to be concerned about economic growth. Small differences in sustained economic growth will have a dramatic impact on the fiscal future of society. If real economic growth averages about 2 percent per year between now and 2050, then, depending on the policy choices we make, government expenditures as a proportion of the economy in 2050 might not be substantially larger than today, and we will still be able to meet the promises made to future beneficiaries.

It would be foolish to assume society will simply grow its way out of the difficult choices that the aging of the population will require. It would be equally foolish to assume that the future will be completely dismal if there is no radical restructuring of government programs. If public policies support the market transitions necessary for economic growth during demographic transitions, then we can afford to meet the challenges of the retirement of the baby boomers.

deficits for the next 75 years, say some economists.[68] This would also help solve any workforce shortages posed by the aging baby boom generation.

"The old model was people worked for 40 or 45 years and then they slipped off into retirement and focused on leisure and recreation," says Freedman of Civic Ventures. "We've said to older people as they moved into their 50s and 60s, please leave the labor market."

The proposed Older Worker Opportunity Act, sponsored by Sen. Herb Kohl, D-Wis., and a bipartisan group of cosponsors, would provide a tax credit of up to 25 percent of a worker's wages to employers who allow workers age 62 and above to participate in a flexible program that allows them to work full or part time while retaining full pension and health-care benefits. But the measure has seen no action, and not everyone is convinced there will be jobs for millions of seniors to continue working.

Ron Manheimer, executive director of the Center for Creative Retirement at the University of North Carolina, Asheville, says that while human resources directors say seniors are loyal and reliable, many employers are not planning to hire them.

There are a number of reasons why employers are not embracing the idea of workers staying on the job longer. Some are concerned that their younger employees will leave if they have less hope of advancement. According to Mary Young, a senior researcher at the Conference Board, 65 percent of the employees who leave IBM do so because they see little hope of promotional opportunities. "That's another reason why holding onto boomers isn't a cure-all," she says.

Other employers are worried that older workers don't always keep their skill sets up to date in an age of rapid technological change, while still others worry about the amount of hours they can count on older workers logging. Workers with long experience have also had years of salary increases and their health-insurance premiums can be more costly.

Finally, says Lynch of Claremont McKenna College, "There isn't a whole lot of evidence for it yet, but I think boomers are going to face age discrimination."

Fiscal Cancer

In Christopher Buckley's satirical novel *Boomsday*, which opens with a mob of young people rioting in front of a Florida gated community "known to harbor early retiring boomers" in protest of a Social Security payroll tax hike, a 29-year-old character suggests a solution to the entitlement funding problem: pay retirees to commit suicide. As an incentive, volunteers could take one last, lavish vacation at government expense, and their children would be exempt from estate taxes. Even so, the government would come out ahead. If only 20 percent of boomers committed suicide, Social Security and Medicare would remain solvent.

In the world of reality, rather than satire, some analysts criticize today's seniors and boomers for what the critics perceive as a selfish insistence on expensive benefits that will have to be paid for by younger workers.

"At nearly every critical juncture, they have preferred the present to the future," wrote former Clinton adviser Paul Begala. "They've put themselves ahead of their parents, ahead of their country, ahead of their children — ahead of our future."[69]

The central question of *Immigrants and Boomers*, a recent book by USC demographer Myers, is whether aging boomers will support programs that benefit younger generations — dominated by other ethnic groups — at the short-term expense of programs that benefit themselves.

"We actually transfer resources from workers up to the elderly, essentially wasting resources," says Myers. "Younger people would have more years of life and could recoup the investment."

The question of whether older, mostly white seniors will support education and other domestic programs used by mostly brown- and black-skinned younger people is becoming increasingly pressing. During the recent congressional debate over the State Children's Health Insurance Program, the House version of the bill would have provided $15 billion more to cover more children who lack insurance. It would have been funded by cutting subsidies to Medicare managed-care plans and providers. The House voted to support the legislation, but the idea proved unpalatable in the Senate, which passed a more modest expansion of the program. Bush vetoed the final bill, however.

MIT economist Diamond notes, "Surveys suggest that young people are very supportive of paying taxes for Medicare and Social Security for their parents," because it removes a potential burden for them. "On the flip side, older people are supportive of education for their grandchildren."

But Medicare and Social Security are entitlement programs, Diamond points out, so spending increases for programs benefiting older people are automatic. Yet Congress must allocate funds annually for programs that primarily benefit younger Americans.

Asked why no one in Congress is taking the lead on reforming entitlement programs, Sen. Kent Conrad, D-N.D., told CBS's "60 Minutes" in July, "It's always easier to defer, to kick the can down the road to avoid making choices. You know, you get in trouble in politics when you make choices."[70]

But Comptroller General Walker warns of the dire consequences of ignoring the entitlement problem: "We suffer from a fiscal cancer," he says. "It is growing within us, and if we do not treat it, it could have catastrophic consequences for our country."[71]

'Sandwich' Generation

Boomers will add to the rising number of seniors — but their parents, in many cases, will still be around. Those 85 and over now make up the fastest-growing segment of the U.S. population, according to the National Institute on Aging. That means that even as the boomers enter what has traditionally been considered old age, they are "sandwiched" between still-living parents and their own children and grandchildren.

A 2005 survey found that 13 million boomers were "deeply involved" in the care of their aging parents, with 25 percent living with their parents.[72] "The children who are caring for the elderly are elderly themselves," says Stanford's Carstensen.

Many boomers already wonder who, in turn, will take care of them when they are frail themselves. That may be particularly true for boomer women, since far more of them are entering old age single — divorced or having never been married — than has traditionally been the case.[73]

"Boomers are quite different from earlier generations as they're approaching this age," says William H. Frey, a demographer at the Brookings Institution. For example, boomer women "are much more likely to have lived independent lives, been head of households and worked."

But there's a great deal of economic inequality within the baby boom generation, he notes, which means many retirees will have a hard time making ends meet. In

Older baby boomers like Marcos Zavala, 59, a locomotive engineer for The Indiana Rail Road Co., pose a dilemma for demographic experts. While many older boomers are expected to retire soon, up to 80 percent of boomers intend to work past 65 to help make ends meet. Two-thirds of the nation's retirees rely on Social Security for at least 50 percent of their income.

addition, Frey says, boomers didn't have as many children as their parents' generation, so they "can't rely on them for support."

As a result, while federal policy makers puzzle over how to pay for entitlement programs, state and local governments are gearing up to provide more services to aging boomers. For example, by 2030 the number of drivers 65 or older could nearly double, to 65 million, according to the GAO.[74] So states and cities are scrambling to enlarge and brighten road signs.

In California, where an elderly driver slammed into an open-air market in 2003, killing 10 people, the Department of Motor Vehicles has launched a pilot program that requires drivers to pass more intensive vision, memory and reflex tests when renewing their licenses. "What we can do is try to identify drivers who can't drive safely," said David Hennessy, a former DMV research program specialist. "This is something we've become especially sensitive to because of the aging of the baby boomers."[75]

Transportation is a key concern for the elderly. Millions of seniors find themselves stranded in the suburbs when they can no longer drive safely. The Denver-area Seniors' Resource Center has responded by offering different transportation modes for seniors, ranging from paratransit — unscheduled rides in vans or cars — to volunteer drivers and taxis.[76]

Other local governments have similar ride-dispatch programs or even training programs to familiarize seniors with public transportation. They are also widening sidewalks to accommodate wheelchairs and encourage walking and, in a few cases, changing zoning laws to allow "granny flats" and other small, one-floor housing units in dense areas (particularly near grocery stores).

An aging population, says Syracuse social work professor Kingson, is a sign that society has successfully fostered an economy that helps people lead long, prosperous lives. "Population aging is not just about the old," he says. "It's about how all of our institutions are going to change."

"The question is, How do we adapt as we get older, and how does society adapt to our needs?" says Achenbaum, the University of Houston historian of aging. "There's no question that we're going to change the meaning of late life."

OUTLOOK

Late Boomers

A decade from now, the oldest boomers will be in their 70s, while the youngest will be well into their 50s. It's almost impossible to predict what their lives will be like and how they will have changed the nature of senior citizenship.

By the time the youngest boomers are in their 60s, their older brothers and sisters may have changed senior housing patterns, workforce participation rates and leisure and recreational activities. Patterns of health and disability may also have changed as medical science continues to make new breakthroughs.

In a few years, Smith of Yankelovich predicts, "We'll probably be talking about one thing especially — that is, a world in which there's an older generation that can expect to live actively past the age of 90."

Even as boomers get older, Smith says, "They have this psychological view of themselves, this youthful mindset, which helps motivate health-service providers to pioneer new solutions to help them stay young a little bit and beat the odds."

Signs already point in that direction. Not only are boomers buying cars aimed at younger drivers, but they also are changing the marketing and packaging of products and services aimed at older people. For instance, many boomers are too vain to wear hearing aids. "To appeal to boomer vanity, many companies are making hearing aids that look more like cousins of Bluetooth or iPod earbuds," said Gordon Wilson, vice president for marketing at Oticon, which manufactures hearing aids.[77]

"Boomers are different from their predecessors and are also different from the generation beyond them," said Washington dermatologist Tina Alster. "They know they can get [cosmetic surgery]. What they're not realistic about is they think they can just come in and do one thing and take away five decades of sin."[78]

Indeed, age does have its consequences. Even optimists like Smith concede there is a downside to living longer. Boomers who had expected to be retired for only a decade or so may start to run out of money as they continue to age. And, although disabilities and frailties are getting pushed farther back in life, they do occur.

"One of the biggest questions for baby boomers is 'Who is going to take care of me?' " says AARP's Rix. "Old age, in the sense of increasing physical problems, is being pushed back, but ultimately more and more people are going to be facing the types of problems that require assistance."

As the senior population grows — both in sheer numbers and as a percentage of the population as a whole — new strains will be put on social services, government budgets and, perhaps, the economy as a whole. Myers, the USC demographer, believes a labor shortage will force employers to adapt their policies to accommodate and retain older workers. He also thinks there will be a side benefit: Society will start to offer better-quality educations to minority groups who traditionally have languished in schools. "We'll be scouting for workers among minority youth," he says. "We haven't worried too much about them before, but suddenly they're going to be precious." Like many observers, Myers worries about the growth in the cost of senior entitlement programs and recommends moving back eligibility ages.

"It's very heard to make changes when the changes you're going to make are seen as painful by the voting public," says MIT economist Diamond. "But the longer you wait, the harder it is to deal with it."

Social scientists can get frustrated at policy makers, who have known for decades that the baby boomers would eventually reach old age. Yet, even though they are on the cusp of retirement age, there appears to be little movement in addressing the core issues.

Employers are not much better prepared, says the Wharton School's Capelli. Even though he doubts that aging boomers will create a labor shortage, he's surprised that employers aren't preparing for the fact that many of their older workers with legacy skills are going to leave.

"The surprise is not that these people are going to retire," he says. "The surprise is that nobody was planning for it."

Whether boomers resort to rocking chairs and playing with their grandchildren or end up changing the nature of old age by living longer, staying healthier and continuing to work past 65, there are so many of them that American society must change in profound ways to this new senior population.

"The question is, 'How do we adapt as we get older and how does society adapt to our needs?'" says Achenbaum, of the University of Houston. "There's no question that we're going to change the meaning of late life."

NOTES

1. Leonard Steinhorn, *The Greatest Generation: In Defense of the Baby Boom* (2006), p. 82.

2. J. Walker Smith and Ann Clurman, *Generation Ageless: How Baby Boomers Are Changing the Way We Live Today . . . and They're Just Getting Started* (2007), p. 97.

3. Leslie M. Harris, ed., *After Fifty: How the Baby Boom Will Redefine the Mature Market* (2003), p. vii.

4. Smith and Clurman, *op. cit.*, p. 89.

5. *Ibid.*, p. 28.

6. *Ibid.*, p. 24.

7. Paul C. Light, *Baby Boomers* (1988), p. 10.

8. Susan Krauss Whitbourne and Sherry L. Willis, eds., *The Baby Boomers Grow Up: Contemporary Perspectives on Midlife* (2006), p. 283.

9. "60-Year-Old Woman Delivers Twin Boys," Fox News, May 24, 2007, www.foxnews.com/story/0,2933,274726,00.html.

10. "Baby Boomers' Retirement Prospects: An Overview," Congressional Budget Office, November 2003.

11. Dennis Cauchon, "Generation Gap? About $200,000," *USA Today*, May 21, 2007, p. 1A.

12. Mindy Fetterman, "Retirement Unfolds in Five Stages for Hearty Boomers," *USA Today*, June 26, 2006, p. 1B.

13. Kathleen Day, "Bankruptcies Rise Fastest for Over-55 Group," *The Washington Post*, April 27, 2007, p. D3.

14. "Baby Boom Generation," Government Accountability Office, July 2006, p. 8.

15. Sharon A. DeVaney and Sophia T. Chiremba, "Comparing the Retirement Savings of the Baby Boomers and Other Cohorts," Bureau of Labor Statistics, March 15, 2005.

16. Sonia Arrison, "80 Is the New 65," *Los Angeles Times*, March 13, 2007, p. A17.

17. For background, see Alan Greenblatt, "Pension Crisis," *CQ Researcher*, Feb 17, 2006, pp. 145-168.

18. Maria L. La Ganga, "More People Over 55 Are Working 9 to 5," *Los Angeles Times*, April 3, 2007, p. B1.

19. Robert B. Friedland and Laura Summer, "Demography Is Not Destiny, Revisited," Georgetown University Center on an Aging Society, March 2005, p. 43.

20. See "Wake-Up Call; David Walker, America's top accountant, going on tour to sound the alarm that America cannot sustain current level of spending," transcript from "60 Minutes," CBS News, July 8, 2007.

21. Steven R. Weisman, "Fed Chief Warns That Entitlement Growth Could Harm Economy," *The New York Times*, Jan. 19, 2007, p. C1.

22. "Baby Boom Generation," *op. cit.*, p. 16.

23. Smith and Clurman, *op. cit.*, p. 35.

24. Sheryl Gay Stolberg, "A Touchy Topic," *The New York Times*, July 6, 2006, p. A1.

25. Nell Henderson, "Aging Is Inevitable, But Boomers Put 'Old' on Hold," *The Washington Post*, Sept. 12, 2007, p. H1.

26. Kim Painter, "Boomers Leap the 60 Hurdle," *USA Today*, Dec. 18, 2006, p. 4D.

27. Joel Achenbach, "The Rise of the Alpha Geezer," *The Washington Post*, Sept. 9, 2007, p. B3.

28. Leslie Walker, "Cross-Training Your Brain to Maintain Its Strength," *The Washington Post*, Sept. 12, 2007, p. H2.

29. Rob Stein, "Baby Boomers Appear to Be Less Healthy Than Parents," *The Washington Post*, April 20, 2007, p. A1.

30. Stephanie Rosenbloom, "The Day the Music Died," *The New York Times*, July 12, 2007, p. G1.

31. Light, p. 23.

32. Herbert S. Klein, "The U.S. Baby Bust in Historical Perspective," in Fred R. Harris, ed., *The Baby Bust: Who Will Do the Work? Who Will Pay the Taxes?* (2006), p. 115.

33. Light, *op. cit.*, p. 23.

34. Steve Gillon, *Boomer Nation: The Largest and Richest Generation Ever and How It Changed America* (2004), p. 1.

35. Light, *op. cit.*, p. 24.

36. For background on the G.I. Bill, see "Record of the 78th Congress (Second Session)," in *Editorial Research Reports*, Dec. 20, 1944, available from *CQ Researcher Plus Archive*, http://cqpress.com.

37. Gillon, *op. cit.*, p. 6.

38. For background, see H. B. Shaffer, "Progress Against Polio," in *Editorial Research Reports*, March 14, 1956, available from *CQ Researcher Plus Archive*, http://cqpress.com.

39. Abigail J. Stewart and Cynthia M. Torges, "Social, Historical and Developmental Influences on Psychology of the Baby Boom at Midlife," in Whitbourne and Willis, *op. cit.*, p. 31.

40. Light, *op. cit.*, p. 121.

41. Whitbourne and Willis, *op. cit.*, p. 12.

42. Landon Y. Jones, *Great Expectations: America and the Baby Boom Generation* (1980), p. 1.

43. Gillon, *op. cit.*, p. 7.

44. Jones, *op. cit.*, p. 52.

45. Steinhorn, *op. cit.*, p. 82.

46. Gillon, *op. cit.*, p. 51.

47. Annie Gottlieb, *Do You Believe in Magic?* (1987), p. 47.

48. Jones, *op. cit.*, p. 99.

49. Tom Wolfe, "The 'Me' Decade and the Third Great Awakening," *New York*, Aug. 23, 1976, p. 26.

50. Harris, *op. cit.*, p. 2.

51. Evan Thomas, "Growing Pains at 40," *Time*, May 19, 1986, p. 22.

52. Jones, *op. cit.*, p. 152.

53. Gillon, *op. cit.*, p. 22.

54. *Ibid.*, p. 117. Also see Roger Thompson, "Baby Boom's Mid-life Crisis," in *Editorial Research Reports*, Jan. 8, 1988, available in *CQ Researcher Plus Archive*, http://library.cqpress.com.

55. Klein, *op. cit.*, p. 173.

56. William Sterling and Stephen Waite, *Boomernomics: The Future of Money in the Upcoming Generational Warfare* (1998), p. 3.

57. Steinhorn, *op. cit.*, p. xiii.

58. Ronald Brownstein, "GOP Takes Politics of '92 Race Personally," *Los Angeles Times*, Aug. 21, 1992.

59. Howard Fineman, "Bring on the Baby Boomers," *Newsweek*, Aug. 26, 1996, p. 18.

60. John Diamond, "Bush: 'They Have Not Led, We Will,' " *Chicago Tribune*, Aug. 4, 2000, p. 1.

61. President Bush, State of the Union address, Jan. 31, 2006, http://www.whitehouse.gov/news/releases/2006/01/20060131-10.html.

62. Jonathan Weisman, "Skepticism of Bush's Social Security Plan Is Growing," *The Washington Post*, March 15, 2005, p. A1.

63. "Social Security's Future — FAQs," Social Security Administration, www.ssa.gov/qa.htm.

64. Jonathan Weisman, "Means Test Sought for Medicare Drug Plan," *The Washington Post*, Oct. 5, 2007, p. A1.

65. Patrick Healy and Robin Toner, "Wary of Past, Clinton Unveils a Health Plan," Sept. 18, 2007, p. A1.

66. Alan Greenblatt, "Gimme Coverage," *Governing*, June 2007, p. 40.

67. Steven R. Weisman, "Fed Chief Warns That Entitlement Growth Could Harm Economy," *The New York Times*, Jan. 19, 2007, p. C1.

68. Walker and Clurman, *op. cit.*, p. 51.

69. Paul Begala, "The Worst Generation," *Esquire*, April 2000.

70. "60 Minutes," *op. cit.*

71. *Ibid.*

72. "Thirteen Million Baby Boomers Care for Ailing Parents, 25% Live With Parents," *SeniorJournal.com*; http://seniorjournal.com/NEWS/Boomers/5-10-19BoomersCare4Parents.htm.

73. Mary Elizabeth Hughes and Angela M. O'Rand, "The Lives and Times of the Baby Boomers," Russell Sage Foundation/Population Research Bureau, 2004, p. 19.

74. William Neikirk, "States Told to Prep for Gray Driver Boom," *Chicago Tribune*, April 12, 2007, p. 3.

75. Rong-Gong Lin II, "DMV Tests a Tough New Test," *Los Angeles Times*, Sept. 30, 2007, p. B1.

76. Christopher Swope, "Stranded Seniors," *Governing*, June 2005, p. 40.

77. Rosenbloom, *op. cit.*, p. G1.

78. Tina Alster, "As Boomers Hit Their 60s, the Clock Takes on a New Face," *The Washington Post*, Sept. 12, 2007, p. H5. Also see David Masci, "Baby Boomers at Midlife," *CQ Researcher*, July 31, 1998, pp. 649-672.

BIBLIOGRAPHY

Books

Freedman, Marc, *Encore: Finding Work That Matters in the Second Half of Life, PublicAffairs*, 2007.
The founder of Civic Ventures, which aims to match up seniors with meaningful work, offers specific examples of workers who have changed the course of their careers.

Gillon, Steve, *Boomer Nation: The Largest and Richest Generation Ever and How It Changed America, Free Press*, 2004.
The History Channel's Gillon writes a sympathetic history of the boomers whose birth, he says, is the "single greatest demographic event in American history."

Jones, Landon Y., *Great Expectations: America and the Baby Boom Generation, Coward, McCann & Geohegan*, 1980.
A journalist's pioneering history of the boomers is still a reliable portrait of the generation's first 35 years.

Smith, J. Walker, and Ann Clurman, *Generation Ageless: How Baby Boomers Are Changing the Way We Live Today . . . and They're Just Getting Started, Collins*, 2007.
As their subtitle suggests, these two executives with the consumer research firm Yankelovich, Inc., believe boomers remain influential and that sectors other than travel and financial services need to recalibrate their offerings to them as they age.

Whitbourne, Susan Krauss, and Sherry L. Willis, eds., *The Baby Boomers Grow Up: Contemporary Perspectives on Midlife* (2006), p. 283.
Fresh research from social scientists about boomer psychology, employment patterns, health and other issues.

Articles

Adler, Jerry, "Hitting 60," *Newsweek*, Nov. 14, 2005, p. 50.
Newsweek kicks off a long series of "Boomer Files" articles about the boomers, their habits and cultural impact.

Begala, Paul, "The Worst Generation," *Esquire*, April 2000.
The political adviser makes the case that boomers have been the most self-indulgent generation in American history.

Conte, Christopher, "Expert Exodus," *Governing*, February 2006, p. 22.
Government workers were hired in abundance in the 1960s and '70s, leaving the public sector with a much older workforce than private companies.

Gross, Jane, "A Grass-Roots Effort to Grow Old at Home," *The New York Times*, Aug. 14, 2007, p. A1.
Seniors are banding together to create neighborhood-based associations that provide everything from medical care to carpentry in an effort to stay longer in their own homes.

Hulbert, Mark, "Baby Boomers Are Cashing In. So What?" *The New York Times*, May 27, 2007, p. 5.
Economists show that although boomers are beginning to liquidate assets, the total size of their investments, such as 401(k) plans, will continue to grow.

Peterson, Jonathan, "At Some Companies, Older Skilled Workers Are Golden," *Los Angeles Times*, Sept. 3, 2007, p. 1.
Since the generation following the boomers is 16 percent smaller, many firms and the government are realizing they'll have to offer incentives to keep boomers on the payroll longer.

Studies and Reports

"Baby Boom Generation: Retirement of Baby Boomers Is Unlikely to Precipitate Dramatic Declines in Market

Returns, but Broader Risks Threaten Retirement Security," *Government Accountability Office*, July 2006, www.gao.gov/new.items/d06718.pdf.
Boomers will have to sell off assets to fund retirement but will not sell all at once, so financial markets won't tank.

DeVaney, Sharon A., and Sophia T. Chiremba, "Comparing the Retirement Savings of the Baby Boomers and Other Cohorts," *Bureau of Labor Statistics*, March 16, 2005, www.bls.gov/opub/cwc/cm20050114ar01p1.htm.
Older baby boomers are more likely than other generational cohorts to hold a retirement account.

Eschtruth, Andrew D., Steven A. Sass and Jean-Pierre Aubry, "Employers Lukewarm About Retaining Older Workers," *Boston College Center for Retirement Research*, May 2007, www.bc.edu/centers/crr/issues/wob_10.pdf.
A quarter of workers now in their 50s will probably want to work after traditional retirement age.

Feinsod, Roselyn, et al., "The Business Case for Workers 50+," *AARP*, Dec. 2005, http://assets.aarp.org/rgcenter/econ/workers_fifty_plus.pdf.
Many Americans plan to work past the retirement age and replacing them would be expensive. Older employees want a mix of benefits and flexibility that a small but growing number of employers are willing to offer.

Frey, William H., "Mapping the Growth of Older America: Seniors and Boomers in the Early 21st Century," *The Brookings Institution*, May 2007, www3.brookings.edu/views/articles/200705frey.pdf.
A demographer finds that "pre-seniors" (55-to-64-year-olds) are now the fastest-growing age group.

Hughes, Mary Elizabeth, and Angela M. O'Rand, "The Lives and Times of the Baby Boomers," *Russell Sage Foundation/Population Research Bureau*, 2004.
Two Duke University sociologists offer an overview of boomers — their educational attainment levels, family lives, income levels, racial divides and their likely futures.

For More Information

Administration on Aging, One Massachussetts Ave., N.W., Suites 4100 and 5100, Washington, DC 20201; (202) 619-0724; www.aoa.gov. Facilitates communication between other federal agencies and older Americans.

AARP, 601 E St., N.W., Washington, DC 20049; (888) 687-2277; www.aarp.org. The leading advocacy organization for older Americans.

Civic Ventures, 139 Townsend St., Suite 505, San Francisco, CA 94107; (415) 430-0141; www.civicventures.org/index.cfm. A think tank and employment incubator that advises older adults and employers about putting experienced Americans to work.

Government Accountability Office, 441 G St., N.W., Washington, DC 20548; (202) 518-3000; http://gao.gov. Congress' investigative arm; publishes studies about the baby boom generation's impact on federal entitlement programs.

National Academy on an Aging Society, 1220 L St., N.W., Suite 901, Washington, DC 20005; (202) 408-3375; www.agingsociety.org/agingsociety/index.html. Conducts research on public policy issues concerning the aging of America.

National Association of Area Aging Agencies, 1730 Rhode Island Ave., N.W., Suite 1200, Washington, DC 20036; (202) 872-0888; www.n4a.org. Umbrella organization for local aging agencies.

National Council on Aging, 1901 L St., N.W., 4th Floor, Washington, DC 20036; (202) 479-1200; www.ncoa.org. Provides a network for sharing information and ideas between more than 14,000 groups providing services to seniors.

National Institute on Aging, Building 31, Room 5C27, 31 Center Dr., MSC 2292, Bethesda, MD 20892; (301) 496-1752; www.nia.nih.gov. Leads the government's scientific effort to study the nature of aging.

Race and Politics

17

Will Skin Color Influence the Presidential Election?

Peter Katel

Republican presidential candidate Sen. John McCain greets supporters at a primary night party in Alexandria, Va., last Feb 5. Some Republicans say the GOP must attract more Latinos and blacks to remain competitive with the Democrats.

From *CQ Researcher*,
July 18, 2008.

W hen the Rev. Martin Luther King Jr. delivered his famous "I Have a Dream" speech at the Lincoln Memorial, capping the historic 1963 March on Washington, he was talking about only the most basic rights. "I have a dream," he thundered, "that one day this nation will rise up and live out the true meaning of its creed: 'We hold these truths to be self-evident: that all men are created equal.'"

Perhaps only in King's inner-most, private dreams did he even entertain the possibility of an African-American running for president, let alone being elected. At the time, standing up for voting rights for black people often meant laying your life on the line.

Yet, 45 years later, to the day, Sen. Barack Obama — a black man — is scheduled to accept the Democratic Party nomination for president. The freshman U.S. senator from Illinois boasts a relatively slim résumé for a major-party presidential candidate: before his Senate stint, eight years in the Illinois legislature and three years of community organizing. Where he most obviously differs from his predecessors, though, is his skin color, the result of having a black Kenyan father and white Kansan mother.

"A lot of black folks, myself included, occasionally pinch ourselves to see if this is really real," says James Rucker of San Francisco, co-founder of ColorOfChange.org, a Web-based network that aims to boost the political presence of African-Americans.

Perhaps adding to the dreamlike quality of the moment, Obama's almost-certain Republican opponent, four-term Sen. John McCain of Arizona, a white, 71-year-old war hero — is running slightly behind in some polls. But even if McCain later moves to

393

Hispanic Population Grew Fastest

The number of Hispanics in the United States has grown by nearly a third since 2000. By contrast, blacks and whites have only grown by 9 and 2 percent, respectively.

Growth in U.S. Population by Ethnicity, 2000-2008

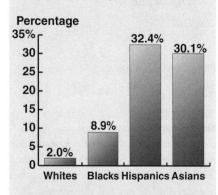

Percentage

Whites 2.0%, Blacks 8.9%, Hispanics 32.4%, Asians 30.1%

Source: William H. Frey, analysis of U.S. Census estimates

the lead, Obama, 46, already has upset expectations rooted in America's complicated and violent racial history.

Obama's strong showing may be as much generational as racial. "We have more racially conservative people being replaced by younger people coming into adulthood who are much more comfortable with the racial and ethnic diversity that characterizes the country today," says Scott Keeter, director of survey research for the nonpartisan Pew Research Center.

Even so, most recent poll results still show a close race. In June, a *Washington Post*-ABC News survey showed Obama with 48 percent support, against 42 percent for McCain. Estimates of electoral votes showed McCain ahead, but by only six votes.[1]

Arguably, Obama should be leaving McCain in the dust. A Republican affiliation is a ticket to the political graveyard these days, as any number of GOP politicians are saying. Former House Speaker Newt Gingrich sees a

"catastrophic collapse in trust for Republicans." Yet Obama and McCain are in "a very competitive race for president," Democratic pollster Peter Hart told *The Wall Street Journal.*[2]

Is Obama's race — as opposed to his relative inexperience or his policy proposals or his personality — holding his numbers down?

A national poll in early July found that Americans disagree on some — but not all — race-related issues. Twenty-nine percent of blacks thought race relations in the U.S. were generally good compared to 55 percent of whites. Yet 70 percent of whites and 65 percent of blacks thought America is ready to elect a black president. As to the candidates themselves, 83 percent of black voters had favorable opinions of Obama compared with 31 percent of whites. And only 5 percent of blacks had favorable opinions of McCain vs. 35 percent of whites.[3]

Obama supporters and the candidate himself are predicting that Republicans inevitably will resort to race. "They're going to try to make you afraid of me. 'He's young and inexperienced and he's got a funny name. And did I mention he's black?' " Obama told a fundraiser in Jacksonville, Fla., in late June.[4]

Republican officials and activists reject the notion that race will be the deciding issue. "I don't believe this presidential election is going to be determined by the race of the candidates," says Minnesota Gov. Tim Pawlenty, a Republican frequently mentioned as a potential vice-presidential running mate for McCain.

Republicans predict, however, that Obama's camp will treat legitimate political challenges as racial attacks. "Every word will be twisted to make it about race," said Sen. Lindsey Graham, R-S.C., a McCain friend and adviser. But GOP attacks on Obama on issues such as national security and the economy, he said, will have "nothing to do with him being an African-American."[5]

Still, no one disputes that race inevitably will affect the election. Race has been intertwined with American history even before nationhood, and racial issues have figured in virtually all past presidential elections for the past half-century — before a major party had a black candidate.

In the politically crucial South — a Republican bastion since 1980 — most white and black voters (when blacks could even register) have always joined opposed parties. When the Democratic Party carried the banner of segregation, blacks tended to be Republicans. After the Democrats aligned themselves with the civil rights movement of the 1960s, the races switched parties.

"The majority [of Southerners] define themselves as conservative," says political scientist Merle Black, a specialist in Southern politics at Emory University in Atlanta. "White moderates have tended to be more Republican than Democratic; that isolates the Democrats with white liberals and African-Americans, who are not a majority in any Southern state."

Democrats Al Gore in 2000 and John Kerry in 2004 each failed to win a single Southern state. But some experts give Obama a strong chance in Virginia — and outside possibilities in North Carolina and Florida. As if to underline the point, Obama opened his post-primary campaign in Virginia on June 5.

Obama's bold move exemplified the approach that has taken him further than any African-American politician in U.S. history.

Indeed, Shelby Steele, a conservative writer of black and white parentage, is disavowing the last part of the subtitle of his recent book, *A Bound Man: Why We Are Excited About Obama and Why He Can't Win*. Steele, a senior fellow at the Hoover Institution at Stanford University in Palo Alto, Calif., says: "I underestimated the hunger in America for what Obama represents — racial transcendence, redemption. He's this wonderful opportunity to prove that we're not a racist society. I thought that would take him a very long way, but I didn't think it would take him all the way, but it may."

However strong that hunger may be, it's not universal. Hard-core race prejudice remains a factor in American life. If Obama wins, "We'll end up slaves. We'll be made slaves just like they was once slaves," Johnny Telvor of Williamson, W. Va., told *The Observer*, a British newspaper. And Victoria Spitzer, an Obama campaign volunteer from Pennsylvania, told *The Washington Post* of even

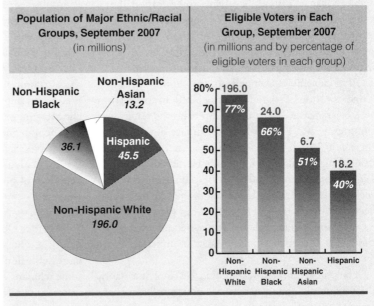

Hispanics Lag in Percentage of Eligible Voters

Hispanics are the largest minority group in the U.S. (left) but have the lowest percentage of eligible voters (right) because so many Hispanics don't have U.S. citizenship or are under age 18.

Population of Major Ethnic/Racial Groups, September 2007 (in millions)

Non-Hispanic Black *36.1*
Non-Hispanic Asian *13.2*
Hispanic *45.5*
Non-Hispanic White *196.0*

Eligible Voters in Each Group, September 2007 (in millions and by percentage of eligible voters in each group)

Non-Hispanic White: 196.0, 77%
Non-Hispanic Black: 24.0, 66%
Non-Hispanic Asian: 6.7, 51%
Hispanic: 18.2, 40%

Source: Pew Hispanic Center, Dec. 6, 2007

uglier comments. "Hang that darky from a tree," she said she was told once as she made phone calls to dozens of prospective primary voters.[6]

Obama argues that the country is indeed ready to rise above America's centuries-old racial divide. "In the history of African-American politics in this country there has always been some tension between speaking in universal terms and speaking in very race-specific terms about the plight of the African-American community," Obama said during a National Public Radio interview in 2007. "By virtue of my background, you know, I am more likely to speak in universal terms."[7]

"Universal" now describes a far more diverse population than the white-majority/black-minority paradigm that prevailed only a few decades ago.

The U.S. Census Bureau calculates the nation's entire minority population — of whom Latinos make up the biggest single component — at 34 percent. (*See sidebar, p. 406.*) "In a single lifetime, we will have gone from a country made up largely of white Europeans to one that looks much more like the rest of the world," writes Simon Rosenberg, president of NDN (formerly New Democratic Network), a liberal think tank and advocacy organization.[8]

Still, old-school racial issues persist. The "post-racial" aura of Obama's candidacy suffered some erosion after a video clip surfaced in March of a fiery black nationalist sermon by Obama's pastor, the Rev. Jeremiah A. Wright Jr. of Trinity United Church of Christ in Chicago, ending with the unforgettable: "God damn America."[9]

After cable news channels put the clip in round-the-clock rotation, Obama disassociated himself from Wright's remarks. When that didn't calm the waters, the Indonesia- and Hawaii-bred candidate gave a major speech on March 18 in Philadelphia, in which he confronted suggestions that his childhood outside the continental United States, and his Ivy League education had sheltered him from the U.S racial drama: "I have never been so naïve as to believe that we can get beyond our racial divisions in a single election cycle, or with a single candidacy — particularly a candidacy as imperfect as my own."[10]

The primary contest was winding to a close. Inevitably, the Wright affair and its aftermath permeated news coverage of the final elections.

In a *Newsweek* poll in May, 21 percent of white registered voters said they didn't think America was ready to elect an African-American president, and 18 percent of non-whites agreed. But pollsters also tried gauging the extent of prejudice, asking white voters only if "we have gone too far in pushing equal rights in this country." Thirty-nine percent said yes.[11]

And in Democratic primary elections in the politically critical states of Ohio and Pennsylvania, as well as in West Virginia and Kentucky, exit polls showed that Obama faced clear resistance among white voters with no more than high-school educations — the standard definition of "working class."

But a Roanoke, Va.-based political consultant who specializes in rural voters argues that Obama's race is a deal-breaker only with a small minority of voters in the Appalachian region that includes Pennsylvania, Ohio and Virginia. "There's one thing that could kill him — his gun record," says David "Mudcat" Saunders. "He's got to come to Jesus on guns. You start taking peoples' handguns, which is how the National Rifle Association

right now is defining him — if he gets branded with that, he's done."[12]

Obama may have weakened his case with rural gun owners with his widely reported comments at a San Francisco fundraising event shortly before the Pennsylvania primary. "You go into some of these small towns in Pennsylvania, and like a lot of small towns in the Midwest, the jobs have been gone now for 25 years, and nothing's replaced them," he told prospective donors. "Each successive administration has said that somehow these communities are gonna regenerate, and they have not. So it's not surprising then that they get bitter, they cling to guns or religion or antipathy to people who aren't like them or anti-immigrant sentiment or anti-trade sentiment as a way to explain their frustrations."[13]

To Obama's foes, the comments confirmed their depiction of him as an arrogant and condescending Ivy Leaguer — someone who aroused class-based suspicion more than racial hostility.

Whether Obama, who grew up fatherless and whose family at one point relied on food stamps, fits the standard definition of "elite" is one question. Another, say some scholars, is whether depictions of negative personal reactions to Obama as working-class pride are a cover. "I don't buy the argument that the racial argument is just a class discussion," says Paula McClain, a specialist in racial politics at Duke University. "For blacks, it doesn't matter how high you get. Millions of middle-class blacks still experience slights."

Obama lost Pennsylvania. But a *Washington Post* reporter traveling through its small towns found voters who agreed with Obama's basic assessment, if not with his wording. "People are sort of bitter, but they're not carrying around guns and causing crimes like he specified," said retired factory worker George Guzzi. "Everyone makes mistakes." Guzzi plans to vote for Obama.[14]

American voters may be more nuanced in their judgments than some pundits think they are. And Obama's influence is undeniable. "No one up until this point has been able to change the dynamics like he has," says Hanes Walton Jr., a political scientist at the Center for Afroamerican and African Studies at the University of Michigan. "Some people would call it a sea change."

As voters debate the impact of race on this year's election, here are some of the key issues being discussed:

Has Republican Party identification with white Southerners cost it support in other regions?

Beginning in the late 1960s, Republican strategists focused on cultivating white Southerners. By the time Ronald Reagan opened his post-nomination presidential campaign in Philadelphia, Miss., in 1980 the Republicans' "Southern strategy" had virtually locked up the white South.

The massive shift of white Democrats to the GOP followed Democratic President Lyndon B. Johnson's victory in passing the Civil Rights Act of 1964 and the Voting Rights Act of 1965, even though some Republicans say opposition to ending segregation played virtually no part in their party's takeover of former Confederate states.

But twin brothers Earl and Merle Black, white political scientists who've spent their careers studying the South, argue that the timing of the rise of Southern Republicanism was no coincidence. Citing data from a long-running research project, "American National Election Studies," the Blacks note that college-educated Southern white Protestants — the backbone of the Republican South — largely reject affirmative action and court-ordered busing to achieve racial balance in schools and say equality has been overemphasized as a goal.[15]

These findings don't point to a vast pool of unreconstructed racism in the South. But they do lend credence to the view that post-civil-rights-era unease among white Southerners fits easily into the modern low-tax, small-government, strong-military ideological package that Reagan assembled and that his Republican successors have continued. "On matters of race, religion, philosophy of government, taxes, national defense and culture," the Blacks write, "[Reagan] gave voice to many of their most cherished conservative values and aspirations as well as their most practical and material interests."[16]

Conservative Republicanism remains the dominant Southern doctrine. But some political analysts argue that its appeal is waning elsewhere. "The political views and social views of white Southerners are so out of step with the rest of the country," says Ruy Teixeira, a political analyst and senior fellow at the Center for American Progress, a think tank founded by former Clinton administration officials. "Voters of similar demographics outside the South tend to be a lot less conservative."

Sen. Barack Obama talks with construction workers at Indiana's University of Evansville on May 5, 2008. Although Obama has encountered resistance from white, working-class voters, 90 percent of the white respondents to a recent survey said they would be comfortable, in principle, with a black president.

AFP/Getty Images/Emmanuel Dunand

McCain, Teixeira says, "would like to move to the center," but most high-level Republicans are in sync, ideologically, with the views of their party's Southern base.

Minnesota Gov. Pawlenty argues that the GOP's nearly all-white demographics reflect no ideological or strategic intent. Rather, he says, "We had success on the traditional formula. Maybe we've gotten a little complacent; maybe we're living a little in the past."

Still, Pawlenty says, Republicans have become "purposeful about reaching out to include candidates who are women and from more diverse backgrounds." This tactic can be more successful than most people realize, he argues. "Areas where socioeconomic challenges exist tend to be heavily represented by Democratic officeholders, but they also happen to be areas that are not doing very well. I always say, 'How is that working out for you? Over time, if we show results, are you willing to at least be open-minded?' It's at least an icebreaker."

Outside the Republican orbit, however, some analysts argue that the party's chances of broadening its base are limited by dependence on its Southern base. "These people are anti-immigration," says David Bositis of the Joint Center for Political and Economic Studies, "which is not the greatest thing in the world to be when the country is exploding with an immigrant population. As soon as they become citizens, they're registering to vote in record numbers. So the Republicans are putting themselves in a position where they're seriously alienating the fastest-growing population group in the country."

Some Republicans agree. Grover Norquist, a conservative activist and president of Americans for Tax Reform, advocates a more energetic GOP effort to attract Latino support and says anti-immigration Republicans aren't helping the cause.

"Some of the smart restrictionists, or 'deportationists,' say, 'Three out of four Hispanics are in the country legally,' " Norquist says. "They won't care if you deport the fourth one.' " But, he adds, the fourth one is "their relative or their neighbor or their friend. When you scare the one out of four, you irritate the three out of four."

But Norquist disputes the view that the anti-immigration campaign waged by Rep. Tom Tancredo, R-Colo., and supported by other top Republicans grows out of the party's Southern history. Nor is the party's poor record in attracting African-Americans the result of any institutional GOP prejudice, he says. "The party has allowed Democrats to make that case," Norquist told a recent conference at the New America Foundation, a liberal think tank. "The modern black church became an organizing tool for the Democratic Party. The Republican Party needs to spend more time doing outreach and pointing out that the Democratic Party is the party that historically has played racial politics. As Bill Clinton and Hillary Clinton have shown, they're perfectly capable of playing racial politics when she's running against Obama."

Can the Democrats attract white, working-class votes outside the South?

Near the end of her contest with Obama for the Democratic nomination, Sen. Clinton suggested that her race gave her an advantage with white, working-class voters in Pennsylvania and Ohio. "I have a much broader base to build a winning coalition on," she said, citing an Associated Press article "that found how Sen. Obama's support among working, hard-working Americans, white Americans, is

weakening again, and how whites in both states who had not completed college were supporting me."[17]

Rep. Charles Rangel, D-N.Y., a Clinton backer and an African-American, later called the remark "the dumbest thing she ever could have said." Clinton herself agreed.

Still, the comment had some basis in exit poll data. Among Ohio and Pennsylvania Democrats with no more than a high-school education, Clinton won 6 in 10 votes. And in Pennsylvania, of the 13 percent of white voters who said race mattered to them, three-quarters voted for Clinton.[18]

Near the end of the primary race in Kentucky, exit polls showed a high level of race-based opposition to Obama. Of the 20 percent of white voters who said race played a part in their decisions, 90 percent voted for Clinton.[19]

White and black Democrats have diverged politically in the past, though not consistently. Since the civil rights era of the 1950s and '60s, the Democratic Party has become the political home for African-Americans. But even before blacks became a national political presence, the Democratic Party identified itself as the voice of working folk. But it also had widespread support from highly educated professionals, such as plaintiffs' lawyers, plus many Hollywood stars and Wall Street financiers.[20]

Links between the party's well-heeled members and its working-class base began unraveling in the late 1960s. In his winning 1980 presidential campaign, Reagan further deepened the divide, cultivating white working-class voters who became known as "Reagan Democrats."

The extent to which race played a role in these defections to the GOP has been debated for decades. But there is no question the Republican Party played up resentment over affirmative action and school busing that was simmering among some whites. By the late 1990s — after three landmark Supreme Court decisions limiting the federal government's role in ordering school desegregation — some of that anger was dying away.

And President Bill Clinton's support for welfare-reform legislation eliminated another racially charged issue from the political agenda.

Today, sensitive to the possibility that affirmative action could reappear as an issue, Obama took care to say last year that he doesn't think his daughters would be good candidates for race-based preferences, given the advantages they're enjoying. Race-based affirmative action should become a "diminishing tool," he said, adding that white students from poor households should get some special consideration in school applications.[21]

Democratic analysts who specialize in working-class issues agree that race can influence voting decisions, but not overwhelmingly.

"There are going to be people who vote against Barack Obama because they're racists — but I don't give a damn about those people," says Saunders, the Virginia-based political strategist. "We ain't going to get the racist vote." He adds, "I'm not saying that if you're a Republican, you're a racist."

Fundamentally, Saunders says, rural and urban working people — white or black — are subject to the same economic and social forces. "We both have problems with education, health care, drug abuse — they've got crack, we've got crystal meth," Saunders says. "None of us can keep our children in our neighborhoods, because there are no jobs." Obama can win votes, Saunders argues, by uniting blacks and whites around these shared problems.

But other trends run counter to the populist vision of a city-rural alliance, say some Republicans with expertise on the subject of working-class Republicans. Minnesota Gov. Pawlenty's four siblings are all "classic Reagan Democrats," he says, including two longtime union members. "They've morphed over the decades in their political views — they're independent and lean Republican," he says. "They don't want their taxes raised, they don't care for too much

Whites and Non-Whites Share Attitudes on Race

About three-quarters of whites and non-whites believe the United States is ready to elect an African-American president. Two-thirds of both groups think Barack Obama would not favor any specific racial group if he were elected president.

Do you think America is ready to elect an African-American president, or not?

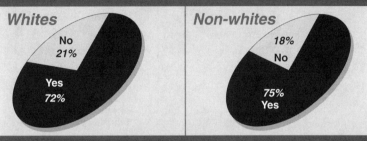

If the choices for president in November are Barack Obama, the Democrat, and John McCain, the Republican, how important will the candidates' race be to your voting decision?

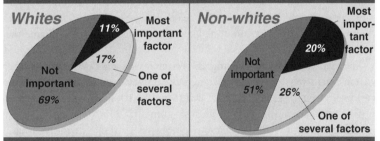

If Barack Obama were to become president, do you think his administration's policies would favor African-Americans and other minorities, would favor whites, or would not favor any group in particular?

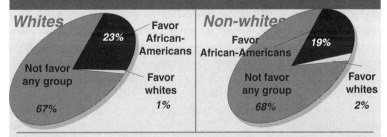

Note: Percentages do not add to 100 because "Don't know" answers are omitted.

Source: Princeton Survey Research Associates International, "Obama and the Race Factor," poll for *Newsweek*, May 23, 2008

Number of Black Elected Officials Skyrocketed

The number of elected black officials in the United States rose to more than 9,000 in 2000 — the most recent available data — up from less than 1,500 in 1970 (graph at left). The biggest gains were in county and municipal offices (bar graphs at right).

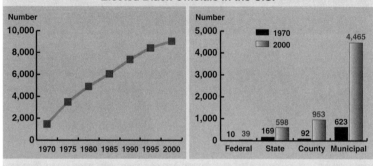

Elected Black Officials in the U.S.

Source: Joint Center for Political and Economic Studies, 2000

Is race a major factor in the presidential election?

Early in Obama's run for the nomination his mixed racial heritage, his upbringing outside the continental United States, even his speaking manner, situated him outside the "black politician" profile. The term "post-racial" floated through news coverage and the blogosphere to describe Obama's candidacy.

NPR commentator Juan Williams, a journalist specializing in racial matters, saluted Obama's effort to move political culture into a new era in which backgrounds such as his have become common. "If black and white voters alike react to Mr. Obama's values, then he will really have taken the nation into post-racial politics," Williams wrote. "Whether he and America will get there is still an open question."[22]

Williams' skepticism turned out to be well-founded. In March, the video of the Rev. Wright's "God damn America" sermon surfaced. The condemnation followed a passage in which Wright enumerated the sins of past colonial powers, leading to a denunciation of the drug war and its effects on African-Americans: "The government gives them the drugs, builds bigger prisons, passes a three-strike law and then wants us to sing 'God Bless America.' No, no, no, not God Bless America. God damn America — that's in the Bible — for killing innocent people."

Obama's Philadelphia speech, in which he said that he couldn't break with Wright even when he disagreed with him, seemed to put the matter to rest. But six weeks later, Wright reappeared on the scene. Speaking at the National Press Club, he stood by another sermon, given after Sept. 11, in which he had declared that the terrorist attack amounted to retribution. "You cannot do terrorism on other people and expect it never to come back on you," Wright said.[23]

As Republican politicians and political commentators kept those remarks in circulation, a Catholic clergyman and longtime Obama supporter, the Rev. Michael Pfelger of Chicago, poked fun in racial terms at Sen. Hillary Rodham Clinton during an appearance at Trinity.

of a liberal agenda socially or economically. They don't want the government taking over the health-care system. My brothers like to hunt and don't like anyone messing with their guns."

The Center for American Progress' Teixeira, who has written extensively from a Democratic perspective about working-class voting, argues that Obama will be trying to get past that standard Republican argument. "His candidacy could revive issues about giveaways to the undeserving poor," Teixeira acknowledges. "But what he mostly wants to talk about is the economy, the war and health care."

Republican activist Norquist, meanwhile, argues against the conventional wisdom that white, working-class voters will respond to fears of further economic decline by peeling away from the GOP. Democrats, Norquist says, are the ones bearing the burden of political disadvantage. "They have a problem with the people they're expecting to pay for their trial lawyer-labor coalition," he says. "And a cultural problem, if you want to count stealing peoples' guns."

Obama has made clear how wide a gulf divides him from working people outside big cities, Norquist says. He cites Obama's widely reported and widely criticized remark that rural voters "cling" to guns and religion. That was, Norquist says, a "snobbish comment."

That episode led Obama to break with Wright and resign from Trinity. Both preachers' views echoed Black Nationalist views — concerning the drug war, for instance — that became commonplace in the 1970s and '80s.

Even so, proclaiming that America is suffering God's righteous wrath has never been a monopoly of black preachers. "I called down damnation on America as 'fallen away from God' at . . . national meetings where I was keynote speaker, including the annual meeting of the ultraconservative Southern Baptist Convention," Frank Schaeffer — an ex-evangelist and son of Francis Schaeffer, a founder of the Christian right — wrote in the wake of the Wright affair. "The top Republican leadership depended on preachers and agitators like us to energize their rank and file. No one called us un-American."[24]

The argument by Schaeffer and others that the wave of condemnation of Wright grew out of a double standard may have encouraged McCain to break ties with two right-wing ministers — the Rev. John C. Hagee and the Rev. Rod Parsley — who had endorsed him. Hagee is a Christian backer of Zionism who called the Holocaust a divine tool for creating Israel, and Parsley called Islam a "false religion."[25]

But McCain's moves didn't seem to take much weight off Obama. For his foes, the entire sequence of events served to link the candidate to old-school racial challenge. "This is a huge story because it contradicts the whole persona and appeal of Obama as a man who transcends race," columnist Charles Krauthammer told *USA Today.* "I think it ought to be explored a lot more deeply."[26]

How openly Republicans might explore the race issue remains uncertain. Bill Clinton still hasn't recovered from the aftershocks of remarks he made after Obama's victory in the South Carolina primary. The ex-president noted, in what sounded like a dismissive tone, that Jesse Jackson had won that state as well. African-Americans accused him of deliberately lumping Obama in with traditional black politicians who never succeeded in gaining major footholds among white voters. Clinton denied any such intent.[27]

Even so, Krauthammer's comments, and others, tell Democratic analysts that Obama will have to openly take on the issue of race once again. "I think he will have to give another speech, as in Philadelphia," says Thomas Schaller, a political scientist at the University of Maryland at Baltimore who specializes in the interplay between race and voting patterns.

Moreover, Schaller acknowledges that race played a role in the extent to which Hillary Clinton beat Obama in the Appalachian region — while he outperformed her among whites in the upper Midwest. Those results don't necessarily predict the course of the general election, he adds. Still, from a political-geography perspective, he says, "It's amazing how they really did slice the Democratic Party right in half."

American history may demonstrate the power of race as a political weapon, but Gov. Pawlenty says the Republican Party has no need for it. A majority of voters will reject Obama's "classic liberal philosophy," he says.

Obama's rhetorical skills give him an advantage over McCain, but McCain trumps him in accomplishments, Pawlenty says. "Everyone says they'll work across party lines; McCain has actually done so," the governor says. "Barack Obama has nothing in his record to suggest that his rhetoric of being a uniting force is consistent with his record."

Former Rep. J. C. Watts, R-Okla., who in 1995-2003, served as the lone black Republican in the House, is skeptical that race won't enter into the campaign. Speaking of a hypothetical match between himself and a white opponent, Watts says, "Operatives and consultants will say, 'You have to drive his numbers down.' Man will always do what is best for man. If it's a matter of making [the opponent] look like he's anti-faith, that's good, or making him look like a racist, that's good."

Consequently, Watts says of Obama, "If the political establishment doesn't try to put him in that box of being a black candidate running for president, as opposed to a Democratic candidate who happens to be black, he has a decent chance."

Democratic analyst Teixeira, however, warns against overplaying race as a factor. "I don't think race is an obstacle in nearly the sense it once would have been. Public opinion data show dramatic liberalization of attitudes."

Teixeira doesn't buy the argument by many academics and political analysts that explicit racist attitudes have been replaced by "symbolic racism" on issues such as public safety. "It's a different breed of cat than old-time racism, and probably should not even be called racist," he says. "If you oppose affirmative action, that doesn't mean you're a racist. If you believe blacks should try harder to get ahead, does that make you a racist?"

BACKGROUND

Change in the South

Race runs through the history of the entire United States, but the drama began in the South.[28]

Following the Civil War, the Republican Party's identification with Abraham Lincoln, who ended slavery, turned Republicans into pariahs among white Southerners, while Democrats became the political mainstays of the system of racial segregation.

The ground under this political arrangement began slowly shifting during the New Deal era, which began with the election of President Franklin D. Roosevelt in 1932. Roosevelt's overwhelming popularity lessened the Democratic Party's reliance on Southern votes in presidential elections.

After World War II, Democrats began openly embracing black voters — that is, black voters outside of the South, where they weren't prevented from voting by poll taxes and other barriers. In 1948, the Democratic presidential nominating convention passed a resolution supporting civil rights instead of states' rights — code words for "Jim Crow" laws mandating racial segregation.

In response, several high-profile Southerners founded the States Rights' Democratic Party — the Dixiecrats. They aimed to defeat Harry S. Truman's bid for the presidency in 1948. Dixiecrat co-founder J. Strom Thurmond, then South Carolina's governor, became the new party's presidential candidate.

Support for Jim Crow was entrenched in the South, but so was loyalty to the Democrats, and the Dixiecrats won only about 25 percent of white Southerners' votes.

The Dixiecrats' defeat gave the Democrats' Southern monopoly a temporary reprieve. Thus, in 1950, every one of the region's 22 senators were Democrats, as were all but two of its 105 House members. Similarly all Southern governors and other statewide elected officials and nearly all state legislators were Democrats, and 80 percent of the registered voters were Democrats.[29]

But in 1952, only 20 percent of eligible Southern black voters were registered.[30]

Civil Rights

The social revolution that would change the Southern political map took shape following the landmark 1954 U.S. Supreme Court's Brown v. Board of Education decision outlawing segregation in public schools.

By the early 1960s, pro-civil rights demonstrations — and retaliatory violence — had spread throughout the South. In 1963 alone, Medgar Evers, the Mississippi field secretary of the National Association for the Advancement of Colored People (NAACP), was assassinated outside his home in Jackson, Miss.; four young black girls were killed in the bombing of a church in Birmingham, Ala.; and peaceful marches by ministers and young people demanding desegregation were met with police clubs, dogs and high-pressure water hoses.

In August of that year, the Rev. King made his "I Have a Dream" speech at the March on Washington for Jobs and Freedom, which attracted some 250,000 people to demand federal civil rights legislation. By then, President John F. Kennedy had formally called for such legislation, abandoning his initial reluctance. But on Nov. 22, 1963, before Congress could take action, JFK was assassinated.

Kennedy's vice president and successor, Johnson, a Southerner who had spent decades in the House and Senate, steered the Civil Rights Act of 1964 to enactment. The law prohibited racial discrimination in schools, employment and in all facilities open to the public.

Southern Democrats in the Senate had mounted a 57-day filibuster against the bill. But a 71-29 vote forced consideration of the bill. Joining to achieve that result were 54 Democrats and 27 Republicans.[31]

When the legislation reached the House (where it had originated before being modified in the Senate), members passed it on a 289-126 vote. On the winning side were 153 Democrats and 136 Republicans. Voting "no" were 35 Republicans and 91 Democrats, all but three of them from the South.[32]

After signing the bill into law on July 2, Johnson told an aide, "I think we just delivered the South to the Republican Party for a long time to come."[33]

The following month, events forced Johnson's Democratic Party into a second repudiation of its Southern political traditions. Delegates from an insurgent, racially integrated group of activists, the Mississippi Freedom Democratic Party (MFDP), demanded to be seated at the party's presidential nominating convention in Atlantic City, N.J., charging the all-white, official delegation had denied the vote to African-Americans.[34]

Despite a compromise in which two MFDP members were seated, most of the regular Mississippi delegates walked out, along with most of their Alabama counterparts.[35]

C H R O N O L O G Y

1948-1965 *Calls for desegregation and civil rights escalate.*

1948 Democrats pass a resolution supporting civil rights. . . . Leading Southern Democrats bolt party to form States' Rights Democratic Party (Dixiecrats).

1952 Only 20 percent of eligible blacks are registered to vote in the South because of Jim Crow restrictions.

1954 U.S. Supreme Court's Brown v. Board of Education ruling outlaws segregation in public schools.

1963 President John F. Kennedy agrees to call for a national civil rights law. . . . Assassination of Kennedy and black civil rights activist Medgar Evers and brutal police repression in Birmingham, Ala., shock nation. . . . The Rev. Martin Luther King Jr. delivers "I Have a Dream" speech.

1964 President Lyndon B. Johnson wins passage of Civil Rights Act. . . . Republican presidential candidate Barry M. Goldwater touts his "no" vote on the legislation while campaigning in the South.

1965 Johnson pushes Congress to pass Voting Rights Act, initiating a vast increase in black voter registration

1968-1992 *Major political realignment along racial lines occurs in South as racial episodes surface regularly in presidential campaigns.*

1968 Republican presidential candidate Richard M. Nixon appeals to Southern resentment about desegregation but doesn't flatly oppose it.

1976 Democratic Georgia Gov. Jimmy Carter wins White House with overwhelming support from black Southerners, who offset his low support among white Southerners.

1980 Ronald Reagan opens his post-convention campaign for president by calling for "states' rights" in Neshoba County, Miss., where three civil rights workers were murdered. . . . Reagan wins 72 percent of white Southern vote.

1988 Independent groups supporting Republican George H. W. Bush for president televise ads featuring black

murderer William "Willie" Horton Jr., who raped a white woman while on furlough; Democrats attack the ads as racially inflammatory. . . . Bush wins 67 percent of white Southern voters.

1992-1996 *Gov. Bill Clinton, D-Ark., shakes up racial politics during his presidential campaign, temporarily eroding Republican hold on the South.*

1992 Clinton criticizes rapper Sister Souljah for what he calls racist comments. . . . Clinton carries four Southern states in presidential election.

1996 Republican presidential candidate Sen. Bob Dole of Kansas attacks affirmative action, prompting Clinton's vow to "mend it, not end it.". . . Clinton wins reelection thanks in part to 84 percent support by black voters.

2000-2008 *Racial politics shift as Republican President George W. Bush ends his second term; Barack Obama launches winning campaign for Democratic nomination.*

2000 Republican primary foes Bush and John McCain support South Carolina Legislature's decision to keep Confederate flag flying over statehouse; McCain later retracts decision. . . . Presidential election vote-counting marked by controversy over disqualification of some black voters in Florida listed as ex-felons. . . . Democrat Al Gore loses every Southern state.

2004 Senate candidate Obama electrifies Democratic National Convention with a speech citing his life story.

2008 Questions about whether Obama is "black enough" give way to skepticism about his appeal to whites. . . . Stung by the Rev. Jeremiah Wright episode, Obama gives major speech on race and history. . . . Republican officials fear political criticism of Obama will be called racist. . . . Obama cuts ties to Wright after provocative new comments. . . . Rumor that Michelle Obama condemned "whitey" proves fraudulent. . . . McCain bids for votes of mostly white women furious at Sen. Hillary Rodham Clinton's primary loss to Obama.

Race-Oriented Debates Invigorate Black Web Sites

Obama draws wide support, but also disagreement.

Barack Obama has vast support among African-Americans, but that doesn't mean everyone agrees with him, or cheers his tactical moves. "Obama is a political opportunist who is driven more by interests than feelings," Marc Lamont Hill, a professor of urban education and American studies at Temple University in Philadelphia, wrote in March during a long-running debate in The Root, a new, black-oriented Web magazine.[1]

When Obama first distanced himself from his former mentor and pastor, the Rev. Jeremiah A. Wright Jr., Hill wrote: "By standing close to Wright, Obama was able to convince local people that he was 'black enough' to represent their political interests. Now that Wright is a political liability rather than a source of street cred, Obama has decided to throw his mentor under the bus to protect his own image."[2]

Melissa Lacewell-Harris, a political science professor at Princeton University, immediately shot back, "I refuse to buy into any Barack bashing on this topic." She added, "I wish we could have a reasoned conversation about race in this country. . . . But I think it is somewhat unfair to ask Obama to perform this same function in the middle of an election with a racially tone-deaf audience."[3]

The Hill-Lacewell-Harris exchanges reflect an explosion of political debate on the black side of the Web, which has been energized by the presidential race. One site, *Black Blog Watch*, simply alerts surfers to new postings.[4]

Much of the commentary scalds the major media for their coverage of racial issues. "First Obama wasn't black enough," blogger and memoirist Ta-Nehisi Coates wrote, responding to a piece in *The New York Times* (by *Times* reporter Marcus Mabry, himself African-American).[5] "Then

he was so black that he couldn't win the nomination. Now the question is 'How black is too black?' "[6]

Writing from a liberal perspective, Coates argued that Obama has been handling the race issue just right: "Obama emphasized race about as much as most black people on the street emphasize race . . . the same issues that keep white folks up at night — the war, the economy, health care — are the same damn issues that keep black folks up at night."[7]

Journalist Marjorie Valbrun questioned his decision to start wearing a flag lapel pin, after some criticized its absence. (*See "At Issue," p. 410.*) "People who don't support you are not going to be swayed by a pin on your lapel," she wrote. "I suspect they point to the flag pin as another reason that they don't like or trust you."[8]

Some commentators are ranging past the views of black Americans, and past Obama himself. Author John McWhorter, a senior fellow at the conservative-leaning Manhattan Institute, argued in a Web video discussion that some white voters were being tagged as racists simply for opposing Obama on the grounds that his appointees would run to the likes of Black Muslim leader Louis Farrakhan. "That's not, to me, racism," said McWhorter, who brutally critiqued hip-hop culture. "That's a kind of ignorance, [a] kind of grand view of history that doesn't take detail into account. But that person doesn't hate black people."[9]

In an exchange on *The New York Times' Bloggingheads* Web site, McWhorter's discussion partner, Brown University economist Glenn Loury, agreed, taking McWhorter's point even further. "Race is a central aspect of my being," said Loury, a conservative turned liberal. "Am I willing to grant that some whites might have their 'race' — I use the word with inverted commas — also to be a constituent aspect of

---

The MFDP grew out of the "Mississippi Summer Project," in which volunteers, including hundreds of white college students, helped African-Americans register to vote. Two of the white volunteers were murdered in Neshoba County, along with a local black civil-rights worker.

Spurred by the killings, Congress in 1965 passed the Voting Rights Act. Within three years, a majority

of African-Americans in the South were registered to vote.

Republican South

The Voting Rights victory followed Johnson's 1964 election — in which he lost the Deep South states of

how they understand themselves? . . . How can you have the blackness genie out of the bottle . . . and not have the whiteness genie out of the bottle?"[10]

Others in the black commentariat were focusing on another kind of white genie.

"Jill Tubman," a pseudonymous blogger on the *Jack and Jill Politics* site, echoed another black Web commentator who ridiculed the discredited rumor that Michelle Obama had denounced "whitey" (*see p. 411*).

Cubans in Miami celebrate on Aug. 1, 2006, after Fidel Castro temporarily handed over power to his brother Raul.

Citing a sitcom from the 1970s, Tubman noted, "The only person I ever heard saying 'honkey' or 'whitey' growing up was George Jefferson on TV. . . . This rumor was started probably by someone who wasn't black."[11]

Black Agenda Report publishes blog-style pieces and longer articles that grow out of left-wing and sometimes black nationalist perspectives. "To make himself acceptable to whites, Obama finds it necessary to shout out how unacceptable he finds the conduct of other Blacks," the site's executive editor, veteran journalist Glen Ford, wrote about Obama's denunciation of male irresponsibility — explicitly including black males. "Can one imagine Obama or any other presidential aspirant repeatedly hectoring any other ethnic group on moral issues? . . . But there are large regions of the white body politic in which it is not only acceptable, but damn near required, that politicians demonstrate their impatience with the alleged moral shortcomings of Black people."[12]

Clearly, whatever the effects of Obama's candidacy on black America, promoting lockstep conformity isn't one of them. One of his toughest, politically conservative critics sees political diversity on the upswing among African-Americans. And he says it promotes — rather than weakens — black identity.

"What black America needs more than anything is individuals," says Shelby Steele, a senior fellow at the Hoover Institution

at Stanford University. "In white America there is this clear right and left division, and people on both sides have legitimacy. We're just getting there in black America, but we are getting there. So I feel very much a member of the group."

[1] See Marc Lamont Hill, "Obama's Response to Jeremiah Wright," *The Root*, March 17, 2008, http://blogs.theroot.com/blogs/downfromthetower/archive/2008/03/17/obama-s-response-to-jeremiah-wright.aspx.

[2] *Ibid.*

[3] See Melissa Harris-Lacewell, "Obama's Response to Wright [Response]," *The Root*, March 18, 2008, http://blogs.theroot.com/blogs/downfromthetower/archive/2008/03/18/obama-s-response-to-wright-response.aspx.

[4] See Courtney Payne, *Black Blog Watch*, www.blackblogwatch.com/v1/index.cfm.

[5] See Marcus Mabry, "Where Whites Draw the Line," *The New York Times*, June 2008, www.nytimes.com/2008/06/08/weekinreview/08mabry.html?_r=1&ref=weekinreview&oref=slogin.

[6] See Ta-Nehisi Coates, *Message to the White Man: We're not Thinking About You*, blog, June 8, 2008, www.ta-nehisi.com/2008/06/message-to-the-white-man-were-not-thinking-about-you.html. Coates is author of *The Beautiful Struggle: A Father, Two Sons, and an Unlikely Road to Manhood* (2008).

[7] *Ibid.*

[8] See Marjorie Valbrun, "A Flag Pin? Come On!" *The Root*, May 16, 2008, www.theroot.com/id/46544.

[9] "Bloggingheads: Is Racism Over?" *The New York Times* video, undated, http://video.on.nytimes.com/?fr_story=4044856890331225e87fadb69 69199e3e28a70c8.

[10] *Ibid.*

[11] See Jill Tubman, "Black People Just Don't Say Whitey . . . Ever," *Jack and Jill Politics*, June 19, 2008, www.jackandjillpolitics.com/2008/06/black-people-just-dont-say-whiteyever.html.

[12] See Glen Ford, "Obama Insults Half a Race," *Black Agenda Report*, June 18, 2008, www.blackagendareport.com/index.php?option=com_content&task=view&id=661&Itemid=1.

Alabama, Georgia, Louisiana, Mississippi and South Carolina to Republican Barry M. Goldwater, R-Ariz.

The failure of a politically skilled Southern Democrat to carry his entire home region signaled that — as Johnson had predicted — Democratic control of the South was eroding.

White Southern hostility to civil rights played a key role in the Republican ascendancy. Goldwater didn't

proclaim opposition to racial integration itself, but he had voted against the civil rights bill — and made sure his Southern audiences knew it. "Forced integration is just as wrong as forced segregation," he said.[36]

Just as important, Goldwater's ally in some of his Southern travels was ex-Dixiecrat Thurmond, by then a South Carolina senator and still a fierce segregationist.

Latinos May Play Crucial Role in Election

But their voting strength lags.

Barack Obama is poised to hand African-Americans a victory in their centuries-old fight for a place in the political sun. But if he wins, it may be voters from another minority group — Latinos — who put him over the top.

Both Obama and Republican nominee John McCain are angling for Latino votes. In early July, Obama was leading McCain among Hispanic voters. McCain himself has a pro-immigration record, but that sets him apart from many in his party.

Other pro-immigration Republicans acknowledge the handicap. "If politicians want to deport your mother, people get this odd view that you don't like them," says veteran GOP strategist Grover Norquist, president of Americans for Tax Reform.

For his part, Obama consistently trailed his primary opponent, Hillary Rodham Clinton, among Latinos. But a summary of May surveys showed Obama registering 62 percent nationwide support among Hispanics nationwide, vs. 29 percent for McCain.[1]

More important, perhaps, Obama was ahead in key swing states. In New Mexico, Colorado and Nevada, as well as Arizona, he was leading McCain 57 percent to 31 percent.[2]

In these states, Hispanics make up sizable shares of the registered voter populations. Hence, Latinos are seen as critical to both parties' fortunes in the swing states (Arizona occupies a special category because it's McCain's home state, where he has enjoyed strong support in the past from Hispanic constituents). In Colorado and Nevada, Hispanics make up 12 percent of the electorate and 37 percent in New Mexico.[3]

In Florida, another possible swing state, where Hispanics account for 14 percent of the voting population, the odds appear tougher for Obama. A poll showed Obama and McCain running virtually even, at 43 percent-42 percent. Cuban-Americans — 45 percent of Florida's Hispanic electorate — traditionally favor Republicans. However, the Cuban-Americans' presence is lessening; they accounted for 90 percent of Florida Hispanic votes in 1988.[4]

Because large numbers of Cuban-Americans vote — a 70 percent turnout is routine — and because they typically vote as a bloc, national interest in Hispanic voting has centered on South Florida.[5]

Along with Latinos' concentration in some key states, their new status as the nation's biggest minority — there are 45.5 million Latinos vs. 40.7 million African-Americans — has given them increased attention this presidential season. Nonetheless, Hispanic voting strength lags behind that of the black population.[6]

The nonpartisan Pew Hispanic Center calculates there were 24 million eligible African-American voters in 2007, or 66 percent of the black population. Among Hispanics, only 40 percent of the Hispanic population — 18 million people — were eligible to vote. The reasons for the low percentage of eligible voters: More than one-third of the Hispanic population is under age 18, and 26 percent aren't citizens.[7] In addition, Latinos (Cuban-Americans excepted) have a weak voting record. In 2004, 47 percent of Latinos nationwide turned out, in contrast with 64 percent for the population as a whole.[8]

"We recognize we must work very hard . . . to do better with Latino voters in the general election," said Federico

(After Thurmond's death, it was revealed that he had fathered a daughter with an African-American woman who had been a maid in Thurmond's parents' home.)[37] In the midst of the race, Thurmond switched his party affiliation to Republican.

Goldwater was the first Republican to receive the votes of a majority — 55 percent — of white Southerners. Since then, every Republican presidential candidate has outpolled his Democratic rival among Southern white voters.

President Richard M. Nixon, in his winning 1968 campaign, appealed to white Southerners' misgivings or outright opposition to civil rights, while avoiding depicting himself as a civil rights enemy. On the advice of Thurmond aide Harry S. Dent, for instance, Nixon favored some "freedom of choice" in school-desegregation plans and opposed mandatory busing.

Democrats were hobbled that year by the insurgent, third-party campaign of former Gov. George C. Wallace of Alabama, who ran a Dixiecrat-style campaign that drew votes from Jim

Peña, an Obama supporter and past secretary of Transportation and Energy in President Bill Clinton's administration.[9]

Tensions between Hispanics and African-Americans could prove problematic as well for the Democrats. A survey late last year showed 44 percent of Latinos reporting they feared blacks "because they are responsible for most of the crime" (50 percent disagreed). And 51 percent of blacks said Latinos were taking jobs, housing and political power from African-Americans (45 percent disagreed).[10]

"There's a lot of angst among blacks about Latinos moving in," says Paula McClain, a Duke University political scientist. But she adds that African-Americans tend not to support anti-immigration activists. "The notion of who's an American — black Americans have dealt with that," she says. "Historically, to be American meant to be white."

McCain hasn't associated himself with the immigration-restriction strain of the political culture, either. He even joined with Democratic icon Sen. Edward M. Kennedy, D-Mass., on a bill that would have allowed illegal immigrants to apply for legal status.

Since then, McCain has said border security must come first. But he's never endorsed the views of Reps. Tom Tancredo, R-Colo., who pushed legislation to build a wall along the Mexican border, and James Sensenbrenner, R-Wis., who tried to make entering the country illegally a felony.[11] Their "strategy has been seen by Hispanics as not just anti-undocumented immigrant but anti-Hispanic," says Simon Rosenberg, president of NDN, a think tank and advocacy organization linked to the Democratic Party.

Latinos tend to rate McCain highly as an individual, says Sergio Bendixen, a Miami-based Democratic pollster specializing in the Latino population. However, "He is definitely not hanging around with people that the Hispanic community respects," Bendixen says, citing the old saw, "Tell me who you go around with, and I'll tell you who you are."

An anti-immigration stance will turn off most Latino voters, Bendixen says, but, beyond that, immigration isn't their main concern. The substantive issues are health insurance, the economy and the Iraq war — all matters on which Hispanics had rated Obama's primary opponent, Hillary Clinton, more highly than Obama. But, Bendixen says, "The issues are so powerful that they are overwhelming whatever lack of comfort or lack of familiarity the Hispanic electorate might have with Sen. Obama."

[1] See Peter Wallsten, "Obama leads in battle for Latino vote," *Los Angeles Times*, June 6, 2008, www.latimes.com/news/politics/la-na-latinos 6-2008jun06,0,5793717.story.

[2] See "Latino voters favor Obama over McCain, according to UW pollsters," University of Washington, June 16, 2008, http://uwnews .washington.edu/ni/article.asp?articleID=42497.

[3] See Paul Taylor and Richard Fry, "Hispanics and the 2008 Election: A Swing Vote?" Pew Hispanic Center, Dec. 6, 2007, p. ii, pewhispanic .org/files/ reports/83.pdf.

[4] *Ibid.*; see also Tal Abbady, "Cuban-American voters make South Florida a logical stop," *South Florida Sun-Sentinel*, www.sun-sentinel .com/news/local/cuba/sfl-flrndcuba20sbmay20,0,3422003.story.

[5] *Ibid.*

[6] See Howard Witt, "Latinos still the largest, fastest-growing minority," *Los Angeles Times*, May 1, 2008, p. A18.

[7] See Taylor and Fry, *op. cit.*, pp. 13-15.

[8] *Ibid.*

[9] Quoted in Alec MacGillis, "Obama Campaign Redoubles Efforts to Reach Hispanic Voters," *The Washington Post*, May 25, 2008, p. A1.

[10] See "Deep Divisions, Shared Destiny: A Poll of African Americans, Hispanics and Asian Americans on Race Relations," *New American Media*, Dec. 12, 2007, pp. 3, 9-10, http://media.newamericamedia. org/images/polls/race/exec_summary.pdf. The survey was conducted for New American Media, a San Francisco-based alliance of ethnic news organizations.

[11] See Kathy Kiely, "GOP leaders oppose immigration felony," *USA Today*, April 4, 2006, ww.usatoday.com/news/washington/2006-04 -12-immigration-congress_x.htm. For background, see Alan Greenblatt, "Immigration Debate," *CQ Researcher*, Feb. 1, 2008, pp. 97-120.

Crow Democrats like himself. Thurmond, meanwhile, was campaigning for Nixon with the message that voters who valued the fading Southern way of life would be better advised to choose Nixon than to waste a vote on Wallace.

As the South realigned, the Democratic Party fought Republican expansion in the South by wooing African-Americans' votes. In 1976, Democrat Jimmy Carter — a former governor of Georgia — won the White House thanks in part to 82 percent support from black Southerners, despite losing most white Southerners to President Gerald R. Ford.

Once Republican Reagan launched his 1980 presidential campaign, he and the party took an overwhelming share of the white Southern Protestant majority. Most of its members now had gone to college and lived in metropolitan areas. Reagan's praise of low taxes and free-market capitalism, coupled with his patriotic rhetoric, found a ready audience.

The civil rights protest era had ended, but memories of the time remained fresh. And Reagan, Democrats said, seemed to exploit white resentment. In fact, in August

1980 he gave his first speech as official Republican presidential nominee in Mississippi's Neshoba County, where the three civil rights workers had been murdered 16 years earlier. Before an almost entirely white crowd, Reagan said: "I believe in states' rights; I believe in people doing as much as they can at the private level."[38]

Democrats seized on Reagan's remark. "You've seen in this campaign the stirrings of hate and the rebirth of code words like 'states' rights' in a speech in Mississippi," said President Carter, whom Reagan was running to unseat.[39]

After Reagan's two-term administration, the GOP became the South's dominant party. But the enfranchisement of African-Americans led to the elections of growing numbers of blacks, virtually all Democrats.

By 1999, 62 percent of America's 8,936 black elected officials served in the 11 states of the Old Confederacy. Mississippi, where 33 percent of the voting-age population was black, led the nation in elected African-Americans, with 850 officeholders.[40] (*See graph, p. 400.*)

Racial Politics

As civil rights laws and affirmative-action programs took effect, supporting "separation of the races" became unacceptable for politicians, except on the fringes.

But racial politics didn't vanish.

When George H. W. Bush, was running for president in 1987-88, his campaign ran a TV ad accusing Massachusetts Gov. Michael Dukakis, the Democratic candidate, of coddling criminals. The controversial ad noted that under a prison furlough program — begun by Dukakis' Republican predecessor — a murderer serving a life sentence without parole raped a woman and slashed her husband after being released for a weekend furlough.[41]

The criminal, William "Willie" Horton, was black, his victim white. Official Bush campaign ads didn't feature Horton's face, though at least one commercial and some fliers produced by independent pro-Bush groups did.

"As a white Southerner, I have always known I had to go the extra mile to avoid being tagged a racist by liberal Northerners," said the late Lee Atwater, Bush's campaign manager, after Bush won. And Roger Ailes, a media consultant to the campaign (now Chairman and CEO of Fox News), said, "I did not do the Willie Horton ad. I thought it was a crude ad and probably would stir up the idea of racism with the media."[42]

Indeed, Democratic leaders accused the Bush campaign of exploiting racist emotions as soon as the explosive Horton ads began appearing. Ensuing news coverage made the campaign's avoidance of Horton's photo irrelevant, because the media frequently showed the image.

In 1992, it was Democratic presidential candidate Bill Clinton who capitalized on a racially charged issue, criticizing a comment made by the rap singer Sister Souljah about the 1992 Los Angeles riots sparked by the acquittal of white police officers who had beaten black motorist Rodney King. Referring to the beating of a white truck driver, she said, "If black people kill black people every day, why not have a week and kill white people?"[43]

She explained later she'd merely been trying to convey the mind-set of young, inner-city blacks. But Clinton equated the comment to what a white racist would say about blacks.[44]

As a leading Democrat, Clinton was praised for drawing the line at offensive speech from one of his party's key voting blocs. Since then, a "Sister Souljah moment" has come to signify precisely that action — especially when a Democrat is dissenting from liberal orthodoxy about a racial issue.[45]

Patriotism and Race

Meanwhile, Clinton kept the faith on a key issue for black Democrats — affirmative action. In February 1995, as he was preparing to fight for reelection amid the first stirrings of the sex scandals that would soon engulf his presidency, the future Republican candidate, Sen. Bob Dole of Kansas, launched an attack on affirmative action. "Why did 62 percent of white males vote Republican in 1994? I think it's because . . . sometimes the best-qualified person does not get the job because he or she may be of one color — and I'm beginning to believe that may not be the way it should be in America."[46]

Seeing a campaign issue in the making, Clinton ordered a high-level review of affirmative-action policies, which gave him the intellectual ammunition to defend them. "When affirmative action is done right, it is flexible, it is fair and it works," he said in July, promising to "mend it, not end it."[47]

Political analysts credited Clinton with lowering the temperature on the issue to the point that affirmative action nearly vanished as a campaign topic. Clinton won reelection thanks in part to 84 percent support among African-Americans.[48]

In the 1999-2000 presidential campaign season, race played a role chiefly in the fight between Texas Gov. George W. Bush and Sen. McCain for the Republican nomination — a fight that spilled over into the larger arena.

Bush and McCain backed South Carolina's decision to keep flying the Confederate flag over the state capitol. The battle pitted Southerners who insisted they were expressing Carolinian pride against African-Americans and white allies, who called talk of heritage a cover for racist sentiment.

Vice President Gore and his Democratic nomination rival, ex-New Jersey Sen. Bill Bradley, attacked the Republicans' stand. Gore noted the flag began flying over the capitol in 1962, during the civil rights protest era, "as a symbol of resistance to justice for African-Americans."[49]

The issue might have remained purely partisan — except that McCain months later reversed course, saying he'd been dishonest. Though some of his ancestors fought for the Confederacy, McCain said, "I don't believe their service, however distinguished, needs to be commemorated in a way that offends, that deeply hurts, people whose ancestors were once denied their freedom by my ancestors."[50]

In another blatantly racial incident during the South Carolina campaign, anonymous opponents of McCain used so-called push polling to suggest that McCain's Bangladeshi-born adopted daughter was his own, illegitimate black child.[51]

A more recent issue with racial dimensions surfaced during the Florida vote-counting controversy following the 2000 presidential election. On Election Day the names of some eligible voters appeared on a list of about 100,000 people said to be dead or to have felony convictions that barred them from casting ballots. Exactly how many eligible voters were kept away isn't known, but the "purge" list, assembled by a contractor for the state of Florida, was disproportionately weighted with African-Americans — 66 percent in Miami-Dade County, and 54 percent in Hillsborough County (Tampa).[52]

The voter-roll purge roused attention because of the closeness of the election, in which 90 percent of black voters who did cast ballots supported Gore. "They rejected the Bush candidacy in a resounding manner," said Bositis of the Joint Center for Political and Economic Studies, "and the events in Florida . . . have convinced them that the election was won because black votes were not counted."[53]

Four years later, Obama, then a relatively unknown Senate candidate, wowed the Democratic National Convention with a speech that touched on his biracial, binational origins, the ties that bind Americans and "the hope of a skinny kid with a funny name who believes that America has a place for him, too."[54]

CURRENT SITUATION

The Women's Vote

McCain and other Republicans are effusively praising Sen. Clinton after her loss — perhaps hoping to attract the votes of her embittered backers.

Their bitterness is seen by some Obama supporters as bordering on racism. Even before she conceded Obama's victory, McCain said, "I admire her and I respect her." "She has inspired generations of American women to believe that they can reach the highest office in this nation."[55]

After the last primary, McCain went further. "The media often overlooked how compassionately she spoke to the concerns and dreams of millions of Americans, and she deserves a lot more appreciation than she sometimes received."[56] The remark resonated with many Clinton backers, who said reporters were swooning for Obama while recycling sexist insults to Clinton.

Most of the anger at the media focused on television, especially cable TV news. News executives and journalists tended to blame the outrage over coverage on the fact that Clinton lost. But "CBS Evening News" Anchor Katie Couric agreed with the critics. "I feel that Sen. Clinton received some of the most unfair, hostile coverage I've ever seen," she said.[57]

Pioneering feminist writer and activist Gloria Steinem argued in *The New York Times* in January that the obstacles confronting Clinton were just as big as those Obama was facing. "What worries me is that he is seen as unifying by his race," Steinem wrote, "while she is seen as divisive by her sex. . . . What worries me is that some women, perhaps especially younger ones, hope to deny or escape the sexual caste system."[58]

McCain is hoping, however, that not all of Clinton's backers will remain loyal to the Democratic Party. The top woman in the McCain campaign, former Hewlett-Packard CEO Carly Fiorina, made a point of appealing to female Democrats in a June TV appearance.

Is race an important factor in the 2008 presidential election?

YES
Marjorie Valbrun
Journalist, contributing writer,
TheRoot.com

Written for *CQ Researcher*, July 2008.

Race is certainly an important factor in the coming election. Is there really any doubt that fascination with the presidential campaign is due largely to the fact that a black candidate has garnered support from voters of all racial stripes and is considered a viable prospect for the White House? This is not necessarily a bad thing. We Americans have been dancing around the subject of race for a long time, and Barack Obama's candidacy offers us a great opportunity to address it.

While John McCain is considered an experienced and able public servant, it is Obama who has struck an emotional chord with those who see his political ascendancy as representational of the American ideal. Many voters are excited by the possibility of electing the country's first black president and the impact it can have on American race relations and on the nation's image internationally.

To be sure, there are also many voters who are uncomfortable with Obama precisely because of his race, and they have not been shy about saying so. Democratic voters have even said in polls and interviews that they would not support Obama because he is a black man. Such views offer further proof that race is a key factor in the election.

Although Obama's candidacy has not been subject to the blatant and ugly race-based tactics that defined past elections involving candidates of different races, he has not been entirely spared of it either. (Who can forget the public furor over Jeremiah Wright?) Still, things seem different this time. Obama's avoidance of racially divisive issues signals that he is more interested in forging racial ties than in refighting the racial battles of the past. This gives voters room to write a new narrative about how race affects our politics. That Obama is a biracial, post-civil-rights-era candidate who pledges to bring Americans of all hues together has made it somewhat easier for us to talk honestly about what keeps us apart.

Pretending race is not an issue in the election won't make it so. Race has a firm hold on the American psyche, and Obama's candidacy has forced white Americans to explore their biases or fears and perhaps come to terms with the idea of a black man occupying the White House. It has also given hope — and some might argue proof — to people of color that the United States is indeed capable of living up to its most noble ideals about equality.

NO
Grover G. Norquist
President, Americans
for Tax Reform

Written for *CQ Researcher*, July 2008

Barack Obama will lose to John McCain in November for many reasons. The color of his skin is not one of those reasons.

Bill and Hillary Clinton argued that many white voters would not vote for Obama because his father was black, and this was offered as a reason for the superdelegates to save the party by snatching the nomination away from Obama and giving it to Hillary.

Bill and Hillary lost that argument. They deserved to. They were wrong.

In early 2008, the Obama groundswell was driven in large part by Obama's content-free call for hope and change and his presentation of himself as a post-racial candidate. He was not Jesse Jackson or Al Sharpton. And if you supported his candidacy, you were making a public statement that you were post-racial also.

Obama faltered when the nation began to see videos of his church and minister that were decidedly not "post-racial." Obama attended a church dripping with racial grievance and bizarre hatred of America — we invented AIDS as genocide. And the replacement minister — who was white — was just as hostile to America as the Rev. Jeremiah Wright.

Then Obama announced at a billionaire's house in San Francisco that he didn't like a Middle America that was "bitter" and "clings" to their guns and religious faith. He doesn't like rural and suburban America, churchgoers and hunters.

Americans do not vote for people who express contempt for them. Hispanics do not vote for Tom Tancredo. Millions of Americans will not vote for Mr. Obama, the snob who looks down at them, their families and communities. He is a snob with a tan, but no one is voting against the tan.

In three years, the 2001 and 2003 tax cuts end. Obama says he wants to let them lapse so your capital gains tax rate will jump from 15 percent to 20 percent. The tax on dividend payments will jump from 15 percent to 35 percent. The top rate for individual taxes will jump from 35 percent to 39.5 percent, and Obama envisions a top rate of 55 percent by extending the Social Security tax to all incomes. A vote for Obama is a vote for the largest tax hike in American history. Also for liberal judges. And gun control. And vast increases in federal spending — beyond the Bush nonsense.

The Democrats often run presidential candidates like this guy: Dukakis, Carter, Mondale, Gore and Kerry. They lose. Changing the color of the liberal won't help. Or hurt.

"No one should take a woman's vote for granted, and the Democratic Party should certainly not take it for granted," she said on "Good Morning America." "I'm a woman, and as a woman, I'm really proud Hillary Clinton ran for president. I am enormously proud of what she did, and frankly, I have enormous sympathy for what she went through."[59]

Feminist Democrats, meanwhile, have been cautioning that McCain would be a bad bet for progressive women. "He voted against legislation that established criminal and civil penalties for those who use threats and violence to keep women from gaining access to reproductive health clinics," wrote Arianna Huffington, founder of *The Huffington Post*, a liberal Web site.[60]

And activist Tim Wise, who writes frequently about racism, authored an essay in the form of a letter to white feminists threatening to vote for McCain or to abstain from voting altogether. Black voters, he said, "would have supported the white woman — hell, for many black folks, before Obama showed his mettle they were downright excited to do so —but you won't support the black man. And yet you have the audacity to insist that it is you who are the most loyal constituency of the Democratic Party, and the ones before whom party leaders should bow down, and whose feet must be kissed? Your whiteness is showing."[61]

The attention being paid to women's political power, meanwhile, may have prompted McCain's cancellation of a June fundraiser in Texas to have been hosted by former gubernatorial candidate Clayton Williams. During his campaign, he had made what he thought was a humorous comparison between weather and rape: "As long as it's inevitable, you might as well lie back and enjoy it."[62]

Targeting Michelle?

Democratic strategists say there are clear indications McCain backers will target Michelle Obama on racial issues. The candidate's outspoken wife, who rose from a working-class family on Chicago's South Side to graduate from Harvard Law School, came under fire early in his campaign for remarks during the Wisconsin primary campaign.

"What we have learned over this year is that hope is making a comeback," she said. "And let me tell you something — for the first time in my adult lifetime, I am really proud of my country. And not just because Barack has done well, but because I think people are hungry for change. And I have been desperate to see our country moving in that direction and just not feeling so alone in my frustration and disappointment. I've seen people who are hungry to be unified around some basic common issues, and it's made me proud."[63]

The next day, McCain's wife, Cindy, told a rally in Wisconsin. "I'm proud of my country. I don't know about you — if you heard those words earlier — I'm very proud of my country."[64]

Since then, Republicans have indicated they will keep reminding voters of Michelle Obama's comments. In June, former Secretary of State Lawrence Eagleburger introduced Cindy McCain at a fundraiser by calling her someone who is "proud of her country, not just once, but always." The audience caught the reference, *Politico* reported.[65]

Most of the commentary Michelle Obama unleashed — not all of it unfavorable — didn't touch on race. But one sympathetic journalist did sense a racial dimension to the emotions behind Mrs. Obama's remark.

"A lot of voters did and will wonder: how could someone who graduated from Princeton and Harvard Law School and won a job at a high-paying Chicago law firm — who was in some way a beneficiary of affirmative action — sound so alienated from her country?" asked *Newsweek* Editor-at-Large Evan Thomas.[66]

He cited her Princeton senior thesis, which examined relations between black Princeton graduates and the larger black community, and revealed the loneliness she had felt. "It is perhaps unsurprising that, for an unguarded moment on the campaign trail, she reflected the alienation she felt at being a working-class black woman at a rich, white man's school long ago."[67]

Obama's thesis did, however, give rise to a slanderous e-mail rumor campaign — one with no apparent links to the McCain camp. The e-mail claimed the thesis "stated that America was a nation founded on 'crime and hatred'" and that whites in America were "ineradicably racist," according to the *Politifact.com* Web site. *Politifact* examined the thesis and said it did not contain those statements.[68]

A subsequent attempt — also evidently unconnected to McCain's campaign — to attack Obama through his wife also focused on race. Conservative broadcaster Rush Limbaugh, blogger Larry Johnson, an ex-CIA agent, and Roger Stone, a former Republican operative, spread word by radio and the Web of a rumor that a tape existed of Michelle giving a talk in which she attacked "whitey."[69]

No such tape has surfaced. After investigating, the Obama campaign said the rumor of the talk was bogus.[70]

OUTLOOK
Changing Attitudes

Students of political and social trends say Obama's candidacy both reflects and stimulates deep changes in Americans' treatment of racial and ethnic differences — and that the changes appear unstoppable.

"It's not just about race," says Bositis of the Joint Center for Political and Economic Studies, citing growing acceptance of gay marriage among young people. "The younger generation is more tolerant. It has grown up with more integration. People under 35 grew up in a world where having overt, negative racial attitudes is not acceptable."

The changes in attitude reflect an underlying demographic shift. By 2050, whites will be outnumbered by blacks, Latinos, Asians and Native Americans, according to the U.S. Census Bureau.[71]

Some Republican politicians see the changes as further evidence that their party is falling behind the times. "The demographics of the country are changing," says Minnesota Gov. Pawlenty. "That doesn't mean you change your philosophy, but our party is going to have to do a better job," including diversifying Republicans' largely white-male candidate ranks.

As the only black Republican in the House during his tenure, former Oklahoma Rep. Watts agrees the GOP should make a stronger effort to reach out to minorities. But he also questions whether politics is the best vehicle for social change, because parties exist to fight for power, using the most effective weapons at hand. "When people say you ought to take the politics out of politics, it wouldn't be politics if you do that — it would be jacks," says Watts.

The Hoover Institution's Steele argues that Obama is bound to disappoint those who see him as the one-man cure for America's racial ills. "People have the illusion that he will be the endgame in terms of our racial conflict. My feeling is that he will be another chapter. He won't resolve anything. White people will realize that a black man in the White House will not save them from the suspicion of being racist."

Steele's skepticism aside, Obama's youthful cadres are changing the national political dynamic, some observers say.

"What you're getting in this election is another youth movement," says the University of Michigan's Walton. "It's not like the youth movement of the '60s; it's in the political arena. The old notion that young people don't vote is going to fall on its face. Young people are not as consumed with iPods and videos as you think. They are caught up in this presidential campaign."

The excitement has caught on abroad as well, and not only among young people. "Everyone is, in fact, impressed with the historical moment, that it is the first time an African-American has won the nomination of a party," said Wamiq Zuberi, editor of *The Business Recorder,* a Pakistani newspaper.[72]

NOTES

1. For electoral vote estimates, see Greg Giroux, "At the Starting Gate, State by State," *CQ Weekly,* June 9, 2008, p. 1513. For the *Washington Post*-ABC News poll, see Dan Balz and Jon Cohen, "Poll Finds Independent Voters Split Between McCain, Obama," *The Washington Post,* June 17, 2008, p. A1.

2. Hart quoted in Jackie Calmes, "Obama Leads McCain, But Race Is Looking Tight," *The Wall Street Journal,* June 12, 2008, p. A8. Gingrich quoted in Jackie Kucinich, "Gingrich warns Republican Party of 'real disaster' this fall," *The Hill,* May 5, 2008, thehill. com/leading-the-news/gingrich-warns-republican-party-of-real-disaster-this-fall-2008-05-06.html.

3. Adam Nagourney and Megan Thee, "Poll Finds Obama Candidacy Isn't Closing Divide on Race," *The New York Times,* July 16, 2008, p. A1. *The New York Times*/CBS News telephone poll was conducted July 7-14 among 1,796 adults, including 1,338 whites and 297 blacks.

4. Quoted in Caren Bohan, "Obama says Republicans will use race to stoke fear," Reuters, June 20, 2008, http://news.yahoo.com/s/nm/20080620/pl_nm/usa_politics_obama_race_dc&printer=1;_ylt=AsqCgl.Al.3gFyN2gkkVh70b.3QA.

5. Quoted in Charles Babington, "Obama braces for race-based ads," The Associated Press, June 23,

2008, http://news.yahoo.com/s/ap/20080623/ap_on_el_pr/obama_racial_ads.

6. Quoted in Kevin Merida, "Racist Incidents Give Some Obama Campaigners Pause," *The Washington Post*, May 13, 2008, p. A1; and Paul Harris, "Democrats in rural strongholds refuse to give backing to Obama," *The Observer*, June 8, 2008, www.guardian.co.uk/world/2008/jun/08/barackobama.hillaryclinton.

7. Quoted in Juan Williams, "Obama's Color Line," *The New York Times*, Nov. 30, 2007, p. A23.

8. See Simon Rosenberg, "On Obama, race and the end of the Southern Strategy," Jan. 4, 2008, www.ndn.org/advocacy/immigration/obama-race-and-end-of.html; and Howard Witt, "Latinos still the largest, fastest-growing minority," *Los Angeles Times*, May 1, 208, p. A18.

9. For a lengthier excerpt of the sermon than the clips commonly broadcast, and a clip of Wright later explaining his language to Bill Moyers of PBS, see "Long excerpt of Wright's 'God Damn America' speech," YouTube [undated], www.youtube.com/watch?v=bV-oI__bHA4.

10. See "Remarks of Senator Barack Obama: 'A More Perfect Union,' " March 18, 2008, www.barackobama.com/2008/03/18/remarks_of_senator_barack_obam_53.php.

11. See "Newsweek Poll, Obama and the Race Factor," *Newsweek*, May 23, 2008, /www.newsweek.com/id/138462.

12. See "On the Second Amendment, Don't Believe Obama," National Rifle Association — Institute for Legislative Action, June 6, 2008, www.nraila.org/Legislation/Federal/Read.aspx?id=3991.

13. For full transcript see Mayhill Fowler, "Obama: No Surprise That Hard-Pressed Pennsylvanians Turn Bitter," *Huffington Post*, April 11, 2008, www.huffingtonpost.com/mayhill-fowler/obama-no-surprise-that-ha_b_96188.html.

14. Quoted in Alec MacGillis, "Maybe Not 'Bitter,' But Aware of the Loss," *The Washington Post*, April 19, 2008, p. A6.

15. See Earl Black and Merle Black, *Divided America: The Ferocious Power Struggle in American Politics* (2007), pp. 84-85.

16. *Ibid.*, pp. 83-84.

17. Quoted in Kathy Kiely and Jill Lawrence, "Clinton makes case for staying in," *USA Today*, May 8, 2008, p. A1.

18. See David Paul Kuhn, "Why Clinton won Pennsylvania," *Politico*, April 23, 2008, www.politico.com/news/stories/0408/9812.html; Katharine Q. Seelye, "The Race Factor in Pa. Primary," *The New York Times*, *The Caucus* blog, April 23, 2008, http://thecaucus.blogs.nytimes.com/2008/04/23/the-race-factor-in-pa-primary/.

19. See "Exit Poll: Whites Back Clinton in Kentucky," MSNBC (The Associated Press), May 20, 2008, www.msnbc.msn.com/id/24736399.

20. See Eric Alterman, "The Hollywood Campaign," *The Atlantic*, September 2004, www.theatlantic.com/doc/200409/alterman; Landon Thomas Jr., "New Role For Rubin: Policy Guru," *The New York Times*, Sept. 8, 2006, p. C1; "Quadrangle, Investment Team," undated, www.quadranglegroup.com/rattner.html.

21. Quoted in Jeff Zeleny, "Obama Says He'd Roll Back Tax Cuts for the Wealthiest," *The New York Times*, May 14, 2007, www.nytimes.com/2007/05/14/us/politics/14talk.html. See also, Jonathan Kaufman, "Fair Enough?" *The Wall Street Journal*, June 14, 2008, p. A1.

22. *Ibid.*

23. Quoted in Peter Nicholas, "Obama's ex-pastor strides back on stage," *Los Angeles Times*, April 29, 2008, p. A1.

24. See Frank Schaeffer, "If Wright is Anti-American, Why Wasn't My Dad?" *beliefnet*, March 18, 2008, http://blog.beliefnet.com/castingstones/2008/03/frank-schaffer-if-wright-is-an.html.

25. See Neela Banerjee and Michael Luo, "McCain Cuts Ties to Pastors Whose Talks Drew Fire," *The New York Times*, May 23, 2008, www.nytimes.com/2008/05/23/us/politics/23hagee.html.

26. Quoted in William M. Welch, "Obama's ties to minister may be 'a big problem,' some say," *USA Today*, March 17, 2008, p. A4.

27. See Katharine Q. Seelye, "Jackson: Not Upset by Clinton Remarks," *The Caucus* blog, *The New York Times*, Jan. 28, 2008, http://thecaucus.blogs.nytimes.com/2008/01/28/jackson-not-upset-by-clinton-remarks/?hp.

28. Except where noted, this subsection is drawn from *ibid.*, and Earl Black and Merle Black, *The Vital South: How Presidents Are Elected* (1992); and Richard M. Valelly, ed., *The Voting Rights Act: Securing the Ballot* (2006).

29. See Black and Black, *Divided America, op. cit.*, p. 74.

30. See *ibid.*, p. 217.

31. See "Senate Votes Cloture on Civil Rights Bill, 71-29," CQ Electronic Library, *CQ Almanac Online Edition*, cqal64-1304621, http://library.cqpress.com/cqalmanac/cqal64-1304621."

32. *Ibid.*

33. Quoted in Black and Black, *The Vital South, op. cit.*, p. 6.

34. See *Congress and the Nation*, CQ Press, Vol. 1 (1945-1964), p. 57.

35. *Ibid.*

36. Quoted in Black and Black, *The Vital South, op. cit.*, p. 152.

37. See Jeffrey Gettleman, "Thurmond Family Struggles With Difficult Truth," *The New York Times*, Dec. 20, 2003, p. A1.

38. Quoted in Douglas E. Kneeland, "Reagan Campaigns at Mississippi Fair," *The New York Times*, Aug. 4, 1980, p. A11.

39. Quoted in Martin Schram, "Carter Said Reagan Injects Racism," *The Washington Post*, Sept. 17, 1980, p. A1.

40. See David A. Bositis, "Black Elected Officials: A Statistical Summary, 1999," Joint Center for Political and Economic Studies, 2000, pp. 10, 12, www.jointcenter.org/publications_recent_publications/black_elected_officials/black_elected_officials_a_statistical_summary_1999.

41. This subsection draws on extensive coverage of the issue by Sidney Blumenthal, "Willie Horton & the Making of an Election Issue," *The Washington Post*, Oct. 28, 1988, p. D1; John Buckley, "The Positive Purpose in Negative Campaigns," *Los Angeles Times*, Oct. 2, 1988, pp. 3, 5; Andrew Rosenthal, "Foes Accuse Bush of Inflaming Racial Tension," *The New York Times*, Oct. 24, 1988, p. A1; Tali Mendelberg, *The Race Card: Campaign Strategy, Implicit Messages, and the Norm of Equality* (2001).

42. Atwater quoted in Blumenthal, *ibid.* Ailes quoted in Josh Barbanel, "Roger Ailes: Master Maker of Fiery Political Darts," *The New York Times*, Oct. 17, 1989, p. B1.

43. Quoted in Jeff Chang, *Can't Stop Won't Stop: A History of the Hip-Hop Generation* (2007), p. 394.

44. For background, see Peter Katel, "Debating Hip-Hop," *CQ Researcher*, June 15, 2007, pp. 529-552.

45. See Joan Vennochi, "Sister Souljah moments," *The Boston Globe*, Sept. 16, 2007, www.boston.com/news/nation/articles/2007/09/16/sister_souljah_moments/; Mickey Kaus, *Kausfiles* (blog); *Slate*, Jan. 22, 2008, www.slate.com/id/2182569/#obamaescape.

46. Quoted in Steven A. Holmes, "On Civil Rights, Clinton Steers Bumpy Course Between Right and Left," *The New York Times*, Oct. 20, 1996, p. A16.

47. *Ibid.*

48. See Michael A. Fleter, "Clinton Move to Center, Cabinet Changes Leave Black Supporters Concerned," *The Washington Post*, Nov. 15, 1996, p. A10.

49. Quoted in James Gerstenzang and Matea Gold, "Gore Looks South as He Stumps in North," *Los Angeles Times*, Feb. 20, 2000, p. A39. See also "Confederate-Flag Battle to Continue in S.C.," *Los Angeles Times* (The Associated Press), June 20, 2000, p. A27.

50. Quoted in "Excerpts From McCain's Remarks on Confederate Flag," *The New York Times*, April 20, 2000, p. A22.

51. Richard H. Davis, "The Anatomy of a Smear," *The Boston Globe*, March 21, 2004. Davis was campaign manager for John McCain in 2000.

52. See Lisa Getter, "Florida Net Too Wide in Purge of Voter Rolls," *Los Angeles Times*, May 21, 2001, p. A1.

53. Quoted in "Can Bush Mend His Party's Rift With Black America?" *The New York Times*, Dec. 17, 2000, Sect. 4, p. 17.

54. See "Transcript: Illinois Senate Candidate Barack Obama," *The Washington Post*, July 27, 2004, www.washingtonpost.com/wp-dyn/articles/A19751-2004Jul27.html.

55. Quoted in "McCain praises Clinton's campaign," CNN, *politicalticker* blog, June 2, 2008, http://politicalticker.blogs.cnn.com/2008/06/02/mccain-praises-clinton%E2%80%99s-campaign.

56. *Ibid.*

57. Quoted in "Couric Gets Honored in D.C.," June 11, 2008, *fishbowlDC*, www.mediabistro.com/fishbowlDC/television/couric_gets_honored_in_dc_86823.asp.

58. See Gloria Steinem, "Women Are Never Front-Runners," *The New York Times*, Jan. 8, 2008, www.nytimes.com/2008/01/08/opinion/08steinem.html.

59. Juliet Eilperin, "McCain, Obama Reaching Out to Female Voters," *The Washington Post*, June 12, 2008, p. A1.

60. See Arianna Huffington, "Unmasking McCain: His Reactionary Record on Reproductive Rights," *Huffington Post*, May 26, 2008, www.huffingtonpost.com/arianna-huffington/unmasking-mccain-his-reac_b_103580.html.

61. See Tim Wise, "Your Whiteness is Showing," *counterpunch*, June 7-8, 2008, www.counterpunch.org/wise06072008.html.

62. See "McCain Cancels Event With Controversial Fundraiser," *ABC Political Radar* blog, June 13, 2008, http://blogs.abcnews.com/politicalradar/2008/06/mccain-cancels.html.

63. See Ariel Alexovich, "Blogtalk: Michelle Obama Under Fire," *The New York Times*, *The Caucus* blog, Feb. 19, 2008, http://thecaucus.blogs.nytimes.com/2008/02/19/blogtalk-michelle-obama-under-fire.

64. See Michael Cooper, "Cindy McCain's Pride," *The New York Times*, *The Caucus* blog, Feb. 19, 2008, http://thecaucus.blogs.nytimes.com/2008/02/19/cindy-mccains-pride.

65. See Carrie Budoff Brown, "Michelle Obama becomes GOP target," *Politico*, June 13, 2008, http://dyn.politico.com/printstory.cfm?uuid=7EC4ACB1-3048-5C12-00B24E3D753ACFCF.

66. See Evan Thomas, "Alienated in the U.S.A.," *Newsweek*, May 13, 2008, www.newsweek.com/id/123024.

67. *Ibid.*

68. See Angie Drobnic Holan, "Digging up dirt on Michelle Obama," *Politifact*, May 30, 2008, www.politifact.com/truth-o-meter/article/2008/may/30/digging-dirt-college-years/. *Politifact* is produced by Congressional Quarterly and *The St. Petersburg Times*.

69. See "Fight the Smears," undated, http://my.barackobama.com/page/content/fightthesmearshome/; "CNN Reliable Sources," June 15, 2008, transcript, http://transcripts.cnn. com/TRANSCRIPTS/0806/15/rs.01.html.

70. *Ibid.*, and Larry Johnson, "The Michelle Obama Diversion," *No Quarter* blog, June 4, 2008, http://noquarterusa.net/blog/2008/06/04/the-michelle-obama-diversion/.

71. See June Kronholz, "Racial Identity's Gray Area," *The Wall Street Journal*, June 12, 2008, p. A10.

72. Quoted in Alan Cowell, "Foreign Reaction to Obama's Claim is Favorable," *The New York Times*, June 5, 2008, www.nytimes.com/2008/06/05/world/05react.html?_r=1&oref=slogin.

BIBLIOGRAPHY

Books

Black, Earl, and Merle Black, *Divided America: The Ferocious Power Struggle in American Politics*, Simon & Schuster, 2007.
Twin-brother political scientists analyze 21st-century political polarization, including its racial dimension.

Obama, Barack, *Dreams From My Father: A Story of Race and Inheritance*, Crown, 2007 (new edition).
Originally published in 1995, the now-presumptive Democratic candidate tells of his search for a place in American culture.

Schaller, Thomas F., *Whistling Past Dixie: How Democrats Can Win Without the South*, Simon & Schuster, 2008.
A University of Maryland political scientist says changing demographics allow the Democrats to win the West.

Steele, Shelby, *A Bound Man: Why We Are Excited About Obama and Why he Can't Win*, Free Press, 2008.

A conservative who shares Obama's mixed racial heritage says Obama is trapped by liberal political culture, which requires him to mask his beliefs to fit the definition of a black politician.

Articles

Bello, Marisol, "Blacks come to terms with Obama-Wright schism," *USA Today*, **May 5, 2008, p. A6.**
African-American churchgoers reflect a variety of opinions concerning the Rev. Wright's effect on Obama's campaign.

Kronholz, June, "Racial Identity's Gray Area," *The Wall Street Journal*, **June 12, 2008, p. A10.**
Obama's mixed racial ancestry reflects the growing diversity of a country where Italians, Slavs and other non-Anglo Saxon peoples used to have to argue to be classified as "white."

McWhorter, John, "Racism in Retreat," *The New York Sun*, **June 5, 2008, www.nysun.com/opinion/racism-in-retreat/79355/.**
An African-American author argues Obama's success so far shows that racism is eroding, even if it hasn't disappeared.

Merida, Kevin, "Incidents Give Some Obama Campaigners Pause," *The Washington Post*, **May 13, 2008, p. A1.**
Obama campaign workers tell of running into frank expressions of racial prejudice.

Mirengoff, Paul, "Loathing of Fear on the Campaign Trail, Part One," *Power Line blog*, **May 14, 2008.**
A conservative blogger rebuts Democratic conventional wisdom that the Republican Party exploits race-based fears.

Rohter, Larry, and Michael Luo, "Groups Respond to Obama's Call for National Discussion About Race," *The New York Times*, **March 20, 2008, p. A21.**
Campaign reporters find Obama's call for dialogue to be generally well-received.

Rosenbaum, Ron, "In Praise of Liberal Guilt," *Slate*, **May 22, 2008, www.slate.com/id/2191906/.**

The author of a book on Hitler and evil argues that conservatives who mock liberals' sensitivity to U.S. racial history are disregarding the moral value of acknowledging guilt.

Schone, Mark, "What role did race play with white Democrats?" *Salon*, **June 3, 2008, www.salon.com/news/feature/2008/06/03/roundtable/index.html.**
The liberal Web magazine sponsors a debate about the extent to which white voters are racist.

Thomas, Evan, "A Memo to Senator Obama," *Newsweek*, **June 2, 2008, p. 21.**
The lead story in a cover report on race in the presidential election says race still haunts American politics.

VandeHei, Jim, and John F. Harris, "Racial problems transcend Wright," *Politico*, **March 19, 2008.**
Top political reporters conclude that Obama's acclaimed Philadelphia speech didn't resolve all his racial problems.

Reports and Studies

"Deep Divisions, Shared Destiny," *New American Media*, **Dec. 12, 2007, http://media.newamericamedia.org/images/polls/race/exec_summary.pdf.**
A report on relations between African-Americans, Latinos and Asian-Americans shows tensions, but also a sense of solidarity.

"Obama Weathers the Wright Storm, Clinton Faces Credibility Problem," *The Pew Research Center for People and the Press*, **March 27, 2008, http://people-press.org/reports/pdf/407.pdf.**
Obama's handling of the Rev. Wright drama won him a largely favorable response, the nonpartisan Pew report concludes.

"Race, Class & Obama," *Princeton Survey Research Associates International*, **April 26, 2008, www.newsweek.com/id/138462.**
Taken for *Newsweek* before the end of the primaries, the poll showed Obama suffering the effects of the Wright episode and facing relatively low support among white working-class voters — but not because of racial prejudice.

For More Information

Black Agenda Report, www.blackagendareport.com. A Web magazine and blog heavy on political reporting and commentary, much of it critical of Obama.

BlackPoliticsontheWeb, (813) 464-7086; http://black-politicsontheweb.com. The site compiles news, avoiding ideological guidelines, and runs reader comments.

ColorofChange.org, http://colorofchange.org/. A Web-based organization that organizes campaigns to e-mail law-makers involved in social-policy and racial-justice issues.

Jack and Jill Politics, www.jackandjillpolitics.com. A blog publishing commentary on a variety of political issues, from a middle-class, or "black bourgeois," perspective.

Joint Center for Political and Economic Studies, 1090 Vermont Ave., N.W., Suite 1100, Washington, DC 20005; (202) 789-3500; www.jointcenter.org. A think tank dedicated to issues critical to the African-American community.

Pew Research Center, 1615 L St., N.W., Suite 700, Washington, DC 20036; (202) 419-4300; http://pewresearch. org/. A nonpartisan organization that tracks public opinion on a wide variety of issues, including race and the presidential election.

The Root, www.theroot.com. Published by Washingtonpost Newsweek Interactive, a black-oriented Web magazine that presents a variety of political viewpoints.

The Obama Presidency

Can Barack Obama Deliver the Change He Promises?

Kenneth Jost and the *CQ Researcher* Staff

The largest crowd in Washington history cheers President Barack Obama after his swearing in on Jan. 20, 2009. An estimated 1.8 million high-spirited, flag-waving people gathered at the Capitol and National Mall, but thousands more were turned away by police due to overcrowding.

From *CQ Researcher*, January 30, 2009.

They came to Washington in numbers unprecedented and with enthusiasm unbounded to bear witness and be a part of history: the inauguration of Barack Hussein Obama on Jan. 20, 2009, as the 44th president of the United States and the first African-American ever to serve as the nation's chief executive.

After taking the oath of office from Chief Justice John G. Roberts Jr., Obama looked out at the estimated 1.8 million people massed at the Capitol and National Mall and delivered an inaugural address nearly as bracing as the subfreezing temperatures.

With hardly the hint of a smile, Obama, 47, outlined the challenges confronting him as the fifth-youngest president in U.S. history. The nation is at war, he noted, the economy "badly weakened" and the public beset with "a sapping of confidence."

"Today I say to you that the challenges we face are real," Obama continued in his 18-minute speech. "They are serious and they are many. They will not be met easily or in a short span of time. But know this, America — they will be met."[1] (*See economy sidebar, p. 428; foreign policy sidebar, p. 434.*)

The crowd received Obama's sobering message with flag-waving exuberance and a unity of spirit unseen in Washington for decades. Despite Democrat Obama's less-than-landslide 7 percentage-point victory over John McCain on Nov. 4, hardly any sign of political dissent or partisan opposition surfaced on Inauguration Day or during the weekend of celebration that preceded it. (*See maps, p. 420; poll, p. 422.*)

"It's life-changing for everyone," said Rhonda Gittens, a University of Florida journalism student, "because of who he is,

Obama Victory Changed Electoral Map

Barack Obama won nine traditionally Republican states in the November 2008 election that George W. Bush had won easily in 2004, and his electoral and popular vote totals were significantly higher than Bush's. In 2004, Bush won with 50.7 percent of the vote to John Kerry's 48.3 percent. By comparison Obama garnered 52.9 percent to Sen. John McCain's 45.7. In the nation's new political map, the Democrats dominate the landscape, with the Republicans clustered in the South, the Plains and the Mountain states.

Presidential Election, 2004

Democrat: John Kerry
Republican: George W. Bush

Total electoral vote:	
Republican	286
Democrat	251

Total popular vote:	
Republican	62,040,610
Democrat	59,028,444

* One "unfaithful" elector voted for John Edwards.

Presidential Election, 2008

Democrat: Barack Obama
Republican: John McCain

Total electoral vote:	
Democrat	365
Republican	173

Total popular vote:	
Democrat	69,456,897
Republican	59,934,814

* Due to the Nebraska's proportional allocation system, McCain received four electoral votes and Obama one.

Source: Federal Election Commission

because of how he represents everyone." Gittens traveled to Washington with some 50 other members of the school's black student union.

The inaugural crowd included tens of thousands clustered on side streets after the U.S. Park Police determined the mall had reached capacity. The crowd was bigger than for any previous inauguration — at least three times larger than when the outgoing president, George W. Bush, had first taken the oath of office eight years earlier. The total number also exceeded independent estimates cited for any of Washington's protest marches or state occasions in the past.*

The spectators came from all over the country and from many foreign lands. "He's bringing change here," said Clayton Preira, a young Brazilian accompanying three fellow students on a two-month visit to the United States. "He's bringing change all over the world." The spectators were of all ages, but overall the crowd seemed disproportionately young. "He really speaks to young people," said Christian McLaren, a white University of Florida student.

Most obviously and most significantly, the crowd was racially and ethnically diverse — just like the new first family. Obama himself is the son of a

---

* Crowd estimates for President Obama's inauguration ranged from 1.2 million to 1.8 million. Commonly cited estimates for other Washington events include: March on Washington for Jobs and Freedom, 1963, 250,000; President John F. Kennedy's funeral, 1963, 800,000; inauguration of President Lyndon B. Johnson, 1965, 1.2 million; Peace Moratorium, 1969, 250,000; Million Man March, 1995, 400,000-800,000; March for Life, 1998, 225,000; March for Women's Lives, 2004, 500,000-800,000.

black Kenyan father and a white Kansan mother. His wife Michelle, he often remarks, carries in her the blood of slaves and of slave owners. Among those behind the first lady on the dais were Obama's half-sister, Maya Soetoro-Ng, whose father was Indonesian, and her husband, Konrad Ng, a Chinese-American. Some of Obama's relatives from Kenya came as well, wearing colorful African garb.

The vast numbers of black Americans often gave the event the air of an old-time church revival. In quieter moments, many struggled to find the words to convey the significance, both historic and personal. "It hasn't sunk in yet," Marcus Collier, a photographer from New York City, remarked several hours later.

David Moses, a health-care supervisor in New York City, carried with him a picture of his late father, who had encouraged him and his brother to join the anti-segregation sit-ins of the early 1960s in their native South Carolina. "It's the culmination of a long struggle," Moses said, "that still has a long way to go."

Shannon Simmons, who had not yet been born when Congress passed major civil rights legislation in the 1960s, brought her 12-year-old daughter from their home in New Orleans. "It's historic," said Simmons, who made monthly contributions to the Obama campaign. "It's about race, but it's more than that. I believe he can bring about change." (*See sidebar, p. 424.*)

For black Americans, old and young alike, the inauguration embodied the lesson that Obama himself had often articulated — that no door need be viewed as closed to any American, regardless of race. For Obama himself, the inauguration climaxed a quest that took him from the Illinois legislature to the White House in only 12 years.

To win the presidency, Obama had to defy political oddsmakers by defeating then-Sen. Hillary Rodham Clinton, the former first lady, for the Democratic nomination and then beating McCain, the veteran Arizona senator and Vietnam War hero. Obama campaigned hard against the Bush administration's record, blaming Bush, among other things, for mismanaging the U.S. economy as well as the wars in Iraq and Afghanistan.

After a nod to Bush's record of service and help during the transition, Obama hinted at some of those criticisms in his address. "The nation cannot prosper long when it favors only the prosperous," he declared, referencing tax cuts enacted in Bush's first year in office that Obama had called for repealing.

On national defense, "we reject the false choice between our safety and our ideals," Obama continued. The Bush administration had come under fierce attack from civil liberties and human rights advocates for aggressive detention and interrogation policies adopted after the Sept. 11, 2001, terrorist attacks on the United States. (*See "At Issue," p. 444.*)

Despite the attacks, Obama also sounded conservative notes throughout the speech, blaming economic woes in part on a "collective failure to make hard choices" and calling for "a new era of responsibility." Republicans in the audience were pleased. "He wasn't pointing fingers just toward Bush," said Rhonda Hamlin, a social worker from Alexandria, Va. "He was pointing fingers toward all of us."

With the inauguration behind him, Obama went quickly to work. Within hours, the administration moved to institute a 120-day moratorium on legal proceedings against the approximately 245 detainees still being held at the Guantánamo Bay Naval Base in Cuba. Obama had repeatedly pledged during the campaign to close the prison; two days later he signed a second decree, ordering that the camp be closed within one year.

Then on his first full day as president, Obama on Jan. 21 issued stringent ethics rules for administration officials and conferred separately with his top economic and military advisers to begin mapping plans to try to lift the U.S. economy out of its yearlong recession and bring successful conclusions to the conflicts in Iraq and Afghanistan.

By then, the Inauguration Day truce in partisan conflict was beginning to break down. House Republicans pointed to a Congressional Budget Office study questioning the likely impact of the Democrats' $825-billion economic stimulus package, weighted toward spending instead of tax cuts. "The money that they're going to throw out the door, at the end of the day, is not going to work," said Rep. Devin Nunes, R-Calif., a member of the tax-writing House Ways and Means Committee. (*See "At Issue," p. 445.*)

The partisan division raised questions whether Democratic leaders could stick to the promised schedule of getting a stimulus plan to Obama's desk for his signature by the time of the Presidents' Day congressional recess in mid-February. More broadly, the Republicans' stance presaged continuing difficulties for Obama as he turned to other ambitious agenda items, including his repeated pledge to overhaul the nation's health-care system. (*See sidebar, p. 438.*)

Public Gives Obama Highest Rating

Barack Obama began his presidency with 79 percent of Americans having a favorable impression of him — higher than the five preceding presidents. George W. Bush entered office with a 62 percent favorability rating; he left with a 33 percent approval rating, lowest of post-World War II presidents except Harry S. Truman and Richard M. Nixon.

Do you have a favorable impression of . . . ?

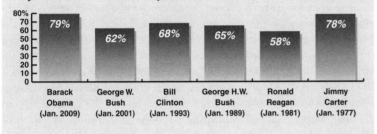

Source: *The Washington Post,* Jan. 18, 2009

Obama included health care in his inaugural litany of challenges, along with education, climate change and technology. For now, those initiatives lie in the future. In the immediate days after his euphoric inauguration, here are some of the major questions being debated:

Is President Obama on the right track in fixing the U.S. economy?

As president-elect, Obama spent his first full week in Washington in early January first warning of trillion-dollar federal budget deficits for years to come and then making urgent appeals for public support for a close to trillion-dollar stimulus to get the economy moving.

Members of Congress from both parties and advocates and economic experts of all persuasions agree on the need for a good-sized federal recovery program for the seriously ailing U.S. economy. And most agree on a prescription that combines spending increases and tax cuts. But there is sharp disagreement as to the particulars between tax-cutting conservatives and pump-priming liberals, with deficit hawks worried that both of the prescribed remedies could get out of hand.

With the plan's price tag then being estimated somewhere around $800 billion, Obama made his first sustained appeal for public support in a somber, half-hour address on Jan. 8 at George Mason University in Fairfax,

Va., outside Washington. Any delay, he warned, could risk double-digit unemployment. He outlined plans to "rebuild America" ranging from alternative energy facilities and new school classrooms to computerized medical records, but he insisted the plan would not entail "a slew of new government programs." He reiterated his campaign promise of a "$1,000 tax cut for 95 percent of working-class families" but made no mention of business tax cuts being included as sweeteners for Republican lawmakers.

Within days, Obama's plan was taking flack from left and right in the blogosphere. Writing on the liberal HuffingtonPost.com, Robert Kuttner, co-editor of *American Prospect* magazine, denounced the spending plan as too small and the business tax cuts as "huge concessions" in a misguided effort at "post-partisanship." From the right, columnist Neal Boortz accused Obama on the conservative TownHall.com of using the economic crisis as "cover for increased government spending that he's been promising since the day he announced his candidacy."

Allen Schick, a professor of economics at the University of Maryland in College Park and formerly an economics specialist with the Congressional Research Service, sees weaknesses with both components of the Obama plan. "We really have no model to deal with the question of what's the right number" for the stimulus, he says. "And we're not even sure that the stimulus will do the job, especially if a lot of the spending is wasteful."

As for the tax cuts, Schick calls them "harebrained, more intended to look good and buy support than to actually get the economy moving." In particular, he criticized a proposed $3,000 jobs credit for employers. "We know from the past that employers don't hire people for just a few shekels," he says. Eventually, the jobs credit was dropped, but the package still includes business tax breaks such as a $16 billion provision to allow businesses to use 2008 and 2009 losses to offset profits for the previous five years instead of two.

Conservatives favor tax cuts, but not the middle-class tax cut that Obama is proposing. "A well-designed tax cut is the only effective short-term stimulus," says J. D. Foster, a senior fellow at the Heritage Foundation. But Foster, who worked in the Office of Management and Budget in the Bush administration, calls either for extending or making permanent Bush's across-the-board rate cuts, which primarily benefited upper-income taxpayers.

From the opposite side, Chad Stone, chief economist with the liberal Center on Budget Policy and Priorities, endorses Obama's approach. "Tax cuts should be focused on people of low and moderate means, who are much more likely to spend the extra money they get," he says.

Academic economists, however, caution that tax cuts may not deliver a lot of bang for the buck in terms of short-term stimulus. Studies indicate that taxpayers pocketed at least one-third of the $500 tax rebate the government disbursed to counteract the 2001 recession.

Advocates and observers on both sides warn that the spending side of the package may also be less effective than hoped if political forces play too large a role in shaping it. "If it goes to pork, if it goes to green jobs that may sound good in the short term but may not have a market response or a market for them, then it's a waste," Paul Gigot, editorial page editor of *The Wall Street Journal*, said on NBC's "Meet the Press" on Jan. 11.

"If the stuff that gets added is not very effective as stimulus or the things that are good get pulled out, that would not be good," says Stone.

For its part, the budget-restraint advocacy group Concord Coalition sees political forces as driving up the total cost of the package — in spending and tax cuts alike — with no regard for the long-term impact. "Nothing is ever taken off the table," says Diane Lim Rogers, the coalition's chief economist.

Rogers complains of "political pressure to come up with tax cuts even though economists are having trouble figuring out whether they're going to do any good." At the same time, she says spending has to be designed "as thoughtfully as possible, not in a way that the federal government ends up literally just throwing money out the door."

A range of experts also call for renewed efforts to solve the mortgage and foreclosure crisis, saying that homeowners are not going to start spending again without confidence-restoring steps. Indeed, Federal Reserve Chairman Ben Bernanke pointedly told a conference in December that steps to reduce foreclosures "should be high on the agenda" in any economic recovery plan.[2]

Despite questions and concerns about the details, however, support for strong action is all but universal. "We have no choice," said Mark Zandi, chief economist of Moody's Economy.com and a former adviser to the McCain campaign, also on "Meet the Press." "If we don't do something like this — a stimulus package, a foreclosure mitigation plan — the economy is going to slide away."

Is President Obama on the right track in Iraq and Afghanistan?

At the start of his presidential campaign in February 2007, candidate Obama was unflinchingly calling for withdrawing all U.S. combat forces from Iraq within 16 months after taking office. But his tone began changing as he neared the Democratic nomination in summer 2008. And in his first extended broadcast interview after the election, President-elect Obama said on NBC's "Meet the Press" on Dec. 7 only that he would summon military advisers on his first day in office and direct them to prepare a plan for "a responsible drawdown."

Obama also did nothing to knock down host Tom Brokaw's forecast of a "residual force" of 35,000 to 50,000 U.S. troops in Iraq through the end of his term. "I'm not going to speculate on the numbers," Obama said, but he went on to promise "a large enough force in the region" to protect U.S. personnel and to "ferret out any terrorist activity." In addition, Obama voiced disappointment with developments in Afghanistan and said that "additional troops" and "more effective diplomacy" would be needed to achieve U.S. goals there.

Many foreign policy observers are viewing Obama's late campaign and post-election stances as a salutary shift from ideology to pragmatism. "It seems very clear that he will not fulfill his initial pledge to withdraw all U.S. forces from Iraq in 16 months — which is only wise," says Thomas Donnelly, a resident fellow on defense and national security issues at the American Enterprise Institute (AEI).

"I personally have been very impressed with [Obama's] thinking and his way of assembling a national security team," says Kenneth Pollack, director of the Brookings Institution's Saban Center for Middle East Policy. "This is not a man who plays by the traditional American political rules."

First Black President Made Race a Non-Issue

Obama's personal attributes swept voters' doubts aside.

Barack Obama took the oath of office the day after this year's Martin Luther King holiday, and he accepted the Democratic presidential nomination last August on the 45th anniversary of King's celebrated "I Have a Dream" speech.

For millions of Americans, Obama's election as the nation's first African-American president seemed to fulfill the promise of King's "dream" of a nation in which citizens "will not be judged by the color of their skin, but by the content of their character."

"Obviously, for an African-American to win the presidency, given the history of this country . . . is a remarkable thing," Obama said after the election. "If you think about grandparents who are alive today who grew up under Jim Crow, that's a big leap."[1]

While Obama clearly benefited from the sacrifices of the civil rights generation — to which he has paid homage — his politics are different from the veterans of that movement. Older black politicians such as the Rev. Jesse Jackson seemed to base their candidacies mainly on issues of particular concern to African-Americans. But black politicians of Obama's generation, such as Massachusetts Gov. Deval Patrick and Newark Mayor Cory Booker (both Democrats), have run on issues of broader concern — in Obama's case, first on the war in Iraq and later on the economic meltdown.

"The successful ones start from the outside by appealing to white voters first, and work back toward their base of black voters," said broadcast journalist Gwen Ifill, author of the new book *The Breakthrough: Politics and Race in the Age of Obama.*[2]

Black voters initially were reluctant to support Obama — polls throughout 2007 showed Sen. Hillary Rodham Clinton with a big lead among African-Americans — but he picked up their support as it became clear he was the first black candidate with a realistic hope of winning the White House. Clinton's support among blacks dropped markedly in the wake of remarks by former President Bill Clinton that many found demeaning.

But many white Democratic voters remained reluctant to support Obama, particularly in Appalachia. Exit polling

during the Pennsylvania primary, for example, showed that 16 percent of whites had considered race in making their pick, with half of those saying they would not support Obama in the fall.[3]

Obama also was bedeviled by videotaped remarks of his pastor, the Rev. Jeremiah Wright, which were incendiary and deemed unpatriotic. But Obama responded with a widely hailed speech on race in March 2008 in which he acknowledged both the grievances of working-class whites and the continuing legacy of economic disadvantages among blacks. Obama said his own life story "has seared into my genetic makeup the idea that this nation is more than the sum of its parts — that out of many, we are truly one."[4]

As the general election campaign got under way, it was clear that race would continue to be a factor. One June poll showed that 30 percent of Americans admit prejudice.[5] And, despite Obama's lead, there was debate throughout the campaign about the so-called Bradley effect — the suggestion that people will lie to pollsters about their true intentions when it comes to black candidates.*

But neither Obama nor Arizona Sen. John McCain, his Republican rival, made explicit pleas based on race, with McCain refusing to air ads featuring Wright. As the campaign wore on, no one forgot that Obama is black — but most doubters put that fact aside in favor of more pressing concerns.

"For a long time, I couldn't ignore the fact that he was black. I'm not proud of that," Joe Sinitski, a 48-year-old Pennsylvania voter, told *The New York Times.* "I was raised to think that there aren't good black people out there."[6] But Sinitski ended up voting for Obama, along with many other whites won over by Obama's personal attributes or convinced that issues such as the economy trumped race.

Exit polls showed that Obama prevailed among those who considered race a significant factor, 53 to 46 percent.[7] "In difficult economic times, people find the price of prejudice is just

---

* The Bradley effect refers to Tom Bradley, an African-American who lost the 1982 race for governor in California despite being ahead in voter polls going into the election.

a little too high," said outgoing North Carolina Gov. Mike Easley, a Democrat.[8]

"The Bradley effect really was not a significant factor, despite much concern, fear and hyperventilation about it leading up to the election," says Scott Keeter, a pollster with the Pew Research Center. "Race was a consideration to people, but what it wasn't, invariably, was a negative consideration for white voters. It was a positive consideration for many white voters who saw Obama as a candidate who could help the country toward racial reconciliation."

Obama carried more white voters than former Vice President Al Gore or Sen. John Kerry of Massachusetts, the two previous Democratic nominees. Still, he could not have prevailed without black and Hispanic voters, particularly in the three Southern states he carried. In Virginia — a state that had voted Republican since 1964 — Obama lost by 21 points among white voters, according to exit polls.

His victory clearly did not bring racial enmity to its end. In December, Chip Saltsman, a candidate for the Republican Party chairmanship, sent potential supporters a CD containing the song "Barack the Magic Negro," a parody popularized by right-wing talk show host Rush Limbaugh during the campaign. And, when Senate Democrats initially balked in January at seating Roland Burris as Obama's replacement, Rep. Bobby Rush, D-Ill, played the race card, warning them not to "hang or lynch the appointee," comparing the move to Southern governors who sought to block desegregation.[9]

But still polls suggest that most Americans believe Obama's presidency will be a boon for race relations. A *USA Today*/Gallup Poll taken the day after the November election showed that two-thirds predicted black-white relations "will eventually be worked out" — by far the highest total in the poll's history.[10]

In the future, white males may no longer be the default inhabitants of America's most powerful position. The present generation and those in the future are likely to grow up thinking it's a normal state of affairs for the country to be led

Michelle Obama holds the Bible used to swear in President Abraham Lincoln as Barack Obama takes the oath of office from Supreme Court Chief Justice John G. Roberts Jr.

AFP/Getty Images/Tim Sloan

by a black president. "For a lot of African-Americans, it already has made them feel better and more positive about the country and American society," says David Bositis, an expert on black voting at the Joint Center for Political and Economic Studies.

"When you ask my kids what they want to be when they grow up, they always say they want to work at McDonald's or Wal-Mart," said Joslyn Reddick, principal at a predominantly black school in Selma, Ala., a city from which King led an historic march for voting rights in 1965.

"Now they will see that an African-American has achieved the highest station in the United States," Reddick said. "They can see for themselves that dreams can come true."[11]

— Alan Greenblatt,
staff writer, *Governing* magazine

[1] Bryan Monroe, "The Audacity of Victory," *Ebony*, January 2009, p. 16.

[2] Sam Fulwood III, "The New Face of America," *Politico.com*, Jan. 13, 2009.

[3] Alan Greenblatt, "Changing U.S. Electorate," *CQ Researcher*, May 30, 2008, p. 459.

[4] The Obama speech, "A More Perfect Union," is at www.youtube.com/watch? v=pWe7wTVbLUU. The text of the March 18, 2008, speech, "A More Perfect Union," is found in *Change We Can Believe In: Barack Obama's Plan to Renew America's Promise* (2008), pp. 215-232.

[5] Jon Cohen and Jennifer Agiesta, "3 in 10 Americans Admit to Race Bias," *The Washington Post*, June 22, 2008, p. A1.

[6] Michael Sokolove," The Transformation," *The New York Times*, Nov. 9, 2008, p. WK1.

[7] John B. Judis, "Did Race Really Matter?" *Los Angeles Times*, Nov. 9, 2008, p. 34.

[8] Rachel L. Swarns, "Vaulting the Racial Divide, Obama Persuaded Americans to Follow," *The New York Times*, Nov. 5, 2008, p. 7.

[9] Clarence Page, "Hiding Behind Black Voters," *Chicago Tribune*, Jan. 4, 2009, p. 24.

[10] Susan Page, "Hopes Are High for Race Relations," *USA Today*, Nov. 7, 2008, p. 1A.

[11] Dahleen Glanton and Howard Witte, "Many Marvel at a Black President," *Chicago Tribune*, Nov. 5, 2008, p. 6.

Cabinet Includes Stars, Superstars and Surprises

President Obama made his Cabinet selections in record time, and his appointees run the gamut of race, ethnic origin, gender, age and even party affiliation. Those in top posts include Sen. Hillary Rodham Clinton at State and Robert Gates continuing at Defense. Besides Gates, one other Republican was chosen: Transportation's Ray LaHood. New Mexico Gov. Bill Richardson's withdrawal left the Commerce post unfilled along with the director of Drug Control Policy. Cabinet-level appointees include four women, two Asian-Americans, two Hispanics and two African-Americans.

Name, Age Department	Date of Nomination	Date of Confirmation	Previous Positions
Hillary Rodham Clinton, 61, State	Dec. 1	Jan. 21	New York U.S. senator (2001-09); first lady (1993-2001); Arkansas first lady (1979-81, 1983-92)
Timothy Geithner, 47, Treasury	Nov. 24	Jan. 26	President, Federal Reserve Bank of New York (2003-09); under secretary, Treasury (1998-2001)
Robert Gates, 65, Defense*	Dec. 1	Dec. 6, 2006 *	Defense secretary (2006-present); director, CIA (1991-93); deputy national security adviser (1989-91)
Eric Holder, 57, Attorney General	Dec. 1		Deputy attorney general (1997-2001); U.S. attorney (1993-97); judge, D.C. Superior Court (1988-93)
Ken Salazar, 53, Interior	Dec. 17	Jan. 20	Colorado U.S. senator (2005-09); Colorado attorney general (1999-2005)
Tom Vilsack, 58, Agriculture	Dec. 17	Jan. 20	Iowa governor (1999-2007); Iowa state senator (1992-99)
Hilda Solis, 51, Labor	Dec. 19		California U.S. representative (2001-09); California state senator (1995-2001)
Tom Daschle, 61, Health & Human Services	Dec. 11		South Dakota U.S. senator (1987-2005); Senate majority leader (2001, 2001-03); South Dakota U.S. representative (1979-87)
Shaun Donovan, 42, Housing and Urban Development	Dec. 13	Jan. 22	Commissioner, New York City Dept. of Housing Preservation and Development (2004-08); deputy assistant secretary, HUD (2000-01)

Obama invited speculation about a shift toward the center by selecting Clinton and Robert Gates as the two Cabinet members on his national security team along with a retired Marine general, James Jones, as national security adviser. (*See chart, left.*) Clinton had voted for the Iraq War in late 2002, though she echoed Obama during the campaign in calling for troop withdrawals. As Bush's secretary of Defense, Gates had overseen the "surge" in U.S. forces during 2007.

"This is a group of people who are very sober, very intelligent, fully aware of the importance of Iraq to America's security interests and of the fragility of the situation there," says Pollack.

Some anti-war activists were voicing concern about Obama's seeming shift within days of his election. "Obama has very successfully branded himself as anti-war, but the fact remains that he's willing to keep a residual force in Iraq indefinitely, [and] he wants to escalate in Afghanistan," said Matthis Chiroux of Iraq Veterans Against the War. "My hope is that he starts bringing home the troops from Iraq immediately, but I think those of us in the anti-war movement could find ourselves disappointed."[3]

Since then, however, criticism of Obama's emerging policies has been virtually non-existent from the anti-war and Democratic Party left. "He seems to be accelerating the withdrawal, which is terrific," says Robert Borosage, co-director of the Campaign for America's Future. Borosage is "concerned" about the residual force in Iraq because of the risk that U.S. troops will become involved in "internecine battles." But he adds, "That's what he's promised, and I think he'll fulfill his promise."

Donnelly and Pollack, however, both view a continuing U.S. role in Iraq as vital. "There's good progress, but a long way to go," says Donnelly. "A huge American role is going to be needed through the four years of the Obama administration." Pollack agrees. "Iraq is far from solved. Whether we like it or not, Iraq is a vital interest for the United States of America."

In his campaign and since, Obama has treated Afghanistan as more important to U.S. interests and harshly criticized the Bush administration for — in his view — ignoring the conflict there. Afghanistan "had had a huge rhetorical place in the Obama campaign," says Donnelly. "The idea being that Afghanistan was the good war, the more important war, and that Iraq was a dead end strategically."

P. J. Crowley, a senior fellow at the liberal think tank Center for American Progress, calls Obama's focus on Afghanistan "correct" but emphasizes the need for a multipronged effort to stabilize and reform the country's U.S.-backed government. "Returning our weight of effort [to Afghanistan] is a right approach," says Crowley, who was spokesman for the National Security Council under President Bill Clinton.

"More troops may help in a narrow sense," Crowley continues, "but I don't think anyone suggests that more troops are the long-term solution in Afghanistan. The insertion of U.S. forces is logical in the short- to mid-term, but it has to be part of a broader strategy."

But Pollack questions the value of any additional U.S. troops at all. "The problems of Afghanistan are not principally military; they are principally political and diplomatic," he says. "Unless this new national security team can create a military mission that is of value to what is ultimately a diplomatic problem, it's going to be tough to justify to the country the commitment of those additional troops."

Name, Age, Department	Date of Nomination	Date of Confirmation	Previous Positions
Ray LaHood, 63, Transportation	Dec. 19	Jan. 22	Illinois U.S. representative (1995-2009); state representative (1982-83)
Steven Chu, 60, Energy	Dec. 15	Jan. 20	Director, Lawrence Berkeley National Laboratory, Dept. of Energy (2004-09); professor, UC-Berkeley (2004-present); Nobel Prize winner, physics (1997)
Arne Duncan, 44, Education	Dec. 16	Jan. 20	C.E.O, Chicago Public Schools (2001-09)
Eric Shinseki, 66, Veterans Affairs	Dec. 7	Jan. 20	Chief of staff, Army (1999-2003)
Janet Napolitano, 51, Homeland Security	Dec. 1	Jan. 20	Arizona governor (2003-09); attorney general (1999-2002)
Rahm Emmanuel, 49, Chief of Staff	Nov. 6	NA	Illinois U.S. representative (2003-09); senior adviser to the president (1993-98)
Lisa Jackson, 46, Environmental Protection Agency	Dec. 15	Jan. 22	Chief of staff, governor of New Jersey (2008-09); commissioner, New Jersey Dept. of Environmental Protection (2006-2008)
Peter Orszag, 40, Office of Management and Budget	Nov. 25	Jan. 20	Director, Congressional Budget Office (2007-08); adviser, National Economic Council (1997-98)
Susan Rice, 44, Ambassador to the United Nations	Dec. 1	Jan. 22	Assistant secretary, State (1997-2001); National Security Council (1993-97)
Ron Kirk, 54, Trade Representative	Dec. 19		Mayor of Dallas (1995-2002)

Department heads are listed in order of succession under Presidential Succession Act; nondepartment heads were given Cabinet-level status.

* Gates was confirmed when first nominated by President George W. Bush and did not have to be re-confirmed.

Compiled by Vyomika Jairam; all photos by Getty Images

Bleak Economy Getting Bleaker

Economists widely agree a stimulus plan is needed.

When Barack Obama took office on Jan. 20, he inherited the most battered U.S. economy since World War II — and one of the shakiest to confront a new president in American history.

And the view from the Oval Office is likely to get bleaker before the gloom begins to lift.

"There are very serious questions on the financial side and apprehension among many parties that there may be more bad news to come," says Kent Hughes, director of the Program on Science, Technology, America and the Global Economy at the Woodrow Wilson Center for Scholars.

Already, Obama has stepped into the worst unemployment picture in 16 years, with the jobless rate at 7.2 percent and 11.1 million people out of work. The economy lost 1.9 million jobs during the last four months of 2008 — 524,000 in December alone.[1]

Economists worry that rising unemployment in manufacturing, construction, retailing and other sectors foreshadows an even more dismal future, at the very least in the short term. Dean Baker, co-director for the Center for Economic and Policy Research, a liberal think tank in Washington, says he expects another million or so jobs to disappear through February, then the pace of job loss to slow if Congress acts to stimulate the economy.

Obama must figure out not only how to get people back to work but also how to restore their confidence in the economy. A punishing credit crisis and cascade of grim news from Wall Street has led consumers to stop spending on everything from restaurant meals to houses and autos.[2]

Home sales have plunged in recent months, foreclosures are hitting record levels and a study by PMI Mortgage Insurance Co. estimates that half of the nation's 50-largest Metropolitan Statistical Areas have an "elevated or high probability" of experiencing lower home prices by the end of the third quarter of 2010 compared to the same quarter of 2008.[3]

Retail sales, a key indicator of consumer confidence, fell in December 2008 for the sixth month in a row, according to the Commerce Department.[4] The International Council of Shopping Centers said chain-store sales in December posted their biggest year-to-year decline since researchers began tracking figures in 1970.[5]

Rebecca Blank, a senior fellow at the Brookings Institution and former member of President Bill Clinton's Council of Economic Advisers, says the unemployment numbers "suggest the economy is still on the way down," and the decline in holiday sales is "surely going to lead to some bankruptcies and belt tightening in the retail sector."

Indeed, such trouble is already occurring. The shopping centers group estimated that 148,000 retail stores closed last year and that more than 73,000 will be shuttered in the first half of 2009.[6] Among the latest examples: Bankrupt electronics chain Circuit City said in January that it was closing its remaining 567 stores, putting some 30,000 employees out of work.

To revive the economy, the new administration — most visibly Obama himself — is urging Congress to quickly approve a stimulus package that could approach $900 billion. Much of the money would likely go toward tax cuts and public infrastructure projects, though how, exactly, the government would allocate it remains a matter of intense political debate.

One thing seems certain, though: The cost of a stimulus package, added to the hundreds of billions of dollars already spent to shore up the nation's flagging financial system, will add to the bulging federal deficit.

"The thing you know for sure is that a stimulus is going to add to the debt, which is [now] quite frightening, and it's going to make it worse," says June O'Neill, an economics professor at the City University of New York's Baruch College

Borosage also worries about an increased U.S. military presence in Afghanistan. "A permanent occupation of Afghanistan is a recipe for defeat," he says.

All of the experts stress that U.S. policy in Afghanistan now plays a secondary part in the fight with the al Qaeda terrorist group, which carried out the 9/11 attacks in the United States. "There is no al Qaeda in Afghanistan," says Donnelly. "Al Qaeda has now reconstituted itself in the tribal areas of northwest Pakistan."

Donnelly questions Afghanistan's importance to U.S. interests altogether but ultimately supports continued U.S. involvement. "The only thing worse than being engaged in Afghanistan," he says, "is turning our backs on it."

and a former director of the Congressional Budget Office (CBO) during the Clinton administration.

In January the CBO projected a $1.2 trillion deficit for the fiscal year. A stimulus plan would add even more pressure on Obama to get federal spending under control. "My own economic and budget team projects that, unless we take decisive action, even after our economy pulls out of its slide, trillion-dollar deficits will be a reality for years to come," Obama said.[7]

Still, a wide spectrum of economists — including conservatives who typically look askance at government spending — agree that a stimulus plan is necessary.

Martin Feldstein, a Harvard University economist and former chair of the Council of Economic Advisers in the Reagan administration, told a House committee in January that stopping the economic slide and restoring "sustainable growth" requires fixing the housing crisis and adopting a "fiscal stimulus of reduced taxes and increased government spending."[8]

Feldstein pointed out that past recessions started after the Federal Reserve raised short-term interest rates to fight inflation. Once inflation was under control, the Fed cut rates, which spurred a recovery. But the current recession is different, Feldstein said: It wasn't caused by the Fed tightening up on fiscal policy, and thus rate cuts haven't succeeded in reviving the economy.

"Because of the dysfunctional credit markets and the collapse of housing demand, monetary policy has had no traction in its attempt to lift the economy," he said.

That poses an especially daunting challenge for Obama.

Baker of the Center for Economic and Policy Research says that the current crisis, occurring amid a broad collapse

The battered economy that confronts President Obama includes record foreclosure rates and plummeting home values. Above, a foreclosed home in Nevada, the state with the nation's highest foreclosure rate.

Getty Images/Ethan Miller

of the financial markets, more closely resembles the Great Depression than any other recession since then.

Most postwar recessions "were the result of the Fed raising rates," says Baker. "That meant we knew how to reverse it. This one, there's not an easy answer to. We're not going to see [another] Great Depression — not double-digit unemployment for a decade." But in terms of the severity of the problem, Baker adds, the Great Depression is the "closest match" to what confronts the new administration.

— Thomas J. Billitteri

[1] Bureau of Labor Statistics, "Employment Situation Summary," Jan. 9, 2009, www.bls.gov/news.release/empsit.nr0.htm.

[2] For coverage of the economic crisis, see the following *CQ Researcher* reports: Thomas J. Billitteri, "Financial Bailout," Oct. 24, 2008, pp. 865-888; Kenneth Jost, "Financial Crisis," May 9, 2008, pp. 409-432; Marcia Clemmitt, "Regulating Credit Cards," Oct. 10, 2008, pp. 817-840; and Marcia Clemmitt, "The National Debt," Nov. 14, 2008, pp. 937-960.

[3] News release, "PMI Winter 2009 Risk Index Indicates Broader Risk Spreading Across Nation's Housing Markets," PMI Mortgage Insurance Co., Jan. 14, 2009.

[4] Bob Willis, "U.S. Economy: Retail Sales Decline for a Sixth Month," Bloomberg, Jan. 14, 2009, www.bloomberg.com.

[5] V. Dion Haynes and Howard Schneider, "A Brutal December for Retailers," *The Washington Post*, Jan. 9, 2009, p. 2D.

[6] *Ibid.*

[7] Quoted in David Stout and Edmund L. Andrews, "$1.2 Trillion Deficit Forecast as Obama Weighs Options," *The New York Times*, Jan. 8, 2009, www.nytimes.com/2009/01/08/business/economy/08deficit.html?scp=2&sq=deficit&st=cse.

[8] Martin Feldstein, "The Economic Stimulus and Sustained Economic Growth," statement to the House Democratic Steering and Policy Committee, Jan. 7, 2009, www.nber.org/feldstein/EconomicStimulusandEconomicGrowthStatement.pdf.

Is President Obama on the right track in winning support for his programs in Congress?

As president of Harvard University, Lawrence Summers clashed so often and so sharply with faculty and others that he was forced out after only five years in office. But when Summers went to Capitol Hill as President-elect Obama's

designee to be top White House economic adviser, the normally self-assured economist told lawmakers that he and other administration officials plan to be all ears.

"All of us have been instructed that when it comes to Congress, to listen and not just talk," Summers told House Democrats in a Jan. 9 meeting to discuss Obama's economic recovery plan.[4]

State Department staffers greet new Secretary of State Hillary Rodham Clinton on her first day of work, Jan. 22, 2009.

Within days after the new Congress was sworn in on Jan. 6, however, lawmakers on both sides of the political aisle were, in fact, taking pot shots at Obama's plan. Republicans were calling for hearings after the plan was unveiled — a move seen as jeopardizing Obama's goal of signing a stimulus bill into law before Congress' mid-February recess. Meanwhile, some Democratic lawmakers were questioning the business tax cuts being considered for the package, calling them examples of what they considered the discredited philosophy of "trickle-down economics."

Despite the criticisms, Obama was upbeat about his relations with Congress in an interview broadcast on ABC's "This Weekend" on Jan. 11. "One of the things that we're trying to set a tone of is that, you know, Congress is a co-equal branch of government," Obama told host George Stephanopoulos. "We're not trying to jam anything down people's throats."

Veteran Congress-watchers in Washington are giving Obama high marks in his dealings with Capitol Hill so far, while also praising Congress for asserting its own constitutional prerogatives.

"Obama is off to a very good start with Congress, and, just as importantly, Congress is off to a good start with him," says Thomas Mann, a senior fellow at the Brookings Institution. "No more [status as a] potted plant for the first branch or an inflated sense of presidential authority by the second, but instead a serious engagement between the players at the opposite ends of Pennsylvania Avenue."

Obama is "in good shape," says Stephen Hess, a senior fellow emeritus at Brookings who began his Washington career as a White House staffer under President Dwight D. Eisenhower in the 1950s. Hess credits Obama in particular with seeking to consult with Republican as well as Democratic lawmakers.

"He was very shrewd after talking with Democrats to talk with Republicans," says Hess, who also teaches at George Washington University. "He has given the opposition the sense that he's open, he's listening. He's reached out to them when he doesn't need them — which of course is the right time to reach out to them."

Norman Ornstein, a resident scholar at the American Enterprise Institute, similarly credits Obama with having gone "further in consulting members of the opposition party than any president I can remember." Writing in the Capitol Hill newspaper *Roll Call*, Ornstein also said Obama is well aware of lawmakers' "issues and sensitivities." For example, Ornstein noted the president-elect's personal apology to Senate Intelligence Committee Chair Dianne Feinstein, D-Calif., for failing to give her advance word in early January of the planned nomination of Leon Panetta to head the Central Intelligence Agency.[5]

The lapse of protocol on the Panetta nomination — which Feinstein later promised to support — may well have been the only avoidable misstep by the Obama team in its dealings with Congress. Criticisms of the economic recovery program as it took shape could hardly have been avoided. And Republican senators naturally looked for ways to find fault with some of Obama's Cabinet nominees — such as their criticism of Attorney General-designate Eric Holder for his role in President Clinton's pardon of fugitive financier Marc Rich and Treasury Secretary-designate Timothy Geithner for his late payment of tens of thousands of dollars in federal income taxes.

A prominent, retired GOP congressman, however, says Obama is doing well so far and predicts the economic crisis may give him a longer than usual pass with lawmakers from both parties. "He has the advantage of a honeymoon, and perhaps the second advantage of the economic conditions of the country, which I think will help the Congress to gather around his program," says Bill Frenzel, a guest scholar at the Brookings Institution and a Minnesota congressman for two decades before his retirement in 1991.

Big-Name Policy 'Czars' Head for West Wing

Appointments may signal decline in Cabinet's influence.

President Barack Obama has tapped several high-profile Washington insiders to fill new and existing senior White House positions, indicating the new administration is shifting policy making from the Cabinet to the influential White House West Wing.

The new so-called policy "czars" include former Sen. Tom Daschle, D-S.D., at the Office of Health Reform (he is also Health and Human Services secretary); former assistant Treasury secretary Nancy Killefer, leading efforts to cut government waste as the nation's first chief performance officer; former Environmental Protection Agency Administrator Carol Browner as the new coordinator of energy and climate policy; and former New York City Council member Adolfo Carrion Jr., who is expected to head the Office of Urban Affairs.

"We're going to have so many czars," said Thomas J. Donohue, president of the U.S. Chamber of Commerce. "It's going to be a lot of fun, seeing the czars and the regulators and the czars and the Cabinet secretaries debate."[1]

In another major West Wing appointment, former Treasury secretary and Harvard President Lawrence Summers becomes director of the existing National Economic Council. In the weeks leading up to the inauguration, analysts noted that Summers, and not then-Treasury secretary-designate Timothy Geithner, was leading then-President-elect Obama's efforts to draft a new financial stimulus package.

But Paul Light, an expert on governance at New York University, questions the role the new "czars" will play. "It's a symbolic gesture of the priority assigned to an issue, and I emphasize the word symbolic," he said. "There've been so many czars over the last 50 years, and they've all been failures. Nobody takes them seriously anymore."[2]

— Vyomika Jairam

---

[1] Michael D. Shear and Ceci Connolly, "Obama Assembles Powerful West Wing; Influential Advisers May Compete With Cabinet," *The Washington Post*, Jan. 14, 2009, p. A1.

[2] Laura Meckler " 'Czars' Ascend at White House," *The Wall Street Journal*, Dec. 15, 2005, p. A6.

"We're talking about both Republicans and Democrats," Frenzel continues. "Democrats are going to want to be independent, and Republicans are going to want to take whacks at him when they can. But I think there is a mood of wanting to help the president when they can for a while."

Ornstein and Hess caution, however, that new presidents cannot expect the honeymoon to last very long. Ornstein writes that Obama's hoped-for supermajority support in Congress "may be doable on stimulus" and "perhaps even on health care." But he says an era of "post-partisan politics" will require "some serious steps" by party leaders and rank-and-file members.

For his part, Hess says Obama may eventually begin to disappoint some within his own party — but not yet. "Democrats will for a while cut him a great deal of slack," Hess explains. "Reason No. 1, he's not George W. Bush. Reason No. 2, they're going to get some of what they want. And reason No. 3, some of those folks have become wiser about the way politics is played in this town."

BACKGROUND

'A Mutt, Like Me'

Barack Obama's inauguration as president represents a 21st-century version of the American dream: the election of a native-born citizen, both black and white, with roots in Kansas and Kenya. Abandoned by his father and later living apart from his mother, Obama was nurtured in his formative years by doting white grandparents and educated in elite schools before turning to community organizing in inner-city Chicago and then to a political career that moved from the Illinois statehouse to the White House in barely 12 years.[6]

Barack Hussein Obama was born in Honolulu on Aug. 4, 1961, to parents he later described in his memoir *Dreams from My Father* as a "white as vanilla" American mother and a "black as pitch" Kenyan father. Barack Obama Sr. and Stanley Ann Dunham married, more or less secretly, after having met as students at the University of Hawaii. Stanley Ann's "moderately liberal" parents

CHRONOLOGY: 1961-2006

1960s-1970s *Obama born to biracial, binational couple; begins education in Indonesia after mother's remarriage, then returns to Hawaii.*

1961 Barack Hussein Obama born on Aug. 4, 1961, in Honolulu; parents Stanley Ann Dunham and Barack Obama Sr. meet as students at University of Hawaii; father leaves family behind two years later for graduate studies at Harvard, return to native Kenya.

1967-1971 Obama's mother remarries, family moves to Indonesia; Obama attends a secular public elementary school with a predominantly Muslim student body until mother decides he should return to Hawaii for schooling.

1971-1979 "Barry" Obama lives with grandparents Stanley and Madelyn Dunham; graduates with honors from Punahou School, one of three black students at the elite private school; enrolls in Occidental College in Los Angeles but transfers later to Columbia University in New York City.

1980s-1990s *Works as community organizer in Chicago, gets law degree, enters politics.*

1983 Obama graduates with degree in political science from Columbia University; floods civil rights organizations with job applications.

1985-1988 Works on housing, employment issues as community organizer in Far South Side neighborhood in Chicago.

Summer 1988 Visits Kenya for first time.

1988-1991 Enrolls in Harvard Law School in fall 1988; graduates in 1991 after serving as president of Harvard Law Review — the first African-American to hold that position.

1992-1995 Returns to Chicago; marries Michelle Robinson in 1992; runs voter registration project; works as lawyer, lecturer at University of Chicago Law School.

1995 Dreams from My Father is published; mother dies just after publication (Nov. 7, 1995).

1996 Elected to Illinois legislature as senator representing Chicago's Hyde Park area; serves for eight years.

2000-2006 *Enters national political stage as U.S. senator, Democratic keynoter.*

2000 Loses badly in Democratic primary for U.S. House seat held by Rep. Bobby Rush.

2002 Opposes then-imminent war in Iraq.

2004 Gains Democratic nomination for U.S. Senate from Illinois. . . . Wins wide praise for keynote address to Democratic National Convention. . . . Elected U.S. senator from Illinois: third African-American to serve in Senate since Reconstruction.

2005-2006 Earns reputation as hard worker in Senate; compiles liberal voting record; manages Democrats' initiative on ethics reform. . . . Audacity of Hope is published (October 2006). . . . Deflects intense speculation about possible presidential bid.

accepted the union. In Kenya — where Barack Sr. already had a wife and child — the family did not. The marriage lasted only two years; Barack left his wife and child behind to go to graduate school at Harvard. Stanley Ann filed for divorce, citing standard legal grounds.

His mother's second marriage, to an Indonesian student, Lolo Soetoro, took young Barry, as he was then called, to his Muslim stepfather's native country at the age of 6. Lolo worked as a geologist in post-colonial Indonesia; his mother taught English. They had a child, Obama's half-sister, Maya. (Maya Soetoro-Ng now teaches high school

history in Honolulu.) Barry attended a predominantly Muslim school that would be falsely depicted as an Islamist madrassa during the 2008 campaign. His mother, meanwhile, taught her son about the civil rights struggles in America and eventually sent him back to Hawaii for schooling. The marriage ended later, a victim of cultural and personality differences.

Barry returned to live with grandparents Stanley and Madelyn Dunham — "Gramps" and "Toot" (her nickname came from the Hawaiian word for grandmother). They provided him the stable, supportive home life that he had

CHRONOLOGY: 2007 - PRESENT

2007 *Obama enters presidential race as underdog to New York Sen. Hillary Rodham Clinton; nearly matches Clinton in "money primary" in advance of Iowa caucuses.*

Feb. 10, 2007 Obama announces candidacy for Democratic nomination for president at rally in Springfield, Ill., three weeks after Clinton, former first lady, joined race; Democratic field eventually includes eight candidates.

March-December 2007 Democratic candidates engage in 17 debates, with no knockout punches; Obama closes gap with Clinton in polls, fundraising.

2008 *Obama gains Democratic nomination after drawn-out contest with Clinton; beats Republican Sen. John McCain as economic issues take center stage.*

January-February Obama scores upset in Iowa caucuses (Jan. 3); Clinton wins New Hampshire primary (Jan. 9); field narrows to two candidates by end of January.

March-April Clinton wins big-state primaries, including Ohio (March 4) and Pennsylvania (April 22); Obama edges ahead in delegates.

May-June Obama gains irreversible lead after Indiana, North Carolina primaries (May 6); clinches nomination after final primaries (June 2).

July Obama goes to Iraq, reaffirms 16-month pullout timetable; speaks at big rally in Berlin, Germany.

August Obama picks Delaware Sen. Joseph R. Biden as running mate; accepts nomination with speech promising

Iraq withdrawal, domestic initiatives; McCain chooses Alaska Gov. Sarah Palin as running mate.

September-October Obama holds his own in three debates with McCain (Sept. 26, Oct. 7, Oct. 15); McCain challenge to go to Washington to push financial bailout plan ends with advantage to Obama.

Nov. 4 Obama victory is signaled with victories in "red states" in East, Midwest; networks declare him winner as polls close in West (11 p.m., Eastern time).

November-December Obama completes Cabinet selections; works on economic recovery plan; vacations in Hawaii.

2009 *Obama inaugurated before largest crowd in Washington history.*

Jan. 5-19 Obama, in Washington, starts public campaign for economic recovery plan. . . . Congress reconvenes with Democrats holding 256-178 majority in House with one vacancy, 57-41 majority in Senate with two seats vacant. . . . More high-level nominations; Commerce post in limbo after Bill Richardson withdraws because of ethics investigation in New Mexico.

Jan. 20 Obama is inaugurated as 44th president; uses inaugural address to detail "serious" challenges at home, abroad; promises that challenges "will be met." . . . President moves quickly over next week to reverse some Bush administration policies; lobbies Congress on economic stimulus package, but Republicans continue to push for less spending, more tax cuts.

---

somewhat lacked so far. He gained admission to the prestigious Punahou School as one of only three black students. His father visited once — Barack's only time spent with him after the divorce — and spoke to one of his son's classes about life in Africa. Obama's mother came back to Hawaii for studies in anthropology, but when she returned to Indonesia for field work Barack chose to stay in Hawaii.

At Punahou, Obama excelled as a student and played with the state championship basketball team his senior year. He graduated in 1979 and enrolled at Occidental

College in Los Angeles. Two years later, he transferred to Columbia University in New York. By now, Obama was well aware of racial issues in the United States — and his ambiguous place in the story. "I learned to slip back and forth between my black and white worlds," he wrote in *Dreams from My Father.* More recently, as president-elect, Obama referred self-deprecatingly to his background. In describing the kind of puppy he would have preferred to get for his two young daughters, but for Malia's allergies, Obama said, "A mutt, like me."

Myriad Global Problems Confront Obama

Two wars, the Middle East and terrorism top the list.

President Barack Obama faces immense foreign-policy challenges — two wars and a turbulent global scene that includes continuing conflict in the Middle East — all against the backdrop of a global economic crisis.

Tens of thousands of U.S. troops are at war in Iraq and Afghanistan. Israel, America's closest Mideast ally, has just suspended a devastating military offensive in the Gaza Strip that could restart at any time. And Islamist terrorism remains a constant threat, with al Qaeda leader Osama bin Laden still at large.[1]

Obama divided his early days in office between wartime matters, the latest Mideast crisis and the economic meltdown. By all indications, he will be walking a tightrope between domestic and international affairs for the forseeable future.

"A president in these circumstances is going to want to do everything possible to ensure that the transformative and ambitious and very difficult projects of domestic policy that have been designated as the priority for this new administration are not inhibited or disrupted by early failures, in counterterrorism or foreign policy," Steve Coll, president and CEO of the New America Foundation, a nonpartisan think tank, told a pre-inauguration conference on security issues.

Obama's inaugural address restated his commitment to withdraw U.S. forces from Iraq, which is more peaceful after more than five years of war but still violent and torn by political intrigue.[2]

In Afghanistan, however, escalating warfare is tied to another source of U.S. worries: Pakistan. Concern escalated in late November following coordinated terrorist attacks on hotels and other sites in Mumbai — India's financial and cultural capital — which were traced to a jihadist group in Pakistan with deep ties to that country's intelligence agency.[3] Some 175 people were killed and 200 wounded.

The group, Lashkar-e-Taiba, also has at least some operational link to al Qaeda and bin Laden, who is believed to be hiding in Pakistan's northern tribal region, bordering Afghanistan. Another al Qaeda ally, the Taliban guerrillas who are fighting the Afghan government and U.S.

and NATO troops in Afghanistan, use Pakistan as a headquarters.[4]

"Moreover," a government commission on weapons of mass destruction and terrorism said in December, "given Pakistan's tense relationship with India, its buildup of nuclear weapons is exacerbating the prospect of a dangerous nuclear arms race in South Asia that could lead to a nuclear conflict."[5]

The other daunting foreign-policy issue facing the new Obama administration — conflict between Israel and the Palestinians — offers slender prospects for peace. "Two states living side by side in peace and security — right now that stands about as much chance as Bozo the Clown becoming president of the United States," says Aaron David Miller, a former Mideast peace adviser to six secretaries of State.

The biggest obstacle, Miller says, is the "broken and dysfunctional" state of the Palestinian national movement. Fatah, the secular party that runs the West Bank, has a negotiating relationship with Israel. Hamas, the elected Islamist party and militia that initially seized power in an anti-Fatah coup in Gaza in 2007, deems Israel illegitimate. Hamas sponsored or tolerated rocket fire into Israel from Gaza but halted rocketing at the beginning of a cease-fire that began in June 2008. But Israel accused Hamas of building up its arsenal and retaliated by limiting the flow of goods into the region. In December, Hamas announced it wouldn't renew the already shaky truce, blaming the Israeli embargo and military moves. From then on, Hamas stepped up rocketing.

Israel's recent 22-day anti-Hamas offensive in Gaza cost some 1,300 Palestinian lives. The Palestinians estimated the civilian death toll at 40 percent to 70 percent of the fatalities; Israel put the toll at about 25 percent of the total. Israeli fatalities totaled 13, including three civilians.[6]

The scale of Israel's Gaza offensive is renewing calls for the U.S. government to change its relationship to Israel. "The days of America's exclusive ties to Israel may be coming to an end," Miller wrote in *Newsweek* in January. Obama, however, reaffirmed his support for Israel in his Jan. 26 interview with the Arabic-language network Al Arabiya.[7]

Those interests also would require devising a response to what the United States believes is a nuclear arms development project by Iran, which supports Hamas politically and financially — a sign, for some, of how all Middle Eastern issues are interconnected.

"One of the great mistakes we have made has been to believe we can compartmentalize these different policies, that we can somehow separate what is happening between Israel and the Palestinians from what's happening in Iraq and what's happening in Iran and what's happening in Egypt and Saudi Arabia and everywhere else in the Middle East," said Kenneth M. Pollack, a senior fellow at the Brookings Institution and former CIA analyst of the region. "Linkage is a reality."[8]

Another set of connections ties past U.S. support for NATO membership by Ukraine and Georgia to chilled U.S. relations with Russia, which views the potential presence of Western military allies — and U.S. missiles — on its borders as hostile.

Despite the Cold War echoes of that dispute, some foreign-affairs experts argue that Obama actually confronts a less perilous international panorama than some of his recent predecessors. "We don't have the Cold War and World War II," says Michael Mandelbaum, director of the foreign policy program at Johns Hopkins University's School of Advanced International Studies. "Those were existential threats. What the incoming president faces are annoying and troublesome, but not existential threats."

That picture could change if jihadist radicals took over nuclear-armed Pakistan. For now, Mandelbaum argues the biggest international and domestic dangers are one and the same — the economic meltdown.

But success for the huge spending package that Obama wants will require participation by China, America's major creditor. "China has been lending us money by buying our bonds," Mandelbaum says. "That huge stimulus package is not going to work unless we get some cooperation from the Chinese."

Palestinians in Gaza search the rubble of their homes for usable items after an Israeli air strike on Jan. 5, 2009.

Getty Images/Ethan Miller

In short, the American way of life very much depends on China, Mandelbaum says: "For what Americans care about, for what matters in the world, the issue of where and how we borrow money for the stimulus and where and how we rebalance the economy dwarfs Gaza in importance, and is more important than Iraq and Afghanistan."

— Peter Katel

[1] For coverage of the Iraq and Afghanistan wars, the Middle East and Islamic fundamentalism, see the following *CQ Researcher* reports: Peter Katel, "Cost of the Iraq War," April 25, 2008, pp. 361-384; Peter Katel, "New Strategy in Iraq," Feb. 23, 2007, pp. 169-192; and Peter Katel, "Middle East Tension," Oct. 27, 2006, pp. 889-912. Also see the following *CQ Global Researcher* reports: Roland Flamini, "Afghanistan on the Brink," June 2007, pp. 125-150; Robert Kiener, "Crisis in Pakistan," December 2008, pp. 321-348; and Sarah Glazer, "Radical Islam in Europe," November 2007, pp. 265-294.

[2] Alissa J. Rubin, "Iraq Unsettled by Political Power Plays," *The New York Times*, Dec. 25, 2008, www.nytimes.com/2008/12/26/world/middleeast/26baghdad.html; and Alissa J. Rubin, "Bombs Kill 5 in Baghdad, but Officials Avoid Harm," *The New York Times*, Jan. 20, 2009, www.nytimes.com/2009/01/21/world/middleeast/21iraq.html.

[3] Jane Perlez and Somini Sengupta, "Mumbai Attack is Test for Pakistan on Curbing Militants," *The New York Times*, Dec. 3, 2008, www.nytimes.com/2008/12/04/world/asia/04pstan.html?scp=5&sq=Mumbai Lashkar ISI&st=cse.

[4] For a summary and analysis, see K. Alan Kronstadt and Kenneth Katzman, "Islamist Militancy in the Pakistan-Afghanistan Border Region and U.S. Policy," Congressional Research Service, Nov. 21, 2008, http://fpc.state.gov/documents/organization/113202.pdf.

[5] See "World at Risk," Commission on the Prevention of Weapons of Mass Destruction Proliferation and Terrorism, December 2008, p. xxiii.

[6] See Steven Erlanger, "Weighing Crimes and Ethics in the Fog of Urban Warfare," *The New York Times*, Jan. 16, 2009, www.nytimes.com/2009/01/17/world/middleeast/17israel.html?scp=1&sq=Gaza civilian death percent&st=cse; Amy Teibel, "Last Israeli troops leave Gaza, completing pullout," The Associated Press, Jan. 21, 2009, http://news.yahoo.com/s/ap/ml_israel_palestinians.

[7] Aaron David Miller, "If Obama Is Serious, He should get tough with Israel," *Newsweek*, Jan. 3, 2009, www.newsweek.com/id/177716.

[8] Quoted in Adam Graham-Silverman, "Conflict in Gaza Strip Presents Immediate Challenge for New President," *CQ Today*, Jan. 20, 2009.

Barack Obama's riveting, highly personal keynote address at the 2004 Democratic National Convention made him an overnight star and presidential contender.

Graduating from Columbia in 1983 with a degree in political science, Obama decided to take on the so-called Reagan revolution by becoming a community organizer — aiming, as he wrote, to bring about "change . . . from a mobilized grass roots." Obama flooded civil rights organizations to no avail until he was hired in 1985 by Gerald Kellman, a white organizer looking for an African-American to help with community development and mobilization in a Far South Side section of Chicago. Obama's three years in Chicago brought him face to face with the gritty realities of urban life and the disillusionment of the disadvantaged. He later described the time as "the best education I ever had."[7]

Obama enrolled in Harvard Law School in 1988.[8] He wrote nothing about the decision in his memoir and has said little about it elsewhere. Before going, he visited Kenya, where his father had died in an automobile accident six years earlier. Obama described enjoying the meeting with his extended family while acutely conscious of the cultural gap. At Harvard, he excelled as a student, played pick-up basketball and had only a limited social life after meeting his future wife, Michelle Robinson, a lawyer he had met while working for a Chicago law firm as a summer associate. His election in 1990 as president of the *Harvard Law Review* — as a compromise between conservative and liberal factions — marked the first time an African-American had held the prestigious position.

His barrier-breaking gained enough attention to get Obama an invitation from a literary agent, Jane Dystel, to write a book.[9] Obama planned to write about race relations, but in the three years of writing it turned into more of a personal memoir. Obama has said he was unmindful of political consequences in the writing and that he rejected a suggestion from one of his editors to delete references to drug use while in college. The book garnered respectable reviews — and the audio version won a Grammy — but no more than middling sales. Obama's mother read page proofs and lived just long enough to see it published. She died of ovarian cancer in November 1995.[10]

Red, Blue and Purple

Obama needed only 10 years to rise from the back benches of the Illinois legislature to a front seat on the national political stage. His political ambition misled him only once: in a failed run for the U.S. House. But he succeeded in other endeavors on the strength of hard work, personal intelligence, political acumen and earnest efforts to bridge the differences of race, class and partisan affiliation.

Obama entered politics in 1995 as the chosen successor of a one-term state senator, Alice Palmer. But he turned on his mentor when she sought re-election after all, following a losing bid in a special election for a U.S. House seat. Obama successfully challenged signatures on Palmer's nominating petitions and had her disqualified (and the other candidates too) to win the Democratic nomination unopposed and eventual election.

As a Democrat in a Republican-controlled legislature and a liberal with no connection to his party's organization, Obama worked to develop personal ties — some formed in a weekly poker game. Among his accomplishments: ethics legislation, a state earned-income tax credit and a measure, backed by law enforcement, to require videotaped interrogations in all capital cases.[11]

After four years in office, Obama decided in 2000 to mount a primary challenge to the popular and much better known Democratic congressman, Bobby Rush. The race was foolhardy from the outset. But — as Obama recounts in his second book, *The Audacity of Hope* — he suffered a grave embarrassment when he failed to return from a family vacation in Hawaii in time to vote on a major gun control bill in a specially called legislative session. Rush won handily.[12] In the 2008 presidential campaign, Obama's absence on the gun control vote was cited along with many other instances when he voted "present" as evidence of risk-averse gamesmanship on his part — a depiction vigorously disputed by the campaign.

His ambition unquenched, Obama began deciding by fall 2002 to run for the U.S. Senate seat then held by Republican Peter Fitzgerald, a vulnerable incumbent who eventually decided not to seek re-election. In October, at the invitation of a peace activist group, he delivered to an anti-war rally in Chicago his now famous speech opposing the then-imminent U.S. war in Iraq. Obama formally entered the Senate race in 2003 as the underdog to multimillionaire Blair Hull and state Comptroller Dan Hynes. But Hull's candidacy collapsed after allegations of abuse against his ex-wife. Hynes ran a lackluster campaign, while Obama waged a determined, disciplined drive that netted him nearly 53 percent of the vote in a seven-way race.[13]

Obama's debut on the national stage came in July 2004 after the presumptive Democratic presidential nominee, Massachusetts Sen. John Kerry, picked him to deliver the keynote address at the party's convention. Obama drafted the speech himself, according to biographer David Mendell. The night before, he told a friend, "My speech is pretty good." It was better than that. Obama wove his personal story together with verbal images of working-class America to lead up to the passage — rebroadcast thousands of times since — envisioning a unified nation instead of the "pundits' " image of monochromatic "Red States" and "Blue States." The speech "electrified the convention hall," *The Washington Post* reported the next day, and made Obama a rising star to be watched.[14]

By the time of the speech, political fortune had already shone on Obama back in Illinois. Divorce files of his Republican opponent in the Senate race, Jack Ryan, made public in June, showed that Ryan had pressured his wife to go with him to sex clubs and have sex in front of others. Ryan, a multimillionaire businessman, resisted pressure to withdraw for more than a month. Once Ryan bowed out — three days after Obama's speech — GOP leaders had to scramble for an opponent. They eventually lured Alan Keyes, a conservative African-American from Maryland, to be the sacrificial lamb in the race. Obama won with a record-setting 70 percent of the vote to take his seat in January 2005 as only the third African-American to serve in the U.S. Senate since Reconstruction.

Obama entered the Senate with the presidency on his mind but also the recognition that he must succeed first in a club with low tolerance for celebrity without substance. A profile in Congressional Quarterly's *Politics in America* published with his presidential campaign under way in 2007 credited Obama with "a reputation as a hard worker, a good listener and a quick study."[15]

With Democrats in the majority, Obama was designated in 2007 to spearhead the party's work on ethics reform — a role that prompted an icy exchange with his future opponent, Sen. McCain, who had expected to work with Democrats on a bipartisan approach. The eventual package included a ban on senators' discounted trips on corporate jets, but not — as Obama had pushed for — outside enforcement of ethics rules.

Obama had more success working with other Republicans, including Oklahoma's Tom Coburn (Internet access to government databases) and Indiana's Richard Lugar (international destruction of conventional weapons). Overall, however, his voting record was solidly liberal and reliably party-line. In the 2008 race, the McCain campaign repeatedly tried to debunk Obama's image of post-partisanship by challenging him to cite a significant example of departing from Democratic Party positions.

'Yes, We Can'

Obama won the Democratic nomination for president in a come-from-behind victory over frontrunner Hillary Clinton on the strength of fundraising prowess, message control and a pre-convention strategy focused on amassing delegates in caucus as well as primary states. He took an even bigger financial advantage into the general election but pulled away from McCain only after the nation's dire economic news in October drove the undecideds decisively toward the candidate promising "change we can believe in."[16]

Despite intense speculation and Obama's evident interest, he decided to run only after heart-to-heart talks with Michelle while vacationing in Hawaii in December 2006. Michelle's reluctance stemmed from the effects on the family and fear for Obama's personal safety. In the end, she agreed — with one stipulation: Obama had to give up smoking. That promise remains a work in progress. In his post-election appearance on NBC's "Meet the Press" on Dec. 7, Obama promised only that, "you will not see any violations" of the White House's no-smoking rule while he is president.

Daschle Appointment Shows Commitment to Health-Care Reforms

But a vote on a specific plan may be delayed until next year.

"The flaws in our health system are pervasive and corrosive. They threaten our health and economic security," said former Sen. Tom Daschle, D-S.D., President Obama's nominee for secretary of Health and Human Services (HHS), at his initial confirmation hearing before the Senate Health, Education, Labor, and Pensions (HELP) Committee on Jan. 8.[1]

Throughout his campaign, Obama promised to make good-quality health care accessible to all Americans. Many observers see his choice of Daschle — who recently coauthored a book laying out a plan for universal insurance coverage — to lead both HHS and a new White House Office of Health Policy as a sign of the new president's commitment to health-care reform, which he has called the key to economic security.[2] "I talk to hardworking Americans every day who worry about paying their medical bills and getting and keeping health insurance for their families," Obama said.[3]

In the final presidential debate on Oct. 15, 2008, Obama laid out the essence of his health overhaul. "If you've got health insurance through your employer, you can keep your health insurance," he said. "If you don't have health insurance, then what we're going to do is to provide you the option of buying into the same kind of federal pool [of private insurance plans] that [Republican presidential nominee] Sen. McCain and I enjoy as federal employees, which will give you high-quality care, choice of doctors at lower costs, because so many people are part of this insured group," Obama said.[4]

In addition, Obama's plan would:

- require insurance companies to accept all applicants, including those with already diagnosed illnesses — or

"preexisting conditions" — that insurers often decline to cover;

- create a federally regulated national "health insurance exchange" where people could buy coverage from a range of approved private insurers and possibly from a public insurance program as well;
- provide subsidies to help lower-income people buy coverage;
- require all children to have health insurance; and
- require employers except small businesses to either provide "meaningful" coverage to workers or pay a percentage of payroll toward the costs of a public plan.[5]

Points of potential controversy include whether all Americans should be required to buy health coverage.

During the presidential primary campaign, Obama sparred with fellow Democratic candidate Sen. Hillary Rodham Clinton, D-N.Y., who called for a mandate on individuals to buy insurance. Obama disagreed, saying, "my belief is that if we make it affordable, if we provide subsidies to those who can't afford it, they will buy it," and that only children's coverage should be required.[6]

But many analysts, including Daschle, point out that unless coverage is required many people will buy it only after they become sick, making it impossible for health insurance to perform its main task — spreading the costs of care among as many people as possible, not just among those who happen to be sick at a given time.

"The only way we can achieve universal coverage is to require everybody to either purchase private insurance or enroll in a public program," Daschle wrote.[7]

Obama entered the race with a speech to an outdoor rally on a cold Feb. 10, 2007, in Springfield, Ill. After acknowledging the "audacity" of his campaign, Obama laid out a platform of reshaping the economy, tackling the health-care crisis and ending the war in Iraq. He started well behind Clinton in the polls and in organization. In the early debates — with eight candidates in all — Obama himself rated his performance as "uneven," according to *Newsweek*'s post-election account.[17] By December, however, Obama had pulled ahead of Clinton in

If Obama ends up authorizing a new government-run insurance plan to compete with private insurers for enrollees, as most Democrats favor, the plan could face tough opposition from Republicans.

"Forcing private plans to compete with federal programs, with their price controls and ability to shift costs to taxpayers, will inevitably doom true competition and could ultimately lead to a single-payer, government-run health-care program," said Sen. Michael Enzi, R-Wyo., the top Republican on the HELP Committee. "Any new insurance coverage must be delivered through private health-insurance plans."[8]

Congressional Democrats stand ready to work with the Obama administration to move health-care reform quickly. Two very influential senators, HELP Committee Chairman Sen. Edward Kennedy, D-Mass., and Finance Committee Chairman Sen. Max Baucus, D-Mont., were already crafting health-reform legislation last year and are expected to begin a strong push for legislation soon. But the press of other business and the time-consuming process of gathering support for a specific plan will put off a vote until the end of this year or the beginning of 2010, predicted Rep. Pete Stark, D-Calif., chairman of the House Ways and Means Health Subcommittee. "I don't think we'll do it in the first 100 days," said Stark.[9]

Ironically, the struggling economy, which leaves many more Americans worried about their jobs and therefore their health coverage, may have opened the door for reform by giving business owners, doctors and others a greater stake in getting more people covered, said Henry Aaron, a senior fellow in economic studies at the centrist Brookings Institution. "Before the economic collapse . . . the odds of national reform were nil," but the nation's economic stress makes it somewhat more likely, especially since Congress has been spending large amounts of money on other industries, Aaron said.[10]

Nevertheless, Aaron and some other analysts say the climate for health-care reform may not be much different from that in 1993 when the tide quickly turned against the Clinton administration's attempt at providing universal health care.

The times are "similar," and despite the desire of many for reform, the details will be painful and will spark push-back, Stuart Butler, vice president of the conservative Heritage Foundation, told PBS' "NewsHour." "When you say, 'We've got to make the system efficient by reducing unnecessary costs' . . . that means people's jobs and . . . doctors are going to rebel against that."[11]

— Marcia Clemmitt

[1] Quoted in "Daschle: Health Care Flaws Threaten Economic Security," CNNPolitics.com, Jan. 8, 2009, www.cnn.com/2009/POLITICS/01/08/daschle.confirmation.

[2] For background see the following *CQ Researcher* reports by Marcia Clemmitt: "Universal Coverage," March 30, 2007, pp. 265-288, and "Rising Health Costs," April 7, 2006, pp. 289-312.

[3] Barack Obama, "Modern Health Care for All Americans," *The New England Journal of Medicine*, Oct. 9, 2008, p. 1537.

[4] Quoted in "In Weak Economy, Obama May Face Obstacles to Health Care Reform," PBS "NewsHour," Nov. 20, 2008, www.pbs.org.

[5] "2008 Presidential Candidate Health Care Proposals: Side-by-Side Summary," health08.org, Kaiser Family Foundation, www.health08.org.

[6] Quoted in Jacob Goldstein, "Clinton and Obama Spar Over Insurance Mandates," *The Wall Street Journal* Health Blog, Feb. 1, 2008, http://blogs.wsj.com.

[7] Quoted in Teddy Davis, "Obama and Daschle at Odds on Individual Mandates," ABC News blogs, Dec. 11, 2008, http://blogs.abcnews.com.

[8] "Enzi Asks Obama Health Cabinet Nominee Daschle Not to Doom Health-Care Competition," press statement, office of Sen. Mike Enzi, Jan. 8, 2009, http://enzi.senate.gov.

[9] Quoted in Jeffrey Young, "Rep. Stark: No Health Reform Vote in Early '09," *The Hill*, Dec. 17, 2008, http://thehill.com.

[10] Quoted in Ben Weyl, "Experts Predict a Health Overhaul Despite Troubled Economy," *CQ Healthbeat*, Dec. 9, 2008.

[11] "In Weak Economy, Obama May Face Obstacles to Health Care Reform," *op. cit.*

some New Hampshire polling and was in a virtual dead-heat in the all-important "money primary."

The Iowa caucuses on Jan. 3, 2007, gave Obama an unexpected win with about 38 percent of the vote and left only two other viable candidates standing: former North Carolina Sen. John Edwards, who came in second; and Clinton, who finished a disappointing third. Five days later, however, Clinton regained her stride with a 3-percentage-point victory over Obama in the first-in-the-nation New Hampshire primary. Edwards' third-place

Vice President Biden Brings Foreign-Policy Savvy

"I want to be the last guy in the room on every important decision."

The inauguration of Joseph R. Biden Jr. as the 47th vice president of the United States caps a journey almost as improbable as Barack Obama's. During seven terms as a U.S. senator from Delaware, Biden has never lived in Washington, instead commuting daily by train from Wilmington. In 1972, at age 29, he became the sixth-youngest senator ever elected, leading many to believe the White House was in his future.

But after two failed presidential campaigns — in 1988 and in the last election — Biden seemed fated to remain a Senate lifer.

Along the way he rose to become chairman of the Judiciary Committee and gained national prominence while leading the confirmation hearings of Supreme Court nominees Robert Bork and Clarence Thomas. He had also served twice as chairman of the Foreign Relations Committee.

Obama's limited time in the Senate and lack of international experience led to increased speculation that he would select Biden as his running mate to bridge the gap. "[Joe Biden is] a leader who sees clearly the challenges facing America in a changing world, with our security and standing set back by eight years of failed foreign policy," Obama said in introducing Biden as his selection on Aug. 23, 2008.

But the new president has yet to clarify the specific role Biden will play in the new administration. The appointment of Hillary Rodham Clinton as secretary of State all but ensures that Biden, despite his impressive résumé, will not be the point man on foreign policy as initially expected.

Nor does anyone expect him to emulate former Vice President Dick Cheney's muscular role. Upon taking office in 2001, Cheney demanded — and President George W. Bush approved — a mandate to give him access to "every table and every meeting," expressing his voice in "whatever area the vice president feels he wants to be active in," recalls former White House Chief of Staff Joshua B. Bolten.[1]

Cheney's push to expand presidential war-making authority is arguably his most lasting legacy, but he also served as a gatekeeper for Supreme Court nominees, editor of tax proposals and arbiter of budget appeals.

While most vice presidents arrive eager to expand the influence of their position, Biden faces the unusual conundrum of figuring out how to scale it back. "The only value of power is the effect, the efficacy of its use," he told *The New York Times*. "And all the power Cheney had did not result in effective outcomes." But without any direct constitutional authority in the executive branch, Biden does not want to return to the days when vice presidents were neither

finish kept him in the race, but he dropped out on Jan. 30 after finishing third in primaries in Florida and his birth state of South Carolina.

The one-on-one between Obama and Clinton continued through May. Clinton bested Obama in a series of supposedly "critical" late-season primaries — notably, Ohio and Pennsylvania — even as Obama pulled ahead in delegates thanks to caucus state victories and also-ran proportional-representation winnings from the primaries. He turned the most serious threat to his campaign — his relationship with the sometimes fiery black minister, Jeremiah Wright — into a plus of sorts with a stirring speech on racial justice delivered in Philadelphia on March

18. With Clinton's "electability" arguments unavailing, Obama mathematically clinched the nomination on June 3 as the two split final primaries in Montana and South Dakota. Clinton withdrew four days later, promising to work hard for Obama's election.

With nearly three months before the convention, Obama went to Iraq and Europe to burnish his national security and foreign policy credentials. His 16-month timetable for withdrawal now essentially matched the Iraqi government's own position — weakening a Republican line of attack. An address to a huge and adoring crowd in Berlin underscored Obama's promise to raise U.S. standing in the world. The McCain campaign countered

seen nor heard. "I don't think the measure is whether or not I accrete the vestiges of power; it matters whether or not the president listens to me."[2]

And although he says he doesn't seek to wield as much influence as Cheney, many don't expect the loquacious Biden to follow Al Gore either, who in 1992 was assigned a defined portfolio by President Bill Clinton to work on environmental and technology matters. "I think his fundamental role is as a trusted counselor," said Obama senior adviser David Axelrod. "I think that when Obama selected him, he selected him to be a counselor and an adviser on a broad range of issues."[3]

And that's exactly how Biden — who at first balked at accepting the position — wants it. "I don't want to have a portfolio," Biden says. "I don't want to be the guy who handles U.S.-Russian relations or the guy who reinvents government."

"I want to be the last guy in the room on every important decision."

"It's irrelevant what the outside world perceives. What is relevant is whether or not I'm value-added," Biden contends. And very few debate his credentials for the position.

"I'm the most experienced vice president since anybody. Anybody ever serve 36 years as a United States senator?" he asks.[4]

But in all likelihood Biden's first move to Washington will surely be his last.

At age 66, he says he has no plans to pursue the presidency, or return to the Senate for that matter, in 2016 — the last full year of a possible second term for Obama. That suggests he'll truly serve Obama's ambitions rather than his own.

"This is in all probability, and hopefully, a worthy capstone in my career," he said.

— Darrell Dela Rosa

Getty Images/Ethan Miller

Newly sworn in Vice President Joseph R. Biden, his wife, Jill, and son Beau greet crowds during the Inaugural Parade.

---

[1] Barton Gellman and Jo Becker, " 'A Different Understanding With the President,' " *The Washington Post*, June 24, 2007, blog.washingtonpost.com/cheney/chapters/chapter_1.

[2] Peter Baker, "Biden Outlines Plans to Do More With Less Power," *The New York Times*, Jan. 14, 2009, www.nytimes.com/2009/01/15/us/politics/15biden.html?_r=1.

[3] Helene Cooper, "For Biden, No Portfolio but the Role of a Counselor," *The New York Times*, Nov. 25, 2008, www.nytimes.com/2008/11/26/us/politics/26biden.html.

[4] Baker, *op. cit.*

---

with an ad mocking Obama's celebrity status. On the eve of the convention, Obama picked Biden as his running mate. The selection won praise as sound, if safe. The four-day convention in Denver (Aug. 25-28) went off without a hitch. Obama's acceptance speech drew generally high marks, but some criticism for its length and predictable domestic-policy prescriptions.

McCain countered the next day by picking Alaska Gov. Sarah Palin as his running mate. The surprise selection energized the GOP base but raised questions among observers and voters about his judgment. For the rest of the campaign, the McCain camp tried but failed to find an Obama weak spot. Obama had already survived personal attacks about ties to Rev. Wright, indicted Chicago developer Tony Rezko and one-time radical William Ayers. He had also fended off attacks for breaking his pledge to limit campaign spending by taking public funds. Improved ground conditions in Iraq shifted the contest from national security — McCain's strength — to the economy: Democratic turf. Obama held his own in three debates and used his financial advantage — he raised a record $742 million in all — to engage McCain not only in battleground states but also in supposedly safe GOP states.

By Election Day, the outcome was hardly in doubt. Any remaining uncertainty vanished when Virginia, Republican since 1968, went to Obama early in the evening. By 9:30, one blog had declared Obama the winner. The networks waited until the polls closed on the West Coast — 11 p.m. in the East — to declare Obama to be the 44th president of the United States. In Chicago's Grant Park, tens of thousands of supporters chanted "Yes, we can," as Obama strode on stage.

"If there is anyone out there," Obama began, "who still doubts that America is a place where all things are possible; who still wonders if the dream of our founders is alive in our time; who still questions the power of our democracy, tonight is your answer."[18]

A Team of Centrists?

President-elect Obama began the 76 days between election and inauguration by hitting nearly pitch-perfect notes in his dealings with official Washington — including President Bush and members of Congress — and with the public at large. Beginning with his first post-election session with reporters, Obama sounded both somber but hopeful in confronting what he continually referred to as the worst economic crisis in generations. He completed his selection of Cabinet appointees in record time before taking an end-of-December vacation with his family in Hawaii. Some discordant notes were sounded as Inauguration Day neared in January. But on the eve of the inauguration, polls showed Obama entering the Oval Office with unprecedented levels of personal popularity and hopeful support. (*See graph, p. 422.*)

Acknowledging the severity of the economic crisis, Obama started the announcement of Cabinet-level appointments on Nov. 24 by introducing an economic team that included New York Federal Reserve Bank President Timothy Geithner to be secretary of the Treasury. Geithner had been deeply involved in the Fed's moves in the financial bailout. Obama also named Summers, who had served as deputy undersecretary of the Treasury in the Clinton administration, as special White House assistant for economic policy.

A week later, Obama introduced a national security team that included Hillary Clinton as secretary of State and Gates as holdover Pentagon chief. Clinton accepted the post only after weighing the offer against continuing in the Senate with possibly enhanced visibility and influence. In addition, the appointment required former President Clinton to disclose donors to his post-presidential foundation to try to reduce potential conflicts of interest with his wife's new role.

Along with Gates, Obama also introduced Gen. Jones, a retired Marine commandant and former North Atlantic Treaty Organization supreme commander, as his national security adviser. He also said that he would nominate Holder, a former deputy attorney general, for attorney general; Gov. Janet Napolitano of Arizona for secretary of Homeland Security; and Susan E. Rice, a former assistant secretary of State, for ambassador to the United Nations with Cabinet rank. Holder was in line to be the first African-American to head the Justice Department.

Other Cabinet nominations followed in rapid succession: New Mexico Gov. Bill Richardson, like Clinton one of the contenders for the Democratic nomination, for Commerce; Gen. Eric Shinseki, a critic of Iraq War policies, for Veterans Affairs; and former Senate Democratic Leader Tom Daschle of South Dakota, for Health and Human Services and a new White House office as health reform czar.

Obama picked Shaun Donovan, commissioner of New York City's housing department, for Housing and Urban Development; outgoing Illinois Rep. Ray LaHood, a Republican, for Transportation; and Chicago public schools Commissioner Arne Duncan, a reformer with good relations with Chicago teacher unions, for Education. Steven Chu, a Nobel Prize-winning scientist and an advocate of measures to reduce global warming, was picked for Energy. Sen. Kenneth Salazar, a Colorado Democrat with a moderate record on environmental and land use issues, was tapped for Interior. Former Iowa Gov. Tom Vilsack, who had supported Clinton for the nomination, was chosen for Agriculture. And Rep. Hilda Solis, a California Democrat and daughter of a union family, was designated for Labor.

As Obama prepared to leave for Hawaii, some supporters were griping about the moderate cast of his selections. "We just hoped the political diversity would have been stronger," Tim Carpenter, executive director of Progressive Democrats of America, told Politico.com. But official Washington appeared to be giving him top marks. *The Washington Post* described the future Cabinet as dominated by "practical-minded centrists who have straddled big policy debates rather than staking out the strongest pro-reform positions."[19]

Obama arrived in Washington on Jan. 4 to enroll daughters Malia, 10, and Natasha ("Sasha"), 7, in the private Sidwell Friends School and begin two hectic work weeks before a long weekend of pre-inaugural events. By then, problems had begun to arise, including a corruption scandal over the selection of Obama's successor in the Senate; the withdrawal of one of his Cabinet nominees; and questions about several of his nominees for top posts.

The Senate seat controversy stemmed from a federal investigation of Illinois Gov. Rod Blagojevich that included tape-recorded comments by the Democratic chief executive that were widely depicted as attempting to sell the appointment for political contributions or other favors. In charging Blagojevich with corruption, U.S. Attorney Patrick Fitzgerald specifically cleared Obama of any involvement. But Obama had been forced to answer questions on the issue from Hawaii and had lined up with Senate Democratic Leader Harry Reid in promising not to seat any Blagojevich appointee. When Blagojevich went ahead and appointed former state Comptroller Roland Burris, an African-American, Reid initially resisted but eventually bowed to the fait accompli and welcomed Burris to the Senate.

Richardson had withdrawn from the Commerce post on Jan. 3 after citing a federal probe into a possible "pay for play" scandal in New Mexico.

Two other Cabinet nominees faced critical questions as Senate confirmation hearings got under way. Treasury Secretary-designate Geithner was disclosed to have failed to pay Social Security and Medicare taxes for several years and to have paid back taxes and interest only after being audited. Attorney General-designate Holder faced questions about his role in recommending that President Clinton pardon fugitive financier Marc Rich and in submitting a pardon application for members of the radical Puerto Rican independence movement FALN. Both seemed headed toward confirmation, however.

CURRENT SITUATION

Moving Quickly

Beginning with his first hours in office, President Obama is moving quickly to put his stamp on government policies by fulfilling campaign promises on such issues as government ethics, secrecy and counterterrorism. Along with the flurry of domestic actions, Obama opened initiatives on the diplomatic front by promising an active U.S. role to promote peace in the Middle East and naming high-level special envoys for the Israeli-Palestinian dispute and the strategically important region of South Asia, including Afghanistan and Pakistan.

In the biggest news of his first days in office, Obama on Jan. 22 signed executive orders to close the Guantánamo prison camp within one year and to prohibit the use of "enhanced" interrogation techniques such as waterboarding by CIA agents or any other U.S. personnel. Human rights groups hailed the actions. "Today is the beginning of the end of that sorry chapter in our nation's history," said Elisa Massimino, executive director and CEO of Human Rights First.

Some Republican lawmakers, however, questioned the moves. "How does it make sense," House GOP Whip Eric Cantor asked, "to close down the Guantánamo facility before there is a clear plan to deal with the terrorists inside its walls?"

An earlier directive, signed late in the day on Jan. 20, ordered Defense Secretary Gates to halt for 120 days any of the military commission proceedings against the remaining 245 detainees at Guantánamo. Separately, Obama directed a review of the case against Ali Saleh Kahlah al-Marri, a U.S. resident and the only person designated as an enemy combatant being held in the U.S.

The ethics and information directives signed on Jan. 21 followed Obama's campaign pledges to limit the "revolving door" between government jobs and lobbyist work and to make government more transparent and accountable.

The new ethics rules bar any executive branch appointees from seeking lobbying jobs during Obama's administration. They also ban gifts from lobbyists to anyone in the administration. Good-government groups praised the new policies as the strictest ethics rules ever adopted. Fred Wertheimer, president of the open-government group Democracy 21, called them "a major step in setting a new tone and attitude for Washington."

On information policy, Obama superseded a Bush administration directive promising legal support for agencies seeking to resist disclosure of government records under the Freedom of Information Act. Instead, Obama called on all agencies to release information whenever possible. "For a long time now, there's been too much secrecy in this city," Obama said at a swearing-in ceremony for senior White House staff.

Obama also signed an executive order aimed at greater openness for presidential records following the

Should Congress and the president create a commission to investigate the Bush administration's counterterrorism policies?

YES

Frederick A. O. Schwarz Jr.
Chief Counsel, Brennan Center for Justice,
New York University School of Law; co-author,
Unchecked and Unbalanced: Presidential
Power in a Time of Terror (*New Press, 2008*)

Written for *CQ Researcher*, January 2009

In his inaugural address, President Obama rejected "as false the choice between our safety and our ideals." Throughout our history, seeking safety in times of crisis has often made it tempting to ignore the wise restraints that make us free and to rush into actions that do not serve the nation's long-term interests. (The Alien and Sedition Acts at the dawn of the republic and the herding of Japanese citizens into concentration camps early in World War II are among many historic examples.) After 9/11 we again overreacted to crisis, this time by descending into practices including torture, extraordinary rendition, warrantless wiretapping and indefinite detention. Each breached American values and thus made America less safe.

Our new president is taking steps to reject these actions. And some say this is all that is needed because we need to look forward. Others clamor for criminal prosecutions because to hold our heads high wrongdoers should be held to account.

But, to me, neither of these positions is right. Prosecution is not likely to be productive, and could well be unfair. At the same time, failure to learn more about how we went wrong poses two dangers: First, if we blind our eyes to the truth, we increase the risk of repetition when the next crisis comes.

Second, clearly and fairly assessing and reporting what went wrong — and right — in our reactions to 9/11 will honor America's commitment to openness and the rule of law. Committing ourselves to a full exploration is consistent with the ethos the new president articulated on his first day in office: "The way to make government responsible is to hold it accountable. And the way to make government accountable is to make it transparent."

For these two reasons, I have recommended that the president and Congress appoint an independent, nonpartisan commission to investigate national counterterrorism policies. This is the best way to achieve accountability and an understanding of how to design an effective counterterrorism policy that comports with fundamental values.

Shortly after his reelection in 1864, President Abraham Lincoln nicely articulated the necessity of learning from the past without seeking punishment: "Let us study the incidents of [recent history], as philosophy to learn wisdom from, and none of them as wrongs to be revenged."

NO

David B. Rivkin Jr. and Lee A. Casey
Washington attorneys who served in the Justice
Department under Presidents Reagan and
George H. W. Bush

Written for *CQ Researcher*, January 2009

A special commission would be both unnecessary and harmful. First, multiple congressional inquiries have already aired and analyzed all of the Bush administration's key legal and policy decisions. Indeed, whether through disclosures, leaks, media and/or congressional investigations, both the process and substance of the administration's war-related decisions have been publicized to an unprecedented extent. If any further inquiry into these policies is necessary, the normal congressional and executive branch investigatory tools are always available, including additional hearings.

Second, a special commission would be fundamentally unfair, beginning — as it would — with the proposition that the Bush policies represent systematic wrongdoing. The Bush policies were based upon well-established case law and reasonable legal extrapolation from the available authorities. Simply because the Supreme Court ultimately decided to change the legal landscape does not mean the Bush administration ignored the law; it did not. Moreover, although there have been many problems and certainly some abuses over the past seven years — Abu Ghraib being a case in point — these have been remarkably rare when compared with past armed conflicts and/or counterterrorism campaigns like the one Britain conducted in Northern Ireland.

A commission would also inevitably involve attacks on career officials in the intelligence community and the departments of Justice and Defense, not merely Bush political appointees. When combined with past investigations, the commission's work would inevitably burden, distract and demoralize the nation's intelligence capabilities. The end result would be the extension of a bureaucratic culture that already favors excessive caution and inaction among our key intelligence and law enforcement officials — the very developments, acknowledged by the 9/11 Commission, as contributing mightily to the analytical, legal and policy failures of 9/11.

Finally, a commission would warp our constitutional fabric and harm civil liberties. While many commissions have operated throughout American history, they have not focused on potential prosecutions. Such a private or quasi-governmental commission would not be constrained by the legal and constitutional limits on Congress and the executive branch, thus raising a host of important constitutional questions.

That the commission's supporters — so determined to vindicate the rights of enemy combatant detainees — seem untroubled by these issues is both ironic and terribly sad.

Will Obama's economic stimulus revive the U.S. economy?

YES
Dean Baker
*Co-director, Center for Economic
and Policy Research*

Written for *CQ Researcher*, January 2009

President Obama's stimulus proposal is a very good start toward rescuing the economy. In assessing the plan, it is vitally important to recognize the seriousness of the downturn. The economy lost an average of more than 500,000 jobs a month in the last three months of 2008. In fact, the actual job loss could have been over 600,000 a month due to the way in which the Labor Department counts jobs in new firms that are not in its survey.

The recent announcements of job loss suggest that the rate of job loss may have accelerated even further. It is possible that we are now losing jobs at the rate of 700,000 a month. This is important, because people must understand the urgency of acting as quickly as possible.

With this in mind, the package being debated does a good job of getting money into the economy quickly. According to the projections of the Congressional Budget Office (CBO), 62 percent of the spending in the package will reach the economy before the end of 2010, with most of the rest coming in 2011. This money will be giving the economy a boost when we need it most.

At this point, there is considerable research on the impact of tax cuts, and the evidence suggests that they do not have nearly as much impact on the economy, primarily because a large portion of any tax cut is saved. According to Martin Feldstein, President Reagan's chief economist, just 10 percent of the tax cuts sent out last spring were spent. The rest was saved. Increased savings can be beneficial to household balance sheets, but savings will not boost the economy right now.

There will also be long-term benefits from President Obama's package. For example, the CBO projected we would save more than $90 billion on medical expenses over the next decade by computerizing medical records, which will be financed through the stimulus. In addition, weatherizing homes and offices and modernizing the electrical grid will substantially reduce our future energy use.

The Obama administration projects that this package will generate close to 4 million jobs, and several independent analysts have arrived at similar numbers. This will not bring the economy back to full employment, but it is still a huge improvement over doing nothing.

The cost of this bill sounds large, but it is important to remember that the need is large. If we were to just do nothing, the economy would continue to spiral downward, with the unemployment rate reaching double-digit levels in the near future.

NO
J. D. Foster
*Norman B. Ture Senior Fellow in the
Economics of Fiscal Policy,
The Heritage Foundation*

Written for *CQ Researcher*, January 2009

President Barack Obama promises to create 3.5 million new jobs by the end of 2010, and that vow provides a clear measure by which to judge whether his policies work.

U.S. employment stood at about 113 million people in December 2008, so the Obama jobs pledge will be met if 116.5 million people are working by the end of 2010. Reaching this goal will require effective stimulus policies — and the only fiscal policy that can come close to reaching the goal is to cut marginal tax rates.

Obama's target for jobs creation was chosen carefully. Employment peaked at about 115.8 million jobs in November 2007. Obama's jobs pledge at that time was to create 2.5 million jobs, for a total of 116.5 million private sector jobs.

The November 2008 jobs report showed a half-million jobs lost, so his job-creating target rose by a half-million, affirming the 116.5 million target. Then last month's jobs report showed another half-million jobs lost, and the president raised the target again to its current 3.5 million total.

To stimulate the economy, Obama and congressional Democrats have focused on massive new spending programs. However, the federal budget deficit is likely to exceed $2.5 trillion over the next two years even before any stimulus is added. If deficit spending were truly stimulative, the economy would be at risk of overheating by now, not sliding deeper into recession.

Additional deficit spending won't be any more effective than the first $2 trillion, because government spending doesn't create additional demand in the economy. Deficit spending must be financed by borrowing, so while government spending increases demand, government borrowing reduces demand. Worse, since the government's likely to borrow between $3 trillion and $4 trillion over the next two years, the enormous waves of government debt will likely drive interest rates up. That would only prolong the recession and weaken the recovery.

An effective fiscal stimulus would defer the massive 2011 tax hike (higher tax rates on dividends and capital gains are scheduled to kick in), and also cut individual and corporate tax rates further to reduce the impediments to starting new businesses, hiring, working and investing.

To meet his goal, President Obama should junk his ideology and the wasteful spending that goes with it and focus on cutting marginal tax rates. That's the only way to hit his jobs creation target.

congressionally established five-year waiting period after any president leaves office. The order supersedes a Bush administration directive in 2001 by giving the incumbent president, not a former president, decision-making authority on whether to invoke executive privilege to prevent release of the former president's records.

On foreign policy, Obama on his first full day in office turned to the fragile cease-fire in Gaza by placing calls to four Mideast leaders: Egyptian President Hosni Mubarak, Israeli Prime Minister Ehud Olmert, Jordanian King Abdullah and Palestinian Authority President Mahmoud Abbas. Obama offered U.S. assistance to try to solidify the ceasefire that had been adopted over the Jan. 17-18 weekend by Israel and Hamas, the ruling party in Gaza.

Israel had begun an offensive against Hamas on Dec. 27 in an effort to halt cross-border rocket attacks into Israel by Hamas supporters. During the transition, Obama had limited himself to a brief statement regretting the loss of life on both sides. White House press secretary Robert Gibbs said Obama used the calls from the Oval Office to pledge U.S. support for consolidating the cease-fire by preventing the smuggling of arms into Hamas from neighboring Egypt. He also promised U.S. support for "a major reconstruction effort for Palestinians in Gaza," Gibbs said.

The next day, Obama took a 10-block ride to the State Department for Hillary Clinton's welcome ceremony as secretary following her 94-2 Senate confirmation on Jan. 21. As part of the event, Clinton announced the appointment of special envoys George Mitchell for the Middle East and Richard Holbrooke for Afghanistan and Pakistan.

In his remarks, Obama renewed support for a two-state solution: Israel and a Palestinian state "living side by side in peace and security." He also promised to refocus U.S. attention on what he called the "perilous" situation in Afghanistan, where he said violence had increased dramatically and a "deadly insurgency" had taken root.

Returning to domestic issues, Obama on Jan. 23 signed — as expected — an order to lift the so-called Mexico City policy prohibiting U.S. aid to any nongovernmental organizations abroad that provide abortion counseling or services. The memorandum instructed Secretary of State Clinton to lift what Obama called the "unwarranted" restrictions. The policy was first put in place by President Ronald Reagan in 1984, rescinded by President Clinton in 1993 and then reinstituted by President Bush in 2001.

After the weekend, Obama reversed another of Bush's policies on Jan. 26 by directing Environmental Protection Agency Administrator Lisa Jackson to reconsider the request by the state of California to adopt automobile emission standards stricter than those set under federal law. In a reversal of past practice, the Bush administration EPA had denied California's waiver request in December 2007. On the same day, Obama instructed Transportation Secretary Ray LaHood to tighten fuel efficiency standards for cars and light trucks beginning with 2011 model cars.

Working With Congress

President Obama is pressing Congress for quick action on an economic stimulus plan even as bipartisan support for a proposal remains elusive. Meanwhile, the new administration is struggling to find ways to make the financial bailout approved before Obama took office more effective in aiding distressed homeowners and unfreezing credit markets.

House Democrats moved ahead with an $825-billion stimulus package after the tax and spending elements won approval in separate, party-line votes by the House Ways and Means Committee on Jan. 22 and the House Appropriations Committee the day before. The full House was scheduled to vote on the package on Jan. 28 after deadline for this issue, but approval was assured given the Democrats' 256-178 majority in the chamber.

Obama used his first weekly address as president on Jan. 24 — now not only broadcast on radio but also posted online as video on YouTube and the White House Web site — to depict his American Recovery and Reinvestment Plan as critical to get the country out of an "unprecedented" economic crisis. The plan, he said, would "jump-start job creation as well as long-term economic growth." Without it, he warned, unemployment could reach double digits, economic output could fall $1 trillion short of capacity and many young Americans could be forced to forgo college or job training.

Without mentioning the tax and spending plan's minimum total cost, Obama detailed a long list of infrastructure improvements to be accomplished in energy, health care, education and transportation. He mentioned a $2,500 college tax credit but did not note other items in the $225 billion in tax breaks included in the plan — either his long-advocated $1,000 tax break for working families or the various business tax cuts added as sweeteners for Republicans.

Republicans, however, remained unconvinced. Replying to Obama's address, House Minority Leader John Boehner called the plan "chock-full of government programs and projects, most of which won't provide immediate relief to our ailing economy." On "Meet the Press" the next day, the Ohio lawmaker again called for more by way of tax cuts, criticized the job-creating potential of Obama's plan and warned of opposition from most House Republicans.

Appearing on another of the Sunday talk shows, McCain told "Fox News Sunday" host Chris Wallace, "I am opposed to most of the provisions in the bill. As it stands now, I would not support it."

On a second front, the principal members of Obama's economic team are assuring Congress of major changes to come in the second stage of the $700-billion financial rescue plan approved last fall. During confirmation hearings, Treasury Secretary-designate Geithner promised the Senate Finance Committee on Jan. 21 to expect "much more substantial action" to address the problem of troubled banks that has chilled both consumer and corporate credit markets since fall 2008.

Geithner's comments on the financial bailout were overshadowed by sharp questions from Republican senators about the nominee's tax problems while working for the International Monetary Fund. For several years, Geithner failed to pay Social Security and Medicare taxes, which the IMF — as an international institution — does not withhold from employees' pay as domestic employers do. Geithner repeatedly apologized for the mistake and pointed to his payment of back taxes plus interest totaling more than $40,000. In the end, the committee voted 18-5 to recommend confirmation; the full Senate followed suit on Jan. 26 in a 60-34 vote.*

On the bailout, Geithner said he would increase the transparency and accountability of the program once he assumed the virtually unfettered responsibility for dispensing the remaining $350 billion. He acknowledged criticisms that so far the program has benefited large financial institutions but done little for small businesses. He also promised to restrict dividends by companies that receive government help.

With many banks still holding billions in troubled assets on their balance sheets, speculation is increasing in Washington and in financial circles about dramatic action by the government. Possible moves include the creation of a government-run "bad bank" to buy distressed assets from financial institutions or even outright nationalization of one or more banks.

"People continue to be surprised by the poor condition of the banks," says Dean Baker, co-director of the Center for Economic and Policy Research, a liberal think tank in Washington. "Whatever plans they may have made a month ago might be seen as inadequate given the severity of the problem of the banking system."

With the stimulus package on the front burner, however, Obama went to Capitol Hill on Jan. 27 for separate meetings to lobby House and Senate Republicans to support the measure. The closed-door session with the full House GOP conference lasted an hour — slightly longer than scheduled, causing the president to be late for the start of the meeting on the other side of the Capitol with Republican senators.

In between meetings, Obama challenged GOP lawmakers to try to minimize partisan differences. "I don't expect 100 percent agreement from my Republican colleagues, but I do hope we can put politics aside," he said.

For their part, House Republican leaders expressed appreciation for the president's visit and his expressed willingness to compromise. But some renewed their opposition to the proposal in its current form. Rep. Tom Price of Georgia, chairman of the conservative House Republican Study Committee, said the proposal "remains rooted in a liberal, big-government ideology."

Obama's meeting with GOP senators came on the same day that the Senate Finance and Appropriations committees were marking up their versions of the stimulus package. The Senate was expected to vote on the proposal over the weekend, giving the two chambers two weeks to iron out their differences if the bill was to reach Obama's desk before the Presidents' Day recess.

OUTLOOK

Peril and Promise

One week after taking office, President Obama is getting high marks from experts on the presidency for carefully stage-managing his first policy initiatives while discreetly moving to set realistic expectations for the months ahead.

---

* Attorney General-designate Holder, Obama's other controversial Cabinet nominee, was expected to be confirmed by the full Senate on Jan. 29 or 30, after deadline for this issue, following the Senate Judiciary Committee's 17-2 vote on Jan. 28 to recommend confirmation.

"He's started out quite impressively," says Fred Greenstein, professor of politics emeritus at Princeton University in New Jersey and the dean of American scholars on the U.S. presidency. "So far, it's been a striking rollout week."

Other experts agree. "The Obama administration has met expectations for the first week," says Meena Bose, chair of the Peter S. Kalikow Center for the Study of the American Presidency at Hofstra University in Hempstead, N.Y. "There's been virtually no drama, which is an indication of how he intends to run his administration."

"The indications are all positive," says Bruce Buchanan, a professor of political science at the University of Texas in Austin and author of several books on the presidency. Like the others, Buchanan says Obama is holding on to popular support while striving either to win over or to neutralize Republicans on Capitol Hill.

The wider world outside Washington, however, is giving Obama no honeymoon in office. The U.S. economy is continuing to lag, while violence and unrest continue to simmer in three global hot spots: Gaza, Iraq and Afghanistan.

On the economy, Obama has initiated a daily briefing from senior adviser Summers in addition to the daily briefing on foreign policy and national security issues. "Frankly," Obama told congressional leaders on Jan. 23, "the news has not been good." The day before, the Commerce Department had reported that new-home construction fell to its slowest pace since reporting on monthly rates began in 1959. On the same day, new claims for unemployment benefits matched the highest level seen in a quarter-century.[20]

Meanwhile, leading U.S. policy makers were giving downbeat assessments of events in Afghanistan and Iraq. In testimony to the Senate Armed Services Committee, Defense chief Gates warned on Jan. 27 to expect "a long and difficult fight" in Afghanistan. A few days earlier, the outgoing U.S. ambassador to Iraq, Ryan Crocker, warned that what he called "a precipitous withdrawal" could jeopardize the country's stability and revive al Qaeda in Iraq. And special envoy Mitchell left Washington for the Mideast on Jan. 26, just as the fragile cease-fire between Hamas and Israel was jeopardized by the death of an Israeli soldier from a roadside bomb and an Israeli air strike in retaliation.

Obama continues to work at the problems with the same kind of message control that served him well in the election. After reaping a full day's worth of mostly favorable news coverage on the Guantánamo issue, the administration began directing laser-like attention to the economy

from Jan. 22 on. For example, the repeal of the Bush administration's ban on funding international groups that perform abortions was announced late on Friday, Jan. 23 — a dead zone for news coverage.

On foreign policy, Obama emphasized the Mitchell and Holbrooke appointments by personally going to the State Department for the announcements. And he underscored the inaugural's outreach to Muslims by granting his first formal television interview as president to the Arabic satellite television network Al Arabiya. Obama called for a new partnership with the Muslim world "based on mutual respect and mutual interest." One of his main tasks, he told the Dubai-based network in an interview aired on Jan. 27, is to communicate that "the Americans are not your enemy."[21]

Obama and his senior aides are also signaling to supporters that some of their agenda items will have to wait. In a pre-inauguration interview with *The Washington Post*, for example, he reiterated his support for a labor-backed bill to make it easier to unionize workers but downgraded it to a post-stimulus agenda item. Similarly, press secretary-designate Gibbs repeated Obama's support for repealing the military's "don't ask, don't tell" policy on homosexuals on the transition's Web site on Jan. 13, but the next day expanded on the answer: "Not everything will get done in the beginning," Gibbs said.[22]

Greenstein and Bose view Obama's inaugural address — which many observers faulted for rhetorical flatness — as a conscious, initial step to lower expectations about the pace of the promised "change we can believe in." Greenstein calls it a "get-down-to-work" address. Obama himself again evoked the inaugural's theme of determination in the face of adversity when he spoke to congressional leaders immediately following the address.

"What's happening today is not about me," Obama said at the joint congressional luncheon on Inauguration Day. "It is about the American people. They understand that we have arrived at a moment of great challenge for our nation, a time of peril, but also extraordinary promise."

"President Obama has done everything he can to tamp down this sense that he somehow walks on water," says Bose. "He has done everything he can to show that he is a man of substance.

"We have to recognize that these challenges aren't going to be met overnight and that we have to have confidence that we're going to meet them," she continues. "Now the question is, 'Can he govern? Can he show results?' "

NOTES

1. The text and video of the inaugural address are available on the redesigned White House Web site: www.whitehouse.gov. Some crowd reaction from Christopher O'Brien of CQ Press' College Division.

2. Quoted in Clea Benson, "An Economy in Foreclosure," *CQ Weekly*, Jan. 12, 2009.

3. Quoted in Aamer Madhani, "Will Obama Stick to Timetable?" *Chicago Tribune*, Nov. 6, 2008, p. 11.

4. Quoted in Shailagh Murray and Paul Kane, "Democratic Congress Shows It Will Not Bow to Obama," *The Washington Post*, Jan. 11, 2009, p. A5.

5. Norman Ornstein, "First Steps Toward 'Post-Partisanship' Show Promise," *Roll Call*, Jan. 14, 2009.

6. For a compact, continuously updated biography, see Barack Obama, www.biography.com. Background also drawn from Barack Obama, *Dreams from My Father: A Story of Race and Inheritance* (2004 ed.; originally published 1995). See also David Mendell, *Obama: From Promise to Power* (2007).

7. Quoted in Serge Kovaleski, "Obama's Organizing Years: Guiding Others and Finding Himself," *The New York Times*, July 7, 2008, p. A1.

8. Background drawn from Jody Kantor, "In Law School, Obama Found Political Voice," *The New York Times*, Jan. 28, 2007, sec. 1, p. 1.

9. Background drawn from Janny Scott, "The Story of Obama, Written by Obama," *The New York Times*, May 18, 2008, p. A1.

10. For a story on his mother's influence on Obama, see Amanda Ripley, "A Mother's Story," *Time*, April 21, 2008, p. 36.

11. See David Jackson and Ray Long, "Showing his bare knuckles: In first campaign, Obama revealed hard-edged, uncompromising side in eliminating party rivals," *Chicago Tribune*, April 4, 2007, p. 1; Rick Pearson and Ray Long, "Careful steps, looking ahead: After arriving in Springfield, Barack Obama proved cautious, but it was clear to many he had ambitions beyond the state Senate," *ibid.*, May 3, 2007, p. 1.

12. See Barack Obama, *The Audacity of Hope: Thoughts on Reclaiming the American Dream* (2006), pp. 105-107.

13. See David Mendell, "Obama routs Democratic foes; Ryan tops crowded GOP field," *Chicago Tribune*, March 17, 2004, p. 1.

14. For the full text of the 2,165-word speech, see http://obamaspeeches.com/002-Keynote-Address-at-the-2004-Democratic-National-Convention-Obama-Speech.htm. For Mendell's account, see *Obama, op. cit.*, pp. 272-285. Obama's conversation with Martin Nesbitt may have been reported first in David Bernstein, "The Speech," *Chicago Magazine*, July 2007; the anecdote is briefly repeated in Evan Thomas, *"A Long Time Coming": The Inspiring, Combative 2008 Campaign and the Historic Election of Barack Obama* (2009), p. 6. For the Post's account, see David S. Broder, "Democrats Focus on Healing Divisions," July 28, 2004, p. A1.

15. *CQ's Politics in America 2008* (110th Congress), www.cnn.com/video/#/video/world/2007/01/22/vause.obama.school.cnn.

16. Some background from Thomas, *op. cit.*

17. *Ibid.*, p. 9.

18. Many versions of the speech are posted on YouTube, including a posting of CNN's coverage.

19. Carpenter was quoted in Carrie Budoff Brown and Nia-Milaka Henderson, "Cabinet: Middle-of-the-roaders' dream?" *Politico*, Dec. 19, 2008; Alec MacGillis, "For Obama Cabinet, a Team of Moderates," *The Washington Post*, Dec. 20, 2008, p. A1.

20. See Kelly Evans, "Home Construction at Record Slow Pace," *The Wall Street Journal*, Jan. 23, 2009, p. A3.

21. See Paul Schemm, "Obama tells Arabic network US 'is not your enemy,'" The Associated Press, Jan. 27, 2009.

22. Obama quoted in Dan Eggen and Michael D. Shear, "The Effort to Roll Back Bush Policies Continues," *The Washington Post*, Jan. 27, 2009, p. A4; Gibbs quoted in, "Obama aide: Ending 'don't ask, don't tell' must wait," CNN.com, Jan. 15, 2009.

BIBLIOGRAPHY

Books by Barack Obama

Dreams from My Father: A Story of Race and Inheritance (Three Rivers Press, 2004; originally published by Times Books, 1995) is a literate, insightful memoir written in the three years after Obama's graduation from Harvard Law School. The three parts chronicle his "origins" from his birth through college, his three years as a community organizer in Chicago and his two-month pre-law school visit to his father's homeland, Kenya.

The Audacity of Hope: Thoughts on Reclaiming the American Dream (Crown, 2006) is a political manifesto written as Obama considered but had not definitively decided on a presidential campaign. The book opens with a critique of the "bitter partisanship" of current politics and an examination of "common values" that could underline "a new political consensus." Later chapters specifically focus on issues of faith and of race. Includes index.

Change We Can Believe In: Barack Obama's Plan to Renew America's Promise (Three Rivers Press, 2008), which includes a foreword by Obama, outlines steps for "reviving our economy," "investing in our prosperity," "rebuilding America's leadership" and "perfecting our union." Also includes texts of seven speeches from his declaration of candidacy on Feb. 7, 2007, to his July 24, 2008, address in Berlin.

Books About Barack Obama

The only objective, full-length biography is ***Obama: From Promise to Power*** (Amistad/Harper Collins, 2007) by David Mendell, the **Chicago Tribune** political reporter who began covering Obama in his first race for the U.S. Senate. An updated version was published in 2008 under the title ***Obama: The Promise of Change.***

Two critical biographies appeared during the 2008 campaign: David Freddoso, ***The Case Against Barack Obama: The Unlikely Rise and Unexamined Agenda of the Media's Favorite Candidate*** (Regnery, 2008); and Jerome Corsi, ***The Obama Nation: Leftist Politics and the Cult of Personality*** (Threshold, 2008). Freddoso, a writer with National Review Online, wrote what one reviewer called a "fact-based critique" depicting Obama as "a fake reformer and a real liberal." Corsi, a conservative author and columnist best known for his

book ***Unfit for Command*** attacking Democratic presidential nominee John Kerry in 2004, came under fierce criticism from the Obama campaign and independent observers for undocumented allegations about Obama's background.

Two post-election books chronicle the 2008 campaign. Evan Thomas, ***"A Long Time Coming": The Inspiring, Combative 2008 Campaign and the Historic Election of Barack Obama*** (Public Affairs, 2009) is the seventh in **Newsweek's** quadrennial titles documenting presidential campaigns on the basis of reporting by a team of correspondents, with some reporting specifically not for publication until after the election. Chuck Todd and Sheldon Gawiser, ***How Barack Obama Won: A State-by-State Guide to the Historic 2008 Presidential Election*** (Vintage, 2009) gives an analytical overview of the campaign and election with detailed voting analyses of every state. A third title, ***Obama: The Historic Journey***, is due for publication Feb. 16 by **The New York Times** and Callaway; the author is Jill Abramson, the **Times'** managing editor, in collaboration with the newspaper's reporters and editors.

Other books include John K. Wilson, ***Barack Obama: The Improbable Quest*** (Paradigm, 2008), an admiring analysis of Obama's political views and philosophy by a lawyer who recalls having been a student in Obama's class on racism and the law at the University of Chicago Law School; Paul Street, ***Barack Obama and the Future of American Politics*** (Paradigm, 2009), a critical depiction of Obama as a "power-conciliating centrist"; and Jabiri Asim, ***What Obama Means: For Our Culture, Our Politics, Our Future*** (Morrow, 2009) a depiction of Obama as creating a new style of racial politics — less confrontational than in the past but equally committed to social justice and more productive of results.

Articles
Purdum, Todd, "Raising Obama," *Vanity Fair*, March 2008.

The magazine's national editor, formerly a *New York Times* reporter, provided an insightful portrait of Obama midway through the 2008 primary season.

Von Drehle, David, "Person of the Year: Barack Obama: Why History Can't Wait," *Time,* **Dec. 29, 2008.**
Time's selection of Obama as person of the year includes an in-depth interview of the president-elect by Managing Editor Richard Stengel, Editor-at-large von Drehle and Time Inc. Editor-in-chief John Huey. The full text is at time.com/obamainterview.

On the Web

The Obama administration unveiled a redesigned White House Web site (www.whitehouse.gov) at 12:01 p.m. on Jan. 20, 2009 — even before President-elect Obama took the oath of office. The "Briefing Room" includes presidential announcements as well as a "Blog" sometimes being updated several times a day. "The Agenda" incorporates Obama's campaign positions, subject by subject. The site includes video of the president's speeches, including the inaugural address as well as the weekly presidential address — previously broadcast only on radio.

For More Information

American Enterprise Institute for Public Policy Research, 1150 17th St., N.W., Washington, DC 20036; (202) 862-5800; www.aei.org. Conservative think tank researching issues on government, economics, politics and social welfare.

Campaign for America's Future, 1825 K St., N.W., Suite 400, Washington, DC 20006; (202) 955-5665; www.ourfuture.org. Advocates progressive policies.

Center for American Progress, 1333 H St., N.W., 10th Floor, Washington, DC 20005; (202) 682-1611; www.americanprogress.org. Left-leaning think tank promoting a government that ensures opportunity for all Americans.

Center for Economic and Policy Research, 1611 Connecticut Ave., N.W., Suite 400, Washington, DC 20009; (202) 293-5380; www.cepr.net. Promotes open debate on key economic and social issues.

Center on Budget and Policy Priorities, 820 First St., N.E., Suite 510, Washington, DC 20002; (202) 408-1080; www.cbpp.org. Policy organization working on issues that affect low- and moderate-income families and individuals.

Concord Coalition, 1011 Arlington Blvd., Suite 300, Arlington, VA 22209; (703) 894-6222; www.concordcoalition.org. Nonpartisan, grassroots organization promoting responsible fiscal policy and spending.

Heritage Foundation, 214 Massachusetts Ave., N.E., Washington, DC 20002; (202) 546-4400; www.heritage.org. Conservative think tank promoting policies based on free enterprise, limited government and individual freedom.

Supporting researchers for more than 40 years

Research methods have always been at the core of SAGE's publishing program. Founder Sara Miller McCune published SAGE's first methods book, *Public Policy Evaluation*, in 1970. Soon after, she launched the *Quantitative Applications in the Social Sciences* series—affectionately known as the "little green books."

Always at the forefront of developing and supporting new approaches in methods, SAGE published early groundbreaking texts and journals in the fields of qualitative methods and evaluation.

Today, more than 40 years and two million little green books later, SAGE continues to push the boundaries with a growing list of more than 1,200 research methods books, journals, and reference works across the social, behavioral, and health sciences. Its imprints—Pine Forge Press, home of innovative textbooks in sociology, and Corwin, publisher of PreK–12 resources for teachers and administrators—broaden SAGE's range of offerings in methods. SAGE further extended its impact in 2008 when it acquired CQ Press and its best-selling and highly respected political science research methods list.

From qualitative, quantitative, and mixed methods to evaluation, SAGE is the essential resource for academics and practitioners looking for the latest methods by leading scholars.

For more information, visit **www.sagepub.com**.